Statistical Concepts

A First Course

Statistical Concepts—A First Course presents the first 10 chapters from *An Introduction to Statistical Concepts, Fourth Edition*. Designed for first and lower-level statistics courses, this book communicates a conceptual, intuitive understanding of statistics that does not assume extensive or recent training in mathematics and only requires a rudimentary knowledge of algebra.

Covering the most basic statistical concepts, this book is designed to help readers really understand statistical concepts, in what situations they can be applied, and how to apply them to data. Specifically, the text covers basic descriptive statistics, including ways of representing data graphically, statistical measures that describe a set of data, the normal distribution and other types of standard scores, and an introduction to probability and sampling. The remainder of the text covers various inferential tests, including those involving tests of means (e.g., *t* tests), proportions, variances, and correlations.

Providing accessible and comprehensive coverage of topics suitable for an undergraduate or graduate course in statistics, this book is an invaluable resource for students undertaking an introductory course in statistics in any number of social science and behavioral science disciplines.

Debbie L. Hahs-Vaughn is Professor of Methodology, Measurement, and Analysis at the University of Central Florida, US. Her research primarily relates to methodological issues when analyzing, and applied research using, complex sample data.

Richard G. Lomax is Professor Emeritus of Educational and Human Ecology at the Ohio State University, US, and former Associate Dean for Research and Administration. His research primarily focuses on early literacy and statistics.

Statistical Concepts

A First Course

Debbie L. Hahs-Vaughn
University of Central Florida

Richard G. Lomax
The Ohio State University

Routledge
Taylor & Francis Group

NEW YORK AND LONDON

First published 2020
by Routledge
52 Vanderbilt Avenue, New York, NY 10017

and by Routledge
2 Park Square, Milton Park, Abingdon, Oxon, OX14 4RN

Routledge is an imprint of the Taylor & Francis Group, an informa business

Library of Congress Cataloging-in-Publication Data
Names: Hahs-Vaughn, Debbie L., author. | Lomax, Richard G., author. | Hahs-Vaughn, Debbie L. Introduction to
    statistical concepts.
Title: Statistical concepts : a first course / Debbie L. Hahs-Vaughn (University of Central Florida), Richard G. Lomax
    (The Ohio State University).
Description: New York, NY : Routledge, 2019.
Identifiers: LCCN 2019013055 (print) | LCCN 2019017022 (ebook) | ISBN 9780429261268 (Ebook) |
    ISBN 9780367203962 (hardback) | ISBN 9780367203993 (pbk.)
Subjects: LCSH: Statistics—Textbooks. | Mathematical statistics—Textbooks.
Classification: LCC QA276.12 (ebook) | LCC QA276.12 .L65 2019 (print) | DDC 519.5—dc23
LC record available at https://lccn.loc.gov/2019013055

ISBN: 978-0-367-20396-2 (hbk)
ISBN: 978-0-367-20399-3 (pbk)
ISBN: 978-0-429-26126-8 (ebk)

Typeset in Palatino
by Apex CoVantage, LLC

Visit the companion website: www.routledge.com/cw/hahs-vaughn

This book is dedicated to our families and to all our former students.

You are statistically significant.

Contents

Preface

Approach

Many individuals have an aversion to statistics, which is quite unfortunate. Statistics is a tool that unleashes great power to the user—the potential to *really* make a difference. Being able to *understand* statistics means that you can critically evaluate empirical research conducted by others and thus better apply what others have found. Being able to *do* statistics means that you contribute to solving problems. We approach the writing of this text with the mindset that we want this text to be an instrument that contributes to your success as a researcher. With the help of this text, you will gain tools that can be used to make a positive contribution in your discipline. Perhaps this is the moment for which you have been created (Esther 4:14)! Consider the use of text as moving one step closer to making the world a better place.

This text is designed for a course in statistics for students in any number of social science and behavioral disciplines—from education to business to communication to exercise science to psychology to sociology and more. The text begins with the most basic introduction to statistics in the first chapter and then proceeds through intermediate statistics. The text is designed for you to become a better prepared researcher and a more intelligent consumer *and* producer of research. We do not assume that you have extensive or recent training in mathematics. Perhaps you have only had algebra, and perhaps that was some time ago. We also do not assume that you have ever had a statistics course. Rest assured; you will do fine.

We believe that a text should serve as an effective instructional tool. You should find this text to be more than a reference book. It is designed to help those who read it really understand statistical concepts, in what situations they can be applied, and how to apply them to data. With that said, there are several things that this text is *not*. This text is not a theoretical statistics book, nor is it a cookbook on computing statistics, nor a statistical software manual. Recipes suggest that there is one effective approach in all situations, and following that approach will produce the same results always. Additionally, recipes tend to be a crutch—followed without understanding how or why you obtain the desired product. As well, knowing how to run a statistics package without understanding the concepts or the output is not particularly useful. Thus, concepts drive the field of statistics, and that is the framework within which this text was approached.

Goals and Content Coverage

Our goals for this text are lofty, but the effort that you put forth in using it and its effects on your learning of statistics are more than worthwhile. First, the text provides comprehensive coverage of topics that could be included in an undergraduate or graduate one- or two-course sequence in statistics. The text is flexible enough so that instructors can select those topics that they desire to cover as they deem relevant in their particular discipline. In other words, chapters and sections of chapters from this text can be included in a statistics course as the instructor sees fit. Most of the popular, as well as many of the lesser-known procedures and models, are described in the text. A particular feature is a thorough discussion of assumptions, the effects of their violation, and how to deal with their violation.

This text represents the first 10 chapters of *An Introduction to Statistical Concepts*. Specifically, the first five chapters of the text cover basic descriptive statistics, including ways of representing data graphically, statistical measures which describe a set of data, the normal distribution and other types of standard scores, and an introduction to probability and sampling. The remainder of the text covers different inferential statistics, dealing with different inferential tests involving means (e.g., *t* tests), proportions, variances, and correlations.

This text also communicates a *conceptual, intuitive* understanding of statistics, which requires only a rudimentary knowledge of basic algebra, and emphasizes the important concepts in statistics. The most effective way to learn statistics is through the conceptual approach. Statistical concepts tend to be easy to learn because (a) concepts can be simply stated, (b) concepts can be made relevant through the use of real-life examples, (c) the same concepts are shared by many procedures, and (d) concepts can be related to one another. This is not to say that the text is void of mathematics, as understanding the math behind the technique blows apart the "black box" of statistics, particularly in a world where statistical software is so incredibly powerful. However, understanding the concepts is the first step in advancing toward a true understanding of statistics.

This text will help you to reach the goal of being a better consumer and producer of research. The following indicators may provide some feedback as to how you are doing. First, there will be a noticeable change in your attitude toward statistics. Thus, one outcome is for you to feel that "Statistics is not half bad" or "This stuff is OK." Second, you will feel comfortable using statistics in your own work. Finally, you will begin to "see the light." You will know when you have reached this highest stage of statistics development when suddenly in the middle of the night you wake up from a dream and say, "Now I get it!" In other words, you will begin to *think* statistics rather than think of ways to get out of doing statistics.

Pedagogical Tools

The text contains several important pedagogical features to allow you to attain these goals. First, each chapter begins with a list of key concepts, which provide helpful landmarks within the chapter. Second, realistic examples from education and the behavioral sciences are used to illustrate the concepts and procedures covered in each chapter. Each example includes an initial vignette, an examination of the relevant procedures and necessary assumptions, how to run SPSS and **R** and develop an APA-style write-up, as well as tables, figures, and annotated SPSS and **R** output to assist you. Third, the text is based on the conceptual approach; that is, material is presented so that you obtain a good understanding of statistical concepts. *If you know the concepts, then you know statistics.* Finally, each chapter ends with three sets of problems—computational, conceptual, and interpretive.

Pay particular attention to the conceptual problems as they provide the best assessment of your understanding of the concepts in the chapter. We strongly suggest using the example datasets and the computational and interpretive problems for additional practice through available statistical software. This will serve to reinforce the concepts covered. Answers to the odd-numbered problems are given at the end of each chapter.

Important Features in This Edition

As noted previously, this text represents the first 10 chapters of *An Introduction to Statistical Concepts*, which is now in its fourth edition. A number of changes were made to the fourth edition text of the text based on the suggestions of reviewers, instructors, teaching assistants, and students, and these are now reflected in *Statistical Concepts: A First Course*. These improvements have been made in order to better achieve the goals of the text. The changes applicable to the chapters in the *First Course* text include the following:

1. The content has been updated and numerous additional references have been provided.
2. To parallel the generation of statistics using SPSS (version 25), script and annotated output using **R** have been included to assist in the generation and interpretation of statistics.
3. Coverage of effect sizes has been expanded, including the use of online tools for computing effect sizes and their confidence intervals.
4. More organizational features (e.g., boxes, tables, figures) have been included to summarize concepts and/or assist in increasing understanding of the material.
5. Additional end-of-chapter problems (conceptual, computational, and interpretive) have been included.
6. A website for the text provides instructor-only access to a test bank (the website continues to offer the datasets, chapter outline, answers to the even-numbered problems, and PowerPoint slides for each chapter, with students granted access to the appropriate elements).

Acknowledgments

We have been blessed beyond measure, and are thankful for so many individuals who have played an important role in our personal and professional lives and, in some way, have shaped this text. Rather than include an admittedly incomplete listing, we just say "thank you" to all of you. A special thank you to all of the terrific students that we have had the pleasure of teaching at the University of Pittsburgh, the University of Illinois at Chicago, Louisiana State University, Boston College, Northern Illinois University, the University of Alabama, The Ohio State University, and the University of Central Florida. For all of your efforts, and the many lights that you have seen and shared with us, this book is for you.

Thanks also to so many wonderful publishing staff that we've had the pleasure of working along the way, first at Lawrence Erlbaum Associates and now at Routledge/Taylor & Francis. Additionally, we are most appreciative of the insightful suggestions provided by the reviewers of this text over the years.

For the users of this text, *you are the reason we write*. Thank you for bringing us along in your research and statistical journey. To those that have contacted us with questions, comments, and suggestions on previous editions of *An Introduction to Statistical Concepts* (the original text from which *Statistical Concepts: A First Course* text was spawned), we are very appreciative. We hope that you will continue to contact us to offer feedback (good and bad).

Last but not least, we extend gratitude to our families, in particular, to Lea and Kristen, and to Mark and Malani. Your unfailing love, understanding, and tolerance during the writing of this text allowed us to cope with such a major project. *You are statistically significant!* Thank you one and all.

DLHV & RGL

Acknowledgments

1

Introduction

Key Concepts

1. *General statistical concepts*

   Population

   Parameter

   Sample

   Statistic

   Descriptive statistics

   Inferential statistics

2. *Variable-related concepts*

   Variable

   Constant

   Categorical variables

   Dichotomous variables

Numerical variables

Discrete variables

Continuous variables

3. *Measurement scale concepts*

Measurement

Nominal scale

Ordinal scale

Interval scale

Ratio scale

Welcome to the wonderful world of statistics! More than ever, statistics are everywhere. Listen to the weather report and you hear about the measurement of variables such as temperature, rainfall, barometric pressure, and humidity. Watch a sporting event and you hear about batting averages, percentage of free throws completed, and total rushing yardage. Read the financial page and you can track the Dow Jones average, the gross national product (GNP), and bank interest rates. Turn to the entertainment section to see movie ratings, movie revenue, or the top 10 best-selling novels. These are just a few examples of statistics that surround you in every aspect of your life. This is not to mention the way statistics have, probably unnoticeably, influenced our everyday lives—just consider the impact that statistics have had the next time you buckle your seatbelt or help a child into their booster seat.

Although you may be thinking that statistics is not the most enjoyable subject on the planet, by the end of this text you will (a) have a more positive attitude about statistics; (b) feel more comfortable using statistics, and thus be more likely to perform your own quantitative data analyses; and (c) certainly know much more about statistics than you do now. In other words, our goal is to equip you with the skills you need to be both a better consumer and producer of research. But be forewarned; the road to statistical independence is not easy. However, we will serve as your guides along the way. When the going gets tough, we will be there to provide you with advice and numerous examples and problems. Using the powers of logic, mathematical reasoning, and statistical concept knowledge, we will help you arrive at an appropriate solution to the statistical problem at hand.

Some students begin statistics courses with some anxiety, or even much anxiety. This could be the result of not having had a quantitative course for some time, apprehension built up by delaying taking statistics, a poor past instructor or course, or less than adequate past success, among other possible reasons. We hope this text will help alleviate any anxiety you may have. This is a good segue to discuss what this text is and what it is not. First, this is not a textbook on only one statistical procedure. This is a text on the application of *many different types of statistics* to a variety of disciplines. If you are looking for a text that goes very deep and into the weeds, so to speak, into just one area of statistics, then please review the Additional Resources sections at the conclusion of the respective chapters of interest. Although we feel we have provided a very comprehensive overview of and introduction into many types of statistics that are covered in the first few statistics courses, we do not pretend to suggest that everything you need to know about any one procedure will be covered in our book. Indeed, we do not know of any text that can make that claim! We do anticipate you will find the text is an excellent starting point, and should you desire to delve deeper, we have offered resources to assist in that endeavor.

Second, the philosophy of the text is on the *understanding of concepts* rather than on the derivation of statistical formulas. In other words, this is not a mathematical statistics textbook. We have written the book with the perspective that it is more important to understand concepts than to solve theorems and derive or memorize various and sundry formulas. If you understand the concepts, you can always look up the formulas if need be. If you do not understand the concepts, then knowing the formulas will only allow you to operate in a cookbook mode without really understanding what you are doing.

Third, the calculator and computer are your friends. These devices are tools that allow you to complete the necessary computations and obtain the results of interest. There is no need to compute equations by hand (another reason why we concentrate on the concepts rather than formulas). If you are performing computations by hand, find a calculator that you are comfortable with; it need not have 800 functions, as the four basic operations, sum, and square root functions are sufficient (one of our personal calculators is one of those little credit card calculators, although we often use the calculator on our computers). If you are using a statistical software program, find one that you are comfortable with (most instructors will have you use a program such as **R**, SPSS, or SAS). In this text, we do walk through basic formulas by hand so that you become acquainted with how the statistical program works and the numbers that are used in it. However, we don't anticipate (nor do we encourage) that you make a practice of working statistics by hand. Throughout the text, we use SPSS and **R** to illustrate statistical applications. Although this book is *not* a guide on all things SPSS and **R**, we do try to provide the tools you need to compute the various statistics. We hope that you will supplement what we provide with your own motivation to learn more about software that can assist you in computing statistics.

Finally, this text will take you from raw data to results using realistic examples. The examples may not always be from a discipline that is like the one you are in, but we hope that you are able to transfer or generalize the illustration to an area in which you more comfortable. These examples can then be followed up using the problems at the end of each chapter. Thus, you will not be on your own, but will have the text, a computer/calculator, as well as your course and instructor, to help guide you.

The intent and philosophy of this text is to be conceptual and intuitive in nature. We have written the text so that students who have completed basic mathematical requirements in high school can be comfortable reading the text. Thus, the text does not require a high level of mathematics, but rather emphasizes the important concepts in statistics. Most statistical concepts really are fairly easy to learn because (a) concepts can be simply stated, (b) concepts can be related to real-life examples, (c) many of the same concepts run through much of statistics, and therefore (d) many concepts can be related.

In this introductory chapter, we describe the most basic statistical concepts. We begin with the question, "What is the value of statistics?" We then look at a brief history of statistics by mentioning a few of the more important and interesting statisticians. Then we consider the concepts of population, parameter, sample, statistic, descriptive and inferential statistics, types of variables, and scales of measurement. Our objectives are that by the end of this chapter you will (a) have a better sense of why statistics are necessary, (b) see that statisticians are an interesting group of people, and (c) have an understanding of several basic statistical concepts.

1.1 What Is the Value of Statistics?

Let us start off with a reasonable rhetorical question: "Why do we need statistics?" In other words, what is the value of statistics, either in your research or in your everyday life? As a way of thinking about these questions, consider the following headlines, which have probably appeared in your local newspaper.

Cigarette Smoking Causes Cancer—Tobacco Industry Denies Charges

A study conducted at Ivy-Covered University Medical School recently published in the *New England Journal of Medicine* has definitively shown that cigarette smoking causes cancer. In interviews with 100 randomly selected smokers and nonsmokers over 50 years of age, 30% of the smokers have developed some form of cancer, while only 10% of the nonsmokers have cancer. "The higher percentage of smokers with cancer in our study clearly indicates that cigarettes cause cancer," said Dr. Jason P. Smythe. On the contrary, "this study doesn't even suggest that cigarettes cause cancer," said tobacco lobbyist Cecil B. Hacker. "Who knows how these folks got cancer; maybe it is caused by the aging process or by the method in which individuals were selected for the interviews," Mr. Hacker went on to say.

North Carolina Congressional Districts Gerrymandered—African Americans Slighted

A study conducted at the National Center for Legal Research indicates that congressional districts in the state of North Carolina have been gerrymandered to minimize the impact of the African American vote. "From our research, it is clear that the districts are apportioned in a racially biased fashion. Otherwise, how could there be no single district in the entire state which has a majority of African American citizens when over 50% of the state's population is African American? The districting system absolutely has to be changed," said Dr. I. M. Researcher. A spokesman for the American Bar Association countered with the statement, "according to a decision rendered by the U.S. Supreme Court in 1999 (No. 98–85), intent or motive must be shown for racial bias to be shown in the creation of congressional districts. The decision states a 'facially neutral law . . . warrants strict scrutiny only if it can be proved that the law was motivated by a racial purpose or object.' The data in this study do not show intent or motive. To imply that these data indicate racial bias is preposterous."

Global Warming—Myth According to the President

Research conducted at the National Center for Global Warming (NCGW) has shown the negative consequences of global warming on the planet Earth. As summarized by Dr. Noble Pryze, "our studies at NCGW clearly demonstrate that if global warming is not halted in the next 20 years, the effects on all aspects of our environment and climatology will be catastrophic." A different view is held by U.S. President Harold W. Tree. He stated in a recent address that "the scientific community has not convinced him that global warming even exists. Why should our administration spend millions of dollars on an issue that has not been shown to be a real concern?"

How is one to make sense of the studies described by these headlines? How is one to decide which side of the issue these data support, so as to take an intellectual stand? In other words, do the interview data clearly indicate that cigarette smoking causes cancer? Do the congressional district percentages of African Americans necessarily imply that there is racial bias? Have scientists convinced us that global warming is a problem? These studies are examples of situations where the appropriate use of statistics is clearly necessary. *Statistics will provide us with an intellectually acceptable method for making decisions in such matters*. For instance, a certain type of research, statistical analysis, and set of results are all necessary to make causal inferences about cigarette smoking. Another type of research, statistical analysis, and set of results are all necessary to lead one to confidently state that the districting system is racially biased or not, or that global warming needs to be dealt with. *The bottom line is that the purpose of statistics, and thus of this text, is to provide you with the tools to make important decisions in an appropriate and confident manner using data.* W. Edwards Deming has been credited with bringing quality to manufacturing (e.g., Gabor, 1990), and he once stated, "In God we trust. All others must have data." These are words to live by! After reading this text, you will not have to trust a statement made by some so-called expert on an issue, which may or may not have any empirical basis or validity; you can make your own judgments based on the statistical analyses of data. For you, the value of statistics can include (a) the ability to read and critique articles in both professional journals and in the popular press, and (b) the ability to conduct statistical analyses for your own research (e.g., thesis or dissertation). We hope that this text will guide you in becoming both a better consumer and better producer of statistics. You are gaining skills that you can use to make a contribution to your field and, more important, make the world a better place. The statistical skills you are gaining through this text are powerful. Use them—wisely!

1.2 Brief Introduction to the History of Statistics

As a way of getting to know the topic of statistics, we want to briefly introduce you to a few famous statisticians. The purpose of this section is not to provide a comprehensive history of statistics, as those already exist (e.g., Heyde, Seneta, Crepel, Feinberg, & Gain, 2001; Pearson, 1978; Stigler, 1986). Rather, the purpose of this section is to show that famous statisticians are not only interesting, but are human beings just like you and me.

One of the fathers of probability (see Chapter 5) is acknowledged to be Blaise Pascal from the late 1600s. One of Pascal's contributions was that he worked out the probabilities for each dice roll in the game of craps, enabling his friend, a member of royalty, to become a consistent winner. He also developed Pascal's triangle, which you may remember from your early mathematics education. The statistical development of the normal or bell-shaped curve (see Chapter 4) is interesting. For many years, this development was attributed to Karl Friedrich Gauss (early 1800s), and was actually known for some time as the Gaussian curve. Later historians found that Abraham DeMoivre actually developed the normal curve in the 1730s. As statistics was not thought of as a true academic discipline until the late 1800s, people like Pascal and DeMoivre were consulted by the wealthy on odds about games of chance and by insurance underwriters to determine mortality rates.

Karl Pearson is one of the most famous statisticians to date (late 1800s to early 1900s). Among his many accomplishments is the Pearson product-moment correlation coefficient still in use today (see Chapter 10). You may know of Florence Nightingale (1820–1910) as an important figure in the field of nursing. However, you may not know of her importance in the field of statistics. Nightingale believed that statistics and theology were linked and that by studying statistics we might come to understand God's laws.

A quite interesting statistical personality is William Sealy Gossett, who was employed by the Guinness Brewery in Ireland. The brewery wanted to select a sample of people from Dublin in 1906 for purposes of taste testing. Gossett was asked how large a sample was needed in order to make an accurate inference about the entire population (see next section). The brewery would not let Gossett publish any of his findings under his own name, so he used the pseudonym of Student. Today the *t* distribution is still known as Student's *t* distribution. Sir Ronald A. Fisher is another of the most famous statisticians of all time. Working in the early 1900s Fisher introduced the analysis of variance (see Chapters 11–16) and Fisher's *z* transformation for correlations (see Chapter 10). In fact, the major statistic in the analysis of variance is referred to as the *F* ratio in honor of Fisher. These individuals represent only a fraction of the many famous and interesting statisticians over the years. For further information about these and other statisticians, we suggest you consult the references noted previously (e.g., Heyde et al., 2001; Pearson, 1978; Stigler, 1986), which provide many interesting stories about statisticians.

1.3 General Statistical Definitions

In this section we define some of the most basic concepts in statistics. Included here are definitions and examples of the following concepts: population, parameter, sample, statistic, descriptive statistics, and inferential statistics.

The first four concepts are tied together, so we discuss them together. A **population** is defined as *all members of a well-defined group*. A population may be large in scope, such as when a population is defined as all of the employees of IBM worldwide. A population may be small in scope, such as when a population is defined as all of the IBM employees at the building on Main Street in Atlanta. *The key is that the population is well defined* such that one could determine specifically who all of the members of the group are and then information or data could be collected from all such members. Thus, if our population is defined as all members working in a particular office building, then our study would consist of collecting data from all employees in that building. It is also important to remember that *you*, the researcher, define the population.

A **parameter** is defined as a *characteristic of a population*. For instance, parameters of our office building example might be the number of individuals who work in that building (e.g., 154), the average salary of those individuals (e.g., $49,569), and the range of ages of those individuals (e.g., 21 to 68 years of age). When we think about characteristics of a population we are thinking about **population parameters**. The two terms are often linked together.

A **sample** is defined as a *subset of a population*. A sample may be large in scope, such as when a population is defined as all of the employees of IBM worldwide and 20% of those individuals are included in the sample. A sample may be small in scope, such as when a population is defined as all of the IBM employees at the building on Main Street in Atlanta and 10% of those individuals are included in the sample. Thus, a sample could be large or small in scope and consist of any portion of the population. *The key is that the sample consists of some, but not all, of the members of the population;* that is, anywhere from one individual to all but one individual from the population is included in the sample. Thus, if our population is defined as all members working in the IBM building on Main Street in Atlanta, then our study would consist of collecting data from a sample of some of the employees in that building. It follows that if we, the researchers, define the population, then we also determine what the sample will be.

A **statistic** is defined as a *characteristic of a sample*. For instance, statistics of our office building example might be the number of individuals who work in the building that we sampled (e.g., 77), the average salary of those individuals (e.g., $54,022), and the range of ages of those individuals (e.g., 25 to 62 years of age). Notice that the statistics of a sample need not be equal to the parameters of a population (more about this in Chapter 5). When we think about characteristics of a sample we are thinking about **sample statistics**. The two terms are often linked together. Thus, we have *population parameters* and *sample statistics*, but no other combinations of those terms exist. The field has become known as "statistics" simply because we are almost always dealing with sample statistics because population data are rarely obtained.

The final two concepts are also tied together, and thus are considered together. The field of statistics is generally divided into two types of statistics: descriptive and inferential. **Descriptive statistics** are defined as *techniques that allow us to tabulate, summarize, and depict a collection of data in an abbreviated fashion.* In other words, the purpose of descriptive statistics is to allow us to talk about (or describe) a collection of data without having to look at the entire collection. For example, say we have just collected a set of data from 100,000 graduate students on various characteristics (e.g., height, weight, gender, grade point average, aptitude test scores). If you were to ask us about the data, we could do one of two things. On the one hand, we could carry around the entire collection of data everywhere we go and when someone asks us about the data simply say, "Here is the data; take a look at them yourself." On the other hand, we could summarize the data in an abbreviated fashion and when someone asks us about the data simply say, "Here is a table and a graph about the data; they summarize the entire collection." So, rather than viewing 100,000 sheets of paper, perhaps we would only have to view two sheets of paper. Because statistics is largely a system of communicating information, descriptive statistics are considerably more useful to a consumer than an entire collection of data. Descriptive statistics are discussed in Chapters 2 through 4.

Inferential statistics are defined as *techniques that allow us to employ inductive reasoning to infer the properties of an entire group or collection of individuals, a population, from a small number of those individuals, a sample.* In other words, the purpose of inferential statistics is to allow us to collect data from a sample of individuals and then infer the properties of that sample back to the population of individuals. In case you have forgotten about logic, inductive reasoning is where you infer from the specific (here the sample) to the general (here the population). For example, say we have just collected a set of sample data from 5000 of the population of 100,000 graduate students on various characteristics (e.g., height, weight, gender, grade point average, aptitude test scores). If you were to ask us about the data, we could compute various sample statistics and then infer with some confidence that these would be similar to the population parameters. In other words, this allows us to collect data from a subset of the population, yet still make inferential statements about the population without collecting data from the entire population. So, rather than collecting data from all 100,000 graduate students in the population, we could collect data on a sample of say 5000 students.

As another example, Gossett (aka Student) was asked to conduct a taste test of Guinness beer for a sample of Dublin residents. Because the brewery could not afford to do this with the entire population of Dublin, Gossett collected data from a sample of Dublin and was able to make an inference from these sample results back to the population. A discussion of inferential statistics begins in Chapter 5. In summary, the field of statistics is roughly divided into descriptive statistics and inferential statistics. Note, however, that many further distinctions are made among the types of statistics, but more about that later.

1.3.1 Statistical Notation

Statistics can be denoted in words or in symbols. Statistical notation that refers to the *population* uses Greek symbols. Statistical notation that refers to the *sample* uses upper- and lowercase letters. Table 1.1 provides a handy reference for the upper and lowercase Greek

TABLE 1.1

Statistical Notation

Greek Alphabet			
Uppercase Letter	**Lowercase Letter**	**Symbol Name**	**Definition and/or What the Symbol Denotes**
A	α	Alpha	Type I error rate (also known as level of significance or significance level)
B	β	Beta	Type II error rate; regression coefficient
Γ	γ	Gamma	Correlation coefficient for ordinal data
Δ	δ	Delta	Standardized effect size
E	ε	Epsilon	Random residual error
Z	ζ	Zeta	Discrete probability distribution
H	η	Eta	When squared, a proportion of variance explained effect size
Θ	θ	Theta	General population parameter
I	ι	Iota	
K	κ	Kappa	A measure of interrater reliability (as in Cohen's kappa)
Λ	λ	Lambda	Probability distribution (as in Wilks' lambda)
M	μ	Mu	Mean
N	ν	Nu	Degrees of freedom
Ξ	ξ	Xi	
O	ο	Omicron	
Π	π	Pi	Population proportion
P	ρ	Rho	Population correlation coefficient
Σ	σ	Sigma	Population standard deviation
T	τ	Tau	Correlation coefficient for ordinal data (as in Kendall's tau); in multilevel modeling, the intercept variance
Υ	υ	Upsilon	Effect size for mediation models
Φ	φ, φ	Phi	Correlation coefficient for binary variables
X	χ	Chi	When squared, a probability distribution
Ψ	ψ	Psi	
Ω	ω	Omega	When squared, a proportion of variance explained effect size
Select Additional Notation			
N	ν		Population and sample size, respectively
	π		Observed probability
	ρ		Sample correlation coefficient
	σ		Sample standard deviation
	τ		Student's *t*
$\overline{X}$		X bar	Sample mean

alphabet, the name of the symbol, and how the symbol is commonly used in statistics. The table also includes additional notation commonly used to denote statistics. We will use many of these symbols throughout the text. This table is provided with a caveat. Unfortunately, statistical notation is not standardized. Should you pick up a different text, it's likely that the authors have used at least some different notation than what has been used in this text. (Argh! How frustrating, right?) Thus, throughout the text we have attempted to clearly indicate what the notation means as it is used.

1.4 Types of Variables

There are several terms we need to define about variables. First, it might be useful to define the term variable. A **variable** is defined as *any characteristic of persons or things that is observed to take on different values*. In other words, the values for a particular characteristic vary across the individuals observed. For example, the annual salary of the families in your neighborhood varies because not every family earns the same annual salary. One family might earn $50,000 while the family right next door might earn $65,000. Thus, the annual family salary is a *variable* because it *varies* across families.

In contrast, a **constant** is defined as *any characteristic of persons or things that is observed to take on only a single value*. In other words, the values for a particular characteristic are the *same* for all individuals or units observed. For example, say every family in your neighborhood has a lawn. Although the nature of the lawns may vary, everyone has a lawn. Thus, whether a family has a lawn in your neighborhood is a constant and therefore would not be a very interesting characteristic to study. *When designing a study, you (i.e., the researcher) can determine what is a constant.* This is part of the process of *delimiting,* or narrowing the scope of, your study. As an example, you may be interested in studying career paths of girls who complete AP science courses. In designing your study, you are only interested in girls, and thus sex would be a constant—you would be delimiting your study to girls. This is not to say that the researcher wholly determines when a characteristic is a constant. It is sometimes the case that we find that a characteristic is a constant *after* we conduct the study. In other words, one of the measures has no variation—everyone or everything scored or remained the same on that particular characteristic.

A number of different typologies are available for describing variables. One typology is categorical (or qualitative) versus numerical (or quantitative), and within numerical, discrete and continuous. A **categorical variable** is a *qualitative variable that describes categories of a characteristic or attribute*. Examples of categorical variables include political party affiliation (Republican = 1, Democrat = 2, Independent = 3), religious affiliation (e.g., Methodist = 1, Baptist = 2, Roman Catholic = 3, etc.), and course letter grade (A = 4, B = 3, C = 2, D = 1, F = 0). A **dichotomous variable** (also known as a *binary variable*) is a special, restricted type of categorical variable and is defined as a *variable that can take on only one of two values*. For example, sex at birth is a variable that can take on the values of male or female and is often coded numerically as 0 (e.g., for males) or 1 (e.g., for females). Other dichotomous variables include pass/fail, true/false, living/dead, and smoker/non-smoker. Dichotomous variables will take on special importance if you later study binary logistic regression.

A **numerical variable** is a quantitative variable. Numerical variables can further be classified as either discrete or continuous. A **discrete variable** is defined as a *variable that can only take on certain values*. For example, the number of children in a family can only take on certain values. Many values are not possible, such as negative values (e.g., the Joneses cannot have –2 children) or decimal values (e.g., the Smiths cannot have 2.2 children). In contrast, a **continuous variable** is defined as a *variable that can take on any value within a certain range, given a precise enough measurement instrument*. For example, the distance between two cities can be measured in miles, with miles estimated in whole numbers. However, given a more precise instrument with which to measure, distance can even be measured down to the inch or millimeter. When considering the difference between a discrete and continuous variable, keep in mind that *discrete variables arise from the counting process* and *continuous variables arise from the measuring process*. For example, the number of students enrolled in your statistics class is a discrete variable. If we were to measure (i.e., count) the number of students in the class, it would not matter if we counted first names alphabetically from A to Z or if we counted beginning with the person sitting in the front row to the last person sitting in the back row—either way, we would arrive at the same value. In other words, how we "measure" (again, in this instance, how we count) the students in the class does not matter—we will always arrive at the same result. In comparison, the value of a continuous variable is dependent on how precise the measuring instrument is. Weighing yourself on a scale that rounds to whole numbers will give us one measure of weight. However weighing on another, more precise, scale that rounds to three decimal places will provide a more precise measure of weight.

Here are a few additional examples. Other discrete variables include number of books owned, number of credit hours enrolled, and number of teachers employed at a school. Other continuous variables include salary (from zero to billions in dollars and cents), age (from zero up, in millisecond increments), height (from zero up, in increments of fractions of millimeters), weight (from zero up, in increments of fractions of ounces), and time (from zero up, in millisecond increments). Variable type is a very important concept in terms of selecting an appropriate statistic, as will be shown later.

1.5 Scales of Measurement

Another concept useful for selecting an appropriate statistic is the scale of measurement of the variables. First, however, we define **measurement** as the *assignment of numerical values to persons or things according to explicit rules*. For example, how do we measure a person's weight? Well, there are rules that individuals commonly follow. Currently weight is measured on some sort of balance or scale in pounds or grams. In the old days weight was measured by different rules, such as the number of stones or gold coins. These explicit rules were developed so that there was a standardized and generally agreed upon method of measuring weight. Thus, if you weighted 10 stones in Coventry, England, then that meant the same as 10 stones in Liverpool, England.

In 1951 the psychologist S.S. Stevens developed four types of measurement scales that could be used for assigning these numerical values. In other words, the type of rule used was related to the measurement scale. The four types of measurement scales are the nominal, ordinal, interval, and ratio scales. They are presented in order of increasing complexity (i.e., *nominal is the simplest* and *ratio is the most complex*) and of increasing information (i.e., *nominal provides the least information* and *ratio provides the most information*) (remembering the mnemonic NOIR might be helpful). It is worth restating the importance of understanding the measurement scales of variables as the measurement scale will dictate what statistical procedures can be performed with the data. While we recommend approaching your analysis by first defining your research question *and then* determining the requisite data and statistical procedure needed, Figures 1.1 and 1.2 may be helpful in understanding how a variable's measurement scale relates to some of the more basic statistical procedures.

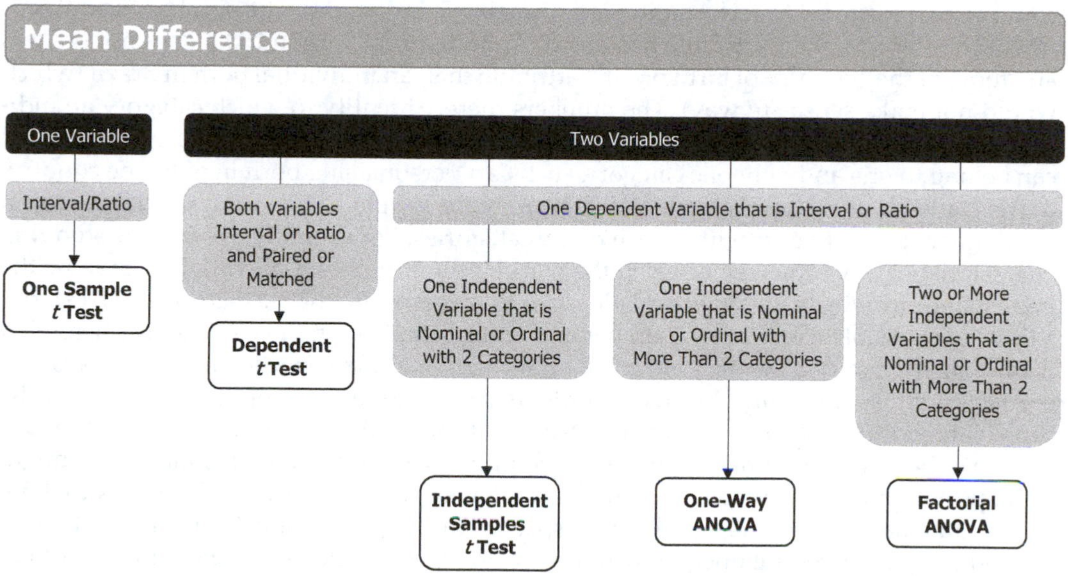

FIGURE 1.1
Flow chart for mean difference tests.

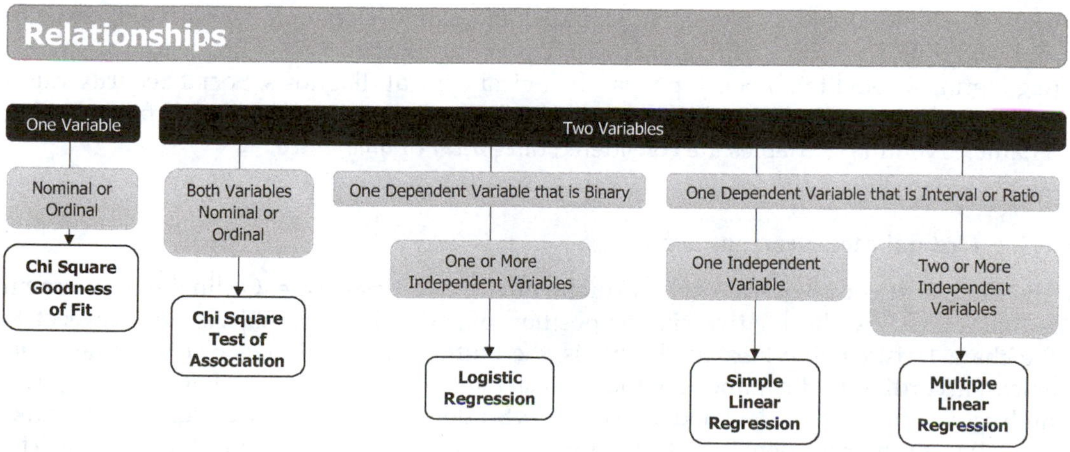

FIGURE 1.2
Flow chart for relationship tests.

1.5.1 Nominal Measurement Scale

The simplest scale of measurement is the **nominal scale**. Here, the units (e.g., individuals or objects) are classified into categories so that all of those in a single category are equivalent with respect to the characteristic being measured. For example, the country of birth of an individual is a nominally scaled variable. Everyone born in France is equivalent with respect to this variable, whereas two people born in different countries (e.g., France and Australia) are not equivalent with respect to this variable. The categories are truly qualitative in nature, not quantitative. Categories are typically given names or numbers. For our example, the country name would be an obvious choice for categories, although numbers could also be assigned to each country (e.g., Brazil = 5, India = 34). The numbers do not represent the amount of the attribute possessed. An individual born in India does not possess any more of the "country of birth origin" attribute than an individual born in Brazil (which would not make sense anyway). The numbers merely identify to which category an individual or object belongs. The categories are also *mutually exclusive*; that is, an individual can belong to one and only one category, such as a person being born in only one country.

The statistics of a nominal scale variable are quite simple as they can only be based on the frequencies that occur within each of the categories. For example, we may be studying characteristics of various countries in the world. A nominally scaled variable could be the hemisphere in which the country is located (Northern, Southern, Eastern, or Western). While it is possible to count the number of countries that belong to each hemisphere, that is all that we can do. *The only mathematical property that the nominal scale possesses is that of equality versus inequality.* In other words, two individuals or objects are either in the same category (equal) or in different categories (unequal). For the hemisphere variable, we can either use the country name or assign numerical values to each country. We might perhaps assign each hemisphere a number alphabetically from 1 to 4. Countries that are in the same hemisphere are equal with respect to this characteristic. Countries that are in different hemispheres are unequal with respect to this characteristic. Again, these particular numerical values are meaningless and could arbitrarily be any values. The numerical values assigned only serve to keep the categories distinct from one another. Many other numerical values could be assigned for the hemispheres and still maintain the equality versus inequality property. For example, the Northern hemisphere could easily be categorized as 1000 and the Southern hemisphere as 2000 with no change in information. Other examples of nominal-scale variables include hair color, eye color, neighborhood, sex, ethnic background, religious affiliation, political party affiliation, type of life insurance owned (e.g., term, whole life), blood type, psychological clinical diagnosis, Social Security number, and type of headache medication prescribed. The term *nominal* is derived from "giving a name." Nominal variables are considered *categorical* or *qualitative*.

1.5.2 Ordinal Measurement Scale

The next most complex scale of measurement is the **ordinal scale**. Ordinal measurement is determined by the relative size or position of individuals or objects with respect to the characteristic being measured. That is, the units (e.g., individuals or objects) are *rank ordered* according to the amount of the characteristic that they possess. For example, say a high school graduating class had 250 students. Students could then be assigned class ranks according to their academic performance (e.g., grade point average) in high school. The student ranked 1 in the class had the highest relative performance and the student ranked 250 had the lowest relative performance.

However, equal differences between the ranks do not imply equal distance in terms of the characteristic being measured. For example, the students ranked 1 and 2 in the class may have a different distance in terms of actual academic performance than the students ranked 249 and 250, even though both pairs of students differ by a rank of 1. In other words, here a rank difference of 1 does not imply the same actual performance distance. The pairs of students may be very, very close or may be quite distant from one another. As a result of *equal differences* not implying *equal distances*, the statistics that we can use are limited due to these unequal intervals. *The ordinal scale then, consists of two mathematical properties: equality versus inequality; and if two individuals or objects are unequal, then we can determine greater than or less than.* That is, if two individuals have different class ranks, then we can determine which student had a greater or lesser class rank. Although the greater than or less than property is evident, an ordinal scale cannot tell us how much greater than or less than because of the unequal intervals. Thus, the student ranked 250 could be farther away from student 249 than the student ranked 2 from student 1.

When we have *untied ranks*, as shown on the left side of Table 1.2, assigning ranks is straightforward. What do we do if there are *tied ranks*? For example, suppose there are two students with the same grade point average of 3.8 as given on the right side of Table 1.1. How do we assign them into class ranks? It is clear that they have to be assigned the same rank, as that would be the only fair method. However, there are at least two methods for dealing with tied ranks. One method would be to assign each of them a rank of 2, as that is the next available rank. However, this method has two problems. First, the sum of the ranks for the same number of scores would be different depending on whether there were ties or not. Statistically, this is not a satisfactory solution. Second, what rank would the next student having the 3.6 grade point average be given, a rank of 3 or 4?

The second and preferred method is to take the average of the available ranks and assign that value to each of the tied individuals. Thus, the two persons tied at a grade point average of 3.8 have as available ranks 2 and 3. Both would then be assigned the average rank of 2.5. Also the three persons tied at a grade point average of 3.0 have as available ranks 5, 6, and 7. These all would be assigned the average rank of 6. You also see in the table that with this method the sum of the ranks for 7 scores is always equal to 28, regardless of the number of ties. Statistically this is a satisfactory solution and the one we prefer whether we are using a statistical software package or hand computations. Other examples of ordinal scale variables include course letter grades (e.g., A, B, C, . . .), order of finish in the Boston Marathon (e.g., 1st, 2nd, 3rd, . . .), socioeconomic status (e.g., low, middle, high), hardness of minerals (1 = softest to 10 = hardest), faculty rank (assistant, associate, and full professor), student class (freshman, sophomore, junior, senior, graduate student), ranking on a personality trait

TABLE 1.2

Untied Ranks and Tied Ranks for Ordinal Data

Untied Ranks		Tied Ranks	
Grade Point Average	Rank	Grade Point Average	Rank
4.0	1	4.0	1
3.9	2	3.8	2.5
3.8	3	3.8	2.5
3.6	4	3.6	4
3.2	5	3.0	6
3.0	6	3.0	6
2.7	7	3.0	6
	Sum = 28		Sum = 28

(e.g., extreme intrinsic to extreme extrinsic motivation), and military rank (e.g., E-1, E-2, E-3, . . .). The term *ordinal* is derived from "ordering" individuals or objects. Ordinal variables are most often considered *categorical* or *qualitative*. We say "most often" because ordinal items are sometimes considered quantitative. In our professional opinion, ordinal items are categorical or qualitative. However, researchers in some disciplines treat ordinal items as quantitative and use them as they would an interval or ratio variable (this won't make much sense yet, but it will soon). We strongly discourage that practice. The only exception may be a situation where an ordinal item has many categories or levels, such as more than 10. In those instances, treating an ordinal item as interval or ratio *may* make sense.

1.5.3 Interval Measurement Scale

The next most complex scale of measurement is the **interval scale**. An interval scale is one where units (e.g., individuals or objects) can be ordered, and equal differences between the values do imply equal distance in terms of the characteristic being measured. That is, *order and distance relationships are meaningful. However, there is no absolute zero point.* Absolute zero, if it exists, implies the total absence of the property being measured. The zero point of an interval scale, if it exists, is arbitrary and does not reflect the total absence of the property being measured. Here, the *zero point merely serves as a placeholder.* For example, suppose that we gave you the final exam in advanced statistics right now. If you were to be so unlucky as to obtain a score of 0, this score does not imply a total lack of knowledge of statistics. It would merely reflect the fact that your statistics knowledge is not that advanced yet (or perhaps the questions posed on the exam just did not capture those concepts that you do understand). You do have some knowledge of statistics, but just at an introductory level in terms of the topics covered so far. Take as an example the Fahrenheit temperature scale, which has a freezing point of 32 degrees. A temperature of zero is not the total absence of heat, just a point slightly colder than 1 degree and slightly warmer than –1 degree.

In terms of the *equal distance* notion, consider the following example. Say that we have two pairs of Fahrenheit temperatures, the first pair being 55 and 60 degrees and the second pair being 25 and 30 degrees. The difference of 5 degrees is the same for both pairs, and is also the same everywhere along the Fahrenheit scale if you are moving in 5 degree intervals. Thus, every 5-degree interval is an equal interval. However, we cannot say that 60 degrees is twice as warm as 30 degrees, as there is no absolute zero. In other words, *we cannot form true ratios of values* (i.e., 60/30 = 2). This property only exists for the ratio scale of measurement. The interval scale has the following mathematical properties: (a) equality versus inequality, (b) greater than or less than if unequal, and (c) equal intervals. Other examples of interval scale variables include the Celsius temperature scale, year (since 1 AD), and arguably, many educational and psychological assessments (both cognitive and noncognitive) (although statisticians have been debating this one for many years; for example, on occasion there is a fine line between whether an assessment is measured along the ordinal or the interval scale, as mentioned previously). Interval variables are considered *numerical* and primarily *continuous.*

1.5.4 Ratio Measurement Scale

The most complex scale of measurement is the **ratio scale**. *A ratio scale has all of the properties of the interval scale, plus an absolute zero point exists.* Here a measurement of 0 indicates a total absence of the property being measured. Due to an absolute zero point existing, true ratios of values can be formed that actually reflect ratios in the amounts of the characteristic being measured. Thus, if concepts such as "one-half as big" or "twice as large" make sense, then that may be a good indication that the variable is ratio in scale.

For example, the height of individuals measured in inches is a ratio-scale variable. There is an absolute zero point of zero height. We can also form ratios such that 6'0" Mark is twice as tall as his 3'0" daughter Malani. The ratio scale of measurement is not observed frequently in education and the behavioral sciences, with certain exceptions. Motor performance variables (e.g., speed in the 100-meter dash as measured in seconds, distance driven in 24 hours as measured in miles or kilometers), elapsed time measured in seconds, calorie consumption, and physiological characteristics (e.g., weight measured in pounds and ounces, height measured in inches, age measured in years and months, and blood pressure measured using a **sphygmomanometer)** are ratio-scale measures. These are all also examples of continuous variables. Discrete variables, those that arise from the counting process, are also examples of ratio variables, because zero indicates an absence of what is measured (e.g., the number of children in a family, the number of trees in a park, pulse rate measured as the number of beats per second). A summary of the measurement scales, their characteristics, and some examples are given in Table 1.3. Ratio variables are considered numerical and can be either discrete or continuous.

TABLE 1.3

Summary of the Scales of Measurement

Scale	Characteristics	Mathematical Property	Examples
Nominal	Classify into categories; categories are given names or numbers, but the numbers are arbitrary.	Equality versus inequality	Hair or eye color, ethnic background, neighborhood (e.g., subdivision name), sex, country of birth, Social Security number, type of life insurance, religious or political affiliation, blood type
Ordinal*	Rank-ordered according to relative size or position	Equality versus inequality Greater or less than if unequal	Letter grades (e.g., A, B, C), order of finish in race (e.g., 1st, 2nd, 3rd), class rank (e.g., freshman, sophomore, junior, senior), socioeconomic status (e.g., low, middle, high), hardness of minerals (e.g., Moh's scale of hardness, 1–10), faculty rank (e.g., assistant, associate, professor), military rank (e.g., E-7, E-8, etc.)
Interval*	Rank-ordered and equal differences between values imply equal distances in the attribute	Equality versus inequality Greater or less than if unequal Equal intervals	Temperature on Fahrenheit scale, most assessment devices (e.g., cognitive or psychological tests)
Ratio*	Rank-ordered, equal intervals, absolute zero allows ratios to be formed	Equality versus inequality Greater or less than if unequal Equal intervals Absolute zero	Speed in 100-meter dash measured in seconds, height measured in inches, weight measured in pounds and ounces, age measured in months, distance driven, elapsed time measured in seconds, pulse rate, blood pressure, calorie consumption

Note: The response scale for an ordinal, interval, or ratio variable can always be collapsed so that it takes on the properties of the measurement scale below it. For example, the responses for an ordinal variable can be collapsed into a binary variable, which then takes on the properties of a nominal variable. The values of an interval or ratio variable can be collapsed into an ordinal variable by grouping the values or further collapsed into a binary variable, which would then take on the properties of an ordinal variable. Takeaway tip: Look at the response scale of the variable before making judgment on the variable's measurement scale. Only then will you truly know the measurement scale.

1.5.5 Summary of Terms

We have defined a number of variable-related terms, including variable, constant, categorical variable, and continuous variable. For a summary of these definitions, see Box 1.1.

BOX 1.1 Summary of Definitions

Term	Definition	Example(s)
Categorical variable	A qualitative variable	Political party affiliation (e.g., Republican, Democrat, Independent)
Constant	Any characteristic of persons or things that is observed to take on only a single value	*Every* unit measured shares the characteristic (this could be any number of examples, but the key is that of all units that are measured, *all* units have the same value on what has been measured; e.g., consider a sample that includes only dancers from the American Ballet Theatre—asking whether the participant is a dancer would produce a constant as the only individuals in the sample are dancers)
Continuous variable	A numerical variable that can take on any value within a certain range, given a precise enough measurement instrument	Distance between two cities measured in miles
Descriptive statistics	Techniques that allow us to tabulate, summarize, and depict a collection of data in an abbreviated fashion	Table or graph summarizing data
Dichotomous variable	A categorical variable that can take on only one of two values	Sex at birth (male, female); questions that require a "yes" or "no" response
Discrete variable	A numerical variable that arises from the counting process that can take on only certain values	Number of children in a family (e.g., 0, 1, 2, 3, 4, . . .)
Inferential statistics	Techniques that allow us to employ inductive reasoning to infer the properties of a population from a sample	One-sample *t* test, independent *t* test, chi square test of association
Numerical variable	A quantitative variable that is either discrete or continuous	Number of children in a family (e.g., 0, 1, 2, 3, 4, . . .); the distance between two cities measured in miles
Parameter	A characteristic of a population	Average salary of a population of individuals
Population	All members of a well-defined group	*All* employees of a particular group
Sample	A subset of a population	*Some* employees of a particular group
Statistic	A characteristic of a sample	Average salary of a sample of individuals
Variable	Any characteristic of persons or things that is observed to take on different values	*Not every* unit measured shares the characteristic (this could be any number of examples, but the key is that of all units that are measured, at least *one* has a different measurement than the others in the sample)

1.6 Additional Resources

A number of excellent resources are available for learning statistics. Throughout the text, we will introduce you to many related to the respective topics for the concepts studied in the individual chapters. Here we offer recommendations for resources that are a bit more general in nature for learning, understanding, and appreciating statistics:

- Designed as a reference tool for manuscript and proposal reviewers, this is a great tool for researchers learning about statistics and wanting to learn more about quantitative data analysis (Hancock & Mueller, 2010)
- A resource that introduces readers to statistical concepts through verse, graphics, and text, with no equations (Keller, 2006)
- An edited text whose contributions from authors address statistical issues (e.g., mediation), methodological issues (e.g., qualitative research, sample size practices), and more (Lance & Vandenberg, 2009)
- Statistical misconceptions related to, among others, probability, estimation, hypothesis testing, ANOVA, and regression are discussed and discarded (Huck, 2016)
- A great additional resource that explains statistics in plain language (Huck, 2012)
- Common statistical conventions, ranging from sample size to bootstrapping to transformations and just about everything in between (Van Belle, 2002)
- A dictionary of statistics and related terms (Vogt, 2005)

Problems ~Go to main points & understand~

Conceptual Problems

1. A mental health counselor is conducting a research study on satisfaction that married couples have with their marriage. In this scenario, "Marital status" (e.g., single, married, divorced, widowed) is which of the following?
   a. Constant
   b. Variable

2. Belle randomly samples 100 library patrons and gathers data on the genre of the "first book" that they checked out from the library. She finds that 85 library patrons checked out a fiction book and 15 library patrons checked out a nonfiction book. Which of the following best characterizes the type of "first book" checked out in this study?
   a. Constant
   b. Variable

3. For interval-level variables, which of the following properties does *not* apply?
   a. A is two units greater than B.
   b. A is greater than B.
   c. A is twice as good as B.
   d. A differs from B.

4. Which of the following properties is appropriate for ordinal, but not for nominal variables?

    a. A differs from B.

    b. A is greater than B.

    c. A is 10 units greater than B.

    d. A is twice as good as B.

5. Which scale of measurement is implied by the following statement: "JoAnn's score is three times greater than Oscar's score?"

    a. Nominal

    b. Ordinal

    c. Interval

    d. Ratio

6. Which scale of measurement is produced by the following survey item: "Which season is your favorite, spring, summer, fall, or winter?"

    a. Nominal

    b. Ordinal

    c. Interval

    d. Ratio

7. A band director collects data on the number of years in which students in the band have played a musical instrument. Which scale of measurement is implied by this scenario?

    a. Nominal

    b. Ordinal

    c. Interval

    d. Ratio

8. Kristen has an IQ of 120. I assert that Kristen is 20% more intelligent than the average person having an IQ of 100. Am I correct?

9. True or false? Population is to parameter as sample is to statistic.

10. True or false? A dichotomous variable is also a categorical variable.

11. True or false? The amount of time spent studying in one week for a population of students is an inferential statistic.

12. A sample of 50 students take an exam and the instructor decides to give the top five scores a bonus of 5 points. Compared to the original set of scores (no bonus), will the ranks of the new set of scores (including the bonus) be exactly the same?

13. Malani and Laila have class ranks of 5 and 6. Ingrid and Toomas have class ranks of 55 and 56. Will the GPAs of Malani and Laila be the same distance apart as the GPAs of Ingrid and Toomas?

14. Aurora is studying sleep disorders in adults. She gathers data on whether they take medication to assist their sleep. Aurora finds that one-third of the adults take medication, and two-thirds do not. Which of the following best characterizes "whether or not medication is taken"?

    a. Constant

    b. Variable

15. A researcher has collected data that compares an intervention program to a comparison program. The researcher finds that the intervention program produces results that are four times better than the comparison program. Which measurement scale is implied and that will allow the researcher to make this type of interpretation? Select all that apply.

    a. Nominal

    b. Ordinal

    c. Interval

    d. Ratio

16. A researcher has access to 22 local health clinics that are part of a network of 56 health clinics in the state. The researcher conducts a study that includes the 22 regional health clinics. In this scenario, the 22 local health clinics are which of the following?

    a. Dichotomous

    b. Interval

    c. Sample

    d. Population

17. A researcher has access to 22 regional health clinics that are part of a network of 56 health clinics in the state. The researcher conducts a study that includes the 22 regional health clinics. In this scenario, the 56 health clinics in the state are which of the following?

    a. Dichotomous

    b. Interval

    c. Sample

    d. Population

18. Which of the following is an example of a dichotomous variable?

    a. Dance type (ballet, contemporary, jazz, lyrical, tap)

    b. Interest (no interest, somewhat interested, much interest)

    c. Total cost (measured in whole dollars ranging from $0 to infinity)

    d. Age (ages < 40 and ages 40+)

19. Which of the following is an example of an ordinal variable?

    a. Dance type (ballet, contemporary, jazz, lyrical, tap)

    b. Interest (no interest, somewhat interested, much interest)

    c. Total cost (measured in whole dollars ranging from $0 to infinity)

    d. Age (ages < 40 and ages 40+)

20. Which of the following is an example of a ratio variable?

    a. Scores on the Myers-Briggs Type Indicator (MBTI) personality inventory

    b. Number of pieces of cake eaten at birthday parties (measured in whole numbers)

    c. Pleasure experienced on vacation (none, some, much)

    d. Types of plants preferred by homeowners (bushes, flowers, grasses, trees)

Answers to Conceptual Problems

1. **a** (All individuals in the study are married, thus the marital status will be "married" for everyone participating; in other words, there is no variation in "marital status" for this particular scenario.)

3. **c** (True ratios cannot be formed with interval variables.)

5. **d** (True ratios can only be formed with ratio variables.)

7. **d** (An absolute value of zero would indicate an absence of what was measured—that is, the number of years playing in a band—and thus ratio is the scale of measure; although an answer of zero is not likely given that the students in the band are those being measured, *if* someone were to respond with an answer of zero, that value would truly indicate "no years playing an instrument.")

9. **True** (There are only population parameters and sample statistics; no other combinations exist.)

11. **False** (Given that this is a population parameter, no inference need be made.)

13. **No** (Class rank is ordinal, and equal intervals are not a characteristic of ordinal variables.)

15. **d** (Ratio variables will allow interpretations such as "four times greater" to be made from the data as they have equal intervals and a true zero point.)

17. **d** (The total population is 56.)

19. **b** (This is a three-point scale, ranked from least to greatest interest, thus it is ordinal; because we cannot tell the distance between each category, it is not interval.)

Computational Problems

1. Rank the following values of the number of books owned, assigning rank 1 to the largest value:

    10   15   12   8   20   17   5   21   3   19

2. Rank the following values of the number of credits earned, assigning rank 1 to the largest value:

    10   16   10   8   19   16   5   21   3   19

3. Rank the following values of the number of pairs of shoes owned, assigning rank 1 to the largest value:

    8   6   3   12   19   7   10   25   4   42

4. A researcher is assisting a colleague with data analysis from a survey. One of the questions asked respondents to indicate the frequency in which they laughed during an average day. In which order should the following responses be ranked, assuming this is an ordinal item and the researcher desires the frequency to be in ascending order?

    o 1–2 times

    o 9 or more times

    o 3–4 times

    o 5–6 times

    o Never

    o 7–8 times

Answers to Computational Problems

1.

Value	Rank
10	7
15	5
12	6
8	8
20	2
17	4
5	9
21	1
3	10
19	3

3.

Value	Rank
8	6
6	8
3	10
12	4
19	3
7	7
10	5
25	2
4	9
42	1

Interpretive Problems

1. Consider the following survey:
   a. What sex was listed on your birth certificate? Male or female?
   b. What is your height in inches?
   c. What is your shoe size (length)?
   d. Do you smoke cigarettes?
   e. Are you left- or right-handed?
   f. Is your mother left- or right-handed?
   g. Is your father left- or right-handed?
   h. How much did you spend at your last hair appointment (in whole dollars, including tip)?
   i. How many songs are downloaded on your phone?
   j. What is your current GPA on a 4.00 scale?
   k. What is your current GPA letter grade (e.g., B, B+, A−, A)?

l. On average, how much exercise do you get per week (in hours)?

m. On average, how much exercise do you get per week (no exercise; 1–2 hours; 3–4 hours, 5–6 hours, 7+ hours)?

n. On a 5-point scale, what is your political view (1 = very liberal, 3 = moderate, 5 = very conservative)?

o. On average, how many hours of TV do you watch per week?

p. How many cups of coffee did you drink yesterday?

q. How many hours did you sleep last night?

r. On average, how many alcoholic drinks do you have per week?

s. Can you tell the difference between Pepsi and Coke? Yes or no?

t. What is the natural color of your hair (black, blonde, brown, red, other)?

u. What is the natural color of your eyes (black, blue, brown, green, other)?

v. How far do you live from this campus (in miles)?

w. How far do you live from this campus (less than 10 miles; 10–70 miles, 71+ miles)?

x. On average, how many books do you read for pleasure each month?

y. On average, how many hours do you study per week?

z. On average, how many hours do you study per week (0–5; 6–10; 11–15; 16–20; 21+)?

aa. Which question on this survey is the most interesting to you?

bb. Which question on this survey is the least interesting?

Possible activities:

i. For each item, determine the most likely scale of measurement (nominal, ordinal, interval, or ratio) and the type of variable [categorical or numerical (if numerical, discrete or continuous)].

ii. Create scenarios in which one or more of the variables in this survey would be a constant, given the delimitations that you define for your study. For example, we are designing a study to measure study habits (as measured by question *y*) for students who *do not* exercise (question *l*). In this sample study, our constant is the number of hours per week that a student exercises (in this case, we are delimiting that to be zero—and thus question *l* will be a constant; all students in our study will have answered question *l* as "zero" indicating that they did not exercise).

iii. Collect data from a sample of individuals. In subsequent chapters you will be asked to analyze this data for different procedures.

Note: An actual sample dataset using this survey is contained on the website (survey1.sav or survey1.csv) and is utilized in later chapters. If you are using the SPSS file, please note that all the variables in the survey1 datafile have been coded as having a measurement scale of "scale" (i.e., interval or ratio). This is not correct, and you will need to determine the most likely scale of measurement of each.

2. The Integrated Postsecondary Education Data System (IPEDS) is just one of many, many public secondary data sources available to researchers. Using 2017 IPEDS

dataset (see https://nces.ed.gov/ipeds/use-the-data; accessible from the text website as IPEDS2017.sav), consider the following possible activities:

i. For each item, determine the most likely scale of measurement (nominal, ordinal, interval, or ratio) and the type of variable (categorical or numerical; if numerical, discrete or continuous). *Note: If you are using the SPSS file, please note that all the variables in IPEDS2017.sav datafile have been coded as having a measurement scale of "scale" (i.e., interval or ratio). This is not correct, and you will need to determine the most likely scale of measurement of each.*

ii. Create scenarios in which one or more of the variables in this survey would be a constant, given the delimitations that you define for your study. For example, we are designing a study to examine institutions who are NCAA/NAIA members for football. In this sample study, our constant is institutional members in NCAA/NAIA for football (in this case, we are delimiting the variable "NCAA/NAIA member for football" [*sport1*] to "yes," which is coded as "1" in the datafile—and thus the "NCAA/NAIA member for football" question will be a constant; all institutions in our study will have answered "NCAA/NAIA member for football" as "yes").

3. The National Health Interview Survey (NHIS*; https://www.cdc.gov/nchs/nhis/) is just one of many, many public secondary data sources available to researchers. Using data from the 2017 NHIS family file (see www.cdc.gov/nchs/nhis/nhis_2017_data_release.htm; accessible from the text website as *NHIS_family2017.sav*), consider the following possible activities:

i. For each item, determine the most likely scale of measurement (nominal, ordinal, interval, or ratio) and the type of variable (categorical or numerical; if numerical, discrete or continuous). *Note: If you are using the SPSS file, please note that all the variables in the NHIS_family2017.sav datafile have been coded as having a measurement scale of "scale" (i.e., interval or ratio). This is not correct, and you will need to determine the most likely scale of measurement of each.*

ii. Create scenarios in which one or more of the variables in this survey would be a constant, given the delimitations that you define for your study. For example, we are designing a study to examine individuals who are living alone. In this sample study, our constant is "family structure." In this case, we are delimiting the variable "family structure" (*FM_STRCP* or *FM_STRP*) to "living alone," which is coded as "11" in the datafile—and thus the family structure question will be a constant; all individuals in our study will have answered family structure as "living alone."

*Should you desire to use the NHIS data for your own research, please access the data directly here as updates to the data may have occurred: www.cdc.gov/nchs/nhis/data-questionnaires-documentation.htm. Also, it is important to note that the NHIS is a *complex sample* (i.e., not a simple random sample). We won't get into the technical aspects of this, but when the data are analyzed to adjust for the sampling design (including non-simple random sampling procedure and disproportionate sampling) the end results are then representative of the intended population. The purpose of the text is not to serve as a primer for understanding complex samples, and thus readers interested in learning more about complex survey designs are referred to any number of excellent resources (Hahs-Vaughn, 2005; Hahs-Vaughn, McWayne, Bulotsky-Shearer, Wen, & Faria, 2011a, 2011b;

Lee, Forthofer, & Lorimor, 1989; Skinner, Holt, & Smith, 1989). Additionally, so as to not complicate matters any more than necessary, the applications in the textbook do not illustrate how to adjust for the complex sample design. As such, if you do not adjust for the complex sampling design, the results that you see should not be interpreted to represent any larger population but only that select sample of individuals who actually completed the survey. I want to stress that the reason why the sampling design has not been illustrated in the textbook applications is because the point of this section of the textbook is to illustrate how to use statistical software to generate various procedures and how to interpret the output and not to ensure the results are representative of the intended population. Please do not let this discount or diminish the need to apply this critical step in your own analyses when using complex survey data as there is quite a large body of research that describes the importance of effectively analyzing complex samples as well as provides evidence of biased results when the complex sample design is not addressed in the analyses (Hahs-Vaughn, 2005, 2006a, 2006b; Hahs-Vaughn et al., 2011a, 2011b; Kish & Frankel, 1973, 1974; Korn & Graubard, 1995; Lee et al., 1989; Lumley, 2004; Pfeffermann, 1993; Skinner et al., 1989).

2

Data Representation

Chapter Outline

Key Concepts

1. Frequencies, cumulative frequencies, relative frequencies, and cumulative relative frequencies
2. Ungrouped and grouped frequency distributions
3. Sample size
4. Real limits and intervals
5. Frequency polygons
6. Normal, symmetric, and skewed frequency distributions
7. Percentiles, quartiles, and percentile ranks

In the first chapter we introduced the wonderful world of statistics. We discussed the value of statistics, met a few of the more well-known statisticians, and defined several basic statistical concepts, including population, parameter, sample, statistic, descriptive and inferential statistics, types of variables, and scales of measurement. In this chapter we begin our examination of descriptive statistics, which we previously defined as techniques that allow us to tabulate, summarize, and depict a collection of data in an abbreviated fashion. We used the example of collecting data from 100,000 graduate students on various characteristics (e.g., height, weight, sex, grade point average, aptitude test scores). Rather than having to carry around the entire collection of data in order to respond to questions, we mentioned that you could summarize the data in an abbreviated fashion through the use of tables and graphs. This way we could communicate features of the data through a few tables or figures without having to carry around the entire dataset.

This chapter deals with the details of the construction of tables and figures for purposes of describing data. Specifically, we first consider the following types of tables: frequency distributions (ungrouped and grouped), cumulative frequency distributions, relative frequency distributions, and cumulative relative frequency distributions. Next we look at the following types of figures: bar graphs, histograms, frequency polygons (or line graphs), cumulative frequency polygons, and stem-and-leaf displays. We also discuss common shapes of frequency distributions. Then we examine the use of percentiles, quartiles, percentile ranks, and box-and-whisker plots. Finally, we look at the use of SPSS and **R** and develop an APA-style paragraph of results. Concepts to be discussed include frequencies, cumulative frequencies, relative frequencies, and cumulative relative frequencies; ungrouped and grouped frequency distributions; sample size; real limits and intervals; frequency polygons; normal, symmetric, and skewed frequency distributions; and percentiles, quartiles and percentile ranks. Our objectives are that by the end of this chapter, you will be able to (a) construct and interpret statistical tables, (b) construct and interpret statistical graphs, and (c) determine and interpret percentile-related information.

2.1 Tabular Display of Distributions

Throughout this text, we will be following a group of superbly talented, creative, and energetic graduate research assistants (Challie Lenge, Ott Lier, Addie Venture, and Oso Wyse) working in their institution's statistics and research lab, fondly known as CASTLE

(Computing and Statistical Technology Laboratory). The students are supervised and mentored by a research methodology faculty member who empowers the group to lead their projects to infinity and beyond, so to speak. With each chapter, we will find the group, or a subset of members thereof, delving into a fantastical statistical journey.

The statistics and research lab at the university serve client within the institution, such as faculty and staff, and outside the institution, including a multitude of diverse community partners. The lab is supervised by a research methodology faculty member and is staffed by the institution's best and brightest graduate students. The graduate students, Addie Venture, Oso Wyse, Challie Lenge, and Ott Lier, have been assigned their first task as research assistants. Dr. Debhard, a statistics professor, has given the group of students quiz data collected from 25 students enrolled in an introductory statistics course and has asked the group to summarize the data. We find Addie taking lead on this project. Given the discussion with Dr. Debhard, Addie has determined that the following four research questions should guide the analysis of the data:

1. What interpretations can be made from the frequency table of quiz scores from students enrolled in an introductory statistics class?
2. What interpretations can be made from graphical representations of quiz scores from students enrolled in an introductory statistics class?
3. What is the distributional shape of the statistics quiz scores?
4. What is the 50th percentile of the quiz scores?

In this section we consider ways in which data can be represented in the form of tables. More specifically, we are interested in how the data for a single variable can be represented (the representation of data for multiple variables is covered in later chapters). The methods described here include frequency distributions (both ungrouped and grouped), cumulative frequency distributions, relative frequency distributions, and cumulative relative frequency distributions.

2.1.1 Frequency Distributions

Let us use an example set of data in this chapter to illustrate ways in which data can be represented. We have selected a small dataset for purposes of simplicity, although datasets are typically larger in size. Note that there is a larger dataset (based on the survey from the Chapter 1 interpretive problem) utilized in the end-of-chapter problems and available on our website as "survey1." As shown in Table 2.1, the smaller dataset consists of a sample of 25 student scores on a statistics quiz, where the maximum score is 20 points. If a colleague asked a question about this data, again a response could be, "Take a look at the data yourself." This would not be very satisfactory to the colleague, as the person would have to eyeball the data to answer the question. Alternatively, one could present the data in the form of a table so that questions could be more easily answered. One question might be: Which score occurred most frequently? In other words, what score occurred more than any other score? Other questions might be: Which scores were the highest and lowest scores in the class? Where do most of the scores tend to fall? In other words, how well did the students

TABLE 2.1

Statistics Quiz Data

9	11	20	15	19	10	19	18	14	12	17	11	13
16	17	19	18	17	13	17	15	18	17	19	15	

TABLE 2.2

Ungrouped Frequency Distribution
of Statistics Quiz Data

X	f	cf	rf	crf
9	1	1	$f/n = 1/25 = .04$	.04
10	1	2	.04	.08
11	2	4	.08	.16
12	1	5	.04	.20
13	2	7	.08	.28
14	1	8	.04	.32
15	3	11	.12	.44
16	1	12	.04	.48
17	5	17	.20	.68
18	3	20	.12	.80
19	4	24	.16	.96
20	1	25	.04	1.00
	$n = 25$		1.00	

tend to do as a class? These and other questions can be easily answered by looking at a **frequency distribution**.

Let us first look at how an **ungrouped frequency distribution** can be constructed for these and other data. By following these steps, we develop the ungrouped frequency distribution as shown in Table 2.2. The first step is to arrange the unique scores on a list from the lowest score to the highest score. The lowest score is 9 and the highest score is 20. Even though scores such as 15 were observed more than once, the value of 15 is only entered in this column once. This is what we mean by unique. Note that if the score of 15 was not observed, it could still be entered as a value in the table to serve as a placeholder within the distribution of scores observed. We label this column as "raw score" or "X," as shown by the first column in the table. **Raw scores** are a set of scores in their original form; that is, the scores have not been altered or transformed in any way. X is often used in statistics to denote a variable, so you see X quite a bit in this text. (As a side note, whenever upper- or lowercase letters are used to denote statistical notation, the letter is always italicized.)

The second step is to determine for each unique score the number of times it was observed. We label this second column as "frequency" or by the abbreviation "f." *The frequency column tells us how many times or how frequently each unique score was observed.* In other words, the **frequency** (f) is simply *count* data. For instance, the score of 20 was only observed one time whereas the score of 17 was observed five times. Now we have some information with which to answer our colleague's question. The most frequently observed score is 17, the lowest score is 9, and the highest score is 20. We can also see that scores tended to be closer to 20 (the highest score) than to 9 (the lowest score).

Two other concepts need to be introduced that are included in Table 2.2. The first concept is **sample size**. At the bottom of the second column you see $n = 25$. From now on, n will be used to denote sample size, that is, the total number of scores obtained for the sample. Thus, because 25 scores were obtained here, then $n = 25$.

The second concept is related to real limits and intervals. Although the scores obtained for this dataset happened to be whole numbers, not fractions or decimals, we still need a system that will cover that possibility. For example, what would we do if a student obtained a score of 18.25? One option would be to list that as another unique score, which would probably be more confusing than useful. A second option would be to include it with one of the other unique scores somehow; this is our option of choice. All researchers use the concepts of **real limits** and **intervals** to cover the possibility of any score being obtained. Each value of X in Table 2.2 can be thought of as being the **midpoint** of an interval. Each interval has an upper and a lower real limit. The **upper real limit** of an interval is halfway between the midpoint of the interval under consideration and the midpoint of the next larger interval. For example, the value of 18 represents the midpoint of an interval. The next larger interval has a midpoint of 19. Therefore the upper real limit of the interval containing 18 would be 18.5, halfway between 18 and 19. The **lower real limit** of an interval is halfway between the midpoint of the interval under consideration and the midpoint of the next smaller interval. Following the example interval of 18 again, the next smaller interval has a midpoint of 17. Therefore, the lower real limit of the interval containing 18 would be 17.5, halfway between 18 and 17. Thus, the interval of 18 has 18.5 as an upper real limit and 17.5 as a lower real limit. Other intervals have their upper and lower real limits as well.

Notice that adjacent intervals (i.e., those next to one another) touch at their respective real limits. For example, the 18 interval has 18.5 as its upper real limit and the 19 interval has 18.5 as its lower real limit. This implies that any possible score that occurs can be placed into some interval and no score can fall between two intervals. If someone obtains a score of 18.25, that will be covered in the 18 interval. The only limitation to this procedure is that because adjacent intervals must touch in order to deal with every possible score, what do we do when a score falls precisely where two intervals touch at their real limits (e.g., at 18.5)? There are two possible solutions. The first solution is to assign the score to one interval or another based on some rule. For instance, we could randomly assign such scores to one interval or the other by flipping a coin. Alternatively, we could arbitrarily assign such scores always into either the larger or smaller of the two intervals. The second solution is to construct intervals such that the number of values falling at the real limits is minimized. For example, say that most of the scores occur at .5 (e.g., 15.5, 16.5, 17.5, etc.). We could construct the intervals with .5 as the midpoint and .0 as the real limits. Thus, the 15.5 interval would have 15.5 as the midpoint, 16.0 as the upper real limit, and 15.0 as the lower real limit. It should also be noted that, strictly speaking, *real limits are only appropriate for continuous variables, but not for discrete variables*. That is, because discrete variables can only have limited values, we probably don't need to worry about real limits (e.g., there is not really an interval for two children). The concept of discrete variables was introduced in Chapter 1. Discrete variables are variables that arise from the counting process.

Finally, the **width** of an interval is defined as the *difference between the upper and lower real limits of an interval*. We can denote this as $w = URL - LRL$, where w is interval width, and URL and LRL are the upper and lower real limits, respectively. In the case of our example interval, we see that $w = URL - LRL = 18.5 - 17.5 = 1.0$. For Table 2.2, then, all intervals have the same interval width of 1.0. For each interval we have a midpoint, a lower real limit that is one-half unit below the midpoint, and an upper real limit that is one-half unit above the midpoint. In general, we want all of the intervals to have the same width for consistency as well as for equal interval reasons. The only exception might be if the largest or smallest intervals were above a certain value (e.g., greater than 20) or below a certain value (e.g., less than 9), respectively.

A frequency distribution with an interval width of 1.0 is often referred to as an **ungrouped frequency distribution**, as the intervals have not been grouped together. Does the interval width always have to be equal to 1.0? The answer, of course, is no. We could group intervals together and form what is often referred to as a **grouped frequency distribution**. For our example data, we can construct a grouped frequency distribution with an interval width of 2.0, as shown in Table 2.3. The largest interval now contains the scores of 19 and 20, the second largest interval the scores of 17 and 18, and so on, down to the smallest interval with the scores of 9 and 10. Correspondingly, the largest interval has a frequency of 5, the second largest interval a frequency of 8, and the smallest interval a frequency of 2. All we have really done is collapse the intervals from Table 2.2, where the interval width was 1.0, into the intervals of width 2.0, as shown in Table 2.3. If we take, for example, the interval containing the scores of 17 and 18, then the midpoint of the interval is 17.5, the *URL* is 18.5, the *LRL* is 16.5, and thus $w = 2.0$. The interval width could actually be any value, including .20 or 100, among other values, depending on what best suits the data.

How does one determine what the proper interval width should be? If there are many frequencies for each score and fewer than 15 or 20 intervals, then an *ungrouped frequency distribution* with an interval width of 1 is appropriate (and this is the default in SPSS for computing frequency distributions). If there are either minimal frequencies per score (say 1 or 2) or a large number of unique scores (say more than 20), then a *grouped frequency distribution* with some other interval width is appropriate. For a first example, say that there are 100 unique scores ranging from 0 to 200. An ungrouped frequency distribution would not really summarize the data very well, as the table would be quite large. The reader would have to eyeball the table and actually do some quick grouping in his or her head so as to gain any information about the data. An interval width of perhaps 10 to 15 would be more useful. In a second example, say that there are only 20 unique scores ranging from 0 to 30, but each score occurs only once or twice. An ungrouped frequency distribution would not be very useful here either, as the reader would again have to collapse intervals in his or her head. Here an interval width of perhaps 2 to 5 would be appropriate.

TABLE 2.3

Grouped Frequency Distribution
of Statistics Quiz Data

X	f
9–10	2
11–12	3
13–14	3
15–16	4
17–18	8
19–20	5
	$n = 25$

Ultimately, deciding on the interval width, and thus the number of intervals, becomes a trade-off between good communication of the data and the amount of information contained in the table. As interval width increases, more and more information is lost from the original data. For the example where scores range from 0 to 200 and using an interval width of 10, some precision in the 15 scores contained in the 30–39 interval is lost. In other words, the reader would not know from the frequency distribution where in that interval the 15 scores actually fall. If you want that information (you may not), you would need to return to the original data. At the same time, an ungrouped frequency distribution for that data would not have much of a message for the reader. Ultimately, the decisive factor is the adequacy with which information is communicated to the reader. There are no absolute rules on how to best group values into intervals. The nature of the interval grouping comes down to whatever form best represents the data. With today's powerful statistical computer software, it is easy for the researcher to try several different interval widths before deciding which one works best for a particular set of data. Note also that the frequency distribution can be used with variables of any measurement scale, from nominal (e.g., the frequencies for eye color of a group of children) to ratio (e.g., the frequencies for the height of a group of adults).

2.1.2 Cumulative Frequency Distributions

A second type of frequency distribution is known as the **cumulative frequency distribution** (*cf*). For the example data, this is depicted in the third column of Table 2.2 and labeled as "*cf*." To put it simply, *the number of cumulative frequencies for a particular interval is the number of scores contained in that interval and all of the smaller intervals*. Thus, the 9 interval contains one frequency and there are no frequencies smaller than that interval, so the cumulative frequency is simply 1. The 10 interval contains one frequency and there is one frequency in a smaller interval, so the cumulative frequency is 2 (i.e., $1 + 1$). The 11 interval contains two frequencies and there are two frequencies in smaller intervals; thus the cumulative frequency is 4 (i.e., $2 + 2$). Then, four people had scores in the 11 interval and smaller intervals. One way to think about determining the cumulative frequency column is to take the frequency column and accumulate downward (i.e., from the top down, yielding 1; $1 + 1 = 2$; $1 + 1 + 2 = 4$; etc.). Just as a check, the *cf* in the largest interval (i.e., the interval largest in value) should be equal to n, the number of scores in the sample, 25 in this case. Note also that the cumulative frequency distribution can be used with variables of measurement scales from ordinal (e.g., with grade level, the cumulative frequency could tell us, among other things, the number of students receiving a B or lower) to interval and ratio (e.g., the number of adults who are 5'7" or shorter), but cannot be used with nominal as there is not at least rank order to nominal data (and thus accumulating information from one nominal category to another does not make sense).

2.1.3 Relative Frequency Distributions

A third type of frequency distribution is known as the relative frequency distribution. For the example data, this is shown in the fourth column of Table 2.2 and labeled as "*rf*." **Relative frequency (*rf*)** is simply *the percentage of scores contained in an interval; it is also known as a proportion or percentage*. Computationally, $rf = f/n$. For example, the percentage of scores occurring in the 17 interval is computed as $rf = f/n = 5/25 = .20$. Relative frequencies take sample size into account, allowing us to make statements about the number of individuals in an interval relative to the total sample. Thus, rather than stating that five individuals had scores in the 17 interval, we could say that 20% of the scores were in that interval. In the popular press, relative frequencies are quite often reported in tables without the frequencies (e.g., "56% of voters agreed with . . . "). Note that the sum of the relative frequencies should be 1.00 (or 100%) within rounding error. Also note that the *relative frequency distribution can be used with variables of all measurement scales*, from nominal (e.g., the percent of children with blue eye color) to ratio (e.g., the percent of adults who are 5'7").

2.1.4 Cumulative Relative Frequency Distributions

A fourth and final type of frequency distribution is known as the cumulative relative frequency distribution. For the example data this is depicted in the fifth column of Table 2.2 and labeled as "*crf*." The number of **cumulative relative frequencies** (*crf*) for a particular interval *is the percentage of scores in that interval and smaller*. Thus, the 9 interval has a relative frequency of .04, and there are no relative frequencies smaller than that interval, so the cumulative relative frequency is simply .04. The 10 interval has a relative frequency of .04 and the relative frequencies less than that interval are .04, so the cumulative relative frequency is .08. The 11 interval has a relative frequency of .08 and the relative frequencies less than that interval total .08, so the cumulative relative frequency is .16. Thus, 16% of the people had scores in the 11 interval and smaller. In other words, *16% of people scored 11 or less*. One way to think about determining the cumulative relative frequency column is to take the relative frequency column and accumulate *downward* (i.e., from the top down, yielding .04; .04 + .04 = .08; .04 + .04 + .08 = .16; etc.). Just as a check, the *crf* in the largest interval should be equal to 1.0, within rounding error, just as the sum of the relative frequencies is equal to 1.0. Also note that the cumulative relative frequency distribution can be used with variables of measurement scales from ordinal (e.g., the percent of students receiving a B or less) to interval and ratio (e.g., the percent of adults who are 5'7" or shorter). As with relative frequency distributions, cumulative relative frequency distributions cannot be used with nominal data.

2.2 Graphical Display of Distributions

In this section we consider several types of graphs for viewing a distribution of scores. Again, we are still interested in how the data for a single variable can be represented, but now in a graphical display rather than a tabular display. The methods described here include the bar graph; histogram; frequency, relative frequency, cumulative frequency and cumulative relative frequency polygons (or line graphs); and stem-and-leaf display. Common shapes of distributions will also be discussed.

2.2.1 Bar Graph

A popular method used for displaying nominal scale data in graphical form is the **bar graph**. As an example, say that we have data on the eye color of a sample of 20 children. Ten children are blue-eyed, six are brown-eyed, three are green-eyed, and one is black-eyed. Note that this is a *discrete* variable rather than a continuous variable. A bar graph for

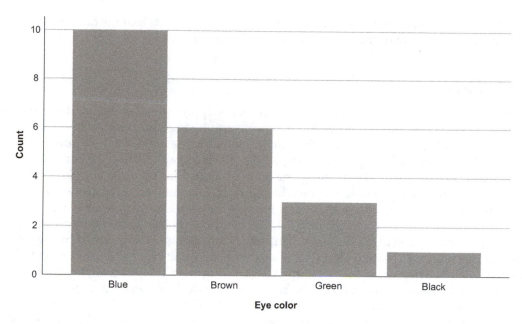

FIGURE 2.1
Bar graph of eye-color data.

this data is shown in Figure 2.1 (generated using the default options in SPSS). The **horizontal axis**, going from left to right on the page, is often referred to in statistics as the **X axis** (for variable X, in this example our variable is *eye color*). On the X axis of Figure 2.1, we have labeled the different eye colors that were observed from individuals in our sample. The order of the colors is not relevant (remember, this is nominal data, so order or rank is irrelevant), but the default happens to be ascending order of how they are labeled in the dataset. In this case, 1 refers to "blue," 2 refers to "brown," 3 refers to "green," and 4 refers to "black." The **vertical axis,** going from bottom to top on the page, is often referred to in statistics as the **Y axis** (the Y label will be more relevant in later chapters when we have a second variable Y). On the Y axis of Figure 2.1, we have labeled the frequencies or the counts. In other words, the number of children who have each eye color is represented on the Y axis. Finally, a bar is drawn for each eye color where the height of the bar denotes the number of frequencies for that particular eye color (i.e., the number of times that particular eye color was observed in our sample). For example, the height of the bar for the blue-eyed category is 10 frequencies. Thus, we see in the graph which eye color is most popular in this sample (i.e., blue) and which eye color occurs least (i.e., black).

Note that the bars are separated by some space and do not touch one another, reflecting the nature of nominal data being discrete. Because there are no intervals or real limits here, we do not want the bars to touch one another, as we will see in a histogram. One could also plot relative frequencies on the Y axis to reflect the percentage of children in the sample who belong to each category of eye color. Here we would see that 50% of the children had blue eyes, 30% brown eyes, 15% green eyes, and 5% black eyes. Another method for displaying nominal data graphically is the pie chart, where the pie is divided into slices whose sizes correspond to the frequencies or relative frequencies of each category. However, for numerous reasons (e.g., contains little information when there are few categories; is unreadable when there are many categories; visually assessing the sizes of each slice is difficult at best), the pie chart is statistically problematic such that Tufte (2001) asserts that the only thing worse than a pie chart is a lot of them. *The bar graph is the recommended graphic for nominal data.*

2.2.2 Histogram

A method somewhat similar to the bar graph that is appropriate for data that are at least ordinal in scale (i.e., ordinal, interval, or ratio) is the **histogram**. Because the data are at least theoretically continuous (even though they may be measured in whole numbers), the main difference in the histogram (as compared to the bar graph) is that the bars touch one another, much like intervals touching one another as real limits. An example of a histogram for the statistics quiz data is shown in Figure 2.2 (generated in SPSS using the default options). As you can see, along the X axis we plot the values of the variable X and along the Y axis the frequencies for each interval. The height of the bar again corresponds to the frequencies for a particular value of X. This figure represents an ungrouped histogram as the interval size is 1. That is, along the X axis *the midpoint of each bar is the midpoint of the interval*; each bar begins on the left at the lower real limit of the interval, the bar ends on the right at the upper real limit, and the bar is 1 unit wide. If we wanted to use an interval size of 2, for example, using the grouped frequency distribution in Table 2.3, then we could construct a grouped histogram in the same way; the differences would be that the bars would be 2 units wide, and the height of the bars would obviously change. Try this one on your own for practice.

One could also plot relative frequencies on the Y axis to reflect the percentage of students in the sample whose scores fell into a particular interval. In reality, all that we have to

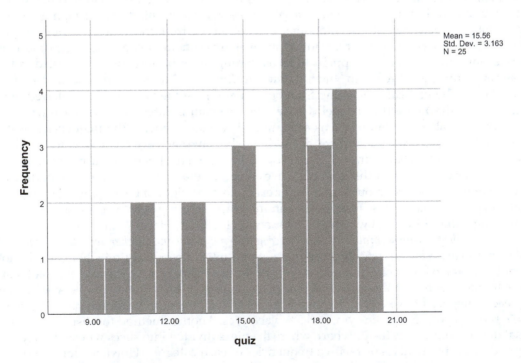

FIGURE 2.2
Histogram of statistics quiz data.

change is the scale of the Y axis. The height of the bars would remain the same regardless of plotting frequencies or relative frequencies. For this particular dataset, each frequency corresponds to a relative frequency of .04.

2.2.3 Frequency Polygon (Line Graph)

Another graphical method appropriate for data that have at least some rank order (i.e., ordinal, interval, or ratio) is the **frequency polygon** (i.e., **line graph**). A polygon is a many-sided figure. The frequency polygon is set up in a fashion similar to the histogram. However, rather than plotting a bar for each interval, points are plotted for each interval and then connected together as shown in Figure 2.3 (generated in SPSS using the default options). The X and Y axes are the same as with the histogram. A point is plotted at the intersection (or coordinates) of the midpoint of each interval along the X axis and the frequency for that interval along the Y axis. Thus, for the 15 interval, a point is plotted at the midpoint of the interval 15.0 and for three frequencies. Once the points are plotted for each interval, we "connect the dots."

One could also plot relative frequencies on the Y axis to reflect the percentage of students in the sample whose scores fell into a particular interval. This is known as the **relative frequency polygon**. As with the histogram, all we have to change is the scale of the Y axis. The position of the polygon would remain the same. For this particular dataset, each frequency corresponds to a relative frequency of .04.

Note also that because the histogram and frequency polygon/line graph each contain the exact same information, Figures 2.2 and 2.3 can be superimposed on one another. If you did this, you would see that the points of the frequency polygon are plotted at the top of each bar of the histogram. There is no advantage of the histogram or frequency polygon

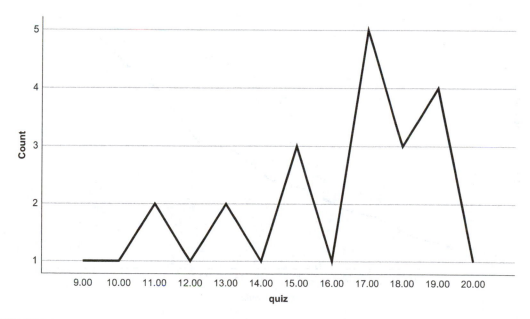

FIGURE 2.3
Frequency polygon (line graph) of statistics quiz data.

over the other; however, the histogram is used more frequently, perhaps because it is a bit easier to visually interpret.

2.2.4 Cumulative Frequency Polygon

Cumulative frequencies of data that have at least some rank order (i.e., ordinal, interval, or ratio), can be displayed as a **cumulative frequency polygon** (sometimes referred to as the **ogive curve**). As shown in Figure 2.4 (generated in SPSS using the default options), the differences between the frequency polygon and the cumulative frequency polygon are that the cumulative frequency polygon (a) involves plotting cumulative frequencies along the *Y* axis, (b) the points should be plotted at the upper real limit of each interval (although SPSS plots the points at the interval midpoints by default), and (c) the polygon cannot be closed on the right-hand side.

Let's discuss each of these differences. First, the *Y* axis represents the cumulative frequencies from the cumulative frequency distribution. The *X* axis is the usual set of raw scores. Second, to reflect the cumulative nature of this type frequency, the points must be plotted at the upper real limit of each interval. For example, the cumulative frequency for the 16 interval is 12, indicating that there are 12 scores in that interval and smaller. Finally, the polygon cannot be closed on the right-hand side. Notice that as you move from left to right in the cumulative frequency polygon, the height of the points always increases or stays the same. Because of the nature of accumulating information, there will never be a decrease in the accumulation of the frequencies. For example, there is an increase in cumulative frequency from the 16 to the 17 interval as five new frequencies are included. Beyond the 20 interval, the number of cumulative frequencies remains at 25, as no new frequencies are included.

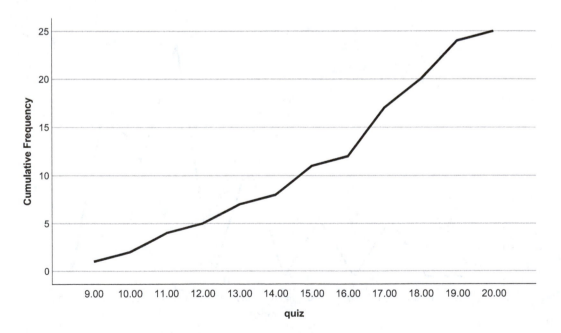

FIGURE 2.4
Cumulative frequency polygon (ogive curve) of statistics quiz data.

One could also plot cumulative relative frequencies on the Y axis to reflect the percentage of students in the sample whose scores fell into a particular interval and smaller. This is known as the **cumulative relative frequency polygon**. All we have to change is the scale of the Y axis to cumulative relative frequency. The position of the polygon would remain the same. For this particular dataset, each cumulative frequency corresponds to a cumulative relative frequency of .04. Thus, a cumulative relative frequency polygon of the example data would look exactly like Figure 2.4, except on the Y axis we plot cumulative relative frequencies ranging from 0 to 1.

2.2.5 Shapes of Frequency Distributions

You will likely encounter several common shapes of frequency distributions, as shown in Figure 2.5. These are briefly described here and more fully in later chapters. Figure 2.5(a) is a **normal distribution** (or bell-shaped curve) where most of the scores are in the center of the distribution, with fewer higher and lower scores. The normal distribution plays a large role in statistics, both for descriptive statistics (as we show beginning in Chapter 4), and particularly as an assumption for many inferential statistics (as we show beginning in Chapter 6). This distribution is also known as **symmetric**, because if we divide the distribution into two equal halves vertically, the left half is a mirror image of the right half (see Chapter 4).

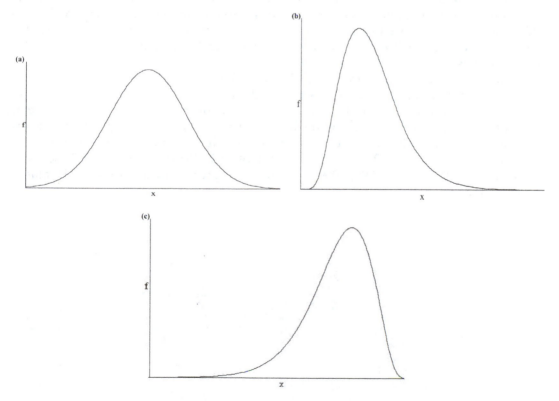

FIGURE 2.5
Common shapes of frequency distributions: (a) normal, (b) positively skewed, and (c) negatively skewed.

Skewed distributions are not symmetric, as the left half is not a mirror image of the right half. Figure 2.5b is a **positively skewed** distribution, where most of the scores are fairly low and there are a few higher scores (see Chapter 4). Figure 2.5c is a **negatively skewed** distribution, where most of the scores are fairly high and there are a few lower scores (see Chapter 4).

2.2.6 Stem-and-Leaf Display

A refined form of the grouped frequency distribution is the **stem-and-leaf display**, developed by Tukey (1977). This is shown in Figure 2.6 (generated in SPSS using the default options in "Explore") for the example statistics quiz data. The stem-and-leaf display was originally developed to be constructed on a typewriter using lines and numbers in a minimal amount of space. In a way, the stem-and-leaf display looks like a grouped type of histogram on its side. The vertical value on the left is the **stem** and, in this example, represents all but the last digit (i.e., the tens digit). The **leaf** represents, in this example, the remaining digit of each score (i.e., the unit's digit). Note that SPSS has grouped values in increments of five. For example, the second line ("1 . 0112334") indicates that there are seven scores from 10 to 14; thus, "1 . 0" means that there is one frequency for the score of 10. The fact that there are two values of "1" that occur in that stem indicates that the score of 11 occurred twice. Interpreting the rest of this stem, we see that 12 occurred once (i.e., there is only one 2 in the stem), 13 occurred twice (i.e., there are two 3s in the stem), and 14 occurred once (i.e., only one 4 in the stem). From the stem-and-leaf display, one can determine every one of the raw scores; this is not possible with a typical grouped frequency distribution (i.e., no information is lost in a stem-and-leaf display). However, with a large sample the display can become rather unwieldy. Consider what a stem-and-leaf display would look like for 100,000 values!

In summary, this section included the most basic types of statistical graphics, although more advanced graphics are described in later chapters. Note, however, that there are a number of publications on how to properly display graphics; that is, "how to do graphics right." While a detailed discussion of statistical graphics is beyond the scope of this text, we recommend a number of publications (e.g., Chambers, 1983; Cleveland, 1994; Hartley, 1992; Howard, 1984; Robbins, 2005; Schmid, 1983; Tufte, 2001; Wainer, 1992, 2000; Wallgren, Wallgren, Persson, Jorner, & Haaland, 1996; Wilkinson, 2005).

```
           quiz Stem-and-Leaf Plot

       Frequency    Stem &  Leaf

           1.00        0  .  9
           7.00        1  .  0112334
          16.00        1  .  5556777778889999
           1.00        2  .  0

       Stem width:       10.00
       Each leaf:           1 case(s)
```

FIGURE 2.6
Stem-and-leaf display of statistics quiz data.

2.3 Percentiles

In this section we consider several concepts and the necessary computations for the area of percentiles, including percentiles, quartiles, percentile ranks, and the box-and-whisker plot. For instance, you might be interested in determining what percentage of the distribution of the GRE-Quantitative subtest fell below a score of 165 or in what score divides the distribution of the GRE-Quantitative subtest into two equal halves.

2.3.1 Percentiles

Let us define a **percentile** as that score below which a certain percentage of the distribution lies. For instance, you may be interested in that score below which 50% of the distribution of the GRE-Quantitative subscale lies. Say that this score is computed as 150; this would mean that 50% of the scores fell below a score of 150. Because percentiles are scores, they are continuous values, and can take on any value of those possible. The 30th percentile could be, for example, the score of 145. For notational purposes, a percentile will be known as P_i, where the i subscript denotes the particular percentile of interest, between 0 and 100. Thus the 30th percentile for the previous example would be denoted as $P_{30} = 145$.

Let us now consider how percentiles are computed. The formula for computing the P_i percentile is

$$P_i = LRL + \left(\frac{(i\%)(n) - cf}{f} \right)(w)$$

where LRL is the lower real limit of the interval containing P_i, $i\%$ is the percentile desired (expressed as a proportion from 0 to 1), n is the sample size, cf is the cumulative frequency less than but not including the interval containing P_i (known as "cf below"), f is the frequency of the interval containing P_i, and w is the interval width.

As an example, consider computing the 25th percentile of our statistics quiz data. This would correspond to that score below which 25% of the distribution falls. For the example data in the form presented in Table 2.2, we can compute P_{25} as follows:

$$P_i = LRL + \left(\frac{(i\%)(n) - cf}{f} \right)(w)$$

$$P_{25} = 12.5 + \left(\frac{(25\%)(25) - 5}{2} \right)(1) = 12.5 + 0.625 = 13.125$$

Conceptually, let us discuss how the equation works. First we have to determine what interval contains the percentile of interest. This is easily done by looking in the *crf* column of the frequency distribution for the interval that contains a *crf* of .25 somewhere within the interval. We see that for the 13 interval the *crf* = .28, which means that the interval spans a *crf* of .20 (the *URL* of the 12 interval) up to .28 (the *URL* of the 13 interval), and thus contains .25. The next largest interval of 14 takes us from a *crf* of .28 up to a *crf* of .32, and thus is too large for this particular percentile. The next smallest interval of 12 takes us from a *crf* of .16 up to a *crf* of .20, and thus is too small. The *LRL* of 12.5 indicates that P_{25} is at least 12.5. The rest of the equation adds some positive amount to the *LRL*.

Next we have to determine how far into that interval we need to go in order to reach the desired percentile. We take *i* percent of *n*, or in this case 25% of the sample size of 25, which is 6.25. So we need to go one-fourth of the way into the distribution, or 6.25 scores, to reach the 25th percentile. Another way to think about this is that because the scores have been rank-ordered from lowest or smallest (top of the frequency distribution) to highest or largest (bottom of the frequency distribution), we need to go 25%, or 6.25 scores, into the distribution from the top (or smallest value) to reach the 25th percentile. We then subtract out all cumulative frequencies smaller than (or below) the interval we are looking in, where *cf* below = 5. Again we just want to determine how far into this interval we need to go, and thus we subtract out all of the frequencies smaller than this interval, or *cf* below. The numerator then becomes 6.25 − 5 = 1.25. Then we divide by the number of frequencies in the interval containing the percentile we are looking for. This forms the ratio of how far into the interval we go. In this case, we needed to go 1.25 scores into the interval and the interval contains two scores; thus the ratio is 1.25 / 2 = .625. In other words, we need to go .625 units into the interval to reach the desired percentile. Now that we know how far into the interval to go, we need to weigh this by the width of the interval. Here we need to go 1.25 scores into an interval containing two scores that is 1 unit wide, and thus we go .625 units into the interval [(1.25 / 2) 1 = .625]. If the interval width was instead 10, then 1.25 scores into the interval would be equal to 6.25 units.

Consider two more worked examples to try on your own, either through statistical software or by hand. The 50th percentile, P_{50}, is

$$P_{50} = 16.500 + \left(\frac{(50\%)(25) - 12}{5}\right)(1) = 16.500 + 0.100 = 16.600$$

and the 75th percentile, P_{75}, is

$$P_{75} = 17.500 + \left(\frac{(75\%)(25) - 17}{3}\right)(1) = 17.500 + 0.583 = 18.083$$

We have only examined a few example percentiles of the many possibilities that exist. For example, we could also have determined $P_{55.5}$ or even $P_{99.5}$. Thus, we could determine any percentile, in whole numbers or decimals, between 0 and 100. Next we examine three particular percentiles that are often of interest, the quartiles.

2.3.2 Quartiles

One common way of dividing a distribution of scores into equal groups of scores is known as **quartiles**. This is done by dividing a distribution into fourths or quartiles where there are four equal groups, each containing 25% of the scores. In the previous examples, we determined P_{25}, P_{50}, and P_{75}, which divided the distribution into four equal groups, from 0 to 25, from 25 to 50, from 50 to 75, and from 75 to 100. *Thus the quartiles are special cases* *of percentiles*. A different notation, however, is often used for these particular percentiles, where we denote P_{25} as Q_1, P_{50} as Q_2, and P_{75} as Q_3. *The Qs represent the quartiles.*

An interesting aspect of quartiles is that they can be used to determine whether a distribution of scores is positively or negatively skewed. This is done by comparing the values of the quartiles as follows. If $(Q_3 - Q_2) > (Q_2 - Q_1)$, then the distribution of scores is *positively skewed* as the scores are more spread out at the high end of the distribution and more bunched up at the low end of the distribution (remember the shapes of the distributions from Figure 2.5). If $(Q_3 - Q_2) < (Q_2 - Q_1)$, then the distribution of scores is negatively skewed as the scores are more spread out at the low end of the distribution and more bunched up at the high end of the distribution. If $(Q_3 - Q_2) = (Q_2 - Q_1)$, then the distribution of scores is obviously not skewed, but is *symmetric* (see Chapter 4). For the example statistics quiz data $(Q_3 - Q_2) = 1.4833$ and $(Q_2 - Q_1) = 3.4750$; thus $(Q_3 - Q_2) < (Q_2 - Q_1)$ and we know that the distribution is negatively skewed. This should already have been evident from examining the frequency distribution in Figure 2.3 as scores are more spread out at the low end of the distribution and more bunched up at the high end. Examining the quartiles is a simple method for getting a general sense of the skewness of a distribution of scores.

2.3.3 Percentile Ranks

Let us define a **percentile rank** as the *percentage of a distribution of scores that falls below (or is less than) a certain score*. For instance, you may be interested in the percentage of scores of the GRE-Quantitative Reasoning subscale that falls below the score of 150. Say that the percentile rank for the score of 150 is computed to be 50; then this would mean that 50% of the scores fell below a score of 150. If this sounds familiar, it should. The 50th percentile was previously stated to be 150. Thus we have logically determined that the percentile rank of 150 is 50. *This is because percentile and percentile rank are actually opposite sides of the same coin.* Many are confused by this and equate percentiles and percentile ranks; however, they are related but different concepts. Recall earlier we said that percentiles are scores. *Percentile ranks are percentages* because they are continuous values and can take on any value from 0 to 100. For notational purposes, a percentile rank will be known as $PR(P_i)$, where P_i is the particular score whose percentile rank, *PR*, you wish to determine. Thus, the percentile rank of the score 150 would be denoted as $PR(150) = 50.00$. In other words, about 50% of the distribution falls below the score of 150.

Let us now consider how percentile ranks are computed. The formula for computing the $PR(P_i)$ percentile rank is

$$PR(P_i) = \left(\frac{cf + \dfrac{f(P_i - LRL)}{w}}{n} \right)(100\%)$$

where $PR(P_i)$ indicates that we are looking for the percentile rank *PR* of the score P_i, *cf* is the cumulative frequency up to but not including the interval containing $PR(P_i)$ (again known as "*cf* below"), *f* is the frequency of the interval containing $PR(P_i)$, *LRL* is the lower real limit of the interval containing $PR(P_i)$, *w* is the interval width, *n* is the sample size, and finally we multiply by 100% to place the percentile rank on a scale from 0 to 100 (and also to remind us that the percentile rank is a percentage).

As an example, consider computing the percentile rank for the score of 17. This would correspond to the percentage of the distribution that falls below a score of 17. For the example data again, using the percentile rank equation we compute $PR(17)$ as follows:

$$PR(17) = \left(\frac{12 + \dfrac{5(17 - 16.5)}{1}}{25} \right)(100\%) = \left(\frac{12 + 2.5}{25} \right)(100\%) = 58.00\%$$

Conceptually, let us discuss how the equation works. First we have to determine what interval contains the percentile rank of interest. This is easily done because we already know the score is 17, and we simply look in the interval containing 17. The *cf* below the 17 interval is 12 and *n* is 25. Thus we know that we need to go at least 12/25, or 48%, of the way into the distribution to obtain the desired percentile rank. We know that $P_i = 17$ and the *LRL* of that interval is 16.5. The interval has five frequencies, so we need to go 2.5 scores into the interval to obtain the proper percentile rank. In other words, because 17 is the midpoint of an interval with width of 1, we need to go halfway, or 2.5/5, of the way into the interval to obtain the percentile rank. In the end, we need to go 14.5/25 (or .58) of the way into the distribution to obtain our percentile rank, which translates to 58%.

As another example, we have already determined that $P_{50} = 16.6000$. Therefore, you should be able to determine on your own that $PR(16.6000) = 50\%$. This verifies that percentiles and percentile ranks are two sides of the same coin. The computation of percentiles identifies a specific score, and you start with the score to determine the score's percentile rank. You can further verify this by determining that $PR(13.1250) = 25.00\%$ and $PR(18.0833) = 75.00\%$. Next we consider the box-and-whisker plot, where quartiles and percentiles are used graphically to depict a distribution of scores.

2.3.4 Box-and-Whisker Plot

A simplified form of the frequency distribution is the **box-and-whisker plot** (often referred to simply as a **box plot**), developed by Tukey (1977). This is shown in Figure 2.7 (generated in SPSS using the default options) for the example data. The box-and-whisker plot was originally developed to be constructed on a typewriter using lines in a minimal amount of space. The **box** in the center of the figure displays the middle 50% of the distribution of scores with the thick black line representing the median. The bottom edge or hinge of the box represents the 25th percentile (or Q_1) (i.e., the bottom or lowest 25% of values). The top edge or hinge of the box represents the 75th percentile (or Q_3) (i.e., the top or highest 25% of values). The middle thick vertical line in the box represents the 50th percentile (also known as Q_2 or the median). The lines extending from the box are known as the **whiskers**. The purpose of the whiskers is to display data outside of the middle 50%. The *bottom whisker* can extend down to the lowest score (as is the case with SPSS using default options), or to the 5th or the 10th percentile (by other means), to display more extreme low scores, and the *top whisker* correspondingly can extend up to the highest score (again, as is the case with SPSS using default options), or to the 95th or 90th percentile (elsewhere), to display more extreme high scores. The choice of where to extend the whiskers is the preference of the researcher and/or the software. Scores that fall beyond the end of the whiskers, known as **outliers** due to their extremeness relative

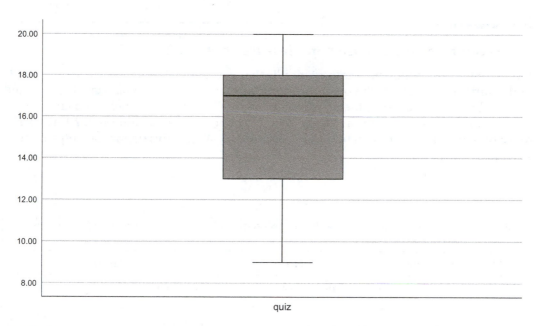

FIGURE 2.7
Box-and-whisker plot of statistics quiz data.

to the bulk of the distribution, are often displayed by dots and/or asterisks. Box-and-whisker plots can be used to examine such things as skewness (through the quartiles), outliers, and where most of the scores tend to fall. *If you turn the boxplot clockwise and compare to the histogram, you'll see similar displays of the distribution*—simply with fewer elements in the boxplot.

Let's talk specifically about some of the elements displayed in Figure 2.7. We see, for example, that the bottom 25% of the distribution (i.e., from the bottom of the box to the bottom whisker) is more spread out than the top 25% of the distribution (i.e., from the top of the box to the top whisker). This indicates that there is more variation in the bottom 25% of values than in the top 25% of values. We can make similar interpretations about the spread of the data comparing area inside the box. For example, there is more variation between Q_1 (i.e., the bottom of the box) and the median (i.e., Q_2) than between the median and Q_3 (i.e., the top of the box). We know this because the space between the median and Q_1 is much more condensed as compared to the space between Q_1 and the median.

Keep the following point in mind when interpreting boxplots: *don't confuse the variation or spread of the data with the percentage of points between the elements of the box.* There is *always* 25% of the distribution between each quartile (e.g., from Q_1 to Q_2 or from Q_2 to Q_3), regardless of how spread out or condensed that area is. Sometimes you may find a quirky boxplot. For example, you might find a boxplot with two whiskers but just one line between them (i.e., no real "box"). This would indicate that there is no variation in the middle 50% of the data; that is, all values, from the 25th to 75th percentile, are the same. As another example, you might find a boxplot where the median is setting on the top of the box. This would indicate that the median and the 75th percentile, all values between, are the same value. In those instances of quirkiness, stay true to what you understand about the boxplot and apply accordingly to your interpretations.

2.4 Recommendations Based on Measurement Scale

We cannot stress enough how important it is that you understand the measurement scale of the variable(s) with which you are working, as that will dictate what statistics can (and cannot) be computed using them. You will use the knowledge of measurement scale in every statistic that you compute. To help in this endeavor, we include Box 2.1 as a summary of which data representation techniques are most appropriate for each type of measurement scale.

BOX 2.1 Appropriate Data Representation Techniques Given the Measurement Scale of the Variable

Measurement Scale	Tables	Figures
Nominal	Frequency distribution	Bar graph
	Relative frequency distribution	
Ordinal, interval, or ratio	Frequency distribution	Histogram
	Cumulative frequency distribution	Frequency polygon
	Relative frequency distribution	Relative frequency polygon
	Cumulative relative frequency distribution	Cumulative frequency polygon
		Cumulative relative frequency polygon
		Stem-and-leaf display
		Box-and-whisker plot

2.5 Computing Tables, Graphs, and More Using SPSS

The purpose of this section is to briefly consider applications of SPSS for the topics covered in this chapter (including important screenshots). We will begin with a brief introduction to SPSS and then demonstrate SPSS procedures for generating frequencies and graphs.

2.5.1 Introduction to SPSS

Before we get into using SPSS, let's go over a few basics. SPSS is one of the most common standard statistical software programs available. Among other nice features of SPSS is that it is user-friendly, particularly compared to many other standard statistical software. Most SPSS users take advantage of the point-and-click interface of SPSS, although you can also use syntax to run statistics in SPSS. While the graphical user interface makes generating statistics in SPSS pretty easy, you need to be aware of a few nuances when working with the program.

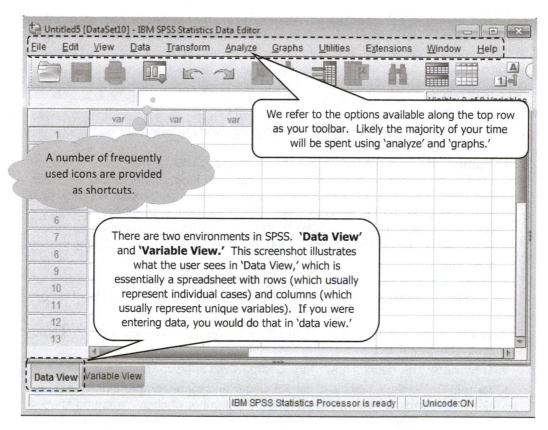

FIGURE 2.8
SPSS Data View interface.

If you use the point-and-click interface (which will be illustrated throughout the text using version 25), then it's important to understand the SPSS environment in which you'll be working. SPSS has two "environments": **Data View** and **Variable View**. Figure 2.8 illustrates what the user sees in *Data View,* which is essentially a spreadsheet with rows (which usually represent individual cases) and columns (which usually represent unique variables). If you were entering data, you would do that in Data View. Even if you haven't used SPSS, Data View probably seems familiar because it's very similar to what you've encountered if you've ever used Excel or a similar spreadsheet.

The second environment in SPSS is Variable View. Figure 2.9 illustrates what the user sees in *Variable View.* Variable View is probably dissimilar to any other software program with which you've worked. This is the environment in SPSS that allows you to refine how your variable(s) are displayed and operationalized. Many options are available in Variable View, and the illustrations in this text don't cover all of them. This isn't to say that you won't need one or more of these options in the future. However, for purposes of the illustrations in the text, we will examine some of the most common options in Variable View: (a) **name**, which is simply the column header that appears in Data View; (b) **label**, which is a longer name that can be provided to better define the variable; and (c) **values**, which connect the numbers assigned to categories with the respective categories for nominal and ordinal variables (e.g., 1 = "morning," 2 = "afternoon").

Variable View offers many options for defining and working with your data:

1. **Name**. This is the column header that will appear in Data View. The name cannot begin with a number or special character, and names cannot include spaces. The name is not limited to a particular length; however, we recommend keeping the name to eight or fewer characters so that it's more efficient to transfer your data into programs that *do* have limitations on length for column headers. If you haven't defined the variable label, then the name will be what appears on your output.

2. **Type**. This defines the type of variable. Variables that are alphanumeric will be "string." Most variables that we will use in the illustrations in the text are "numeric."

3. **Width**. For string variables, width refers to the maximum number of characters. The default is 8.

4. **Decimals**. This defines how many decimals will appear. The default is 2.

5. **Label**. The variable label is usually a longer and more comprehensive description of the variable. There is no limit on the number of characters, and spaces, numbers, and special characters can be used. Keep in mind that the variable label will be what appears on your output, so longer is fine, but concise is still a good guideline.

6. **Values**. Values are used most often only for nominal and ordinal variables. This is where you define the categories of the numeric values. The "value" is the number of the category and the "label" is what that number represents. For example, 1 may refer to "morning" and 2 may refer to "afternoon." The values and labels must be defined and added for each category of your variable. In some cases, missing values for interval and ratio variables are defined in "values" (e.g., −7 = "don't know," −8 = "refused to answer," −9 = "logical skip").

7. **Missing**. Should there be missing data, this is where you can define how it is coded. If the missing data item is simply an empty cell in your spreadsheet, there is nothing you need to do here. However, if a missing data item has been coded as a unique value (e.g., 99 or −9), then it is important that you define that value as missing. Failure to do so will result in that value being picked up as a legitimate value. Missing values can be defined as unique (i.e., discrete) or by providing the range within which all values are missing (e.g., low of −9 to high of −6).

8. **Column**. The width of the column is defined here. The default is 8.

9. **Align**. This sets the alignment of your columns (left, center, right).

10. **Measure**. The measurement scale of your variable is defined here. Interval and ratio are defined as "scale," with options for nominal and ordinal as well.

11. **Role**. The role is how the variable will be used. The default is "input," which refers to an independent variable. "Target" is a dependent variable. "Both" indicates the variable can be used as either an independent or a dependent variable. Defining the role is not required. However, some dialogs in SPSS support predefined roles. When using those dialog menus, variables that meet the requisite role are automatically displayed in the destination list.

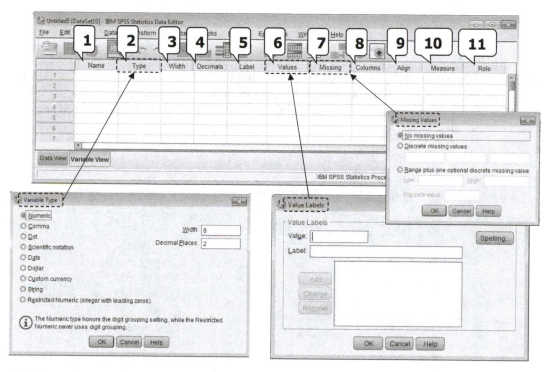

FIGURE 2.9
SPSS Variable View interface.

An additional feature of SPSS that is important to know is how the datafiles and output operate. The *datafile* (or *dataset* as we often call it) is the actual raw data—those rows and columns of data in spreadsheet form. Datasets in SPSS are saved as **.sav** files. Once you have data (i.e., a .sav file) and generate a statistic using that data, a new page will appear, and that is your output. *If you want to save your output (and we recommend doing that!), then you must save your output page separately from your dataset*. Saving the dataset does *not* save your output, and saving your output does *not* save your dataset. Output files have an extension of **.spv**. We will repeat this because it's that important—*saving your dataset file does not save your output in SPSS*. In SPSS, the data exist independent of any output that is generated using it. Don't know whether you need to save your output? Our best recommendation is this: If in doubt, just save it! Err on the side of caution. You can always delete the file later.

Referring back to Figure 2.8, it is also important to know that you can use the options in the top toolbar regardless of which environment you are in (Data View or Variable View), and even if you are on the output page. SPSS offers quite a bit of flexibility in being able to access and use the toolbar from any view.

These are just a few tips on the nuances of using SPSS. The more you use SPSS, as with any software, the better you will understand the functionalities, shortcuts, and more. We encourage you to experiment in SPSS. You can't break it, so to speak, so explore what it has to offer. The illustrations in the text are just a starting point but will hopefully whet your appetite to learn more about the software to allow you to become a better researcher.

2.5.2 Frequencies

Step 1. For the types of tables discussed in this chapter, in SPSS go to "Analyze" in the top pulldown menu, then "Descriptive Statistics," and then select "Frequencies." Following the steps (A–C) in the screenshot for "FREQUENCIES: Step 1" in Figure 2.10 will produce the "Frequencies" dialog box.

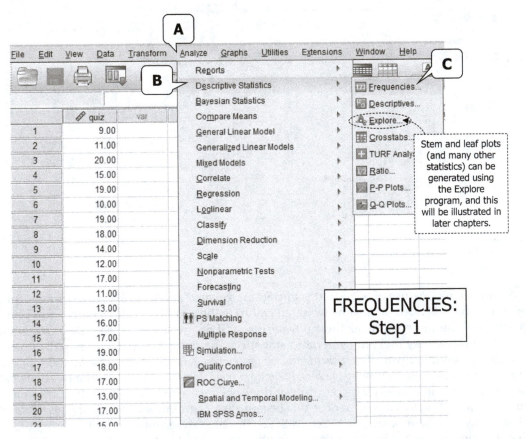

FIGURE 2.10
FREQENCIES: Step 1.

Step 2. The Frequencies dialog box will open (see screenshot for "FREQUENCIES: Step 2" in Figure 2.11). From this main Frequencies dialog box, click the variable of interest from the list on the left (e.g., "quiz") and move it into the "Variables" box by clicking the arrow button. By default, there is a checkmark in the box "Display frequency tables," and we will keep this checked; this will generate a table of frequencies, relative frequencies, and cumulative relative frequencies. Four buttons are listed on the right side of the Frequencies dialog box: "Statistics," "Charts," "Format," and "Style." Let's first talk about options available through Statistics and then about Charts. Format and Style provide options for aesthetics (e.g., ordering by ascending or descending values, formatting the cell background and text), and we won't go into detail on those (however, you are encouraged to explore these on your own).

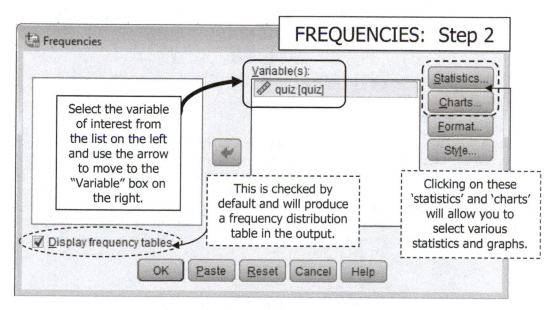

FIGURE 2.11
FREQUENCIES: Step 2.

Step 3a. If you click on the Statistics button from the main Frequencies dialog box, a new box labeled "Frequencies: Statistics" will appear (see the screenshot for "FREQUENCIES: Step 3a" in Figure 2.12). From here, you can obtain quartiles and selected percentiles as well as numerous other descriptive statistics simply by placing a checkmark in the boxes for the statistics that you want to generate. For better accuracy when generating the median, quartiles and percentiles, check the box "Values are group midpoints." However, note that these values are not always as precise as those from the formula given earlier in this chapter and *not* taking this step doesn't mean your results will be incorrect.

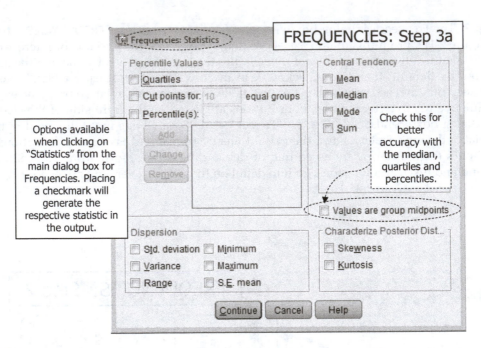

FIGURE 2.12
FREQUENCIES: Step 3a.

Step 3b. If you click on the Charts button from the main Frequencies dialog box, a new box labeled "Frequencies: Charts" will appear (see the screenshot for "FREQUENCIES: Step 3b" in Figure 2.13). From here, you can select options to generate bar graphs, pie charts, or histograms. If you select bar graphs or pie charts, you can plot either frequencies or percentages (relative frequencies). Thus the Frequencies program enables you to do much of what this chapter has covered. In addition, stem-and-leaf plots are available in the Explore program (see "Frequencies: Step 1" for a screenshot on where the Explore program can be accessed).

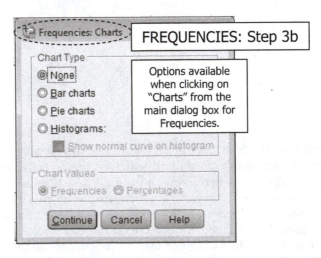

FIGURE 2.13
FREQUENCIES: Step 3b.

2.5.3 Graphs

SPSS can generate multiple types of graphs. We will examine how to generate histograms, boxplots, bar graphs, and more using the Graphs procedure in SPSS.

2.5.3.1 Histograms

Step 1. For other ways to generate the types of graphical displays covered in this chapter, go to "Graphs" in the top pulldown menu. From there, select "Legacy Dialogs," then "Histogram" (see the screenshot for "GRAPHS: Step 1" in Figure 2.14). Another option for creating a histogram, which we will not illustrate but that uses an interactive drag-and-drop system, starting again from the Graphs option in the top pulldown menu, is to select "Chart Builder."

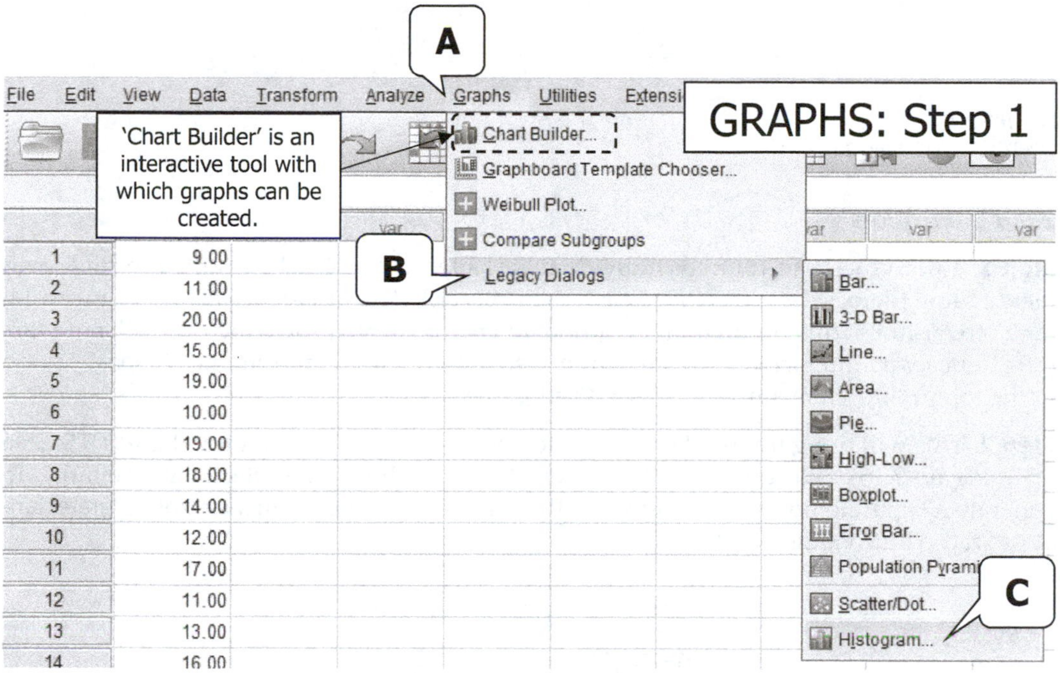

FIGURE 2.14
GRAPHS: Step 1.

Step 2. Following Step 1 will bring up the "Histogram" dialog box (see the screenshot for "HISTOGRAMS: Step 2" in Figure 2.15). Click the variable of interest (e.g., "quiz") and move it into the "Variable(s)" box by clicking the arrow. Place a checkmark in "Display normal curve," and then click "OK." This will generate the same histogram as was produced through the Frequencies program already mentioned and will overlay a normal curve.

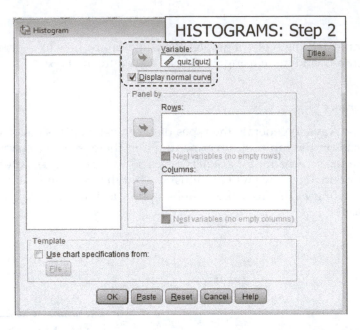

FIGURE 2.15
HISTOGRAMS: Step 2.

2.5.3.2 *Boxplots*

Step 1. To produce a boxplot for individual variables, click "Graphs" in the top pulldown menu. From there, select "Legacy Dialogs," then "Boxplot" (see "GRAPHS: Step 1," Figure 2.14, for a screenshot of this step). Another option for creating a boxplot, which we will not illustrate but uses an interactive drag-and-drop system, starting again from the "Graphs" option in the top pulldown menu, is to select "Chart Builder."

Step 2. This will bring up the "Boxplot" dialog box (see the screenshot for "BOXPLOTS: Step 2" in Figure 2.16). Select the "Simple" option (this will already be selected by default). To generate a separate boxplot for individual variables, click the "Summaries of separate variables" radio button, then click "Define."

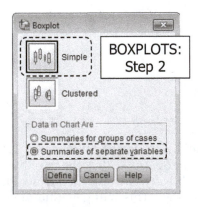

FIGURE 2.16
BOXPLOTS: Step 2.

Step 3. This will bring up the "Define simple boxplot: Summaries . . ." dialog box (see the screenshot for "BOXPLOTS: Step 3" in Figure 2.17). Click the variable of interest (e.g., "quiz") into the "Boxes Represent" box. Then click "OK." This will generate a boxplot.

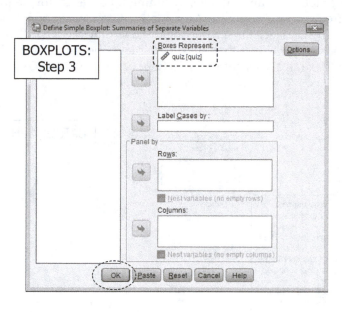

FIGURE 2.17
BOXPLOTS: Step 3.

2.5.3.3 Bar Graphs

Step 1. To produce a bar graph for individual variables, select "Graphs" from the top pull-down menu. From there, select "Legacy Dialogs," then "Bar" (see "GRAPHS: Step 1" in Figure 2.14 for a screenshot of this step).

Step 2. From the main "Bar Chart" dialog box, select "Simple" (which will be selected by default), and click the "Summaries for groups of cases" radio button (see "BAR GRAPHS: Step 2" in Figure 2.18 for a screenshot of this step).

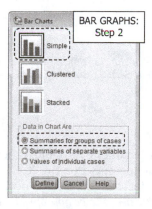

FIGURE 2.18
BAR GRAPHS: Step 2.

Step 3. A new box labeled "Define Simple Bar: Summaries . . ." will appear. Click the variable of interest (e.g., "eye color") and move it into the "Variable" box by clicking the arrow button. Then a decision must be made for how the bars will be displayed. Several types of displays for bar graph data are available, including "N of cases" for frequencies, "Cum. N" for cumulative frequencies, "% of cases" for relative frequencies, and "Cum. %" for cumulative relative frequencies (see the screenshot for "BAR GRAPHS: Step 3" in Figure 2.19). The most common bar graph is one that simply displays the frequencies (i.e., selecting the radio button for "N of cases"). Once your selections are made, click "OK." This will generate a bar graph.

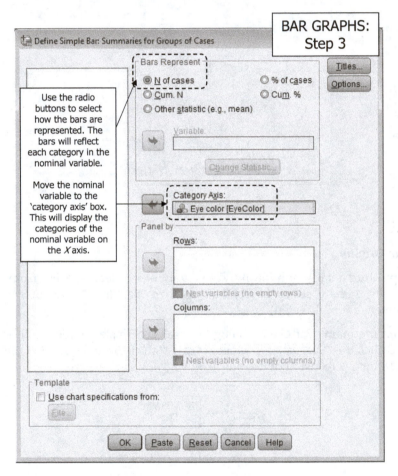

FIGURE 2.19
BAR GRAPHS: Step 3.

Additionally, if you have more than one variable, more complex bar graphs can be created. The categories can continue to appear on the X axis; however, the bars can represent other statistics using the "Other statistic (e.g., mean)" option (Figure 2.20). *Keep in mind that the measurement scale of the variable needs to be appropriate for the statistic that you are computing.* Thus, for example, if you want the bars to represent the mean of a second variable, the second variable should be at least interval in scale.

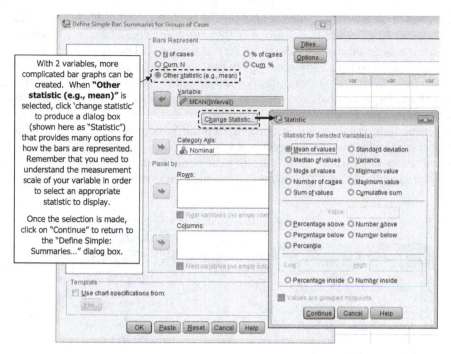

FIGURE 2.20
Bar graph option with multiple variables.

2.5.3.3 Frequency Polygons

Step 1. Frequency polygons, or line graphs, can be generated by clicking on "Graphs" in the top pulldown menu. From there, select "Legacy Dialogs," then "Line" (see "GRAPHS: Step 1" in Figure 2.14 for a screenshot of this step).

Step 2. From the main "Line Charts" dialog box, select "Simple" (which will be selected by default), and click the "Summaries for groups of cases" (which will be selected by default) radio button (see the screenshot for "FREQUENCY POLYGONS: Step 2" in Figure 2.21).

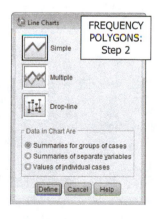

FIGURE 2.21
FREQUENCY POLYGONS: Step 2.

Step 3. A new box labeled "Define Simple Line: Summaries . . ." will appear. Click the variable of interest (e.g., "quiz") and move it into the "Variable" box by clicking the arrow button. Then a decision must be made for how the lines will be displayed. Several types of displays for line graph (i.e., frequency polygon) data are available, including "N of cases" for frequencies, "Cum. N" for cumulative frequencies, "% of cases" for relative frequencies, and "Cum. %" for cumulative relative frequencies (see the screenshot for "FREQUENCY POLYGONS: Step 3" in Figure 2.22). Additionally, other statistics can be selected through the "Other statistic (e.g., mean)" option (similar to what was illustrated with the bar graphs). The most common frequency polygon is one that simply displays the frequencies or counts for the values in the variable (i.e., selecting the radio button for "N of cases"). Once your selections are made, click "OK." This will generate a frequency polygon.

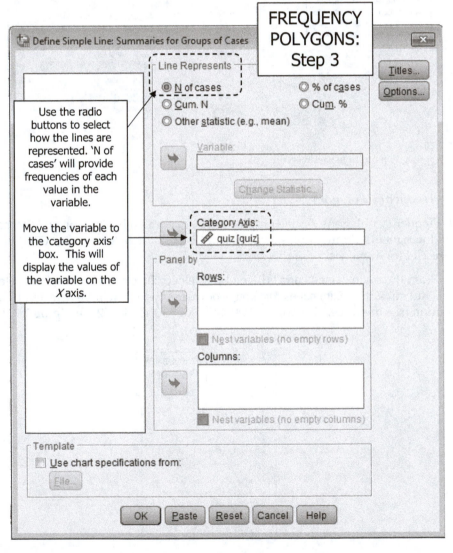

FIGURE 2.22
FREQUENCY POLYGONS: Step 3.

Graphs can also be generated in SPSS using Chart Builder (click on "Graphs" in the top pulldown menu and then go to "Chart Builder"). This is an interactive tool that allows researchers to drag and drop variables and types of graphs (e.g., bar, line, boxplots, and more) to build the figure. On the right side, "Element Properties" and "Chart Appearance" provide researchers with aesthetic options. Should you not choose to use Chart Builder to create your graph, you still have the ability to adapt the look of your graph by double-clicking on the graph in your output. This will allow you to access Chart Editor and make aesthetic alterations to your figure.

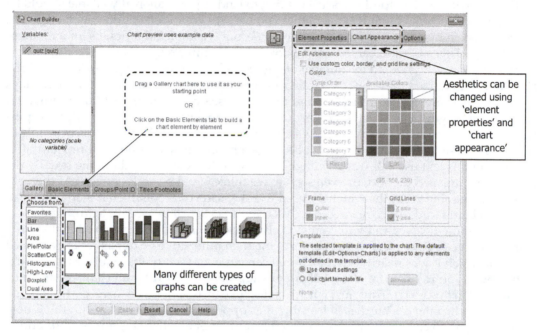

FIGURE 2.23
Chart Builder.

2.6 Computing Tables, Graphs, and More Using R

2.6.1 Introduction to R

The purpose of this section is to briefly consider applications of **R** for the topics covered in this chapter. We will begin with a brief introduction to **R** and then describe **R** procedures for frequencies and graphs.

R is a freely accessible open source software environment that operates on both Windows and Mac platforms. *Open source* means that anyone can contribute to the environment, and thus a plethora of exciting tools have been, and will continue to be, developed in **R**. We will interject here that we have a love–hate relationship with **R**. By being free and open source, **R** is broad and deep in terms of the tools available, with more being added almost daily. Additionally, the **R** community is unparalleled for the help and support offered to users. On the other hand, **R** does not operate in a point-and-click environment. Rather, **R** operates using command language and users have to write "scripts" (i.e., code or syntax) to *tell* **R** what to do, and **R** is very finicky in its prose. At this point, you may be asking: "Why in the world would I want to subject myself to the torture of having to write commands to generate statistics when just learning statistics is hard enough?" Great question, and we've asked ourselves the same question! If you ask around to a few **R** users, what you'll often find is that many **R** users avoided **R** for as long as they could, but when they finally gave it a shot (or perhaps *had* to give it a shot as the **R** environment was the only tool accessible for a particular statistic needed), were actually quite pleased—or at least were able to endure **R** sufficiently so that they saw the value in it and continued to use it. We've already mentioned a few benefits of **R**, and the fact that it's free, extremely powerful, open source, and overflowing with helpful users just waiting to lend support are really all that should be needed to convince you that **R** is a tool that you need in your toolkit. You may have heard the assertion, "Do something for 21 days and it becomes a habit." (Pardon us for a momentary detour: This assertion came from a book published in 1960 by Dr. Maxwell Maltz, a plastic surgeon, who studied the number of days it took amputees to adjust to losing a limb. Dr. Maltz generalized these results to other major life events, and the assertion of 21 days for a habit was almost set in stone. More recently, research suggests that habit formation takes much longer than 21 days, and is quite varied depending on the task. For our purposes, we're going with Dr. Maltz! Now let's get back on track!) We apply this principle to **R** and say, "Use **R** for 9 chapters and it becomes a habit" (okay, it's not 21, but 9 of the 10 chapters in this text use **R**!). We encourage you to give **R** a shot throughout the text. By the time you've finished the text, or even sooner, we think you'll be an **R** convert. At the very least, you'll be able to say that you have used **R** and it is in your toolkit! That is no small feat!

All that being said, we're not necessarily saying that **R** will be easy to learn. Again, ask around to a few **R** users and you'll most likely quickly come to understand that there is a learning curve to **R**, one that is steeper for some than others (we've ourselves experienced points at which it was nearly vertical). If you can get over the hump, so to speak, in using **R**, however, you're home free (remember our suggestion to try **R** for all chapters in which it's covered in this text?). Thus, just when you feel like throwing in the towel on **R**, don't do it. Stick with it. Take the hurdles in learning **R** as opportunities to connect with the **R** help community, and keep going. We have offered a number of excellent resources at the end of the chapter to help in learning more about **R**. We hope that the **R** sections in this textbook will provide a smooth transition into the **R** environment and will whet your appetite to learn more about **R**. We want to remind you that what we have provided is an introduction to **R** for the various statistics generated in the text. Keep in mind that this text is *not* meant to serve as a comprehensive resource for all things **R**. There *are* resources that serve in that capacity, and we will offer a few of those at the conclusion of this chapter. However, this textbook is first and foremost a resource for learning about statistical concepts, which is supplemented with resources for computing statistics using both SPSS and **R**. With that introduction, let's get rolling in **R**!

2.6.1.1 R Basics

You need to understand a few basic things about **R** before we delve into writing commands. **R** is a base package. Similar to SPSS, Mplus, and many other software programs, there is a base package **R**, to which additional modules (called *packages* in the **R** environment) can be added. The packages written for **R** are stored in the Comprehensive **R** Archive Network (CRAN). There are identical versions of CRAN, called CRAN "mirrors," all around the world. Thus, when you first download **R**, you have to select from which mirror you want to download. What most **R** users do is to select a CRAN location that is geographically close to them, or at least in their same time zone.

2.6.1.2 *Downloading R and RStudio*

R can be downloaded from www.r-project.org. When you click "download **R**," you will be asked from which CRAN mirror you want to download. Many **R** users work directly from the original **R** environment. We prefer using **R** from **RStudio**. The makers of RStudio claim that it "makes **R** easier to use" by providing a console within which to work, visualization space, debugging, and more—and we agree. We have used **R** (version 3.5.1) through RStudio (version 1.1.456) in a Windows platform throughout the text. To download RStudio, download **R** first and then visit www.rstudio.com and click "download." The RStudio Desktop open source license can be downloaded for free. That is the version that has been used throughout the text.

When you use **R** through RStudio, you'll see that you will have access to four quadrants (see Figure 2.24). The top-left quadrant is the **source editor window**. This is where you will write and execute scripts or commands (i.e., syntax or code). The bottom-left quadrant is the **console**, and this is where the output will appear once you run a command (the exceptions are graphs and figures, which display in the bottom-right quadrant). When you open RStudio, the console will autopopulate with information—one very important piece of information is contained within the first line, and that is the version of **R** that is being used by RStudio. In Windows, the current version is the default. However, you may find yourself in a

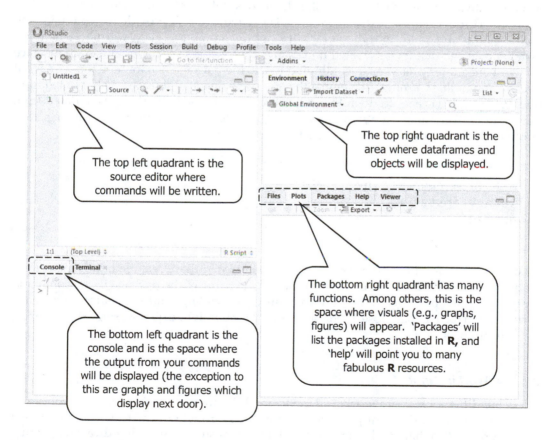

FIGURE 2.24
RStudio.

situation where you want to run an older version of **R**, as not all packages run in all versions of **R**. To override which version of **R** is being used, go to "Tools" in RStudio's top toolbar and select "Global options." If not already selected, click "general" in the left navigational menu. The version of **R** that is being used is displayed. Click the button labeled "change" to display other options of **R** available on your computer and to select the specific version of **R** that you want to work with. You can install previous released of **R** by visiting the CRAN project website (https://cran.r-project.org/bin/windows/base/old/). The top-right quadrant is where you will see the list of dataframes and objects (you'll learn about these soon) that you have called up to work with. The bottom-right quadrant is the visualization space (i.e., graphs and plots that are generated will appear in this quadrant), and also where you can find the list of **R** packages installed, update packages, and link to various help tools.

2.6.1.3 Packages

Again, base **R** has a number of functionalities in it ready to use, but there are lots of great packages available that provide additional functionality. Accessing and using a package is a two-step process. The package has to first be installed (using the *install.packages("PackageNameHere")* command), and then the package has to be called into the library (using the *library(PackageNameHere)* command). Packages only need be installed once (i.e., once installed, always installed). However, they have to be called into the library each time they are used. Throughout the text, as a package is needed, we will provide the commands to both install it and call it into the library. It's not uncommon to get a warning when you install a package that it was created under an earlier version of **R**. Only in a rare instance will you encounter problems in continuing to use the package, so don't be too worried if you encounter this warning. Remember that packages, just like software, get updated from time to time. This is easy to do in RStudio using the *update* icon. **R** also gets updated from time to time. You can efficiently, and painlessly, update **R** by running the following script. You will want to copy all your packages to the new version of **R**.

```
install.packages("installr")
library(installr)
updateR()
```

Let us digress for a moment. Previously we mentioned that **R** can be quite persnickety. Notice that quotation marks are used to enclose the name of the package in the command for installing the package but not in the command for calling it into the library. Yes, that's correct—you have to pay close attention to little details in **R** like quotation marks, commas, capitalization, etc.

2.6.1.4 Working in R

There are different ways to work in **R**, none of which are necessarily right or wrong, and different users have different preferences. However, throughout the text we have guided your work in **R** so that you begin your work by establishing a **working directory**. Within that working directory, your files and scripts will be stored. We have found that to be the easiest way to keep track of your files and stay organized.

Throughout the text, we will refer to objects and functions. An **object** is something created from a **function.** Many times, a function will be running a statistical procedure (e.g., generating an ANOVA or a regression model), but a function could also be generating a table or creating a variable or more. An object is what results from that function (e.g., the results of the ANOVA model, the table, or the variable). Throughout the text, we will try to remind you what is the object versus the function but generally this takes the form in **R** command language as the following: *object <- function*, where the object appears to the left of <- and the function appears to the right of <-. You might be wondering why this is important. Creating objects from functions is not necessarily a requirement, but it can make life much easier when you want to extend the results from your function to something else. This is because rather than writing the entire function again (e.g., an entire ANOVA or regression model), you simply have to write the name of your object. As you will see, some functions are short and sweet, whereas others are long and tedious. Naming your function as an object is particularly helpful in the case of the latter!

Although data can be created in **R**, the data examples provided in the text use comma-separated (.csv) files. Command language is provided in the illustrations to bring the .csv file into the **R** environment. We have done this because it is usually the case that the data that we work with already exist in spreadsheet form (e.g., Excel, SPSS, SAS). And if the data do not already exist, we encourage you to use a spreadsheet tool to create the dataset and then bring it into the **R** environment. Once the data are brought into **R**, it is called a **dataframe**. There are lots of ways to work with data in dataframes (e.g., recoding variables, creating new variables), and you'll be introduced to quite a few of those in the examples throughout the text. If you manipulate your dataframe, you may want to save it and export it out of the **R** environment. That's easy to do using the *write.csv(DataframeName, "FileName.csv")* command. This command, along with a few other "staples," are provided in Box 2.2. RStudio has a number of time-saving shortcuts. You can access these directly in RStudio by going to "Tools" in the top menu, and then selecting "keyboard shortcuts help." You'll find that some are the same as what you're accustomed in other environments (e.g., in Windows, Ctrl+O to open, Ctrl+S to save).

BOX 2.2 Need-to-Know Commands in R

Command	Functionality
install. packages("PackageNameHere")	Installs a package into **R**. Once a package is installed, it remains installed in **R**. However, each time it is used, the user needs to call it in using the library command. (*Note: Quotation marks around the package name are required.*)
library(PackageNameHere)	Calls a package into **R** so that it can be used. Each time a package is used, it must be called into the **R** environment using the library command.
getwd()	**R** is always directed to a directory on your computer. To find out which directory it is pointed to, run this "get working directory" command. We will assume that we need to change the working directory, and will use the next line of code to set the working directory to the desired path.

(continued)

(continued)

Command	Functionality
setwd("E:/Folder")	Establishes a working directory that points to a specific folder that is designated by the user. (Momentary detour: If you don't know where a file is located, right-click on the file and go to "properties." The "location" in properties will provide the specific file location.) *(Note: Quotation marks around the folder are required.)*
DataframeName <- read.csv ("DatasetName.csv")	Renames the dataset to whatever is designated to the left of the <-. *(Note: Quotation marks around the file name are required.)*
names(DataframeName)	Lists the names of the variables in the dataframe (this output is provided in the console).
View(DataframeName)	Calls the dataframe into RStudio (i.e., creates a tab in the source editor where the user can see the actual spreadsheet view of the data).
write.csv(DataframeName, "FileName.csv")	Exports the dataframe from **R** into a comma separated file.

Now that you've been provided the basics of **R**, let's dive in! Next we consider **R** for various tables, graphs, and more. The **R** code is only those lines of text that are included in the boxes. The remainder is annotation, provided here to help you understand what the various lines of code are doing. We will preface this by reading in our data. We will be using both the quiz data and the eye color data. These reside in two separate data files, so we will read them in separately using the following code (Figure 2.25). One additional tip as we're getting started. . . . When you run script in **R**, do *not* highlight the command and then hit run. *Rather, simply place your cursor anywhere in the command that you want to run and then hit the run icon (or Ctrl+Enter).* This is especially helpful when you have very long lines of code, and it will prevent you from failing to highlight parts of it.

```
getwd()
```

R is always directed to a directory on your computer. To find out which directory it is pointed to, run this "get working directory" command. We will assume that we need to change the working directory, and will use the next line of code to set the working directory to the desired path.

```
setwd("E:/Folder")
```

Change what is in parentheses to your file location. Also, if you are copying the directory name, it will copy in slashes. You will need to change the slash (i.e., \) to a forward slash (i.e., /). Additionally, note that you need the name of your folder location in quotation marks.

```
Ch2_quiz <- read.csv("Ch2_quiz.csv")
Ch2_eye <- read.csv("Ch2_eye.csv")
```

FIGURE 2.25
Getting Started in **R**.

This command reads your data into **R**. What's to the left of the <- will be what you want to call the dataframe in **R**. In this example, we're calling the first **R** dataframe "Ch2_quiz." What's to the right of the <- tells **R** to find this particular .csv file. In this example, our file is called "Ch2_quiz.csv." Make sure the extension (i.e., .csv) is there. Also note that you need this in quotation marks. We are reading in the eye color data similarly.

```
names(Ch4_quiz)
names(Ch2_eye)
```

This command will display in the console a list of variable names for each dataframe as follows:

```
# names(Ch2_quiz)
[1] "quiz"
```

```
# names(Ch2_eye)
[1] "EyeColor"
```

This is a good check to make sure your data have been read in correctly.

```
View(Ch2_quiz)
View(Ch2_eye)
```

This command will let you view the dataset in spreadsheet format in R Studio. It will be set as an additional tab in the upper-left quadrant in RStudio so you can toggle to it from any other open file.

```
Ch2_eye$color <- factor(Ch2_eye$EyeColor,
                        labels = c("blue",
                                   "brown",
                                   "green",
                                   "black"))
```

This will create a new variable in our dataframe named "color" that is a nominal variable with four categories with labels of the eye colors. The colors are listed in order of their values. For example, "blue" is 1 and "brown" is 2.

```
summary(Ch2_quiz)
```

The *summary* command will produce basic descriptive statistics on all the variables in our dataframe. This is a great way to quickly check to see if the data have been read in correctly and get a feel for your data, if you haven't already. The output from the summary statement for this dataframe looks like this:

```
      quiz
Min.    : 9.00
1st Qu.:13.00
Median :17.00
Mean    :15.56
3rd Qu.:18.00
Max.    :20.00
```

```
levels(Ch2_eye$color)
```

This command will output the categories in our nominal variable as follows:

```
[1] "blue" "brown" "green" "black"
```

FIGURE 2.25 (continued)
Getting started in **R**.

2.6.2 Frequencies

```
install.packages("plyr")
```

Frequencies can be generated using many different packages in **R**. This command will install the *plyr* package that we can use to generate frequencies.

```
library(plyr)
```

This command will load the *plyr* package.

```
count(Ch2_eye$color)
```

The *count* function will generate a frequency table for the variable "color" in our dataframe "Ch2_eye."

```
      x freq
1  blue   10
2 brown    6
3 green    3
4 black    1
```

FIGURE 2.26
Frequencies.

2.6.3 Graphs

2.6.3.1 Histograms

```
hist(Ch2_quiz$quiz,
     main = "Histogram of Quiz Scores",
     xlab = "Quiz Score", ylab = "Frequency")
```

The *hist* function will produce a histogram using the variable "quiz" from the "Ch4_quiz" dataframe (i.e., "ch2_quiz$quiz"). The histogram will include "Histogram of Quiz Scores" as the title (i.e., main = "Histogram of Quiz Scores"), with the X axis being labeled "Quiz Score" (i.e., *xlab = "Quiz Score"*) and the Y axis being labeled "Frequency" (i.e., *ylab = "Frequency"*).

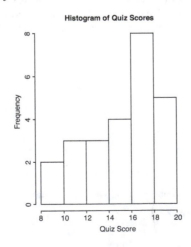

FIGURE 2.27
Histograms.

```
install.packages("ggplot2")
```

Histograms can be made using many different packages in **R**. This command will install the *ggplot2* package that we can use to create various graphs and plots, including a histogram.

```
library(ggplot2)
```

This command will load the *ggplot2* package.

```
qplot(Ch2_quiz$quiz, geom="histogram")
```

We can generate a very simple histogram using this command.

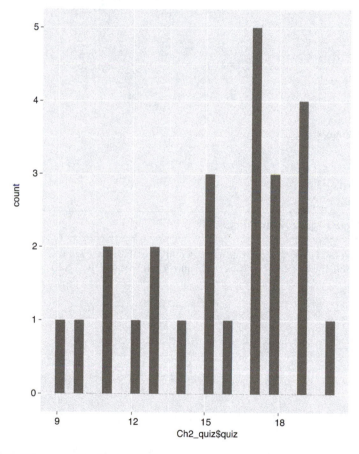

```
qplot(Ch2_quiz$quiz, geom="histogram",
      binwidth=0.8,
          main = "Histogram for Quiz Score",
      xlab = "Score", ylab = "Count",
      fill=I("gray"),
      col=I("white"))
```

FIGURE 2.27 (continued)
Histograms.

We can add a few commands to change the width of the bars (i.e., *binwidth = 0.8*), color of the bars (i.e., *fill = I("gray")*), and outline of the bars (i.e., *col = I("white")*). We can also add a title (i.e., *main = "Histogram for Quiz Score"*) and change the *X* and *Y* axes (*xlab = "Score," ylab = "Count"*).

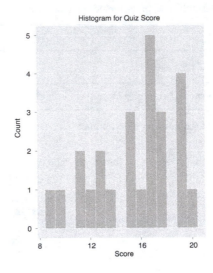

FIGURE 2.27 (continued)
Histograms.

2.6.3.2 *Boxplots*

```
boxplot(Ch2_quiz$quiz,ylab="Score")
```

The *boxplot* function can be used to generate a boxplot. In parentheses, we tell **R** which variable in our dataframe to compute the boxplot (i.e., "Ch2_quiz$quiz") and we label the *Y* axis as "Score."

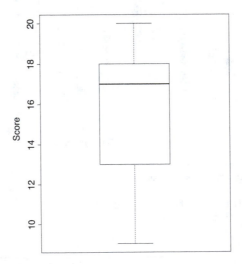

FIGURE 2.28
Boxplots.

2.6.3.3 *Bar Graphs*

```
eyecounts <- table(Ch2_eye$color)
```

To generate a bar graph, we first need to create a table of counts of our variable. We do this using the *table* function. If we run only the command, *table(Ch2_eye$color)*, we see the counts for the categories in our variable, but we are not creating an object:

```
blue brown green black
  10     6     3     1
```

By adding "eyecounts <-" to the command, we are creating an object called "eyecounts" that we can use to create our bar graph in the following command.

```
barplot(eyecounts,
        main= "Bar Graph of Eye Color",
        xlab = "Eye Color",
        ylab = "Count",
        col = "gray")
```

This command will create a bar graph using the counts from "eyecounts." The graph will be titled based on the *main* command (i.e., "Bar Graph of Eye Color"). The *X* axis will be labeled "Eye Color," and the *Y* axis will be labeled "Count." The color of the bars will be gray.

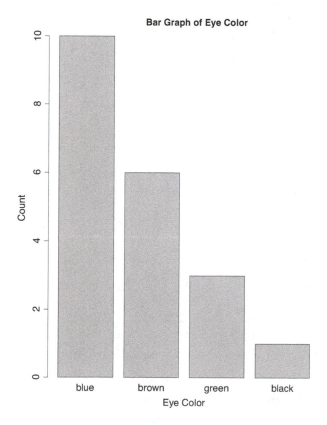

FIGURE 2.29
Bar graphs.

2.6.3.4 Frequency Polygons

```
plot(Ch2_quiz$quiz,
     type = "o",
     xlab = "Score",
     ylab = "Count",
     main = "Line Graph")
```

We use the *plot* function and define the dataframe and variable for which we want to create the line graph (i.e., "Ch2_quiz$quiz"). The graph will be titled based on how we define the *main* command (i.e., "Line Graph"). The X axis will be labeled "Score," and the Y axis will be labeled "Count." The *type = "o"* tells **R** to draw both the lines and points in the graph ("p" would draw only points and "l" would draw only lines).

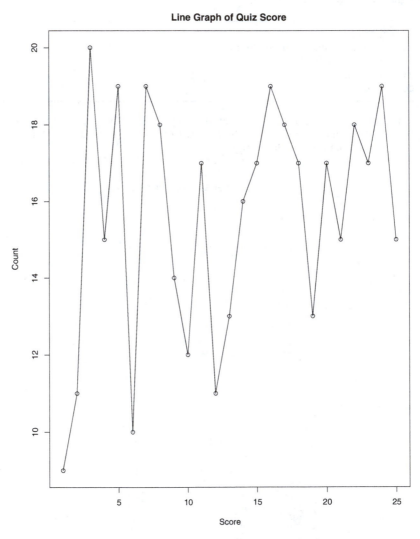

FIGURE 2.30
Frequency polygons (aka line graphs).

2.7 Research Question Template and Example Write-Up

Depending on the purpose of your research study, you may or may not write a research question that corresponds to your descriptive statistics. If the end result of your research paper is to present results from inferential statistics, it may be that your research questions correspond only to those inferential questions, and thus no question is presented to represent the descriptive statistics. That is quite common. On the other hand, if the ultimate purpose of your research study is purely descriptive in nature, then writing one or more research questions that correspond to the descriptive statistics is not only entirely appropriate, but (in most cases) absolutely necessary. At this time, let us revisit our graduate research assistant, Addie Venture, who was introduced at the beginning of the chapter. As you may recall, her task was to summarize data from 25 students enrolled in Dr. Debhard's statistics course. The questions that Addie developed based on consultation with Dr. Debhard included the following:

1. What interpretations can be made from the frequency table of quiz scores from students enrolled in an introductory statistics class?
2. What interpretations can be made from graphical representations of quiz scores from students enrolled in an introductory statistics class?
3. What is the distributional shape of the statistics quiz scores?
4. What is the 50th percentile of the quiz scores?

A template for writing descriptive research questions for summarizing data follows. Note that these are just a few examples. Given the multitude of descriptive statistics that can be generated, these are not meant to be exhaustive:

What interpretations can be made from the table of [variable]? What interpretations can be made from the graphical representation of [variable]? What is the distributional shape of the [variable]? What is the 50th percentile of [variable]?

Next, we present an APA-like paragraph summarizing the results of the statistics quiz data example:

As shown in Table 2.2 and Figure 2.2, scores ranged from 9 to 20, with more students achieving a score of 17 than any other score (20%). From Figure 2.2 we also know that the distribution of scores was negatively skewed, with the bulk of the scores being at the high end of the distribution. Skewness was also evident as the quartiles were not equally spaced, as shown in Figure 2.7. Thus, overall the sample of students tended to do rather well on this particular quiz, although a few low scores should be troubling (as 20% did not pass the quiz and suggest the need for some remediation).

2.8 Additional Resources

Throughout the chapter, we've shared a number of resources related to graphing. As you step into learning statistical software, a number of excellent tools are available to help you:

- An increasing number of books are available for learning **R** (e.g., Crawley, 2013; Rahlf, 2017; Wickham & Grolemund, 2017). Wickham and Grolemund (2017) is also available online at https://r4ds.had.co.nz.
- As mentioned in the text, the **R** user community is both large and immensely helpful. The following websites are a few places you can start when you need **R** support:
  - o **R** cookbook: www.cookbook-r.com
  - o Datacamp: www.datacamp.com
  - o Stackoverflow: https://stackoverflow.com/questions/tagged/r
  - o Comprehensive **R** Archive Network (CRAN): https://cran.r-project.org
  - o Learning **R** in **R**: https://swirlstats.com
- Discussion lists are one of the quickest ways to find support; users of SPSS can join the SPSS listserv to post questions or search the archives (https://listserv.uga.edu/cgi-bin/wa?A0=SPSSX-L).

Problems

Conceptual Problems

1. For a distribution where the 50th percentile is 100, what is the percentile rank of 100?
   a. 0
   b. .50
   c. 50
   d. 100

2. Which of the following frequency distributions will generate the same relative frequency distribution?

X	f	Y	f	Z	f
100	2	100	6	100	8
99	5	99	15	99	18
98	8	98	24	98	28
97	5	97	15	97	18
96	2	96	6	96	8

   a. *X* and *Y* only
   b. *X* and *Z* only
   c. *Y* and *Z* only
   d. *X*, *Y*, and *Z*
   e. None of the above

3. Which of the following frequency distributions will generate the same cumulative relative frequency distribution?

X	f	Y	f	Z	f
100	2	100	6	100	8
99	5	99	15	99	18
98	8	98	24	98	28
97	5	97	15	97	18
96	2	96	6	96	8

   a. X and Y only
   b. X and Z only
   c. Y and Z only
   d. X, Y, and Z
   e. None of the above

4. True or false? In a histogram, 48% of the area lies below the score whose percentile rank is 52.

5. Which of the following would be the preferred method of graphing data pertaining to the ethnicity of a sample?
   a. Histogram
   b. Frequency polygon
   c. Cumulative frequency polygon
   d. Bar graph

6. True or false? The proportion of scores between Q_1 and Q_3 may be less than .50.

7. The values of Q_1, Q_2, and Q_3 in a positively skewed population distribution are calculated. What is the expected relationship between $(Q_2 - Q_1)$ and $(Q_3 - Q_2)$?
   a. $(Q_2 - Q_1)$ is greater than $(Q_3 - Q_2)$.
   b. $(Q_2 - Q_1)$ is equal to $(Q_3 - Q_2)$.
   c. $(Q_2 - Q_1)$ is less than $(Q_3 - Q_2)$.
   d. Cannot be determined without examining the data.

8. True or false? If the percentile rank of a score of 72 is 65, we can say that 35% of the scores exceed 72.

9. True or false? In a negatively skewed distribution, the proportion of scores between Q_1 and Q_2 is less than .25.

10. A group of 200 sixth-grade students was given a standardized test and obtained scores ranging from 42 to 88. If the scores tended to "bunch up" in the low 80s, the shape of the distribution would be which of the following?
   a. Symmetrical
   b. Positively skewed
   c. Negatively skewed
   d. Normal

11. Which of the following is the preferred method of graphing data on the eye color of a sample?

     a. Bar graph

     b. Frequency polygon

     c. Cumulative frequency polygon

     d. Relative frequency polygon

12. If $Q_2 = 60$, then what is P_{50}?

     a. 50

     b. 60

     c. 95

     d. Cannot be determined with the information provided.

13. True or false? With the same data and using an interval width of 1, the frequency polygon and histogram will display the same information.

14. A researcher develops a histogram based on an interval width of 2. Can she reconstruct the raw scores using only this histogram? Yes or No?

15. True or false? $Q_2 = 50$ for a positively skewed variable and $Q_2 = 50$ for a negatively skewed variable. Given this, Q_1 will be the same for both variables.

16. Which of the following statements is *correct* for a continuous variable?

     a. The proportion of the distribution below the 25th percentile is 75%.

     b. The proportion of the distribution below the 50th percentile is 25%.

     c. The proportion of the distribution above the third quartile is 25%.

     d. The proportion of the distribution between the 25th and 75th percentile is 25%.

17. For a dataset with four unique values (55, 70, 80, and 90), the relative frequency for the value 55 is 20%, the relative frequency for 70 is 30%, the relative frequency for 80 is 20%, and the relative frequency for 90 is 30%. What is the cumulative relative frequency for the value 70?

     a. 20%

     b. 30%

     c. 50%

     d. 100%

18. In examining data collected over the past 10 years, researchers at a theme park find the following for 5000 first-time guests: 2250 visited during the summer months; 675 visited during the fall; 1300 visited during the winter; and 775 visited during the spring. What is the relative frequency for guests who visited during the spring?

     a. .135

     b. .155

     c. .260

     d. .450

19. A researcher is analyzing student enrollment data for the last academic year for all public postsecondary institutions in the United States. The researcher has data on the number of graduate students enrolled in at least six credit hours per semester,

a variable measured in whole numbers. Which of the following graphs would be appropriate to use to graph this variable? Select all that apply.

   a. Bar graph

   b. Boxplot

   c. Histogram

   d. Stem-and-leaf plot

20. Data have been collected on how often adults feel they "eat healthy" during an average week. Responses include: "all the time," "most of the time," "sometimes," and "never." Which of the following graphs would be appropriate to use to graph this variable? Select all that apply.

   a. Bar graph

   b. Boxplot

   c. Histogram

   d. Stem-and-leaf plot

21. Your statistics professor requires you to submit a report that includes a boxplot. The following variables are available in your dataset. Which of the following would be appropriate for graphing a boxplot? Select all that apply.

   a. Dollar amount of donations to charitable organizations reported on last year's taxes (measured in whole dollars)

   b. Favorite vacation destination (responses of "beach," "mountain," "city," "other")

   c. Home ownership (responses of "own," "rent," "other")

   d. Number of days per week that at least 30 minutes of exercise is achieved (responses of 0, 1, 2, 3, 4, 5, 6, 7)

22. Your statistics professor requires you to submit a report that includes a boxplot. The following variables are available in your dataset. Which of the follwoing would be appropriate for computing a relative frequency distribution? Select all that apply.

   a. Dollar amount of donations to charitable organizations reported on last year's taxes (measured in whole dollars)

   b. Favorite vacation destination (responses of "beach," "mountain," "city," "other")

   c. Home ownership (responses of "own," "rent," "other")

   d. Number of days per week that at least 30 minutes of exercise is achieved (responses of 0, 1, 2, 3, 4, 5, 6, 7)

23. Which of the following is a correct interpretation of the 30th percentile?

   a. The value at which 30% of the distribution is above.

   b. The value at which 30% of the distribution is below.

   c. The value at which 70% of the distribution is above.

   d. Two values, between which 70% of the distribution falls.

Answers to Conceptual Problems

1. c (Percentile and percentile rank are two sides of the same coin; if the 50th percentile = 100, then $PR(100) = 50$.)

3. a (For 96, $crf = .09$ for both X and Y and $crf = .10$ for Z.)

5. **d** (Ethnicity is not continuous, so only a bar graph is appropriate.)
7. **c** (See Section 2.2.3.)
9. **False** (The proportion is .25 by definition.)
11. **a** (Eye color is nominal and not continuous.)
13. **True** (With the same interval width, each is based on exactly the same information.)
15. **False** (It is most likely that Q_1 will be *smaller* for the negatively skewed variable.)
17. **c** (If the relative frequency for the value 55 is 20% and for 70 is 30%, the cumulative relative frequency for the value 70 is 50%.)
19. **b, c, d** (Graduate student enrollment, measured in whole numbers, is a ratio variable; thus all graphs listed except bar graphs can be applied.)
21. **a, d** (Dollar amount donated to charity and number of days exercised are both ratio variables, thus boxplots can be computed using them.)
23. **b** (30% of the distribution is below the value reflected in the 30th percentile.)

Computational Problems

1. The following scores were obtained from a statistics exam.

50.00	43.00	48.00	46.00	47.00	48.00	47.00
47.00	44.00	46.00	47.00	45.00	43.00	45.00
45.00	44.00	45.00	45.00	46.00	42.00	46.00
44.00	49.00	47.00	43.00	47.00	46.00	
47.00	48.00	41.00	47.00	46.00	49.00	
47.00	46.00	49.00	50.00	44.00	44.00	
45.00	50.00	41.00	43.00	49.00	48.00	

Using an interval size of 1, construct or compute each of the following:
    a. Frequency distribution
    b. Relative frequency distribution
    c. Cumulative relative frequency distribution
    d. Histogram
    e. Frequency polygon
    f. Cumulative frequency polygon
    g. Quartiles
    h. P_{10} and P_{90}
    i. Box-and-whisker plot
    j. Stem-and-leaf display

2. The following data were obtained from classroom observations and reflect the number of times that preschool children shared during an 8-hour period.

4	8	10	5	12	10	14	5
10	14	12	14	8	5	0	8
12	8	12	5	4	10	8	5

Using an interval size of 1, construct or compute each of the following:
a. Frequency distribution
b. Cumulative frequency distribution
c. Relative frequency distribution
d. Cumulative relative frequency distribution
e. Histogram and frequency polygon
f. Cumulative frequency polygon
g. Quartiles
h. P_{10} and P_{90}
i. $PR(10)$
j. Box-and-whisker plot
k. Stem-and-leaf display

3. A sample distribution of variable X is as follows:

X	f
2	1
3	2
4	5
5	8
6	4
7	3
8	4
9	1
10	2

Calculate or draw each of the following for the sample distribution of X:
a. Q_1
b. Q_2
c. Q_3
d. $P_{44.5}$
e. Box-and-whisker plot
f. Histogram (ungrouped)

4. A sample distribution of aptitude scores is as follows:

X	f
70	1
75	2
77	3
79	2
80	6
82	5
85	4
90	4
96	3

Calculate or draw each of the following for the sample distribution of X:

a. Q_1

b. Q_2

c. Q_3

d. $P_{44.5}$

e. $PR(82)$

f. Box-and-whisker plot

g. Histogram (ungrouped)

5. Using the rollercoaster data (ch2_rollercoaster.sav or ch2_rollercoaster.csv), drawn from the Roller Coaster Database (https://rcdb.com/), compute the following for the variable "number of steel sit down rollercoasters" ("SteelSitDown") using statistical software.

a. Frequency distribution

b. Relative frequency distribution

c. Cumulative relative frequency distribution

d. Histogram

e. Quartiles

f. P_{10} and P_{90}

g. Box-and-whisker plot

h. Stem-and-leaf display

Selected Answers to Computational Problems

1. a–c. Frequency distributions, relative frequency distribution, and cumulative relative frequency distribution

   Using SPSS, your frequency distribution (labeled "frequency"), relative frenquency distribution (labeled "percent"), and cumulative relative frequency (labeled "cumulative percent") would appear like this:

		Frequency	Percent	Valid Percent	Cumulative Percent
Valid	41.00	2	4.4	4.4	4.4
	42.00	1	2.2	2.2	6.7
	43.00	4	8.9	8.9	15.6
	44.00	5	11.1	11.1	26.7
	45.00	6	13.3	13.3	40.0
	46.00	7	15.6	15.6	55.6
	47.00	9	20.0	20.0	75.6
	48.00	4	8.9	8.9	84.4
	49.00	4	8.9	8.9	93.3
	50.00	3	6.7	6.7	100.0
	Total	45	100.0	100.0	

Score

d. Histogram

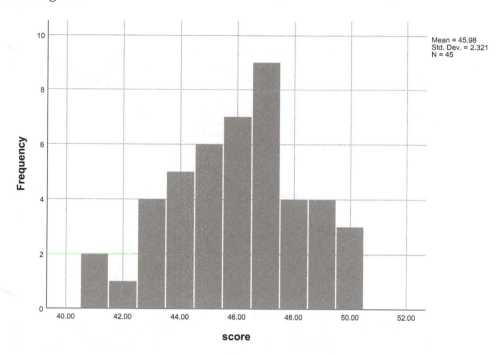

e. Frequency polygon

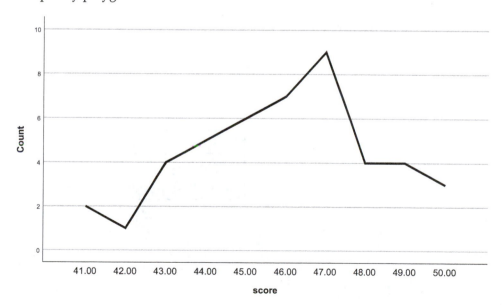

f.   Cumulative frequency polygon

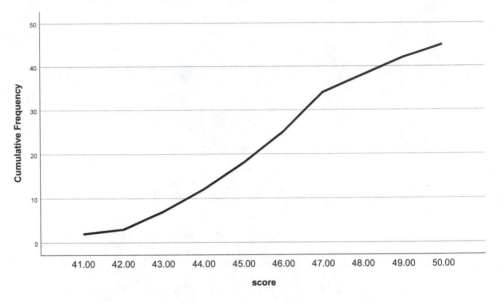

g. $Q_1 = 44.3182$, $Q_2 = 46.1250$, $Q_3 = 47.6538$. Computed using the "Values are group midpoints" option; not using "Values are group midpoints" will result in the following: $Q_1 = 44$, $Q_2 = 46$, $Q_3 = 47.50$.

h. $P_{10} = 42.80$, $P_{90} = 49.1429$. Computed using the "Values are group midpoints" option; not using "Values are group midpoints" will result in the following: $P_{10} = 43$, $P_{90} = 49$.

j.   Box-and-whisker plot

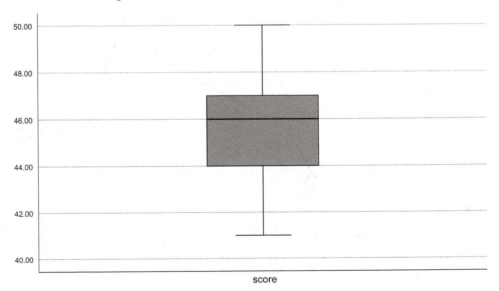

k. Stem-and-leaf display

```
Frequency Stem & Leaf
   2.00      41 .   00
   2.00      42 .   00
   4.00      43 .   0000
   5.00      44 .   00000
   6.00      45 .   000000
   8.00      46 .   00000000
  11.00      47 .   00000000000
   4.00      48 .   0000
   5.00      49 .   00000
   3.00      50 .   000
```

3. a–c. $Q_1 = 4.308$, $Q_2 = 5.50$, $Q_3 = 7.286$. Computed using the "Values are group mid-points" option; not using "Values are group midpoints" will result in the following: $Q_1 = 4$, $Q_2 = 5$, $Q_3 = 7.25$.

d. $P_{44.5} = 5.225$

e. Box-and-whisker plot

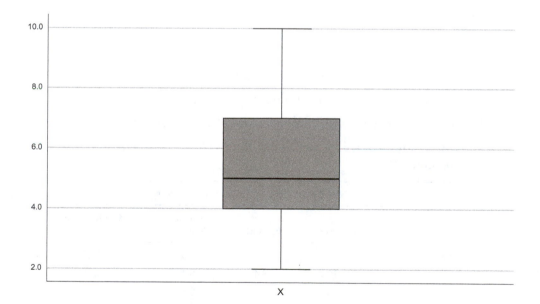

g. Histogram

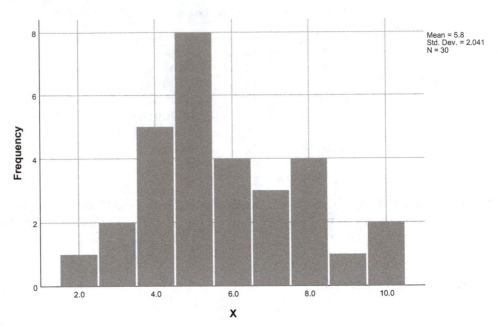

5. Given the Ch2_rollercoaster data, we find:

a. Frequency distribution (column labeled "frequency")

b. Relative frequency distribution (column labeled "percent")

c. Cumulative relative frequency distribution (column labeled "cumulative relative frequency")

		Number of steel sit down rollercoasters		
		Frequency	**Percent**	**Valid Percent**	**Cumulative Percent**
Valid	1	21	17.6	17.6	17.6
	2	10	8.4	8.4	26.1
	3	3	2.5	2.5	28.6
	4	12	10.1	10.1	38.7
	5	3	2.5	2.5	41.2
	6	8	6.7	6.7	47.9
	7	1	.8	.8	48.7
	8	4	3.4	3.4	52.1
	9	4	3.4	3.4	55.5
	10	2	1.7	1.7	57.1

Number of steel sit down rollercoasters			
	Frequency	Percent	Valid Percent	Cumulative Percent
11	4	3.4	3.4	60.5
12	4	3.4	3.4	63.9
13	3	2.5	2.5	66.4
14	1	.8	.8	67.2
15	1	.8	.8	68.1
16	1	.8	.8	68.9
17	1	.8	.8	69.7
18	3	2.5	2.5	72.3
20	3	2.5	2.5	74.8
22	1	.8	.8	75.6
26	3	2.5	2.5	78.2
28	2	1.7	1.7	79.8
36	1	.8	.8	80.7
37	1	.8	.8	81.5
39	1	.8	.8	82.4
40	1	.8	.8	83.2
41	1	.8	.8	84.0
46	1	.8	.8	84.9
47	1	.8	.8	85.7
48	1	.8	.8	86.6
50	1	.8	.8	87.4
51	1	.8	.8	88.2
53	1	.8	.8	89.1
61	1	.8	.8	89.9
72	1	.8	.8	90.8
81	1	.8	.8	91.6
89	1	.8	.8	92.4
94	1	.8	.8	93.3
115	1	.8	.8	94.1
145	1	.8	.8	95.0
158	1	.8	.8	95.8
165	1	.8	.8	96.6
184	1	.8	.8	97.5
204	1	.8	.8	98.3
575	1	.8	.8	99.2
1176	1	.8	.8	100.0
Total	119	100.0	100.0	

d.   Histogram

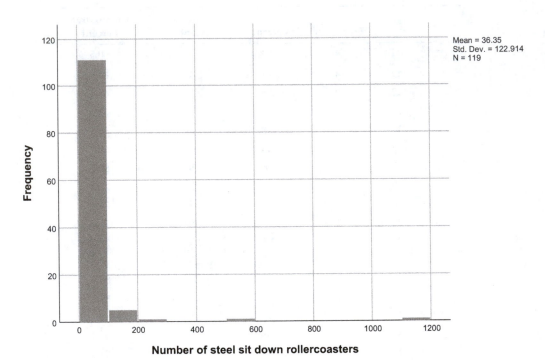

e.   Quartiles (noted as 25th, 50th, and 75th percentiles)

f. P_{10} and P_{90}

Statistics		
Number of steel sit down rollercoasters		
N	Valid	119
	Missing	0
Percentiles	10	1.00
	25	2.00
	50	8.00
	75	22.00
	90	72.00

g. Box-and-whisker plot

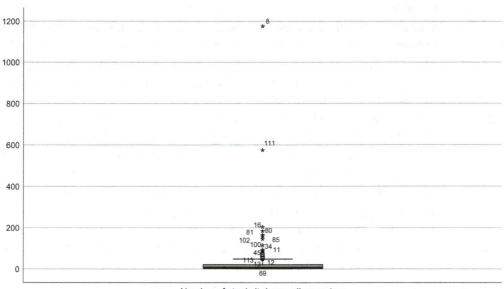

Number of steel sit down rollercoasters

h. Stem-and-leaf display

```
Number of steel sit down rollercoasters Stem-and-Leaf Plot

Frequency   Stem & Leaf
   46.00      0 . 11111111111111111111111222222222233344444444444
   20.00      0 . 55566666666788889999
   14.00      1 . 00111122223334
    6.00      1 . 567888
    4.00      2 . 0002
    5.00      2 . 66688
     .00      3 .
    3.00      3 . 679
    2.00      4 . 01
    3.00      4 . 678
   16.00  Extremes  (>=50)

Stem width:      10
Each leaf:        1 case(s)
```

Interpretive Problems

1. Select two variables from the survey1 dataset on the website, one that is nominal and one that is not.
   a. Write research questions that will be answered from this data using descriptive statistics (you may want to review the research question template in this chapter).
   b. Construct the relevant tables and figures to answer the questions you posed.
   c. Write a paragraph that summarizes the findings for each variable (you may want to review the writing template in this chapter).

2. Select two variables from the Integrated Postsecondary Education Data System dataset (IPEDS2017) on the website, one that is nominal and one that is not.
   a. Write research questions that will be answered from this data using descriptive statistics (you may want to review the research question template in this chapter).
   b. Construct the relevant tables and figures to answer the questions you posed.
   c. Write a paragraph that summarizes the findings for each variable (you may want to review the writing template in this chapter).

3. Select two variables from the NHIS_family2017* dataset on the website, one that is nominal and one that is not.
   a. Write research questions that will be answered from this data using descriptive statistics (you may want to review the research question template in this chapter).
   b. Construct the relevant tables and figures to answer the questions you posed.
   c. Write a paragraph that summarizes the findings for each variable (you may want to review the writing template in this chapter).

*Should you desire to use the NHIS data for your own research, please access the data directly here as updates to the data may have occurred: www.cdc.gov/nchs/nhis/data-questionnaires-documentation.htm. See additional information regarding this in chapter one.

3

Univariate Population Parameters
and Sample Statistics

Chapter Outline

Key Concepts

1. Summation
2. Central tendency
3. Outliers
4. Dispersion
5. Exclusive versus inclusive range
6. Deviation scores
7. Bias

In Chapter 2, we began our discussion of descriptive statistics, previously defined as techniques that allow us to tabulate, summarize, and depict a collection of data in an abbreviated fashion. We considered various methods for representing data for purposes of communicating something to the reader or audience. In particular, we were concerned with ways of representing data in an abbreviated fashion through both tables and figures.

In this chapter, we delve more into the field of descriptive statistics in terms of three general topics. First, we examine **summation notation**, which is important for much of the chapter, and to some extent, the remainder of the text. Second, *measures of central tendency* allow us to boil down a set of scores into a single value, a point estimate, which somehow represents the entire set. The most commonly used measures of central tendency are the mode, median, and mean. Finally, *measures of dispersion* provide us with information about the extent to which the set of scores varies—in other words, whether the scores are spread out quite a bit or are pretty much the same. The most commonly used measures of dispersion are the range (exclusive and inclusive ranges), H spread, and variance and standard deviation. In summary, concepts to be discussed in this chapter include summation, central tendency, and dispersion. Within this discussion, we also address outliers and bias. Our objectives are that by the end of this chapter, you will be able to do the following: (a) understand and utilize summation notation, (b) determine and interpret the three commonly used measures of central tendency, and (c) determine and interpret commonly used measures of dispersion.

3.1 Summation Notation

A superbly talented and motivated group of graduate students are working in the statistics lab. We now find Oso Wyse tasked with his first lead role.

The graduate students in the statistics lab, Addie Venture, Oso Wyse, Challie Lenge, and Ott Lier, have been assigned their first task as research assistants. Dr. Debhard, a statistics professor, has given the group of students quiz data collected from 25 students enrolled in an introductory statistics course and has asked the group to summarize the data. Dr. Debhard was pleased with the descriptive analysis and presentation of results previously shared and is now working with Oso Wyse to conduct additional analyses related to the following research questions: *How can quiz scores of students enrolled in an introductory statistics class be summarized using measures of central tendency? How can quiz scores of students enrolled in an introductory statistics class be summarized using measures of dispersion?*

Many areas of statistics, including many methods of descriptive and inferential statistics, require the use of summation notation. Say we have collected heart rate scores from 100 students. Many statistics require us to develop "sums" or "totals" in different ways. For example, what is the simple sum, or total, of all 100 heart rate scores? **Summation** (i.e., addition) is not only quite tedious to do computationally by hand, but we also need a system of notation to communicate how we have conducted this summation process. This section describes such a notational system.

For simplicity let us utilize a small set of scores, keeping in mind that this system can be used for a set of numerical values of any size. In other words, while we speak in terms of "scores," this could just as easily be a set of heights, distances, ages, or other measures. Specifically, in this example we have a set of five ages: 7, 11, 18, 20, and 24. Recall from Chapter 2 the use of X to denote a variable. Here we define X_i as the score for variable X (in this example, age) for a particular individual or object i. The subscript i serves to identify one individual or object from another. These scores would then be denoted as follows: $X_1 = 7$, $X_2 = 11$, $X_3 = 18$, $X_4 = 20$, and $X_5 = 24$. To interpret $X_1 = 7$ means that for variable X and individual 1, the value of the variable "age" is 7. In other words, individual 1 is 7 years of age. With five individuals measured on age, then $i = 1, 2, 3, 4$, or 5. However, with a large set of values this notation can become quite unwieldy, so as shorthand we abbreviate this as $i = 1, \ldots, 5$, meaning that X ranges or goes from $i = 1$ to $i = 5$.

Next we need a system of notation to denote the summation or total of a set of scores. The standard notation used is $\sum_{i=a}^{b} X_i$ where $\sum$ is the Greek capital letter sigma and means "the sum of," X_i is the variable we are summing across for each of the i individuals, $i = a$ indicates that a is the lower limit (or beginning) of the summation (i.e., the first value with which we begin our addition), and b indicates the upper limit (or end) of the summation (i.e., the last value added). For our example set of ages, the sum of all of the ages would be denoted as $\sum_{i=1}^{5} X_i$ in shorthand version and as follows in longhand version:

$$\sum_{i=1}^{5} X_i = X_1 + X_2 + X_3 + X_4 + X_5$$

In narrative, this is simply saying "sum all five Xs, from X_1 to X_5." For the example data, the sum of all of the ages is computed as follows:

$$\sum_{i=1}^{5} X_i = X_1 + X_2 + X_3 + X_4 + X_5 = 7 + 11 + 18 + 20 + 24 = 80$$

Thus, the sum of the age variable across all five individuals is 80.

For large sets of values, the longhand version is rather tedious, and thus the shorthand version is almost exclusively used. A general form of the longhand version is as follows:

$$\sum_{i=a}^{b} X_i = X_a + X_{a+1} + \ldots + X_{b-1} + X_b$$

The ellipse notation (i.e., . . .) indicates that there are as many values in between the two values on either side of the ellipse as are necessary. The ellipse notation is then just shorthand for "there are some values in between here." The most frequently used values for a and b with sample data are $a = 1$ and $b = n$ (as you may recall, n is the notation used to represent our sample size). *Thus, the most frequently used summation notation for sample data is* $\sum_{i=1}^{n} X_i$. Reading this, we can say that we are summing all X_i from 1 to n, where n denotes the sample size. Thus, we are summing all X_i in the entire dataset.

3.2 Measures of Central Tendency

One method for summarizing a set of scores is to construct a single index or value that can somehow be used to represent the entire collection of scores. In this section we consider the three most popular indices, known as **measures of central tendency**. Although other indices exist, the most popular ones are the mode, the median, and the mean.

3.2.1 The Mode

The simplest method to use for measuring central tendency is the mode. The **mode** is defined as *that value in a distribution of scores that occurs most frequently*. An easy way to remember the definition of the mode is to associate "mode" with "most," as that what the mode represents—the value or category (in the case of nominal or ordinal variables) that occurs most often. Consider the example frequency distributions of the number of hours of TV watched per week, as shown in Table 3.1. In distribution $f(a)$ the mode is easy to determine, as the interval for value 8 contains the most scores, three (i.e., the mode number of hours of TV watched is 8). In distribution $f(b)$ the mode is a bit more complicated as two adjacent intervals each contain the most scores; that is, the 8- and 9-hour intervals each contain three scores. Strictly speaking, this distribution is *bimodal*, that is, containing two modes, one at 8 and one at 9. This is our personal preference for reporting this particular situation. However, because the two modes are in adjacent intervals, some individuals make an arbitrary decision to average these intervals and report the mode as 8.5.

Distribution $f(c)$ is also bimodal; however, here the two modes at 7 and 11 hours are not in adjacent intervals. Thus, one cannot justify taking the average of these intervals, as the average of 9 hours, $7+11)/2$, is not representative of the most frequently occurring score. The score of 9 occurs less than any other score observed. We recommend reporting both modes here as well. Obviously, there are other possible situations for the mode (e.g., trimodal distribution), but these examples cover the basics. As one further example, the example data on the statistics quiz from Chapter 2 are shown in Table 3.2 and are used to illustrate the methods in this chapter. The mode is equal to 17 because that interval contains more scores (five) than any other interval. Note also that the mode is determined in

TABLE 3.1

Example Frequency Distributions

X	$f(a)$	$f(b)$	$f(c)$
6	1	1	2
7	2	2	3
8	3	3	2
9	2	3	1
10	1	2	2
11	0	1	3
12	0	0	2

TABLE 3.2

Frequency Distribution of Statistics Quiz Data

X	f	cf	rf	crf
9	1	1	.04	.04
10	1	2	.04	.08
11	2	4	.08	.16
12	1	5	.04	.20
13	2	7	.08	.28
14	1	8	.04	.32
15	3	11	.12	.44
16	1	12	.04	.48
17	5	17	.20	.68
18	3	20	.12	.80
19	4	24	.16	.96
20	1	25	.04	1.00
	$n = 25$		1.00	

precisely the same way whether we are talking about the population mode (i.e., the population parameter) or the sample mode (i.e., the sample statistic).

Let's turn to a discussion of the general characteristics of the mode, as well as whether a particular characteristic is an advantage or a disadvantage in a statistical sense. The first characteristic of the mode is *it is simple to obtain*. The mode is often used as a quick-and-dirty method for reporting central tendency. This is an obvious advantage.

The second characteristic is that the mode *does not always have a unique value*. We saw this in distributions *f*(b) and *f*(c) of Table 3.1. This is generally a disadvantage, as we initially stated we wanted a single index that could be used to represent the collection of scores. The mode cannot guarantee a single index.

Third, the mode is *not a function of all of the scores in the distribution*, and this is generally a disadvantage. The mode is strictly determined by which score or interval contains the most frequencies. In distribution *f*(a), as long as the other intervals have fewer frequencies than the interval for value 8, then the mode will always be 8. That is, if the interval for value 8 contains three scores and all of the other intervals contain less than three scores, then the mode will be 8. The number of frequencies for the remaining intervals is not relevant as long as it is less than three. Also, the location or value of the other scores is not taken into account.

The fourth characteristic of the mode is that it is *difficult to deal with mathematically*. For example, the mode is not very stable from one sample to another, especially with small samples. We could have two nearly identical samples except for one score, which can alter the mode. For example, in distribution *f*(a) if a second similar sample contains the same scores except that an 8 is replaced with a 7, then the mode is changed from 8 to 7. Thus changing a single score can change the mode, and this is considered to be a disadvantage.

A fifth and final characteristic is the mode *can be used with a variable of any type of measurement scale*, from nominal to ratio, and *is the only measure of central tendency appropriate for nominal data*.

3.2.2 The Median

A second measure of central tendency represents a concept that you are already familiar with. *The **median** is that score which divides a distribution of scores into two equal parts.* In other words, one-half of the scores fall below the median and one-half of the scores fall above the median. We already know this from Chapter 2 as the 50th percentile or Q_2. In other words, the 50th percentile, or Q_2, represents the median value. The formula for computing the median is

$$Median = LRL + \left(\frac{50\%(n) - cf}{f} \right)(w)$$

where the notation is the same as previously described in Chapter 2. Just as a reminder, *LRL* is the lower real limit of the interval containing the median, 50% is the percentile desired, n is the sample size, cf is the cumulative frequency of all intervals less than but not including the interval containing the median (cf below), f is the frequency of the interval containing the median, and w is the interval width. For the example quiz data, the median is computed as follows:

$$Median = 16.5 + \left(\frac{50\%(25) - 12}{5} \right)(1) = 16.5 + 0.10 = 16.60$$

Occasionally, you will run into simple distributions of scores where the median is easy to identify. *If you have an odd number of untied scores, then the median is the middle-ranked score.* For an example, say we have measured individuals on the number of autographed jerseys owned and find values of 1, 3, 7, 11, and 21. For this data, the median is 7 (e.g., 7 autographed jerseys is the middle-ranked value or score). *If you have an even number of untied scores, then the median is the average of the two middle-ranked scores.* For example, a different sample reveals the following number of autographed jerseys owned: 1, 3, 5, 11, 21, and 32. The two middle scores are 5 and 11, and thus the median is the average of 8 autographed jerseys owned; that is, $(5 + 11)/2$. *In most other situations where there are tied scores, the median is not as simple to locate and first equation is necessary.* Note also that the median is computed in precisely the same way whether we are talking about the population median (i.e., the population parameter) or the sample median (i.e., the sample statistic).

The general characteristics of the median are as follows. First, *the median is not influenced by extreme scores* (scores far away from the middle of the distribution are known as **outliers**). Because the median is defined conceptually as the middle score, the actual size of an extreme score is not relevant. For the example statistics quiz data, imagine that the extreme score of 9 was somehow actually 0 (e.g., incorrectly scored). The median would still be 16.6, as half of the scores are still above this value and half below. Because the extreme score under consideration here still remained below the 50th percentile, the median was not altered. This characteristic is an advantage, particularly when extreme scores are observed. As another example using salary data, say that all but one of the individual salaries is below $100,000 and the median is $50,000. The remaining extreme observation has a salary of $5,000,000. The median is not affected by this millionaire—the extreme individual is simply treated as every other observation above the median, no more or no less than, say, the salary of $65,000.

A second characteristic is that *the median is not a function of all of the scores*. Because we already know that the median is not influenced by extreme scores, we know that the median does not take such scores into account. Another way to think about this is to examine the first equation for the median. The equation only deals with information for the interval containing the median. The specific information for the remaining intervals is not relevant so long as we are looking in the median-contained interval. We could, for instance, take the top 25% of the scores and make them even more extreme (say we add 10 bonus points to the top quiz scores). The median would remain unchanged. As you have probably surmised, this characteristic is generally thought to be a disadvantage. If you really think about the first two characteristics, no measure could possibly possess both. That is, if a measure is a function of all of the scores, then extreme scores must also be taken into account. If a measure does not take extreme scores into account, like the median, then it cannot be a function of all of the scores.

A third characteristic is that *the median is difficult to deal with mathematically*, a disadvantage as with the mode. The median is somewhat unstable from sample to sample, especially with small samples.

As a fourth characteristic, *the median always has a unique value*, another advantage. This is unlike the mode, which does not always have a unique value.

Finally, the fifth characteristic of the median is that *it can be used with all types of measurement scales except the nominal*. Nominal data cannot be ranked, and thus percentiles (including the 50th percentile, i.e., the median) are inappropriate.

3.2.3 The Mean

The final measure of central tendency to be considered is the mean, also known as the *arithmetic mean* or *average* (although the term "average" is used rather loosely by laypeople). Note that there are different types of means; we will generally be concerned only with the arithmetic mean. Statistically, we define the **mean** as *the sum of all of the scores divided by the number of scores*. Thought of in those terms, you may have been computing the mean for many years, and may not have even known it.

The **population mean** is denoted by μ (lowercase Greek mu) and computed as follows:

$$\mu = \frac{\sum_{i=1}^{N} X_i}{N}$$

For sample data, the **sample mean** is denoted by $\bar{X}$ (read "X bar") and computed as follows:

$$\bar{X} = \frac{\sum_{i=1}^{n} X_i}{n}$$

For the example quiz data, the sample mean is computed as follows:

$$\bar{X} = \frac{\sum_{i=1}^{n} X_i}{n} = \frac{389}{25} = 15.56$$

Here are the general characteristics of the mean. First, *the mean is a function of every score*, which is a definite advantage in terms of a measure of central tendency representing all of the data. If you look at the numerator of the mean, you see that all of the scores are clearly taken into account in the sum.

The second characteristic of the mean is that *it is influenced by extreme scores*. Because the numerator sum takes all of the scores into account, it also includes the extreme scores, which is (or at least can be) a disadvantage. Let us return for a moment to a previous example of salary data where all but one of the individuals has an annual salary under $100,000, and the one outlier is making $5,000,000. Because this one outlying value is so extreme, the mean will be greatly influenced. In fact, the mean could easily fall somewhere between the second highest salary and the millionaire, which does not represent well the collection of scores.

Third, *the mean always has a unique value*, another advantage. As we will see, many inferential statistics use the mean in their calculation. Thus, since the mean generates a unique value, we are able to use that value as both a way to summarize data but also to make inferences to a larger population.

Fourth, *the mean is easy to deal with mathematically*. The mean is the most stable measure of central tendency from sample to sample, and because of that is the measure most often used in inferential statistics (as we show in later chapters).

Finally, the fifth characteristic of the mean is that *it is only appropriate for interval and ratio measurement scales*. This is because the mean implicitly assumes equal intervals, which of course the nominal and ordinal scales do not possess.

3.2.4 Summary of Measures of Central Tendency

To summarize, some of the distinguishing features of the measures of central tendency are as follows:

1. The mode is the only appropriate measure for nominal data.
2. The median and mode are both appropriate for ordinal data (and conceptually the median fits the ordinal scale as both deal with ranked scores).
3. All three measures (mode, median, and mean) are appropriate for interval and ratio data.

As discussed, each measure of central tendency has advantages and disadvantages. A summary of the advantages and disadvantages of each measure is presented in Box 3.1.

BOX 3.1 Advantages and Disadvantages of Measures of Central Tendency

Measure of Central Tendency	Advantages	Disadvantages
Mode	Quick and easy method for reporting central tendency Can be used with any measurement scale of variable	Does not always have a unique value Not a function of all scores in the distribution Difficult to deal with mathematically due to its instability
Median	Not influenced by extreme scores Has a unique value Can be used with ordinal, interval, and ratio measurement scales of variables	Not a function of all scores in the distribution Difficult to deal with mathematically due to its instability Cannot be used with nominal data

Measure of Central Tendency	Advantages	Disadvantages
Mean	Function of all scores in the distribution	Influenced by extreme scores
	Has a unique value	Cannot be used with nominal or ordinal variables
	Easy to deal with mathematically	
	Can be used with interval and ratio measurement scales of variables	

We began our discussion of measures of central tendency by stating that *other indices exist*; however, the most popular ones are the mode, the median, and the mean. You may be wondering what those other indices are! While the *arithmetic mean* is the most common mean, and the one with which we are generally concerned, it is not the only mean, and it should not be confused with other types of means. Other means that you may encounter include the harmonic mean, trimmed mean, winsorized mean, and more. Huck (2016) provides a concise discussion on understanding the most common measures of central tendency relative to other statistics you may encounter.

3.3 Measures of Dispersion

In the previous section, we discussed one method for summarizing a collection of scores, the measures of central tendency. Central tendency measures are useful for describing a collection of scores in terms of a single index or value (with one exception: the mode for distributions that are not unimodal). However, what do they tell us about the distribution of scores? Consider the following example. If we know that a sample has a mean of 50, what do we know about the distribution of scores? Can we infer from the mean what the distribution looks like? Are most of the scores fairly close to the mean of 50, or are they spread out quite a bit? Perhaps most of the scores are within 2 points of the mean. Perhaps most are within 10 points of the mean. Perhaps most are within 50 points of the mean. Do we know? The answer, of course, is that the mean provides us with no information about what the distribution of scores looks like, and any of the possibilities mentioned, and many others, can occur. The same goes if we only know the mode or the median.

Another method for summarizing a set of scores is to construct an index or value that can be used to describe the amount of *spread* amongst the collection of scores. In other words, we need measures that can be used to determine whether the scores fall fairly close to the central tendency measure, are fairly well spread out, or are somewhere in between. In this section we consider the four most popular such indices, which are known as **measures of dispersion** (i.e., the extent to which the scores are dispersed or spread out). Although other indices exist, the most popular ones are the range (exclusive and inclusive), *H* spread, variance, and standard deviation.

3.3.1 The Range

The simplest measure of dispersion is the **range**. The term *range* is one that is in common use outside of statistical circles, so you have some familiarity with it already. For instance, say you are at the mall shopping for a new pair of shoes. You find six stores have the same pair of shoes that you really like, but the prices vary somewhat. At this point you might actually make the statement "the price for these shoes ranges from $59 to $75." In a way you are talking about the range.

Let us be more specific as to how the range is measured. In fact, there are actually two different definitions of the range, exclusive and inclusive, which we consider now. The **exclusive range** is defined as *the difference between the largest and smallest scores in a collection of scores*. For notational purposes, the exclusive range (ER) is shown as $ER = X_{max} - X_{min}$, where X_{max} is the largest or maximum score obtained, and X_{min} is the smallest or minimum score obtained. For the shoe example then, $ER = X_{max} - X_{min} = 75 - 59 = 16$. In other words, the actual exclusive range of the scores is 16 because the price varies from 59 to 75 (in dollar units).

A limitation of the exclusive range is that it fails to account for the width of the intervals being used. For example, if we use an interval width of one dollar, then the 59 interval really has 59.5 as the upper real limit and 58.5 as the lower real limit. If the least expensive shoe is $58.95, then the exclusive range covering from $59 to $75 actually *excludes* the least expensive shoe. Hence, the term exclusive range means *that scores can be excluded from this range*. The same would go for a shoe priced at $75.95, as it would fall outside of the exclusive range at the high end of the distribution.

Because of this limitation, a second definition of the range was developed, known as the *inclusive range*. As you might surmise, the inclusive range takes into account the interval width so that all scores are *included* in the range. The **inclusive range** is defined as *the difference between the upper real limit of the interval containing the largest score and the lower real limit of the interval containing the smallest score in a collection of scores*. For notational purposes, the inclusive range (IR) is shown as $IR = URL$ of $X_{max} - LRL$ of X_{min}. If you think about it, what we are actually doing is extending the range by one-half of an interval at each extreme, one-half an interval width at the maximum value and one-half an interval width at the minimum value. In notational form $IR = ER + w$. For the shoe example, using an interval width of 1, then $IR = URL$ of $X_{max} - LRL$ of $X_{min} = 75.5 - 58.5 = 17$. In other words, the actual inclusive range of the scores is 17 (in dollar units). If the interval width was instead 2, then we would add 1 unit to each extreme rather than the .5 unit that we previously added to each extreme. The inclusive range would instead be 18. For the example quiz data (presented in Table 3.2), note that the exclusive range is 11 and the inclusive range is 12 (as interval width is 1).

Finally, we need to examine the general characteristics of the range (they are the same for both definitions of the range). First, *the range is simple to compute*, which is a definite advantage. One can look at a collection of data and almost immediately, even without a computer or calculator, determine the range.

The second characteristic is that *the range is influenced by extreme scores*, a disadvantage. Because the range is computed from the two most extreme scores, this characteristic is quite obvious. This might be a problem, for instance, if all of the salary data range from $10,000 to $95,000 except for one individual with a salary of $5,000,000. Without this outlier the exclusive range is $85,000. With the outlier the exclusive range is $4,990,000. Thus, the millionaire's salary has a drastic impact on the range.

Third, *the range is only a function of two scores*, another disadvantage. Obviously the range is computed from the largest and smallest scores, and thus is only a function of those two scores. The spread of the distribution of scores between those two extreme scores is not at all taken into account. In other words, for the same maximum ($5,000,000) and minimum ($10,000) salaries, the range is the same whether the salaries are mostly near the maximum salary, mostly near the minimum salary, or spread out evenly.

The fourth characteristic is that *the range is unstable from sample to sample,* another disadvantage. Say a second sample of salary data yielded the exact same data except for the maximum salary now being a less extreme $100,000. The range is now dramatically different. Also, in statistics we tend to worry about measures that are not stable from sample to sample, as this implies that the results are not very reliable.

Finally, the range is appropriate for *data that are ordinal, interval, or ratio in measurement scale.*

3.3.2 *H* Spread

The next measure of dispersion is *H* spread, a variation on the range measure with one major exception. Although the range relies upon the two extreme scores, resulting in certain disadvantages, *H* spread relies upon the difference between the third and first quartiles. To be more specific, **H spread** is defined as $Q_3 - Q_1$, *the simple difference between the third and first quartiles.* The term *H* spread was developed by Tukey (1977), *H* being short for "hinge" from the box-and-whisker plot; it is also known as the **interquartile range**.

For the example statistics quiz data (presented in Table 3.2), we already determined in Chapter 2 that $Q_3 = 18.0833$ and $Q_1 = 13.1250$. Therefore, $H = Q_3 - Q_1 = 18.0833 - 13.1250 = 4.9583$. *H* measures the range of the middle 50% of the distribution. *The larger the value, the greater the spread in the middle of the distribution.* The size or magnitude of any of the range measures takes on more meaning when making comparisons across samples. For example, you might find with salary data that the range of salaries for middle management is smaller than the range of salaries for upper management. As another example, we might expect the salary range to increase over time.

What are the characteristics of *H* spread? The first characteristic is that *H is unaffected by extreme scores,* an advantage. Because we are looking at the difference between the third and first quartiles, extreme observations will be outside of this range. Second, *H is not a function of every score,* a disadvantage. The precise placement of where scores fall above Q_3, below Q_1, and between Q_3 and Q_1 is not relevant. All that matters is that 25% of the scores fall above Q_3, 25% fall below Q_1, and 50% fall between Q_3 and Q_1. Thus, *H* is not a function of very many of the scores at all, just those around Q_3 and Q_1. Third, *H is not very stable from sample to sample,* another disadvantage, especially in terms of inferential statistics and one's ability to be confident about a sample estimate of a population parameter. Finally, *H is appropriate for all scales of measurement except for nominal.*

3.3.3 Deviational Measures

In this section we examine deviation scores, population variance and standard deviation, and sample variance and standard deviation, all methods that deal with deviations from the mean.

3.3.3.1 *Deviation Scores*

In the last category of measures of dispersion are those that utilize deviations from the mean. Let us define a **deviation score** as the *difference between a particular raw score and the mean of the collection of scores* (population or sample, either will work). For *population data* we define a deviation as $d_i = X_i - \mu$. In other words, we can compute the deviation from the mean for each individual or object. Consider the credit card dataset as shown in Table 3.3.

TABLE 3.3

Credit Card Dataset

X	$X - \mu$	$(X - \mu)^2$
1	−5	25
5	−1	1
6	0	0
8	2	4
10	4	16
$\Sigma = 30$	$\Sigma = 0$	$\Sigma = 46$
$N = 5$		
$\mu = 6$		

To make matters simple, we only have a small population of data, five values to be exact. The first column lists the raw scores, which are in this example the number of credit cards owned for five individuals and, at the bottom of the first column, indicates the sum ($\Sigma = 30$), population size ($N = 5$), and population mean ($\mu = 6.0$). The second column provides the deviation scores for each observation from the population mean and, at the bottom of the second column, indicates the sum of the deviation scores, denoted by

$$\sum_{i=1}^{N} \left(X_i - \mu \right)$$

From the second column we see that two of the observations have positive deviation scores as their raw score is above the mean, one observation has a zero deviation score as that raw score is at the mean, and two other observations have negative deviation scores as their raw score is below the mean. However, when we sum the deviation scores, we obtain a value of zero. This will always be the case, as follows:

$$\sum_{i=1}^{N} \left(X_i - \mu \right) = 0$$

The positive deviation scores will exactly offset the negative deviation scores. *Thus, any measure involving simple deviation scores will be useless in that the sum of the deviation scores will always be zero, regardless of the spread of the scores.*

What other alternatives are there for developing a deviational measure that will yield a sum other than zero? One alternative is to take the absolute value of the deviation scores (i.e., where the sign is ignored). Unfortunately, however, this is not very useful mathematically in terms of deriving other statistics, such as inferential statistics. As a result, this deviational measure is rarely used in statistics.

3.3.3.2 *Population Variance and Standard Deviation*

So far we found the sum of the deviations and the sum of the absolute deviations not to be very useful in describing the spread of the scores from the mean. What other alternative might be useful? As shown in the third column of Table 3.3, one could square the deviation scores to remove the sign problem. The sum of the squared deviations is shown at the bottom of the column as $\Sigma = 46$ and denoted as

$$\sum_{i=1}^{N}\left(X_i - \mu\right)^2$$

As you might suspect, with more scores, the sum of the squared deviations will increase. So we have to weigh the sum by the number of observations in the population. This yields a deviational measure known as the **population variance**, which is denoted as σ^2 (sigma squared) and computed by the following formula:

$$\sigma^2 = \frac{\sum_{i=1}^{N}\left(X_i - \mu\right)^2}{N}$$

For the credit card example, $\sigma^2 = (46/5) = 9.2$. We refer to this particular formula for the population variance as the **definitional formula**, as conceptually that is how we define the variance. *Conceptually, the variance is a measure of the area of a distribution, and, more specifically, the spread of the distribution from the mean.* That is, the more spread out the scores, the more area or space the distribution takes up and the larger the variance. *The variance may also be thought of as an average distance from the mean.* The variance has nice mathematical properties and is useful for deriving other statistics, such as inferential statistics.

The **computational formula** for the population variance is

$$\sigma^2 = \frac{(N)\left[\sum_{i=1}^{N}X_i^2\right] - \left[\sum_{i=1}^{N}X_i\right]^2}{N^2}$$

This method is computationally easier to deal with than the definitional formula. Imagine if you had a population of 100 scores. Using hand computations, the definitional formula would take considerably more time than the computational formula. With the computer this is a moot point, obviously. But, if you do have to compute the population variance by hand, then the easiest formula to use is the computational one.

Exactly how does this formula work? The numerator is three basic terms: (a) the population size (N), (b) the sum of all X_i^2 (i.e., square each X_i and then sum those squared values), and (c) the squared sum of all X_i (i.e., sum all the X_i and then square that summed value). The denominator is simply the squared population size.

Let's look at this again. For the first summation in the numerator, we square each score first, then sum all the squared scores. This value is then multiplied by the population size. For the second summation in the numerator, we sum all the scores first, then square the summed scores. After subtracting the values computed in the numerator, we divide by the squared population size.

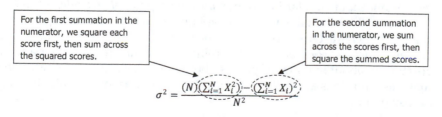

For the first summation in the numerator, we square each score first, then sum across the squared scores.

For the second summation in the numerator, we sum across the scores first, then square the summed scores.

$$\sigma^2 = \frac{(N)\left(\sum_{i=1}^{N}X_i^2\right) - \left(\sum_{i=1}^{N}X_i\right)^2}{N^2}$$

The two quantities derived by the summation operations in the numerator are computed in much different ways and generally yield different values.

Let us return to the credit card dataset and see if the computational formula actually yields the same value for σ^2 as the definitional formula did earlier ($\sigma^2 = 9.2$). The computational formula shows σ^2 to be:

$$\sigma^2 = \frac{(N)\left(\sum_{i=1}^{N} X_i^2\right) - \left(\sum_{i=1}^{N} X_i\right)^2}{N^2} = \frac{(5)(226) - (30)^2}{(5)^2} = \frac{1130 - 900}{25} = 9.20$$

which is precisely the value we computed previously.

A few individuals (none of us, of course) are a bit bothered about the variance for the following reason. Say you are measuring the height of children in inches. The raw scores are measured in terms of inches, the mean is measured in terms of inches, but the variance is measured in terms of inches squared. *Squaring the scale is bothersome to some as the scale is no longer in the original units of measure, but rather a squared unit of measure*—making interpretation a bit difficult. To generate a deviational measure in the original scale (i.e., inches), we can take the square root of the variance. This is known as the **standard deviation**, and it is the final measure of dispersion we discuss. The **population standard deviation** is defined as the *positive square root of the population variance* and is denoted by sigma, σ $\left(i.e., \sigma = \sqrt{\sigma^2}\right)$.

The standard deviation, then, is measured *in the original scale* (i.e., in this example, inches). For the credit card data, the standard deviation is computed as follows:

$$\sigma = \sqrt{\sigma^2} = \sqrt{9.2} = 3.0332$$

What are the major characteristics of the population variance and standard deviation? First, the variance and standard deviation *are a function of every score*, an advantage. An examination of either the definitional or computational formula for the variance (and standard deviation as well) indicates that all of the scores are taken into account, unlike the range or H spread.

Second, therefore, the variance and standard deviation *are affected by extreme scores*, a disadvantage. As we said earlier, if a measure takes all of the scores into account, then it must take into account the extreme scores as well. Thus, a child much taller than all of the rest of the children will dramatically increase the variance, as the area or size of the distribution will be much more spread out. Another way to think about this is the size of the deviation score for such an outlier will be large, and then it will be squared, and then summed with the rest of the deviation scores. Thus, an outlier can really increase the variance. Also, it goes without saying that it is always a good idea when using the computer to verify your data. A data entry error can cause an outlier and therefore a larger variance (e.g., that child coded as 700 inches tall instead of 70 will surely inflate your variance).

Third, the variance and standard deviation *are only appropriate for interval and ratio measurement scales*. Like the mean, this is due to the implicit requirement of equal intervals.

A fourth and final characteristic of the variance and standard deviation is *they are quite useful for deriving other statistics*, particularly in inferential statistics, another advantage. In fact, Chapter 9 is all about making inferences about variances, and many other inferential statistics make assumptions about the variance. Thus, the variance is quite important as a measure of dispersion.

It is also interesting to compare the measures of central tendency with the measures of dispersion, as they do share some important characteristics. *The mode and the range share certain characteristics.* Both only take some of the data into account, are simple to compute, and are unstable from sample to sample. *The median shares certain characteristics with H spread.* These are not influenced by extreme scores, are not a function of every score, are difficult to deal with mathematically due to their instability from sample to sample, and can be used with all measurement scales except the nominal scale. *The mean shares many characteristics with the variance and standard deviation.* These all are a function of every score, are influenced by extreme scores, are useful for deriving other statistics, and are only appropriate for interval and ratio measurement scales.

To complete this section of the chapter, we take a look at the sample variance and standard deviation and how they are computed for large samples of data (i.e., larger than our credit card dataset).

3.3.3.3 Sample Variance and Standard Deviation

Most of the time we are interested in computing the sample variance and standard deviation; we also often have large samples of data with multiple frequencies for many of the scores. Here we consider these last aspects of the measures of dispersion. Recall when we computed the sample statistics of central tendency. The computations were exactly the same as with the population parameters (although the notation for the population and sample means was different). There are also no differences between the sample and population values for the range, or H spread. However, there *is* a difference between the sample and population values for the variance and standard deviation, as we see next.

Recall the definitional formula for the population variance:

$$\sigma^2 = \frac{\sum_{i=1}^{N}\left(X_i - \mu\right)^2}{N}$$

Why not just take this equation and convert everything to sample statistics? In other words, we could simply change N to n and μ to $\overline{X}$. What could be wrong with that? The answer is that there is a problem that prevents us from simply changing the notation in the formula from population notation to sample notation.

Here is the problem. First, the sample mean, $\overline{X}$, may not be exactly equal to the population mean, μ. In fact, for most samples, the sample mean will be somewhat different from the population mean. Second, we cannot use the population mean because it is unknown (in most instances anyway). Instead, we have to substitute the sample mean into the equation (i.e., the sample mean, $\overline{X}$, is the sample estimate for the population mean, μ). Because the sample mean is different from the population mean, the deviations will all be affected. Also, the sample variance that would be obtained in this fashion would be a biased estimate of the population variance. In statistics, **bias** means that *something is systematically off*. In this case, the sample variance obtained in this manner would be systematically too small.

In order to obtain an unbiased sample estimate of the population variance, the following adjustments have to be made in the definitional and computational formulas, respectively:

$$s^2 = \frac{\sum_{i=1}^{n}\left(X_i - \bar{X}\right)^2}{n-1}$$

$$s^2 = \frac{(n)\left[\sum_{i=1}^{n}X_i^2\right]-\left[\sum_{i=1}^{n}X_i\right]^2}{n(n-1)}$$

In terms of the notation, s^2 is the **sample variance,** n has been substituted for N, and $\bar{X}$ has been substituted for μ. These changes are relatively minor and expected. The major change is in the denominator, where instead of N for the definitional formula we have $n - 1$, and instead of N^2 for the computational formula we have $n(n - 1)$. *This turns out to be the correction that early statisticians discovered was necessary to obtain an unbiased estimate of the population variance.*

The following two points should be noted: (a) when sample size is relatively large (e.g., $n = 1000$), the correction will be quite small; and (b) when sample size is relatively small (e.g., $n = 5$), the correction will be quite a bit larger. One suggestion is that when computing the variance on a calculator or computer, you might want to be aware of whether the sample or population variance is being computed, as it can make a difference (typically the sample variance is computed). The sample standard deviation is denoted by s and computed as the positive square root of the sample variance, s^2 (i.e., $s = \sqrt{s^2}$).

For our example statistics quiz data (presented in Table 3.2), we have multiple frequencies for many of the raw scores that need to be taken into account. A simple procedure for dealing with this situation when performing hand computations is shown in Table 3.4. Here we see that in the third and fifth columns the scores and squared scores are multiplied by their respective frequencies. This allows us to take into account, for example, that the score of 19 occurred four times. Note for the fifth column that the frequencies are not squared; only the scores are squared. At the bottom of the third and fifth columns are the sums we need to compute the parameters of interest.

TABLE 3.4

Sums for Statistics Quiz Data

X	f	fX	X²	fX²
9	1	9	81	81
10	1	10	100	100
11	2	22	121	242
12	1	12	144	144
13	2	26	169	338
14	1	14	19	196
15	3	45	225	675
16	1	16	256	256
17	5	85	289	1445
18	3	54	324	972
19	4	76	361	1444
20	1	20	400	400
	n = 25	Σ = 389		Σ = 6293

We compute the **sample mean** as follows:

$$\bar{X} = \frac{\sum_{i=1}^{n} fX_i}{n} = \frac{389}{25} = 15.5600$$

The **sample variance** is computed to be:

$$s^2 = \frac{(n)\left[\sum_{i=1}^{n} fX_i^2\right] - \left[\sum_{i=1}^{n} fX_i\right]^2}{n(n-1)}$$

$$s^2 = \frac{(25)(6293) - (389)^2}{25(25-1)} = \frac{157,325 - 151,321}{600} = \frac{6004}{600} = 10.0067$$

Therefore, the **sample standard deviation** is

$$s = \sqrt{s^2} = \sqrt{10.0067} = 3.1633$$

One concluding thought related to our discussion of variance is that it is common to want to interpret the value of the variance as "large" or "small." Keep in mind that the spread of the distribution is only large or small relative to the size of the mean, for example. A standard deviation of 1 sounds tiny, however relative to a mean of .05 it's huge! There are no conventions on interpreting the size of a variance or standard deviation. Rather, report these values as descriptive statistics in connection with the mean and do not try to interpret the magnitude of the dispersion.

3.3.4 Summary of Measures of Dispersion

To summarize the measures of dispersion then:

1. The range and H spread are the only appropriate measures for ordinal data.
2. The range, H spread, variance, and standard deviation can be used with interval or ratio measurement scales.
3. There are no measures of dispersion appropriate for nominal data.

A summary of the advantages and disadvantages of each measure is presented in Box 3.2.

BOX 3.2 Advantages and Disadvantages of Measures of Dispersion

Measure of Dispersion	Advantages	Disadvantages
Range	Simple to compute	Influenced by extreme scores
	Can be used with ordinal, interval and ratio measurement scales of variables	Function of only two scores
		Unstable from sample to sample
		Cannot be used with nominal data

(continued)

(continued)

Measure of Dispersion	Advantages	Disadvantages
H spread	Unaffected by extreme scores Can be used with ordinal, interval, and ratio measurement scales of variables	Not a function of all scores in the distribution Difficult to deal with mathematically due to its instability Cannot be used with nominal data
Variance and standard deviation	Function of all scores in the distribution Useful for deriving other statistics Can be used with interval and ratio measurement scales of variables	Influenced by extreme scores Cannot be used with nominal or ordinal variables

3.3.5 Recommendations Based on Measurement Scale

A summary of when these descriptive statistics are most appropriate for each of the scales of measurement is shown in Box 3.3. Throughout the text we emphasize that it is the researcher's responsibility to understand the data and its measurement scale so that the appropriate statistics can be generated given the measurement scale of the data.

BOX 3.3 Appropriate Descriptive Statistics

Measurement Scale	Measure of Central Tendency	Measure of Dispersion
Nominal	Mode	
Ordinal	Mode	Range
	Median	*H* spread
Interval/ratio	Mode	Range
	Median	*H* spread
	Mean	Variance and standard deviation

3.4 Computing Sample Statistics Using SPSS

The purpose of this section is to see what SPSS has to offer in terms of computing measures of central tendency and dispersion. In fact, SPSS provides us with many different ways to obtain such measures. The three tools that we have found to be most useful for generating descriptive statistics covered in this chapter are Explore, Descriptives, and Frequencies.

3.4.1 Explore

Step 1. The first tool, Explore, can be invoked by clicking "Analyze" in the top pulldown menu, then "Descriptive Statistics," and then "Explore." Following the screenshot in Figure 3.1 will produce the Explore dialog box. For brevity, we have not reproduced this initial screenshot when we discuss the Descriptives and Frequencies programs; however, you can see in Figure 3.1 where they can be found on the pulldown menus.

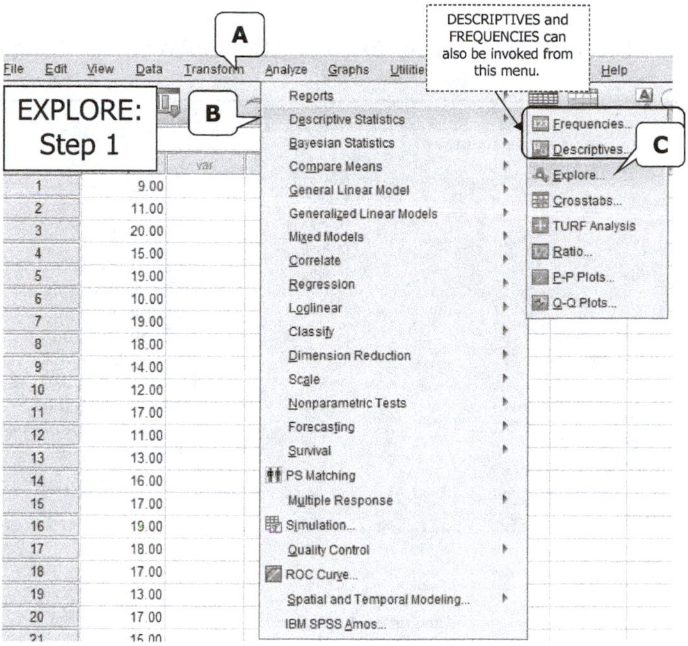

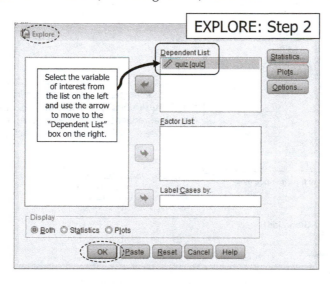

FIGURE 3.1
EXPLORE: Step 1.

Step 2. Next, from the main Explore dialog box, click the variable of interest from the list on the left (e.g., "quiz"), and move it into the "Dependent List" box by clicking the arrow button (see screenshot for "EXPLORE: Step 2" in Figure 3.2). Then click the "OK" button.

FIGURE 3.2
EXPLORE: Step 2.

This will automatically generate the mean, median (approximate), variance, standard deviation, minimum, maximum, exclusive range, and interquartile range (*H*), as well as many other statistics, some of which will be covered in later chapters. The SPSS output from Explore is shown in the top panel of Table 3.5.

TABLE 3.5

Select Output for Statistics Quiz Data using "Explore," "Descriptives," and "Frequencies" Options in SPSS

Descriptives

			Statistic	Std. Error
quiz	Mean		15.5600	.63267
	95% Confidence Interval for Mean	Lower Bound	14.2542	
		Upper Bound	16.8658	
	5% Trimmed Mean		15.6778	
	Median		17.0000	
	Variance		10.007	
	Std. Deviation		3.16333	
	Minimum		9.00	
	Maximum		20.00	
	Range		11.00	
	Interquartile Range		5.00	
	Skewness		-.598	.464
	Kurtosis		-.741	.902

This is an example of the output generated using the "**Explore**" procedure in SPSS. By default, a stem-and-leaf plot and boxplot are also generated from "Explore" (but are not presented here).

Descriptive Statistics

	N	Range	Minimum	Maximum	Mean	Std. Deviation	Variance
quiz	25	11.00	9.00	20.00	15.5600	3.16333	10.007
Valid N (listwise)	25						

This is an example of the output generated using the "**Descriptives**" procedure in SPSS.

Statistics

quiz

N	Valid	25
	Missing	0
Mean		15.5600
Median		16.3333[a]
Mode		17.00
Std. Deviation		3.16333
Variance		10.007
Range		11.00

a. Calculated from grouped data.

This is an example of the output generated using the "**Frequencies**" procedure in SPSS. By default, a frequency table is also generated from "Frequencies" (but is not presented here).

Note the footnote: The median was computed using grouped data by requesting *values are group midpoints.*

Statistics

quiz

N	Valid	25
	Missing	0
Mean		15.5600
Median		17.0000
Mode		17.00
Std. Deviation		3.16333
Variance		10.007
Range		11.00

When computed without *values are group midpoints,* the value of the median is slightly different.

3.4.2 Descriptives

Step 1. The second tool we consider is Descriptives. It can also be accessed by going to "Analyze" in the top pulldown menu, then selecting "Descriptive Statistics," and then "Descriptives" (see Figure 3.1, "EXPLORE: Step 1," for a screenshot of this step).

Step 2. This will bring up the Descriptives dialog box (see the "Descriptives: Step 2" screenshot in Figure 3.3). From the main Descriptives dialog box, click the variable of interest (e.g., "quiz") and move into the "Variable(s)" box by clicking on the arrow. Next, click the "Options" button.

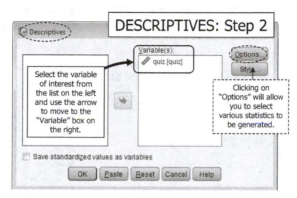

FIGURE 3.3
DESCRIPTIVES: Step 2.

Step 3. A new box called "Descriptives: Options" will appear (see the "DESCRIPTIVES: Step 3" screenshot in Figure 3.4), and you can simply place a checkmark in the boxes for the statistics that you want to generate. By default, the mean, standard deviation, minimum, and maximum are selected. From illustrative purposes, we will also select the variance and range. After making your selections, click "Continue." You will then be returned to the main Descriptives dialog box. From there, click "OK." The SPSS output from the Descriptives tool is shown in the middle panel of Table 3.5.

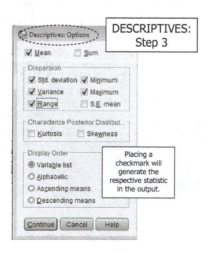

FIGURE 3.4
DESCRIPTIVES: Step 3.

3.4.3 Frequencies

Step 1. The final program to consider is Frequencies. Go to "Analyze" in the top pulldown menu, then "Descriptive Statistics," and then select "Frequencies" (see Figure 3.1, "EXPLORE: Step 1," for a screenshot of this step).

Step 2. The Frequencies dialog box will open (see the screenshot for "FREQUENCIES: Step 2" in Figure 3.5). From this main Frequencies dialog box, click the variable of interest from the list on the left (e.g., "quiz") and move it into the "Variables" box by clicking on the arrow button. By default, there is a checkmark in the box for "Display frequency tables," and we will keep this checked. Selecting "Display frequency tables" will generate a table of frequencies, relative frequencies, and cumulative relative frequencies. Then click on "Statistics" located in the top-right corner.

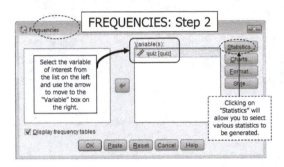

FIGURE 3.5
FREQUENCIES: Step 2.

Step 3. A new dialog box labeled "Frequencies: Statistics" will appear (see screenshot for "FREQUENCIES: Step 3"). Here you can obtain the mean, median (approximate), mode, variance, standard deviation, minimum, maximum, and exclusive range (among others). In order to obtain the closest approximation to the median, check the "Values are group midpoints" box, as shown. However, it should be noted that these values are not always as precise as those from the formula given earlier in this chapter, and your results will not be incorrect should you not select this option. After making your selections, click "Continue." You will then be returned to the main Frequencies dialog box. From there, click "OK." The SPSS output from the Frequencies tool is shown in the bottom panel of Table 3.5.

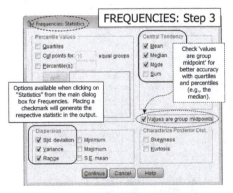

FIGURE 3.6
FREQUENCIES: Step 3.

3.5 Computing Sample Statistics Using R

Next we consider **R** for computing the mean, median, mode, standard deviation, variance, range, minimum, and maximum. The commands are provided within the blocks with additional annotation to assist you in understanding how each command works. Should you want to write reminder notes and annotation to yourself as you write the commands in **R** (and we highly encourage doing so), remember that any text that follows a hashtag (i.e., #) is annotation only and not part of the **R** code. Thus, you can write annotations directly into **R** with hashtags. We encourage this practice so that when you call up the commands in the future you'll understand what the various lines of code are doing. You may think you'll remember what you did. However, trust us. There is a good chance that you won't. Thus, consider it best practice when using **R** to annotate heavily!

3.5.1 Reading Data into R

We will first read in our data (Figure 3.7). We will be using the quiz data that we have used previously.

```
getwd()
```

R is always pointed to a directory on your computer. To find out which directory it is pointed to, run this "get working directory" command. We will assume that we need to change the working directory, and will use the next line of code to point the working directory to the desired path.

```
setwd("E:/Folder")
```

To set the working directory, use the *setwd* function and change what is in quotation marks here to your file location. Also, if you are copying the directory name, it will copy in slashes. You will need to change the slash (i.e., \) to a forward slash (i.e., /). Note that you need your destination name within quotation marks in the parentheses.

```
Ch3_quiz <- read.csv("Ch3_quiz.csv")
```

The *read.csv* function reads your data into **R**. What's to the left of the <- will be what you want to call the data in **R**. In this example, we're calling the dataframe "Ch3_quiz." What's to the right of the <- tells **R** to find this particular .csv file. In this example, our file is called "Ch3_quiz.csv." Make sure the extension (i.e., .csv) is included in your script. Also note that you need the name of your file in quotation marks within the parentheses.

```
names(Ch3_quiz)
```

The *names* function will produce a list of variable names for each dataframe as follows. This is a good check to make sure your data have been read in correctly.

```
[1] "quiz"
```

```
View(Ch3_quiz)
```

The *View* function will let you view the dataset in spreadsheet format in RStudio.

FIGURE 3.7
Reading data into **R**.

3.5.2 Generating Sample Statistics

Similar to SPSS, statistics can be generated in **R** in a number of different ways. The *summary* function will produce a number of helpful statistics, including the mean, median, minimum, and maximum, as well as the 1st and 3rd quartiles (which we will learn about soon) (Figure 3.8).

```
summary(Ch3_quiz)
```

The *summary* function will produce basic descriptive statistics on all the variables in your dataframe. This is a great way to quickly check to see if the data have been read in correctly and get a feel for your data, if you haven't already. The output from the summary statement for this dataframe looks like this:

```
        quiz
Min.    : 9.00
1st Qu.:13.00
Median :17.00
Mean    :15.56
3rd Qu.:18.00
Max.    :20.00
```

FIGURE 3.8
Summary function in **R**.

We can also use the *pastecs* package to generate similar statistics (Figure 3.9).

```
install.packages("pastecs")
library(pastecs)
```

To use a package in **R**, we first have to install the package using the *install.package* function. The name of the package is placed in quotation marks within parentheses. Once the package is installed, we call it into our **R** library so we can access its functionalities using the *library* function.

```
stat.desc(Ch3_quiz$quiz)
```

The function we will use is *stat.desc*, and we define, within parentheses, the dataframe (i.e., "Ch3_quiz") and variable (i.e., "quiz") for which we want to generate the descriptive statistics. The script *Ch3_quiz$quiz* tells **R** to use the variable "quiz" from the "Ch3_quiz" dataframe. The output from this function includes the number of cases in our dataframe (i.e., sample size; *nbr.val*), the number of null values (*nbr.null*), the number of missing values (*nbr.na*), the minimal value (*min*), the maximal value (*max*), the range (*range*, which is computed as max-min), and the sum of all nonmissing values (*sum*). What we are most likely interested in are the values of the median (*median*), mean (*mean*), standard error of the mean (*SE.mean*; we will learn about this in an upcoming chapter), 95% confidence interval of the mean (*CI.mean.0.95*), variance (*var*), standard deviation, (*std.dev*), and coefficient of variation (*coef.var*).

nbr.val	nbr.null	nbr.na
25.0000000	0.0000000	0.0000000

min	max	range
9.0000000	20.0000000	11.0000000

sum	median	mean
389.0000000	17.0000000	15.5600000

FIGURE 3.9
Summary statistics using the *pastecs* package.

```
 SE.mean CI.mean.0.95           var
0.6326663    1.3057591  10.0066667

   std.dev      coef.var
3.1633316    0.2032989
```

FIGURE 3.9 (continued)
Summary statistics using the *pastecs* package.

If we want to produce just one statistic, such as the mean, standard deviation, or variance, we can generate those values with the following scripts (Figure 3.10). The first part of the script defines the function (i.e., *mean, sd, var*) to compute the mean, standard deviation, or variance, respectively. What is enclosed in parentheses tells **R** which dataframe (i.e., "Ch3_quiz") and which variable within that dataframe (i.e., "quiz") to use to compute the statistics. These terms are separated by a $.

```
mean(Ch3_quiz$quiz)
sd(Ch3_quiz$quiz)
var(Ch3_quiz$quiz)
```

The *mean, sd,* and *var* functions can be used to generate, respectively, the mean, standard deviation, and variance. The script *Ch3_quiz$quiz* tells **R** to use the variable "quiz" from the "Ch3_quiz" dataframe. The output follows.

```
# mean(Ch3_quiz$quiz)
[1] 15.56

# sd(Ch3_quiz$quiz)
[1] 3.163332

# var(Ch3_quiz$quiz)
[1] 10.00667
```

FIGURE 3.10
Sample statistics.

3.6 Research Question Template and Example Write-Up

As we stated in Chapter 2, depending on the purpose of your research study, you may or may not write a research question that corresponds to your descriptive statistics. If the end result of your research paper is to present results from inferential statistics, it may be that your research questions correspond only to those inferential questions, and thus no question is presented to represent the descriptive statistics. That is quite common. On the other hand, if the ultimate purpose of your research study is purely descriptive in nature, then writing one or more research questions that correspond to the descriptive statistics is not only entirely appropriate but (in most cases) absolutely necessary. At this time, let us revisit our graduate research assistant, Oso Wyse, who was working with Dr. Debhard. As you may recall, his task was to summarize data from 25 students enrolled in a statistics course. The questions with which Oso was assisting Dr. Debhard were as follows: *How can quiz scores of students enrolled in an introductory statistics class be summarized using measures of central tendency? How can quiz scores of students enrolled in an introductory statistics class be summarized using measures of dispersion?*

The following is a template for writing descriptive research questions for summarizing data with measures of central tendency and dispersion:

How can [variable] be summarized using measures of central tendency? How can [variable] be summarized using measures of dispersion?

Next, we present an APA-like paragraph summarizing the results of the statistics quiz data example answering the questions posed to Marie.

As shown in Table 3.5, scores ranged from 9 to 20. The mean was 15.56, the approximate median was 17.00 (or 16.33 when calculated from grouped data), and the mode was 17.00. Thus, the scores tended to lump together at the high end of the scale. A negatively skewed distribution is suggested given that the mean was less than the median and mode. The exclusive range was 11, *H* spread (interquartile range) was 5.0, variance was 10.007, and standard deviation was 3.1633. From this we can tell that the scores tended to be quite variable. For example, the middle 50% of the scores had a range of 5 (*H* spread), indicating that there was a reasonable spread of scores around the median. Thus, despite a high "average" score, there were some low-performing students as well. These results are consistent with those described in Section 2.4.

3.7 Additional Resources

In the previous chapters, we have mentioned a number of excellent resources for learning statistics. As we are still in the early stages of learning statistics, there are no additional resources that we suggest here. Rather, we refer you back to those chapters for supplemental resources for statistics as well as statistical software.

Problems

Conceptual Problems

1. Adding just one or two extreme scores to the low end of a large distribution of scores will have a greater effect on:

    a. Q than on the variance.

    b. the variance than on Q.

    c. the mode than on the median.

    d. none of the above.

2. Which of the following is true of the variance of a distribution of scores?
   a. It is always 1.
   b. It can be any number—negative, zero, or positive.
   c. It can be any number greater than zero.
   d. It can be any number equal to or greater than zero.

3. A 20-item statistics test was graded using the following procedure: a correct response is scored +1, a blank response is scored 0, and an incorrect response is scored −1. The highest possible score is +20; the lowest score possible is −20. Because the variance of the test scores for the class was −3, we can conclude which of the following?
   a. The class did very poorly on the test.
   b. The test was too difficult for the class.
   c. Some students received negative scores.
   d. A computational error was made.

4. Adding just one or two extreme scores to the high end of a large distribution of scores will have a greater effect on:
   a. the mode than on the median.
   b. the median than on the mode.
   c. the mean than on the median.
   d. none of the above.

5. True or false? In a negatively skewed distribution, the proportion of scores between Q_1 and the median is less than .25.

6. True or false? Median is to ordinal as mode is to nominal.

7. I assert that it is appropriate to utilize the mean in dealing with class-rank data. Am I correct?

8. For a perfectly symmetrical distribution of data, the mean, median, and mode are calculated. I assert that the values of all three measures are necessarily equal. Am I correct?

9. In a distribution of 100 scores, the top 10 examinees received an additional bonus of 5 points. Compared to the original median, I assert that the median of the new (revised) distribution will be the same value. Am I correct?

10. A set of eight scores was collected and the variance was found to be zero. I assert that a computational error must have been made. Am I correct?

11. For a set of 10 test scores, which of the following values will be different when computing the sample statistic as compared to the population parameter?
    a. Mean
    b. H
    c. Range
    d. Variance

12. True or false? The inclusive range will be greater than the exclusive range for any dataset.

13. For a set of IQ test scores, the median was computed to be 95 and Q_1 to be 100. I assert that the statistician is to be commended for her work. Am I correct?

14. A physical education teacher is conducting research related to elementary children's time spent in physical activity. As part of his research, he collects data from schools related to the number of minutes that they require children to participate in physical education classes. She finds that the most frequently occurring number of minutes required for children to participate in physical education classes is 22.00 minutes. Which measure of central tendency does this statement represent?

    a. Mean

    b. Median

    c. Mode

    d. Range

    e. Standard deviation

15. A physical education teacher is conducting research related to elementary children's time spent in physical activity. As part of his research, he collects data from schools related to the number of minutes that they require children to participate in physical education classes. He finds that the fewest number of minutes required per week is 15 minutes and the maximum number of minutes is 45. Which measure of dispersion do these values reflect?

    a. Mean

    b. Median

    c. Mode

    d. Range

    e. Standard deviation

16. A physical education teacher is conducting research related to elementary children's time spent in physical activity. As part of his research, he collects data from schools related to the number of minutes that they require children to participate in physical education classes. He finds that 50% of schools required 20 or more minutes of participation in physical education classes. Which measure of central tendency does this statement represent?

    a. Mean

    b. Median

    c. Mode

    d. Range

    e. Standard deviation

17. One item on a survey of incoming college students asks students to indicate if they plan to live within a 50-mile radius of the university. Responses to the question include "yes," "maybe," or "no." The researcher who gathers this data computes the variance of this variable. Is this appropriate given the measurement scale of this variable? Yes or no?

18. A marriage and family counselor randomly samples 250 clients and collects data on the number of hours they spent in counseling during the past year. What is the most stable measure of central tendency to compute given the measurement scale of this variable?

    a. Mean

    b. Median

c. Mode

d. Range

e. Standard deviation

19. A report issued by a research think tank states that the average teenager spends 9 hours per day on social media. Which measure is reflected in this statement?

a. Mean

b. Median

c. Mode

d. Range

e. Standard deviation

20. A researcher is analyzing data from a patient registry. One of the variables is patient response to the question, "Does your family have a history of this disease?" Responses are "yes" or "no." Which measure of central tendency can the researcher use to analyze data from this question? Select all that apply.

a. Median

b. Mean

c. Mode

d. None of the above

21. A researcher has collected survey data from adults who have visited the Maldives. One of the items asked is, "How many vacations do you take per year?" Responses included: 0–1, 2–3, 4–5, 6 or more. Which of the following measures of central tendency and dispersion would be appropriate given the measurement scale of this variable? Select all that apply.

a. Mean

b. Median

c. Mode

d. Range

e. Standard deviation

22. A researcher is examining the relationship between daytime light exposure and energy expenditure. Subjects are randomly assigned to three light conditions (continuous warm white light, continuous blue-enriched white light, or intermittent warm white and blue-enriched white light). Energy expenditure is measured using indirect calorimetry (i.e., the amount of oxygen consumed and carbon dioxide produced), with values recorded to the third decimal place. The researcher wishes to compute measures of central tendency and dispersion on energy expenditure. Which of the following measures of central tendency and dispersion would be appropriate given the measurement scale of this variable? Select all that apply.

a. Mean

b. Median

c. Mode

d. Range

e. Standard deviation

23.   A researcher is examining the relationship between tourism development and economic growth. Economic growth is measured by a country's gross domestic product (GDP) (measured in whole numbers). The researcher wishes to compute measures of central tendency and dispersion on GDP. Which of the following measures of central tendency and dispersion would be appropriate given the measurement scale of this variable? Select all that apply.

a.   Mean

b.   Median

c.   Mode

d.   Range

e.   Standard deviation

Answers to Conceptual Problems

1.   **b** (It will affect variance the most.)

3.   **d** (The variance cannot be negative.)

5.   **False** (That proportion is always .25.)

7.   **No** (Class rank is ordinal, so the mean is inappropriate.)

9.   **Yes** (Middle score is still the same.)

11.   **d** (Variance has two different formulas.)

13.   **No** (By nature of the median being the second quartile, the median must be larger than the first quartile; fire the statistician.)

15.   **d** (Range, as it is computed as the difference between the two extreme values in the data.)

17.   **No** (Interval or ratio data must be used to compute the variance.)

19.   **a** (The average is also the mean.)

21.   **b, c, d** (With responses of 0–1, 2–3, 4–5, 6 or more, this is an ordinal measurement scale, and thus mean and standard deviation are not appropriate.)

23.   **a, b, c, d, e** (Given the continuous scale of GDP in this example, suggesting a ratio variable, all measures of central tendency and dispersion can be computed.)

Computational Problems

1.   The following scores were obtained from a statistics exam.

50.00	44.00	41.00	43.00	43.00
47.00	49.00	49.00	47.00	42.00
45.00	48.00	41.00	45.00	46.00
44.00	46.00	46.00	46.00	49.00
47.00	50.00	47.00	47.00	44.00
47.00	48.00	45.00	46.00	48.00
45.00	46.00	43.00	44.00	47.00
43.00	45.00	47.00	49.00	45.00
44.00	47.00	50.00	48.00	46.00

Assuming an interval width of 1, compute the following:

a. Mode

b. Median

c. Mean

d. Interquartile range

e. Variance

f. Standard deviation

2. Given a negatively skewed distribution with a mean of 10, a variance of 81, and $N = 500$, what is the numerical value of the following?

$$\sum_{i=1}^{N}(X_i - \mu)$$

3. The following data were obtained from classroom observations and reflect the number of times that preschool children shared during an 8-hour period.

4	8	10	5	12	10	14	5
10	14	12	14	8	5	0	8
12	8	12	5	4	10	8	5

Assuming an interval width of 1, compute the following:

a. Mode

b. Median

c. Mean

d. Interquartile range

e. Variance

f. Standard deviation

4. A sample distribution of aptitude scores is as follows:

X	f
70	1
75	2
77	3
79	2
80	6
82	5
85	4
90	4
96	3

Assuming an interval width of 1, compute the following:

a. Mode

b. Median

c. Mean

d. Interquartile range

    e. Variance

    f. Standard deviation

5. A sample of 30 test scores are as follows:

X	f
8	1
9	4
10	3
11	7
12	9
13	0
14	0
15	3
16	0
17	0
18	2
19	0
20	1

Compute each of the following statistics.

    a. Mode

    b. Median

    c. Mean

    d. Interquartile range

    e. Variance

    f. Standard deviation

6. Without doing any computations, which of the following distributions has the largest variance?

X	f	Y	f	Z	f
15	6	15	4	15	2
16	7	16	7	16	7
17	9	17	11	17	13
18	9	18	11	18	13
19	7	19	7	19	7
20	6	20	4	20	2

7. Without doing any computations, which of the following distributions has the largest variance?

X	f	Y	f	Z	f
5	3	5	1	5	6
6	2	6	0	6	2
7	4	7	4	7	3
8	3	8	3	8	1
9	5	9	2	9	0
10	2	10	1	10	7

8. A researcher has pulled data from the National Oceanic and Atmospheric Administration's (NOAA) Significant Volcanic Eruption Database (www.ngdc.noaa.gov/nndc/servlet/ShowDatasets?dataset=102557&search_look=50&display_look=50) and is examining volcanos that occurred between 2000 and 2018. Using the Ch2_volcano.sav data, answer the following questions.

   a. What type of volcano occurred most often (use "VolcanoType")?

   b. How many deaths occurred most often (use "Deaths")?

   c. What was the range, standard deviation, and average elevation of the volcanos that erupted (use "VolcanoElevation")?

9. A researcher has pulled country-level data from the rollercoaster census report (https://rcdb.com/) and is examining rollercoasters within North American countries. Using the Ch2_rollercoaster.sav data, answer the following questions.

   a. What is the range, standard deviation, and average number of sit-down rollercoasters (use "SitDown")?

   b. What is the mean, median, and standard deviation for steel rollercoasters (use "Steel")?

   c. How can the median number of steel rollercoasters be interpreted?

Answers to Computational Problems

1. Mode = 47, median = 46.00 (46.125 if computed using "values at group midpoints"), mean = 45.9778, interquartile range = 3.50 variance = 5.386, standard deviation = 2.32075.

3. Mode = multiple modes exist, 5 is the smallest mode; median = 8.0 (8.6667 if calculated using "values at group midpoint"), mean = 8.4583, interquartile range = 7.0, variance = 14.085, standard deviation = 3.75302.

5. Mode = 12, median = 11.5 (11.4375 if computed using "values at group midpoint"), mean = 12, interquartile range = 13, variance = 8.0690, standard deviation = 2.8406.

7. Distribution Z. It has more extreme scores than the other distributions.

9. Using the Ch2_rollercoaster.sav data, we find:

   a. The range is 574, SD = 187.717, and the average number of sit-down rollercoasters is 77.00.

   b. Mean = 86.56; median = 5; standard deviation = 213.429.

   c. The median is 5. This indicates that one-half of the countries in North America have fewer than five steel rollercoasters and one-half have more than five steel rollercoasters.

Interpretive Problem

1. Select one interval or ratio variable from the survey1 sample dataset on the website.

   a. Calculate all of the measures of central tendency and dispersion discussed in this chapter that are appropriate for this measurement scale.

   b. Write an APA-style paragraph that summarizes the findings.

2. Select one ordinal variable from the survey1 sample dataset on the website.

   a. Calculate the measures of central tendency and dispersion discussed in this chapter that are appropriate for this measurement scale.

   b. Write an APA-style paragraph that summarizes the findings.

4

The Normal Distribution and Standard Scores

Chapter Outline

Key Concepts

1. Normal distribution (family of distributions, unit normal distribution, area under the curve, points of inflection, asymptotic curve)

2. Standard scores (z, T, IQ)

3. Symmetry

4. Skewness (positively skewed, negatively skewed)

5. Kurtosis (leptokurtic, platykurtic, mesokurtic)

6. Moments around the mean

In Chapter 3, we continued our discussion of descriptive statistics, which were defined as techniques that allow us to tabulate, summarize, and depict a collection of data in an abbreviated fashion. We considered the following three topics: summation notation (method for summing a set of scores), measures of central tendency (measures for boiling down a set of scores into a single value used to represent the data), and measures of dispersion (measures dealing with the extent to which a collection of scores vary).

In this chapter, we delve more into the field of descriptive statistics in terms of three additional topics. First, we consider the most commonly used distributional shape, the normal distribution. Although in this chapter we discuss the major characteristics of the normal distribution and how it is used descriptively, in later chapters we see how the normal distribution is used inferentially as an assumption for certain statistical tests. Second, several types of standard scores are considered. To this point we have looked at raw scores and deviation scores. Here we consider scores that are often easier to interpret, known as *standard scores*. Third, we examine two other measures useful for describing a collection of data, namely skewness and kurtosis. As we show shortly, *skewness* refers to the lack of symmetry of a distribution of scores and kurtosis refers to the *peakedness* of a distribution of scores. Finally, we provide a template for writing research questions, develop an APA-style paragraph of results for an example dataset, and also illustrate the use of SPSS and **R**. Concepts to be discussed include the normal distribution (i.e., family of distributions, unit normal distribution, area under the curve, points of inflection, asymptotic curve), standard scores (e.g., z, T, IQ), symmetry, skewness (positively skewed, negatively skewed), kurtosis (leptokurtic, platykurtic, mesokurtic), and moments around the mean. Our objectives are that by the end of this chapter, you will be able to (a) understand the normal distribution and utilize the normal table; (b) determine and interpret different types of standard scores, particularly z scores; and (c) understand and interpret skewness and kurtosis statistics.

4.1 The Normal Distribution and How It Works

You may remember the following research scenario that was first introduced in Chapter 2. We will revisit our talented group of graduate students in this chapter as they continue to explore the data.

The graduate students in the statistics lab, Addie Venture, Oso Wyse, Challie Lenge, and Ott Lier, have been assigned their first task as research assistants. Dr. Debhard, a statistics professor, has given the group of students quiz data collected from 25 students enrolled in an introductory statistics course and has asked the group to summarize the data. Working now with Challie Lenge, Dr. Debhard has asked Challie to revisit the following research question related to distributional shape: *What is the distributional shape of the statistics quiz score?* Additionally, Dr. Debhard has asked Challie to standardize the quiz score and compare student 1 to student 3 relative to the mean. The corresponding research question that Challie is provided for this analysis is as follows: *In standard deviation units, what is the relative standing to the mean of student 1 compared to student 3?*

Recall from Chapter 2 that there are several commonly seen distributions. The most commonly observed and used distribution is the *normal distribution*. It has many uses, both in descriptive and inferential statistics, as we will show. In this section, we discuss the history of the normal distribution and the major characteristics of the normal distribution.

4.1.1 History

Let us first consider a brief history of the normal distribution. From the time that data were collected and distributions examined, a particular bell-shaped distribution occurred quite often for many variables in many disciplines (e.g., many physical, cognitive, physiological, and motor attributes). This has come to be known as the **normal distribution**. Back in the 1700s, mathematicians were called on to develop an equation that could be used to approximate the normal distribution. If such an equation could be found, then the probability associated with any point on the curve could be determined, and the amount of space or area under any portion of the curve could also be determined. For example, one might want to know what the probability of being taller than 6'2" would be for a male, given that height is normally shaped for each gender. Until the 1920s the development of this equation was commonly attributed to Karl Friedrich Gauss. Until that time this distribution was known as the *Gaussian curve*. However, in the 1920s, Karl Pearson found this equation in an earlier article written by Abraham DeMoivre in 1733 and renamed the curve as the "normal distribution." Today the normal distribution is obviously attributed to DeMoivre. The history of statistics is quite fascinating, and we encourage those interested to explore any number of resources to learn more (e.g., Koren, 1970; Stigler, 1986).

4.1.2 Characteristics

The normal distribution has seven important characteristics. Because the normal distribution occurs frequently, features of the distribution are standard across all normal distributions. This **standard curve** allows us to make comparisons across two or more normal distributions as well as look at areas under the curve, as becomes evident.

4.1.2.1 Standard Curve

First, the normal distribution is a standard curve because *it is always (a) symmetric around the mean, (b) unimodal, and (c) bell-shaped*. As shown in Figure 4.1, if we split the distribution in one-half at the mean (μ), the left-hand half (below the mean) is the mirror image of the right-hand half (above the mean). Also, the normal distribution has only one mode (i.e., unimodal), and the general shape of the distribution is bell shaped (some even call it the *bell-shaped curve*). Given these conditions, the mean, median, and mode will always be equal to one another for any normal distribution. (We will see later, however, that rarely do we encounter *perfectly* normal distributions where the mean, median, and mode are exactly equal to each other. Indeed, in our many combined years of generating statistics, we cannot necessarily recall a time when that happened! Rather, we will examine the range in which a distribution can be considered normal.)

4.1.2.2 Family of Curves

Second, there is no single normal distribution, but rather *the normal distribution is a family of curves*. For instance, one particular normal curve has a mean of 100 and a variance of

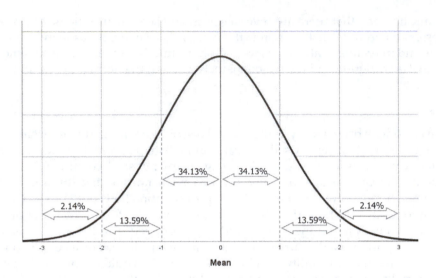

FIGURE 4.1
The normal distribution.

225 (recall that the standard deviation is the square root of the variance, thus the standard deviation in this instance is 15). This normal curve is exemplified by the Wechsler Intelligence Scales. Another specific normal curve has a mean of 50 and a variance of 100 (and thus a standard deviation of 10). This normal curve is used with most behavior rating scales. *In fact, there are an infinite number of normal curves, one for every distinct pair of values for the mean and variance.* Every member of the family of normal curves has the same characteristics; however, the scale of X, the mean of X, and the variance (and standard deviation) of X can differ across different variables and/or populations.

To keep the members of the family distinct, we use the following notation. If the variable X is normally distributed, we write $X \sim N(\mu, \sigma^2)$. This is read as, "X is distributed normally with population mean μ and population variance σ^2." This is the general notation; for notation specific to a particular normal distribution, the mean and variance values are given. For our examples, the Wechsler Intelligence Scales are denoted by $X \sim N(100,225)$, whereas the behavior rating scales are denoted by $X \sim N(50,100)$. Narratively speaking, therefore, the Wechsler Intelligence Scale is distributed normally with a population mean of 100 and population variance of 225. A similar interpretation can be made on the behavior rating scale.

4.1.2.3 Unit Normal Distribution

Third, there is one particular member of the family of normal curves that deserves additional attention. This member has a mean of 0 and a variance (and standard deviation) of 1, and thus is denoted by $X \sim N(0,1)$. This is known as the **unit normal distribution** ("unit" referring to the variance of 1) or as the **standard unit normal distribution**. On a related matter, let us define a z score as follows:

$$z_i = \frac{\left(X_i - \mu\right)}{\sigma}$$

The numerator of this equation is actually a deviation score, previously described in Chapter 3, and indicates how far above or below the mean an individual's score falls. *When we* divide the deviation from the mean (i.e., the numerator) by the standard deviation (i.e., denominator), the value derived indicates how many deviations above or below the mean a unit's score falls. If one individual has a z score of +1.00, then the person falls one standard deviation above the mean on that particular measure. If another individual has a z score of –2.00, then that person falls two standard deviations below the mean on that particular measure. There is more to say about this as we move along in this section.

4.1.2.4 Area

The fourth characteristic of the normal distribution is the ability to determine any area under the curve. *Specifically, we can determine the area above any value, the area below any value, or the area between any two values under the curve.* Let us chat about what we mean by *area*. If you return to Figure 4.1, areas for different portions of the curve are listed. Here, **area** is defined as *the percentage or amount of space of a distribution, either above a certain score, below a certain score, or between two different scores*. For example, we see that the area between the mean and one standard deviation above the mean is 34.13%. In other words, roughly one-third of the entire distribution falls into that region. The entire area under the curve then represents 100%, and smaller portions of the curve represent somewhat less than that.

For example, say you wanted to know what percentage of adults had an IQ score greater than 120, or what percentage of adults had an IQ score less than 107, or what percentage of adults had an IQ score between 107 and 120. How can we compute these areas under the curve? A table of the unit normal distribution has been developed for this purpose. Although similar tables could also be developed for every member of the normal family of curves, these are unnecessary, as any normal distribution can be converted to a unit normal distribution. The **unit normal table** is given in Table A.1 in the Appendix.

Turn to Appendix Table A.1 now and familiarize yourself with its contents. To help illustrate, a portion of the table is presented in Figure 4.2. The first column simply lists the values of z. These are standardized scores on the X axis. Note that the values of z only range from 0 to 4.0. There are two reasons for this. First, values above 4.0 are rather unlikely, as the area under that portion of the curve is negligible (less than .003%). Second, values below 0 (i.e., negative z scores) are not really necessary to present in the table, as the normal distribution is symmetric around the mean of 0. Thus, that portion of the table would be redundant and is not shown here (we show how to deal with this situation for some example problems in a bit).

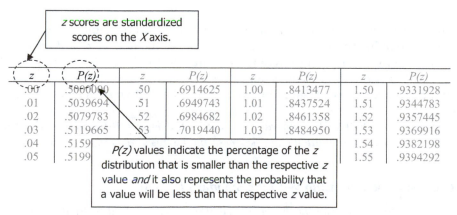

z	P(z)	z	P(z)	z	P(z)	z	P(z)
.00	.5000000	.50	.6914625	1.00	.8413477	1.50	.9331928
.01	.5039694	.51	.6949743	1.01	.8437524	1.51	.9344783
.02	.5079783	.52	.6984682	1.02	.8461358	1.52	.9357445
.03	.5119665	.53	.7019440	1.03	.8484950	1.53	.9369916
.04	.5159					1.54	.9382198
.05	.5199					1.55	.9394292

z scores are standardized scores on the X axis.

P(z) values indicate the percentage of the z distribution that is smaller than the respective z value *and* it also represents the probability that a value will be less than that respective z value.

FIGURE 4.2
Portion of z table.

The second column, labeled $P(z)$, gives the area below the respective value of z. In other words, the area between that value of z and the most extreme left-hand portion of the curve (i.e., -4, or negative infinity, on the far negative or left-hand side of zero). So if we wanted to know what the area was below $z = +1.00$, we would look in the first column under $z = 1.00$ and then look in the second column, $P(z)$, to find the area of .8413. *This value, .8413, represents the percentage of the distribution that is smaller than z of +1.00. It also represents the probability that a score will be smaller than z of +1.00.* In other words, about 84% of the distribution is less than z of $+1.00$ *and* the probability that a value will be less than z of $+1.00$ is about 84%. More examples are considered later in this section.

4.1.2.5 Transformation to Unit Normal Distribution

A fifth characteristic is that *any normally distributed variable, regardless of the mean and variance, can be converted into a unit normally distributed variable.* Thus, our Wechsler Intelligence Scales, as denoted by $X \sim N(100,225)$, can be converted into $z \sim N(0,1)$. Conceptually this transformation is done by moving the curve along the X axis until it is centered at a mean of 0 (by subtracting out the original mean) and then by stretching or compressing the distribution until it has a variance of 1 (remember, however, that the shape of the distribution does not change during the standardization process, only those values on the X axis). This allows us to make the same interpretation about any individual's score on any normally distributed variable. If $z = +1.00$, then for *any* variable this implies that the individual falls one standard deviation above the mean.

This also allows us to make comparisons between two different individuals or cases or across two different variables. If we wanted to make comparisons between two different individuals on the same variable X, then rather than comparing their individual raw scores, X_1 and X_2, we could compare their individual z scores, z_1 and z_2, where

$$z_1 = \frac{(X_1 - \mu)}{\sigma}$$

and

$$z_2 = \frac{(X_2 - \mu)}{\sigma}$$

This is the reason we only need the unit normal distribution table to determine areas under the curve rather than a table for every member of the normal distribution family. In another situation we may want to compare scores on the Wechsler Intelligence Scales, $X \sim N(100,225)$, to scores on behavior rating scales, $X \sim N(50,100)$, for the same individual. We would convert to z scores again for two variables, and then direct comparisons could be made.

It is important to note that in standardizing a variable, it is only the values on the X axis that change. The shape of the distribution (e.g., skewness and kurtosis) remains the same.

4.1.2.6 Constant Relationship With the Standard Deviation

The sixth characteristic is that *the normal distribution has a constant relationship with the standard deviation.* Consider Figure 4.1 again. Along the X axis we see values represented in standard deviation increments. In particular, from left to right, the values shown are three, two, and one standard deviation units below the mean; the mean; and one, two, and three standard deviation units above the mean. Under the curve, we see the percentage of scores that are under different portions of the curve. For example, the area between the mean and one standard deviation above or below the mean is 34.13%. The area between one standard deviation and two standard deviations on the same side of the mean is 13.59%, the area between two and three standard deviations on the same side is 2.14%, and the area beyond three standard deviations is .13%.

In addition, three other areas are often of interest. The area within one standard deviation of the mean, from one standard deviation below the mean to one standard deviation above the mean, is approximately 68% (or roughly two-thirds of the distribution). The area within two standard deviations of the mean, from two standard deviations below the mean to two standard deviations above the mean, is approximately 95%. The area within three standard deviations of the mean, from three standard deviations below the mean to three standard deviations above the mean, is approximately 99%. In other words, nearly all of the scores will be within two or three standard deviations of the mean for any normal curve.

4.1.2.7 Points of Inflection and Asymptotic Curve

The seventh and final characteristic of the normal distribution is as follows. *The points of inflection are where the curve changes from sloping down (concave) to sloping up (convex).* These **points of inflection** occur precisely at one standard deviation unit *above* and *below* the mean. This is more a matter of mathematical elegance than a statistical application. The curve also never touches the X axis. This is because with the theoretical normal curve, all values from negative infinity to positive infinity have a nonzero probability of occurring. Thus, while the curve continues to slope ever-downward toward more extreme scores, it approaches, but never quite touches, the X axis. The curve is referred to here as being **asymptotic**. This allows for the possibility of extreme scores.

4.1.2.8 Examples

Now for the long-awaited examples for finding area using the unit normal distribution. These examples require the use of Table A.1 in the Appendix, the z table. Our personal preference is to start by drawing a picture of the normal curve so that the proper area is visualized. Let us consider four examples of finding the area below a certain value of z: (a) below $z = -2.50$; (b) below $z = 0$; (c) below $z = 1.00$; and (d) between $z = -2.50$ and $z = 1.00$.

To determine the value below $z = -2.50$, we draw a picture as shown in Figure 4.3a. We draw a vertical line at the value of z, then shade in the area we want to find. In this example, that represents $z \leq -2.50$. Because the shaded region is relatively small, we know the area must be considerably smaller than .50. In the unit normal table we already know negative values of z are not included. However, because the normal distribution is symmetric, we know the area *below* −2.50 is the same as the area *above* +2.50. Thus, we look up the area below +2.50 and find the value of .9938. This indicates that about 99.38% of the distribution is below $z = +2.50$ and what remains in the distribution is $z \geq +2.50$. Thus, we can subtract .9938 from 1.0000 and find the value of .0062, or .62%, very small area indeed, which represents the area of the distribution where $z \geq +2.50$ as well as $z \leq -2.50$.

How do we determine the area *below* $z = 0$ (i.e., the mean)? As shown in Figure 4.3b, we already know from reading this section that the area has to be .5000, or one-half of the total

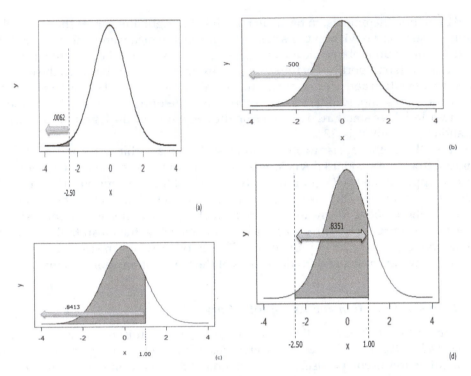

FIGURE 4.3

Examples of area under the unit normal distribution: (a) area below $z = -2.5$, (b) area below $z = 0$, (c) area below $z = 1.0$, (d) area between $z = -2.5$ and $z = 1.0$.

area under the curve. However, looking in the table again for the area below $z = 0$, we find the area is .5000. How do we determine the area below $z = 1.00$? As shown in Figure 4.3c, this region exists on both sides of zero and actually constitutes two smaller areas, the first area below 0 and the second area between 0 and 1. For this example we use the table directly and find the value of .8413. We leave you with two other problems to solve on your own. First, what is the area below $z = 0.50$ (answer: .6915)? Second, what is the area below $z = 1.96$ (answer: .9750)?

Because the unit normal distribution is symmetric, finding the area *above* a certain value of z is solved in a similar fashion as the area *below* a certain value of z. We need not devote any further attention to that particular situation. However, how do we determine the area *between* two values of z? This is a little different and needs some additional discussion. Consider as an example finding the area between $z = -2.50$ and $z = 1.00$, as depicted in Figure 4.3 (d). Here we see that the shaded region consists of two smaller areas, the area between the mean ($z = 0$) and -2.50 and the area between the mean ($z = 0$) and 1.00. Using the table again, we find the area *below* 1.00 is .8413 and the area *below* -2.50 is .0062. Thus, the shaded region is the difference, as computed by $.8413 - .0062 = .8351$. Thus, the area between $z = -2.50$ and $z = 1.00$ is about 83.51% of the distribution. On your own, determine the area between $z = -1.27$ and $z = 0.50$ (answer: .5895).

Finally, what if we wanted to determine areas under the curve for values of X rather than z? The answer here is simple, as you might have guessed. First, we convert the value of X to a z score, and then we use the unit normal table to determine the area. Because the normal curve is standard for all members of the family of normal curves, the scale of the variable, X or z, is irrelevant in terms of determining such areas. In the next section we deal more with such transformations.

4.2 Standard Scores and How They Work

We have already devoted considerable attention to z scores, which are one type of standard score. In this section we describe an application of z scores leading up to a discussion of other types of standard scores. As we show, the major purpose of standard scores is to place scores on the same standard scale so that comparisons can be made across individuals and/or variables. Without some standard scale, comparisons across individuals and/or variables would be difficult to make. Examples are coming right up.

4.2.1 *z* Scores

You have just interviewed for your dream job. As part of your interview, you completed a cognitive ability assessment (which measured problem-solving skills and ability to learn and understand instructions) and a motivation index (designed to measure work engagement motivation). On the cognitive ability assessment, you receives a score of 75 and on the motivation index you receive a score of 60. The natural question to ask is, "Which performance was the stronger one?" The suspense is killing you! No information about any of the following is available: maximum score possible, mean of the candidates who were interviewed (or any other central tendency measure), or standard deviation of the candidates who were interviewed (or any other dispersion measure). It is possible, and quite likely, that the two assessments had a different number of possible points, different means, and/or different standard deviations. How can we possibly answer our question?

The answer, of course, is to use z scores if the data are assumed to be normally distributed, once the relevant information is obtained. Let us take a minor digression before we return to answer our question in more detail. Recall the formula for standardizing variable X into a z score:

$$z_i = \frac{(X_i - \mu_X)}{\sigma_X}$$

where the X subscript has been added to the mean and standard deviation for purposes of clarifying which variable is being considered. If variable X is the number of items correct on a test, then the numerator is the deviation of the student's raw score from the class mean (i.e., the numerator is a deviation score as previously defined in Chapter 3), measured in terms of items correct, and the denominator is the standard deviation of the class, measured in terms of items correct. Because both the numerator and denominator are measured in terms of items correct, the resultant z score is measured in terms of no units (as the units of the numerator and denominator essentially cancel out). *Given that z scores have no units (i.e., the z score is interpreted as the number of standard deviation units above or below the mean), this allows us to compare two different raw score variables with different scales, means, and/or standard deviations.* By converting our two variables to z scores, the transformed variables are now on the same z score scale with a mean of 0 and a variance and standard deviation of 1.

Let us return to our previous situation where the cognitive ability score is 75 and the motivation index score is 60. In addition, we are provided with information that the standard deviation for the cognitive ability is 15 and the standard deviation for the motivation index is 10. Consider the following three examples. In the first example, the means are 60 for the cognitive ability assessment and 50 for the motivation index. The z scores are then computed as follows:

$$z_i = \frac{(X_i - \mu)}{\sigma}$$

$$z_{cognitive\ ability} = \frac{(75 - 60)}{15} = 1.0$$

$$z_{motivation} = \frac{(60 - 50)}{10} = 1.0$$

The conclusion for the first example is that the performance on both instruments is the same; that is, you scored one standard deviation above the mean on both assessments.

In the second example, the means are 60 for the cognitive ability assessment and 40 for the motivation index. The z scores are then computed as follows:

$$z_{cognitive\ ability} = \frac{(75 - 60)}{15} = 1.0$$

$$z_{motivation} = \frac{(60 - 40)}{10} = 2.0$$

The conclusion for the second example is that performance is better on the motivation index; that is, you scored two standard deviations above the mean for the motivation index and only one standard deviation above the mean for the cognitive ability assessment.

In the third example, the means are 60 for the cognitive ability assessment and 70 for the motivation index. The z scores are then computed as follows:

$$z_{cognitive\ ability} = \frac{(75 - 60)}{15} = 1.0$$

$$z_{motivation} = \frac{(60 - 70)}{10} = -1.0$$

The conclusion for the third example is that performance is better on the cognitive ability assessment; that is, you scored one standard deviation above the mean for the cognitive ability assessment and one standard deviation below the mean for the motivation index. These examples serve to illustrate a few of the many possibilities, depending on the particular combinations of raw score, mean, and standard deviation for each variable.

Let us conclude this section by mentioning the major characteristics of z scores. The first characteristic is that z scores provide us with *comparable distributions,* as we just saw in the previous examples. Second, z scores take into account *the entire distribution of raw scores.* All raw scores can be converted to z scores such that every raw score will have a corresponding z score. Third, we can evaluate an individual's performance *relative to the scores in the distribution*. For example, saying that an individual's score is one standard deviation above the mean is a measure of relative performance. This implies that approximately 84% of the scores will fall below the performance of that individual. Finally, *negative values* (i.e., below 0) and *decimal values* (e.g., z = 1.55) *are obviously possible* (and will most certainly occur) with z scores. On the average, about one-half of the z scores for any distribution will be negative and some decimal values are quite likely. This last characteristic is bothersome to some individuals and has led to the development of other types of standard scores, as described in the next section.

4.2.2 Other Types of Standard Scores

Over the years, other standard scores besides z scores have been developed, either to alleviate the concern over negative and/or decimal values associated with z scores or to obtain a particular mean and standard deviation. Let us examine some common examples. The first additional standard score is known as the *T* score and is used in tests such as most behavior rating scales, as previously mentioned. The **T scores** have a mean of 50 and a standard deviation of 10. A second additional standard score is known as the **IQ score** and is used in the Wechsler Intelligence Scales. The IQ score has a mean of 100 and a standard deviation of 15 (the Stanford-Binet Intelligence Scales have a mean of 100 and a standard deviation of 16). Entrance exams are also standardized scores but with means and standard deviations that differ from 0 and 1, respectively.

Say we want to develop our own type of standard score, where we determine in advance the mean and standard deviation that we would like to have. How would that be done? Given that the equation for z scores is as follows:

$$z_i = \frac{\left(X_i - \mu_X\right)}{\sigma_X}$$

then algebraically the following can be shown:

$$X_i = \mu_X + \sigma_X z_i$$

If, for example, we want to develop our own "stat" standardized score, then the following equation would be used:

$$stat_i = \mu_{start} + \sigma_{start} Z_i$$

where $stat_i$ is the "stat" standardized score for a particular individual i, μ_{stat} is the desired mean of the "stat" distribution, and σ_{stat} is the desired standard deviation of the "stat" distribution. If we want to have a mean of 10 and a standard deviation of 2, then our equation becomes

$$stat_i = 10 + 2z_i$$

We would then have the computer simply plug in a z score and compute an individual's "stat" score. Thus, a z score of 1.0 would yield a "stat" standardized score of 12.0.

Consider a realistic example where we have a raw score variable we want to transform into a standard score, and we want to control the mean and standard deviation. For example, we have statistics midterm raw scores with 225 points possible. We want to develop a standard score with a mean of 50 and a standard deviation of 5. We also have scores on other variables that are on different scales with different means and different standard deviations (e.g., statistics final exam scores worth 175 points, a set of 20 lab assignments worth a total of 200 points, a statistics performance assessment worth 100 points). We can standardize each of those variables by placing them on the same scale with the same mean and same standard deviation, thereby allowing comparisons across variables. This is precisely the rationale used by testing companies and researchers when they develop standard scores. In short, from z scores we can develop a T, IQ, "stat," or any other type of standard score. Examples of types of standard scores are summarized in Box 4.1.

BOX 4.1 Examples of Types of Standard Scores

Standard Score	Distribution*
Z (unit normal)	$N(0,1)$
College Entrance Examination Board (CEEB) score	$N(500,10{,}000)$
T score	$N(50,100)$
Weschler intelligence scale	$N(100,225)$
Stanford-Binet intelligence scale	$N(100,256)$

$*N\left(\mu,\sigma^2\right)$

4.3 Skewness and Kurtosis Statistics

In previous chapters we discussed the distributional concepts of symmetry, skewness, central tendency, and dispersion. In this section we more closely define symmetry as well as the statistics commonly used to measure skewness and kurtosis.

4.3.1 Symmetry

Conceptually, we define a distribution as being **symmetric** *if when we divide the distribution precisely in one-half, the left-hand half is a mirror image of the right-hand half.* That is, the distribution above the mean is a mirror image of the distribution below the mean. To put it another way, a distribution is **symmetric around the mean** if for every score that is q units below the mean, there is a corresponding score that is q units above the mean.

Two examples of symmetric distributions are shown in Figure 4.4. In Figure 4.4a, we have a normal distribution, which is clearly symmetric around the mean. In Figure 4.4b, we have a symmetric distribution that is bimodal, unlike the previous example. From these and other numerous examples, we can make the following two conclusions. First, if a distribution is *symmetric*, then the mean is equal to the median. Second, if a distribution is

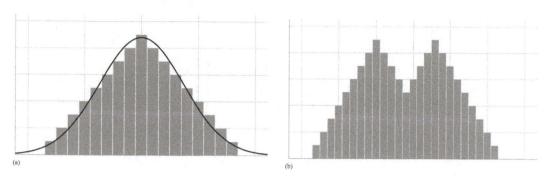

FIGURE 4.4
Symmetric distributions: (a) normal distribution and (b) bimodal distribution.

symmetric and unimodal, then the mean, median, and mode are all equal. This indicates we can determine whether a distribution is symmetric by simply comparing the measures of central tendency.

4.3.2 Skewness

We define **skewness** as *the extent to which a distribution of scores deviates from perfect symmetry.* This is important because perfectly symmetrical distributions rarely occur with actual sample data (i.e., "real" data). A skewed distribution is known as being **asymmetrical.** As shown in Figure 4.5, there are two general types of skewness, distributions that are negatively skewed, as in Figure 4.5a, and those that are positively skewed, as in Figure 4.5b. *Negatively skewed distributions, which are skewed to the left, occur when most of the scores are toward the high end of the distribution and only a few scores are toward the low end.* If you make a fist with your thumb pointing to the left (skewed to the left), you have graphically defined a negatively skewed distribution. For a negatively skewed distribution, we also find the following: mode > median > mean. This indicates that we can determine whether a distribution is negatively skewed by simply comparing the measures of central tendency.

Positively skewed distributions, which are skewed to the right, occur when most of the scores are toward the low end of the distribution and only a few scores are toward the high end. If you make a fist with your thumb pointing to the right (skewed to the right), you have visually defined a positively skewed distribution. For a positively skewed distribution, we also find the following: mode < median < mean. This indicates that we can determine whether a distribution is positively skewed by simply comparing the measures of central tendency.

The most commonly used measure of skewness is known as γ_1 (Greek letter gamma), which is mathematically defined as follows:

$$\gamma_1 = \frac{\sum_{i=1}^{N} z_i^3}{N}$$

where we take the z score for each individual, cube it (i.e., z_i^3), sum across all N individuals, and then divide by the number of individuals N. This measure is available in nearly all computer packages, so hand computations are not necessary. The characteristics of this measure of skewness are as follows: (a) a perfectly symmetrical distribution has a skewness

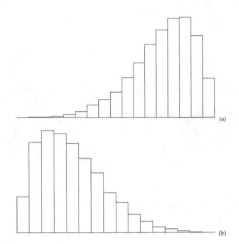

FIGURE 4.5
Skewed distributions: (a) negatively skewed distribution and (b) positively skewed distribution.

value of 0, (b) the range of values for the skewness statistic is approximately from −3 to +3, (c) negatively skewed distributions have negative skewness values, and (d) positively skewed distributions have positive skewness values.

You will rarely, if ever, find a distribution that has a skewness statistic that is exactly equal to zero. In other words, most distributions have some degree of skew. Different conventions are available for determining how extreme skewness can be and still retain a relatively normal distribution. One simple guideline is that skewness values within ±2.0 are considered relatively normal, with more liberal researchers applying a ±3.0 guideline, and more conservative researchers using ±1.0. Another recommendation for determining how extreme a skewness value must be for the distribution to be considered nonnormal is as follows: Skewness values outside the range of plus or minus two standard errors of skewness suggest a distribution that is nonnormal. Applying this suggestion, if the standard error of skewness is .85, then anything outside of −2(.85) to +2(.85), or −1.7 to +1.7, would be considered nonnormal. It is important to note that this second recommendation is sensitive to small sample sizes and should only be considered as a general guide. When we delve into inferential statistics (see Chapter 6), we will discuss how we can use skew and kurtosis divided by their standard errors to determine what is statistically significantly different from normal—but we'll save that conversation for a few more chapters! ☺ A summary of items related to skewness is provided in Box 4.2.

BOX 4.2 Summary of Skewness

Property	Characteristic	Conventions
Negatively skewed distributions (i.e., skewed left) occur when most of the scores are toward the high end of the distribution and only a few scores are toward the low end/ Negative skew = mode > median > mean	A perfectly symmetrical distribution has a skewness value of 0. The range of values for the skewness statistic is approximately from −3 to +3.	*Liberal convention:* skewness within ±3.0 are normal *Moderate convention:* skewness within ±2.0 are normal.

Property	Characteristic	Conventions
Positively skewed distributions (i.e., skewed right) occur when most of the scores are toward the low end of the distribution and only a few scores are toward the high end Positive skew = mode < median < mean	Negatively skewed distributions have negative skewness values. Positively skewed distributions have positive skewness values. Skewness can be computed on variables that are interval or ratio in scale.	*Conservative convention:* skewness within skewness within ±1.0 are normal. Skewness values outside the range of ±2 standard errors of skewness suggest a distribution that is nonnormal.

4.3.3 Kurtosis

Kurtosis is the fourth and final property of a distribution (often referred to as the **moments around the mean**). *These four properties are central tendency (first moment), dispersion (second moment), skewness (third moment), and kurtosis (fourth moment).* **Kurtosis** is conceptually defined as the "peakedness" of a distribution (*kurtosis* is Greek for "peakedness"). Some distributions are rather flat and others have a rather sharp peak. Specifically, the three general types of peakedness are shown in Figure 4.6. A distribution that is very peaked is

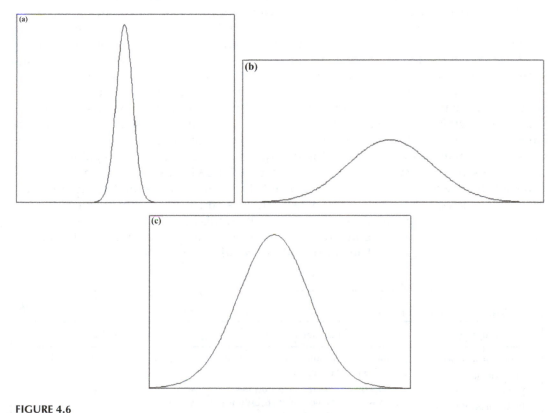

FIGURE 4.6
Distributions of different kurtoses: (a) leptokurtic distribution, (b) platykurtic distribution, (c) mesokurtic distribution.

known as being **leptokurtic** (*lepto* meaning "slender" or "narrow"; Figure 4.6a). A distribution that is relatively flat is known as being **platykurtic** (*platy* meaning "flat" or "broad"; Figure 4.6b). A distribution that is somewhere in between, such as a normal distribution, is known as being **mesokurtic** (*meso* meaning "intermediate"; Figure 4.6c).

The most commonly used measure of kurtosis is known as γ_2, which is mathematically defined as

$$\gamma_2 = \frac{\sum_{i=1}^{N} z_i^4}{N} - 3$$

where we take the z score for each unit, take it to the fourth power (being the fourth moment), sum across all N individuals, divide by the number of individuals N, and then subtract 3. This measure is available in nearly all computer packages, so hand computations are not necessary. The characteristics of this measure of kurtosis are as follows: (a) a perfectly mesokurtic distribution, which would be a normal distribution, has a kurtosis value of 0; (b) platykurtic distributions have negative kurtosis values (being flat rather than peaked); and (c) leptokurtic distributions have positive kurtosis values (being peaked). Kurtosis values can range from negative to positive infinity, and kurtosis can be computed on variables that are interval or ratio in scale.

Similar to skewness, you will rarely, if ever, find a distribution that has a kurtosis statistic that is exactly equal to zero. In other words, most distributions have some degree of kurtosis. Different conventions are available for determining how extreme kurtosis can be and still retain a relatively normal distribution. One simple guideline is that kurtosis values within ±2.0 are considered relatively normal, with more conservative researchers applying a ±3.0 guideline, and more stringent researchers using ±1.0. A suggestion for determining how extreme a kurtosis value may be for the distribution to be considered nonnormal is as follows: Kurtosis values outside the range of ±2.0 standard errors of kurtosis suggest a distribution that is nonnormal. Applying this criteria, if the standard error of kurtosis is 1.20, then anything outside of (−2.00) (1.20) to (+2.00) (1.20), or −2.40 to +2.40, would be considered nonnormal. It is important to note that this second guideline (i.e., ±2.0 *SE*) is sensitive to small sample sizes and should only be considered as a general guide.

Skewness and kurtosis statistics are useful for the following two reasons: (a) as descriptive statistics used to describe the shape of a distribution of scores, and (b) in inferential statistics, which often assume a normal distribution, so the researcher has some indication of whether the assumption has been met (more about this beginning in Chapter 6). Skewness and kurtosis are appropriate to compute only on variables that are interval or ratio in scale. A summary of items related to kurtosis is provided in Box 4.3.

BOX 4.3 Summary of Kurtosis

Property	Characteristics	Conventions
Leptokurtic, peaked Mesokurtic, neither peaked nor flat Platykurtic, flat	Leptokurtic distributions have positive kurtosis values (being peaked). A perfectly mesokurtic distribution, which would be a normal distribution, has a kurtosis value of 0.	*Liberal convention:* kurtosis within ±3.0 are normal. *Moderate convention:* kurtosis within ±2.0 are normal.

Property	Characteristics	Conventions
	Platykurtic distributions have negative kurtosis values (being flat rather than peaked). Kurtosis values can range from negative to positive infinity. Kurtosis can be computed on variables that are interval or ratio in scale.	*Conservative convention:* kurtosis within ±1.0 are normal. Kurtosis values outside the range of ±2 standard errors of kurtosis suggest a distribution that is nonnormal.

4.4 Computing Graphs and Standard Scores Using SPSS

Here we review what SPSS has to offer for examining distributional shape and computing standard scores. The following tools have proven to be quite useful for these purposes: Explore, Descriptives, Frequencies, Graphs, and Transform.

4.4.1 Explore

Step 1. Explore can be invoked by clicking "Analyze" in the top pulldown menu, then "Descriptive Statistics," and then "Explore." Following the screenshot for "EXPLORE: Step 1" in Figure 4.7 produces the Explore dialog box. For brevity, we have not reproduced this initial screenshot when we discuss the Descriptives and Frequencies tools; however, you see here where they can be found from the pulldown menus.

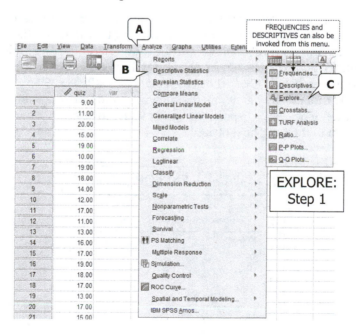

FIGURE 4.7
EXPLORE: Step 1.

Step 2. Next, from the main Explore dialog box, click the variable of interest from the list on the left (e.g., "quiz"), and move it into the "Dependent List" box by clicking the arrow button. Next, click the "Statistics" button located in the top-right corner of the main dialog box (Figure 4.8).

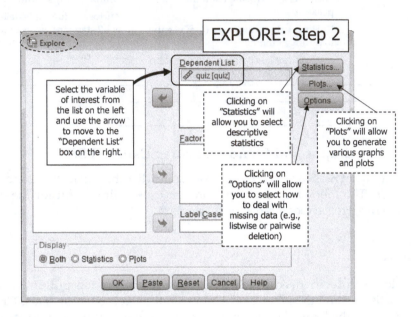

FIGURE 4.8
EXPLORE: Step 2.

Step 3. A new box labeled "Explore: Statistics" will appear. Simply place a checkmark in the "Descriptives" box. Should you desire to use an alpha other than .05 (i.e., 95% confidence interval for the mean), then that change can be made here. For this illustration, we will keep the default 95%. Next click "Continue." You will then be returned to the main Explore dialog box. From there, click "OK." The screenshot for "EXPLORE: Step 3" is shown in Figure 4.9. This will automatically generate the skewness and kurtosis values, as well as measures of central tendency and dispersion, which were covered in Chapter 3. The output from this is shown in the top panel of Table 3.5.

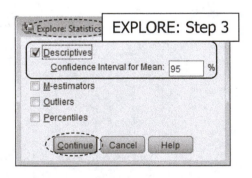

FIGURE 4.9
EXPLORE: Step 3.

4.4.2 Descriptives

Step 1. The second tool to consider is Descriptives. It can also be accessed by going to "Analyze" in the top pulldown menu, then selecting "Descriptive Statistics," and then "Descriptives" (see Figure 4.7, "EXPLORE: Step 1," for a screenshot of these steps).

Step 2. This will bring up the Descriptives dialog box (see Figure 4.10 for a screenshot of "Descriptives: Step 2"). From the main Descriptives dialog box, click the variable of interest (e.g., "quiz") and move into the "Variable(s)" box by clicking the arrow. If you want to obtain z scores for this variable for each case (e.g., person or object that was measured—your unit of analysis), check the "Save standardized values as variables" box located in the bottom-left corner of the main Descriptives dialog box. This will insert a new variable into your dataset for subsequent analysis (see the screenshot in Figure 4.12 for how this will appear in Data View). Next, click on the "Options" button.

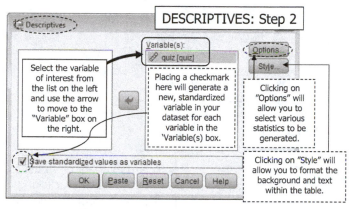

FIGURE 4.10
DESCRIPTIVES: Step 2.

		quiz	Zquiz
	1	9.00	-2.07376
	2	11.00	-1.44152
	3	20.00	1.40358
	4	15.00	-.17703
	5	19.00	1.08746
	6	10.00	-1.75764
	7	19.00	1.08746
	8	18.00	.77134
	9	14.00	-.49315
	10	12.00	-1.12540
	11	17.00	.45522
	12	11.00	-1.44152
	13	13.00	-.80927
	14	16.00	.13909
	15	17.00	.45522
	16	19.00	1.08746
	17	18.00	.77134
	18	17.00	.45522
	19	13.00	-.80927
	20	17.00	.45522

DESCRIPTIVES: Saving Standardized Variable

If "Save standardized values as variables" was checked on the main "Descriptives" dialog box, a new standardized variable will be created.

By default, this variable name is the name of the original variable prefixed with a "Z" (denoting its standardization).

It is computed using the unit normal formula:

$$z = \frac{X - \mu}{\sigma}$$

FIGURE 4.11
Standardized variable (first 20 cases).

Step 3. A new box called "Descriptives: Options" will appear (see Figure 4.12 for the screen-shot of "DESCRIPTIVES: Step 3"), and you can simply place a checkmark in the boxes for the statistics that you want to generate. This will allow you to obtain the skewness and kurtosis values, as well as measures of central tendency and dispersion discussed in Chapter 3. After making your selections, click on "dfw Continue." You will then be returned to the main Descriptives dialog box. From there, click "OK."

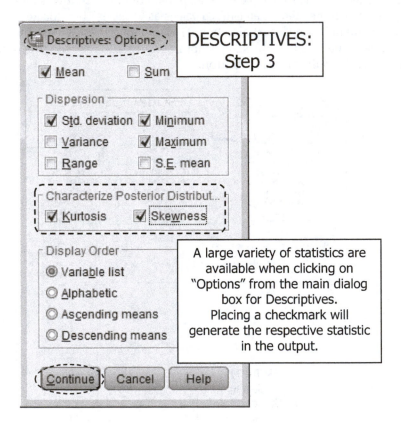

FIGURE 4.12
DESCRIPTIVES: Step 3.

4.4.3 Frequencies

Step 1. The third tool to consider is Frequencies, which is also accessible by clicking "Analyze" in the top pulldown menu, then clicking "Descriptive Statistics," and then selecting "Frequencies" (see Figure 4.7, "EXPLORE: Step 1," for a screenshot of these steps).

Step 2. This will bring up the Frequencies dialog box. Click the variable of interest (e.g., "quiz") into the "Variable(s)" box, then click the "Statistics" button (see Figure 4.13, "FRE-QUENCIES: Step 2," for a screenshot of these steps).

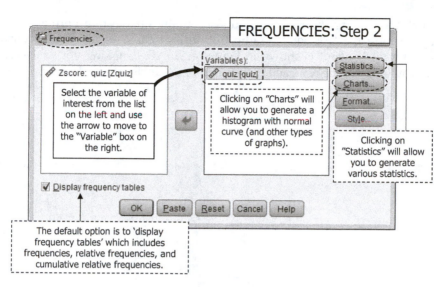

FIGURE 4.13
FREQUENCIES: Step 2.

Step 3. A new box labeled "Frequencies: Statistics" will appear. Again, you can simply place a checkmark in the boxes for the statistics that you want to generate (see Figure 4.14, "FREQUENCIES: Step 3," for a screenshot of these steps). Here you can obtain the skewness and kurtosis values, as well as measures of central tendency and dispersion from Chapter 3.

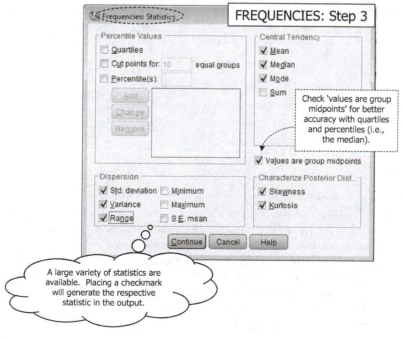

FIGURE 4.14
FREQUENCIES: Step 3.

If you click the "Charts" button, you can also obtain a histogram with a normal curve overlay by clicking the "Histogram" radio button and checking the "With normal curve" box. This histogram output is shown in Figure 4.15. After making your selections, click "Continue." You will then be returned to the main Frequencies dialog box. From there, click "OK."

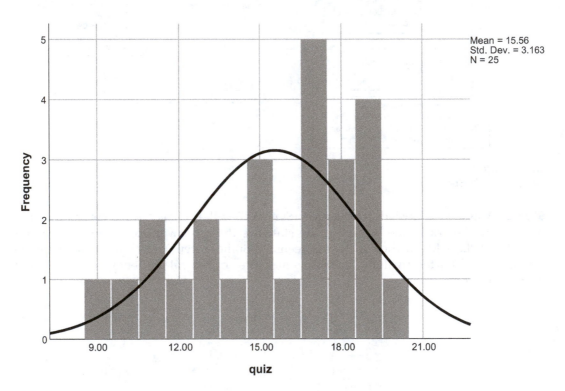

FIGURE 4.15
Histogram of statistics quiz data with normal distribution overlay.

4.4.4 Graphs

Two other tools also yield a histogram with a normal curve overlay. Both can be accessed by first going to "Graphs" in the top pulldown menu. From there, select "Legacy Dialogs," then "Histogram." Simply move the variable of interest into the "variable" box and place a check in the appropriate box if you want to display a normal curve .

Another option for creating a histogram, starting again from the "Graphs" option in the top pulldown menu, is to select "Chart Builder." Chart Builder allows researchers to drag and drop variable(s) and select the type of graph from a menu, with options for defining the elements of the graph (such as displaying the normal curve) (see Figure 4.16, "GRAPHS: Step 1," for a screenshot of these steps).

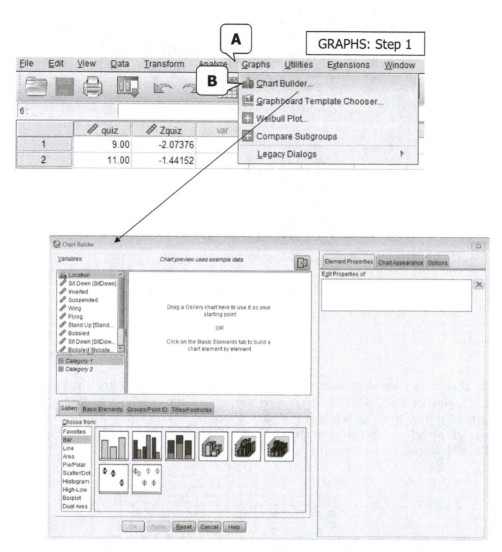

FIGURE 4.16
GRAPHS: Step 1.

4.4.5 Transform

Step 1. A final tool that comes in handy is for transforming variables, such as creating a standardized version of a variable (most notably standardization *other* than the application of the unit normal formula, where the unit normal standardization can be easily performed as seen previously by using Descriptives). Go to "Transform" from the top pulldown menu, and then select "Compute Variables." A dialog box labeled "Compute Variables" will appear (see Figure 4.17, "TRANSFORM: Step 1," for a screenshot of these steps). SPSS offers a number of different mathematical formulas, and researchers can also write their own equation.

FIGURE 4.17
TRANSFORM: Step 1.

Step 2. The "Target Variable" is the name of the new variable you are creating and the "Numeric Expression" box is where you insert the commands of which original variable to transform and how to transform it (e.g., "stat" variable). When you are done defining the formula, simply click "OK" to generate the new variable in the datafile (see Figure 4.18, "TRANSFORM: Step 2," for a screenshot of these steps).

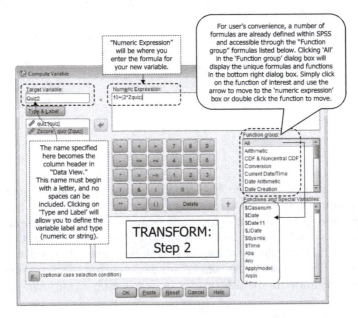

FIGURE 4.18
TRANSFORM: Step 2.

4.5 Computing Graphs and Standard Scores Using R

Next we consider **R** for various statistics and graphs. The scripts are provided within the blocks with additional annotation to assist in understanding how the commands work. Should you want to write reminder notes and annotation to yourself as you write the commands in **R** (and we highly encourage doing so), remember that any text that follows a hashtag (i.e., #) is annotation only and not part of the **R** code. Thus, you can write annotations directly into **R** with hashtags. We encourage this practice so that when you call up the commands in the future, you'll understand what the various lines of code are doing. You may think you'll remember what you did. However, trust us. There is a good chance that you won't. Thus, consider it best practice when using **R** to annotate heavily!

4.5.1 Reading Data into R

We will first read in our data (Figure 4.19). We will be working with the Ch4_quiz.csv data.

```
getwd()
```

R is always pointed to a directory on your computer. To find out which directory it is pointed to, run this "get working directory" command. We will assume that we need to change the working directory, and will use the next line of code to set the working directory to the desired path.

```
setwd("E:/Folder")
```

To set the working directory, use the *setwd* function and change what is in quotation marks here to your file location. Also, if you are copying the directory name, it will copy in slashes. You will need to change the slash (i.e., \) to forward slash (i.e., /). Note that you need your destination name within quotation marks in the parentheses.

```
Ch4_quiz <- read.csv("Ch4_quiz.csv")
```

The *read.csv* function reads your data into **R**. What's to the left of the <- will be what you want to call the data in **R**. In this example, we're calling the **R** dataframe "Ch4_quiz." What's to the right of the <- tells **R** to find this particular csv file. In this example, our file is called "Ch4_quiz.csv." Make sure the extension (i.e., .csv) is included in your script. Also note that you need the name of your file in quotation marks within the parentheses.

```
names(Ch4_quiz)
```

The *names* function will produce a list of variable names for each dataframe as follows. This is a good check to make sure your data has been read in correctly.

```
[1] "quiz"
```

```
View(Ch4_quiz)
```

The *View* function will let you view the dataset in spreadsheet format in RStudio.

```
summary(Ch4_quiz)
```

FIGURE 4.19
Reading data into **R**.

The *summary* function will produce basic descriptive statistics on all the variables in your dataframe. This is a great way to quickly check to see if the data have been read in correctly and get a feel for your data, if you haven't already. The output from the summary statement for this dataframe looks like this:

```
        quiz
Min.   : 9.00
1st Qu.:13.00
Median :17.00
Mean   :15.56
3rd Qu.:18.00
Max.   :20.00
```

FIGURE 4.19 (continued)
Reading data into **R**.

4.5.2 Generating Skewness and Kurtosis

```
install.packages("e1071")
```

The *install.packages* function will install the *e1071* package that we will use to generate skewness and kurtosis. Note that the name of the package needs to be placed within quotation marks in the script.

```
library(e1071)
```

We only need to install the package once; however, we need to call it into our library each time we use it. The *library* function will load the *e1071* package into our library.

```
skewness(Ch4_quiz$quiz, type=3)
skewness(Ch4_quiz$quiz, type=2)
skewness(Ch4_quiz$quiz, type=1)
```

The *skewness* command will generate skewness statistics on the variable(s) we specify. In this example, we are using the variable "quiz" from the dataframe "Ch4_quiz," and we indicate this in **R** by the script *Ch4_quiz$quiz*. The *type=script* defines how skewness is calculated. Specifying *type=2* will use the algorithm that is used by SPSS. Readers interested in learning more, including the algorithms for each of the three methods, are encouraged to review Joanes and Gill (1998). We see that using *type=2* our skew is −.598.

```
# skewness(Ch4_quiz$quiz, type=3)
[1] -0.5280266

# skewness(Ch4_quiz$quiz, type=2)
[1] -0.5978562

# skewness(Ch4_quiz$quiz, type=1)
[1] -0.5613697
```

```
kurtosis(Ch4_quiz$quiz, type=3)
kurtosis(Ch4_quiz$quiz, type=2)
kurtosis(Ch4_quiz$quiz, type=1)
```

The *kurtosis* function will generate kurtosis statistics on the variable(s) we specify. In this example, we are using the variable "quiz" from the dataframe "Ch4_quiz," and we indicate this in **R** by the script *Ch4_quiz$quiz*. The "type=script" defines how kurtosis is calculated. Specifying "type=2" will use the algorithm that is used by SPSS. Readers interested in learning more, including the algorithms for each of the three methods, are encouraged to review Joanes and Gill (1998). We see that using *type=2* our kurtosis is −.741.

FIGURE 4.20
Generating skewness and kurtosis.

```
# kurtosis(Ch4_quiz$quiz, type=3)
[1] -1.002001

# kurtosis(Ch4_quiz$quiz, type=2)
[1] -0.741478

# kurtosis(Ch4_quiz$quiz, type=1)
[1] -0.8320318
```

FIGURE 4.20 (continued)
Generating skewness and kurtosis.

4.5.3 Generating a Histogram

```
hist(Ch4_quiz$quiz,
     main = "Histogram of Quiz Scores",
     xlab = "Quiz Score", ylab = "Frequency")
```

The *hist* function will produce a histogram using the variable "quiz" from the "Ch4_quiz" dataframe. The histogram will include "Histogram of Quiz Scores" as the title (generated based on main = "Histogram of Quiz Scores"), with the X axis being labeled "Quiz Score" (i.e., *xlab = "Quiz Score"*) and the Y axis being labeled "Frequency" (i.e., *ylab = "Frequency"*).

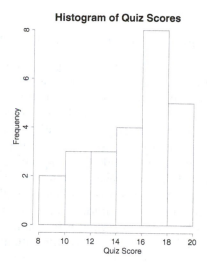

FIGURE 4.21
Generating a histogram.

4.5.4 Creating a Standardized Variable

```
Ch4_quiz$Zquiz <- scale(Ch4_quiz$quiz)
```

To create a new standardized variable in our dataframe, we use the *scale* function. The script to the left of <- (i.e., "Ch4_quiz$Zquiz") tells **R** to create a new variable in the dataframe "Ch4_quiz" that is called "Zquiz." In parentheses, we are telling **R** to use the variable "quiz" from our dataframe "Ch4_quiz" to create the standardized variable (i.e., "Ch4_quiz$quiz").

FIGURE 4.22
Creating a standardized variable.

```
View(Ch4_quiz)
```

We use the *View* function to confirm that our new variable has been created and added to our dataframe by displaying the dataframe in RStudio.

```
summary(Ch4_quiz)
```

We use the *summary* function to generate basic descriptive statistics on our variable. We see that the mean of our new standardized variable, "Zquiz.v1," is 0, which is expected!

```
quiz                    Zquiz.V1
Min.    : 9.00    Min.    :-2.0737630
1st Qu.:13.00    1st Qu.:-0.8092734
Median :17.00    Median : 0.4552163
Mean    :15.56    Mean    : 0.0000000
3rd Qu.:18.00    3rd Qu.: 0.7713387
Max.    :20.00    Max.    : 1.4035835
```

FIGURE 4.22 (continued)
Creating a standardized variable.

4.6 Research Question Template and Example Write-Up

As stated in the previous chapter, depending on the purpose of your research study, you may or may not write a research question that corresponds to your descriptive statistics. If the end result of your research paper is to present results from inferential statistics, it may be that your research questions correspond only to those inferential questions, and thus no question is presented to represent the descriptive statistics. That is quite common. On the other hand, if the ultimate purpose of your research study is purely descriptive in nature, then writing one or more research questions that correspond to the descriptive statistics is not only entirely appropriate, but (in most cases) absolutely necessary.

It is time again to revisit our graduate research assistant, Challie Lenge, who was reintroduced at the beginning of the chapter. As a reminder, Challie was working with Dr. Debhard, a statistics professor. Challie's task was to continue to summarize data from 25 students enrolled in a statistics course, this time paying particular attention to distributional shape and standardization. The questions posed this time by Dr. Debhard were as follows: *What is the distributional shape of the statistics quiz score? In standard deviation units, what is the relative standing to the mean of student 1 compared to student 3?* The following is a template for writing a descriptive research question for summarizing distributional shape (this may sound familiar as this was first presented in Chapter 2 when we initially discussed distributional shape). This is followed by a template for writing a research question related to standardization.

What is the distributional shape of the [variable]? In standard deviation units, what is the relative standing to the mean of [unit 1] compared to [unit 3]?

Next, we present an APA-style paragraph summarizing the results of the statistics quiz data example answering the questions posed to Marie.

The skewness value is −.598 (*SE* = .464) and the kurtosis value is −.741 (*SE* = .902). Skewness and kurtosis values within the range of ±2 (*SE*) are generally considered normal. Given our values, skewness is within the range of −.928 to +.928 and kurtosis is within the range of −1.804 and +1.804, and these would be considered normal. Another convention is that the skewness and kurtosis values should fall within an absolute value of 2.0 to be considered normal. Applying this rule, normality is still evident. The histogram with a normal curve overlay is depicted in Figure 4.15. Taken with the skewness and kurtosis statistics, these results indicate that the quiz scores are reasonably normally distributed. There is a slight negative skew such that there are more scores at the high end of the distribution than a typical normal distribution. There is also a slight negative kurtosis indicating that the distribution is slightly flatter than a normal distribution, with a few more extreme scores at the low end of the distribution. Again, however, the values are within the range of what is considered a reasonable approximation to the normal curve.

Prior to standardization, student 1 had a score of 9 and student 3 had a score of 20. The quiz score data were standardized using the unit normal formula. After standardization, student 1's score was −2.07 and student 3's score was 1.40. This suggests that student 1 was slightly more than two standard deviation units below the mean on the statistics quiz score while student 3 was nearly 1.5 standard deviation units above the mean.

4.7 Additional Resources

In the previous chapters, we have mentioned a number of excellent resources for learning statistics. As we are still in the early stages of learning statistics, there are no additional resources that we suggest that are specifically related to normal distributions and standard scores. Rather, we refer you back to earlier chapters for supplemental resources for statistics as well as statistical software.

Problems

Conceptual Problems

1. For which of the following distributions will the skewness value be zero?
   a. $N(0,1)$
   b. $N(0,2)$
   c. $N(10,50)$
   d. All of the above
2. For which of the following distributions will the kurtosis value be zero?
   a. $N(0,1)$
   b. $N(0,2)$
   c. $N(10,50)$
   d. All of the above

3. A set of 400 scores is approximately normally distributed with a mean of 65 and a standard deviation of 4.5. Approximately 95% of the scores would fall between which range of scores?

    a. 60.5 and 69.5

    b. 56 and 74

    c. 51.5 and 78.5

    d. 64.775 and 65.225

4. What is the percentile rank of 60 in the distribution of $N(60,100)$?

    a. 10

    b. 50

    c. 60

    d. 100

5. The skewness value is calculated for a set of data and is found to be equal to +2.75. This indicates that the distribution of scores is which of the following?

    a. Highly negatively skewed

    b. Slightly negatively skewed

    c. Symmetrical

    d. Slightly positively skewed

    e. Highly positively skewed

6. The kurtosis value is calculated for a set of data and is found to be equal to +2.75. This indicates that the distribution of scores is which of the following?

    a. Mesokurtic

    b. Platykurtic

    c. Leptokurtic

    d. Cannot be determined

7. True or false? For a normal distribution, all percentiles above the 50th must yield positive z scores.

8. True or false? If one knows the raw score, the mean, and the z score, then one can calculate the value of the standard deviation.

9. True or false? In a normal distribution, a z score of 1.0 has a percentile rank of 34.

10. True or false? The mean of a normal distribution of scores is always 1.

11. If in a distribution of 200 IQ scores, the mean is considerably above the median, then the distribution is which of the following?

    a. Negatively skewed

    b. Symmetrical

    c. Positively skewed

    d. Bimodal

12. Which of the following is indicative of a distribution that has a skewness value of −3.98 and a kurtosis value of −6.72?

    a. A left tail that is pulled to the left and a very flat distribution

    b. A left tail that is pulled to the left and a distribution that is neither very peaked nor very flat

c. A right tail that is pulled to the right and a very peaked distribution

d. A right tail that is pulled to the right and a very flat distribution

13. Which of the following is indicative of a distribution that has a kurtosis value of +4.09?

a. Leptokurtic distribution

b. Mesokurtic distribution

c. Platykurtic distribution

d. Positive skewness

e. Negative skewness

14. For which of the following distributions will the kurtosis value be greatest?

A	f	B	f	C	f	D	f
11	3	11	4	11	1	11	1
12	4	12	4	12	3	12	5
13	6	13	4	13	12	13	8
14	4	14	4	14	3	14	5
15	3	15	4	15	1	15	1

a. Distribution A

b. Distribution B

c. Distribution C

d. Distribution D

15. The distribution of variable X has a mean of 10 and is positively skewed. The distribution of variable Y has the same mean of 10 and is negatively skewed. I assert that the medians for the two variables must also be the same. Am I correct?

16. True or false? The variance of z scores is always equal to the variance of the raw scores for the same variable.

17. True or false? The mode has the largest value of the central tendency measures in a positively skewed distribution.

18. Which of the following represents the highest performance in a standard normal distribution?

a. P_{90}

b. $z = +1.00$

c. Q_3

d. $IQ = 115$

19. A student came home with two test scores, $z = +1$ in math and $z = -1$ in biology. For which test did the student perform better?

20. A psychologist analyzing data from creative intelligence scores finds a relatively normal distribution with a population mean of 100 and population standard deviation of 10. When standardized into a unit normal distribution, what is the mean of the (standardized) creative intelligence scores?

a. 0

b. 70

    c. 100

    d. Cannot be determined from the information provided

21. A distribution has the following parameters: mean = 6, median = 4, mode = 2. Which of the following is suggested?

    a. Negatively skewed distribution

    b. Normal distribution

    c. Positively skewed distribution

    d. Cannot be determined from these values

22. A distribution has the following parameters: mean = 10, median = 16, mode = 20. Which of the following is suggested?

    a. Negatively skewed distribution

    b. Normal distribution

    c. Positively skewed distribution

    d. Cannot be determined from these values

23. What is the percentile rank of a standardized normal score of 2.0?

    a. 2nd percentile

    b. 34th percentile

    c. 50th percentile

    d. 98th percentile

24. What is the percentile rank of a standardized normal score of −2.0?

    a. 2nd percentile

    b. 34th percentile

    c. 50th percentile

    d. 98th percentile

25. Which of the following graphs reflects a negatively skewed distribution?

a.

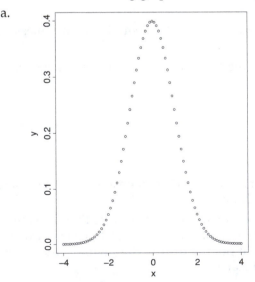

b.

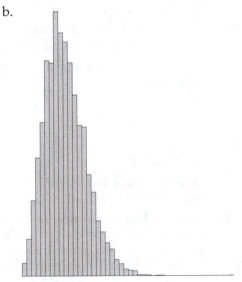

c.

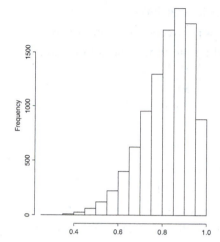

d.

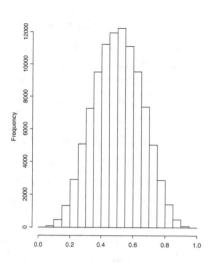

Answers to Conceptual Problems

1. **d** (Skewness is zero for normal.)
3. **b** (±2.0 standard deviations.)
5. **e** (High positive value = high positive skew.)
7. **True** (Mean = median for a normal distribution, so above the 50th percentile = positive z.)
9. **False** ($z = +1.00$ is the 84th percentile.)
11. **c** (Positively skewed: mode < median < mean.)
13. **a** (The large positive kurtosis value indicates a very peaked, or leptokurtic, distribution.)
15. **No** (The median for distribution X must be larger.)
17. **False** (The mean has the largest value in that situation.)
19. **Math** (84th percentile in math, 16th percentile in biology.)
21. **c** (With mean = 6, median = 4, mode = 2, the mean > median > mode; this suggests a positively skewed distribution.)
23. **d** (A standardized normal score of 2.0 has a percentile rank of approximately 98.)
25. **c** (Negatively skewed distributions have tails that are pulled to the left of the distribution.)

Computational Problems

1. Give the numerical value for each of the following descriptions concerning normal distributions by referring to the table for $N(0,1)$.
   a. The proportion of the area below $z = -1.66$
   b. The proportion of the area between $z = -1.03$ and $z = +1.03$
   c. The 5th percentile of $N(20,36)$
   d. The 99th percentile of $N(30,49)$
   e. The percentile rank of the score 25 in $N(20,36)$

    f.   The percentile rank of the score 24.5 in $N(30,49)$

    g.   The proportion of the area in $N(36,64)$ between the scores of 18 and 42

2.   Give the numerical value for each of the following descriptions concerning normal distributions by referring to the table for $N(0,1)$.

    a.   The proportion of the area below $z = -.80$

    b.   The proportion of the area between $z = -1.49$ and $z = +1.49$

    c.   The 2.5th percentile of $N(50,81)$

    d.   The 50th percentile of $N(40,64)$

    e.   The percentile rank of the score 45 in $N(50,81)$

    f.   The percentile rank of the score 53 in $N(50,81)$

    g.   The proportion of the area in $N(36,64)$ between the scores of 19.7 and 45.1

3.   Give the numerical value for each of the following descriptions concerning normal distributions by referring to the table for $N(0,1)$.

    a.   The proportion of the area below $z = +1.50$

    b.   The proportion of the area between $z = -.75$ and $z = +2.25$

    c.   The 15th percentile of $N(12,9)$

    d.   The 80th percentile of $N(100,000,5000)$

    e.   The percentile rank of the score 300 in $N(200,2500)$

    f.   The percentile rank of the score 61 in $N(60,9)$

    g.   The proportion of the area in $N(500,1600)$ between the scores of 350 and 550

4.   Using the Ch6.HW4.sav data, compute and interpret the distributional shape for the variables "learning strategies" and "coping strategies" based on mean, median, mode, skew, kurtosis, and histograms.

Answers to Computational Problems

1.   a = .0485; b = .6970; c = 10.16; d = 46.31; e = approximately 79.67%; f = approximately 21.48%; g = 76.12%

3.   a = .9332; b = .7611; c = 8.91; d = 100059.40; e = approximately 97.72%; f = approximately 62.93%; g = 20%

Interpretive Problems

1.   Select one interval or ratio variable from the survey1 dataset on the website (e.g., one idea is to select the same variable you selected for the interpretive problem from Chapter 3).

    a.   Determine the measures of central tendency, dispersion, skewness, and kurtosis.

    b.   Write a paragraph that summarizes the findings, particularly commenting on the distributional shape.

2.   Use the same variable selected in the previous problem, and standardize it.

    a.   Determine the measures of central tendency, dispersion, skewness, and kurtosis for the standardized variable.

    b.   Compare and contrast the differences between the standardized results and unstandardized results.

5

Introduction to Probability and Sample Statistics

Chapter Outline

Key Concepts

1. Probability

2. Inferential statistics

3. Simple random sampling (with and without replacement)

4. Sampling distribution of the mean

5. Variance and standard error of the mean (sampling error)

6. Confidence intervals (point vs. interval estimation)

7. Central limit theorem

In Chapter 4 we extended our discussion of descriptive statistics. We considered the following three general topics: the normal distribution, standard scores, and skewness and kurtosis. In this chapter we begin to move from descriptive statistics into inferential statistics (in which normally distributed data plays a major role). The two basic topics described in this chapter are (a) probability and (b) sampling and estimation. First, as a brief introduction to probability, we discuss the importance of probability in statistics, define probability in a conceptual and computational sense, and discuss the notion of intuition versus probability. Second, under sampling and estimation, we formally move into inferential statistics by considering the following topics: simple random sampling (and briefly other types of sampling), and estimation of population parameters and sampling distributions. Concepts to be discussed include probability, inferential statistics, simple random sampling (with and without replacement), sampling distribution of the mean, variance and standard error of the mean (sampling error), confidence intervals (point vs. interval estimation), and central limit theorem. Our objectives are that by the end of this chapter, you will be able to (a) understand the most basic concepts of probability; (b) understand and conduct simple random sampling; and (c) understand, determine, and interpret the results from the estimation of population parameters via a sample.

5.1 Brief Introduction to Probability

The area of probability became important and began to be developed during the Middle Ages (17th and 18th centuries) when royalty and other well-to-do gamblers consulted with mathematicians for advice on games of chance. For example, in poker if you hold two jacks, what are your chances of drawing a third jack? Or in craps, what is the chance of rolling a 7 with two dice? During that time, probability was also used for more practical purposes, such as to help determine life expectancy to underwrite life insurance policies. Considerable development in probability has obviously taken place since that time. In this section, we discuss the importance of probability, provide a definition of probability, and consider the notion of intuition versus probability. Although there is much more to the topic of probability, here we simply discuss those aspects of probability necessary for the remainder of the text. For additional information on probability, take a look at texts by Rudas (2004) or Tijms (2004).

5.1.1 Importance of Probability

Let us first consider why probability is important in statistics. A researcher is out collecting some sample data from a group of individuals (e.g., students, parents, teachers, voters, corporations, animals, etc.). Some descriptive statistics are generated from the sample data. Say the sample mean, $\overline{X}$, is computed for several variables (e.g., number of hours of study time per week, grade point average, confidence in a political candidate, widget sales, animal food consumption). To what extent can we generalize from these sample statistics to their corresponding population parameters? For example, if the mean amount of study time per week for a given sample of graduate students is $\overline{X} = 10$ hours, to what extent are we able to generalize to the population of graduate students on the value of the population mean, μ?

As we see, beginning in this chapter, inferential statistics involve making an inference about population parameters from sample statistics. We would like to know (a) how much uncertainty exists in our sample statistics, as well as (b) how much confidence to place in our sample statistics. These questions can be addressed by assigning a probability value to an inference. As we show beginning in Chapter 6, probability can also be used to make statements about areas under a distribution of scores (e.g., the normal distribution). First, however, we need to provide a definition of probability.

5.1.2 Definition of Probability

In order to more easily define probability, consider a simple example of rolling a six-sided die (as there are dice with different numbers of sides). Each of the six sides, of course, has anywhere from one to six dots. Each side has a different number of dots. What is the probability of rolling a 4? Technically, there are six possible outcomes or events that can occur. One can also determine how many times a specific outcome or event actually can occur. These two concepts are used to define and compute the probability of a particular outcome or event by

$$p(A) = \frac{S}{T}$$

where $p(A)$ is the probability that outcome or event A will occur, S is the number of times that the specific outcome or event A can occur, and T is the total number of outcomes or events possible. Let us revisit our example, the probability of rolling a 4. A 4 can occur only once, thus $S = 1$; and six possible values can be rolled, thus $T = 6$. Therefore, the probability of rolling a 4 is determined by

$$p(4) = \frac{S}{T} = \frac{1}{6}$$

This assumes, however, that the die is *unbiased*, which means that the die is fair and that the probability of obtaining any of the six outcomes is the same. For a fair, unbiased die, the probability of obtaining any outcome is $1/6$. Gamblers have been known to possess an unfair, biased die such that the probability of obtaining a particular outcome is different from $1/6$ (e.g., to cheat their opponent by shaving one side of the die).

Consider one other classic probability example. Imagine you have an urn (or other container). Inside of the urn and out of view are a total of nine balls (thus $T = 9$). Six of the balls are red (event A; $S = 6$), and the other three balls are green (event B; $S = 3$). Your task is to draw one ball out of the urn (without looking) and then observe its color. The probability of each of these two events occurring on the *first draw* is as follows:

$$p(A) = \frac{S}{T} = \frac{6}{9} = \frac{2}{3}$$

$$p(B) = \frac{S}{T} = \frac{3}{9} = \frac{1}{3}$$

Thus, the probability of drawing a red ball on the first draw is $2/3$ and the probability of drawing a green ball is $1/3$.

Two notions become evident in thinking about these examples. *First, the sum of the probabilities for all distinct or independent events is precisely one.* In other words, if we take each distinct event and compute its probability, then the sum of those probabilities must be equal to one so as to account for all possible outcomes. *Second, the probability of any given event (a) cannot exceed one, and (b) cannot be less than zero.* Part (a) should be obvious in that the sum of the probabilities for all events cannot exceed one, and therefore the probability of any one event cannot exceed one either (it makes no sense to talk about an event occurring more than all of the time). An event would have a probability of one if no other event can possibly occur, such as the probability that you are currently breathing. For part (b) no event can have a negative probability (it makes no sense to talk about an event occurring less than never); however, an event could have a zero probability if the event can never occur. For instance, in our urn example, one could never draw a purple ball (as only red and green balls are possibilities).

5.1.3 Intuition vs. Probability

At this point you are probably thinking that probability is an interesting topic. However, without extensive training to think in a probabilistic fashion, people tend to let their intuition guide them. This is all well and good, except that intuition can often guide you to a different conclusion than probability. Let us examine two classic examples to illustrate this dilemma. The first classic example is known as the "birthday problem." Imagine you are in a room of 23 people. You ask each person to write down their birthday (month and day) on a piece of paper. What do you think is the probability that in a room of 23 people at least two will have the same birthday?

Assume first that we are dealing with 365 different possible birthdays, where leap year (February 29) is not considered. Also assume the sample of 23 people is randomly drawn from some population of people. Taken together, this implies that each of the 365 different possible birthdays has the same probability (i.e., 1/365). An intuitive thinker might have the following thought processing. "There are 365 different birthdays in a year and there are 23 people in the sample. Therefore, the probability of two people having the same birthday must be close to zero." We have tried this on our introductory classes often and students' guesses are usually around zero.

Intuition has led us astray and we have not used the proper thought processing. True, there are 365 days and 23 people. However, the question really deals with *pairs of people*. The number of different possible pairs of people is fairly large (i.e., person 1 with 2, 1 with 3, etc.); specifically, the total number of different pairs of people is equal to $n(n-1)/2 = 23(22)/2 = 253$. But all we need is for one *pair* to have the same birthday. While the probability computations are a little complex (see Appendix 5.A at the end of the chapter), the probability that at least two individuals will have the same birthday in a group of 23 is equal to .507. *That's right, about one-half of the time, a group of 23 people will have 2 or more with the same birthday.* Our introductory classes typically have between 20 and 40 students. More often than not, we are able to find two students with the same birthday. One year one of us wrote each birthday on the board so that students could see the data. The first two students selected actually had the same birthday, so our point was very quickly shown. What was the probability of that event occurring?

The second classic example is the "gambler's fallacy," sometimes referred to as the "law of averages." This works for any game of chance, so imagine you are flipping a coin. Obviously there are two possible outcomes from a coin flip, heads and tails. Assume the coin is fair and unbiased such that the probability of flipping a head is the same as flipping a tail, that is, .5. After flipping the coin nine times, you have observed a tail every time. What is the probability of obtaining a head on the next flip?

An intuitive thinker might have the following thought processing. "I have just observed a tail each of the last nine flips. According to the law of averages, the probability of observing a head on the next flip must be near certainty. The probability must be nearly one." We also try this on our introductory students and their guesses are almost always near one.

Intuition has led us astray once again, as we have not used the proper thought processing. True, we have just observed nine consecutive tails. However, the question really deals with the *probability of the 10th flip being a head*, not the probability of obtaining 10 consecutive tails. The probability of a head is always .5 with a fair, unbiased coin. The coin has no memory; thus, the probability of tossing a head after nine consecutive tails is the same as the probability of tossing a head after nine consecutive heads, .5. In technical terms, *the probabilities of each event (each toss) are independent of one another.* In other words, the probability of flipping a head is the same regardless of the preceding flips. This is not the same as the probability of tossing 10 consecutive heads, which is rather small (approximately .0010). So when you are gambling at the casino and have lost the last nine games, do not believe that you are guaranteed to win the next game. You can just as easily lose game 10 as you did game 1. The same goes if you have won a number of games. You can just as easily win the next game as you did game 1. To some extent, the casinos count on their customers playing the gambler's fallacy to make a profit.

5.2 Sampling and Estimation

In Chapter 3 we spent some time discussing sample statistics, including the measures of central tendency and dispersion. In this section we expand upon that discussion by defining inferential statistics, describing different types of sampling, and then moving into the implications of such sampling in terms of estimation and sampling distributions.

Consider the situation where we have a population of graduate students. **Population parameters** (which are characteristics of a population) could be determined, such as the population size (N), the population mean (μ), the population variance (σ^2), and the population standard deviation (σ). Through some method of sampling, we then take a sample of students from this population. **Sample statistics**, which are just characteristics of a sample, could be determined, such as the sample size (n), the sample mean ($\bar{X}$), the sample variance (s^2), and the sample standard deviation (s).

How often do we actually ever deal with population data? Except when dealing with very small, well-defined populations, we almost never deal with population data. (There are always exceptions; however, our experience dictates that it is almost always the case that we are working with sample data.) The main reason for this is cost, in terms of time, personnel, and economics. *This means then that we are almost always dealing with sample data.* With descriptive statistics, dealing with sample data is very straightforward, and we only need to make sure we are using the appropriate sample statistic equation. However, what if we want to take a sample statistic and make some generalization about its relevant population parameter? For example, you have computed a sample mean on grade point average (GPA) of $\bar{X} = 3.25$ for a sample of 25 graduate students at State University. You would like to make some generalizations from this sample mean to the population mean (μ) at State University. How do we do this? To what extent can we make such a generalization? How confident are we that this sample mean actually represents the population mean?

This brings us to the field of inferential statistics. We define **inferential statistics** as *statistics that allow us to make an inference or generalization from a sample to the population.* In terms of reasoning, *inductive reasoning* is used to infer from the specific (the sample) to the general (the population). Thus, inferential statistics is the answer to all of our preceding questions about generalizing from sample statistics to population parameters. *How* the sample is derived, however, is important in determining to what extent the statistical results we derive can be inferred from the sample back to the population. Thus, it is important to spend a little time talking about simple random sampling, the only sampling procedure that directly allows generalizations to be made from the sample to the population. Although there are statistical means to correct for non-simple random samples, they are beyond the scope of this textbook. Researchers may wish to refer to references, such as Skinner, Holt, and Smith (1989). In the remainder of this section, and in much of the remainder of this text, we take up the details of inferential statistics for many different procedures.

5.2.1 Simple Random Sampling

A sample can be drawn from a population in several different ways. In this section we introduce simple random sampling, which is a commonly used type of sampling. It is also assumed for many inferential statistics (beginning in Chapter 6), as it is the only sampling procedure that *directly* allows generalizations to be made from the sample to the population. **Simple random sampling** is defined as the *process of selecting sample observations from a population so that each observation has an equal and independent probability of being selected*. If the sampling process is truly random, then (a) each observation in the population has an equal chance of being included in the sample, and (b) each observation selected into the sample is independent of (or not affected by) every other selection. Thus, a volunteer or "street-corner" sample would not meet the first condition because members of the population who do not frequent that particular street corner have no chance of being included in the sample.

In addition, if the selection of spouses *required* the corresponding selection of their respective mates, then the second condition would not be met. For example, if the selection of Mr. Joe Smith III also required the selection of his wife, then these two selections are not independent of one another. Because we selected Mr. Joe Smith III, we must also therefore select his wife. Note that through independent sampling it is possible for Mr. Smith and his wife to both be sampled, but it is not required. *Thus, independence implies that each observation is selected without regard to any other observation sampled.*

We also would fail to have equal and independent probability of selection if the sampling procedure employed was something other than a simple random sample—because it is only with a simple random sample that we have met the conditions of equal probability and independence. (Although there are statistical means to correct for nonsimple random samples, they are beyond the scope of this textbook.) This concept of **independence** is an important assumption that we will become acquainted with more in the remaining chapters. If we have independence, then generalizations from the sample back to the population can be made (you may remember this as *external validity*, which was likely introduced in your research methods course) (see Figure 5.1). Because of the connection between simple

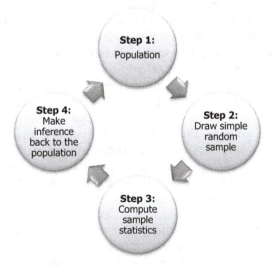

FIGURE 5.1
Cycle of inference.

random sampling and independence, let us expand our discussion on the two types of simple random sampling.

5.2.1.1 Simple Random Sampling with Replacement

There are two specific types of simple random sampling. **Simple random sampling with replacement** is conducted as follows. The first observation is selected from the population into the sample, and that observation is then replaced back into the population. The second observation is selected and then replaced in the population. This continues until a sample of the desired size is obtained. *The key here is that each observation sampled is placed back into the population and could be selected again.*

This scenario makes sense in certain applications and not in others. For example, return to our coin-flipping example where we now want to flip a coin 100 times (i.e., a sample size of 100). How does this operate in the context of sampling? We flip the coin (e.g., heads) and record the result. This "head" becomes the first observation in our sample. This observation is then placed back into the population. Then a second observation is made and is placed back into the population. This continues until our sample size requirement of 100 is reached. In this particular scenario we always sample with replacement, and we automatically do so even if we have never heard of sampling with replacement. If no replacement took place, then we could only ever have a sample size of two, one "head" and one "tail."

5.2.1.2 Simple Random Sampling Without Replacement

In other scenarios, sampling with replacement does not make sense. For example, say we are conducting a poll for the next major election by randomly selecting 100 students (the sample) from among all students who attend a local university (the population). As each student is selected into the sample, they are removed and cannot be sampled again. It simply would make no sense if our sample of 100 students only contained 78 different students due to replacement (as some students were polled more than once). Our polling example represents the other type of simple random sampling, this time *without replacement*. **Simple random sampling without replacement** is conducted in a similar fashion except that *once an observation is selected for inclusion in the sample, it is not replaced and cannot be selected a second time.*

5.2.1.3 Other Types of Sampling

Several other types of sampling are possible. These other types of sampling include convenience sampling (i.e., volunteer or "street-corner" sampling previously mentioned), systematic sampling (e.g., select every 10th observation from the population into the sample), cluster sampling (i.e., sample groups or clusters of observations and include all members of the selected clusters in the sample), stratified sampling (i.e., sampling within subgroups or strata to ensure adequate representation of each strata), and multistage sampling (e.g., stratify at one stage and randomly sample at another stage or randomly select clusters, and then within clusters, randomly select individual units). These types of sampling are beyond the scope of this text, and the interested reader is referred to sampling texts (e.g., Fink, 2002; Jaeger, 1984; Kalton, 1983; Levy & Lemeshow, 2011; Sudman, 1976).

5.2.2 Estimation of Population Parameters and Sampling Distributions

Take as an example the situation where we select one random sample of n females (e.g., $n = 20$), measure their weight, and then compute the mean weight of the sample. We find the mean of this first sample to be 102 pounds and denote it by $\bar{X}_1 = 102$, where the subscript identifies the first sample. This one sample mean is known as a **point estimate** of the population mean, μ, as it is simply one value or point. We can then proceed to collect weight data from a second sample of n females and find that $\bar{X}_2 = 110$. Next we collect weight data from a third sample of n females and find that $\bar{X}_3 = 119$. Imagine that we go on to collect such data from many other samples of size n and compute a sample mean for each of those samples.

5.2.2.1 Sampling Distribution of the Mean

At this point we have a *collection of sample means*, which we can use to construct a frequency distribution of sample means. This frequency distribution is formally known as the **sampling distribution of the mean**. To better illustrate this new distribution, let us take a very small population from which we can take many samples. Here we define our population of observations as follows: 1, 2, 3, 5, 9 (in other words, we have five values in our population). As the entire population is known here, we can better illustrate the important underlying concepts. We can determine that the population mean $\mu_X = 4$ and the population variance $\sigma_X^2 = 8$, where X indicates the variable we are referring to. Let us first take all possible samples from this population of size 2 (i.e., $n = 2$) with replacement. As there are only five observations, there will be 25 possible samples, as shown in the upper portion of Table 5.1, called "Samples." Each entry represents the two observations for a particular sample. For instance, in row 1 and column 4, we see 1,5. This indicates that the first observation is a 1 and the second observation is a 5. If sampling was done without replacement, then the diagonal of the table from upper left to lower right would not exist. For instance, a 1,1 sample could not be selected if sampling without replacement.

Now that we have all possible samples of $n = 2$, let us compute the sample means for each of the 25 samples. The sample means are shown in the middle portion of Table 5.1, called "Sample means." Just eyeballing the table, we see the means range from 1 to 9 with numerous different values in between. We then compute the mean of the 25 sample means to be 4, as shown in the bottom portion of Table 5.1, called "Mean of the sample means."

This is a matter for some discussion, so consider the following three points. *First, the distribution of $\bar{X}$ for all possible samples of size n is known as the sampling distribution of the mean.* In other words, if we were to take all of the "sample mean" values in Table 5.1 and construct a histogram of those values, then that is what is referred to as a *sampling distribution of the mean*. It is simply the distribution (i.e., histogram) of all the sample mean values. *Second, the mean of the sampling distribution of the mean for all possible samples of size n is equal to $\mu_{\bar{X}}$.* As the mean of the sampling distribution of the mean is denoted by $\mu_{\bar{X}}$ (the mean of the $\bar{X}s$), then we see for the example that $\mu_{\bar{X}} = \mu_X = 4$. In other words, the mean of the sampling distribution of the mean is simply the average of all of the sample means in Table 5.1. The mean of the sampling distribution of the mean will always be equal to the population mean.

Third, we define sampling error in this context as the difference (or deviation) between a particular sample mean and the population mean, denoted as $\bar{X} - \mu_X$. A positive sampling error indicates a sample mean greater than the population mean, where the sample mean is known as an *overestimate* of the population mean. A *zero sampling error* indicates a sample mean exactly *equal* to the population mean. A *negative sampling error* indicates a sample mean less than

TABLE 5.1

All Possible Samples and Sample Means for $n = 2$ From the Population of 1, 2, 3, 5, 9

First Observation		Second Observation			
Samples	1	2	3	5	9
1	1,1	1,2	1,3	1,5	1,9
2	2,1	2,2	2,3	2,5	2,9
3	3,1	3,2	3,3	3,5	3,9
5	5,1	5,2	5,3	5,5	5,9
9	9,1	9,2	9,3	9,5	9,9
			Sample means		
1	1.0	1.5	2.0	3.0	5.0
2	1.5	2.0	2.5	3.5	5.5
3	2.0	2.5	3.0	4.0	6.0
5	3.0	3.5	4.0	5.0	7.0
9	5.0	5.5	6.0	7.0	9.0
	$\sum \bar{X} = 12.5$	$\sum \bar{X} = 15.0$	$\sum \bar{X} = 17.5$	$\sum \bar{X} = 22.5$	$\sum \bar{X} = 32.5$

Mean of the sample means:

$$\mu_{\bar{X}} = \frac{\sum \bar{X}}{number\ of\ samples} = \frac{100}{25} = 4.0$$

Variance of the sample means:

$$\sigma_{\bar{x}}^2 = \frac{\left(number\ of\ samples\right)\left(\sum X^{-2}\right) - \left(\sum \bar{X}\right)^2}{\left(number\ of\ samples\right)^2} = \frac{(25)(500) - (100)^2}{(25)^2} = \frac{(25)(500) - 10,000}{(625)} = 4.0$$

the population mean, where the sample mean is known as an *underestimate* of the population mean. As a researcher, *we want the sampling error to be as close to zero as possible to suggest that the sample reflects the population well.*

5.2.2.2 Variance Error of the Mean

Now that we have a measure of the mean of the sampling distribution of the mean, let us consider the variance of this distribution. We define the variance of the sampling distribution of the mean, known as the **variance error of the mean**, as $\sigma_{\bar{X}}^2$. This will provide us with a dispersion measure of the extent to which the sample means vary and will also provide some indication of the confidence we can place in a particular sample mean. The variance error of the mean is computed as

$$\sigma_{\bar{X}}^2 = \frac{\sigma_X^2}{n}$$

where σ_X^2 is the population variance of X and n is the sample size. For the example, we have already determined that $\sigma_X^2 = 8$ and that $n = 2$; therefore,

$$\sigma_{\bar{X}}^2 = \frac{\sigma_X^2}{n} = \frac{8}{2} = 4$$

This is verified in the bottom portion of Table 5.1, "Variance of the sample means," where the variance error is computed from the collection of sample means.

What will happen if we *increase* the size of the sample? If we increase the sample size to $n = 4$, then the variance error is reduced to 2. Thus we see that *as the size of the sample* n *increases, the magnitude of the sampling error decreases*. Why? Conceptually, as sample size increases, we are sampling a larger portion of the population. In doing so, we are also obtaining a sample that is likely more representative of the population. In addition, the larger the sample size, the less likely it is to obtain a sample mean that is far from the population mean. Thus, *as sample size increases, we hone in closer and closer to the population mean and have less and less sampling error.*

For example, say we are sampling from a voting district with a population of 5000 voters. A survey is developed to assess how satisfied the district voters are with their local state representative. Assume the survey generates a 100-point satisfaction scale. First we determine that the population mean of satisfaction is 75. Next we take samples of different sizes. For a sample size of 1, we find sample means that range from 0 to 100 (i.e., each mean really only represents a single observation). For a sample size of 10, we find sample means that range from 50 to 95. For a sample size of 100, we find sample means that range from 70 to 80. We see then that *as sample size increases, our sample means become closer and closer to the population mean, and the variability of those sample means becomes smaller and smaller.*

5.2.2.3 Standard Error of the Mean

We can also compute the standard deviation of the sampling distribution of the mean, known as the **standard error of the mean**, by

$$\sigma_{\bar{X}} = \frac{\sigma_X}{\sqrt{n}}$$

Thus, for our example we have

$$\sigma_{\bar{X}} = \frac{\sigma_X}{\sqrt{n}} = \frac{2.8284}{\sqrt{2}} = 2$$

Because the applied researcher typically does not know the population variance, the population variance error of the mean and the population standard error of the mean can be estimated by the following, respectively:

$$s_{\bar{X}}^2 = \frac{s_X^2}{n}$$

and

$$s_{\bar{X}} = \frac{s_X}{\sqrt{n}}$$

5.2.2.4 Confidence Intervals

Thus far we have illustrated how a sample mean is a point estimate of the population mean and how a variance error gives us some sense of the variability among the sample means. Putting these concepts together, we can also build an **interval estimate** for the population mean to give us a sense of how confident we are in our particular sample mean. We can form a **confidence interval** around a particular sample mean as follows. As we learned in Chapter 4, for a normal distribution 68% of the distribution falls within one standard deviation of the mean. A 68% confidence interval (CI) of a sample mean can be formed as follows:

$$68\% \ CI = \bar{X} \pm (1.00)(\sigma_{\bar{X}})$$

Conceptually, this means that if we form 68% confidence intervals for 100 sample means, then 68 of those 100 intervals would contain or include the population mean (it does *not* mean that there is a 68% probability of the interval containing the population mean—the interval either contains it or does not). Because the applied researcher typically only has one sample mean and does not know the population mean, he or she has no way of knowing if this one confidence interval actually contains the population mean or not. If one wanted to be more confident in a sample mean, then a 90% CI, a 95% CI, or a 99% CI could be formed as follows:

$$90\% \ CI = \bar{X} \pm (1.645)(\sigma_{\bar{X}})$$

$$95\% \ CI = \bar{X} \pm (1.96)(\sigma_{\bar{X}})$$

$$99\% \ CI = \bar{X} \pm (2.5758)(\sigma_{\bar{X}})$$

Thus, for the 90% CI, the population mean will be contained in 90 out of 100 CIs; for the 95% CI, the population mean will be contained in 95 out of 100 CIs; and for the 99% CI, the population mean will be contained in 99 out of 100 CIs. The critical values of 1.645, 1.96, and 2.5758 come from the standard unit normal distribution table (Table A.1 in the Appendix) and indicate the width of the confidence interval. The earlier example of a 68% CI refers to the standard unit normal distribution table as well, with $z \simeq .84$. *Wider confidence intervals, such as the 99% CI, enable greater confidence.* For example, with a sample mean of 70 and a standard error of the mean of 3, the following confidence intervals result: 68% CI = (67, 73) [i.e., ranging from 67 to 73]; 90% CI = (65.065, 74.935); 95% CI = (64.12, 75.88); and 99% CI = (62.2726, 77.7274). We can see here that to be assured that 99% of the confidence intervals contain the population mean, then our interval must be wider (i.e., ranging from about 62.27 to 77.73, or a range of about 15) than the confidence intervals that are lesser (e.g., the 95% confidence interval ranges from 64.12 to 75.88, or a range of about 11).

In general, a confidence interval for any level of confidence (i.e., #% CI) can be computed by the following general formula:

$$\#\% \ CI = \bar{X} \pm (z_{CV})(\sigma_{\bar{X}})$$

where z_{cv} is the critical value taken from the standard unit normal distribution table for that particular level of confidence, and the other values are as before.

5.2.2.5 Central Limit Theorem

In our discussion of confidence intervals, we used the normal distribution to help determine the width of the intervals. Many inferential statistics assume the population distribution is normal in shape. Because we are looking at sampling distributions in this chapter, does the shape of the original population distribution have any relationship to the sampling distribution of the mean we obtain? For example, if the population distribution is nonnormal, what form does the sampling distribution of the mean take (i.e., is the sampling distribution of the mean also nonnormal)? There is a nice concept, known as the central limit theorem, to assist us here. The **central limit theorem** *states that as sample size* n *increases, the sampling distribution of the mean from a random sample of size* n *more closely approximates a normal distribution. If the population distribution is normal in shape, then the sampling distribution of the mean is also normal in shape. If the population distribution is not normal in shape, then the sampling distribution of the mean becomes more nearly normal as sample size increases.* This concept is graphically depicted in Figure 5.2.

The top row of Figure 5.2 depicts two population distributions, the left one being normal and the right one being positively skewed. The remaining rows are for the various sampling distributions, depending on the sample size. The second row shows the sampling distributions of the mean for $n = 1$. Note that these sampling distributions look precisely like the population distributions, as each observation is literally a sample mean. The next row gives the sampling distributions for $n = 2$; here we see for the skewed population that the sampling distribution is slightly less skewed. This is because the more extreme observations are now being averaged in with less extreme observations, yielding less extreme means. For $n = 4$ the sampling distribution in the skewed case is even less skewed than for $n = 2$. Eventually we reach the $n = 25$ sampling distribution, where the sampling distribution for the skewed case is nearly normal and nearly matches the sampling distribution for the normal case. This phenomenon will occur for other nonnormal population distributions as well (e.g., negatively skewed). The moral of the story here is a good one. *If the population*

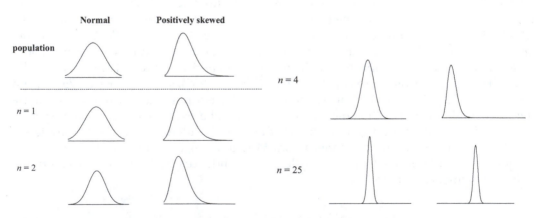

FIGURE 5.2
Central limit theorem for normal and positively skewed population distributions.

distribution is nonnormal, then this will have minimal effect on the sampling distribution of the mean except for rather small samples. This can come into play with inferential statistics when the assumption of normality is not satisfied, as we see in later chapters.

5.3 Additional Resources

This chapter is meant to serve as a concise and general introduction to probability, sampling, and related concepts. For readers who want more in-depth and comprehensive coverage, numerous superb references are available to assist in learning more about concepts introduced in this chapter. A number of these have already been cited. Additional resources you may wish to consider include the following:

- Probabilities in the context of everyday examples (Olofsson, 2007).
- A general introduction to probability and statistics (Kinney, 2015).
- An edited work that is a compilation of papers related to teaching and learning probability, valuable both to those teaching probability as well as those learning probability (Batanero & Chernoff, 2018).

Appendix 5.a: Probability That at Least Two Individuals Have the Same Birthday

This probability can be shown by either of the following equations. Note that there are $n = 23$ individuals in the room. One method is as follows:

$$1 - \left(\frac{(365)(364)(363)\ldots(365 - n + 1)}{365^n} \right) = 1 - \left(\frac{(365)(364)(363)\ldots(343)}{365^{23}} \right) = .507$$

An equivalent method is as follows:

$$1 - \left[\left(\frac{365}{365} \right)\left(\frac{364}{365} \right)\left(\frac{363}{365} \right)\ldots\left(\frac{365 - n + 1}{365} \right) \right] = 1 - \left[\left(\frac{365}{365} \right)\left(\frac{364}{365} \right)\left(\frac{363}{365} \right)\ldots\left(\frac{343}{365} \right) \right] = .507$$

Problems

Conceptual Problems

1. The standard error of the mean is which of the following?
   a. Standard deviation of a sample distribution
   b. Standard deviation of the population distribution
   c. Standard deviation of the sampling distribution of the mean
   d. Mean of the sampling distribution of the standard deviation

2. An unbiased six-sided die is tossed on two consecutive trials and the first toss results in a "2." What is the probability that a "2" will result on the second toss?
    a. Less than 1/6
    b. 1/6
    c. Greater than 1/6
    d. Cannot be determined

3. An urn contains 9 balls: 3 green, 4 red, and 2 blue. What is the probability that a ball selected at random is blue?
    a. 2/9
    b. 5/9
    c. 6/9
    d. 7/9

4. Sampling error is which of the following?
    a. The amount by which a sample mean is greater than the population mean
    b. The amount of difference between a sample statistic and a population parameter
    c. The standard deviation divided by the square root of n
    d. When the sample is not drawn randomly

5. What does the central limit theorem state?
    a. The means of many random samples from a population will be normally distributed.
    b. The raw scores of many natural events will be normally distributed.
    c. z scores will be normally distributed.
    d. None of the above

6. True or false? For a normal population, the variance of the sampling distribution of the mean increases as sample size increases.

7. True or false? All other things being equal, as the sample size increases, the standard error of a statistic decreases.

8. I assert that the 95% CI has a larger (or wider) range than the 99% CI for the same parameter using the same data. Am I correct?

9. I assert that the 90% CI has a smaller (or more narrow) range than the 68% CI for the same parameter using the same data. Am I correct?

10. I assert that the mean and median of any random sample drawn from a symmetric population distribution will be equal. Am I correct?

11. A random sample is to be drawn from a symmetric population with mean 100 and variance 225. I assert that the sample mean is more likely to have a value larger than 105 if the sample size is 16 than if the sample size is 25. Am I correct?

12. A gambler is playing a card game where the known probability of winning is .40 (win 40% of the time). The gambler has just lost 10 consecutive hands. What is the probability of the gambler winning the next hand?
    a. Less than .40
    b. Equal to .40
    c. Greater than .40
    d. Cannot be determined without observing the gambler

13. On the evening news, the anchorwoman announces that the state's lottery has reached $72 billion and reminds the viewing audience that there has not been a winner in over 5 years. In researching lottery facts, you find a report that states the probability of winning the lottery is 1 in 2 million (i.e., a very, very small probability). What is the probability that you will win the lottery?

    a. Less than 1 in 2 million
    b. Equal to 1 in 2 million
    c. Greater than 1 in 2 million
    d. Cannot be determined without additional statistics

14. True or false? The probability of being selected into a sample is the same for every individual in the population for the convenient method of sampling.

15. Malani is conducting research on elementary teacher attitudes toward changes in mathematics standards. Malani's population consists of all elementary teachers within one district in the state. Malani wants her sampling method to be such that every teacher in the population has an equal and independent probability of selection. Which of the following is the most appropriate sampling method?

    a. Convenience sampling
    b. Simple random sampling with replacement
    c. Simple random sampling without replacement
    d. Systematic sampling

16. True or false? Sampling error increases with larger samples.

17. If a population distribution is highly positively skewed, then the distribution of the sample means for samples of size 500 will be:

    a. highly negatively skewed.
    b. highly positively skewed.
    c. approximately normally distributed.
    d. Cannot be determined without further information

18. A dance studio has 35 competitive dancers and four competition teams with the following numbers of dancers on each team: mini troupe, 6; junior company, 9; apprentice, 8; and senior, 12. The probability that one dancer selected at random will be from junior company is equal to which of the following?

    a. 6/35
    b. 8/35
    c. 9/35
    d. 12/35

19. Mark is conducting research on the effects of the concussion protocol in professional football. Mark's population consists of all active professional football players in the National Football League (NFL). He wants to make sure that football players in both the the NFL's conferences (AFC and NFC) are proportionally represented. Which of the following sampling methods would be most appropriate?

    a. Convenience sampling
    b. Simple random sampling without replacement
    c. Stratified sampling
    d. Systematic sampling

20. A game of chance is offered at a fall festival with multiple prizes available, including the grand prize, a 7-day Caribbean cruise on the Disney Cruise Line. To enter to win, adults filled out an entry form with their name and contact information. The entry forms were dropped into container. Once a winning entry was selected, it was returned to the container. Which type of sampling methods is suggested by this example?

    a. Convenience sampling

    b. Simple random sampling with replacement

    c. Simple random sampling without replacement

    d. Systematic sampling

21. The previous football season's average number of points scored per game is computed for each college in the Southeastern Conference (SEC). A sports analyst computes a frequency distribution of these mean values. Which of the following has the sports analyst computed?

    a. Confidence interval

    b. Sampling distribution of the mean

    c. Sampling error

    d. Standard error of the mean

22. Probability is important to statistics because it enables which of the following?

    a. To describe a sample

    b. To generalize from a sample to a population

    c. To infer from a group to an individual

    d. To prove an idea is correct

Answers to Conceptual Problems

1. **c** (See definition in Section 5.2.2.)

3. **a** (2 out of 9.)

5. **a** (See Section 5.2.2.)

7. **True** (Less sampling error as n increases.)

9. **False** (90% CI has a wider range than 68% CI.)

11. **Yes** (Extreme mean more likely with smaller n.)

13. **b** (Probability of winning the lottery is the same for each attempt, regardless of how long it has been since a winner was announced.)

15. **c** (For all teachers to have an equal and independent probability of being selected, the sampling procedure must be a type of simple random sampling; the nature of Malani's research is such that this should be done without replacement, as she would not want to survey the same teacher twice.)

17. **c** (Due to the central limit theorem with large size samples.)

19. **c** (To ensure that football players in both the NFL's conferences, the AFC and the NFC, are proportionally represented, stratified sampling can be used where the conference—AFC and NFC—is the strata, within which the sampling would occur.)

21. **b** (The sampling distribution of the mean is the frequency distribution of the sample means; in this case, the frequency distribution of the average number of points scored for all football games for SEC teams during the past season.)

Computational Problems

1. The population distribution of variable X, the number of pets owned, consists of the five values of 1, 4, 5, 7, and 8.

   a. Calculate the values of the population mean and variance.

   b. List all possible samples of size 2 where samples are drawn with replacement.

   c. Calculate the values of the mean and variance of the sampling distribution of the mean.

2. The following is a random sampling distribution of the mean number of children for samples of size 3, where samples are drawn with replacement.

Sample mean	f
1	1
2	2
3	4
4	2
5	1

   a. What is the population mean?

   b. What is the population variance?

   c. What is the mean of the sampling distribution of the mean?

   d. What is the variance error of the mean?

3. In a study of the entire student body of a large university, if the standard error of the mean is 20 for $n = 16$, what must the sample size be to reduce the standard error to 5?

4. A random sample of 13 statistics texts had a mean number of pages of 685 and a standard deviation of 42. Calculate the standard error of the mean, then calculate the 95% CI for the mean length of statistics texts.

5. A random sample of 10 high schools employed a mean number of guidance counselors of 3 and a standard deviation of 2. Calculate the standard error of the mean, then calculate the 90% CI for the mean number of guidance counselors.

6. A random sample of average systolic blood pressure from patients at 10 general practitioners were recorded as follows. Calculate the standard error of the mean given the following data:

115	122	125	126	117
120	118	130	112	124

Selected Answers to Computational Problems

1. a. Population mean = 5; population variance = 6;

   b. Construct table of possible sample means as in Table 5.1.

   c. Mean of the sampling distribution of the mean = 5; variance of the sampling distribution of the mean = 3.

3. If the standard error of the mean is 20 and we want to reduce it to 5, that means we are reducing the standard error of the mean by 1/4 but holding the standard deviation of X constant. Our equation is $s_{\bar{X}} = s_X / \sqrt{n}$. Thus, $20 = s_X / \sqrt{15}$, and therefore

$S_X = 80$. When the standard error of the mean if 5, given $S_X = 80$, we have: $5 = 80/\sqrt{n}$, which is $5\sqrt{n} = 80$. Dividing each side by 5 and squaring to remove the square root, that is, $\left(\sqrt{n}\right)^2 = \left(80/5\right)^2$, we need a sample size of 256 to reduce the standard error to 5, holding the standard deviation of X constant at 80.

5.   Standard error of the mean = .6325; 90% CI = 1.9595 to 4.0405.

Interpretive Problems

1.   Take a six-sided die, where the population values are obviously 1, 2, 3, 4, 5, and 6. Take 20 samples, each of size 2 (e.g., every two rolls is one sample). For each sample calculate the mean. Then determine the mean of the sampling distribution of the mean and the variance error of the mean. Compare your results to those of your colleagues.

2.   You will need 20 plain M&M candy pieces and one cup. Put the candy pieces in the cup and toss them onto a flat surface. Count the number of candy pieces that land with the "M" facing up. Write down that number. Repeat these steps five times. These steps will constitute *one sample*. Next, generate four additional samples (i.e., repeat the process of tossing the candy pieces, counting the "Ms," and writing down that number). Then determine the mean of the sampling distribution of the mean and the variance error of the mean. Compare your results to those of your colleagues.

6

Introduction to Hypothesis Testing: Inferences About a Single Mean

Chapter Outline

Key Concepts

1. Null or statistical hypothesis versus scientific or research hypothesis

2. Type I error (α), type II error (β), and power ($1 - \beta$)

3. Two-tailed versus one-tailed alternative hypotheses

4. Critical regions and critical values

5. z test statistic

6. Confidence interval around the mean

7. t test statistic

8. t distribution, degrees of freedom, and table of t distributions

In Chapter 5 we began to move into the realm of inferential statistics. There we considered the following general topics: probability, sampling, and estimation. In this chapter we move totally into the domain of inferential statistics, where the concepts involved in probability, sampling, and estimation can be implemented. The overarching theme of the chapter is the use of a statistical test to make inferences about a single mean. In order to properly cover this inferential test, a number of basic foundational concepts are described in this chapter. Many of these concepts are utilized throughout the remainder of this text. Thus, even though there are likely lots of new concepts introduced in this chapter, a large portion of them will resurface in the remaining chapters (i.e., you'll be able to continue to apply what you learn in this chapter).

The topics described in the chapter include the following: types of hypotheses; types of decision errors; level of significance (α); overview of steps in the decision-making process; inferences about μ when σ is known; Type II error (β) and power ($1 - \beta$); statistical versus practical significance; and inferences about μ when σ is unknown. Concepts to be discussed include the following: the null or statistical hypothesis versus the scientific or research hypothesis; Type I error (α), Type II error (β), and power ($1 - \beta$); two-tailed versus one-tailed alternative hypotheses; critical regions and critical values; the z test statistic; the confidence interval around the mean; the t statistic; and the t distribution, degrees of freedom, and table of t distributions. Our objectives are that by the end of this chapter, you will be able to (a) understand the basic concepts of hypothesis testing; (b) utilize the normal and t tables; and (c) understand, determine, and interpret the results from the z test, t test, and confidence interval procedures.

6.1 Inferences About a Single Mean and How They Work

6.1.1 Characteristics

You may remember Ott Lier and his graduate student colleagues from previous chapters as they have assisted in solving various statistical dilemmas. We see Ott has now been tasked with quite an interesting project.

Ott Lier has greatly enjoyed working with his colleagues on various statistical projects in which they have been involved through the stats lab. Ott and his group completed their first tasks as research assistants—determining a number of descriptive statistics on data. The faculty advisor for the statistical lab has been contacted by a community partner, Coach Wesley, the local hockey coach, who is interested in examining team skating performance. Ott has been assigned to the project. After consulting with Coach Wesley, Ott determines the most appropriate research question to be the following: *Is the mean skating speed of the hockey team different from the league mean speed of 12 seconds?* Ott suggests a one-sample test of means as the test of inference. His task is to assist Coach Wesley in generating the test of inference to answer his research question.

6.1.1.1 Types of Hypotheses

Hypothesis testing is a decision-making process where two possible decisions are weighed in a statistical fashion. In a way, this is much like any other decision involving two possibilities, such as whether to carry an umbrella with you today or not. In statistical decision-making, the two possible decisions are known as **hypotheses**. Sample data are then used to help us select one of these decisions. The two types of hypotheses competing against one another are known as the **null** or **statistical hypothesis**, denoted by H_0, and the **scientific, alternative,** or **research hypothesis**, denoted by H_1.

The null or statistical hypothesis is *a statement about the value of an unknown population parameter.* Considering the statistical procedure we are discussing in this chapter, the one-sample mean test, one example null hypothesis, H_0, might be that the population mean IQ score is 100, which we denote as

$$H_0: \mu = 100 \quad \text{or} \quad H_0: \mu - 100 = 0$$

Mathematically, both of these equations say the same thing. The version on the left is the more traditional form of the null hypothesis involving a single mean. However, the version on the right makes clear to the reader why the term "null" is appropriate; that is, there is no difference, or a "null" difference, between the population mean and the hypothesized mean value of 100. In general, the **hypothesized mean value** is denoted by μ_0 (here $\mu_0 = 100$). Another H_0 might be that statistics exam population means are the same for male and female students, which we denote as

$$H_0: \mu_1 - \mu_2 = 0$$

where μ_1 is the population mean for males and μ_2 is the population mean for females. Here there is no difference, or a "null" difference, between the two population means. The test of the difference between two means is presented in Chapter 7. As we move through subsequent chapters, we become familiar with null hypotheses that involve other population parameters such as proportions, variances, and correlations.

The null hypothesis is basically set up by the researcher in an attempt to reject the null hypothesis in favor of our own personal scientific, alternative, or research hypothesis. In other words, the scientific hypothesis is what we believe the outcome of the study will be, based on previous theory and research. *Thus, we are trying to reject the null hypothesis and find evidence in favor of our scientific hypothesis.* The scientific hypotheses (alternative hypotheses) H_1, for our two examples are:

$$H_1: \mu \neq 100 \quad \text{or} \quad H_1: \mu - 100 \neq 0$$

and

$$H_1: \mu_1 - \mu_2 \neq 0 \quad \text{or} \quad H_1: \mu_1 \neq \mu_2$$

Based on the sample data, *hypothesis testing involves making a decision as to whether the null or the research hypothesis is supported.* Because we are dealing with sample statistics in our decision-making process, and trying to make an inference back to the population parameter(s), *there is always some risk of making an incorrect decision.* In other words, the sample data might lead us to make a decision that is not consistent with the population. We might decide to take an umbrella and it does not rain, or we might decide to leave the umbrella at home and it rains. Thus, as in any decision, the possibility always exists that an incorrect decision may be made. *This uncertainty is due to sampling error,* which we will see can be described by a probability statement. That is, because the decision is made based on sample data, the sample may not be very representative of the population, and therefore leads us to an incorrect decision. If we had population data, we would always make the correct decision about a population parameter. Because we usually do not, we use inferential statistics to help make decisions from sample data and infer those results back to the population. The nature of such decision errors and the probabilities we can attribute to them are described in the next section.

6.1.1.2 Types of Decision Errors

In this section we consider more specifically the types of decision errors that might be made in the decision-making process. First an example decision-making situation is presented. This is followed by a decision-making table whereby the types of decision errors are easily depicted.

6.1.1.2.1 Example Decision-Making Situation

Let us propose an example decision-making situation using an instrument that measures adult intelligence. It is known somehow that the population standard deviation of the instrument is 15 (i.e., $\sigma^2 = 225$, $\sigma = 15$). (In the real world it is rare that the population standard deviation is known, and we return to reality later in the chapter when the basic concepts have been covered. But for now, assume that we know the population standard deviation.) Our null and alternative hypotheses, respectively, are as follows:

$$H_0: \mu = 100 \quad \text{or} \quad H_0: \mu - 100 = 0$$
$$H_1: \mu \neq 100 \quad \text{or} \quad H_1: \mu - 100 \neq 0$$

Thus, we are interested in testing whether the population mean for the intelligence instrument is equal to 100, our hypothesized mean value, or not equal to 100.

Next we take several random samples of individuals from the adult population. We find for our first sample $\overline{Y}_1 = 105$ (i.e., denoting the mean for sample 1). Eyeballing the information for sample 1, the sample mean is one-third of a standard deviation above the hypothesized value, which we determine by computing a z score of $(105 - 100)/15 = .3333$, so our conclusion would probably be that we fail to reject H_0. In other words, if the population mean actually is 100, then we believe that one is quite likely to observe a sample mean of 105. Thus, our decision for sample 1 is that we fail to reject H_0; however, there is some likelihood or probability that our decision is incorrect.

We take a second sample and find $\overline{Y}_2 = 115$ (i.e., denoting the mean for sample 2). Eyeballing the information for sample 2, the sample mean is one standard deviation above the hypothesized value, based on $z = (115 - 100)/15 = 1.0000$, so our conclusion would probably be that we fail to reject H_0. In other words, if the population mean actually is 100, then we believe that it is somewhat likely to observe a sample mean of 115. Thus, our decision for sample 2 is that we fail to reject H_0. However, there is an even greater likelihood or probability that our decision is incorrect than was the case for sample 1; this is because the sample mean is further away from the hypothesized value.

We take a third sample and find $\overline{Y}_3 = 190$ (i.e., denoting the mean for sample 3). Eyeballing the information for sample 3, the sample mean is six standard deviations above the hypothesized value, based on $z = (190 - 100)/15 = 6.0000$, so our conclusion would probably be to reject H_0. In other words, if the population mean actually is 100, then we believe that it is quite unlikely to observe a sample mean of 190. Thus our decision for sample 3 is to reject H_0; however, there is some small likelihood or probability that our decision is incorrect.

6.1.1.2.1 Decision-Making Table

Let us consider Table 6.1 as a mechanism for sorting out the possible outcomes in the statistical decision-making process. The table consists of the general case and a specific case. First, in part (a) of the table, we have the possible outcomes for the general case. For the state of nature or reality (i.e., how things really are in the population), there are two distinct possibilities, as depicted by the rows of the table: either H_0 is *indeed true* or H_0 is *indeed false*. In other words, according to the real-world conditions in the population, either H_0 is actually true or H_0 is actually false. Admittedly, we usually do not know what the state of nature truly is; however, it does exist in the population data. It is the state of nature that we are trying to best approximate when making a statistical decision based on sample data.

For our statistical decision, there are two distinct possibilities, as depicted by the columns of the table: either we *fail to reject* H_0 or we *reject* H_0. In other words, based on our sample data, we either fail to reject H_0 or reject H_0. As our goal is *usually* to reject H_0 in favor of our research hypothesis, we prefer to say "fail to reject" rather than "accept." "Accept" implies you are willing to throw out your research hypothesis and admit defeat based on one sample (i.e., this is the absolute and final truth). "Fail to reject" implies you still have some hope for your research hypothesis, despite evidence from a single sample to the contrary (i.e., there is some evidence that supports the null but you are not assuming this is the absolute and final truth).

If we look inside of the table, we see four different outcomes based on a combination of our statistical decision and the state of nature. Consider the first row of the table where H_0

TABLE 6.1

Statistical Decision Table

	Decision	
State of nature (reality)	**Fail to reject H_0**	**Reject H_0 (reality)**
(a) Geeral Case		
H_0 is true	Correct decision: $(1 - \alpha)$	Type I error: α
H_0 is false	Type II error: β	Correct decision: $(1 - \beta) = $ power

	Decision	
State of nature (reality)	**Fail to reject H_0**	**Reject H_0 (reality)**
(b) Example Rain Case		
H_0 is true (no rain)	Correct decision (do not take umbrella and no umbrella needed): $(1 - \alpha)$	Type I error (take umbrella but umbrella not needed): α
H_0 is false (rains)	Type II error (do not take umbrella and get wet): β	Correct decision (take umbrella and stay dry): $(1 - \beta) = $ power

is in actuality true. First, if H_0 is true and we fail to reject H_0, then we have made a correct decision; that is, we have *correctly failed to reject a true H_0*. The probability of this first outcome is known as $1 - \alpha$, where α represents alpha. Second, if H_0 is true and we reject H_0, then we have made a decision error known as a **Type I error**. That is, we have *incorrectly rejected a true H_0*; this is also referred to as a **false positive**. Our sample data has led us to a different conclusion than the population data would have. The probability of this second outcome is known as alpha (α). Therefore, if H_0 is actually true, then our sample data lead us to one of two conclusions: either we correctly fail to reject H_0 or we incorrectly reject H_0. The sum of the probabilities for these two outcomes when H_0 is true is equal to 1; that is, $(1 - \alpha) + \alpha = 1$.

Consider now the second row of the table where H_0 is in actuality false. First, if H_0 is really false and we fail to reject H_0, then we have made a decision error known as a **Type II error**. That is, we have *incorrectly failed to reject a false H_0*, also referred to as a **false negative**. Our sample data has led us to a different conclusion than the population data would have. The probability of this outcome is known as beta (β). Second, if H_0 is really false and we reject H_0, then we have made a correct decision; that is, we have *correctly rejected a false H_0*. The probability of this second outcome is known as $1 - \beta$, or power (to be more fully discussed later in this chapter). Therefore, if H_0 is actually false, then our sample data lead us to one of two conclusions: either we incorrectly fail to reject H_0 or we correctly reject H_0. The sum of the probabilities for these two outcomes when H_0 is false is equal to 1; that is, $\beta + (1 - \beta) = 1$.

Consider the following specific case, as shown in part (b) of Table 6.1. We wish to test the following hypotheses about whether it will rain tomorrow:

$$H_0\text{: no rain tomorrow}$$

$$H_1\text{: rains tomorrow}$$

We collect some sample data from prior years for the same month and day, and go to make our statistical decision. Our two possible statistical decisions are (a) we do not believe it will rain tomorrow, and therefore do not bring an umbrella with us, or (b) we do believe it will rain tomorrow, and therefore do bring an umbrella.

Again, there are four potential outcomes. First, if H_0 is really true (no rain) and we do not carry an umbrella, then we have made a correct decision as no umbrella is necessary (probability = $1 - \alpha$). Second, if H_0 is really true (no rain) and we carry an umbrella, then we have made a Type I error, and we carry an umbrella around all day when we do not need to (probability = α). Third, if H_0 is really false (rains) and we do not carry an umbrella, then we have made a Type II error and we get wet (probability = β). Fourth, if H_0 is really false (rains) and we carry an umbrella, then we have made the correct decision, as the umbrella keeps us dry (probability = $1 - \beta$).

Let us make two concluding statements about the decision table. First, one can never prove the truth or falsity of H_0 in a single study. One only gathers evidence in favor of or in opposition to the null hypothesis. Something is proven in research when an entire collection of studies or evidence reaches the same conclusion time and time again. Scientific proof is difficult to achieve in the social and behavioral sciences, and we should not use the terms "prove" or "proof" loosely. As researchers, we gather multiple pieces of evidence that eventually lead to the development of one or more theories. When a theory is shown to be unequivocally true (i.e., in all cases), then proof has been established.

Second, let us consider the decision errors in a different light. One can totally eliminate the possibility of a Type I error by deciding to *never* reject H_0. That is, if we always fail to reject H_0 (do not ever carry an umbrella), then we can never make a Type I error (carry an unnecessary umbrella). Although this strategy sounds fine, it totally takes the decision-making power out of our hands. With this strategy we do not even need to collect any sample data, as we have already decided to never reject H_0.

One can totally eliminate the possibility of a Type II error by deciding to *always* reject H_0. That is, if we always reject H_0 (always carry an umbrella), then we can never make a Type II error (get wet without an umbrella). Although this strategy also sounds fine, it totally takes the decision-making power out of our hands. With this strategy we do not even need to collect any sample data as we have already decided to always reject H_0. Taken together, one can never totally eliminate the possibility of both a Type I and a Type II error. No matter what decision we make, there is always some possibility of making a Type I and/or Type II error. Therefore as researchers, our job is to make conscience decisions in designing and conducting our study and in analyzing the data so that the possibility of decision error is minimized. And, as we will see in the next section, it is the researcher's judgment on how to balance Type I versus Type II errors.

6.1.1.2.2 A Little History

Neyman and Pearson (1933) presented the term "hypothesis testing" as a contrast with "significance testing," which was coined by Fisher (thus, referring to "significance level" as "Type I error" actually has mixed these two approaches, among other ways the two have mixed). The approach by Neyman and Pearson includes two competing hypotheses, the null *and* the alternative hypotheses, whereas the approach by Fisher includes *just* the null hypothesis. This explicit specification of an alternative hypothesis distinguishes the approaches of Fisher and Neyman and Pearson and, more important, introduced probabilities associated with committing two kinds of errors related to the null hypothesis (i.e., Type I and Type II). The approach by Neyman and Pearson also introduced the concept of statistical power. Because Fisher's approach has no alternative hypothesis, Type II error and power are irrelevant. As stated by (Fisher, 1935, p. 474), "'Errors of the second kind' are committed only by those who misunderstand the nature and application of tests of significance."

Fisher and Neyman and Pearson also viewed inductive reasoning differently. Fisher was centered on rejection of the null hypothesis, whereas Neyman and Pearson conceptualized inductive behavior, which was irrespective of the beliefs in either the null or alternative hypothesis. Rather, establishing rules for making decisions between the two hypotheses was their focus: "To accept a hypothesis H means only to decide to take action A rather than action B. This does not mean that we necessarily believe that the hypothesis H is true . . . [Rejecting H] . . . means only that the rule prescribes action B and does not imply that we believe that H is false" (Neyman, 1950, pp. 259–260). The Neyman–Pearson approach recognizes the costs of committing a Type I or Type II error when accepting or rejecting the null hypothesis, with these costs being context dependent, and thus based on the judgment of the researcher. At the same time, they noted that control of Type I errors was most important (Neyman, 1950). Balancing between Type I and Type II error was critical to Neyman and Pearson (1933), and they provided an example to illustrate:

In a scientific investigation we may be testing some new hypothesis H_0 . . . The hypothesis is perhaps novel and important, and we do not wish to throw it aside lightly . . . .

[W]e shall therefore be inclined to give H_0 the benefit of the doubt, and fix the level of rejection low ... perhaps .01 or less. On the other hand we may be analyzing the results of a series of experiments designed to detect possible factors which may modify the working of a standard law. In this case we shall be watching carefully for any signs of divergence from the standard hypotheses H_0, and shall allow [Type I error] to be large—perhaps .10—in order than the risk of error II may be reduced. The importance of finding some new line of development here outweighs any loss due to certain waste of effort in starting on a false trail.

(pp. 497–498)

6.1.1.3 *Level of Significance (α)*

We have already stated that a Type I error occurs when the decision is to reject H_0 when in fact H_0 is actually true. We defined the probability of a Type I error as α, which is also known as the *level of significance* or *significance level*. We now examine α as a basis for helping us make statistical decisions. Recall from a previous example that the null and alternative hypotheses, respectively, are as follows:

$$H_0: \mu = 100 \quad \text{or} \quad H_0: \mu - 100 = 0$$

$$H_1: \mu \neq 100 \quad \text{or} \quad H_1: \mu - 100 \neq 0$$

Thus, we need a mechanism for deciding how far away a sample mean needs to be from the hypothesized mean value of $\mu_0 = 100$ in order to reject H_0. In other words, at a certain point or distance away from 100, we will decide to reject H_0. We use α to determine that point for us, where in this context α is known as the **level of significance**. Figure 6.1a shows a sampling distribution of the mean where the hypothesized value μ_0 is depicted at the center of the distribution. Toward both tails of the distribution, we see two shaded regions known as the **critical regions**, or regions of rejection. The combined area of the two shaded regions is equal to α, and thus the area of either the upper or the lower tail critical region is equal to a/2 (i.e., we split α into one-half by dividing by 2). If the sample mean is far enough away from the hypothesized mean value, μ_0, that it falls into either critical region, then our statistical decision is to *reject H_0*. In this case our decision is to reject H_0 at the α level of significance. If, however, the sample mean is close enough to μ_0 that it falls into the unshaded region (i.e., not into either critical region), then our statistical decision is to *fail to reject H_0*. The **critical values** are the *precise points on the X axis at which the critical regions are divided from the unshaded region*. Determining critical values is discussed later in this chapter.

Note that under the alternative hypothesis, H_1, we are willing to reject H_0 when the sample mean is either significantly greater than or significantly less than the hypothesized mean value μ_0. This particular alternative hypothesis is known as a *nondirectional alternative hypothesis*, as no direction is implied with respect to the hypothesized value; that is, *we will reject the null hypothesis in favor of the alternative hypothesis in either direction, either above or below the hypothesized mean value*. This also results in what is known as a *two-tailed test of significance* in that we are willing to reject the null hypothesis in either tail or critical region.

Two other alternative hypotheses are also possible, depending on the researcher's scientific hypothesis, which are known as *directional alternative hypotheses*. One directional alternative is that the *population mean is greater than the hypothesized mean value*, also known as a *right-tailed test*, as denoted by:

$$H_1: \mu > 100 \quad \text{or} \quad H_1: \mu - 100 > 0$$

Mathematically, both of these equations say the same thing. With a right-tailed alternative hypothesis, the entire region of rejection is contained in the upper tail, with an area of α, known as a one-tailed test of significance (and specifically the right tail). If the sample mean is significantly greater than the hypothesized mean value of 100, then our statistical decision is to reject H_0. If, however, the sample mean falls into the unshaded region, then our statistical decision is to fail to reject H_0. This situation is depicted in Figure 6.1b.

A second directional alternative is that the *population mean is less than the hypothesized mean value*, also known as a left-tailed test, as denoted by:

$$H_1: \mu < 100 \quad \text{or} \quad H_1: \mu - 100 < 0$$

Mathematically, both of these equations say the same thing. With a left-tailed alternative hypothesis, the entire region of rejection is contained in the lower tail, with an area of α, also known as a one-tailed test of significance (and specifically the left tail). If the

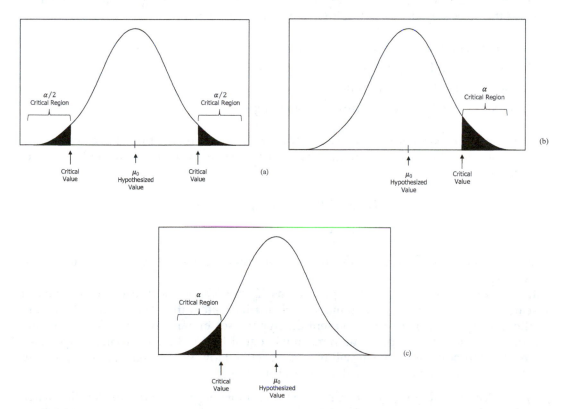

FIGURE 6.1
Alternative hypotheses and critical regions.

sample mean is significantly less than the hypothesized mean value of 100, then our statistical decision is to reject H_0. If, however, the sample mean falls into the unshaded region, then our statistical decision is to fail to reject H_0. This situation is depicted in Figure 6.1c.

The potential for misuse exists for the different alternatives, which we consider to be an ethical matter. For example, say that a researcher conducts a one-tailed test with an upper-tail critical region and fails to reject H_0. However, the researcher notices that the sample mean is considerably below the hypothesized mean value and then decides to change the alternative hypothesis to either a nondirectional test or a one-tailed test in the other tail. This is unethical, as the researcher has examined the data and changed the alternative hypothesis. The moral of the story is this: *If there is previous and consistent empirical evidence to use a specific directional alternative hypothesis, then you should do so. If, however, there is minimal or inconsistent empirical evidence to use a specific directional alternative, then you should not. Instead, you should use a nondirectional alternative.* Once you have decided which alternative hypothesis to go with, then you need to stick with it for the duration of the statistical decision. If you find contrary evidence, then report it, as it may be an important finding, but do not change the alternative hypothesis in midstream.

6.1.1.4 Overview of Steps in the Decision-Making Process

Before we get into the specific details of conducting the test of a single mean, we want to discuss the basic steps for hypothesis testing of any inferential test:

1. State the null and alternative hypotheses.
2. Select the level of significance (i.e., alpha, α).
3. Calculate the test statistic value.
4. Make a statistical decision (reject or fail to reject H_0).

Step 1: State the null and alternative hypotheses. Recall from our previous example that the null and nondirectional alternative hypotheses, respectively, for a two-tailed test are as follows:

$$H_0: \mu = 100 \quad \text{or} \quad H_0: \mu - 100 = 0$$
$$H_1: \mu \neq 100 \quad \text{or} \quad H_1: \mu - 100 \neq 0$$

One could also choose one of the other directional alternative hypotheses described previously.

If we choose to write our null hypothesis as $H_0: \mu = 100$, we would want to write our research hypothesis in a consistent manner: $H_1: \mu \neq 100$ (rather than $H_1: \mu - 100 \neq 0$). In publication, many researchers opt to present the hypotheses in narrative form (e.g., "the null hypothesis states that the population mean will equal 100, and the alternative hypothesis states that the population mean will not equal 100"). How you present your hypotheses (mathematically or using statistical notation) is up to you.

Step 2: Select a level of significance, α. Two things must be taken into consideration when selecting a level of significance. The first is the cost associated with making a Type I error, which is what α really is. Recall that alpha is the probability of rejecting the null hypothesis if in reality the null hypothesis is true. When a Type I error is made, that means evidence is building in favor of the research hypothesis (which is actually false). Let us take an example of a new drug. To test the efficacy of the drug, an experiment is conducted where some individuals take the new drug, whereas others receive a placebo. The null hypothesis, stated nondirectionally, would essentially indicate that the effects of the drug and placebo are the same. Rejecting that null hypothesis would mean that the effects are not equal—suggesting that perhaps this new drug, which in reality is not any better than a placebo, is being touted as effective medication. That is obviously problematic and potentially very hazardous!

Thus, if there is a relatively high cost associated with a Type I error—for example, such that lives are lost, as in the medical profession—then one would want to select a relatively small level of significance (e.g., .01 or smaller). A small alpha would translate to a very small probability of rejecting the null if it were really true (i.e., a small probability of making an incorrect decision). If there is a relatively low cost associated with a Type I error—for example, such that children have to eat the second-rated candy rather than the first—then selecting a larger level of significance may be appropriate (e.g., .05 or larger). Costs are not always known, however. A second consideration is the level of significance commonly used in your field of study. In many disciplines the .05 level of significance has become the standard (although no one seems to have a really good rationale). This is true in many of the social and behavioral sciences. Thus, you would do well to consult the published literature in your field to see if some standard alpha is commonly used and to consider it for your own research.

Here is a good point to interject a little history as well as new developments. We just stated that .05 is the standard alpha in many disciplines, and this is generally attributed to Fisher (1925) when he developed analysis of variance procedures. Later, Fisher (1926), acknowledged the use of other alpha levels, stating,

---

If one in twenty does not seem high enough odds, we may, if we prefer it, draw the line at one in fifty (the 2 per cent point), or one in a hundred (the 1 per cent point). Personally, the writer prefers to set a low standard of significance at the 5 per cent point, and ignore entirely all results which fail to reach this level. A scientific fact should be regarded as experimentally established only if a properly designed experiment rarely fails to give this level of significance.

(p. 504)

Many scholars who have studied the history of probability feel the selection of an alpha of .05 as the cutoff is arbitrary (Cowles & Davis, 1982). Cowles and Davis (1982) argue that the reason why the adoption of .05 was appropriate to early statisticians and why it prevailed was due to its consideration as a concept of probability. Alpha of .05 was justified as a criterion for judging outcomes, as generally, people feel that an event that occurs 5% of the time is a rare event *and* they are comfortable assigning a nonchance cause to an event that occurs that infrequently (Cowles & Davis, 1982).

Approaching 100 years in use, there is obviously a long history in the application of an alpha of .05. However, a number of scholars argue that the threshold should be changed from .05 to .005, claiming that "statistical standards of evidence for claiming new discoveries in many fields of science are simply too low. Associating 'statistically significant' findings with $p < .05$ results in a high rate of false positives even in the absence of other experimental, procedural and reporting problems" (Benjamin et al., 2018, p. 5). Others argue that simply adjusting the alpha level will not solve the problem but may actually have adverse effects (Crane, 2018). Some scholars argue that getting rid of significance testing altogether is needed (Trafimow et al., 2018). Bayesian methods are one attractive alternative to null hypothesis significance testing (Cristea & Ioannidis, 2018). Still others suggest using probability values (i.e., p) on a scale of 0 (completely incompatible) to 1 (completely compatible) or replacing the p value with a scale that is more intuitive, such as a likelihood ratio (Amrhein & Greenland, 2018).

This is just a tip of the iceberg. As this likely illustrates, there is quite a robust discussion in the research community on this topic. Our philosophy is that your research question should *always* guide your statistical approach and analysis. In some instances, a frequentist perspective, which applies parametric inference and within which this text is framed, is needed. In other instances, Bayesian statistics are more appropriate. In still other instances, neither is needed. This text provides many useful tools for conducting statistics. However, we do not claim these to be the only tools you will ever need. Rather, we hope that this text whets your appetite to learn other approaches, such as Bayesian statistics, so that you can make informed decisions on how best to approach a particular research problem.

Step 3: Calculate the test statistic. For the one-sample mean test, we will compute the sample mean $\bar{Y}$ and compare it to the hypothesized value μ_0. This allows us to determine the size of the difference between $\bar{Y}$ and μ_0, and subsequently the probability associated with the difference. The larger the difference, the more likely it is that the sample mean really differs from the hypothesized mean value and the larger the probability associated with the difference.

Step 4: Make a statistical decision regarding the null hypothesis, H_0. That is, a decision is made whether to reject H_0 or to fail to reject H_0. If the difference between the sample mean and the hypothesized value is large enough relative to the critical value (we will talk about critical values in more detail later), then our decision is to reject H_0. If the difference between the sample mean and the hypothesized value is not large enough relative to the critical value, then our decision is to fail to reject H_0. This is the basic four-step process for hypothesis testing of any inferential test. The specific details for the test of a single mean are given in the following section.

6.1.1.5 Inferences About μ When σ Is Known

In this section we examine how hypotheses about a single mean are conducted when the population standard deviation is known. Specifically we consider the z test, an example illustrating use of the z test, and how to construct a confidence interval around the mean.

6.1.1.5.1 The z Test

Recall from Chapter 4 the definition of a **z score** as

$$z = \frac{Y_i - \mu}{\sigma_Y}$$

where Y_i is the score on variable Y for individual i, μ is the population mean for variable Y, and σ_Y is the population standard deviation for variable Y. The z score is used to tell us how many standard deviation units an individual's score is from the mean.

In the context of this chapter, however, we are concerned with the extent to which a sample mean differs from some hypothesized mean value. We can construct a variation of the z score for testing hypotheses about a single mean. In this situation we are concerned with the sampling distribution of the mean (introduced in Chapter 5), so the equation must reflect means rather than raw scores. Our z score equation for testing hypotheses about a single mean becomes the following:

$$z = \frac{\bar{Y} - \mu_0}{\sigma_{\bar{Y}}}$$

where $\bar{Y}$ is the sample mean for variable Y, μ_0 is the hypothesized mean value for variable Y, and $\sigma_{\bar{Y}}$ is the population standard error of the mean for variable Y. From Chapter 5, recall that the population standard error of the mean $\sigma_{\bar{Y}}$ is computed by

$$\sigma_{\bar{Y}} = \frac{\sigma_Y}{\sqrt{n}}$$

where σ_Y is the population standard deviation for variable Y and n is sample size. Thus, the numerator of the z score equation is the difference between the sample mean and the hypothesized value of the mean, and the denominator is the standard error of the mean. *What we are really determining here is how many standard deviation (or standard error) units the sample mean is from the hypothesized mean.* Henceforth, we call this variation of the z score the **test statistic for the test of a single mean**, also known as the **z test**. This is the first of several test statistics we describe in this text; every inferential test requires some test statistic for purposes of testing hypotheses.

We need to make a statistical assumption regarding this hypothesis-testing situation. We assume that z is normally distributed with a mean of 0 and a standard deviation of 1. This is written statistically as $z \sim N(0,1)$ following the notation we developed in Chapter 4. Thus, the assumption is that z follows the unit normal distribution (in other words, the shape of the distribution is approximately normal). An examination of our test statistic z reveals that only the sample mean can vary from sample to sample. The hypothesized value and the standard error of the mean are constant for every sample of size n from the same population.

In order to make a statistical decision, the critical regions need to be defined. Because the test statistic is z and we have assumed normality, then the relevant theoretical distribution we compare the test statistic to is the *unit normal distribution*. We previously discussed this distribution in Chapter 4, and the table of values is given in Table A.1 in the Appendix. If the alternative hypothesis is nondirectional, then there would be two critical regions—one in the upper tail and one in the lower tail. Here we would split the area of the critical region, known as α, in two. If the alternative hypothesis is directional, then there would only be one critical region, either in the upper tail or in the lower tail, depending on which direction one is willing to reject H_0.

6.1.1.5.2 An Example

Let us illustrate use of this inferential test through an example. We are interested in testing whether the population of undergraduate students from Awesome State University (ASU) have a mean intelligence test score different from the hypothesized mean value of $\mu_0 = 100$. (Remember that the hypothesized mean value does not come from our sample, but from another source; in this example, let us say that this value of 100 is the national norm as presented in the technical manual of this particular intelligence test.)

Our first step in hypothesis testing is to state the hypothesis. A nondirectional alternative hypothesis is of interest as we simply want to know if this population has a mean intelligence different from the hypothesized value, either greater than or less than. Thus, the null and alternative hypotheses can be written, respectively, as follows:

$$H_0: \mu = 100 \quad \text{or} \quad H_0: \mu - 100 = 0$$
$$H_1: \mu \neq 100 \quad \text{or} \quad H_1: \mu - 100 \neq 0$$

A sample mean of $\bar{Y} = 103$ is observed for a sample of $n = 100$ ASU undergraduate students. From the development of this intelligence test, we know that the theoretical population standard deviation is $\sigma_Y = 15$ (again, for purposes of illustration, let us say that the population standard deviation of 15 was noted in the technical manual for this test).

Our second step is to select a level of significance. The standard level of significance in this field is the .05 level; thus, we perform our significance test at $\alpha = .05$.

The third step is to compute the test statistic value. To compute our test statistic value, first we compute the standard error of the mean (the denominator of our test statistic formula) as follows with the population standard deviation of 15 and a sample size of 100 (values of which were given previously):

$$\sigma_{\bar{Y}} = \frac{\sigma_Y}{\sqrt{n}} = \frac{15}{\sqrt{100}} = 1.50$$

Then we compute the test statistic z, where the numerator is the difference between the mean of our sample $\left(\bar{Y} = 103\right)$ and the hypothesized mean value ($\mu_0 = 100$) and the denominator is the standard error of the mean:

$$z = \frac{\bar{Y} - \mu_0}{\sigma_{\bar{Y}}} = \frac{103 - 100}{1.50} = 2.00$$

Finally, in the last step we make our statistical decision by comparing the test statistic z to the critical values. To determine the critical values for the z test, we use the unit normal distribution in Table A.1 in the Appendix. Because $\alpha = .05$ and we are conducting a nondirectional test, we need to find critical values for the upper and lower tails, where the area of each of the two critical regions is equal to .025 (i.e., splitting alpha in half: $\alpha/2$ or $.05/2 = .025$). From the unit normal table we find these critical values to be +1.96 (the point on the X axis where the area above that point is equal to .025) and −1.96 (the point on the X axis where the area below that point is equal to .025). As shown in Figure 6.2, the test statistic $z = 2.00$ falls into the upper-tail critical region, just slightly larger than the upper-tail critical value of +1.96. Our decision is to reject H_0 and conclude that the ASU population from which the sample was selected has a mean intelligence score that is statistically significantly different from the hypothesized mean of 100 at the .05 level of significance.

A more precise way of thinking about this process is to determine the **exact probability** of observing a sample mean that differs from the hypothesized mean value. From the unit

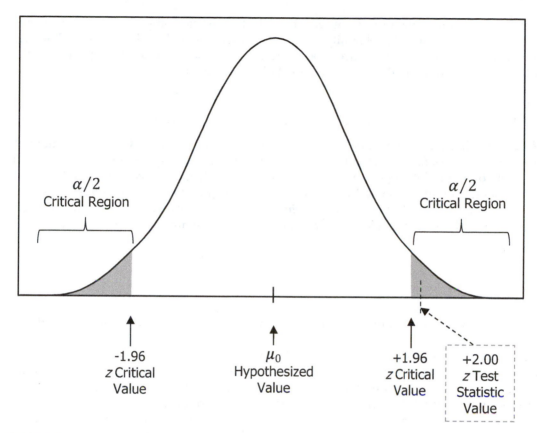

FIGURE 6.2

normal table, the area above $z = 2.00$ is equal to .0228. Therefore, the area below $z = -2.00$ is also equal to .0228. Thus, the probability, p, of observing, by chance, a sample mean of 2.00 or more standard errors (i.e., $z = 2.00$) from the hypothesized mean value of 100, in either direction, is two times the observed probability level, or $p = (2)(.0228) = .0456$. To put this in the context of the values in this example, there is a relatively small probability (less than 5%) of observing a sample mean of 103 just by chance if the true population mean is really 100. As this exact probability ($p = .0456$) is smaller than our level of significance $\alpha = .05$, we reject H_0. Thus, there are two approaches to dealing with probability. One approach is a decision based solely on the critical values. We reject or fail to reject H_0 at a given α level, but no other information is provided. The other approach is a decision based on comparing the exact probability to the given α level. We reject or fail to reject H_0 at a given α level, but we also have information available about the closeness or confidence in that decision.

For this example, the findings in a publication would be reported based on comparing the p value to alpha and reported either as $z = 2$ ($p < .05$) or as $z = 2$ ($p = .0456$). (You may want to refer to the style manual relevant to your discipline, such as the *Publication Manual for the American Psychological Association* (2010), for information on which is the recommended reporting style.) Obviously, the conclusion is the same with either approach; it is just a matter of how the results are reported. Most statistical computer programs, including SPSS, report the exact probability so that the readers can make a decision based on their own selected level of significance. These programs do not provide the critical value(s), which are only found in the appendices of statistics textbooks.

6.1.1.5.3 Constructing Confidence Intervals Around the Mean

Recall our discussion from Chapter 5 on confidence intervals (CI). Confidence intervals are often quite useful in inferential statistics for providing the researcher with an interval estimate of a population parameter. Although the sample mean gives us a point estimate (i.e., just one value) of a population mean, a confidence interval *gives us an interval estimate of a population mean and allows us to determine the accuracy or precision of the sample mean*. For the inferential test of a single mean, a confidence interval around the sample mean $\bar{Y}$ is formed from

$$\bar{Y} \pm z_{cv}\sigma_{\bar{Y}}$$

where z_{cv} is the critical value from the unit normal distribution and $\sigma_{\bar{Y}}$ is the population standard error of the mean.

Confidence intervals are typically formed for nondirectional or two-tailed tests, as shown in the equation. *A confidence interval will generate a lower and an upper limit*. If the hypothesized mean value falls within the lower and upper limits, then we would fail to reject H_0. In other words, if the hypothesized mean is contained in (or falls within) the confidence interval around the sample mean, then we conclude that the sample mean and the hypothesized mean are not significantly different and that the sample mean could have come from a population with the hypothesized mean; that is, we *fail to reject H_0*. If the hypothesized mean value falls outside the limits of the interval, then we would *reject H_0*. Here we conclude that it is unlikely that the sample mean could have come from a population with the hypothesized mean.

One way to think about CIs is as follows. Imagine we take 100 random samples of the same sample size n, compute each sample mean, and then construct each 95% confidence interval. Then we can say that 95% of these CIs will contain the population parameter and 5% will not. In short, 95% of similarly constructed CIs will contain the population parameter. It should also be mentioned that at a particular level of significance, one will always obtain the same statistical decision with both the hypothesis test and the confidence interval. The two procedures use precisely the same information. The hypothesis test is based on a point estimate; the CI is based on an interval estimate, providing the researcher with quite a bit more information.

For the ASU example situation, the 95% CI would be computed by

$$\bar{Y} \pm z_{cv}\sigma_{\bar{Y}} = 103 \pm (1.96)(1.50) = 103 \pm 2.94 = (100.06, 105.94)$$

Thus, the 95% confidence interval ranges from 100.06 to 105.94. Because the interval does not contain the hypothesized mean value of 100, we reject H_0 (the same decision we arrived at by walking through the steps for hypothesis testing). Thus, it is quite unlikely that our sample mean could have come from a population distribution with a mean of 100.

6.1.1.8 *Inferences About μ When σ Is Unknown*

We have already considered the inferential test involving a single mean when the population standard deviation σ is known. However, rarely is σ known to the applied researcher. When σ is unknown, then the z test is no longer appropriate. In this section we consider the following: the test statistic for inferences about the mean when the population standard deviation is unknown, the t distribution, the t test, and an example using the t test.

6.1.1.8.1 A New Test Statistic, t

What is the applied researcher to do then when σ is unknown? The answer is to estimate σ by the sample standard deviation s. This changes the standard error of the mean to be

$$s_{\bar{Y}} = \frac{s_Y}{\sqrt{n}}$$

Now we are estimating two population parameters: (1) the population mean, μ_Y, is being estimated by the sample mean, $\bar{Y}$; and (2) the population standard deviation, σ_Y, is being estimated by the sample standard deviation, s_Y. Both $\bar{Y}$ and s_Y can vary from sample to sample. Thus, although the sampling error of the mean is taken into account explicitly in the z test, we also need to take into account the sampling error of the standard deviation, which the z test does not at all consider.

We now develop a new inferential test for the situation where σ is unknown. The test statistic is known as the **t test** and is computed as follows:

$$t = \frac{\bar{Y} - \mu_0}{s_{\bar{Y}}}$$

The t test was developed by William Sealy Gossett, also known by the pseudonym Student, mentioned in Chapter 1. The unit normal distribution cannot be used here for the unknown σ situation. A different theoretical distribution must be used for determining critical values for the t test, known as the **t distribution**.

6.1.1.8.2 The t Distribution

The t distribution is the theoretical distribution used for determining the critical values of the t test. Like the normal distribution, the t distribution is actually a *family of distributions*. A different t distribution exists for each degrees of freedom. However, before we look more closely at the t distribution, some discussion of the **degrees of freedom** concept is necessary.

As an example, say we know a sample mean $\bar{Y} = 6$ for a sample size of $n = 5$. How many of those five observed scores are free to vary? The answer is that four scores are free to vary. If the four known scores are 2, 4, 6, and 8 and the mean is 6, then the remaining score must be 10. The remaining score is not free to vary, but is already totally determined. We see this in the following equation where, to arrive at a solution of 6, the sum in the numerator must equal 30, and Y_5 must be 10.

$$\bar{Y} = \frac{\sum_{i=1}^{n} Y_i}{n} = \frac{\sum_{i=1}^{5} Y_i}{5} = \frac{2+4+6+8+Y_5}{5} = 6$$

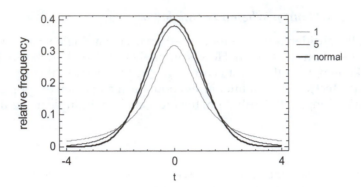

FIGURE 6.3
Several members of the family of *t* distributions.

Therefore, the number of degrees of freedom is equal to 4 in this particular case, and $n - 1$ in general. For the *t* test being considered here, we specify the degrees of freedom as $v = n - 1$ (where v is the Greek letter nu). We use v often in statistics to denote some type of degrees of freedom.

Another way to think about degrees of freedom is that we know the sum of the deviations from the mean must equal zero (recall the unsquared numerator of the variance conceptual formula). For example, if $n = 10$, there are 10 deviations from the mean. Once the mean is known, only 9 of the deviations are free to vary. A final way to think about this is that, in general, $df = (n - \text{number of restrictions})$. For the one-sample *t* test, because the population variance is unknown, we have to estimate it resulting in one restriction. Thus, $df = (n - 1)$ for this particular inferential test.

Several members of the family of *t* distributions are shown in Figure 6.3. The distribution for $v = 1$ has thicker tails than the unit normal distribution and a shorter peak. This indicates that there is considerable sampling error of the sample standard deviation with only 2 observations (as $v = 2 - 1 = 1$). For $v = 5$, the tails are thinner and the peak is taller than for $v = 1$. As the degrees of freedom increase, the *t* distribution becomes more nearly normal. For $v = 4$ (i.e., infinity), the *t* distribution is precisely the unit normal distribution.

A few important characteristics of the *t* distribution are worth mentioning. First, like the unit normal distribution, the mean of any *t* distribution is 0, and the *t* distribution is symmetric around the mean and unimodal. Second, unlike the unit normal distribution, which has a variance of 1, the variance of a *t* distribution is equal to

$$\sigma^2 = \frac{v}{v-2} \text{ for } v > 2$$

Thus, the variance of a *t* distribution is somewhat greater than 1, but approaches 1 as v increases.

The table for the *t* distribution is given in Table A.2 in the Appendix, and a snapshot of the table is presented in Figure 6.6 for illustration purposes. In looking at the table, each column header has two values. The top value is the significance level for a **one-tailed test**, denoted by α_1. Thus, if you were doing a one-tailed test at the .05 level of significance, you want to look in the second column of numbers. The bottom value is the significance level for a **two-tailed test**, denoted by α_2. Thus, if you were doing a two-tailed test at the .05 level

ν	$\alpha_1=.10$ $\alpha_2=.20$	.05 .10	.025 .050	.01 .02	.005 .010	.0025 .0050	.001 .002	.0005 .0010
1	3.078	6.314	12.706	31.821	63.657	127.32	318.31	636.62
2	1.886	2.920	4.303	6.965	9.925	14.089	22.327	31.598
3	1.638	2.353	3.182	4.541	5.841	7.453	10.214	12.924
...	...	...	...	...	...	...	...	...

FIGURE 6.4
Snapshot of t distribution table.

of significance, you want to look in the third column of numbers. The rows of the table denote the various degrees of freedom, ν.

Thus, if ν = 3, meaning $n = 4$, you want to look in the third row of numbers. If ν = 3 for $\alpha_1 = .05$, the tabled value is 2.353. This value represents the 95th percentile point in a t distribution with 3 degrees of freedom. This is because the table only presents the upper tail percentiles. Given that the t distribution is symmetric around 0, the lower-tail percentiles are the same values except for a change in sign. The 5th percentile for 3 degrees of freedom then is −2.353. Thus, for a right-tailed directional hypothesis the critical value will be +2.353 and for a left-tailed directional hypothesis the critical value will be −2.353.

If ν = 120 for $\alpha_1 = .05$, then the tabled value is 1.658. Thus, as sample size and degrees of freedom increase, the value of t decreases. *This makes it easier to reject the null hypothesis when sample size is large* (and thus one of the criticisms of null hypothesis significance testing).

6.1.1.8.3 The t Test

Now that we have covered the theoretical distribution underlying the test of a single mean for an unknown σ, we can go ahead and look at the inferential test. First, the null and alternative hypotheses for the t test are written in the same fashion as for the z test presented earlier. Thus, for a two-tailed test we have the same notation as previously presented:

$$H_0: \mu = 100 \quad \text{or} \quad H_0: \mu - 100 = 0$$
$$H_1: \mu \neq 100 \quad \text{or} \quad H_1: \mu - 100 \neq 0$$

The test statistic t is determined as follows:

$$t = \frac{\bar{Y} - \mu_0}{s_{\bar{Y}}}$$

The critical values for the t distribution are obtained from the t table in Table A.2 in the Appendix, where you take into account the α level, whether the test is one or two tailed, and the degrees of freedom ($\nu = n - 1$). If the test statistic falls into a critical region, as defined by the critical values, then our conclusion is to *reject H_0*. If the test statistic does not fall into a critical region, then our conclusion is to *fail to reject H_0*. For the t test the critical values depend on the sample size, whereas for the z test the critical values do not.

As was the case for the z test, for the t test a confidence interval for μ_0 can be developed. The $(1 - \alpha)\%$ confidence interval is formed from

$$\bar{Y} \pm t_{cv} s_{\bar{Y}}$$

where t_{cv} is the critical value from the t table. If the hypothesized mean value m_0 is not contained in the interval, then our conclusion is to *reject H_0*. If the hypothesized mean value μ_0 is contained in the interval, then our conclusion is *fail to reject H_0*. The confidence interval procedure for the t test then is comparable to that for the z test.

6.1.1.8.4 An Example

Let us consider the entire t test process using the example that we saw earlier with Ott Lier in the opening scenario. A hockey coach wanted to determine whether the mean skating speed of his team differed from the hypothesized league mean speed of 12 seconds. The hypotheses are developed as a *two-tailed test* and written as follows:

$$H_0: \mu = 12 \quad \text{or} \quad H_0: \mu - 12 = 0$$

$$H_1: \mu \neq 12 \quad \text{or} \quad H_1: \mu - 12 \neq 0$$

Skating speed around the rink was timed for each of 16 players (data are given in Table 6.2 and on the website as "ch6skatingtime"). The mean speed of the team was $\bar{Y} = 10$ seconds with a standard deviation of $s_Y = 1.7889$ seconds. The standard error of the mean is then computed as follows:

$$s_{\bar{Y}} = \frac{s_Y}{\sqrt{n}} = \frac{1.7889}{\sqrt{16}} = 0.4472$$

We wish to conduct a t test at $\alpha = .05$, where we compute the test statistic t as

$$t = \frac{\bar{Y} - \mu_0}{s_{\bar{Y}}} = \frac{10 - 12}{0.4472} = -4.4722$$

We turn to the t table in Table A.2 in the Appendix and determine the critical values based on $\alpha_2 = .05$ and $v = 15$ degrees of freedom. The critical values are +2.131, which defines the upper-tail critical region, and −2.131, which defines the lower-tail critical region. Given that the test statistic t (i.e., −4.4722) falls into the lower-tail critical region (i.e., the test statistic is less than the lower-tail critical value), our decision is to *reject H_0* and conclude that the mean skating speed of this team is statistically significantly different from the hypothesized league mean speed at the .05 level of significance. A **95% confidence interval** can be computed as follows:

$$\bar{Y} \pm t_{cv} s_{\bar{Y}} = 10 \pm (2.131)(0.4472) = 10 \pm .9530 = (9.0470, 10.9530)$$

As the confidence interval does not contain the hypothesized mean value of 12, our conclusion is again to reject H_0. Thus, there is evidence to suggest that the mean skating speed of the team differs from the hypothesized league mean speed of 12 seconds.

TABLE 6.2

SPSS Output for Skating Example

Raw data: 8, 12, 9, 7, 8, 10, 9, 11, 13.5, 8.5, 10.5, 9.5, 11.5, 12.5, 9.5, 10.5

6.1.2 Sample Size

We will start our discussion of sufficient sample size for the one-sample t test by noting that there is a difference in having a sample size that produces *sufficiently powered results* as compared to a sample size that will produce *robust results*. **Robust results** mean that the results are still relatively accurate even if there are some violations of assumptions. Having robust results does *not* equate, necessarily, to having a sufficiently powered test (i.e., being able to detect a statistically significant difference if it exists). It is possible to have robust results for an underpowered test (i.e., assumptions are met, but the sample size is not large enough for detecting a difference if it is there). And it is also possible to have a sufficiently powered test that does not produce robust results (i.e., sample size is sufficient for detecting a difference if it is there, but assumptions have been violated). It is a common myth that a sample size of 30 is sufficient for conducting a one-sample t test (or generally any of the three t tests). We have also seen researchers say that a sample size of 20 is sufficient. Other researchers say that as long as the normality assumption is met, regardless of the sample size, the results will be robust. *We do not condone going by any of these suggested guidelines for determining sample size.* There are no conventions that we recommend for sample size. Rather, we encourage researchers to conduct a power analysis to determine the sample size needed for sufficient power.

6.1.3 Power

In this section we complete our discussion of Type II error (β) and power ($1 - \beta$). First, we return to our rain example and discuss the entire decision-making context. Then we describe the factors that determine power.

6.1.3.1 *The Full Decision-Making Context*

Previously, we defined Type II error as the probability of failing to reject H_0 when H_0 is really false. In other words, in reality H_0 is false, yet we made a decision error and did not reject H_0. The probability associated with a Type II error is denoted by β . **Power** is a related concept and is defined as the *probability of rejecting* H_0 *when* H_0 *is really false*. In other words, in reality H_0 is false, and we made the correct decision to reject H_0. The probability associated with power is denoted by ($1 - \beta$). Let us return to our "rain" example to describe Type I and Type II errors and power more completely.

The full decision-making context for the rain example is given in Figure 6.5. The distribution on the left-hand side of the figure is the sampling distribution when H_0 is true, meaning in reality it does not rain. The vertical line represents the critical value for deciding whether to carry an umbrella or not. To the left of the vertical line we do not carry an umbrella, and to the right side of the vertical line we do carry an umbrella. For the no-rain sampling distribution on the left, there are two possibilities. *First, we do not carry an umbrella and it does not rain.* This is the *unshaded* portion under the no-rain sampling distribution to the left of the vertical line. This is a *correct decision*, and the probability associated with this decision is $1 - \alpha$. *Second, we do carry an umbrella and it does not rain.* This is the *shaded* portion under the no-rain sampling distribution to the right of the vertical line. This is an *incorrect decision*, a Type I error, and the probability associated with this decision is $\alpha/2$ in either the upper or lower tail, and α collectively.

The distribution on the right-hand side of the figure is the sampling distribution when H_0 is false, meaning in reality it does rain. For the rain sampling distribution, there are two

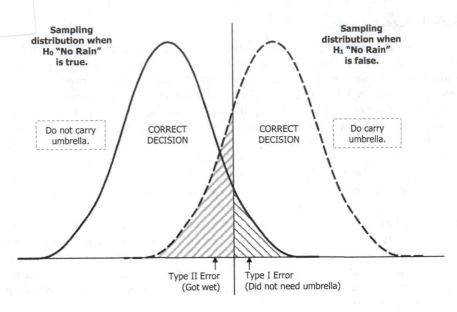

FIGURE 6.5
Sampling distributions for the rain case.

possibilities. *First, we do carry an umbrella and it does rain*. This is the *unshaded* portion under the rain sampling distribution to the right of the vertical line. This is a *correct decision* and the probability associated with this decision is $1 - \beta$, or power. *Second, we do not carry an umbrella and it does rain*. This is the *shaded* portion under the rain sampling distribution to the left of the vertical line. This is an *incorrect decision*, a Type II error, and the probability associated with this decision is β.

As a second illustration, consider again the example intelligence test situation. This situation is depicted in Figure 6.6. The distribution on the left-hand side of the figure is the sampling distribution of $\bar{Y}$ when H_0 is true, meaning in reality $\mu = 100$. The distribution on the right-hand side of the figure is the sampling distribution of $\bar{Y}$ when H_1 is true, meaning in reality $\mu = 115$ (and in this example, while there are two critical values, only the right tail matters as that relates to the H_1 sampling distribution). The vertical line represents the critical value for deciding whether to reject the null hypothesis or not. To the left of the vertical line we do not reject H_0 and to the right of the vertical line we reject H_0. For the H_0 is true sampling distribution on the left, there are two possibilities. First, we do not reject H_0 and H_0 is really true. This is the *unshaded* portion under the H_0 is true sampling distribution to the *left* of the vertical line. This is a *correct decision* and the probability associated with this decision is $1 - \alpha$. Second, we reject H_0 and H_0 is true. This is the *shaded* portion under the H_0 is true sampling distribution to the *right* of the vertical line. This is an *incorrect decision*, a Type I error, and the probability associated with this decision is $\alpha/2$ in either the upper or lower tail, and α collectively.

The distribution on the right-hand side of the figure is the sampling distribution when H_0 is false, and in particular, when $H_1: \mu = 115$ is true. This is a specific sampling distribution when H_0 is false, and other possible sampling distributions can also be examined (e.g., $\mu = 85$, 110, etc.). For the $H_1: \mu = 115$ is true sampling distribution, there are two possibilities. First, we do reject H_0 as H_0 is really false, and $H_1: \mu = 115$ is really true. This is the *unshaded* portion under the $H_1: \mu = 115$ is true sampling distribution to the right of the vertical line.

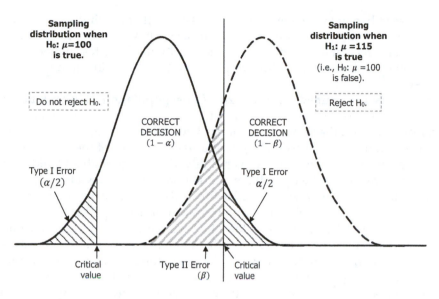

FIGURE 6.6
Sampling distributions for the intelligence test case.

This is a *correct decision*, and the probability associated with this decision is $1 - \beta$, or power. Second, we do not reject H_0, H_0 is really false, and H_1: $\mu = 115$ is really true. This is the *shaded* portion under the H_1: $\mu = 115$ is true sampling distribution to the left of the vertical line. This is an *incorrect decision*, a Type II error, and the probability associated with this decision is β.

6.1.3.2 Power Determinants

Power is determined by five different factors: (1) level of significance, (2) sample size, (3) population standard deviation, (4) difference between the true population mean μ and the hypothesized mean value μ_0, and (5) directionality of the test (i.e., one- or two-tailed test). Let us talk about each of these factors in more detail.

First, power is determined by the level of significance, α. As α increases, power increases. Thus, if α increases from .05 to .10, then power will increase. This would occur in Figure 6.6 if the vertical line were shifted to the left (thus creating a larger critical region and thereby making it easier to reject the null hypothesis). This would increase the alpha level and also increase power. This factor is under the control of the researcher as the researcher is the one to establish α.

Second, power is determined by sample size. As sample size n increases, power increases. Thus, if sample size increases, meaning we have a sample that consists of a larger proportion of the population, this will cause the standard error of the mean to decrease, as there is less sampling error with larger samples. In our figure, this would also result in the vertical line being moved to the left (again thereby creating a larger critical region and thereby making it easier to reject the null hypothesis). In addition, because a larger sample yields a smaller standard error, it will be easier to reject H_0 (all else being equal) as sample size increases, and the confidence intervals generated will also be narrower. This factor is *theoretically* under the control of the researcher. In theory, researchers have access to populations that are sufficient for drawing the sample size needed for sufficient power.

In practice, researchers may have access to populations that are limited in size, and thus regardless of what sample size is needed for sufficient power, they simply don't have a population that meets that requirement. In the latter situation, the researcher may consider adjustments on other factors that influence power so that they can still have a sufficiently powered test.

Third, power is determined by the size of the population standard deviation, σ. Although not under the researcher's control, as the population standard deviation increases, power decreases. Thus, if the population standard deviation *increases*, meaning the variability in the population is larger, this will cause the standard error of the mean to increase as there is more sampling error with larger variability. In our figure, this would result in the vertical line being moved to the right. If the population standard deviation *decreases*, meaning the variability in the population is smaller, this will cause the standard error of the mean to decrease as there is less sampling error with smaller variability. This would result in the vertical line in our figure being moved to the left. Considering, for example, the one-sample mean test, the standard error of the mean is the denominator of the test statistic formula. When the standard error term decreases, the denominator is smaller, and thus the test statistic value becomes larger (and thereby easier to reject the null hypothesis).

Fourth, power is determined by the difference between the true population mean, μ, and the hypothesized mean value, μ_0. Although not always under the researcher's control (only in true experiments), as the difference between the true population mean and the hypothesized mean value increases, power increases. Thus, if the difference between the true population mean and the hypothesized mean value is large, it will be easier to correctly reject H_0. This would result in greater separation between the two sampling distributions. In other words, the entire H_1 is true sampling distribution would be shifted to the right. Consider, for example, the one-sample mean test. The numerator is the difference between the means. The larger the numerator (holding the denominator constant), the more likely it will be to reject the null hypothesis.

Finally, power is determined by directionality and type of statistical procedure—whether we conduct a one- or a two-tailed test as well as the type of test of inference. There is greater power in a one-tailed test, such as when μ > 100, than in a two-tailed test. In a one-tailed test the vertical line in our figure will be shifted to the left, creating a larger rejection region. This factor is *theoretically* under the researcher's control, however it may be hard to justify a one-tailed test if there is a complete absence of theory to support directionality. There is also often greater power in conducting parametric as compared to nonparametric tests of inference (we will talk more about parametric vs. nonparametric tests in later chapters). This factor is under the researcher's control to some extent depending on the scale of measurement of the variables and the extent to which the assumptions of parametric tests are met.

Power has become of much greater interest and concern to the applied researcher in recent years. We begin by distinguishing between *a priori* **power**, when power is determined as a study is being planned or designed (i.e., prior to the study), and **post hoc power**, when power is determined after the study has been conducted and the data analyzed.

For *a priori* power, if you want to ensure a certain amount of power in a study, then you can determine what sample size would be needed to achieve such a level of power. This requires the input of characteristics such as alpha level; the estimated effect size, which requires knowledge of difference between the true population mean (μ) and the hypothesized mean value (μ_0), as well as the standard deviation; and one- versus two-tailed test. Alternatively, one could determine power given each of those characteristics. This can be done by either using statistical software (e.g., G*Power), or by using tables, with the most definitive collection of tables being in Cohen (1988).

For post hoc power (also called *observed power*), most statistical software packages (e.g., SPSS, SAS) will compute this as part of the analysis for many types of inferential statistics (e.g., analysis of variance). However, even though post hoc power is routinely reported in some journals, it has been found to have some flaws. For example, Hoenig and Heisey (2001) concluded that it should not be used to aid in interpreting nonsignificant results. They found that low power may indicate a small effect (e.g., a small mean difference) rather than an underpowered study. Thus, increasing sample size may not make much of a difference. Yuan and Maxwell (2005) found that observed power is almost always biased (too high or too low), except when true power is .50. Therefore, we do not recommend the sole use of post hoc power to determine sample size in the next study; rather, we recommended that CIs be used in addition to post hoc power. (An example presented later in this chapter will use G*Power to illustrate both *a priori* sample size requirements given desired power and post hoc power analysis.)

6.1.4 Effect Size

We have discussed the inferential test of a single mean in terms of statistical significance. However, are statistically significant results always *practically* (or *clinically*) *important*? In other words, if a result is statistically significant, should we make a big deal out of this result in a practical or clinical sense? Regardless of the results of the null hypothesis significance test, are the results clinically important such that they make a difference? Consider again the simple example where the null and alternative hypotheses are as follows.

$$H_0: \mu = 100 \quad \text{or} \quad H_0: \mu - 100 = 0$$

$$H_1: \mu \neq 100 \quad \text{or} \quad H_1: \mu - 100 \neq 0$$

A sample mean intelligence test score of $\bar{Y} = 101$ is observed for a sample size of $n = 2000$ and a known population standard deviation of $\sigma_Y = 15$. If we perform the test at the .01 level of significance, we find we are able to reject H_0 even though the observed mean is only 1 unit away from the hypothesized mean value. The reason is, because the sample size is rather large, a rather small standard error of the mean is computed $\left(\sigma_{\bar{Y}} = 0.3354 \right)$, and we thus reject H_0 because the test statistic ($z = 2.9815$) exceeds the critical value ($z = 2.5758$). Holding the mean and standard deviation constant, if we had a sample size of 200 instead of 2000, the standard error becomes much larger $\left(\sigma_{\bar{Y}} = 1.0607 \right)$, and we thus fail to reject H_0 because the test statistic ($z = 0.9428$) does not exceed the critical value ($z = 2.5758$). From this example we can see how the sample size can drive the results of the hypothesis test, and how it is possible that statistical significance can be influenced simply as an artifact of sample size.

Should we make a big deal out of an intelligence test sample mean that is 1 unit away from the hypothesized mean intelligence? In other words, does this difference have practical significance—is it clinically important? The answer is "maybe not." If we gather enough sample data, any small difference, no matter how small, can wind up being statistically significant. Larger samples are simply more likely to yield statistically significant results. On the other hand, *practical or clinical significance is not entirely a statistical matter*. It is also a matter for the substantive field under investigation. Thus, the meaningfulness of a "small difference" (or a moderate or large one) is for the substantive area to determine. All that inferential statistics can really determine is statistical significance. However, we should always keep practical or clinical significance in mind when interpreting our findings.

As we have already noted, in recent years, a major debate has been ongoing in the statistical community about the role of significance testing. The debate centers on whether null hypothesis significance testing (NHST) best suits the needs of researchers. At one extreme, some argue that NHST is fine as is. At the other extreme, others argue that NHST should be totally abandoned. In the middle, yet others argue that NHST should be supplemented with measures of effect size, which are metrics for practical or clinical significance. In this text we have taken the middle road believing that more information is a better choice. Many other researchers agree with this, and if you follow the American Psychological Association (APA) style guide (2020), you'll find that they agree as well:

APA, for example, stresses that *NHST is but a starting point* and that additional reporting elements, such as effect sizes, confidence intervals, and extensive description are needed to convey the most complete meaning of the results. . . . [C]omplete reporting of all tested hypotheses and estimates of appropriate effect sizes and confidence intervals are the *minimum expectations* for all APA journals.

(p. 87, italics added for emphasis)

6.1.4.1 Cohen's Delta

Let us now formally introduce the notion of **effect size**, which again *are metrics for practical or clinical significance*. While there are a number of different measures of effect size, the most commonly used measure is **Cohen's delta (δ)** for population data or *d* for sample data (Cohen, 1988). For the *population case* of the one-sample mean test, Cohen's δ is computed as follows:

$$\delta = \frac{\mu - \mu_0}{\sigma}$$

For the corresponding *sample case*, **Cohen's *d*** is computed as follows:

$$d = \frac{\bar{Y} - \mu_0}{s}$$

Using the skating time example presented earlier, we find the following:

$$d = \frac{10 - 12}{1.7889} = -1.118$$

For the one-sample mean test, *d* indicates how many standard deviations the sample mean is from the hypothesized mean. Thus, if *d* = 1.0, the sample mean is one standard deviation away from the hypothesized mean. In this example, *d* indicates that there is slightly more than one standard deviation difference between our sample mean skating speed and the hypothesized mean value. The negative value for *d* is simply a reflection of the fact that our sample skating speed is less than what we hypothesized and that our sample is about one standard deviation quicker than what was hypothesized.

Cohen has proposed the following subjective standards for the social and behavioral sciences as a convention for interpreting *d*: small effect size, *d* = .2; medium effect size, *d* = .5; large effect size, *d* = .8. Applying Cohen's subjective standards for interpreting the size of your effect should always be a last resort. Rather, a good starting place for interpreting the size of an effect is to translate that effect back into a comparison within your study. In other words, contextualize the effect with your own sample. For example, if you find an effect size of 1.0, you can say that there is one standard deviation difference between your sample mean and the hypothesized mean value. More specifically, you can say that 84% of the cases in your sample will be above the hypothesized mean (recall the normal distribution and when $z = 1.0$, 84% of the distribution is below that value?). Researchers may want to review online resources for interpreting Cohen's d (e.g., http://rpsychologist.com/d3/cohend/, an interactive tool that provides multiple types of interpretation given d). Interpretation of effect size can also be made based on a comparison to similar studies; what is considered a "small" effect using Cohen's rule of thumb may actually be quite large in comparison to other related studies that have been conducted. In lieu of a comparison to other studies, such as in those cases where there are no or minimal related studies, then Cohen's subjective standards may be considered.

6.1.4.2 Confidence Intervals for Cohen's Delta

Computing **confidence intervals for effect sizes** is also valuable. The benefit in creating confidence intervals for effect size values is similar to that of creating confidence intervals for parameter estimates—*confidence intervals for the effect size provide an added measure of precision that is not obtained from knowledge of the effect size alone.* Computing confidence intervals for effect size indices, however, is not as straightforward as simply plugging in known values into a formula. This is because d is a function of both the population mean and population standard deviation (Finch & Cumming, 2009), and the noncentrality parameter comes into play. Without going deep into the weeds, we'll provide an overview into the noncentrality parameter and what it means in relation to confidence intervals for effect sizes [readers who wish to learn more may want to consult Smithson (2003)]. A central t distribution occurs when we subtract the true population mean from the sample mean. A **noncentral t distribution** is not distributed around zero but around some other point, which is referred to as the **noncentrality parameter (ncp)**. If $\mu = \mu_0$, then ncp is 0 and the distribution is a central t. Effect size d is a linear function of the noncentrality parameter, and thus putting confidence limits on ncp will allow us to compute confidence intervals for effect size d.

A nice online calculator for computing the one-sample t test confidence interval for effect size d using the noncentrality parameter is available at https://effect-size-calculator.herokuapp.com (Uanhoro, 2017). As we see in Figure 6.7, five inputs are required: sample mean, population mean (where the population mean is the hypothesized mean value), sample standard deviation, sample size, and confidence interval (i.e., the complement of alpha). Cohen's d is -1.118, as noted previously as well, with confidence intervals of -1.734 and $-.477$. Putting this in context of our skating example, if multiple random samples were drawn from the population, 95% of the samples could expect, at minimum, about one-half and, at maximum, up to nearly 2 standard deviation units quicker skating speed relative to the hypothesized mean of 12.

Interested readers are referred to appropriate sources to learn more about confidence intervals for d (e.g., Algina & Keselman, 2003; Algina, Keselman, & Penfield, 2005; Cumming & Calin-Jageman, 2017; Cumming & Finch, 2001).

While a complete discussion of issues discussed in this section is beyond this text, further information on effect sizes can be seen in special sections of *Educational and Psychological Measurement* (April 2001; August 2001), Grissom and Kim (2005), and Grissom and Kim (2012), among many other resources, while additional material on NHST can be viewed in Harlow, Mulaik, and Steiger (1997) and a special section of *Educational and Psychological*

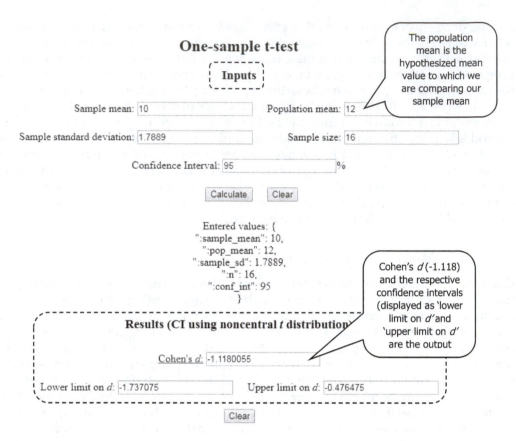

FIGURE 6.7
Effect size *d* and confidence interval of *d*.

Measurement (October 2000). Additionally, style manuals (e.g., American Psychological Association, 2020) often provide useful guidelines on reporting effect size.

6.1.5 Assumptions

In order to use the theoretical *t* distribution to determine critical values, we must assume that $Y_i \sim N(\mu, \sigma^2)$ (i.e., *Y* is approximately normally distributed with a population mean, μ, and population variance, σ^2) and that the observations are independent of each other (also referred to as being "independent and identically distributed," or IID). Thus, there are two assumptions for the one-sample *t* test: independence and normality.

6.1.5.1 Independence

In terms of the assumption of *independence*, this means that the measurements for each unit in our sample have not been influenced by the measurements of the other units and that they are not related in any way. This assumption is met when the cases or units in a sample have been *randomly sampled* from the population. Thus, the extent to which this assumption is met is dependent on the sampling design. In reality, random selection is often difficult in education and the social sciences, and may or may not be feasible for a particular study.

6.1.5.2 Normality

In terms of the distribution of scores on Y, we assume that the population of scores on Y is normally distributed with some population mean, μ, and some population variance, σ^2. The most important assumption for the t test is **normality** of the population. Conventional research has shown that the t test is very robust to nonnormality for a two-tailed test except for very small samples (e.g., $n < 5$). The t test is not as robust to nonnormality for a one-tailed test, even for samples as large as 40 or more (Noreen, 1989; Wilcox, 1993). Recall from Chapter 5 on the central limit theorem that when sample size increases, the sampling distribution of the mean becomes more nearly normal. As the shape of a population distribution may be unknown, conservatively one would do better to conduct a two-tailed test when sample size is small, unless some normality evidence is available.

However, more recent research suggests that small departures from normality can inflate the standard error of the mean (as the standard deviation is larger) (Basu & DasGupta, 1995; Wilcox, 2003, 2012). This can reduce power and also affect control over Type I error. Thus, a cavalier attitude about ignoring nonnormality may not be the best approach, and if nonnormality *is* an issue, other procedures, such as the nonparametric Kolmogorov-Smirnov one-sample test, should be considered.

Many different tools can be used for testing the assumption of normality, and researchers should approach testing this assumption as collecting multiple forms of evidence to best understand the extent to which the assumption was met. Sample statistics, such as skewness and kurtosis, can be reviewed. Values within an absolute value of 2.0 suggest evidence of normality. We can also divide the skew and kurtosis values by their standard errors to get *standardized skew and kurtosis* values. We can compare those values to a critical value (e.g., ± 1.65 if $\alpha = .10$; ± 1.96 if $\alpha = .05$; ± 2.06 if $\alpha = .01$) and determine if there is statistically significant skew and/or kurtosis. **D'Agostino's test** (D'Agostino, 1970) can be used to examine the null hypothesis that skewness equals zero, with a statistically significant D'Agostino's test indicating that there is statistically significant skewness. For kurtosis, we can use the **Bonett-Seier test for Geary's kurtosis** (Bonett & Seier, 2002). The null hypothesis states that data should have a Geary's kurtosis value equal to $\sqrt{2/\pi} = .7979$. Thus, a statistically significant Bonett-Seier test for Geary's kurtosis would indicate that there is statistically significant kurtosis. Thus, with these tests, as with the Kolmogorov-Smirnov (K-S) and the Shapiro-Wilk (S-W), we do *not* want to find statistically significant results.

A few other statistics can be used to gauge normality as well. Quantile-quantile (Q-Q) plots are also often examined to determine evidence of normality. Q-Q plots are graphs that depict quantiles of the sample distribution to quantiles of the theoretical normal distribution. Points that fall on or closely to the diagonal line of the Q-Q plot suggest evidence of normality. The detrended normal Q-Q plot is another graph that can be reviewed. This plot provides evidence of normality when the points exhibit little or no pattern around zero (the horizontal line); however, due to subjectivity in determining the extent of a pattern, this graph can often be difficult to interpret. Thus, in many cases, you may wish to rely more heavily on the other forms of evidence of normality. A summary of several different types of evidence for examining normality is provided in Box 6.1.

BOX 6.1 Evidence for Testing the Assumption of Normality

Evidence	Interpretation for Providing Evidence of Normality
Boxplot	Normality suggested when the quartiles are relatively evenly distributed with no outliers.
Histogram	Normality suggested with a relatively bell-shaped curve.
Skewness	Values within an absolute value of 2.0 suggest evidence of normality.
Kurtosis	Values within an absolute value of 2.0 suggest evidence of normality.
Standardized skew and standardized kurtosis	Divide the skew and kurtosis values by their standard errors to get standardized skew and kurtosis values. Compare those values to a critical value (e.g., ± 1.65 if $\alpha = .10$; ± 1.96 if $\alpha = .05$; ± 2.06 if $\alpha = .01$). Standardized skew and kurtosis that are less than the critical value suggest evidence of normality.
D'Agostino's test	Tests the null hypothesis that skewness equals zero, with a statistically significant D'Agostino's test indicating that there is statistically significant skewness.
Bonett-Seier test for Geary's kurtosis	Tests the null hypothesis that data should have a Geary's kurtosis value equal to $\sqrt{2/\pi} = .7979$. A statistically significant test indicates that there is statistically significant kurtosis.
Quantile-quantile (Q-Q) plots	Plots that depict quantiles of the sample distribution to quantiles of the theoretical normal distribution. Points that fall on or closely to the diagonal line of the Q-Q plot suggest evidence of normality.
Detrended quantile-quantile plot	Evidence of normality is provided when the points exhibit little or no pattern around zero (the horizontal line).
Kolmogorov-Smirnov (K-S) and Shapiro-Wilk (S-W) tests	K-S and S-W are formal tests of normality. K-S is conservative; S-W test is usually considered more powerful and is recommended for use with small sample sizes ($n < 50$). Non-statistically significant K-S and S-W results are interpreted to say that our distribution is *not* statistically significantly different than a normal distribution.

6.2 Computing Inferences About a Single Mean Using SPSS

Here we consider what SPSS has to offer in the way of testing hypotheses about a single mean. As with most statistical software, the *t* test is included as an option in SPSS, but the *z* test is not. Thus, instructions for determining the one-sample *t* test using SPSS are presented first.

Step 1. To conduct the one-sample *t* test, go to "Analyze" in the top pulldown menu, then select "Compare Means," and then select "One-Sample T Test." Following the steps in the screenshot shown in Figure 6.8 produces the "One-Sample T Test" dialog box.

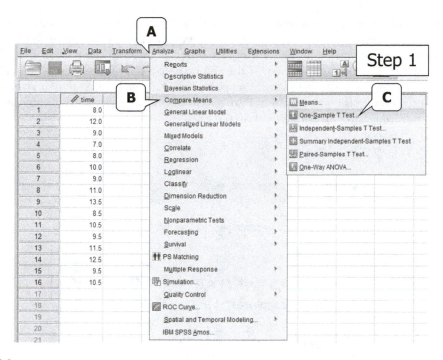

FIGURE 6.8
Step 1: One-sample *t* test.

Step 2. Next, from the main "One-Sample T Test" dialog box, click the variable of interest from the list on the left (e.g., "time"), and move it into the "Test Variable" box by clicking the arrow button. At the bottom right of the screen is a box for "Test Value," where you indicate the hypothesized value (e.g., "12") (see the screenshot in Figure 6.9). It's obviously very important not to fail to input your hypothesized value as doing so will test against the default, which is zero!

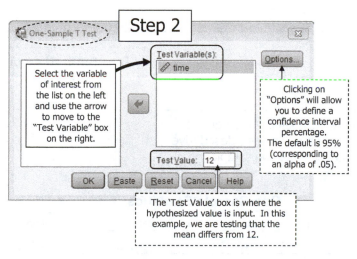

FIGURE 6.9
Step 2: One-sample *t* test.

Step 3 (optional). The default alpha level in SPSS is .05, and thus the default corresponding confidence interval is 95%. If you wish to test your hypothesis at an alpha level other than .05 (and thus obtain confidence intervals other than 95%), then click the "Options" button located in the top-right corner of the main dialog box. From here, the confidence interval percentage can be adjusted to correspond to the alpha level at which your hypothesis is being tested (see the screenshot in Figure 6.10). For purposes of this example, the test has been generated using an alpha level of .05.

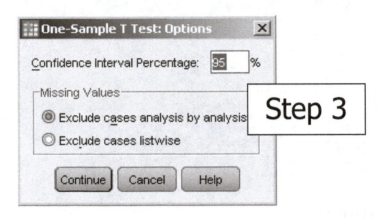

FIGURE 6.10
Step 3: One-sample *t* test.

The one-sample *t* test output for the skating example is provided in Table 6.3.

TABLE 6.3
SPSS Output for Skating Example

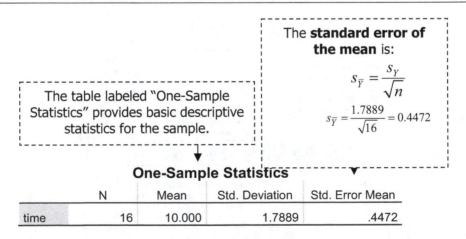

The **standard error of the mean** is:

$$s_{\bar{Y}} = \frac{s_Y}{\sqrt{n}}$$

$$s_{\bar{Y}} = \frac{1.7889}{\sqrt{16}} = 0.4472$$

The table labeled "One-Sample Statistics" provides basic descriptive statistics for the sample.

One-Sample Statistics

	N	Mean	Std. Deviation	Std. Error Mean
time	16	10.000	1.7889	.4472

TABLE 6.3 (continued)
SPSS Output for Skating Example

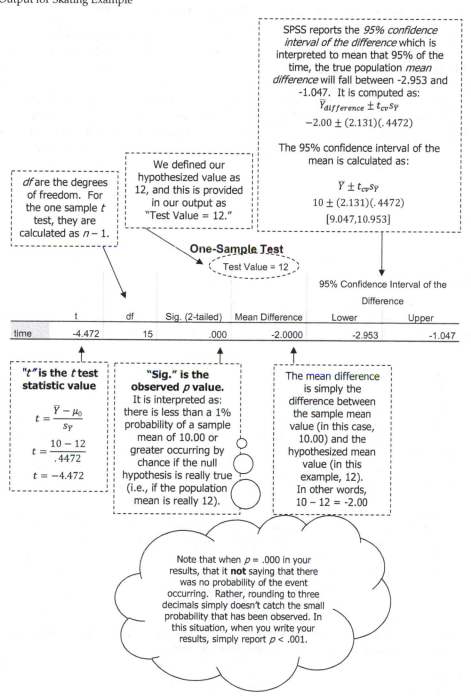

SPSS reports the *95% confidence interval of the difference* which is interpreted to mean that 95% of the time, the true population *mean difference* will fall between -2.953 and -1.047. It is computed as:

$$\overline{Y}_{difference} \pm t_{cv}s_{\overline{Y}}$$

$$-2.00 \pm (2.131)(.4472)$$

The 95% confidence interval of the mean is calculated as:

$$\overline{Y} \pm t_{cv}s_{\overline{Y}}$$

$$10 \pm (2.131)(.4472)$$

$$[9.047, 10.953]$$

We defined our hypothesized value as 12, and this is provided in our output as "Test Value = 12."

df are the degrees of freedom. For the one sample *t* test, they are calculated as $n-1$.

One-Sample Test

Test Value = 12

95% Confidence Interval of the Difference

	t	df	Sig. (2-tailed)	Mean Difference	Lower	Upper
time	-4.472	15	.000	-2.0000	-2.953	-1.047

"*t*" is the *t* test statistic value

$$t = \frac{\overline{Y} - \mu_0}{s_{\overline{Y}}}$$

$$t = \frac{10 - 12}{.4472}$$

$$t = -4.472$$

"Sig." is the observed *p* value. It is interpreted as: there is less than a 1% probability of a sample mean of 10.00 or greater occurring by chance if the null hypothesis is really true (i.e., if the population mean is really 12).

The mean difference is simply the difference between the sample mean value (in this case, 10.00) and the hypothesized mean value (in this example, 12). In other words, $10 - 12 = -2.00$.

Note that when $p = .000$ in your results, that it **not** saying that there was no probability of the event occurring. Rather, rounding to three decimals simply doesn't catch the small probability that has been observed. In this situation, when you write your results, simply report $p < .001$.

6.3 Computing Inferences About a Single Mean Using R

Next we consider **R** for the one-sample *t* test. The scripts are provided within the blocks with additional annotation to assist in understanding how the commands work. Should you want to write reminder notes and annotation to yourself as you write the commands in **R** (and we highly encourage doing so), remember that any text that follows a hashtag (i.e., #) is annotation only and not part of the **R** script. Thus, you can write annotations directly into **R** with hashtags. We encourage this practice so that when you call up the commands in the future, you'll understand what the various lines of code are doing. You may think you'll remember what you did. However, trust us. There is a good chance that you won't. Thus, consider it best practice when using **R** to annotate heavily!

6.3.1 Reading Data into R

```
getwd()
```

R is always pointed to a directory on your computer. To find out which directory it is pointed to, run this "get working directory" command. We will assume that we need to change the working directory, and will use the next line of code to set the working directory to the desired path.

```
setwd("E:/Folder")
```

To set the working directory, use the *setwd* function and change what is in quotation marks here to your file location. Also, if you are copying the directory name, it will copy in slashes. You will need to change the slash (i.e., \) to forward slash (i.e., /). Note that you need your destination name within quotation marks in the parentheses.

```
Ch6_skate <- read.csv("Ch6_skate.csv")
```

The *read.csv* function reads your data into **R**. What's to the left of the <- will be what the data will be called in **R**. In this example, we're calling the **R** dataframe "Ch6_skate." What's to the right of the <- tells **R** to find this particular .csv file. In this example, our file is called "Ch6_skate.csv." Make sure the extension (i.e., .csv) is included in your script. Also note that the name of your file should be in quotation marks within the parentheses.

```
names(Ch6_skate)
```

The *names* function will produce a list of variable names for each dataframe as follows. This is a good check to make sure your data have been read in correctly.

FIGURE 6.11
Reading data into **R**.

```
[1] "time"
```

```
View(Ch6_skate)
```

The *View* function will let you view the dataset in spreadsheet format in RStudio.

```
summary(Ch6_skate)
```

The *summary* function will produce basic descriptive statistics on all the variables in your dataframe. This is a great way to quickly check to see if the data have been read in correctly and get a feel for your data, if you haven't already. The output from the summary statement for this dataframe looks like this:

```
         time
Min.    : 7.000
1st Qu.: 8.875
Median : 9.750
Mean    :10.000
3rd Qu.:11.125
Max.    :13.500
```

FIGURE 6.11 (continued)
Reading data into **R**.

6.3.2 Generating the One-Sample *t* Test

```
install.packages("devtools")
```

We will use the *devtools* package in **R** to compute our one sample *t* test. The *install.packages* function will install the package. We only need to install the package once.

```
library(devtools)
```

Once the package is installed, we load it into our library using the *library* function, and we will need to load it into the library whenever we start a new session in **R**.

```
Ch6_onet <- t.test(Ch6_skate$time,
                   mu = 12,
                   alternative = "two.sided")
```

We use the *t.test* function to generate the one sample *t* test. We use the variable *time* from our dataframe, *Ch6_skate*. We are testing our sample mean to a hypothesized mean of 12 (i.e., *mu* = 12). And we are conducting a two-tailed test (i.e., *alternative* = "*two.sided*"). We are creating an object named *Ch6_onet* from the model we generate.

FIGURE 6.12
Generating the One-Sample *t* Test

Ch6_onet

This script will output the results from our one sample *t* test into the RStudio console. We see our test statistic value, $t = -4.4721$, with 15 degrees of freedom, and a *p* value of < .001 (specifically $p = .0004475$). The 95% confidence interval of the mean is 9.05 to 10.95. The mean of our variable is 10 and is provided in the 'sample estimates' output.

```
        One Sample t-test

data: Ch6_skate$time

t = -4.4721, df = 15, p-value = 0.0004475

alternative hypothesis: true mean is not equal to 12

95 percent confidence interval:
  9.046787 10.953213

sample estimates:
mean of x
      10
```

FIGURE 6.12 (continued)
Generating the One-Sample *t* Test

6.4 Data Screening

Recall that the one-sample *t* test rests on two assumptions: independence of observations and normality. In terms of data screening to examine the extent to which assumptions were met, we will focus on normality, as independence is a matter of sampling method.

6.4.1 Generating Normality Evidence

As alluded to earlier in the chapter, understanding the distributional shape of your variable, specifically the extent to which normality is a reasonable assumption, is important. In earlier chapters, we saw how we could use the Explore tool in SPSS to generate a number of useful descriptive statistics. In conducting our one-sample *t* test, we can again use Explore to examine the extent to which the assumption of normality is met for our sample distribution. As the general steps for accessing Explore from the top toolbar in SPSS have been presented in previous chapters (e.g., Chapter 4), they will not be reiterated here. Thus, we will begin from the main dialog box. We first move the variable of interest to the "Dependent List" box in the main Explore dialog box. Next, click "Plots" in the upper-right corner. Place a checkmark in the boxes for "Normality plots with tests" and also for "Histogram" (see the screenshot in Figure 6.13a).

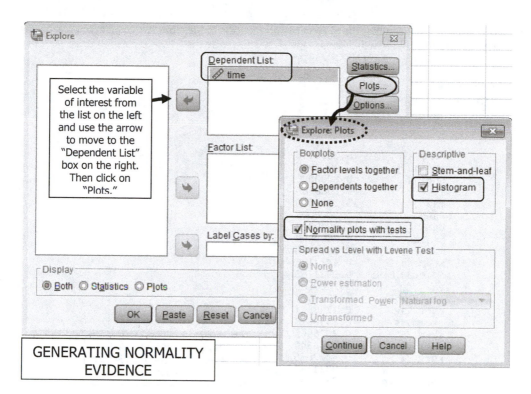

GENERATING NORMALITY
EVIDENCE

Working in **R**, we can generate normality evidence as well.

```
install.packages("pastecs")
```

The *install.packages* function will install the *pastecs* package, which we will use to generate various forms of normality evidence.

```
library(pastecs)
```

The *library* function will load the *pastecs* package.

```
stat.desc(Ch6_skate,
          norm = TRUE)
```

The *stat.desc* function will generate normality indices on all variables in the dataframe as follows (had we wanted to generate for specific variables, rather than "Ch6_skate," our script would have read "Ch6_skate$VariableName"). We see skew (.25) and kurtosis (−.98) *(wait—these aren't the same values as what we found with SPSS; if that's what you're thinking, hold that thought!)*, along with $SW = .98$, $p = .98$ for the "time" variable. All indicate that the assumption of normality has been met. As we will see later, we can divide the skew and kurtosis values by their standard errors to get a standardized value that can be used to determine if the skew and/or kurtosis is statistically different from zero. Because this output provides "2SE," we would simply divide this value by 2 to arrive at the standard error.

FIGURE 6.13a
Generating normality evidence.

Note: You may have noticed that the skewness and kurtosis values that we've just generated differ from what we found in SPSS, which was skew = .299 and kurtosis = −.483. *This is because there are different ways to calculate skewness and kurtosis.*

FIGURE 6.13a (continued)
Generating normality evidence.

```
                            time
nbr.val          16.0000000
nbr.null          0.0000000
nbr.na            0.0000000
min               7.0000000
max              13.5000000
range             6.5000000
sum             160.0000000
median            9.7500000
mean             10.0000000
SE.mean           0.4472136
CI.mean.0.95      0.9532132
var               3.2000000
std.dev           1.7888544
coef.var          0.1788854
skewness          0.2456618
skew.2SE          0.2176665
kurtosis         -0.9766846
kurt.2SE         -0.4477026
normtest.W        0.9821789
normtest.p        0.9784739
```

> Shapiro Wilk's is labeled *normtest.W.* The *p* value for Shapiro Wilk's is *normtest.p.*

Let's use another package in **R** to calculate these statistics with different algorithms.

```
install.packages("e1071")
```

The *install.packages* function will install the *e1071* package that we will use to generate skewness and kurtosis. (If this package is already installed on your computer, you only need to load it into your library, which is the next command.)

```
library(e1071)
```

The *library* function will load the *e1071* package.

```
skewness(Ch4_quiz$quiz, type=3)
skewness(Ch4_quiz$quiz, type=2)
skewness(Ch4_quiz$quiz, type=1)
```

The *skewness* function will generate skewness statistics on the variable(s) we specify. The *type=* script defines how skewness is calculated. Specifying *type=2* will use the algorithm that is used by SPSS. Readers interested in learning more, including the algorithms for each of the three methods, are encouraged to review Joanes and Gill (1998). We see that using *type=2*, our skew is .299, the same value as generated using SPSS.

```
# skewness(Ch6_skate$time, type=3)
[1] 0.2456618
```

FIGURE 6.13b
Generating normality evidence.

```
# skewness(Ch6_skate$time, type=2)
[1] 0.2994734

# skewness(Ch6_skate$time, type=1)
[1] 0.2706329
```

```
kurtosis(Ch6_skate$time, type=3)
kurtosis(Ch6_skate$time, type=2)
kurtosis(Ch6_skate$time, type=1)
```

The *kurtosis* function will generate kurtosis statistics on the variable(s) we specify. The *type=* script defines how kurtosis is calculated. Specifying *type=2* will use the algorithm that is used by SPSS. Readers interested in learning more, including the algorithms for each of the three methods, are encouraged to review Joanes and Gill (1998). We see that using *type=2*, our kurtosis is −.483, the same value as generated using SPSS.

```
# kurtosis(Ch6_skate$time, type=3)
[1] -0.9766846

# kurtosis(Ch6_skate$time, type=2)
[1] -0.4833448

# kurtosis(Ch6_skate$time, type=1)
[1] -0.6979167
```

FIGURE 6.13b (continued)
Generating normality evidence.

6.4.2 Interpreting Normality Evidence

We have already developed a good understanding of how to interpret some forms of evidence of normality, including skewness and kurtosis, histograms, and boxplots. Using data from the hockey team, the histogram suggests relative normality (see Figure 6.14).

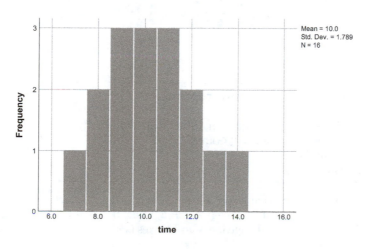

FIGURE 6.14
Histogram and boxplot.

Working in **R**, we can use the *ggplot2* package to produce a histogram.

```
install.packages("ggplot2")
```

The *install.packages* function will install the *ggplot2* package that we can use to create various graphs and plots. If this package is already installed on your computer, you can skip this step and just load it into your library (if not already loaded!).

```
library(ggplot2)
```

The *library* function will load the *ggplot2* package.

```
qplot(Ch6_skate$time, geom="histogram")
```

We can generate a very simple histogram, as seen in Figure 6.14b, using the *qplot* function, where "Ch6_skate$time" represents the variable "time" from our dataframe "Ch6_skate." The command *geom=histogram* tells **R** to generate a histogram.

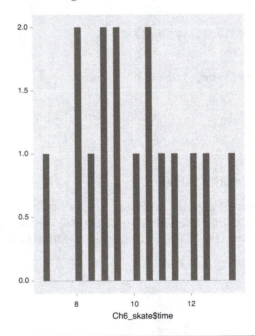

```
qplot(Ch6_skate$time, geom="histogram",
      binwidth=0.5,
          main = "Histogram for Skating Time",
      xlab = "Time", ylab = "Count",
      fill=I("gray"),
      col=I("white"))
```

We can add a few commands to change the width of the bars (i.e., *binwidth = 0.5*), color of the bars (i.e., *fill = I("gray")*), and outline of the bars (i.e., *col=I("white")*). We can also add a title (i.e., *main = "Histogram for Skating Time"*) and change the X and Y axes (*xlab = "Time", ylab = "Count"*).

FIGURE 6.14 (continued)
Histogram and boxplot.

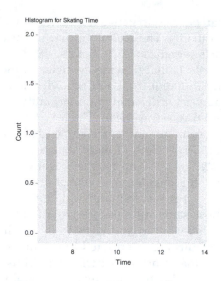

```
boxplot(Ch6_skate$time,ylab="Time")
```

We can also generate a boxplot of the "time" variable from the "Ch6_skate" dataframe using the *boxplot* function. We change the Y axis with the script *ylab = "Time."*

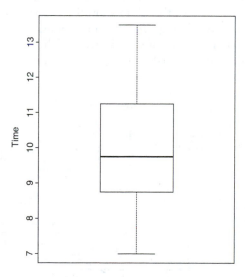

FIGURE 6.14 (continued)
Histogram and boxplot.

The skewness statistic is .299 and kurtosis is −.483—both within the range of an absolute value of 2.0, suggesting some evidence of normality. We can divide the skew and kurtosis values by their standard errors to get standardized skew and kurtosis values. We can review those values to a critical value (e.g., ±1.65 if alpha = .10; ±1.96 if alpha = .05; ±2.06 if alpha = .01) and determine if there is statistically significant skew and/or kurtosis. In this example, the standardized skew and kurtosis values are .530 and −.443, respectively. Both are well under ±1.96 (given alpha = .05), suggesting normality.

A few other statistics can be used to gauge normality as well. Using SPSS, we can obtain two statistical tests of normality. The **Kolmogorov-Smirnov (K-S)** (Chakravart, Laha, & Roy, 1967) with Lilliefor's significance (Lilliefors, 1967) and the **Shapiro-Wilk (S-W)** (Shapiro & Wilk, 1965) are tests that provide evidence of the extent to which our sample distribution is statistically different from a normal distribution. The K-S test tends to be conservative and lacks power for detecting nonnormality; thus, it is is not recommended (D'Agostino, Belanger, & D'Agostino, 1990). The S-W test is considered the more powerful of the two for testing normality and is recommended for use with small sample sizes ($n < 50$) (D'Agostino et al., 1990). Both of these statistics are generated from the selection of "Normality plots with tests." The output for the K-S and S-W tests is presented in Figure 6.15. As we have learned in this chapter, when the observed probability (i.e., p value which is reported in SPSS as "Sig.") is less than our stated alpha level, then we reject the null hypothesis. We follow those same rules of interpretation here. When testing the K-S and S-W for normality, we do *not* want to find statistically significant results. Nonstatistically significant K-S and S-W results are interpreted to say that our distribution is *not* statistically significantly different than a normal distribution. Thus, regardless of which test (K-S or S-W) we examine, both provide the same evidence—our sample distribution is not statistically significantly different than what would be expected from a normal distribution.

Working in **R**, **D'Agostino's test** (D'Agostino, 1970) can be used to examine the null hypothesis that skewness equals zero. Thus, a statistically significant D'Agostino's test would indicate that there is statistically significant skewness. For kurtosis, we can use the **Bonett-Seier test for Geary's kurtosis** (Bonett & Seier, 2002) for data that are normally distributed. The null hypothesis states that data should have a Geary's kurtosis value equal to $\sqrt{2/\pi} = .7979$. Thus, a statistically significant Bonett-Seier test for Geary's kurtosis would indicate that there is statistically significant kurtosis. Thus, with these tests, as with K-S and S-W, we do *not* want to find statistically significant results.

Descriptives

		Statistic	Std. Error
time	Mean	10.000	.4472
	95% Confidence Interval for Mean — Lower Bound	9.047	
	95% Confidence Interval for Mean — Upper Bound	10.953	
	5% Trimmed Mean	9.972	
	Median	9.750	
	Variance	3.200	
	Std. Deviation	1.7889	
	Minimum	7.0	
	Maximum	13.5	
	Range	6.5	
	Interquartile Range	2.8	
	Skewness	.299	.564
	Kurtosis	-.483	1.091

> **Skewness divided by its standard error provides a standardized value that also can be examined for normality evidence.** If alpha = .05, values of skewness divided by its standard error that are greater than ±1.96 indicate statistically significant skew. For skew we see: $.299/.564 = .530$
>
> We can apply this to kurtosis and the standard error of kurtosis as well. For kurtosis we see: $-.483/1.091 = -.443$

Tests of Normality

	Kolmogorov-Smirnov[a]			Shapiro-Wilk		
	Statistic	df	Sig.	Statistic	df	Sig.
time	.110	16	.200*	.982	16	.978

*. This is a lower bound of the true significance.

a. Lilliefors Significance Correction

FIGURE 6.15
Skewness and kurtosis and Shapiro-Wilk's test of normality.

Working in **R**, we saw in Figure 6.13 how we could generate Shapiro-Wilk's test using the *stat.desc* function from the *pastecs* package. Should we want to generate *just* the S-W test, we can run the following script.

```
shapiro.test(Ch6_skate$time)
```

```
        Shapiro-Wilk normality test

data: Ch6_skate$time
W = 0.98218, p-value = 0.9785
```

Normality can also be tested in **R** using Agostino's test for skewness and the Bonett-Seier test for Geary's kurtosis.

```
install.packages("moments")
library(moments)
```

To conduct Agostino's test, we first have to install the *moments* package and then load it into our library. The null hypothesis for this test is that skewness equals zero. Thus, a statistically significant Agostino's test would indicate that there is statistically significant skewness.

```
agostino.test(Ch6_skate$time)
```

The function *agostino.test* is generated using the variable "time" from our "Ch6_skate" dataframe. The results suggest evidence of normality as $p = .5762$, greater than alpha.

```
        D'Agostino skewness test

data: Ch6_skate$time
skew = 0.2706, z = 0.5590, p-value = 0.5762
alternative hypothesis: data have a skewness
```

```
bonett.test((Ch6_skate$time))
```

The *bonett.test* function, using the "time" variable from our "Ch6_skate" dataframe, performs the Bonett-Seier test for Geary's kurtosis for data that are normally distributed. The null hypothesis states that data should have a Geary's kurtosis value equal to $\sqrt{2/\pi} = .7979$. The results suggest evidence of normality as $p = .531$, greater than alpha.

```
        Bonett-Seier test for Geary kurtosis
data: (Ch6_skate$time)
tau = 1.4375, z = -0.6265, p-value = 0.531
alternative hypothesis: kurtosis is not equal to sqrt(2/pi)
```

FIGURE 6.15 (continued)
Skewness and kurtosis and Shapiro-Wilk's test of normality.

Quantile-quantile (Q-Q) plots are also often examined to determine evidence of normality. Q-Q plots are graphs that depict quantiles of the sample distribution to quantiles of the theoretical normal distribution. Points that fall on or closely to the diagonal line suggest evidence of normality. The Q-Q plot of our hockey skating time provides another form of evidence of normality (see Figure 6.16).

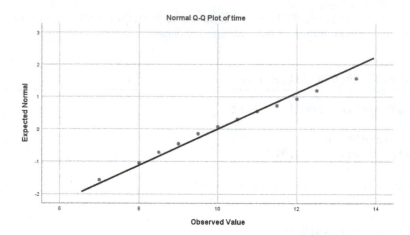

Working in **R**, we can generate a Q-Q plot with the following script, again using the *ggplot2* package.

```
qplot(sample=time, data = Ch6_skate)
```

The *qplot* function will generate a Q-Q plot using our variable "time" (i.e., using the script *sample=time*) from the dataframe "Ch6_skate" (i.e., *data = Ch6_skate*).

FIGURE 6.16
Q-Q plot.

The detrended normal Q-Q plot shows deviations of the observed values from the theoretical normal distribution. Evidence of normality is suggested when the points exhibit little or no pattern around zero (the horizontal line); however, due to subjectivity in determining the extent of a pattern, this graph can often be difficult to interpret. Thus, in many cases you may wish to rely more heavily on the other forms of evidence of normality. For a summary of normality evidence, please see Box 6.1 presented previously.

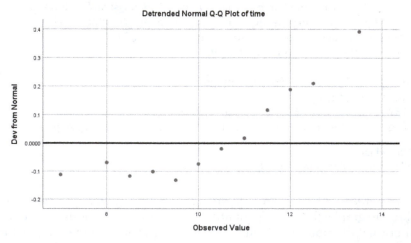

FIGURE 6.17
Detrended normal Q-Q plot.

6.5 Power Using G*Power

In our discussion of power presented earlier in this chapter, we indicated that the sample size to achieve a desired level of power can be determined *a priori* (before the study is conducted) as well as post hoc (after the study is conducted) using statistical software or power tables. One freeware program for calculating power is G*Power (www.psycho.uni-duesseldorf. de/abteilungen/aap/gpower3/) which can be used to compute both *a priori* sample size and post hoc power analyses (among other things). Using the results of the one-sample *t* test just conducted, let us utilize G*Power to first determine the required sample size given various estimated parameters and then compute the post hoc power of our test.

6.5.1 *A Priori* Power

Step 1. As shown in the screenshot for Step 1 in Figure 6.18, several decisions need to be made from the initial G*Power screen. First, the correct test family needs to be selected. In our case, we conducted a one-sample *t* test; therefore, the default selection of "t tests" is the correct test family. Next, we need to select the appropriate statistical test. We use the arrow to toggle to "Means: Difference from constant (one sample case)."

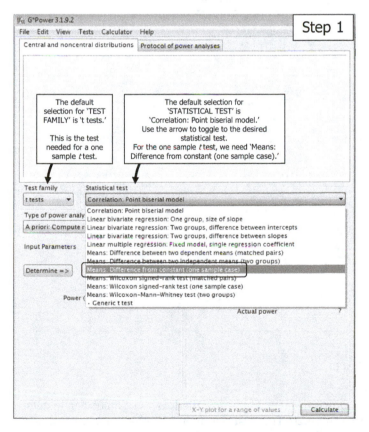

FIGURE 6.18
A priori power: Step 1.

Step 2. The type of power analysis is selected. As shown in the screenshot in Figure 6.19, the options for the type of power analysis are shown in the drop-down menu "Type of power analysis." The default is "A priori: Compute required sample size—given α, power, and effect size." For this example, we will first compute the *a priori* sample size (i.e., the default option), and then we will compute post hoc power. Note that there are three additional forms of power analysis that can be conducted using G*Power: "Compromise," "criterion," and "sensitivity."

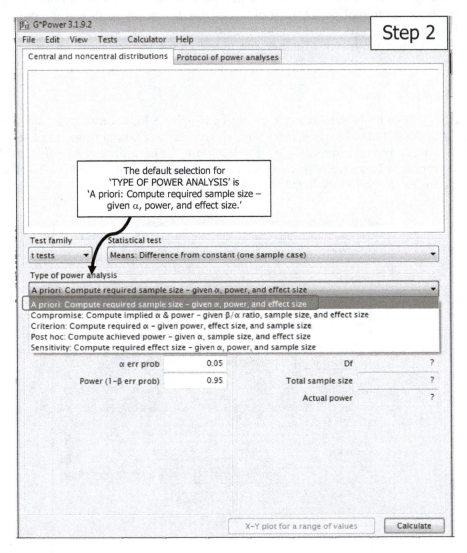

FIGURE 6.19
A priori power: Step 2.

Step 3. The input parameters are specified in the "Input Parameters" box shown in the screenshot in Figure 6.20. The first parameter is whether your test is one tailed (i.e., directional) or two tailed (i.e., nondirectional). In this example we have a two-tailed test, so we use the arrow to toggle "Tail(s)" to "Two." For *a priori* power, we have to indicate the anticipated effect size. The best estimate of effect size that you can anticipate on achieving is usually to rely on previous studies that have been conducted that are similar to yours. In G*Power, the default effect size is $d = .50$. For the purposes of this example, we will use the default. The alpha level must also be defined. The default significance level in G*Power is .05, which is the alpha level we will be use for our example. The desired level of power must also be defined. The G*Power default for power is .95. Many researchers in the social sciences indicate that a desired power of .80 or above is usually desired. Thus .95 may be higher than what many would consider sufficient power. For purposes of this example, however, we will use the default power of .95. Once the parameters are specified, simply click on "Calculate" to generate the *a priori* power statistics.

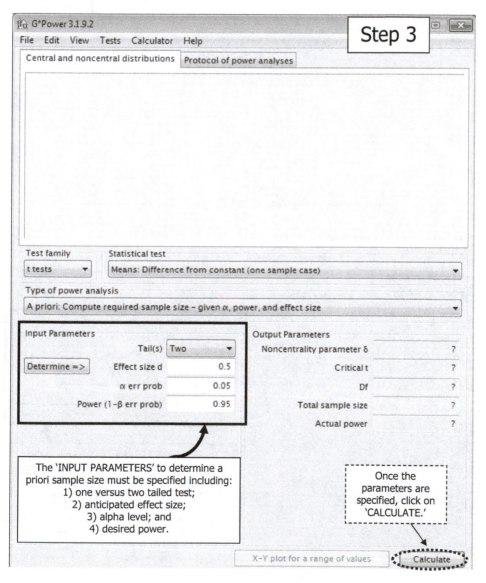

FIGURE 6.20
A priori power: Step 3.

Step 4. The output parameters provide the relevant statistics given the input specified (see the screenshot in Figure 6.21). In this example, we were interested in determining the *a priori* sample size given a two-tailed test, with an anticipated effect size of .50, an alpha level of .05, and desired power of .95. *Based on those criteria, the required sample size for our one-sample* t *test is 54.* In other words, if we have a sample size of 54 individuals or cases in our study, testing at an alpha level of .05, with a two-tailed test, and achieving a moderate effect size of .50, then the power of our test will be .95—the probability of rejecting the null hypothesis when it is really false will be 95%.

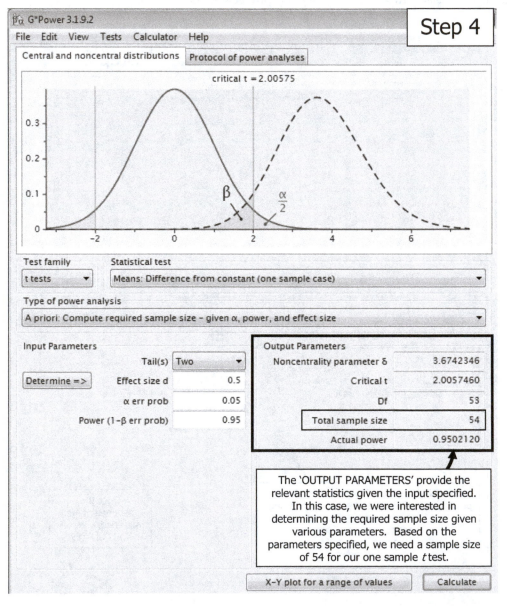

FIGURE 6.21
A priori power: Step 4.

If we had anticipated a smaller effect size, say .20 rather than .50, but left all of the other input parameters the same, the required sample size needed to achieve a power of .95 increases greatly—from 54 to 327 (see the screenshot in Figure 6.22). This demonstrate that there is less power with smaller effect sizes.

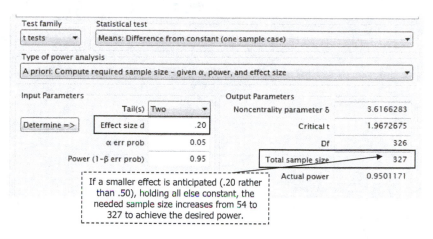

FIGURE 6.22
Change in power based on size of effect.

6.5.2 Post Hoc Power

Now, let us use G*Power to compute post hoc power. Step 1, as presented earlier for *a priori* power, remains the same; thus we will start from Step 2. See the screenshots in Figure 6.23.

Step 2. The type of power analysis needs to be selected from the "Type of power analysis" menu. In this case, you would select "Post hoc: Compute achieved power—given α, sample size, and effect size."

Step 3. You specify the input parameters. The first parameter is the selection of whether your test is one tailed (i.e., directional) or two tailed (i.e., nondirectional). In this example, we have a two-tailed test so we use the arrow to toggle to "Tail(s) to "Two." The achieved or observed effect size was −1.118. The alpha level we tested at was .05, and the actual sample size was 16. Once the parameters are specified, simply click on "Calculate" to generate the achieved power statistics.

Step 4. The output parameters provide the relevant statistics given the input specified. In this example, we were interested in determining post hoc power given a two-tailed test, with an observed effect size of −1.118, an alpha level of .05, and sample size of 16. Based on those criteria, the post hoc power is .986. In other words, with a sample size of 16 skaters in our study, testing at an alpha level of .05, with a two-tailed test, and observing a large effect size of −1.118, then the power of our test is .986—the probability of rejecting the null hypothesis when it is really false is about 99%, an excellent level of power. Keep in mind that conducting power analysis *a priori* is highly recommended so that you avoid a situation where, post hoc, you find that the sample size was not sufficient to reach the desired power (given the observed effect size and alpha level).

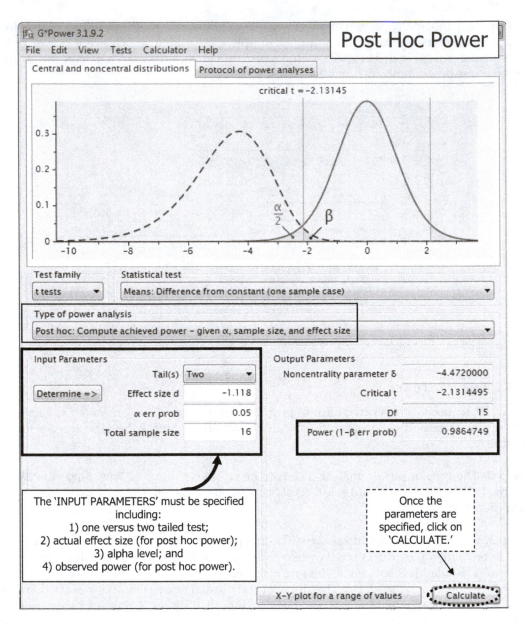

FIGURE 6.23
Post hoc power.

6.6 Research Question Template and Example Write-Up

Let us revisit our graduate research assistant, Ott Lier, who was working with Coach Wesley, a local hockey coach, to assist in analyzing his team's data. As a reminder, Ott's task was to assist Coach Wesley in generating the test of inference to answer the following research question: *Is the mean skating speed of our hockey team different from the league mean speed of 12 seconds?* Ott suggested a one-sample test of means as the test of inference. A template for writing a research question for a one-sample test of inference (i.e., one-sample *t* test) follows:

Is the mean of [sample variable] different from [hypothesized mean value]?

It may be helpful to preface the results of the one-sample *t* test with information we gathered to examine the extent to which the assumption of normality was met. This assists the reader in understanding that you were thorough in data screening prior to conducting the test of inference.

The distributional shape of skating speed was examined to determine the extent to which the assumption of normality was met. Skewness (.299, *SE* = .564) and kurtosis (−.483, *SE* = 1.091) were within the range of an absolute value of 2, suggesting evidence of normality. Standardized skew and kurtosis (.530 and −.443, respectively, calculated as skew or kurtosis divided by their standard errors) were not statistically significant, providing further evidence of normality. The Shapiro-Wilk test of normality (*W* = .982, *df* = 16, *p* = .978) suggests that normality is a reasonable assumption. Additional tests, including D'Agostino's test for skewness (*z* = .559, *p* = .576) and the Bonett-Seier test for Geary's kurtosis (*z* = −.627, *p* = .531) suggested evidence of normality. Visually, a relatively bell-shaped distribution displayed in the histogram (reflected similarly in the boxplot) as well as a Q-Q plot with points adhering closely to the diagonal line also suggest evidence of normality. Additionally, the boxplot did not suggest the presence of any potential outliers. These indices suggest evidence that the assumption of normality was met.

An additional assumption of the one sample *t* test is the assumption of independence. This assumption is met when the cases in our sample have been randomly selected from the population. This is an often overlooked, but important, assumption for researchers when presenting the results of their test. One or two sentences are usually sufficient to indicate if this assumption was met.

Because the skaters in this sample represented a random sample, the assumption of independence was met.

It is also desirable to include a measure of effect size. Recall our formula for computing the effect size, *d*, presented earlier in the chapter. Plugging in the values for our skating example, we find an effect size of −1.118, interpreted according to Cohen's (1988) guidelines as a large effect.

$$d = \frac{\bar{Y} - \mu_0}{s} = \frac{10 - 12}{1.7889} = -1.118$$

Remember that for the one-sample mean test, d indicates how many standard deviations the sample mean is from the hypothesized mean. Thus with an effect size of -1.118, there are nearly one and one-quarter standard deviation units between our sample mean and the hypothesized mean. The negative sign simply indicates that our sample mean was the smaller mean (as it is the first value in the numerator of the formula). In this particular example, the negative effect is desired as it suggests the team's average skating time is quicker than the league mean. Using Uanhoro's online calculator (Uanhoro, 2017), we find the confidence interval for the effect size of $(-1.7371, -0.4765)$.

Here is an example APA-style paragraph of results for the skating data (remember that this will be prefaced by the paragraph reporting the extent to which the assumptions of the test were met).

A one sample t test was conducted at an alpha level of .05 to answer the research question: *Is the mean skating speed of a hockey team different from the league mean speed of 12 seconds?* The null hypothesis stated that the team mean speed would not differ from the league mean speed of 12. The alternative hypothesis stated that the team average speed would differ from the league mean. Based on a random sample of 16 skaters, there was a mean time of 10 seconds and a standard deviation of 1.7889 seconds. When compared against the hypothesized mean of 12 seconds, the one-sample t test was shown to be statistically significant ($t = -4.472$, $df = 15$, $p < .001$). Therefore, the null hypothesis that the team average time would be 12 seconds was rejected. This provides evidence to suggest that the sample mean skating time for this particular team was statistically different from the hypothesized mean skating time of the league. Additionally, the effect size d was -1.118 (*CI* $-1.7371, -0.4765$), generally interpreted as a large effect (Cohen, 1988), and indicating that there is more than a one standard deviation difference between the team and league mean skating times, with the team speed quicker than the league speed. The post hoc power of the test, given the sample size, two-tailed test, alpha level, and observed effect size, was .986.

6.7 Additional Resources

A number of resources are available for learning more about statistics and how to interpret statistics. In addition to those already cited, Huck (2000) is an excellent general resource to assist in learning more about statistics and how to interpret statistics

---

Problems

Conceptual Problems

1. In hypothesis testing, the probability of failing to reject H_0 when H_0 is false is denoted by which of the following?

    a. α

    b. $1 - \alpha$

    c. β

    d. $1 - \beta$

2.   The probability of observing the sample mean (or some value greater than the sample mean) by chance if the null hypothesis is really true is denoted by which of the following?

    a. a

    b. Level of significance

    c. p value

    d. Test statistic value

3.   When testing the following hypothesis at a .05 level of significance with the t test, where is the rejection region?

$$H_0 : \mu \geq 100$$

$$H_1 : \mu < 100$$

    a. Upper tail

    b. Lower tail

    c. Both the upper and lower tails

    d. Cannot be determined

4.   A research question asks, "Is the mean age of children who enter preschool different from 48 months?" Which of the following is implied?

    a. Left-tailed test

    b. Right-tailed test

    c. Two-tailed test

    d. Cannot be determined based on this information

5.   If the 90% CI does not include the value for the parameter being estimated in H_0, then which of the following is a correct statement?

    a. H_0 cannot be rejected at the .10 level

    b. H_0 can be rejected at the .10 level

    c. A Type I error has been made

    d. A Type II error has been made

6.   Other things being equal, which of the following values of t is least likely to result for a two-tailed test when H_0 is true?

    a. 2.67

    b. 1.00

    c. 0.00

    d. -1.96

    e. -2.70

7.   Which of the following is the fundamental difference between the z test and the t test for testing hypotheses about a population mean?

    a. Only z assumes the population distribution be normal.

    b. z is a two-tailed test whereas t is one-tailed.

   c. Only t becomes more powerful as sample size increases.

   d. Only z requires the population variance be known.

8. True or false? If one fails to reject a true H_0, one is making a Type I error.

9. Which of the following is a correct interpretation of d?

   a. Alpha level

   b. Confidence interval

   c. Effect size

   d. Observed probability

   e. Power

10. A one-sample t test is conducted at an alpha level of .10. The researcher finds a p value of .08 and concludes that the test is statistically significant. Is the researcher correct?

11. When testing the following hypothesis at the .01 level of significance with the t test a sample mean of 301 is observed. I assert that if I calculate the test statistic and compare it to the t distribution with $n - 1$ degrees of freedom, then it is possible to reject H_0. Am I correct?

$$H_0: \mu \geq 295$$

$$H_1: \mu < 295$$

12. I assert that H_0 can be rejected with 100% confidence if the sample consists of the entire population. Am I correct?

13. I assert that the 95% CI has a larger width than the 99% CI for a population mean using the same data. Am I correct?

14. True or false? A 90% CI will have a smaller width than a 95% CI for a population mean using the same data.

15. I assert that the critical value of z for a test of a single mean will increase as the sample size increases. Am I correct?

16. True or false? The mean of the t distribution increases as degrees of freedom increase.

17. True or false? It is possible that the results of a one-sample t test and for the corresponding CI will differ for the same dataset and level of significance.

18. True or false? The width of the 95% CI does not depend on the sample mean.

19. The null hypothesis is a numerical statement about which of the following?

   a. An unknown parameter

   b. A known parameter

   c. An unknown statistic

   d. A known statistic

20. A research question asks, "To what extent does the average aptitude for success onboarding employees higher than 78?" Which of the following is implied?

   a. Left-tailed test

   b. Right-tailed test

   c. Two-tailed test

   d. Cannot be determined based on this information

21. In hypothesis testing, the probability of rejecting H_0 when H_0 is true is denoted by which of the following?

    a. α

    b. $1 - \alpha$

    c. β

    d. $1 - \beta$

22. A one-sample t test is conducted at an alpha level of .05. The researcher finds a p value of .10. Which of the following is a correct interpretation of these results?

    a. Results are not statistically significant.

    b. Results are statistically significant.

    c. Cannot be determined without additional information.

    d. Both a and b, depending on the situation.

23. A one-sample t test is conducted at an alpha level of .01. The researcher finds a p value of .05. Which of the following is a correct interpretation of these results?

    a. Results are not statistically significant.

    b. Results are statistically significant.

    c. Cannot be determined without additional information.

    d. Both a and b, depending on the situation.

24. Effect size measures provide which of the following?

    a. Inferences from the sample to population

    b. Level of confidence

    c. Practical significance

    d. Probability of rejecting the null hypothesis when it is false

25. A researcher computes a one-sample t test and finds an effect size $d = .75$. Which of the following is a correct interpretation of this effect?

    a. About 75% of the sample means will fall between the lower and upper levels.

    b. The probability of rejecting the null hypothesis is about 75%.

    c. There is evidence of normality.

    d. There is three-quarter of one standard deviation between the sample and hypothesized means.

Answers to Conceptual Problems

  1. **c** (Beta is the probability of failing to reject the null hypothesis when the null hypothesis is false.)

  3. **b** (Willing to reject only if sample mean is less than 100.)

  5. **b** (Reject when CI does not contain parameter value.)

  7. **d** (z is based on known population variance, t is not.)

  9. **c** (d is an effect size index, a measure of practical significance.)

 11. **No** (Cannot reject when sample mean is in opposite direction of region of rejection.)

 13. **No** (The range will be wider for the 99% CI.)

15.   **No** (The critical value of z does not depend on sample size.)

17.   **False** (They will always agree.)

19.   **a** (The null hypothesis is always about an unknown population parameter, hence the term inferential statistics.)

21.   **a** (Alpha, α, is the probability of falsely rejecting the null hypothesis when it is really true.)

23.   **b** ($p <$ alpha so reject the null hypothesis.)

25.   **d** (d is a standardized mean difference effect size, and a d of .75 indicates three-quarters of one standard deviation between the sample and hypothesized means.)

Computational Problems

1.   Using the same data and the same method of analysis, the following hypotheses are tested about whether mean height is 72 inches. Researcher A uses the .05 level of significance, and Researcher B uses the .01 level of significance.

$$H_0 : \mu = 72$$

$$H_1 : \mu \neq 72$$

  a.   If Researcher A rejects H_0, what is the conclusion of Researcher B?
  b.   If Researcher B rejects H_0, what is the conclusion of Researcher A?
  c.   If Researcher A fails to reject H_0, what is the conclusion of Researcher B?
  d.   If Researcher B fails to reject H_0, what is the conclusion of Researcher A?

2.   Give a numerical value for each of the following descriptions by referring to a t table.
  a.   Percentile rank of $t_5 = 1.476$
  b.   Percentile rank of $t_{10} = 3.169$
  c.   Percentile rank of $t_{21} = 2.518$
  d.   Mean of the distribution of t_{23}
  e.   Median of the distribution of t_{23}
  f.   Variance of the distribution of t_{23}
  g.   90th percentile of the distribution of t_{27}

3.   Give a numerical value for each of the following descriptions by referring to a t table.
  a.   Percentile rank of $t_5 = 2.015$
  b.   Percentile rank of $t_{20} = 1.325$
  c.   Percentile rank of $t_{30} = 2.042$
  d.   Mean of the distribution of t_{10}
  e.   Median of the distribution of t_{10}
  f.   Variance of the distribution of t_{10}
  g.   95th percentile of the distribution of t_{14}

4.   The following random sample of weekly student expenses is obtained from a normally distributed population of undergraduate students with unknown parameters:

68	56	76	75	62	81	72	69	91	84
49	75	69	59	70	53	65	78	71	87
71	74	69	65	64					

a. Test the following hypothesis at the .05 level of significance:

$$H_0 : \mu = 74$$

$$H_1 : \mu \neq 74$$

b. Construct a 95% confidence interval.

5. The following random sample of hours spent per day answering email is obtained from a normally distributed population of community college faculty with unknown parameters:

2	3.5	4	1.25	2.5	3.25	4.5	4.25	2.75	3.25
1.75	1.5	2.75	3.5	3.25	3.75	2.25	1.5	1.25	3.25

a. Test the following hypothesis at the .05 level of significance:

$$H_0 : \mu = 3.0$$

$$H_1 : \mu \neq 3.0$$

b. Construct a 95% confidence interval.

6. In the population it is hypothesized that flags have a mean usable life of 100 days. Twenty-five flags are flown in the city of Tuscaloosa and are found to have a sample mean usable life of 200 days with a standard deviation of 216 days. Does the sample mean in Tuscaloosa differ from that of the population mean?

a. Conduct a two-tailed t test at the .01 level of significance.

b. Construct a 99% confidence interval.

7. A researcher is examining IPEDS data (https://nces.ed.gov/ipeds/use-the-data). The researcher is interested in knowing if the mean number of students enrolled exclusively in distance education courses in 2016 differs from 600. Use the Ch6_IPEDS data with the variable "DE2016." Using statistical software, test at alpha = .05 and report the appropriate test results.

8. A researcher is examining IPEDS data (https://nces.ed.gov/ipeds/use-the-data) from land grant institutions. The researcher is interested in knowing if the mean number of students enrolled exclusively in distance education courses in 2012 differs from 350. Use the Ch6_IPEDS data with the variable "DE2012." Using statistical software, test at alpha = .05 and report the appropriate test results.

Answers to Computational Problems

1. a. B may or may not reject as B's level of significance is more stringent than A's.
   b. A also rejects as A's level of significance is more liberal than B's.
   c. B also fails to reject. If it's not significant at .05, it won't be significant at a smaller alpha.
   d. A may or may not fail to reject as A's alpha level is more liberal than B's.
3. a. 95th
   b. 90th
   c. 97.5th
   d. 0

   e.   0

   f.   1.25

   g.   1.761

5.   a. $t = -.884$, critical values $= -2.093$ and $+ 2.093$, and thus fail to reject H_0.

   b.   (2.3265, 3.2735) includes hypothesized value of 3.0, and thus fail to reject H_0.

7.   The mean number of students at land grant institutions who were enrolled exclusively in distance education courses in 2016 was 678.73 ($SD = 758.233$). This value is not statistically significantly different than the hypothesized value of 600, $t = .893$, $df = 73$, $p = .375$.

Interpretive Problem

1.   Using the survey1 data (accessible from the website) and SPSS or **R**, conduct a one-sample t test to determine whether the mean number of songs downloaded to a phone [SONGS] significantly differs from 25 at the .05 level of significance. Test for the extent to which the assumption of normality has been met. Calculate an effect size as well as post hoc power. Then write an APA-style paragraph reporting your results.

2.   Using the survey1 data (accessible from the website) and SPSS or **R**, conduct a one-sample t test to determine whether the mean number of hours slept [SLEEP] is significantly different from 8 at the .05 level of significance. Test for the extent to which the assumption of normality has been met. Calculate an effect size as well as post hoc power. Then write an APA-style paragraph reporting your results.

3.   A researcher has pulled country-level data from the rollercoaster census report (https://rcdb.com/census.htm) and is examining rollercoasters within North American countries. Using the Ch2_rollercoaster data (accessible from the website) and SPSS or **R**, conduct a one-sample t test to determine whether the mean number of steel rollercoasters [STEEL] is significantly different from 50 at the .05 level of significance. Test for the extent to which the assumption of normality has been met. Calculate an effect size as well as post hoc power. Then write an APA-style paragraph reporting your results.

7

Inferences About the Difference Between Two Means

Chapter Outline

Key Concepts

1. Independent versus dependent samples
2. Sampling distribution of the difference between two means
3. Standard error of the difference between two means
4. Parametric versus nonparametric tests

In Chapter 6 we introduced hypothesis testing and ultimately considered our first inferential statistic, the one-sample t test. There we examined the following general topics: types of hypotheses, types of decision errors, level of significance, steps in the decision-making process, inferences about a single mean when the population standard deviation is known (the z test), power, statistical versus practical significance, and inferences about a single mean when the population standard deviation is unknown (the t test).

In this chapter we consider inferential tests involving the difference between two means. In other words, our research question is the extent to which two sample means are statistically different and, by inference, the extent to which their respective population means are different. Several inferential tests are covered in this chapter, depending on whether the two samples are selected in an independent or dependent manner, and on whether the statistical assumptions are met. More specifically, the topics described include the following inferential tests: for two independent samples, the independent t test, the Welch t' test, and the Mann-Whitney-Wilcoxon test; for two dependent samples, the dependent t test and the Wilcoxon signed ranks test. We use many of the foundational concepts covered in Chapter 6. New concepts to be discussed include the following: independent versus dependent samples; the sampling distribution of the difference between two means; and the standard error of the difference between two means. Our objectives are that by the end of this chapter, you will be able to: (a) understand the basic concepts underlying the inferential tests of two means, (b) select the appropriate test, and (c) determine and interpret the results from the appropriate test.

7.1 Inferences About Two Independent Means and How They Work

Remember our very capable quad of graduate students who work in the stats lab? Let's see what Oso Wyse and Addie Venture have in store now . . .

The stats lab has been humming with research project requests from faculty and the community. The latest request comes from Dr. Nightingale, a local nurse practitioner, who is studying cholesterol levels of adults and how they differ based on sex. Oso Wyse has been assigned to the project and suggests the following research question: *Is there a mean difference in cholesterol level between males and females?* Oso suggests an independent samples t test as the test of inference. His task is then to assist Dr. Nightingale in generating the test of inference to answer the research question.

Addie Venture has been asked to consult with the institution's swimming coach, Coach Bryant, who works with the community and various swimming programs that are offered through their local Parks & Recreation Department. Coach Bryant has just conducted an intensive 2-month training program for a group of 10 swimmers. He wants to determine if, on average, their time in the 50-meter freestyle event is different after the training. The following research question is suggested by Addie: *Is there a mean difference in swim time for the 50-meter freestyle event before participation in an intensive training program as compared to swim time for the 50-meter freestyle event after participation in an intensive training program?* Addie suggests a dependent samples *t* test as the test of inference. Her task is then to assist Coach Bryant in generating the test of inference to answer his research question.

Before we proceed to inferential tests of the difference between two means, a few new concepts need to be introduced. The new concepts are the difference between the selection of independent samples and dependent samples, the hypotheses to be tested, and the sampling distribution of the difference between two means.

7.1.1 Independent vs. Dependent Samples

The first new concept to address is to make a distinction between the selection of **independent samples** and **dependent samples**. *Two samples are independent when the method of sample selection is such that those individuals selected for sample 1 do not have any relationship to those individuals selected for sample 2.* In other words, the selection of individuals to be included in the two samples are unrelated or uncorrelated such that they have absolutely nothing to do with one another. You might think of the samples as being selected totally separate from one another. Because the individuals in the two samples are independent of one another, their scores on the dependent variable, Y, should also be independent of one another. The independence condition leads us to consider, for example, the **independent samples *t* test**. (This should not, however, be confused with the assumption of independence, which was introduced in the previous chapter. The assumption of independence still holds for the independent samples *t* test, and we will talk later about how this assumption can be met with this particular procedure.)

Two samples are dependent when the method of sample selection is such that those individuals selected for sample 1 do have a relationship to those individuals selected for sample 2. In other words, the selections of individuals to be included in the two samples *are* related or correlated. You might think of the samples as being selected simultaneously such that there are actually pairs of individuals. Consider the following two typical examples. First, if the same individuals are measured at two points in time, such as during a pretest and a posttest, then we have two dependent samples. The scores on Y at time 1 will be correlated with the scores on Y at time 2 because the same individuals are assessed at both time points. *Second, if units are selected that are paired or matched in some way such that measurements will be matched (e.g., husband–wife pairs, twins), then we have two dependent samples.* For example, if a particular wife is selected for the study, then her corresponding husband is also automatically selected—this is an example where individuals are paired or matched in some way such that they share characteristics that makes the score of one person related to (i.e., dependent on) the score of the other person. In both examples we have natural pairs of individuals or scores. The dependence condition leads us to consider the **dependent samples *t* test**, alternatively known as the **correlated samples *t* test** or the **paired samples *t* test**. As we show in this chapter, whether the samples are independent or dependent determines the appropriate inferential test.

7.1.2 Hypotheses

The hypotheses to be evaluated for detecting a difference between two means are as follows. The null hypothesis, H_0, for a *nondirectional* test is that there is no difference between the two population means, which we denote as the following:

$$H_0: \mu_1 - \mu_2 = 0 \quad \text{or} \quad H_0: \mu_1 = \mu_2$$

where μ_1 is the population mean for sample 1 and μ_2 is the population mean for sample 2. Mathematically, both equations say the same thing. The version on the left makes it clear to the reader why the term "null" is appropriate; that is, there is no difference, or a "null" difference, between the two population means. The version on the right indicates that the population mean of sample 1 is the same as the population mean of sample 2, which is another way of saying that there is no difference between the means (i.e., they are the same). The *nondirectional* scientific or alternative hypothesis, H_1, is that there is a difference between the two population means, which we denote as follows:

$$H_1: \mu_1 - \mu_2 \neq 0 \quad \text{or} \quad H_1: \mu_1 \neq \mu_2$$

The null hypothesis, H_0, will be rejected here in favor of the alternative hypothesis, H_1, if the population means are different. As we have not specified a direction on H_1, we are willing to reject either if μ_1 is greater than μ_2 or if μ_1 is less than μ_2. This alternative hypothesis results in a two-tailed test.

Directional alternative hypotheses can also be tested if we believe μ_1 is greater than μ_2, denoted as follows:

$$H_1: \mu_1 - \mu_2 > 0 \quad \text{or} \quad H_1: \mu_1 > \mu_2$$

In this case, the equation on the left tells us that when μ_2 is subtracted from μ_1, a positive value will result (i.e., μ_1 is larger in value than μ_2, and thus results in some value greater than zero). The equation on the right makes it somewhat clearer what we hypothesize.

Or if we believe μ_1 is less than μ_2, the directional alternative hypotheses will be denoted as we see here:

$$H_1: \mu_1 - \mu_2 < 0 \quad \text{or} \quad H_1: \mu_1 < \mu_2$$

In this case, the equation on the left tells us that when μ_2 is subtracted from μ_1, a negative value will result (i.e., μ_1 is smaller in value than μ_2, and thus results in some value less than zero). The equation on the right makes it somewhat clearer what we hypothesize. Regardless of how they are denoted, directional alternative hypotheses result in a one-tailed test.

The underlying sampling distribution for these tests is known as the *sampling distribution of the difference between two means*. This makes sense, as the hypotheses examine the extent to which two sample means differ. The mean of this sampling distribution is zero, as that is the hypothesized difference between the two population means $\mu_1 - \mu_2$. The more the two sample means differ, the more likely we are to reject the null hypothesis. As we show later, the test statistics in this chapter all deal in some way with the difference between the two means and with the standard error (or standard deviation) of the difference between two means.

7.1.3 Characteristics of Tests of Difference Between Two Independent Means

In this section, three inferential tests of the difference between two independent means are described: the independent t test, the Welch t' test, and the Mann-Whitney-Wilcoxon test. The section concludes with a list of recommendations.

7.1.3.1 The Independent t Test

The test statistic for the **independent t test** is known as t and is denoted by the following formula:

$$t = \frac{\bar{Y}_1 - \bar{Y}_2}{s_{\bar{Y}_1 - \bar{Y}_2}}$$

where $\bar{Y}_1$ and $\bar{Y}_2$ are the means for sample 1 and sample 2, respectively, and $s_{\bar{Y}_1 - \bar{Y}_2}$ is the *standard error of the difference between two means*. This standard error is the *standard deviation of the sampling distribution of the difference between two means* and is computed as follows:

$$s_{\bar{Y}_1 - \bar{Y}_2} = s_p \sqrt{\frac{1}{n_1} + \frac{1}{n_2}}$$

where s_p is the *pooled standard deviation* computed as

$$s_p = \sqrt{\frac{(n_1 - 1)(s_1^2) + (n_2 - 1)(s_2^2)}{n_1 + n_2 - 2}}$$

and where s_1^2 and s_2^2 are the sample variances for groups 1 and 2, respectively, and n_1 and n_2 are the sample sizes for groups 1 and 2, respectively. Conceptually, the standard error $s_{\bar{Y}_1 - \bar{Y}_2}$ is a pooled standard deviation weighted by the two sample sizes; more specifically, the two sample variances are weighted by their respective sample sizes and then pooled. This is conceptually similar to the standard error for the one-sample t test, which you will recall from Chapter 6 as

$$s_{\bar{Y}} = \frac{s_Y}{\sqrt{n}}$$

where we also have a standard deviation weighted by sample size. If the sample variances are not equal, as the test assumes, then you can see why we might not want to take a pooled or weighted average (i.e., as it would not represent well the individual sample variances).

The test statistic t is then compared to a critical value(s) from the t distribution. For a two-tailed test, from Table A.2 in the Appendix we would use the appropriate α_2 column depending on the desired level of significance and the appropriate row depending on the degrees of freedom. The *degrees of freedom* for this test are $n_1 + n_2 - 2$. Conceptually, we lose one degree of freedom from each sample for estimating the population variances (i.e., there are two restrictions along the lines of what was discussed in Chapter 6). The *critical values* are denoted as $\pm_{\alpha_2} t_{n_1+n_2-2}$. The subscript α_2 of the critical values reflects the fact that this is a two-tailed test, and the subscript $n_1 + n_2 - 2$ indicates this particular degrees of freedom. (Remember that the critical value can be found based on the knowledge of the degrees of freedom and whether it is a one- or two-tailed test.) If the test statistic falls into either critical region, then we reject H_0; otherwise, we fail to reject H_0.

For a one-tailed test, from Table A.2 in the Appendix we would use the appropriate α_1 column depending on the desired level of significance and the appropriate row depending on the degrees of freedom. The degrees of freedom are again $n_1 + n_2 - 2$. The critical value is denoted as $+_{\alpha_1} t_{n_1+n_2-2}$ for the alternative hypothesis $H_1: \mu_1 - \mu_2 > 0$ (i.e., right-tailed test, so the critical value will be positive), and as $-_{\alpha_1} t_{n_1+n_2-2}$ for the alternative hypothesis $H_1: \mu_1 - \mu_2 < 0$ (i.e., left-tailed test, and thus a negative critical value). If the test statistic t falls into the appropriate critical region, then we reject H_0; otherwise, we fail to reject H_0.

7.1.3.1.1 Confidence Interval

For the two-tailed test, a $(1 - \alpha)\%$ confidence interval can also be examined. The confidence interval is formed as follows:

$$\left(\overline{Y}_1 - \overline{Y}_2\right) \pm \left(_{\alpha_2} t_{n_1+n_2-2}\right)\left(s_{\overline{Y}_1 - \overline{Y}_2}\right)$$

If the confidence interval contains the hypothesized mean difference of 0, then the conclusion is to *fail to reject H_0*; otherwise, we *reject H_0*. The interpretation and use of CIs is similar to that of the one-sample test described in Chapter 6. Imagine we take 100 random samples from each of two populations and construct 95% CIs. Then 95% of the CIs will contain the true population mean difference $\mu_1 - \mu_2$ and 5% will not. In short, 95% of similarly constructed CIs will contain the true population mean difference.

7.1.3.1.2 Example of the Independent *t* Test

Let us now consider an example where the independent *t* test is implemented. Recall from Chapter 6 the basic steps for hypothesis testing for any inferential test: (1) State the null and alternative hypotheses; (2) select the level of significance (i.e., alpha, α); (3) calculate the test statistic value; and (4) make a statistical decision (reject or fail to reject H_0). We will follow these steps again in conducting our independent *t* test.

In our example, samples of 8 female and 12 male middle-age adults are randomly and independently sampled from the populations of female and male middle-age adults, respectively. Each individual is given a cholesterol test through a standard blood sample. *The null hypothesis to be tested is that males and females have equal cholesterol levels. The alternative hypothesis is that males and females will not have equal cholesterol levels*, thus necessitating a *nondirectional* or *two-tailed test*. We will conduct our test using an alpha level of .05. The raw data and summary statistics are presented in Table 7.1. For the female sample (sample 1) the mean and variance are 185.0000 and 364.2857, respectively, and for the male sample (sample 2) the mean and variance are 215.0000 and 913.6363, respectively.

TABLE 7.1

Cholesterol Data for Independent Samples

Female (Sample 1)	Male (Sample 2)
205	245
160	170
170	180
180	190
190	200
200	210
210	220
165	230
	240
	250
	260
	185
$\overline{Y}_1 = 185.0000$	$\overline{Y}_2 = 215.0000$
$s_1^2 = 364.2857$	$s_2^2 = 913.6363$

In order to compute the test statistic t, we first need to determine the standard error of the difference between the two means. The pooled standard deviation is computed as

$$s_p = \sqrt{\frac{(n_1 - 1)(s_1^2) + (n_2 - 1)(s_2^2)}{n_1 + n_2 - 2}}$$

$$s_p = \sqrt{\frac{(8-1)(364.2857) + (12-1)(913.6363)}{8 + 12 - 2}} = 26.4575$$

and the standard error of the difference between two means is computed as

$$s_{\overline{Y}_1 - \overline{Y}_2} = s_p \sqrt{\frac{1}{n_1} + \frac{1}{n_2}} = 26.4575 \sqrt{\frac{1}{8} + \frac{1}{12}} = 12.0752$$

The test statistic t can then be computed as

$$t = \frac{\overline{Y}_1 - \overline{Y}_2}{s_{\overline{Y}_1 - \overline{Y}_2}} = \frac{185 - 215}{12.0752} = -2.4844$$

The next step is to use Table A.2 in the Appendix to determine the critical values. As there are 18 degrees of freedom $(n_1 + n_2 - 2) = 8 + 12 - 2 = 18$, using $\alpha = .05$ and a two-tailed or

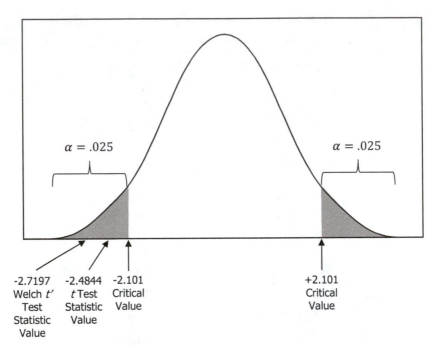

FIGURE 7.1
Critical regions and test statistics for the cholesterol example.

nondirectional test, we find the critical values using the appropriate α_2 column to be +2.101 and −2.101. Because the test statistic falls beyond the critical values as shown in Figure 7.1, we therefore *reject the null hypothesis* that the means are equal in favor of the nondirectional alternative that the means are not equal. Thus, we conclude that the mean cholesterol levels for males and females are *not* equal at the .05 level of significance (denoted by $p < .05$).

The 95% confidence interval can also be examined. For the cholesterol example, the confidence interval is formed as follows:

$$\left(\bar{Y}_1 - \bar{Y}_2\right) \pm \left(_{\alpha_2} t_{n_1 + n_2 - 2}\right)\left(s_{\bar{Y}_1 - \bar{Y}_2}\right) = \left(185 - 215\right) \pm \left(2.101\right)\left(12.0752\right)$$
$$= \left(-30\right) \pm \left(25.3700\right) = \left(-55.3700, -4.6300\right)$$

Because the confidence interval does not contain the hypothesized mean difference value of zero, then we would again reject the null hypothesis and conclude that the mean difference in cholesterol levels for males and females was not equal to zero at the .05 level of significance ($p < .05$). In other words, there is evidence to suggest that the males and females differ, on average, on cholesterol level. More specifically, the mean cholesterol level for males is greater than the mean cholesterol level for females.

7.1.3.2 The Welch t′ Test

The **Welch t′ test** is usually appropriate when the population variances are unequal and the sample sizes are unequal. The Welch t′ test assumes that the scores on the dependent variable Y are normally distributed in each of the two populations and are independent.

The test statistic is known as t' and is denoted by

$$t' = \frac{\bar{Y}_1 - \bar{Y}_2}{s_{\bar{Y}_1 - \bar{Y}_2}} = \frac{\bar{Y}_1 - \bar{Y}_2}{\sqrt{s_{\bar{Y}_1}^2 + s_{\bar{Y}_2}^2}} = \frac{\bar{Y}_1 - \bar{Y}_2}{\sqrt{\dfrac{s_1^2}{n_1} + \dfrac{s_2^2}{n_2}}}$$

where $\bar{Y}_1$ and $\bar{Y}_2$ are the means for samples 1 and 2, respectively, and $s_{\bar{Y}_1}^2$ and $s_{\bar{Y}_2}^2$ are the variance errors of the means for samples 1 and 2, respectively. Here we see that the denominator of this test statistic is conceptually similar to the one-sample t and the independent t test statistics. The *variance errors of the mean* are computed for each group by

$$s_{\bar{Y}_1}^2 = \frac{s_1^2}{n_1}$$

$$s_{\bar{Y}_2}^2 = \frac{s_2^2}{n_2}$$

where s_1^2 and s_2^2 are the sample variances for groups 1 and 2, respectively. The square root of the variance error of the mean is the standard error of the mean (i.e., $s_{\bar{Y}_1}$ and $s_{\bar{Y}_2}$). *Thus we see that rather than take a pooled or weighted average of the two sample variances as we did with the independent t test, the two sample variances are treated separately.*

The test statistic t' is then compared to a critical value(s) from the t distribution in Table A.2 in the Appendix. We again use the appropriate α column depending on the desired level of significance and whether the test is one- or two-tailed (i.e., α_1 and α_2), and the appropriate row for the degrees of freedom. The degrees of freedom for this test are a bit more complicated than for the independent t test. The degrees of freedom are adjusted from $n_1 + n_2 - 2$ for the independent t test to the following value for the Welch t' test:

$$\nu = \frac{\left(s_{\bar{Y}_1}^2 + s_{\bar{Y}_2}^2\right)^2}{\dfrac{\left(s_{\bar{Y}_1}^2\right)^2}{n_1 - 1} + \dfrac{\left(s_{\bar{Y}_2}^2\right)^2}{n_2 - 1}}$$

The degrees of freedom, ν, are approximated by rounding to the nearest whole number prior to using the table. If the test statistic falls into a critical region, then we reject H_0; otherwise, we fail to reject H_0.

For the two-tailed test, a $(1 - \alpha)\%$ confidence interval can also be examined. The confidence interval is formed as follows:

$$\left(\bar{Y}_1 - \bar{Y}_2\right) \pm {}_{\alpha_2}t_\nu \left(s_{\bar{Y}_1 - \bar{Y}_2}\right)$$

If the confidence interval contains the hypothesized mean difference of zero, then the conclusion is to *fail to reject H_0*; otherwise, we *reject H_0*. Thus, interpretation of this CI is the same as with the independent t test.

Consider again the example cholesterol data where the sample variances were somewhat different and the sample sizes were different. The *variance errors of the mean* are computed for each sample as follows:

$$s_{\bar{Y}_1}^2 = \frac{s_1^2}{n_1} = \frac{364.2857}{8} = 45.5357$$

$$s_{\bar{Y}_2}^2 = \frac{s_2^2}{n_2} = \frac{913.6363}{12} = 76.1364$$

The t' test statistic is computed as

$$t' = \frac{\bar{Y}_1 - \bar{Y}_2}{s_{\bar{Y}_1 - \bar{Y}_2}} = \frac{185 - 215}{\sqrt{45.5357 + 76.1364}} = \frac{-30}{11.0305} = -2.7197$$

Finally, the degrees of freedom, v, are determined to be

$$v = \frac{\left(s_{\bar{Y}_1}^2 + s_{\bar{Y}_2}^2\right)^2}{\dfrac{\left(s_{\bar{Y}_1}^2\right)^2}{n_1 - 1} + \dfrac{\left(s_{\bar{Y}_2}^2\right)^2}{n_2 - 1}} = \frac{\left(45.5357 + 76.1364\right)^2}{\dfrac{\left(45.5357\right)^2}{8 - 1} + \dfrac{\left(76.1364\right)^2}{12 - 1}} = 17.9838$$

which is rounded to 18, the nearest whole number. The degrees of freedom remain 18 as they were for the independent t test, and thus the critical values are still +2.101 and −2.101. Because the test statistic falls beyond the critical values shown in Figure 7.1, we therefore reject the null hypothesis that the means are equal in favor of the alternative that the means are not equal. Thus, as with the independent t test, with the Welch t' test we conclude that the mean cholesterol levels for males and females are not equal at the .05 level of significance. In this particular example, then, we see that the unequal sample variances and unequal sample sizes did not alter the outcome when comparing the independent t test result with the Welch t' test result. However, note that the results for these two tests may differ with other data.

Finally, the 95% confidence interval can be examined. For the example, the confidence interval is formed as follows:

$$\left(\bar{Y}_1 - \bar{Y}_2\right) \pm {}_{\alpha_2}t_v\left(s_{\bar{Y}_1 - \bar{Y}_2}\right) = (185 - 215) \pm (2.101)(11.0305)$$
$$= (-30) \pm (23.1751) = (-53.1751, -6.8249)$$

Because the confidence interval does not contain the hypothesized mean difference value of zero, then we would again reject the null hypothesis and conclude that the mean gender difference was not equal to zero at the .05 level of significance ($p < .05$).

7.1.3.3 Recommendations

The following four recommendations are made regarding the two independent samples case. Although there is not total consensus in the field, our recommendations take into account, as much as possible, the available research and statistical software.

First, if the *normality assumption is satisfied*, the following recommendations are made: (a) the independent *t* test is recommended when the homogeneity of variance assumption is met (i.e., equal variance assumption is met and there is either an equal, balanced or unequal, unbalanced number of observations in the sample); (b) the independent *t* test is recommended when the homogeneity of variance assumption is not met and when there are an equal number of observations in the samples (i.e., balanced design but equal variance assumption is violated); and (c) the Welch *t'* test is recommended when the homogeneity of variance assumption is not met and when there are an unequal number of observations in the samples (i.e., unbalanced design and equal variance assumption is violated).

Second, if the *normality assumption is not satisfied*, the following recommendations are made: (a) if the homogeneity of variance assumption is met, then the independent *t* test using ranked scores (Conover & Iman, 1981), rather than raw scores, is recommended; and (b) if homogeneity of variance assumption is *not* met, then the Welch *t'* test using ranked scores is recommended, regardless of whether there are an equal number of observations in the samples. Using ranked scores means you rank order the observations from highest to lowest regardless of group membership, then conduct the appropriate *t* test with ranked scores rather than raw scores.

Third, the dependent *t* test is recommended when there is some dependence between the groups (e.g., matched pairs or the same individuals measured on two occasions), as described later in this chapter.

Fourth, the nonparametric Mann-Whitney-Wilcoxon test is *not* recommended under any circumstances. Among the disadvantages of this test are that (a) the critical values are not extensively tabled, (b) tied ranks can affect the results and no optimal procedure has yet been developed (Wilcox, 1986), and (c) Type I error appears to be inflated regardless of the status of the assumptions (Zimmerman, 2003). For these reasons the Mann-Whitney-Wilcoxon test is not further described here. Note that most major statistical packages, including SPSS, have options for conducting the independent *t* test, the Welch *t'* test, and the Mann-Whitney-Wilcoxon test. Alternatively, one could conduct the Kruskal-Wallis nonparametric one-factor analysis of variance, which is also based on ranked data, and which is appropriate for comparing the means of two or more independent groups. This test is considered more fully in the later discussion of analysis of variance (ANOVA). These recommendations are summarized in Box 7.1.

7.1.4 Sample Size of the Independent *t* Test

We will start our discussion of sufficient sample size for the independent *t* test with the same thing that we began the discussion in Chapter 6: Remember that there is a difference in having a sample size that produces *sufficiently powered results* as compared to a sample size that will produce *robust results*. **Robust results** mean that the results are still relatively accurate even if there are some violations of assumptions. Having robust results does *not* equate, necessarily, to having a sufficiently powered test (i.e., being able to detect

---

BOX 7.1 Recommendations for the Independent and Dependent Samples Tests Based on
Meeting or Violating the Assumption of Normality

Assumption	Independent Samples Tests	Dependent Samples Tests
Normality is met.	Use the independent *t* test when homogeneity of variances is met.	Use the dependent *t* test.
	Use the independent *t* test when homogeneity of variances is *not* met, but there are equal sample sizes in the groups.	
	Use the Welch *t'* test when homogeneity of variances is *not* met and there are unequal sample sizes in the groups.	
Normality is *not* met.	Use the independent *t* test with ranked scores when homogeneity of variances is met.	Use the dependent *t* test with ranked scores or alternative procedures, including bootstrap methods, trimmed means, medians, or Stein's method.
	Use the Welch *t'* test with ranked scores when homogeneity of variances is *not* met, regardless of equal or unequal sample sizes in the groups.	Use the Wilcoxon signed ranks test when data are both nonnormal and have extreme outliers.
	Use the Kruskal-Wallis nonparametric procedure.	Use the Friedman nonparametric procedure.

---

a statistically significant difference if it exists). It's possible to have robust results for an underpowered test (i.e., assumptions are met, but the sample size is not large enough for detecting a difference if it's there). And it's also possible to have a sufficiently powered test that does not produce robust results (i.e., sample size is sufficient for detecting a difference if it's there, but assumptions have been violated). A common myth is that a sample size of 30 is sufficient for conducting an independent *t* test (or generally any of the three *t* tests). We've also seen researchers say that a sample size of 20 is sufficient. Other researchers say that as long as the normality assumption is met, regardless of the sample size, the results will be robust. *We do not condone going by any of these suggested guidelines for determining sample size.* There are no conventions that we recommend for sample size. Rather, we encourage researchers to conduct a power analysis to determine the sample size needed for sufficient power.

7.1.5 Power of the Independent *t* Test

Power for the independent *t* test can be determined based on reviewing power tables or using statistical software (e.g., G*Power).

7.1.6 Effect Size of the Independent *t* Test

Several effect size indices can be computed for the independent *t* test. We will examine standardized mean difference effects and proportion of variance accounted for.

7.1.6.1 Standardized Mean Difference

We extend Cohen's (1988) sample measure of effect size, *delta* or *d*, from Chapter 6 to the two independent samples situation. Here we compute the **standardized mean difference**, *d*, as follows:

$$d = \frac{\overline{Y}_1 - \overline{Y}_2}{s_p}$$

The numerator of the formula is the difference between the two sample means. The denominator is the pooled standard deviation, for which the formula was presented previously. Cohen (1988) originally used n_1 and n_2 to compute s_p. However, Hedges and Olkin (1985) used $n_1 - 1$ and n_{2-1} to compute s_p, as we have done.

A **bias corrected effect size** (Hedges, 1981) for small sample sizes (e.g., $n < 50$) is computed as follows, where $df = n_1 + n_2 - 2$.

$$g = \left(\frac{\overline{Y}_1 - \overline{Y}_2}{s_p} \right) \left(1 - \frac{3}{(4)(df) - 1} \right)$$

The correction factor, $\left(1 - \dfrac{3}{(4)(df) - 1} \right)$, will always less than 1.0. Thus, the **sample size adjusted Hedge's g** will always be less than *d*. The correction factor will always be close to 1.0 unless the *df* are very small (e.g., < 10) (Hedges, 1981).

The effect size *d* is measured in standard deviation units, and again we use Cohen's proposed subjective standards for interpreting *d*: small effect size, $d = .2$; medium effect size, $d = .5$; large effect size, $d = .8$. Conceptually, this is similar to *d* in the one-sample case from Chapter 6. The effect size *d* is considered a standardized group difference type of effect size (Huberty, 2002).

Alternative methods are available for computing the standardizer (i.e., the denominator). Rather than the pooled standard deviation, the standard deviation of just one of the groups (typically the control group) can be used as the denominator (Glass, 1976), and this is often referred to as Glass's *d*, or d_G. Glass's *d* has been recommended when the homogeneity of variance assumption is not met (Olejnik & Algina, 2000). As noted by Olejnik and Algina (2000, p. 246), when the equal variances assumption is violated, *the researcher will have to select one standard deviation that expresses the contrast on the scale the researcher thinks is most important or will have to report the mean difference standardized by several standard deviations and discussion the implications of these figures.*

7.1.6.2 Strength of Association

Other types of effect sizes can be computed for independent *t* test results. One such effect size index measures strength of association; that is, the amount of variation in the dependent variable that can be explained or accounted for by the independent variable. For the independent *t* test, we will examine **eta squared (η^2)** and **omega squared (ω^2)**.

For the independent t test, **eta squared (η^2)** can be calculated as follows:

$$\eta^2 = \frac{t^2}{t^2 + df} = \frac{t^2}{t^2 + (n_1 + n_2 - 2)}$$

The numerator is the squared t test statistic value and the denominator is the sum of the squared t test statistic value and the degrees of freedom. Values for eta squared range from 0 to +1.00, where values closer to one indicate a stronger association. In terms of what this effect size tells us, as noted earlier, eta squared is interpreted as the *proportion of variance accounted for in the dependent variable by the independent variable* and indicates the degree of the relationship between the independent and dependent variables. If we use Cohen's (1988) metric for interpreting eta squared: small effect size, $\eta^2 = .01$; moderate effect size, $\eta^2 = .06$; large effect size, $\eta^2 = .14$.

Omega squared (ω^2) can be computed for the independent t test as follows:

$$\omega^2 = \frac{t^2 - 1}{t^2 + N - 1}$$

The interpretation for omega squared is the same as for eta squared: The *proportion of variance accounted for in the dependent variable by the independent variable* and indicates the degree of the relationship between the independent and dependent variables. If we use Cohen's (1988) metric for interpreting omega squared: small effect size, $\omega^2 = .01$; moderate effect size, $\omega^2 = .06$; large effect size, $\omega^2 = .14$.

7.1.6.3 An Example

The effect size, d, using the pooled standard deviation for the standandardizer for the example examined previously is computed as follows:

$$d = \frac{\overline{Y}_1 - \overline{Y}_2}{s_p} = \frac{185 - 215}{26.4575} = -1.1339$$

Computing the sample size adjusted Hedge's g, we find:

$$g = \left(\frac{\overline{Y}_1 - \overline{Y}_2}{s_p}\right)\left(1 - \frac{3}{(4)(df) - 1}\right) = \left(\frac{185 - 215}{26.4575}\right)\left(1 - \frac{3}{(4)(18) - 1}\right) = (-1.1339)(.9577)$$

$$g = -1.0860$$

According to Cohen's recommended subjective standards, this would certainly be a rather large effect size, as the difference between the two sample means is larger than one standard deviation. Rather than d, had we wanted to compute eta squared or omega squared, we would have also found a large effect:

$$\eta^2 = \frac{t^2}{t^2 + df} = \frac{(-2.4844)^2}{(-2.4844)^2 + 18} = .2553$$

$$\omega^2 = \frac{t^2 - 1}{t^2 + N - 1} = \frac{(-2.4844)^2 - 1}{(-2.4844)^2 + 20 - 1} = .2055$$

An eta squared value of .26 and omega squared of .21 both indicate a large relationship between the independent and dependent variables, with eta squared suggesting that 26% of the variance in the dependent variable (i.e., cholesterol level) accounted for by the independent variable (i.e., sex) and omega squared indicating that about 21% of the variance is accounted for.

7.1.6.4 Confidence Intervals for Cohen's Delta

As we learned in the previous chapter, computing confidence intervals for effect sizes is also valuable. The benefit in creating confidence intervals for effect size values is similar to that of creating confidence intervals for parameter estimates—*confidence intervals for the effect size provide an added measure of precision that is not obtained from knowledge of the effect size alone.* Computing confidence intervals for effect size indices, however, is not as straightforward as simply plugging in known values into a formula. This is because d is a function of both the population mean and population standard deviation (Finch & Cumming, 2009), and the noncentrality parameter comes into play. We refer you back to Chapter 6 for a refresher on this.

A nice online calculator for computing the independent t test confidence interval for effect size d using the noncentrality parameter is available at https://effect-size-calculator.herokuapp.com (Uanhoro, 2017). As we see in Figure 7.2, seven inputs are required: sample mean for each group, sample standard deviation for each group, sample size for each group, and confidence interval (i.e., the complement of alpha). Cohen's d (in absolute value terms; note that we input the larger mean as sample 1 in the online calculator, resulting in a positive effect size but we could have just as easily input the smaller mean as sample 1 and we'll see the effect of this using the Campbell online calculator) is 1.139, as noted previously as well, with confidence intervals of .1533 and 2.0877. Putting this in context of our cholesterol example, if multiple random samples were drawn from the population, 95% of the samples could expect males to have, at minimum, about .15 and, at maximum, over 2 standard deviation units higher cholesterol as compared to females.

Note that while we are provided the additional effect size measure, $r_{equivalent}$, on our output, Rosenthal and Rubin (2003, p. 496) provide a number of limitations to consider when using this effect and refer to it as a "first-aid kit" rather than ideal. Specifically, $r_{equivalent}$ is designed for situations in which the actual study is close in form to the canonical study and, in the case of the independent t test, when the sample size is so small or the data so nonnormal that other effect size indices would not be robust (Rosenthal & Rubin, 2003). There are other limitations noted, however these are the critiques applicable when considering this effect in the context of the independent t test.

Another online calculator for computing all types of effect sizes and their confidence intervals is provided by Dr. David B. Wilson and is available through the Campbell Collaboration (see https://campbellcollaboration.org/research-resources/effect-size-calculator.html). Although designed for use when conducting meta-analyses, the online calculator comes in handy whenever an effect size and its CI are desired. Let's look at the example using the cholesterol data for males and females. We enter the means, standard deviations, and sample sizes of the two groups. Using Campbell's effect size calculator, we find *d* computed to be −1.1339 and the 95% CI of (−2.095, −1728) (see Figure 7.2). Because the confidence interval does not contain 0, our null value (i.e., reflecting no relationship),

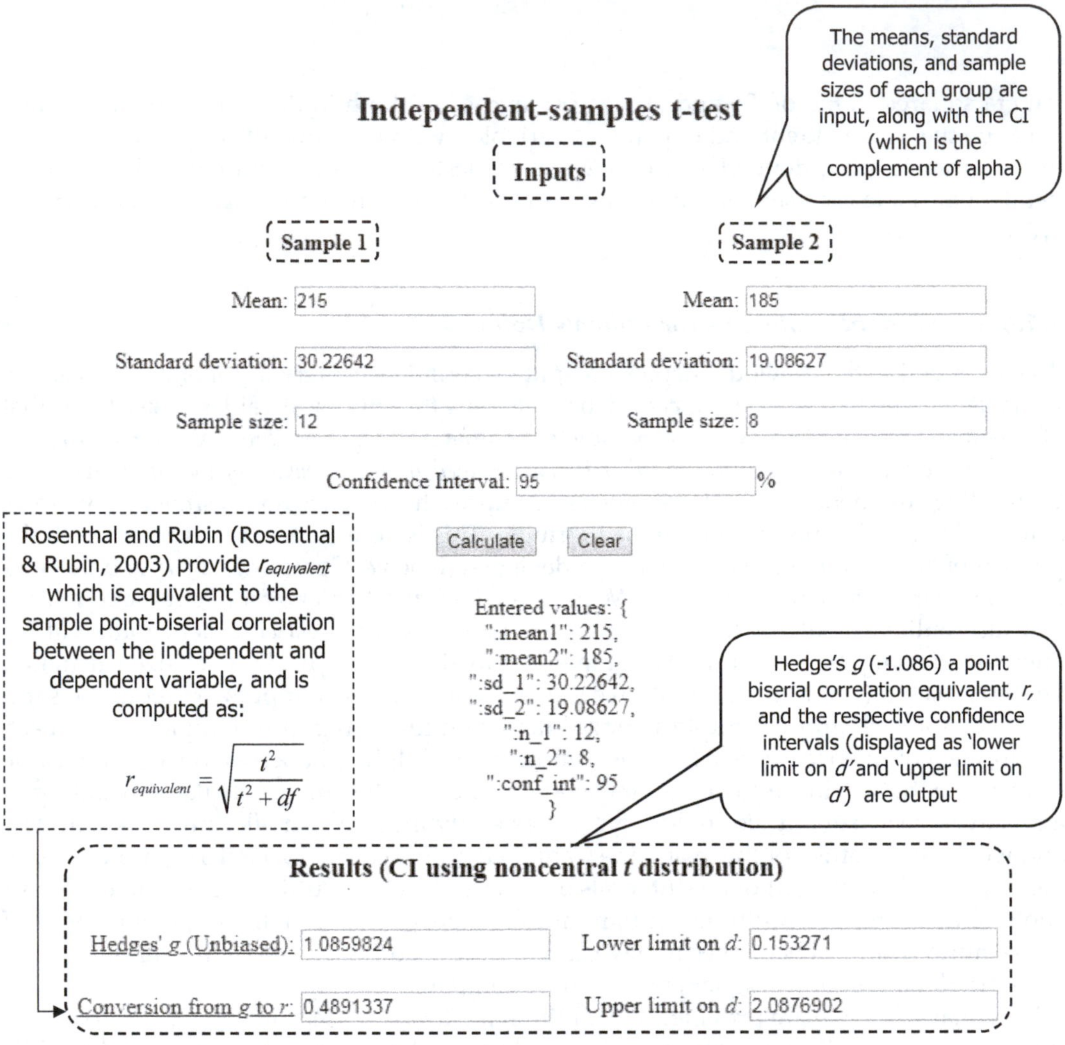

Using Campbell's online effect size calculator, we can compute *d* and it's confidence interval.

FIGURE 7.2
Effect size *d* and confidence interval of *d*.

Source: R. Rosenthal & D. B. Rubin. (2003). r-sub(equivalent): A simple effect size indicator. *Psychological Methods*, 8(4), 492–496.

Practical Meta-Analysis Effect Size Calculator
David B. Wilson, Ph.D., George Mason University

HOME	
EFFECT SIZE TYPE	**Means, Standard Deviations, and Sample Sizes**
+ Standardized Mean Difference (d)	

Means, Standard Deviations, and Sample Sizes

	Mean	SD	N
Treatment	185	19.08627	8
Control	215	30.22642	12
	Calculate	Reset	
d =	-1.1339		
95% C.I. =	-2.095	-0.1728	
v =	0.2405		

Effect size type list:
MEANS AND STANDARD DEVIATIONS
T-TEST, UNEQUAL SAMPLE SIZES
T-TEST, EQUAL SAMPLE SIZES
F-TEST, 2-GROUP, UNEQUAL SAMPLE SIZES
F-TEST, 2-GROUP, EQUAL SAMPLE SIZES
T-TEST P-VALUE, EQUAL SAMPLE SIZES
T-TEST P-VALUE, UNEQUAL SAMPLE SIZES
MEANS AND STANDARD ERRORS
2 BY 2 FREQUENCY TABLE
BINARY PROPORTIONS

FIGURE 7.2 (continued)
Effect size d and confidence interval of d.

this provides evidence to suggest a statistically significant difference in cholesterol levels between males and females.

Interested readers are referred to appropriate sources to learn more about confidence intervals for d (e.g., Algina & Keselman, 2003; Algina, Keselman, & Penfield, 2005; Cumming & Calin-Jageman, 2017; Cumming & Finch, 2001).

7.1.6.4 Recommendations for Effect Size of the Independent t Test

A number of excellent resources are available for learning more about effect size (e.g., Cohen, 1988; Cortina & Nouri, 2000; Grissom & Kim, 2012), and we encourage researchers to review these resources for better understanding effect size. We will offer a few general recommendations for effect size as follows (see Box 7.2), along with a summary of some common effect size measures for two independent groups in Table 7.2:

1. If you are reporting a standardized mean difference, always report the standardizer with which you have computed the effect size (or better yet, just include the formula for your effect size). There is not a consensus in the field on notation for effect size, and thus reporting d may imply different calculations to different researchers.
2. For very small samples, use sample size corrected Hedge's g.
3. When the assumption of equal variances is met, report d or Hedge's g that is corrected for small sample sizes.
4. When the assumption of equal variances is *not* met, do not use the pooled standard deviation. Rather, adhere to the recommendation of Glass (1976) and select the standard deviation for one of the groups as the standardizer.
5. Because nonnormality can unduly influence standardized mean difference effect size estimates, selecting an effect size index that does not require normality is recommended in cases where the assumption of normality is violated (Grissom & Kim, 2012).

TABLE 7.2

Independent *t* Test Effect Sizes and Interpretations

Effect Size	Interpretation
Omega squared (ω^2) and eta squared (η^2)	Proportion of total variability in the dependent variable that is accounted for by the factor (i.e., independent variable) • Small effect = .01 • Medium effect = .06 • Large effect = .14
Cohen's *d* and Hedge's *g* for small samples	The number of standard deviation units for which the groups differ • Small effect = .20 • Medium effect = .50 • Large effect = .80

BOX 7.2 Recommendations for Reporting Effect Size with the Independent *t* Test

Condition	Recommendation
Reporting standardized mean difference	Always report the standardizer (i.e., denominator) with which you have computed the effect size or, even better, include the formula for your effect size.
Very small samples	Report sample size corrected Hedge's *g*.
Assumption of equal variances is met	Report *d* or sample size corrected Hedge's *g*.
Assumption of equal variances is *not* met	Report *d* using the standard deviation for one of the groups as the standardizer (not the pooled standard deviation).
Assumption of normality is *not* met	Select an effect size index that does not require normality.

7.1.7 Assumptions of the Independent *t* Test

The assumptions of the independent *t* test are that the scores on the dependent variable *Y* (a) are *normally distributed* within each of the two populations, (b) are *independent*, and (c) have *equal population variances* (known as *homogeneity of variance* or *homoscedasticity*). (The assumptions of normality and independence should sound familiar as they were introduced as we learned about the one-sample *t* test.) When these assumptions are not met, other procedures may be more appropriate, as we also show later.

7.1.7.1 Normality

Let us being with a discussion of normality. The normality assumption is made because we are dealing with a *parametric inferential test*. **Parametric tests** assume a particular underlying theoretical population distribution, in this case, the normal distribution. **Nonparametric tests** do not assume a particular underlying theoretical population distribution. For the independent *t* test, *the assumption of normality is met when the dependent variable is normally* *distributed for each sample (i.e., each category or group) of the independent variable.* Conventional wisdom tells us the following about nonnormality. When the normality assumption is violated with the independent t test, the effects on Type I and Type II errors are minimal when using a two-tailed test (e.g., Glass, Peckham, & Sanders, 1972; Sawilowsky & Blair, 1992). When using a one-tailed test, violation of the normality assumption is minimal for samples larger than 10 and disappears for samples of at least 20 (Sawilowsky & Blair, 1992; Tiku & Singh, 1981). However, more recent research in situations where the groups have unequal sample sizes and the distributions for the groups differ in skewness, t is not asymptotically correct.(Cressie & Whitford, 1986). Additionally, Wilcox (2003) indicates that power for both the independent t and Welch t' can be reduced even for slight departures from normality, with outliers also contributing to the problem. Wilcox recommends several procedures not readily available and beyond the scope of this text (such as bootstrap methods, trimmed means, medians). Keep in mind, though, that the independent t test is fairly robust to nonnormality in most situations. Additionally, Wilcox (2017) suggests that t is robust to Type I errors when the group distributions are equal (e.g., the same skew across all groups).

The simplest methods for detecting violation of the normality assumption are graphical methods, such as stem-and-leaf plots, box plots, histograms, or Q-Q plots, as well as statistical procedures such as the Shapiro-Wilk test (1965) and skewness and kurtosis statistics.

7.1.7.2 Independence

The independence assumption is also necessary for the independent t test. *The assumption of independence is met when there is random assignment of individuals to the two groups or categories of the independent variable.* Random assignment to the two samples being studied provides for greater internal validity—the ability to state with some degree of confidence that the independent variable caused the outcome (i.e., the dependent variable). If the independence assumption is *not* met, then probability statements about the Type I and Type II errors will not be accurate; in other words, the probability of a Type I or Type II error may be increased as a result of the assumption not being met. Zimmerman (1997) found that Type I error was affected even for relatively small relations or correlations between the samples (i.e., even as small as .10 or .20).

In general, the assumption can be met by (a) keeping the assignment of individuals to groups separate through the design of the experiment (specifically random assignment—not to be confused with random selection), and (b) keeping the individuals separate from one another through experimental control so that the scores on the dependent variable Y for sample 1 do not influence the scores for sample 2. Zimmerman also stated that independence can be violated for supposedly independent samples due to some type of matching in the design of the experiment (e.g., matched pairs based on sex, age, and weight). If the observations are not independent, then the dependent t test, discussed later in the chapter, may be appropriate.

When considering random assignment to groups, it is important to consider the size of the sample that is being randomized. Hsu (1989) identified conditions under which equivalence is likely to be attained with random assignment. In particular, Hsu noted that the probability of groups being *nonequivalent* after random assignment increases as the number of nuisance variables increase and generally decreases as total sample size increases. For example, with a sample size of 24, the probability of nonequivalence for two groups randomly assigned is about 22% with one nuisance variable but increases to 53% with three nuisance variables. It is only at samples of about 40 in size that randomization appears to be an effective method of creating equivalent groups considering the maximum number of nuisance variables examined by Hsu (1989). The take-home message from this is the following: *Don't assume that random assignment to groups will achieve equivalence with samples of less than 40.*

7.1.7.3 Homogeneity of Variance

Of potentially more serious concern is violation of the homogeneity of variance assumption. Homogeneity of variance is met when the variances of the dependent variable for the two samples (i.e., the two groups or categories of the independent variables) are the same. Research has shown that the effect of heterogeneity (i.e., unequal variances) is minimal when the sizes of the two samples, n_1 and n_2, are equal *and* the assumption of normality holds; this is not the case when the sample sizes are not equal. When the larger variance is associated with the smaller sample size (e.g., group 1 has the larger variance and the smaller n), then the actual (i.e., observed) α level is larger than the nominal (i.e., stated) α level. In other words, if you set alpha at .05, then you are not really conducting the test at the .05 level, but at some larger value. When the larger variance is associated with the larger sample size (e.g., group 1 has the larger variance and the larger n), then the actual alpha level is smaller than the nominal alpha level. In other words, if you set alpha at .05, then you are not really conducting the test at the .05 level, but at some smaller value. When there are equal sample sizes and the assumption of normality is violated, the results from a t test will not be robust unless the distributions of the group are equal (e.g., each group has the same degree of skew) (Wilcox, 2017). One can use statistical tests to detect violation of the homogeneity of variance assumption, although the most commonly used tests are somewhat problematic. These tests include Hartley's F_{max} test (for equal ns, but sensitive to nonnormality; it is the unequal ns situation that we are concerned with anyway), Cochran's test (for equal ns, but even more sensitive to nonnormality than Hartley's test; concerned with unequal ns situation anyway), Levene's test, which is provided by default in SPSS (for equal ns, but sensitive to nonnormality; concerned with unequal ns situation anyway), the Bartlett test (for unequal ns, but very sensitive to nonnormality), the Box-Scheffé-Anderson test (for unequal ns, fairly robust to nonnormality), and the Browne-Forsythe test (for unequal ns, more robust to nonnormality than the Box-Scheffé-Anderson test and therefore recommended). When the variances are unequal and the sample sizes are unequal, the usual method is to use the Welch t' test as an alternative to the independent t test, as described in the next section. Inferential tests for evaluating homogeneity of variance are more fully considered in Chapter 9.

7.1.7.4 Conditions of the Independent t Test

In addition to meeting the assumptions of the test, we also must consider the measurement scales of the variables used as they must also be appropriate for the statistical procedure to which they are applied. Because this is a test of means, the *dependent variable* must be measured on an *interval or ratio scale*. The *independent variable*, however, must be *nominal or ordinal*, and only two categories or groups of the independent variable can be used with the independent t test. (If you continue your statistical journey, you will likely learn about analysis of variance, which can accommodate an independent variable with *more* than two categories.) It is *not* a condition of the independent *t* test that the sample sizes of the two groups be the same. *An unbalanced design (i.e., unequal sample sizes) is perfectly acceptable.* An unbalanced design is only a concern in the event that the assumption of homogeneity is violated. If you find yourself in that situation, please refer to the previous discussion on measures that can be taken.

7.2 Inferences About Two Dependent Means and How They Work

In this section, two inferential tests of the difference between two dependent means are described, the dependent *t* test and briefly the Wilcoxon signed ranks test. The section concludes with a list of recommendations.

7.2.1 Characteristics of the Dependent *t* Test

As you may recall, the **dependent *t* test** is appropriate to use when there are two samples that are dependent; that is, the individuals in sample 1 have some relationship to the individuals in sample 2. Although there are several methods for computing the test statistic *t*, the most direct method and the one most closely aligned conceptually with the one-sample *t* test is as follows:

$$t = \frac{\overline{d}}{s_{\overline{d}}}$$

where $\overline{d}$ is the **mean difference**, and $s_{\overline{d}}$ is the **standard error of the mean difference**. Conceptually, this test statistic looks just like the one-sample *t* test statistic, except now the notation has been changed to denote that we are dealing with *difference scores* rather than raw scores.

The **standard error of the mean difference** is computed by

$$s_{\overline{d}} = \frac{s_d}{\sqrt{n}}$$

where s_d is the standard deviation of the difference scores (i.e., like any other standard deviation, only this one is computed from the difference scores rather than raw scores), and *n* is the total number of pairs. Conceptually, this standard error looks just like the standard error for the one-sample *t* test. If we were doing hand computations, we would compute a difference score for each pair of scores (i.e., $Y_1 - Y_2$). For example, if sample 1 were wives and sample 2 were their husbands, then we calculate a difference score for each couple. From this set of difference scores, we then compute the mean of the difference scores $\overline{d}$ and standard deviation of the difference scores, s_d. This leads us directly into the computation of the *t* test statistic. Note that although there are *n* scores in sample 1, *n* scores in sample 2, and thus 2*n* total scores, there are only *n* difference scores, which is what the analysis is actually based upon.

The test statistic t is then compared with a critical value(s) from the t distribution. For a two-tailed test, from Table A.2 in the Appendix we would use the appropriate α_2 column depending on the desired level of significance and the appropriate row depending on the degrees of freedom. The *degrees of freedom for this test are $n - 1$*, where n represents the difference score. Conceptually, we lose one degree of freedom from the number of differences (or pairs) because we are estimating the population variance (or standard deviation) of the difference. Thus, there is one restriction along the lines of our discussion of degrees of freedom in Chapter 6. The critical values are denoted as $\pm_{\alpha_2} t_{n-1}$. The subscript, α_2, of the critical values reflects the fact that this is a two-tailed test, and the subscript $n - 1$ indicates the degrees of freedom. If the test statistic falls into either critical region, then we reject H_0; otherwise, we fail to reject H_0.

For a one-tailed test, from Table A.2 in the Appendix we would use the appropriate α_1 column depending on the desired level of significance and the appropriate row depending on the degrees of freedom. The degrees of freedom are again $n - 1$. The critical value is denoted as $+_{a_1} t_{n-1}$ for the alternative hypothesis where the difference in means is greater than zero, that is, $H_1: \mu_1 - \mu_2 > 0$, and as $-_{a_1} t_{n-1}$ for the alternative hypothesis where the difference in means is less than zero, that is, $H_1: \mu_1 - \mu_2 < 0$. If the test statistic t falls into the appropriate critical region, then we reject H_0; otherwise, we fail to reject H_0.

7.2.1.1 Confidence Interval for the Dependent t Test

For the two-tailed test, a $(1 - \alpha)\%$ confidence interval can also be examined. The confidence interval is formed as follows:

$$\bar{d} \pm \left(_{\alpha_2} t_{n-1}\right)\left(s_{\bar{d}}\right)$$

If the confidence interval contains the hypothesized mean difference of 0, then the conclusion is to fail to reject H_0; otherwise, we reject H_0. The interpretation of these confidence intervals is the same as those previously discussed for the one-sample t test and the independent t test.

7.2.1.2 Example of the Dependent t Test

Let us consider an example for purposes of illustrating the dependent t test. Ten young swimmers participated in an intensive 2-month training program. Prior to the program, each swimmer was timed during a 50-meter freestyle event. Following the program, the same swimmers were timed in the 50-meter freestyle event again. This is a classic pretest–posttest design. For illustrative purposes, we will conduct a two-tailed test. However, a case might also be made for a one-tailed test as well, in that the coach might want to see improvement only. However, conducting a two-tailed test allows us to examine the confidence interval for purposes of illustration. The raw scores, the difference scores, and the mean and standard deviation of the difference scores are shown in Table 7.3. The pretest mean time was 64 seconds, and the posttest mean time was 59 seconds.

To determine our test statistic value, t, first we compute the standard error of the mean difference as follows:

$$s_{\bar{d}} = \frac{s_d}{\sqrt{n}} = \frac{2.1602}{\sqrt{10}} = 0.6831$$

TABLE 7.3

Swimming Data for Dependent Samples

Swimmer	Pretest Time (in seconds)	Posttest Time (in seconds)	Difference (d)
1	58	54	$(58 - 54) = 4$
2	62	57	5
3	60	54	6
4	61	56	5
5	63	61	2
6	65	59	6
7	66	64	2
8	69	62	7
9	64	60	4
10	72	63	9
			$\bar{d} = 5.0000$
			$s_d = 2.1602$

Next, using this value for the denominator, the test statistic t is then computed as follows:

$$t = \frac{\bar{d}}{s_{\bar{d}}} = \frac{5}{0.6831} = 7.3196$$

We then use Table A.2 in the Appendix to determine the critical values. Because there are 9 degrees of freedom ($n - 1 = 10 - 1 = 9$), using $\alpha = .05$ and a two-tailed or nondirectional test we find the critical values using the appropriate α_2 column to be $+2.262$ and -2.262. Because the test statistic falls beyond the critical values, as shown in Figure 7.3, we reject the null hypothesis that the means are equal in favor of the nondirectional alternative that the means are not equal. Thus, we conclude that the mean swimming performance changed from pretest to posttest at the .05 level of significance (observed $p <$ nominal alpha of .05).

The 95% confidence interval is computed to be the following:

$$\bar{d} \pm \left({}_{\alpha_2} t_{n-1} \right) \left(s_{\bar{d}} \right) = 5 \pm (2.262)(0.6831) = 5 \pm (1.5452) = (3.4548, 6.5452)$$

Because the confidence interval does not contain the hypothesized mean difference value of zero, we would again reject the null hypothesis and conclude that the mean pretest–postttest difference was not equal to zero at the .05 level of significance (observed $p <$ nominal alpha of .05).

7.2.1.3 Recommendations

The following three recommendations are made regarding the two dependent samples case. First, the dependent t test is recommended when the normality assumption is met.

Second, the dependent t test using ranks (Conover & Iman, 1981) is recommended when the normality assumption is not met. Here you rank order the difference scores from

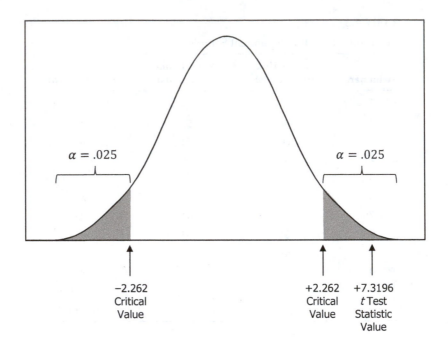

FIGURE 7.3
Critical regions and test statistic for the swimming example.

highest to lowest, then conduct the test on the ranked difference scores rather than on the raw difference scores. However, more recent research by Wilcox (2003) indicates that power for the dependent t can be reduced even for slight departures from normality. Wilcox recommends several procedures beyond the scope of this text (bootstrap methods, trimmed means, medians, Stein's method). Keep in mind, though, that the dependent t test is fairly robust to nonnormality in most situations.

Third, the nonparametric Wilcoxon signed ranks test is recommended when the data are nonnormal with extreme outliers (one or a few observations that behave quite differently from the rest). However, among the disadvantages of this test are that (a) the critical values are not extensively tabled and two different tables exist depending on sample size, and (b) tied ranks can affect the results and no optimal procedure has yet been developed (Wilcox, 1995). For these reasons the details of the Wilcoxon signed ranks test are not described here. Note that most major statistical packages, including SPSS, include options for conducting the dependent t test and the Wilcoxon signed ranks test. Alternatively, one could conduct the Friedman nonparametric one-factor analysis of variance, also based on ranked data, and which is appropriate for comparing two or more dependent sample means. These recommendations are summarized in Box 7.1.

7.2.2 Sample Size of the Dependent t Test

A common myth is that a sample size of 30 is sufficient for conducting a dependent t test (or generally any of the three t tests). *We do not condone going by this rule.* Rather, we encourage researchers to conduct a power analysis to determine the sample size needed for sufficient power.

7.2.3 Power of the Dependent *t* Test

Power for the dependent *t* test can be determined based on reviewing power tables or using statistical software (e.g., G*Power).

7.2.4 Effect Size of the Dependent *t* Test

The effect size for the dependent *t* test can be measured using Cohen's (1988) *d*, computed as follows:

$$\text{Cohen's } d = \frac{\bar{d}}{s_d}$$

where Cohen's *d* is simply used to distinguish among the various uses and slight differences in the computation of *d*. Interpretation of the value of *d* would be the same as for the one-sample *t* and the independent *t* tests discussed earlier—specifically, the number of standard deviation units for which the mean(s) differ(s).

The effect size for the example examined previously is computed to be the following:

$$\text{Cohen's } d = \frac{\bar{d}}{s_d} = \frac{5}{2.1602} = 2.3146$$

which is interpreted as there is approximately a two and one-third standard deviation difference between the pretest and posttest mean swimming times, a very large effect size according to Cohen's subjective standard. See Table 7.4 for guidelines on interpreting Cohen's *d*.

7.2.4.1 Confidence Intervals for Cohen's Delta

As we learned in the previous chapter, computing *confidence intervals for effect sizes* is also valuable. The benefit in creating confidence intervals for effect size values is similar to that of creating confidence intervals for parameter estimates—*confidence intervals for the effect size provide an added measure of precision that is not obtained from knowledge of the effect size alone.* Computing confidence intervals for effect size indices, however, is not as straightforward as simply plugging in known values into a formula. This is because *d* is a function of

TABLE 7.4

Dependent *t* Test Effect Size and Interpretation

Effect Size	Interpretation
d	The number of standard deviation units in which the groups differ • Small effect = .20 • Medium effect = .50 • Large effect = .80

both the population mean and population standard deviation (Finch & Cumming, 2009), and the noncentrality parameter comes into play. We refer you back to Chapter 6 for a refresher on this.

A nice online calculator for computing the dependent *t* test confidence interval for effect size *d* using the noncentrality parameter is available at https://effect-size-calculator.herokuapp.com (Uanhoro, 2017). As shown in Figure 7.4, seven inputs are required: sample mean for each group, sample standard deviation for each group, number of pairs (i.e., sample size), the bivariate correlation between measures (*r*, which we will learn about in more detail in an

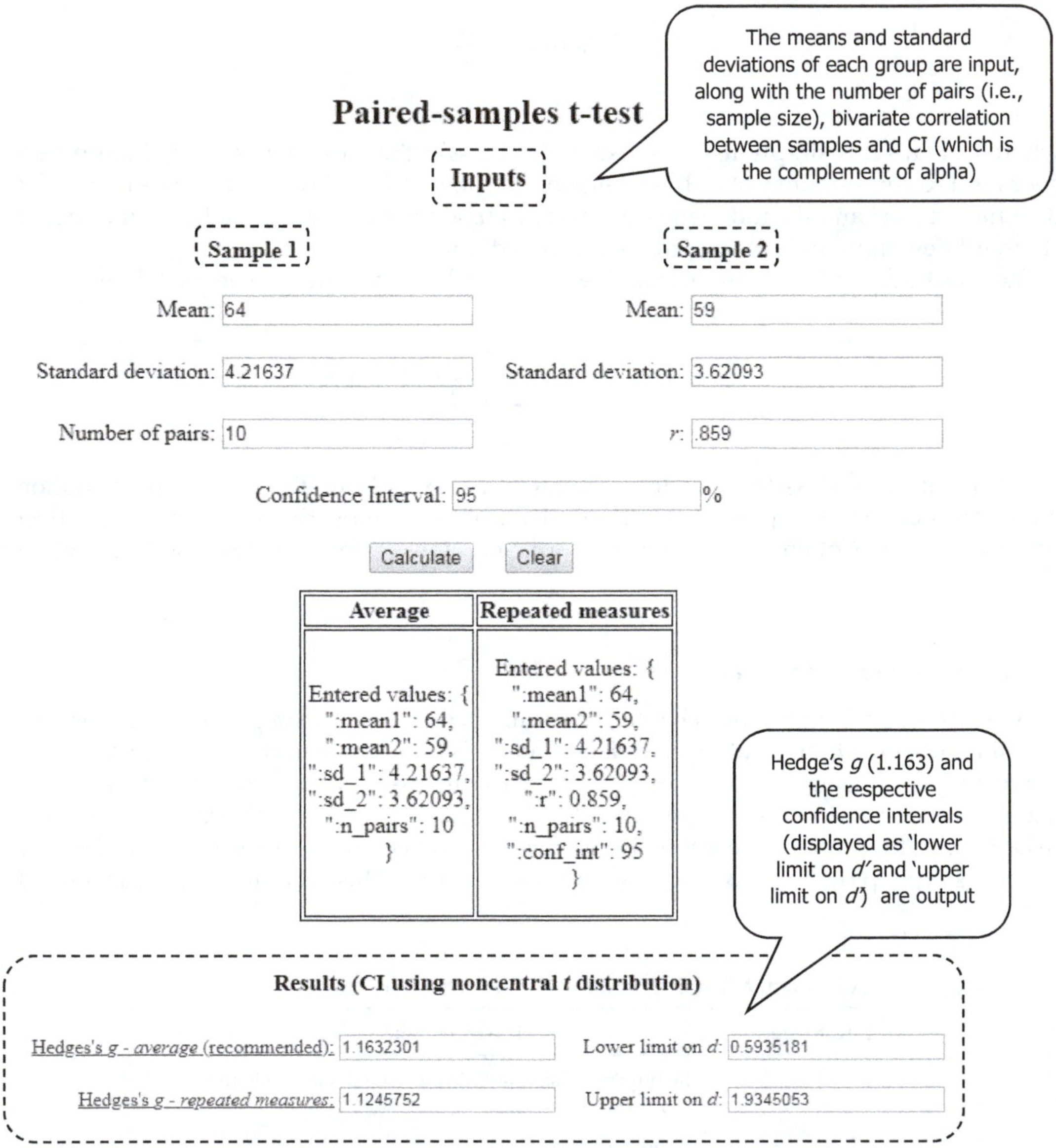

Paired-samples t-test

Inputs

> The means and standard deviations of each group are input, along with the number of pairs (i.e., sample size), bivariate correlation between samples and CI (which is the complement of alpha)

Sample 1

Mean: 64

Standard deviation: 4.21637

Number of pairs: 10

Sample 2

Mean: 59

Standard deviation: 3.62093

r: .859

Confidence Interval: 95 %

Calculate   Clear

Average	Repeated measures
Entered values: { ":mean1": 64, ":mean2": 59, ":sd_1": 4.21637, ":sd_2": 3.62093, ":n_pairs": 10 }	Entered values: { ":mean1": 64, ":mean2": 59, ":sd_1": 4.21637, ":sd_2": 3.62093, ":r": 0.859, ":n_pairs": 10, ":conf_int": 95 }

> Hedge's *g* (1.163) and the respective confidence intervals (displayed as 'lower limit on *d*' and 'upper limit on *d*') are output

Results (CI using noncentral *t* distribution)

Hedges's *g - average* (recommended): 1.1632301   Lower limit on *d*: 0.5935181

Hedges's *g - repeated measures*: 1.1245752   Upper limit on *d*: 1.9345053

FIGURE 7.4
Effect size *d* and confidence interval of *d*.

upcoming chapter), and confidence interval (i.e., the complement of alpha). Hedge's *g* is 1.1632, with confidence intervals for *d* of .5935 and 1.9345. Putting this in context of our swimming example, if multiple random samples were drawn from the population, 95% of the samples could expect the posttest swimming speed to have, at minimum, about .60 and, at maximum, nearly two standard deviation units faster swim time as compared to speed at pretest.

7.2.5 Assumptions of the Dependent *t* Test

The assumptions of the dependent *t* test include: normality, independence, and homogeneity of variance. These should sound familiar as they are the same assumptions as those for the independent *t* test. As you will see, however, how we approach estimating evidence of these assumptions differs.

7.2.5.1 Normality

For the dependent *t* test, the assumption of normality is met when the *difference scores* are normally distributed. Normality of the difference scores can be examined as discussed previously—graphical methods (such as stem-and-leaf plots, box plots, histograms, and/or Q-Q plots), statistical procedures such as the Shapiro-Wilk test (1965), and skewness and kurtosis statistics.

7.2.5.2 Independence

The assumption of independence is met when the cases in our sample have been *randomly selected* from the population. If the independence assumption is *not* met, then probability statements about the Type I and Type II errors will not be accurate; in other words, the probability of a Type I or Type II error may be increased as a result of the assumption not being met.

7.2.5.3 Homogeneity of Variance

Homogeneity of variance refers to *equal variances of the two populations*. In later chapters we will examine procedures for formally testing for equal variances. For the moment, *if the ratio of the smallest to largest sample variance is within 1:4, then we have evidence to suggest the assumption of homogeneity of variances is met*. Research has shown that the effect of heterogeneity (i.e., unequal variances) is minimal when the sizes of the two samples, n_1 and n_2, are equal, as is the case with the dependent *t* test by definition (unless there are missing data).

7.2.5.4 Conditions of the Dependent t Test

First, we need to determine the conditions under which the dependent *t* test is appropriate. Because this is a test of means, *both variables* on the matched pair must be measured on an *interval or ratio scale*. For example, the same individuals may be measured at two points in time on the same interval-scaled pretest and posttest, or some matched pairs (e.g., twins or husbands–wives) may be assessed with the same ratio-scaled measure (e.g., weight measured in pounds).

7.3 Computing Inferences About Two Independent Means Using SPSS

Instructions for determining the independent samples *t* test using SPSS are presented first. The data-screening section provides additional steps for examining the assumption of normality for the independent *t* test.

Step 1. In order to conduct an independent *t* test, your dataset needs to include one dependent variable *Y* that is measured on an interval or ratio scale (e.g., "cholesterol") as well as a grouping variable *X* that is measured on a nominal or ordinal scale (e.g., "gender"). For the grouping variable, if there are more than two categories available, only two categories can be selected (or multiple categories must be collapsed so there are only two categories) when running the independent *t* test (the analysis of variance is required for examining more than two categories). To conduct the independent *t* test, go to the "Analyze" in the top pulldown menu, select "Compare Means," and then select "Independent-Samples T Test." Following the steps in the screenshot in Figure 7.5 produces the "Independent-Samples T Test" dialog box.

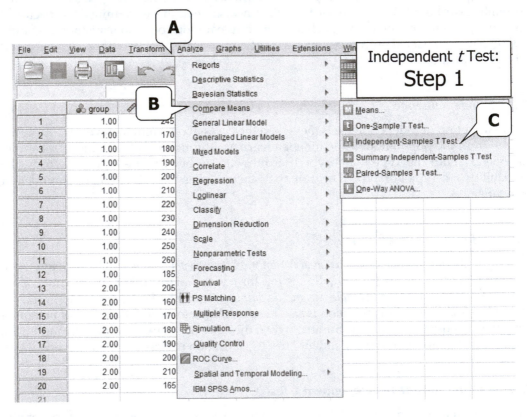

FIGURE 7.5
Independent *t* test: Step 1.

Step 2. Next, from the main "Independent-Samples T Test" dialog box, click the dependent variable (e.g., "cholesterol") and move it into the "Test Variable" box by clicking the arrow button. Next, click the grouping variable (e.g., "gender") and move it into the "Grouping

Variable" box by clicking the arrow button. You will notice that there are two question marks next to the name of your grouping variable. This is SPSS letting you know that you need to define (numerically) which two categories of the grouping variable you want to include in your analysis. To do that, click "Define Groups."

Note on changing the alpha level. The default alpha level in SPSS is .05, and thus the default corresponding confidence interval is 95%. If you wish to test your hypothesis at an alpha level other than .05 (and thus obtain confidence intervals other than 95%), click the "Options" button located in the top-right corner of the main dialog box (see Step 2 in the screenshot in Figure 7.6). From here, the confidence interval percentage can be adjusted to correspond to the alpha level at which you wish your hypothesis to be tested (see Step 3 in the screenshot in Figure 7.7). (For purposes of this example, the test has been generated using an alpha level of .05.)

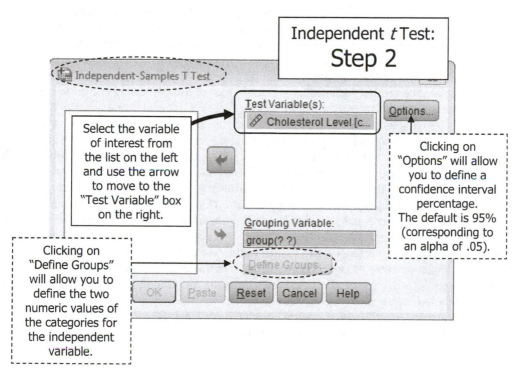

FIGURE 7.6
Independent *t* test: Step 2.

Step 3. From the "Define Groups" dialog box, enter the numeric value designated for each of the two categories or groups of your independent variable. Where it says "Group 1," type in the value designated for your first group (e.g., 1, which in our case indicated that the individual was a female), and where it says "Group 2" type in the value designated for your second group (e.g., 2, in our example, a male) (see Step 3 in the screenshot in Figure 7.7).

Click "Continue" to return to the original dialog box (see the screenshot in Figure 7.6) and then click "OK" to run the analysis.

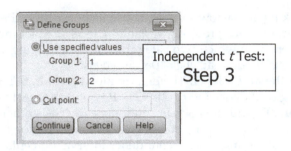

FIGURE 7.7
Independent *t* test: Step 3.

7.3.1 Interpreting the Output for Inferences About Two Independent Means

The first portion of Table 7.5 provides various descriptive statistics for each group, while the bottom box gives the results of the requested procedure. The following three different inferential tests are automatically provided: (1) Levene's test of the homogeneity of variance assumption (the first two columns of results), (2) the independent *t* test (which SPSS calls "Equal Variances Assumed"; the top row of the remaining columns of results), and (3) the Welch *t'* test (which SPSS calls "Equal Variances Not Assumed"; the bottom row of the remaining columns of results).

The first interpretation that must be made is for *Levene's test of equal variances*. We must interpret Levene's test first as the results for Levene's dictates whether the *t* test results are based on equal variances or unequal variances (which is the Welch *t'* test). The assumption of equal variances is met when Levene's test is *not* statistically significant, which is interpreted as the variances of the two groups are equal. We can determine statistical significance for Levene's test by reviewing the *p* value for the *F* test. In this example, the *p* value is .090, greater than our alpha level of .05, and thus not statistically significant. *Thus, Levene's test tells us that the variance for cholesterol level for males is not statistically significantly different than the variance for cholesterol level for females, and this provides evidence of meeting the assumption of equal variances.* Having met the assumption of equal variances, the values in the rest of the table will be drawn from the row labeled "Equal Variances Assumed." Had we *not* met the assumption of equal variances (*p* < alpha for Levene's test), we would report Welch *t'* results for which the statistics are presented on the row labeled "Equal Variances Not Assumed."

After determining that the variances are equal, the next step is to examine the results of the independent *t* test. The *t* test statistic value is 2.484 and the associated *p* value is .023. *Because*

TABLE 7.5

SPSS Results for Independent *t* Test

> The table labeled "Group Statistics"
> provides basic descriptive statistics for the
> dependent variable by group.

Group Statistics

	Gender	N	Mean	Std. Deviation	Std. Error Mean
Cholesterol Level	Male	12	215.0000	30.22642	8.72562
	Female	8	185.0000	19.08627	6.74802

TABLE 7.5 (continued)

SPSS Results for Independent *t* Test

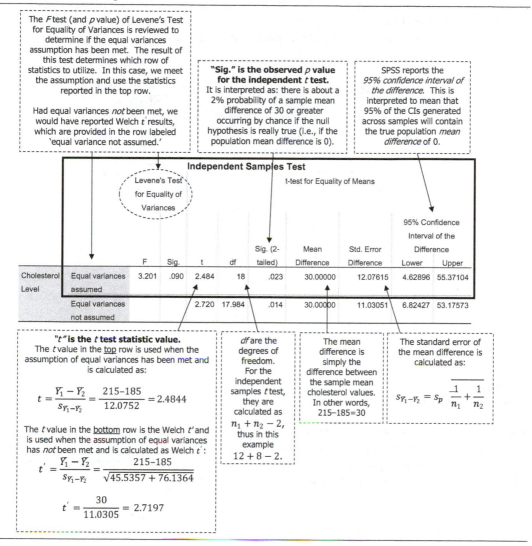

The *F* test (and *p* value) of Levene's Test for Equality of Variances is reviewed to determine if the equal variances assumption has been met. The result of this test determines which row of statistics to utilize. In this case, we meet the assumption and use the statistics reported in the top row.

Had equal variances *not* been met, we would have reported Welch *t'* results, which are provided in the row labeled 'equal variance not assumed.'

"Sig." is the observed *p* value for the independent *t* test. It is interpreted as: there is about a 2% probability of a sample mean difference of 30 or greater occurring by chance if the null hypothesis is really true (i.e., if the population mean difference is 0).

SPSS reports the *95% confidence interval of the difference*. This is interpreted to mean that 95% of the CIs generated across samples will contain the true population *mean difference* of 0.

Independent Samples Test

Levene's Test for Equality of Variances

t-test for Equality of Means

		F	Sig.	t	df	Sig. (2-tailed)	Mean Difference	Std. Error Difference	95% Confidence Interval of the Difference	
									Lower	Upper
Cholesterol Level	Equal variances assumed	3.201	.090	2.484	18	.023	30.00000	12.07615	4.62896	55.37104
	Equal variances not assumed			2.720	17.984	.014	30.00000	11.03051	6.82427	53.17573

"*t*" is the *t* test statistic value. The *t* value in the <u>top</u> row is used when the assumption of equal variances has been met and is calculated as:

$$t = \frac{\bar{Y}_1 - \bar{Y}_2}{s_{\bar{Y}_1 - \bar{Y}_2}} = \frac{215 - 185}{12.0752} = 2.4844$$

The *t* value in the <u>bottom</u> row is the Welch *t'* and is used when the assumption of equal variances has *not* been met and is calculated as Welch *t'*:

$$t' = \frac{\bar{Y}_1 - \bar{Y}_2}{s_{\bar{Y}_1 - \bar{Y}_2}} = \frac{215 - 185}{\sqrt{45.5357 + 76.1364}}$$

$$t' = \frac{30}{11.0305} = 2.7197$$

df are the degrees of freedom. For the independent samples *t* test, they are calculated as $n_1 + n_2 - 2$, thus in this example $12 + 8 - 2$.

The mean difference is simply the difference between the sample mean cholesterol values. In other words, $215 - 185 = 30$

The standard error of the mean difference is calculated as:

$$s_{\bar{Y}_1 - \bar{Y}_2} = s_p \sqrt{\frac{1}{n_1} + \frac{1}{n_2}}$$

the observed probability, *p*, is less than our nominal alpha of .05, we reject the null hypothesis. There is a statistically significant difference between groups, and there is evidence to suggest that the mean cholesterol level for males is different than the mean cholesterol level for females.

7.4 Computing Inferences About Two Dependent Means Using SPSS

Next, instructions for determining the dependent samples *t* test using SPSS are presented. The data-screening section provides additional steps for examining the assumptions of normality and homogeneity for the dependent *t* test.

Step 1. To conduct a dependent *t* test, your dataset needs to include the two variables (i.e., for the paired samples) whose means you wish to compare (e.g., pretest and posttest). To conduct the dependent *t* test, go to the "Analyze" in the top pulldown menu, then select "Compare Means," and then select "Paired-Samples T Test." Following the steps in the screenshot in Figure 7.8 produces the "Paired-Samples T Test" dialog box.

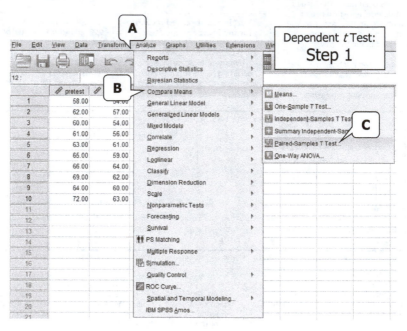

FIGURE 7.8
Dependent *t* test: Step 1.

Step 2. Click both variables (e.g., pretest and posttest as Variable 1 and Variable 2, respectively) and move them into the "Paired Variables" box by clicking the arrow button. Both variables should now appear in the box, as shown in the screenshot for Step 2 in Figure 7.9. Then click "OK" to run the analysis and generate the output.

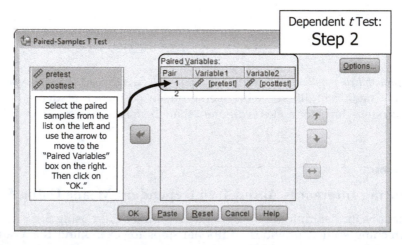

FIGURE 7.9
Dependent *t* test: Step 2.

7.4.1 Interpreting the Output for Inferences About Two Dependent Means

The output appears in Table 7.6, where again the top box provides descriptive statistics, the middle box provides a bivariate correlation coefficient for the two variables, and the bottom box gives the results of the dependent *t* test procedure. In terms of our test of inference, with a test statistic value of 7.319 and *p* of .000, we reject the null hypothesis. There is a statistically significant pre to post mean swim time.

TABLE 7.6

SPSS Results for Dependent *t* Test

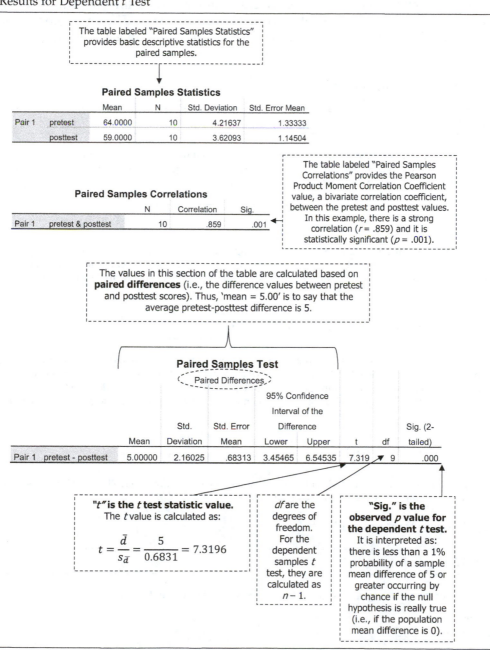

The table labeled "Paired Samples Statistics" provides basic descriptive statistics for the paired samples.

Paired Samples Statistics

		Mean	N	Std. Deviation	Std. Error Mean
Pair 1	pretest	64.0000	10	4.21637	1.33333
	posttest	59.0000	10	3.62093	1.14504

The table labeled "Paired Samples Correlations" provides the Pearson Product Moment Correlation Coefficient value, a bivariate correlation coefficient, between the pretest and posttest values. In this example, there is a strong correlation ($r = .859$) and it is statistically significant ($p = .001$).

Paired Samples Correlations

		N	Correlation	Sig.
Pair 1	pretest & posttest	10	.859	.001

The values in this section of the table are calculated based on **paired differences** (i.e., the difference values between pretest and posttest scores). Thus, 'mean = 5.00' is to say that the average pretest-posttest difference is 5.

Paired Samples Test

Paired Differences

		Mean	Std. Deviation	Std. Error Mean	95% Confidence Interval of the Difference Lower	95% Confidence Interval of the Difference Upper	t	df	Sig. (2-tailed)
Pair 1	pretest - posttest	5.00000	2.16025	.68313	3.45465	6.54535	7.319	9	.000

"*t*" is the *t* test statistic value. The *t* value is calculated as:

$$t = \frac{\bar{d}}{s_{\bar{d}}} = \frac{5}{0.6831} = 7.3196$$

df are the degrees of freedom. For the dependent samples *t* test, they are calculated as $n - 1$.

"Sig." is the observed *p* value for the dependent *t* test. It is interpreted as: there is less than a 1% probability of a sample mean difference of 5 or greater occurring by chance if the null hypothesis is really true (i.e., if the population mean difference is 0).

7.5 Computing Inferences About Two Independent Means Using R

Next we consider **R** for the dependent *t* test. The scripts are provided within the blocks with additional annotation to assist in understanding how the commands work. Should you want to write reminder notes and annotation to yourself as you write the commands in **R** (and we highly encourage doing so), remember that any text that follows a hashtag (i.e., #) is annotation only and not part of the **R** script. Thus, you can write annotations directly into **R** with hashtags. We encourage this practice so that when you call up the commands in the future, you'll understand what the various lines of code are doing. You may think you'll remember what you did. However, trust us. There is a good chance that you won't. Thus, consider it best practice when using **R** to annotate heavily!

7.5.1 Reading Data into R

```
getwd()
```

R is always pointed to a directory on your computer. To find out which directory it is pointed to, run this "get working directory" function. We will assume that we need to change the working directory, and will use the next line of code to set the working directory to the desired path.

```
setwd("E:/Folder")
```

To set the working directory, use the *setwd* function and change what is in quotation marks here to your file location. Also, if you are copying the directory name, it will copy in slashes. You will need to change the slash (i.e., \) to a forward slash (i.e., /). Note that you need your destination name within quotation marks in the parentheses.

```
Ch7_cholesterol <- read.csv("Ch7_cholesterol.csv")
```

The *read.csv* function reads our data into **R**. What's to the left of the <- will be what the data will be called in **R**. In this example, we're calling the **R** dataframe "Ch7_cholesterol." What's to the right of the <- tells **R** to find this particular .csv file. In this example, our file is called "Ch7_cholesterol.csv." Make sure the extension (i.e., .csv) is included in your script. Also note that the name of your file should be in quotation marks within parentheses.

```
names(Ch7_cholesterol)
```

The *names* function will produce a list of variable names for each dataframe as follows. This is a good check to make sure your data have been read in correctly.

```
[1] "group" "cholesterol"
```

```
View(Ch7_cholesterol)
```

The *View* function will let you view the dataset in spreadsheet format in RStudio.

FIGURE 7.10
Reading data into **R**.

```
Ch7_cholesterol$group <- factor(Ch7_cholesterol$group,
                                labels = c("male",
                                            "female"))
```

The *factor* function renames our "group" variable as nominal (i.e., "factor") with two groups or categories with labels of "male" and "female." Had we wanted to create a new variable rather than rename our variable, we would have defined "Ch7_cholesterol$NewName" rather than "Ch7_cholesterol$group" to the left of <- (i.e., as the first portion of this script).

```
levels(Ch7_cholesterol$group)
```

The *levels* function will output the categories in our "group" variable as follows:

```
[1] "male" "female"
```

```
summary(Ch7_cholesterol)
```

The *summary* function will produce basic descriptive statistics on all the variables in our dataframe. This is a great way to quickly check to see if the data have been read in correctly and to get a feel for your data, if you haven't already. The output from the summary statement for this dataframe looks like this. Because the variable "group" is nominal, our output includes only the frequencies of cases within the categories.

```
    group     cholesterol
male  :12   Min.    :160.0
female: 8   1st Qu.:180.0
            Median :200.0
            Mean    :203.0
            3rd Qu.:222.5
            Max.    :260.0
```

FIGURE 7.10 (continued)
Reading data into **R**.

7.5.2 Generating the Independent *t* and Welch *t′* Tests

Working in **R**, we will first generate the independent *t* test assuming equal variances.

```
Ch7_indT <- t.test(cholesterol ~ group,
                   data=Ch7_cholesterol,
                   conf.level = .95,
                   var.equal=TRUE)
```

The *t.test* function will generate the independent *t* test with "cholesterol" as the dependent variable and "group" as the independent variable from the dataframe "Ch7_cholesterol." We are testing to an alpha of .05 (i.e., "conf.level = .95") and assuming the variances are equal (i.e., "var.equal = TRUE"). Based on the results of Levene's test (see data-screening section), we have met this assumption. We are creating an object from the results of this test, and we're naming that object "Ch7_indT."

FIGURE 7.11
Generating the independent *t* and Welch *t′* tests.

```
Ch7_indT
```

This script will generate the output from the test we just conducted. We see our test statistic is 2.4842, with 18 degrees of freedom, and p value of .02. The 95% confidence interval of the mean difference is 4.63 to 55.37. The averages for both male ($M = 215$) and female ($F = 185$) are also presented, labeled "sample estimates."

```
        Two Sample t-test
data: cholesterol by group
t = 2.4842, df = 18, p-value = 0.02305

alternative hypothesis: true difference in means is not equal to 0

95 percent confidence interval:
  4.628956 55.371044

sample estimates:
  mean in group male     mean in group female
                 215                      185
```

Next, let's generate results of the Welch t' test.

```
Ch7_indT2 <- t.test(cholesterol ~ group,
                    data=Ch7_cholesterol,
                    conf.level = .95,
                    var.equal=FALSE)
```

The *t.test* function with "var.equal = FALSE" will generate the Welch t' test with "*cholesterol*" as the dependent variable, "*group*" as the independent variable, and an alpha of .05 (i.e., "conf.level = .95"). This test assumes the variances are *not* equal (i.e., "var.equal = FALSE"). For illustrative purposes, we will generate these results. However, we met the assumption of equal variances, and thus do not need the results from Welch t'.

```
Ch7_indT2
```

This script will generate output from the test we just conducted as follows using Welch t'. We see that our test statistic is 2.7197, with 18 degrees of freedom, and p value of .014. The 95% confidence interval of the mean difference is 6.824 to 53.176. The averages for both male ($M = 215$) and female ($F = 185$) are also presented.

```
        elch Two-Sample t Test

data: cholesterol by group
t = 2.7197, df = 17.984, p-value = 0.01406

alternative hypothesis: true difference in means is not equal to 0

95 percent confidence interval:
  6.824267 53.175733
```

FIGURE 7.11 (continued)
Generating the independent t and Welch t' tests.

```
sample estimates:
  mean in group male mean in group female
                 215                    185
```

Finally, let's generate effect size indices.

```
install.packages("compute.es")
```

The *install.packages* function will install the *compute.es* package that will be used to generate various effect size values.

```
library(compute.es)
```

The *library* function will load the *compute.es* package.

```
compute.es::tes(2.484236, n.1 =12,
                n.2 =8,
                level=95)
```

We will compute the effect size using the value of the *t* test statistic, sample size of each group, and confidence level. In parentheses, we enter the test statistic value from the independent *t* test that we just generated (i.e., 2.48236), along with sample sizes of the groups using the *n.1* and *n.2* script (male *n* = 12; female *n* = 8), and the alpha level ("level = 95" for an alpha of .05). A lot of information is provided, but we are most interested in the effect size estimate and their confidence intervals (provided in brackets). We are provided a number of different effect size estimates, but we are primarily interested in Cohen's *d* (the first estimate, 1.13) and Hedge's *g* (the second estimate, 1.09). Both of these estimates also include the confidence intervals for the respective effect size.

Mean Differences ES:

```
d [ 95 %CI] = 1.13 [ 0.1 , 2.16 ]
   var(d) = 0.24
   p-value(d) = 0.03
   U3(d) = 87.16 %
   CLES(d) = 78.87 %
   Cliff's Delta = 0.58
g [ 95 %CI] = 1.09 [ 0.1 , 2.07 ]
   var(g) = 0.22
   p-value(g) = 0.03
   U3(g) = 86.13 %
   CLES(g) = 77.87 %
```

```
Correlation ES:
```

```
r [ 95 %CI] = 0.51 [ 0.05 , 0.79 ]
   var(r) = 0.03
   p-value(r) = 0.03
```

```
z [ 95 %CI] = 0.56 [ 0.05 , 1.07 ]
   var(z) = 0.06
   p-value(z) = 0.03
```

FIGURE 7.11 (continued)
Generating the independent *t* and Welch *t'* tests.

```
Odds Ratio ES:

OR [ 95 %CI] = 7.82 [ 1.21 , 50.67 ]
  p-value(OR) = 0.03

Log OR [ 95 %CI] = 2.06 [ 0.19 , 3.93 ]
  var(lOR) = 0.79
  p-value(Log OR) = 0.03

Other:

NNT = 2.41
Total N = 20
```

FIGURE 7.11 (continued)
Generating the independent *t* and Welch *t'* tests.

7.6 Computing Inferences About Two Dependent Means Using R

Next we consider **R** for the dependent *t* test. As noted previously, the scripts are provided within the blocks with additional annotation to assist in understanding how the commands work.

7.6.1 Reading Data Into R

```
getwd()
```

R is always pointed to a directory on your computer. To find out which directory it is pointed to, run this "get working directory" function. We will assume that we need to change the working directory, and will use the next line of code to set the working directory to the desired path.

```
setwd("E:/Folder")
```

To set the working directory, use the *setwd* function and change what is in quotation marks here to your file location. Also, if you are copying the directory name, it will copy in slashes. You will need to change the slash (i.e., \) to a forward slash (i.e., /). Note that you need your destination name within quotation marks in the parentheses.

```
Ch7_swim <- read.csv("Ch7_swim.csv")
```

The *read.csv* function reads our data into **R**. What's to the left of the <- will be what the data will be called in **R**. In this example, we're calling the **R** dataframe "Ch7_swim." What's to the right of the <- tells **R** to find this particular .csv file. In this example, our file is called "Ch7_swim.csv." Make sure the extension (i.e., .csv) is included in your script. Also note that the name of your file should be in quotation marks within the parentheses.

FIGURE 7.12
Reading data into **R** for the dependent *t* test.

```
names(Ch7_swim)
```

The *names* function will produce a list of variable names for each dataframe as follows. This is a good check to make sure your data have been read in correctly.

```
[1] "pretest" "posttest"
```

```
View(Ch7_swim)
```

The *View* function will let you view the dataset in spreadsheet format in RStudio.

```
summary(Ch7_swim)
```

The *summary* function will produce basic descriptive statistics on all the variables in our dataframe. This is a great way to quickly check to see if the data have been read in correctly and to get a feel for your data, if you haven't already. The output from the summary statement for this dataframe looks like this.

```
   pretest            posttest
Min.   :58.00     Min.   :54.00
1st Qu.:61.25     1st Qu.:56.25
Median :63.50     Median :59.50
Mean   :64.00     Mean   :59.00
3rd Qu.:65.75     3rd Qu.:61.75
Max.   :72.00     Max.   :64.00
```

```
Ch7_swim$differ <- Ch7_swim$pretest-Ch7_swim$posttest
```

We can write a script to create a new variable computed as the difference between the pretest and posttest. In our script, what's to the left of <- tells **R** to create a new variable, "differ," and place it into our dataframe, "Ch7_swim." This variable, "differ," is computed as the pretest minus the posttest (i.e., "Ch7_swim$pretest—Ch7_swim$posttest"). In other words, what's the right of <- is the formula for computing the difference score.

```
View(Ch7_swim)
```

The *View* function will let us view the dataset in spreadsheet format in RStudio.

FIGURE 7.12 (continued)
Reading data into **R** for the dependent *t* test.

7.6.2 Generating the Dependent *t* Test

```
Ch7_depT <- t.test(Ch7_swim$pretest, Ch7_swim$posttest,
                   paired=TRUE)
```

The *t.test* function with "paired=TRUE" will generate the dependent *t* test, pairing the pretest and posttest variables from the "Ch7_swim" dataframe. It will call the object "Ch7_depT."

FIGURE 7.13
Generating the dependent *t* test.

```
Ch7_depT
```

This script will generate output from the test we just conducted. We see that our test statistic is 7.3193, with 9 degrees of freedom, and p value of < .001. The 95% confidence interval of the mean difference is 3.45 to 6.54. The mean of the differences is 5.

Paired t-test

data: `Ch7_swim$pretest` and `Ch7_swim$posttest`

t = 7.3193, df = 9, p-value = 4.472e-05

alternative hypothesis: true difference in means is not equal to 0

95 percent confidence interval:
 3.454652 6.545348

sample estimates:
mean of the differences
                      5

FIGURE 7.13 (continued)
Generating the dependent t test.

7.7 Data Screening

We will begin data screening with examining the extent to which the assumptions of the independent t test were met. This will be following by data screening for the assumptions of the dependent t test.

7.7.1 Data Screening for the Independent t Test

The assumptions for the independent t test that we need to examine via data screening include the *normality* of the distribution of the dependent variable by categories of the independent variable and *homogeneity of variances*. Recall that the assumption of independence is required as well; however, as noted earlier, that is not an assumption with which data will be used to assess the extent to which the assumption is met.

7.7.1.1 Normality for the Independent t Test

Let's first examine the assumption of normality of the distribution of the dependent variable by categories of the independent variable. As alluded to earlier in the chapter, understanding the distributional shape, specifically the extent to which normality is a reasonable assumption, is important. *For the independent t test, the distributional shape for the dependent variable should be normally distributed for each category/group of the independent variable.* As with our one-sample t test, we can again use Explore to examine the extent to which the assumption of normality is met.

The general steps for accessing Explore have been presented in previous chapters (e.g., Chapter 4), and they will not be reiterated here. Normality of the dependent variable must be examined for each category of the independent variable, so we must tell SPSS to split the examination of normality by group. Click the dependent variable (e.g., cholesterol) and move it into the "Test Variable" box by clicking on the arrow button. Next, click the grouping variable (e.g., gender) and move it into the "Factor List" box by clicking on the arrow button. The procedures for selecting normality statistics were presented in Chapter 6, and they remain the same here: click "Plots" in the upper-right corner. Place a checkmark in the boxes for "Normality plots with tests" and also for "Histogram." Then click "Continue" to return to the main Explore dialog screen. From there, click "OK" to generate the output.

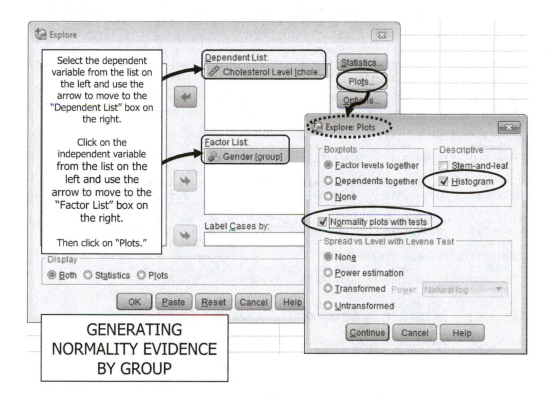

Working in **R**, we can generate similar normality evidence.

```
install.packages("pastecs")
```

The *install.packages* function will install the *pastecs* package which we will use to generate various forms of normality evidence.

```
library(pastecs)
```

The *library* function will load the *pastecs* package.

FIGURE 7.14
Generating normality evidence by group.

```
by(Ch7_cholesterol$cholesterol, Ch7_cholesterol$group,
    stat.desc,
    basic = FALSE,
    norm=TRUE)
```

The *by* function will generate descriptive statistics (i.e., "stat.desc") for our dependent variable, "cholesterol," split by our independent variable, "gender" (i.e., "by(Ch7_cholesterol$cholesterol, Ch7_cholesterol$group"). The command *basic=FALSE* will remove a lot of descriptive statistic estimates that we won't use for examining normality. We could have easily said *basic=TRUE* and generated what we needed plus a lot more. The command *norm=TRUE* will generate statistics related to normality.

Skew and kurtosis are both within the range of normal for both males and females. We see our output as follows, where we have skew and kurtosis along with its standard error. Skew and kurtosis divided by its standard error can be reviewed to a critical value of 1.96 (alpha = .05) to determine statistical significance (where values greater than about 2 indicate statistically significant nonnormality). *Note:* You may have noticed that the skewness and kurtosis value that we've just generated differs from what we found in SPSS. *This is because there are different ways to calculate skewness and kurtosis.* Let's use another package in **R** to calculate these statistics with different algorithms.

Shapiro-Wilk's test statistic is labeled "normtest.W" in the output. The *p* value for Shapiro-Wilk's is labeled "normtest.p." For both males and females, the results are not statistically significant.

```
Ch7_cholesterol$group: male
       median            mean       SE.mean  CI.mean.0.95             var
  215.0000000     215.0000000     8.7256154    19.2049499     913.6363636

      std.dev        coef.var      skewness       skew.2SE        kurtosis
   30.2264183       0.1405880     0.0000000      0.0000000      -1.6316706

     kurt.2SE      normtest.W     normtest.p
   -0.6620715       0.9486328     0.6170905
```

Shapiro Wilk's is labeled *normtest.W.* The *p* value for Shapiro Wilk's is *normtest.p.*

```
Ch7_cholesterol$group: female
       median            mean       SE.mean  CI.mean.0.95             var
  185.0000000     185.0000000     6.7480156    15.9565213     364.2857143

      std.dev        coef.var      skewness       skew.2SE        kurtosis
   19.0862703       0.1031690     0.0000000      0.0000000      -1.8661332

     kurt.2SE      normtest.W     normtest.p
   -0.6300756       0.9309643     0.5248938
```

Shapiro Wilk's is labeled *normtest.W.* The *p* value for Shapiro Wilk's is *normtest.p.*

```
install.packages("e1071")
```

The *install.packages* function will install the *e1071* package which we will use to generate skewness and kurtosis.

```
library(e1071)
```

The *library* function will load the *e1071* package.

```
Ch7_female <-Ch7_cholesterol[ which(Ch7_cholesterol$group=='female'), ]
Ch7_female
Ch7_male <- Ch7_cholesterol[ which(Ch7_cholesterol$group=='male'), ]
Ch7_male
```

FIGURE 7.14 (continued)
Generating normality evidence by group.

With this script, we split our dataframe by "group" and create new dataframes consisting of observations of only females or males, respectively, "Ch7_female" and "Ch7_male."

```
skewness(Ch7_female$cholesterol, type=3)
skewness(Ch7_female$cholesterol, type=2)
skewness(Ch7_female$cholesterol, type=1)
```

The *skewness* function will generate skewness statistics on the variable(s) we specify. The *type=* script defines how skewness is calculated. Specifying *type=2* will use the algorithm that is used by SPSS. Readers interested in learning more, including the algorithms for each of the three methods, are encouraged to review Joanes and Gill (1998). We see that using *type=2*, our skew is the same value as generated using SPSS.

```
# skewness(Ch7_female$cholesterol, type=3)
[1] 0

# skewness(Ch7_female$cholesterol, type=2)
[1] 0

# skewness(Ch7_female$cholesterol, type=1)
[1] 0
```

```
kurtosis(Ch7_female$cholesterol, type=3)
kurtosis(Ch7_female$cholesterol, type=2)
kurtosis(Ch7_female$cholesterol, type=1)
```

The *kurtosis* function will generate kurtosis statistics on the variable(s) we specify. The *type=* script defines how kurtosis is calculated. Specifying *type=2* will use the algorithm that is used by SPSS. Readers interested in learning more, including the algorithms for each of the three methods, are encouraged to review Joanes and Gill (1998). We see that using *type=2*, our kurtosis is the same value as generated using SPSS.

```
# kurtosis(Ch7_female$cholesterol, type=3)
[1] -1.866133

# kurtosis(Ch7_female$cholesterol, type=2)
[1] -1.789965

# kurtosis(Ch7_female$cholesterol, type=1)
[1] -1.519031
```

FIGURE 7.14 (continued)
Generating normality evidence by group.

7.7.1.1.1 Interpreting Normality Evidence

We have already developed a good understanding of how to interpret some forms of evidence of normality, including skewness and kurtosis, histograms, and boxplots. As we examine the "Descriptives" table (see Figure 7.15), we see the output for the cholesterol statistics is separated for male (top portion) and female (bottom portion). The skewness statistic of cholesterol level for the males is .000 and kurtosis is −1.446—both within the range of an absolute value of 2.0, suggesting some evidence of normality of the dependent variable for males. Evidence of normality for the distributional shape of cholesterol level

Descriptives

	Gender			Statistic	Std. Error
Cholesterol Level	Male	Mean		215.0000	8.72562
		95% Confidence Interval for Mean	Lower Bound	195.7951	
			Upper Bound	234.2049	
		5% Trimmed Mean		215.0000	
		Median		215.0000	
		Variance		913.636	
		Std. Deviation		30.22642	
		Minimum		170.00	
		Maximum		260.00	
		Range		90.00	
		Interquartile Range		57.50	
		Skewness		.000	.637
		Kurtosis		-1.446	1.232
	Female	Mean		185.0000	6.74802
		95% Confidence Interval for Mean	Lower Bound	169.0435	
			Upper Bound	200.9565	
		5% Trimmed Mean		185.0000	
		Median		185.0000	
		Variance		364.286	
		Std. Deviation		19.08627	
		Minimum		160.00	
		Maximum		210.00	
		Range		50.00	
		Interquartile Range		37.50	
		Skewness		.000	.752
		Kurtosis		-1.790	1.481

FIGURE 7.15
Normality evidence.

for females is also present: skewness = .000 and kurtosis is −1.790. For illustrative purposes, let's take the largest skew or kurtosis value and divide by the standard error. This would be kurtosis for females: −1.790/1.481 = −1.21. This is a standardized value that can be used to determine if the kurtosis is statistically different from zero. Relative to a critical value of ± 1.96, −1.21 does not fall in the rejection region, thus kurtosis is not statistically significantly different from zero. Because all other skew and kurtosis values were less than −1.790, we know that all skew and kurtosis statistics provide evidence of normality.

The histogram of cholesterol level for males is not exactly what most researchers would consider a classic normally shaped distribution (see Figure 7.16). Although the histogram of cholesterol level for females is not presented here, it follows a similar distributional shape.

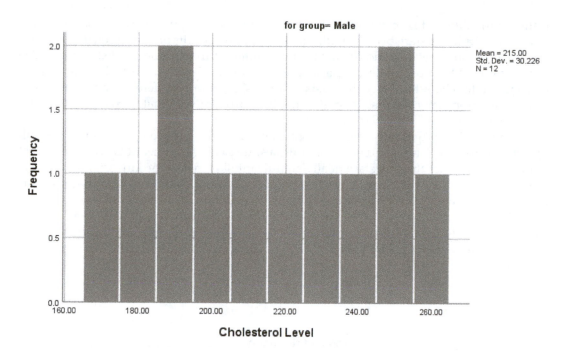

Working in **R,** we can compute histograms for each group.

```
Ch7_female <-Ch7_cholesterol[ which(Ch7_cholesterol$group=='female'), ]
Ch7_female

Ch7_male <- Ch7_cholesterol[ which(Ch7_cholesterol$group=='male'), ]
Ch7_male
```

First, we split our data by the grouping variable, "group," and create two new dataframes to work with, "Ch7_female" and "Ch7_male."

```
hist(Ch7_female$cholesterol)
hist(Ch7_male$cholesterol)
```

The *hist* function will compute a histogram for the variable "cholesterol" from each of the new dataframes.

FIGURE 7.16
Histogram of cholesterol level for males.

A few other statistics can be used to gauge normality as well, providing evidence of the extent to which our sample distribution is statistically different from a normal distribution. As we learned previously, the Kolmogorov-Smirnov (K-S) (Chakravart, Laha, & Roy, 1967) with Lilliefor's significance (Lilliefors, 1967) and the Shapiro-Wilk (S-W) (Shapiro & Wilk, 1965) are tests that provide evidence of the extent to which our sample distribution is statistically different from a normal distribution. The K-S test tends to be conservative and lacks power for detecting nonnormality, so it is not recommended (D'Agostino, Belanger, & D'Agostino, 1990). The S-W test is considered the more powerful of the two for testing normality and is recommended for use with small sample sizes ($n < 50$) (D'Agostino et al., 1990). Nonstatistically significant K-S and S-W results are interpreted to say that our distribution is *not* statistically significantly different than a normal distribution. The output for the Shapiro-Wilk test is presented in Figure 7.17 and suggests that our sample distribution for cholesterol level is not statistically significantly different than what would be expected from a normal distribution—and this is true for both males ($SW = .949$, $df = 12$, $p = .617$) and females ($SW = .931$, $df = 8$, $p = .525$).

Working in **R**, D'Agostino's test (D'Agostino, 1970) can be used to examine the null hypothesis that skewness equals zero. Thus, a statistically significant D'Agostino's test would indicate that there is statistically significant skewness. For kurtosis, we can use the Bonett-Seier test for Geary's kurtosis (Bonett & Seier, 2002) for data that are normally distributed. The null hypothesis states that data should have a Geary's kurtosis value equal to $\sqrt{2/\pi} = .7979$. Thus, a statistically significant Bonett-Seier test for Geary's kurtosis would indicate that there is statistically significant kurtosis. Thus, with these tests, as with K-S and S-W, we do *not* want to find statistically significant results.

Tests of Normality

	Gender	Kolmogorov-Smirnov[a]			Shapiro-Wilk		
		Statistic	df	Sig.	Statistic	df	Sig.
Cholesterol Level	Male	.129	12	.200*	.949	12	.617
	Female	.159	8	.200*	.931	8	.525

*. This is a lower bound of the true significance.

a. Lilliefors Significance Correction

Working in **R**, we saw in Figure 7.14 how we could generate the Shapiro-Wilk test using the *stat.desc* function in the *pastecs* package. Another way to test for normality is D'Agostino's test for skewness and the Bonett-Seier test for Geary's kurtosis.

```
install.packages("moments")
library(moments)
```

To conduct D'Agostino's test, we first have to install the *moments* package and then load it into our library. The null hypothesis for this test is that skewness equals zero. Thus, a statistically significant Agostino's test would indicate that there is statistically significant skewness.

```
agostino.test(Ch7_male$cholesterol)
agostino.test(Ch7_female$cholesterol)
```

The function *agostino.test* is generated using the variable "cholesterol" from our split files, "Ch7_male" and "Ch7_female." The results suggest evidence of normality as $p = 1.00$, greater than alpha.

FIGURE 7.17
Shapiro-Wilk test of normality results.

```
agostino.test(Ch7_male$cholesterol)

        D'Agostino skewness test

data: Ch7_male$cholesterol
skew = 0, z = 0, p-value = 1
alternative hypothesis: data have a skewness

 agostino.test(Ch7_female$cholesterol)

        D'Agostino skewness test

data:  Ch7_female$cholesterol
skew = 0, z = 0, p-value = 1
alternative hypothesis: data have a skewness
```

```
bonett.test((Ch7_male$cholesterol))
bonett.test((Ch7_female$cholesterol))
```

The *bonett.test* function, using the "cholesterol" variable from our split files, "Ch7_male" and "Ch7_female," performs the Bonett-Seier test for Geary's kurtosis for data that are normally distributed. The null hypothesis states that data should have a Geary's kurtosis value equal to $\sqrt{2/\pi} = .7979$. The results suggest evidence of normality for the distribution of males and females as $p = .115$ and $p = .1181$, respectively, both greater than alpha.

bonett.test((Ch7_male$cholesterol))

```
        Bonett-Seier test for Geary kurtosis

data:  (Ch7_male$cholesterol)
tau = 25.8333, z = -1.5759, p-value = 0.115
alternative hypothesis: kurtosis is not equal to sqrt(2/pi)
```

bonett.test((Ch7_female$cholesterol))

```
        Bonett-Seier test for Geary kurtosis

data: (Ch7_female$cholesterol)
tau = 16.2500, z = -1.5626, p-value = 0.1181
alternative hypothesis: kurtosis is not equal to sqrt(2/pi)
```

FIGURE 7.17 (continued)
Shapiro-Wilk test of normality results.

Quantile-quantile (Q-Q) plots are also often examined to determine evidence of normality. Q-Q plots are graphs that plot quantiles of the theoretical normal distribution against quantiles of the sample distribution. Points that fall on or close to the diagonal line suggest evidence of normality. Similar to what we saw with the histogram, the Q-Q plot of cholesterol level for both males and females (although the latter is not shown here) suggests some nonnormality. Keep in mind that we have a relatively small sample size. Thus interpreting the visual graphs (e.g., histograms and Q-Q plots) can be challenging, although we have plenty of other evidence for normality.

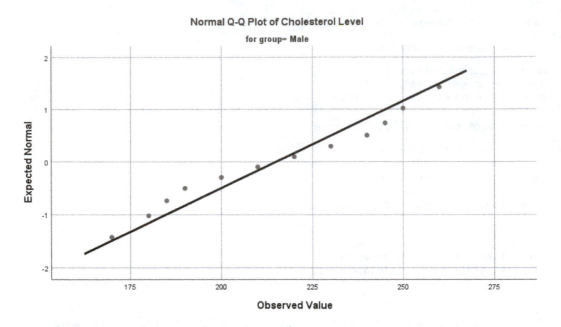

Working in **R**, we can use the *ggplot2* package to produce the Q-Q plot.

```
install.packages("ggplot2")
```

The *install.packages* function will install the *ggplot2* package that we can use to create various graphs and plots.

```
library(ggplot2)
```

The *library* function will load the *ggplot2* package.

```
qplot(sample=cholesterol, data = Ch7_female)
qplot(sample=cholesterol, data = Ch7_male)
```

The *qplot* function will generate a Q-Q plot using the variable "cholesterol" from the dataframes specified in "data =" which correspond to data from females and males, respectively.

FIGURE 7.18
Q-Q plot of cholesterol level for males.

Examination of the boxplots suggests a relatively normal distributional shape of choles-terol level for both males and females and no outliers for either group.

Considering the forms of evidence we have examined, skewness and kurtosis statistics, the Shapiro-Wilk test, and the boxplots, all suggest normality is a reasonable assumption. Although the histograms and Q-Q plots suggest some nonnormality, this is somewhat expected given the small sample size. Generally, we can be reasonably assured we have met the assumption of normality of the dependent variable for each group of the independent variable. Additionally, recall that when the assumption of normality is violated with the independent *t* test, the effects on Type I and Type II errors are minimal when using a two-tailed test, as we are conducting here (e.g., Glass et al., 1972; Sawilowsky & Blair, 1992).

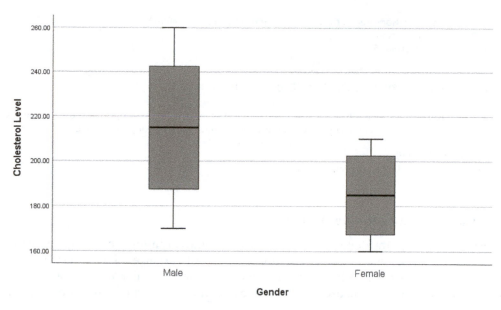

Working in **R**, we can generate a boxplot by groups using the following script.

```
boxplot(Ch7_cholesterol$cholesterol~Ch7_cholesterol$group)
```

The *boxplot* function can be used to generate a boxplot. In parentheses, we tell **R** which variable in our dataframe to use to compute the boxplot (i.e., "Ch7_cholesterol$cholesterol") and to split the boxplot by our grouping variable, "Ch7_cholesterol$group."

FIGURE 7.19
Boxplot of cholesterol level by gender.

7.7.1.2 Homogeneity of Variance for the Independent t Test

Testing for the assumption for equal variances is provided by default in SPSS with the independent *t* test. More specifically, it is provided as "Levene's Test for Equality of Variances" in the output. See Table 7.3. Levene's test can also be generated in **R**.

```
install.packages(car)
```

We use the *install.packages* function to install the *car* package, which we will use to generate Levene's test.

```
library(car)
```

The *library* function will load the *car* package into our library.

```
leveneTest(Ch7_cholesterol$cholesterol,
           Ch7_cholesterol$group)
```

The *leveneTest* function is used to generate Levene's test by variable "group" on the variable "cholesterol."

FIGURE 7.20
Generating Levene's test for equal variances in **R**.

```
Levene's Test for Homogeneity of Variance (center = mean)
      Df F value Pr(>F)
group 1 3.2007 0.09045
      18
---
Signif. codes: 0 '***' 0.001 '**' 0.01 '*' 0.05 '.' 0.1 ' ' 1
```

We read this output as $F(1,18) = 3.20$, $p = .09$, indicating that we have met the assumption of equal variances. Thus, we can generate the independent *t* test assuming the variances of the groups are equal.

FIGURE 7.20 (continued)
Generating Levene's test for equal variances in **R**.

7.7.2 Data Screening for the Dependent *t* Test

The assumptions for the dependent *t* test that we need to examine include normality of the distribution of the difference scores and homogeneity of variances. Recall that the assumption of independence is required as well; however, as noted earlier, that is not an assumption with which data will be used to assess the extent to which the assumption is met.

7.7.2.1 Normality for the Dependent t Test

Let's start with using the Explore option to examine normality of the distribution of the difference scores. As with the other *t* tests we have studied, understanding the distributional

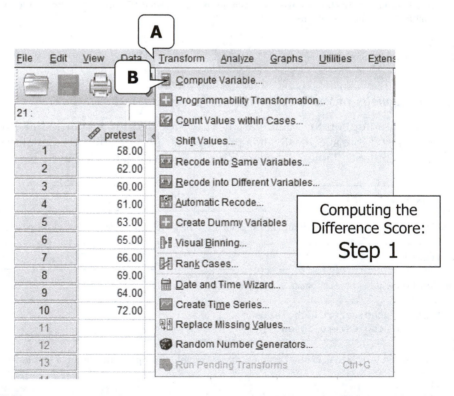

FIGURE 7.21
Computing the difference score: Step 1.

shape and the extent to which normality is a reasonable assumption is important. For the dependent *t* test, the distributional shape for the *difference scores* should be normally distributed. Thus, we first need to create a new variable in our dataset to reflect the difference scores (in this case, the difference between the pre- and posttest values). To do this, go to "Transform" in the top pulldown menu, then select "Compute Variable." Following the screenshot of Step 1 in Figure 7.21 produces the "Compute Variable" dialog box.

From the "Compute Variable" dialog screen, we can define the column header for our variable by typing in a name in the "Target Variable" box (no spaces, no special characters, and cannot begin with a numeric value). The formula for computing our difference score is inserted in the "Numeric Expression" box. To create this formula: (1) click "pretest" in the left list of variables and use the arrow key to move it into the "Numeric Expression" box; (2) use your keyboard or the mathematical operators within the dialog box to insert a minus sign (i.e., dash) after "pretest" in the "Numeric Expression" box; (3) click "posttest" in the left list of variables and use the arrow key to move it into the "Numeric Expression" box; and (4) click "OK" to create the new difference score variable in your dataset.

We can again use Explore to examine the extent to which the assumption of normality is met for the distributional shape of our newly created difference score. The general steps for accessing Explore (see, for example, Chapter 4) and for generating normality evidence for one variable (see Chapter 6) have been presented in previous chapters, and they will not be reiterated here.

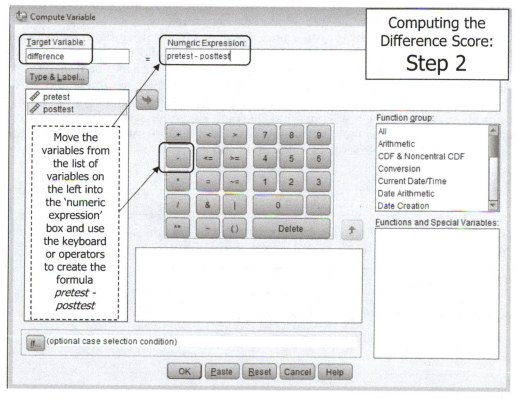

FIGURE 7.22
Computing the difference score: Step 2.

Working in **R**, we can create a new variable in our dataset that reflects the difference score.

```
Ch7_swim$differ <- Ch7_swim$pretest-Ch7_swim$posttest
```

This script will create a new variable named "differ" in the "Ch7_swim" dataframe. This variable, "differ," is computed as the pretest minus the posttest (i.e., "Ch7_swim$pretest—Ch7_swim$posttest").

```
View(Ch7_swim)
```

The *View* function will let us view the dataframe and see the new variable that was created.

FIGURE 7.22 (continued)
Computing the difference score: Step 2.

7.7.2.1.1 Interpreting Normality Evidence for the Dependent *t* Test

We have already developed a good understanding of how to interpret some forms of evidence of normality, including skewness and kurtosis, histograms, and boxplots. The skewness statistic for the difference score is .248 and kurtosis is .050—both within the range of an absolute value of 2.0, suggesting one form of evidence of normality of the differences.

The histogram for the difference scores (not presented here) is not necessarily what most researchers would consider a normally shaped distribution. Our formal test of normality, the Shapiro-Wilk (SW) test (Shapiro & Wilk, 1965) suggests that our sample distribution for differences is not statistically significantly different than what would be expected from a normal distribution ($W = .956$, $df = 10$, $p = .734$). Similar to what we saw with the histogram, the Q-Q plot of differences suggests some nonnormality in the tails (as the farthest points are not falling on the diagonal line). Keep in mind that we have a small sample size. Thus interpreting the visual graphs (e.g., histograms and Q-Q plots) can be difficult. Examination of the boxplot suggests a relatively normal distributional shape with no outliers. Considering the forms of evidence we have examined, skewness and kurtosis, Shapiro-Wilk's test of normality, and boxplots, all suggest that normality is a reasonable assumption. Although the histograms and Q-Q plots suggested some nonnormality, this is somewhat expected given the small sample size. Generally, we can be reasonably assured we have met the assumption of normality of the difference scores.

```
install.packages("pastecs")
```

The *install.packages* function will install the *pastecs* package which we will use to generate various forms of normality evidence.

```
library(pastecs)
```

The *library* function will load the *pastecs* package.

```
stat.desc(Ch7_swim,
          norm = TRUE)
```

FIGURE 7.23
Generating and interpreting normality evidence for the dependent *t* test in **R**.

The *stat.desc* function will generate normality indices on all variables in the dataframe as follows. We see skew (.18) and kurtosis (−.99), along with *SW* = .96, *p* = .73 for the difference score. All indicate the assumption of normality has been met. We review the ratio of the variances of the pretest (17.78) and posttest (13.11) to determine that we have met the assumption of equal variances.

	pretest	posttest	differ
nbr.val	10.00000000	10.00000000	10.0000000
nbr.null	0.00000000	0.00000000	0.0000000
nbr.na	0.00000000	0.00000000	0.0000000
min	58.00000000	54.00000000	2.0000000
max	72.00000000	64.00000000	9.0000000
range	14.00000000	10.00000000	7.0000000
sum	640.00000000	590.00000000	50.0000000
median	63.50000000	59.50000000	5.0000000
mean	64.00000000	59.00000000	5.0000000
SE.mean	1.33333333	1.14503760	0.6831301
CI.mean.0.95	3.01620955	2.59025501	1.5453475
var	**17.77777778**	**13.11111111**	4.6666667
std.dev	4.21637021	3.62092683	2.1602469
coef.var	0.06588078	0.06137164	0.4320494
skewness	0.44024834	−0.12638397	**0.1785510**
skew.2SE	0.32039363	−0.09197677	0.1299417
kurtosis	−0.97879688	−1.64689744	**−0.9887755**
kurt.2SE	−0.36679699	−0.61716281	−0.3705364
normtest.W	0.97233926	0.93703314	**0.9555691**
normtest.p	0.91164605	0.52049701	**0.7344122**

> Shapiro Wilk's is labeled *normtest.W*. The *p* value for Shapiro Wilk's is *normtest.p*.

Note: You may have noticed that the skewness and kurtosis value that we've just generated differs from what we found in SPSS. *This is because there are different ways to calculate skewness and kurtosis.* Let's use another package in **R** to calculate these statistics with different algorithms.

```
install.packages("e1071")
```

The *install.packages* function will install the *e1071* package that we will use to generate skewness and kurtosis.

```
library(e1071)
```

The *library* function will load the *e1071* package.

```
skewness(Ch7_swim$differ, type=3)
skewness(Ch7_swim$differ, type=2)
skewness(Ch7_swim$differ, type=1)
```

The *skewness* function will generate skewness statistics on the variable(s) we specify. The *type=* defines how skewness is calculated. Specifying *type=2* will use the algorithm that is used by SPSS. Readers interested in learning more, including the algorithms for each of the three methods, are encouraged to review Joanes and Gill (1998). We see that using *type=2*, our skew is the same value as generated using SPSS.

```
# skewness(Ch6_skate$time, type=3)
[1] 0.2456618

# skewness(Ch6_skate$time, type=2)
[1] 0.2994734

# skewness(Ch6_skate$time, type=1)
[1] 0.2706329
```

FIGURE 7.23 (continued)
Generating and interpreting normality evidence for the dependent *t* test in **R**.

```
kurtosis(Ch7_swim$differ, type=3)
kurtosis(Ch7_swim$differ, type=2)
kurtosis(Ch7_swim$differ, type=1)
```

The *kurtosis* function will generate kurtosis statistics on the variable(s) we specify. The *type=* defines how kurtosis is calculated. Specifying *type=2* will use the algorithm that is used by SPSS. Readers interested in learning more, including the algorithms for each of the three methods, are encouraged to review Joanes and Gill (1998). We see that using *type=2*, our kurtosis is the same value as generated using SPSS.

```
# kurtosis(Ch6_skate$time, type=3)
[1] -0.9766846
```

```
# kurtosis(Ch6_skate$time, type=2)
[1] -0.4833448
```

```
# kurtosis(Ch6_skate$time, type=1)
[1] -0.6979167
```

We saw in Figure 7.17 how we could generate additional tests for normality, including D'Agostino's test for skewness and the Bonett-Seier test for Geary's kurtosis.

```
install.packages("moments")
library(moments)
```

To conduct D'Agostino's test, we first have to install the *moments* package and then load it into our library. (Remember that a package needs to be installed only once but loaded when you start a new session in **R**.) The null hypothesis for this test is that skewness equals zero. Thus, a statistically significant Agostino's test would indicate that there is statistically significant skewness.

```
agostino.test(Ch7_swim$differ)
```

The function *agostino.test* is generated using the variable *differ* from our dataframe, "Ch7_swim." The results suggest evidence of normality of the difference score as $p = .7087$, greater than alpha.

```
# agostino.test(Ch7_swim$differ)

        D'Agostino skewness test

data: Ch7_swim$differ
skew = 0.2091, z = 0.3737, p-value = 0.7087
alternative hypothesis: data have a skewness
```

```
bonett.test((Ch7_swim$differ))
```

The *bonett.test* function, using the "differ" variable from our dataframe, "Ch7_swim," performs the Bonett-Seier test for Geary's kurtosis for data that are normally distributed. The null hypothesis states that data should have a Geary's kurtosis value equal to $\sqrt{2/\pi} = .7979$. The results suggest evidence of normality for the distribution of the difference score as $p = .7767$, greater than alpha.

```
# bonett.test((Ch7_swim$differ))

        Bonett-Seier test for Geary kurtosis

data: (Ch7_swim$differ)
tau = 1.6000, z = 0.2836, p-value = 0.7767
alternative hypothesis: kurtosis is not equal to sqrt(2/pi)
```

FIGURE 7.23 (continued)
Generating and interpreting normality evidence for the dependent *t* test in **R**.

7.7.2.2 *Homogeneity of Variance for the Dependent* t *Test*

We also need to examine evidence for meeting equal variances, or more specifically homogeneity of variance of the difference scores. Without conducting a formal test of equality of variances (as we do in Chapter 9), a rough benchmark for having met the assumption of homogeneity of variances when conducting the dependent *t* test is that the *ratio of the smallest to largest variance of the paired samples is no greater than 1:4 to decrease the chance of a Type I error. Recent research suggests that a variance ratio lower than 1.5 should be used as convention in the presence of heterogeneity with unequal sample sizes* (Blanca, Alarcón, Arnau, Bono, & Bendayan, 2018). The variance can be computed easily by any number of procedures in SPSS (refer back to Chapter 3, for example), and these steps will not be repeated here. For our paired samples, the variance of the pretest score is 17.778 and the variance of the posttest score is 13.111—well within the range of 1:4 suggesting that homogeneity of variances is reasonable.

7.8 G*Power

Using the results of the independent samples *t* test just conducted, let's use G*Power to compute the post hoc power of our test.

7.8.1 Post Hoc Power for the Independent *t* Test Using G*Power

The first thing that must be done when using G*Power for computing post hoc power is to select the correct test family. In our case, we conducted an independent samples *t* test, therefore the default selection of "t tests" is the correct test family. Next, we need to select the appropriate statistical test. We use the arrow to toggle to "Means: Difference between two independent means (two groups)." The "Type of power analysis" then needs to be selected. To compute post hoc power, we need to select "Post hoc: Compute achieved power—given α, sample size, and effect size."

The "Input Parameters" must then be specified. The first parameter is the selection of whether the test is one tailed (i.e., directional) or two tailed (i.e., nondirectional). In this example, we have a two-tailed test, so we use the arrow to toggle to "Two." We can input our observed effect size, d, or we can also use the pop-out calculator to compute the effect size d. Using the pop-out calculator, our effect size is 1.19 (note that the pop-out calculator does not use the pooled standard deviation as the standardizer). The alpha level we tested at was .05, and the sample size for females was 8 and for males, 12. Once the parameters are specified, simply click "Calculate" to generate the achieved power statistics.

The "Output Parameters" provide the relevant statistics given the input just specified. In this example, we were interested in determining post hoc power given a two-tailed test, with an observed effect size of 1.18, an alpha level of .05, and sample sizes of 8 (females) and 12 (males). Based on those criteria, the post hoc power was .69. In other words, with a sample size of 8 female and 12 males in our study, testing at an alpha level of .05 and observing a large effect of 1.19, then the power of our test was .69—the probability of rejecting the null hypothesis when it is really false will be 69%, which is only moderate power (minimally acceptable power is generally about 80%). Keep in mind that conducting power analysis *a priori* is recommended so that you avoid a situation where, post hoc, you find that the sample size was not sufficient to reach the desired power (given the observed effect size and alpha level). We were fortunate in this example in that we were still able to detect a statistically significant difference in cholesterol levels between males and females; however, we will likely not always be that lucky!

How does power change if a different effect size value is input? We know that power is a function of many elements, one of which is effect size. More specifically, holding all else constant in the power calculation, larger effect sizes will produce greater power. Let's look at this in the context of the example illustrated in this chapter. Recall that the achieved or observed effect size (in absolute value) calculated using the *pooled standard deviation* (as computed via Hedges and Olkin (1985) using n_1-1 and n_2-1 to compute s_p) as the standardizer was 1.1339. In computing post hoc power, had we used the pooled standard deviation via Hedges and Olkin as the standardizer in our effect size input (i.e., an observed effect size of 1.1339), our post hoc power would be .65, slightly less than what we obtained when we used Cohen's pooled standard deviation formula (i.e., using n_1 and n_2 to compute s_p). The observed Hedge's *g* with bias correction for small samples was 1.0860. Had we used the bias corrected effect size *g*, our post hoc power would be only about .61. Thus, we see that larger effects produce greater power!

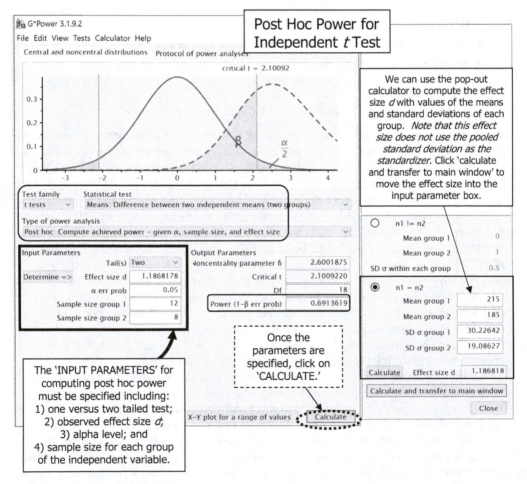

FIGURE 7.24
Independent *t* test: *Post hoc* power.

7.8.2 Post Hoc Power for the Dependent *t* Test Using G*Power

Now, let us use G*Power to compute post hoc power for the dependent *t* test. First, the correct test family needs to be selected. In our case, we conducted an dependent samples *t* test, therefore the default selection of "t tests" is the correct test family. Next, we need to select the appropriate statistical test. We use the arrow to toggle to "Means: Difference between two dependent means (matched pairs)." The "Type of power analysis" desired then needs to be selected. To compute post hoc power, we need to select "Post hoc: Compute achieved power— given α, sample size, and effect size."

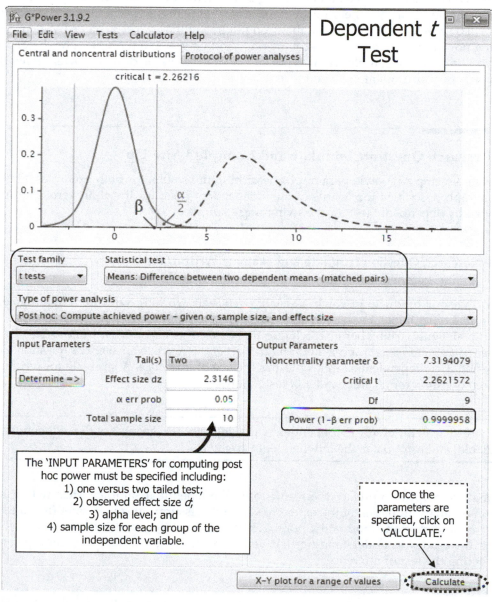

FIGURE 7.25
Dependent *t* test: *Post hoc* power.

The "Input Parameters" must then be specified. The first parameter is the selection of whether your test is one tailed (i.e., directional) or two tailed (i.e., nondirectional). In this example, we have a two-tailed test, so we use the arrow to toggle to "Two." The achieved or observed effect size was 2.3146. The alpha level we tested at was .05, and the total sample size was 10. Once the parameters are specified, simply click "Calculate" to generate the achieved power statistics.

The "Output Parameters" provide the relevant statistics given the input specified. In this example, we were interested in determining post hoc power given a two-tailed test, with an observed effect size of 2.3146, an alpha level of .05, and total sample size of 10. Based on those criteria, the post hoc power was .99. In other words, with a total sample size of 10, testing at an alpha level of .05 and observing a large effect of 2.3146, then the power of our test was greater than .99—the probability of rejecting the null hypothesis when it is really false will be greater than 99%, about the strongest power that can be achieved. Again, conducting power analysis *a priori* is recommended so that you avoid a situation where, post hoc, you find that the sample size was not sufficient to reach the desired power (given the observed effect size and alpha level).

7.9 Research Question Template and Example Write-Up

Next we develop APA-style paragraphs describing the results for both examples. First is a paragraph describing the results of the independent *t* test for the cholesterol example, followed by dependent *t* test for the swimming example.

7.9.1 Research Question Template and Example Write-Up for the Independent *t* Test

Recall that our graduate research assistant, Oso, was working with Dr. Nightingale, a local nurse practitioner, to assist in analyzing cholesterol levels. His task was to assist Dr. Nightingale with writing her research question (*Is there a mean difference in cholesterol level between males and females?*) and generating the test of inference to answer her question. Oso suggested an independent-samples *t* test as the test of inference. A template for writing a research question for an independent *t* test follows:

Is there a mean difference in [dependent variable] between [group 1 of the independent variable] and [group 2 of the independent variable]?

It may be helpful to preface the results of the independent-samples *t* test with information on an examination of the extent to which the assumptions were met (recall there are three assumptions: normality, homogeneity of variances, and independence). This assists the reader in understanding that you were thorough in data screening prior to conducting the test of inference.

An independent samples *t* test was conducted to determine if the mean cholesterol level of males differed from females. The assumption of normality was tested and met for the distributional shape of the dependent variable (cholesterol level) for *females*. Review of the Shapiro-Wilk test for normality ($SW = .931, df = 8, p = .525$), D'Agostino's skewness test ($z = 0, p = 1$), Bonett-Seier test for Geary's kurtosis ($z = -1.5626, p = .1181$), and skewness ($.000, SE = .752$) and kurtosis ($-1.790, SE = 1.481$) statistics suggested that normality of cholesterol levels for females was a reasonable assumption.

Similar results were found for *male* cholesterol levels. Review of the Shapiro-Wilk test for normality ($W = .949, df = 12, p = .617$), D'Agostino's skewness test ($z = 0, p = 1$), Bonett-Seier test for Geary's kurtosis ($z = -1.5759, p = .115$), and skewness ($.000, SE = .637$) and kurtosis ($-1.446, SE = 1.232$) statistics suggested that normality of males cholesterol levels was a reasonable assumption. Standardizing skew and kurtosis by dividing by their standard errors and comparing to a critical value of ± 1.96, we find nonstatistically significant skew and kurtosis. This provides further evidence of normality.

The boxplots suggested a relatively normal distributional shape (with no outliers) of cholesterol levels for both males and females. The Q-Q plots and histograms suggested some minor nonnormality for both male and female cholesterol levels. Due to the small sample, this was anticipated. Although normality indices generally suggest the assumption is met, even if there are slight departures from normality, the effects on Type I and Type II errors will be minimal given the use of a two-tailed test (Glass et al., 1972; Sawilowsky & Blair, 1992). According to Levene's test, the homogeneity of variance assumption was satisfied ($F = 3.2007, p = .090$). Because there was not random assignment of the individuals to gender, the assumption of independence was not met creating a potential for an increased probability of a Type I or Type II error.

It is also desirable to include a measure of effect size. Recall our formula for computing the effect size, d, presented earlier in the chapter. Plugging in the values for our cholesterol example, we find an effect size d (in absolute value terms) of 1.1339 and Hedge's g of 1.0860, both of which are interpreted according to Cohen's (1988) guidelines as a large effect. Given the small sample size, we will report Hedge's g, as calculated here, along with the respective confidence intervals that were found earlier using the online calculator. (Remember that the sign for the effect size is simply an artifact of which group is entered into the numerator equation first; had the cholesterol level for females been entered as $\bar{Y}_1$, the effect size would be positive. The sign of the effect doesn't change the interpretation; it only reflects which group happens to be larger or smaller.)

$$g = \left(\frac{\bar{Y}_1 - \bar{Y}_2}{s_p}\right)\left(1 - \frac{3}{(4)(df) - 1}\right) = \left(\frac{215 - 185}{26.4575}\right)\left(1 - \frac{3}{(4)(18) - 1}\right) = (1.1339)(.9577)$$

$$g = 1.0860$$

Keep in mind that for the two-sample mean test, standardized mean difference effects indicates how many standard deviations the mean of sample 1 is from the mean of sample 2. Thus, with an effect size g of 1.0860, there is more than one standard deviation unit between the mean cholesterol levels of males as compared to females. The positive sign simply indicates that group 1 (i.e., males) has the larger mean (as it is the first value in the numerator of the formula; in our case, the mean cholesterol level of males).

Here is an APA-style example paragraph of results for the cholesterol level data (remember that this will be prefaced by the paragraph reporting the extent to which the assumptions of the test were met).

Cholesterol data were gathered from samples of 12 males and 8 females, with a female sample mean of 185 ($SD = 19.09$) and a male sample mean of 215 ($SD = 30.22$). The independent t test indicated that the cholesterol means were statistically significantly different for males and females ($t = 2.4842$, $df = 18$, $p = .023$). Thus, the null hypothesis that the cholesterol means were the same by gender was rejected at the .05 level of significance. The effect size g (Hedge's sample size adjusted effect size) was 1.09 (CI .15, 2.09) and d was 1.13 (CI −.17, −2.10). Using Cohen's (1988) guidelines, this is interpreted as a large effect. The results provide evidence to support the conclusion that males and females differ in cholesterol levels, on average. More specifically, males were observed to have higher cholesterol levels, on average, than females.

Parenthetically, notice that the results of the Welch t' test were the same as for the independent t test (Welch $t' = 2.720$, rounded $df = 18$, $p = .014$). Thus any deviation from homogeneity of variance did not affect the results.

7.9.2 Research Question Template and Example Write-Up for the Dependent t Test

Addie, as you recall, was also working with Coach Bryant, a local swimming coach, to assist in analyzing freestyle swimming time before and after swimmers participated in an intensive training program. Addie suggested a research question (*Is there a mean difference in swim time for the 50-meter freestyle event before participation in an intensive training program as compared to swim time for the 50-meter freestyle event after participation in an intensive training program?*) and assisted in generating the test of inference (specifically the dependent t test) to answer her question. A template for writing a research question for a dependent t test follows:

Is there a mean difference in [paired sample 1] as compared to [paired sample 2]?

It may be helpful to preface the results of the dependent samples t test with information on the extent to which the assumptions were met (recall there are three assumptions: normality, homogeneity of variance, and independence). This assists the reader in understanding that you were thorough in data screening prior to conducting the test of inference.

A dependent samples t test was conducted to determine if there was a difference in the mean swim time for the 50-meter freestyle before participation in an intensive training program as compared to the mean swim time for the 50-meter freestyle after participation in an intensive training program. The assumption of normality was tested and met for the distributional shape of the paired differences. Review of the Shapiro-Wilk test for normality ($SW = .956$, $df = 10$, $p = .734$) and skewness (.248, $SE = .687$) and kurtosis (.050, $SE = 1.334$) statistics suggested that normality of the paired differences was reasonable. Standardizing skew and kurtosis by dividing by their standard errors and comparing to a critical value of ±1.96, we find nonstatistically significant skew and kurtosis. Additional tests, including D'Agostino's test for skewness ($z = .3737, p = .7087$) and the Bonett-Seier test for Geary's kurtosis ($z = .2836, p = .7767$) suggested further evidence of normality.

The boxplot suggested a relatively normal distributional shape and there were no outliers present. The Q-Q plot and histogram suggested minor nonnormality. Due to the small sample, this was anticipated. Homogeneity of variance was tested by reviewing the ratio of the raw score variances. The ratio of the smallest (posttest = 13.111) to largest (pretest = 17.778) variance was less than 1:4 therefore there is evidence of the equal variance assumption. The individuals were not randomly selected, therefore the assumption of independence was not met creating a potential for an increased probability of a Type I or Type II error.

It is also important to include a measure of effect size. Recall our formula for computing the effect size, d, presented earlier in the chapter. Plugging in the values for our swimming example, we find an effect size d of 2.3146, which is interpreted according to Cohen's (1988) guidelines as a large effect.

$$\text{Cohen's } d = \frac{\overline{d}}{s_d} = \frac{5}{2.1602} = 2.3146$$

With an effect size of 2.3146, there are about two and a third standard deviation units between the pretraining mean swim time and the posttraining mean swim time. Using Uanhoro's online calculator (Uanhoro, 2017), we find Hedge's g to be 1.1632 with a confidence interval of (.5935, 1.9345).

Here is an APA-style example paragraph of results for the swimming data (remember that this will be prefaced by the paragraph reporting the extent to which the assumptions of the test were met).

The pretest and posttest data were collected from a sample of 10 swimmers, with a pretest mean of 64 seconds ($SD = 4.22$) and a posttest mean of 59 seconds ($SD = 3.62$). Thus, swimming times decreased from pretest to posttest. The dependent t test was conducted to determine if this difference was statistically significantly different from zero, and the results indicate that the pretest and posttest means were statistically different ($t = 7.32, df = 9, p < .001$). The null hypothesis that the freestyle swimming means were the same at both points in time was rejected at the .05 level of significance. The effect size d (calculated as the mean difference divided by the standard deviation of the difference) was 2.3146. Hedge's g was computed to be 1.16 (CI .59, 1.9). Using Cohen's (1988) guidelines, this is interpreted as a large effect. The results provide evidence to support the conclusion that the mean 50-meter freestyle swimming time prior to intensive training is different than the mean 50-meter freestyle swimming time after intensive training. The effect size d suggests almost a 2 1/2 standard deviation unit difference between pre and post (i.e., post swim time was nearly 2 1/2 standard deviation units quicker than pre swim time).

7.10 Additional Resources

A number of resources are available for learning more about statistics and how to interpret statistics. In addition to those already cited, Huck (2000) is an excellent general resource to assist in learning more about statistics and how to interpret statistics.

Problems

Conceptual Problems

1. When H_0 is true, the difference between two independent sample means is a function of which of the following?
   a. Degrees of freedom
   b. Standard error
   c. Sampling distribution
   d. Sampling error

2. The denominator of the independent t test is known as the standard error of the difference between two means, and may be defined as which of the following?
   a. The difference between the two group means
   b. The amount by which the difference between the two group means differs from the population mean
   c. The standard deviation of the sampling distribution of the difference between two means
   d. All of the above
   e. None of the above

3. In the independent t test, what does the homoscedasticity assumption state?
   a. The two population means are equal
   b. The two population variances are equal
   c. The two sample means are equal
   d. The two sample variances are equal

4. True or false? Sampling error increases with larger samples.

5. True or false? At a given level of significance, it is possible that the significance test and the confidence interval results will differ for the same dataset.

6. I assert that the critical value of t required for statistical significance is smaller (in absolute value) when using a directional rather than a nondirectional test. Am I correct?

7. If a 95% CI from an independent t test ranges from −.13 to +1.67, I assert that the null hypothesis would not be rejected at the .05 level of significance. Am I correct?

8. The mathematic ability of 10 preschool children was measured when they entered their first year of preschool and then again in the spring of their kindergarten year. To test for pre to post mean differences, which of the following tests would be used?

    a. Independent *t* test

    b. Dependent *t* test

    c. *z* test

    d. None of the above

9. A researcher collected data to answer the following research question: Are there mean differences in science test scores for middle school students who participate in school-sponsored athletics as compared to students who do not participate? Which of the following tests would be used to answer this question?

    a. Independent *t* test

    b. Dependent *t* test

    c. *z* test

    d. None of the above

10. True or false? The number of degrees of freedom for an independent *t* test with 15 females and 25 males is 40.

11. I assert that the critical value of *t*, for a test of two dependent means, will increase as the samples become larger. Am I correct?

12. Which of the following is NOT an assumption of the independent *t* test?

    a. Normality

    b. Independence

    c. Equal sample sizes

    d. Homogeneity of variance

13. For which of the following assumptions of the independent *t* test is evidence provided in the SPSS output by default?

    a. Normality

    b. Independence

    c. Equal sample sizes

    d. Homogeneity of variance

14. A researcher conducts an independent *t* test with balanced samples, equal variances, and a total sample size of 12. Which of the following standardized mean differences measures of effect is recommended?

    a. Cohen's *d*

    b. Eta squared

    c. Glass's *d*

    d. Hedge's *g*

15. A researcher is computing a dependent *t* test to examine the difference between a pre- and post-assessment. Which of the following is used to examine the assumption of normality with the dependent *t* test?

    a. Both variables (i.e., pre- and post-assessment)

    b. The dependent variable

    c. The dependent variable by each category of the independent variable

    d. The pre- to post-assessment difference score

16. The denominator of the dependent *t* test is known as the standard error of the mean difference, and may be defined as which of the following?
    a. The difference between the two group means
    b. The amount by which the difference between the two group means differs from the population mean
    c. The standard deviation of the sampling distribution of the mean difference
    d. All of the above
    e. None of the above

17. True or false? The degrees of freedom lost with a dependent *t* test are greater than the degrees of freedom lost with an independent *t* test.

Answers to Conceptual Problems

1. **d** (If the population means are equal, then the difference between the two sample means is only due to sampling error.)

3. **b** (The assumption of equal variances stated that the variances of the populations are equal.)

5. **False** (They will always agree for constant alpha.)

7. **Yes** (The CI contains zero.)

9. **a** (The independent *t* test is appropriate to use for testing mean differences between groups, as is the case here.)

11. **No** (It will decrease, as shown in Table A.2 in the Appendix.)

13. **d** (Homogeneity of variances, via Levene's test, is provided by default in SPSS when conducting the independent *t* test.)

15. **d** (The assumption of normality with the dependent *t* test can be examined using the difference score; in this example, that would be the pre- to post-assessment difference.)

17. **False** (The degrees of freedom lost with a dependent *t* test (i.e., $n - 1$), are *less* than the degrees of freedom lost with an independent *t* test, (i.e., $n_1 + n_2 - 2$).)

Computational Problems

1. The following two independent samples of older and younger adults were measured on an attitude towards violence test:

Sample 1 (Older Adult) Data			Sample 1 (Younger Adult) Data		
42	36	47	45	50	57
35	46	37	58	43	52
52	44	47	43	60	41
51	56	54	49	44	51
55	50	40	49	55	56
40	46	41			

a. Test the following hypothesis at the .05 level of significance.

$$H_0: \mu_1 - \mu_2 = 0$$
$$H_1: \mu_1 - \mu_2 \neq 0$$

b. Construct a 95% CI.

2. The following two independent samples of male and female undergraduate students were measured on an English literature quiz:

Sample 1 (Male) Data			Sample 1 (Female) Data		
5	7	8	9	9	11
10	11	11	13	15	18
13	15		19	20	

a. Test the following hypothesis at the .05 level of significance.

$$H_0: \mu_1 - \mu_2 = 0$$
$$H_1: \mu_1 - \mu_2 \neq 0$$

b. Construct a 95% CI.

3. The following two independent samples of preschool children (who were demographically similar but differed in Head Start participation) were measured on teacher-reported social skills during the spring of kindergarten.

Sample 1 (Head Start) Data			Sample 1 (Non–Head Start) Data		
18	14	12	15	12	9
16	10	17	10	18	12
20	16	19	11	8	11
15	13	22	13	10	14

a. Test the following hypothesis at the .05 level of significance.

$$H_0: \mu_1 - \mu_2 = 0$$
$$H_1: \mu_1 - \mu_2 \neq 0$$

b. Construct a 95% CI.

4. The following is a random sample of paired values of weight measured before (time 1) and after (time 2) a weight-reduction program:

Pair	1	2
1	127	130
2	126	124
3	129	135
4	123	127
5	124	127
6	129	128
7	132	136
8	125	130
9	135	131
10	126	128

a. Test the following hypothesis at the .05 level of significance.

$$H_0: \mu_1 - \mu_2 = 0$$
$$H_1: \mu_1 - \mu_2 \neq 0$$

b. Construct a 95% CI.

5. Individuals were measured on the number of words spoken during the 1 minute prior to exposure to a confrontational situation. During the 1 minute after exposure, the individuals were again measured on the number of words spoken. The data are as follows:

Person	Pre	Post
1	60	50
2	80	70
3	120	80
4	100	90
5	90	100
6	85	70
7	70	40
8	90	70
9	100	60
10	110	100
11	80	100
12	100	70
13	130	90
14	120	80
15	90	50

a. Test the following hypothesis at the .05 level of significance.

$$H_0: \mu_1 - \mu_2 = 0$$
$$H_1: \mu_1 - \mu_2 \neq 0$$

b. Construct a 95% CI.

6. The following is a random sample of scores on an attitude toward family planning scale for husband (sample 1) and wife (sample 2) pairs:

Pair	1	2
1	1	3
2	2	3
3	4	6
4	4	5
5	5	7
6	7	8
7	7	9
8	8	10

a. Test the following hypothesis at the .05 level of significance.

$$H_0: \mu_1 - \mu_2 = 0$$
$$H_1: \mu_1 - \mu_2 \neq 0$$

b. Construct a 95% CI.

7. For two dependent samples, test the hypothesis below at the .05 level of significance. Sample statistics: $n = 121$; $\bar{d} = 10$; $s_d = 45$.

$$H_0: \mu_1 - \mu_2 \leq 0$$
$$H_1: \mu_1 - \mu_2 > 0$$

8. For two dependent samples, test the hypothesis below at the .05 level of significance. Sample statistics: $n = 25$; $\bar{d} = 25$; $s_d = 14$.

$$H_0: \mu_1 - \mu_2 \leq 0$$
$$H_1: \mu_1 - \mu_2 > 0$$

9. Use the Ch7_ER.sav data to test the hypothesis that the anxiety of emergency room doctors differs from the anxiety of doctors who work in other areas of the hospital. Test at alpha = .05 and report the appropriate test results based on the extent to which the assumption of equal variances is met.

10. A researcher is examining IPEDS data (https://nces.ed.gov/ipeds/use-the-data) from land grant institutions. The researcher is interested in knowing if the mean number of students enrolled exclusively in distance education courses between 2012

and 2016 has changed. Use the Ch7_IPEDS.sav data. Test at alpha = .05 and report the appropriate test results.

Answers to Computational Problems

1. a. $t = -2.110$, critical values are approximately -2.041 and $+2.041$, reject H_0.
    b. $(-9.24377, -.15623)$, does not include hypothesized value of 0, reject H_0.

3. a. $t = -3.185$, critical values are -2.074 and $+2.074$, reject H_0.
    b. $(-6.742, -1.4248)$, does not include hypothesized value of 0, reject H_0.

5. a. $t = 4.117$, critical values are -2.145 and $+2.145$, reject H_0.
    b. $(9.7396, 30.9271)$, does not include hypothesized value of 0, reject H_0.

7. $t = 2.4444$, critical value is 1.658, reject H_0.

9. The assumption of equal variances is violated, $F = 9.39$, $p = .002$, thus we report Welch t'. There is a statistically significant difference in mean anxiety for doctors in the ER ($M = 26.63$, $SD = 4.41$) as compared to doctors who do not teach in the ER ($M = 24.13$, $SD = 5.48$), Welch $t' = -3.511$, $df = 174.20$, $p < .001$.

Interpretive Problems

1. Using the survey1 dataset from the website, use SPSS or **R** to conduct an independent t test, where gender is the grouping variable and the dependent variable is a continuous variable of interest to you. Test for the extent to which the assumptions have been met. Calculate an effect size as well as post hoc power. Then write an APA-style paragraph describing the results.

2. Using the survey1 dataset accessible from the website, use SPSS or **R** to conduct an independent t test, where the grouping variable is whether or not the person could tell the difference between Pepsi and Coke and the dependent variable is a continuous variable of interest to you. Test for the extent to which the assumptions have been met. Calculate an effect size as well as post hoc power. Then write an APA-style paragraph describing the results.

3. Using the Ch2_volcano dataset accessible from the website, use SPSS or **R** to conduct an independent t test, where the grouping variable is "stratovolcano" and the dependent variable is a continuous variable of interest to you. Test for the extent to which the assumptions have been met. Calculate an effect size as well as post hoc power. Then write an APA-style paragraph describing the results.

8

Inferences About Proportions

Chapter Outline

Key Concepts

1. Proportion
2. Sampling distribution and standard error of a proportion
3. Contingency table
4. Chi-square distribution
5. Observed versus expected proportions

In Chapters 6 and 7 we considered testing inferences about means, first for a single mean (Chapter 6) and then for two means (Chapter 7). The major concepts discussed in those chapters that are applicable throughout the rest of the text include the following: types of hypotheses, types of decision errors, level of significance, power, confidence intervals, effect sizes, sampling distributions, and standard errors. While we previously examined inferences about a single mean, inferences about the difference between two independent means, and inferences about the difference between two dependent means, in this chapter we consider inferential tests involving proportions. We define a *proportion* as the percentage of scores falling into particular categories. Thus, the tests described in this chapter deal with variables that are categorical in nature and thus are *nominal* or *ordinal* in terms of measurement scale (see Chapter 1), or have been collapsed from higher level variables into nominal or ordinal variables (e.g., high and low scorers on an achievement test; although, generally, collapsing interval or ratio into categorical is not good practice as much information is lost in the process).

The tests that we cover in this chapter are considered **nonparametric** procedures, also sometimes referred to as *distribution-free* procedures, as there is no requirement that the data adhere to a particular distribution (e.g., normal distribution). Nonparametric procedures are often *less preferable* than parametric procedures (e.g., *t* tests, which assume normality of the distribution) for the following reasons: (a) parametric procedures are often robust to assumption violations, in other words, the results are often still interpretable even if there may be assumption violations; (2) nonparametric procedures have lower power relative to sample size, in other words, rejecting the null hypothesis if it is false requires a larger sample size with nonparametric procedures; and (3) the types of research questions that can be addressed by nonparametric procedures are often quite simple (e.g., while complex interactions of many different variables can be tested with parametric procedures such as factorial analysis of variance, this cannot be done with nonparametric procedures). Nonparametric procedures can still be valuable to use given the measurement scale(s) of the variable(s) and the research question. However, at the same time it is important that researchers recognize the limitations in using these types of procedures.

Research questions to be asked of proportions include the following examples:

1. Is the quarter in my hand a fair or biased coin; in other words, over repeated samples, is the proportion of heads equal to .50 or not?
2. Is there a difference between the proportions of Republicans and Democrats who support the local school bond issue?
3. Is there a relationship between education level (e.g., less than high school diploma, high school graduate, some college, college graduate) and type of criminal offense (e.g., petty theft, rape, murder); in other words, is the proportion of one education level different from another in terms of the types of crimes committed?

Several inferential tests are covered in this chapter, depending on (a) whether there are one or two samples, (b) whether the two samples are selected in an independent or dependent manner, and (c) whether there are one or more categorical variables. More specifically, the topics described include the following inferential tests: testing whether a single proportion is different from a hypothesized value; testing whether two independent proportions are different; testing whether two dependent proportions are different; and the chi-square goodness-of-fit test and chi-square test of association. We use many of the foundational concepts previously covered in Chapters 6 and 7. New concepts to be discussed include the following: proportion; sampling distribution and standard error of a proportion; contingency table; chi-square distribution; and observed versus expected frequencies. Our objectives are that by the end of this chapter, you will be able to (a) understand the basic concepts underlying tests of proportions, (b) select the appropriate test, and (c) determine and interpret the results from the appropriate test.

8.1 What Inferences About Proportions Involving the Normal Distribution Are and How They Work

A superbly talented set of four graduate students have been expertly completing research projects through their work in the statistics lab. We find the group, once again, ready for a challenge!

The statistics lab has been contracted to work with Dr. Senata, the Director of the Undergraduate Services Office at Ivy Covered University, and Dr. Walnut, a lobbyist from a state that is considering legalizing gambling. Challie Lenge will be advising Dr. Senata, and Addie Venture will be working with Dr. Walnut.

In conversation with Challie, Dr. Senata shares that she recently read a report that provided national statistics on the proportion of students that major in various disciplines. Dr. Senata wants to know if there are similar proportions at their institution. Dr. Senata suggests the following research question: *Are the sample proportions of undergraduate student college majors at Ivy Covered University in the same proportions of those nationally?* Challie suggests a chi-square goodness of fit test as the test of inference. Her task is then to assist Dr. Senata in generating the test of inference to answer her research question.

Addie is consulting with Dr. Walnut, a lobbyist who is lobbying against legalizing gambling in his state. Dr. Walnut wants to determine if there is a relationship between level of education and stance on a proposed gambling amendment. Addie suspects that the proportions supporting gambling vary as a function of their education level. The following research question is suggested by Addie: *Is there an association between level of education and stance on gambling?* Addie suggests a chi-square test of association as the test of inference. Her task is then to assist Dr. Walnut in generating the test of inference to answer the research question.

This section deals with concepts and procedures for testing inferences about proportions that involve the normal distribution. Following a discussion of the concepts related to tests

of proportions, inferential tests are presented for situations when there is a single proportion, two independent proportions, and two dependent proportions.

8.1.1 Characteristics

Let us examine in greater detail the concepts related to tests of proportions. First, a **proportion** represents *the percentage of individuals or objects that fall into a particular category*. For
instance, the proportion of individuals who support a particular political candidate might
be of interest. Thus the variable here is a dichotomous, categorical, nominal variable, as
there are only two categories represented, support or do not support the candidate.

For notational purposes, we define the **population proportion**, π (pi), as

$$\pi = \frac{f}{N}$$

where f is the *number of frequencies in the population who fall into the category of interest* (e.g.,
the number of individuals in the population who support the candidate), and N is the total
number of units (e.g., individuals) in the population. For example, if the population consists of 100 individuals and 58 support the candidate, then $\pi = .58$ (i.e., 58/100). If the proportion is multiplied by 100%, this yields the percentage of individuals in the population
who support the candidate, which in the example would be 58%. At the same time, $1 - \pi$
represents the population proportion of individuals who do *not* support the candidate,
which for this example would be $1 - .58 = .42$. If this is multiplied by 100%, this yields the
percentage of individuals in the population who do not support the candidate, which in
the example would be 42%.

In a fashion, the population proportion is conceptually similar to the population mean
if the category of interest (support of candidate) is coded as 1 and the other category
(not support) is coded as 0. In the case of the example with 100 individuals, there are 58
individuals coded 1, 42 individuals coded 0, and therefore the mean (i.e., the proportion
of cases coded as 1) would be .58. To this point then we have π representing the population proportion of individuals *supporting* the candidate and $1 - \pi$ representing the
population proportion of individuals *not supporting* the candidate.

The **population variance of a proportion** can be determined by $\sigma^2 = \pi(1 - \pi)$. Thus, the
population standard deviation of a proportion is $\sigma = \sqrt{\pi(1-\pi)}$. These provide us with
measures of variability that represent the extent to which the individuals in the population
vary in their support of the candidate. For the example population then, the variance is
computed to be $\sigma^2 = \pi(1 - \pi) = .58(1 - .58) = .58(.42) = .2436$ and the standard deviation is
$\sigma = \sqrt{\pi(1-\pi)} = \sqrt{.58(1-.58)} = \sqrt{.58(.42)} = .4936$.

For the *population parameters*, we now have the population proportion (or mean), the
population variance, and the population standard deviation. The next step is to discuss the
corresponding *sample statistics* for the proportion. The **sample proportion**, p, is defined as

$$p = \frac{f}{n}$$

where f is the *number of frequencies in the sample that fall into the category of interest*
(e.g., the number of individuals who support the candidate), and n is the *total number of*

units (e.g., individuals) in the sample. The sample proportion p is thus a *sample estimate* of the population proportion, π. One way we can estimate the population variance is by the sample variance $s^2 = p(1 - p)$ and the population standard deviation of a proportion can be estimated by the sample standard deviation $s = \sqrt{p(1-p)}$.

The next concept to discuss is the sampling distribution of the proportion. This is comparable to the sampling distribution of the mean discussed in Chapter 5. If one were to take many samples, and for each sample compute the sample proportion p, then we could generate a distribution of p. This is known as the **sampling distribution of the proportion**. For example, imagine that we take 50 samples of size 100 and determine the proportion for each sample. That is, we would have 50 different sample proportions each based on 100 observations. If we construct a frequency distribution of these 50 proportions, then this is actually the sampling distribution of the proportion.

In theory, the sample proportions for this example could range from .00 ($p = 0/100$) to 1.00 ($p = 100/100$), given that there are 100 observations in each sample. One could also examine the variability of these 50 sample proportions. That is, we might be interested in the extent to which the sample proportions vary. We might have, for one example, most of the sample proportions falling near the mean proportion of .60. This would indicate for the candidate data that (a) the samples generally support the candidate, as the average proportion is .60, and (b) the support for the candidate is fairly consistent across samples, as the sample proportions tend to fall close to .60. Alternatively, in a second example, we might find the sample proportions varying quite a bit around the mean of .60, say ranging from .20 to .80. This would indicate that (a) the samples generally support the candidate again, as the average proportion is .60, and (b) the support for the candidate is not very consistent across samples, leading one to believe that some groups support the candidate and others do not.

The variability of the sampling distribution of the proportion can be determined as follows. The *population variance of the sampling distribution of the proportion* is known as the **variance error of the proportion**, denoted by σ_p^2. The **variance error** is computed as

$$\sigma_p^2 = \frac{\pi(1-\pi)}{n}$$

where π is again the population proportion and n is sample size (i.e., the number of observations in a single sample).

The *population standard deviation of the sampling distribution of the proportion* is known as the **standard error of the proportion**, denoted by σ_p. The **standard error** is an index of how variable a sample statistic (in this case, the sample proportion) is when multiple samples of the same size are drawn, and is computed as follows:

$$\sigma_p = \sqrt{\frac{\pi(1-\pi)}{n}}$$

This situation is quite comparable to the sampling distribution of the mean discussed in Chapter 5. There we had the variance error and standard error of the mean as measures of the variability of the sample means.

Technically speaking, the binomial distribution is the exact sampling distribution for the proportion; **binomial** here refers to a categorical variable with two possible categories, which is certainly the situation here. *However, except for rather small samples, the normal distribution is a reasonable approximation to the binomial distribution and is therefore typically used.* The reason we can rely on the normal distribution is due to the *central limit theorem*, previously discussed in Chapter 5. For proportions, the central limit theorem states that as sample size n increases, the sampling distribution of the proportion from a random sample of size n more closely approximates a normal distribution. If the population distribution is normal in shape, then the sampling distribution of the proportion is also normal in shape. If the population distribution is not normal in shape, then the sampling distribution of the proportion becomes more nearly normal as sample size increases. As previously shown in Figure 5.2 in the context of the mean, *the bottom line is that if the population is nonnormal, this will have a minimal effect on the sampling distribution of the proportion except for rather small samples.*

Because nearly always the applied researcher only has access to a single sample, the population variance error and standard error of the proportion must be estimated. The sample variance error of the proportion is denoted by s_p^2 and computed as

$$s_p^2 = \frac{p(1-p)}{n}$$

where p is again the sample proportion and n is sample size. The sample standard error of the proportion is denoted by s_p and computed as

$$s_p = \sqrt{\frac{p(1-p)}{n}}$$

8.1.1.1 Inferences About a Single Proportion

In the first inferential testing situation for proportions, the researcher would like to know whether the population proportion is equal to some hypothesized proportion or not. This is comparable to the one-sample t test described in Chapter 6 where a population mean was compared against some hypothesized mean. Now, we are examining a population proportion compared to some hypothesized proportion.

First, the hypotheses are stated. The hypotheses to be evaluated for detecting whether a population proportion differs from a hypothesized proportion are as follows. The *null hypothesis*, H_0, is that there is no difference between the population proportion, π, and the hypothesized proportion, π_0, which we denote as

$$H_0: \pi = \pi_0$$

Here there is no difference, or a "null" difference, between the population proportion and the hypothesized proportion. For example, if we are seeking to determine whether the quarter you are flipping is a biased coin or not, then a reasonable hypothesized value would be .50, as an unbiased coin should yield "heads" about 50% of the time.

The *nondirectional, scientific, or alternative hypothesis*, H_1, is that there *is* a difference between the population proportion, π, and the hypothesized proportion, π_0, which we denote as

$$H_1 : \pi \neq \pi_0$$

The null hypothesis, H_0, will be rejected here in favor of the alternative hypothesis, H_1, if the population proportion is different from the hypothesized proportion. As we have not specified a direction on H_1, we are willing to reject H_0 either if π is greater than π_0 or if π is less than π_0. This alternative hypothesis results in a two-tailed test. Directional (or one-tailed) alternative hypotheses can also be tested if we believe either that π is greater than π_0 or that π is less than π_0. In either case, the more the resulting sample proportion differs from the hypothesized proportion, the more likely we are to reject the null hypothesis.

Second, we then compute the test statistic z as

$$z = \frac{p - \pi_0}{s_{\hat{p}}} = \frac{p - \pi_0}{\sqrt{\dfrac{\pi_0\left(1 - \pi_0\right)}{n}}}$$

where $s_{\hat{p}}$ is estimated based on the hypothesized proportion π_0.

Third, the test statistic z is then compared to a critical value(s) from the unit normal distribution. For a two-tailed test, the critical values are denoted as $\pm_{\alpha/2}z$ and are found in Table A.1 in the Appendix. If the test statistic z falls into either critical region, then we reject H_0; otherwise, we fail to reject H_0. For a one-tailed test, the critical value is denoted as $+_{\alpha}z$ for the alternative hypothesis H_1: $\pi > \pi_0$ (i.e., a right-tailed test) and as $-_{\alpha}z$ for the alternative hypothesis H_1: $\pi < \pi_0$ (i.e., a left-tailed test). If the test statistic z falls into the appropriate critical region, then we reject H_0; otherwise, we fail to reject H_0.

For the two-tailed test, a $(1 - \alpha)\%$ confidence interval can also be examined. The confidence interval is formed as follows:

$$p \pm {}_{\alpha/2}z\left(s_{\hat{p}}\right)$$

where p is the observed sample proportion, $\pm_{\alpha/2}z$ is the tabled critical value, and $s_{\hat{p}}$ is the sample standard error of the proportion. If the confidence interval contains the hypothesized proportion π_0, then the conclusion is to fail to reject H_0; otherwise, we reject H_0. The interpretation of confidence intervals described in this chapter is the same as those in Chapter 7.

Simulation research has shown that this confidence interval procedure works fine for small samples when the sample proportion is near .50; that is, the normal distribution is a reasonable approximation in this situation. However, as the sample proportion moves closer to 0 or 1, larger samples are required for the normal distribution to be reasonably approximate. Alternative approaches have been developed that appear to be more widely applicable. The interested reader is referred to Ghosh (1979) and Wilcox (1996).

8.1.1.1.1 An Example

Let us consider an example to illustrate use of the test of a single proportion. We follow the basic steps for hypothesis testing that we applied in previous chapters. These steps include:

1. State the null and alternative hypotheses.
2. Select the level of significance (i.e., alpha, α).
3. Calculate the test statistic value.
4. Make a statistical decision (reject or fail to reject H_0).

Suppose a researcher conducts a survey in a city that is voting on whether or not to have an elected school board. Based on informal conversations with a small number of influential citizens, the researcher is led to hypothesize that 50% of the voters are in favor of an elected school board. Through use of a scientific poll, the researcher would like to know whether the population proportion is different from this hypothesized value; thus, a nondirectional, two-tailed alternative hypothesis is utilized. The null and alternative hypotheses are denoted as follows:

$$H_0: \pi = \pi_0$$
$$H_1: \pi \neq \pi_0$$

If the null hypothesis is *rejected*, this would indicate that scientific polls of larger samples yield different results than what was anticipated based on informal conversations and are important in this situation. If the null hypothesis is *not rejected*, this would indicate that informal conversations with a small sample are just as accurate as a scientific larger-sized sample.

A random sample of 100 voters is taken and 60 indicate their support of an elected school board (i.e., $p = .60$). In an effort to minimize the Type I error rate, the significance level is set at $\alpha = .01$. The test statistic z is computed as

$$z = \frac{p - \pi_0}{\sqrt{\dfrac{\pi_0(1-\pi_0)}{n}}} = \frac{.60 - .50}{\sqrt{\dfrac{.50(1-.50)}{100}}} = \frac{.10}{\sqrt{\dfrac{.50(.50)}{100}}} = \frac{.10}{.05} = 2.00$$

Note that the final value for the denominator is the standard error of the proportion (i.e., $s_{\hat{p}} = .0500$), which we will need for computing the confidence interval. From Table A.1 in the Appendix, we determine the critical values to be $\pm_{\alpha/2}z = \pm_{.005}z = 2.58$, in other words, the z value that corresponds to the $P(z)$ value closest to .995 is when z is equal to 2.58. As the test statistic (i.e., $z = 2.000$) does not exceed the critical values (i.e., ± 2.58) and thus fails to fall into a critical region, our decision is to *fail to reject H_0*. Our conclusion then is that the accuracy of the scientific poll is not any different from the hypothesized value of .50 as determined informally. In other words, the proportion of individuals who stated during informal conversations that they would be in favor of an elected school board is similar to the proportion of individuals who would be in favor in the sample.

The 99% confidence interval for the example would be computed as follows:

$$p \pm {}_{\alpha/2}z\left(s_{\hat{p}}\right) = .60 \pm (2.58)(.05) = .60 \pm .129 = (.471, .729)$$

Because the confidence interval contains the hypothesized value of .50, our conclusion is to fail to reject H_0 (the same result found when we conducted the statistical test). The conclusion derived from the test statistic is always consistent with the conclusion derived from the confidence interval. We can interpret the confidence interval as follows: 99% of similarly constructed CIs will contain the hypothesized value of .50.

8.1.1.2 Inferences About Two Independent Proportions

In our second inferential testing situation for proportions, the researcher would like to know whether the population proportion for one group is different from the population proportion for a second independent group. This is comparable to the independent t test described in Chapter 7 where one population mean was compared to a second independent population mean. Once again we have two independently drawn samples, as discussed in Chapter 7.

First, the hypotheses to be evaluated for detecting whether two independent population proportions differ are as follows. The *null hypothesis, H_0,* is that there is no difference between the two population proportions, π_1 and π_2, which we denote as

$$H_0: \pi_1 - \pi_2 = 0$$

Here there is no difference, or a "null" difference, between the two population proportions. For example, a researcher wants to determine how shift work (i.e., working outside traditional 9 a.m. to 5 p.m. hours, such as an afternoon shift, 3 p.m. to 11 p.m., or a night shift, 11 p.m. to 7 a.m.) may impact sleep. Thus, we may be seeking to determine whether the proportion of adults who work in shifts (relative to those that don't work in shifts) who have sleep disorders (relative to not having a sleep disorder) is equal to the proportion of adults who work in shifts (relative to those that don't work in shifts) who *do not* have sleep disorders. In this example, we have two variables, each with two categories: shift work status (job requires shift work, job does not require shirt work) and sleep disorder status (has sleep disorder, does not have sleep disorder). As we will see later, this tests of proportions for independent samples can be conducted with categorical variables with more than two categories or levels.

The *nondirectional, scientific,* or *alternative hypothesis, H_1,* is that there is a difference between the population proportions, π_1 and π_2, which we denote as

$$H_1: \pi_1 - \pi_2 \neq 0$$

The null hypothesis, H_0, will be rejected here in favor of the alternative hypothesis, H_1, if the population proportions are different. As we have not specified a direction on H_1, we are willing to reject either if π_1 is greater than π_2 or if π_1 is less than π_2. This alternative hypothesis results in a two-tailed test. Directional alternative hypotheses can also be tested if we believe either that π_1 is greater than π_2 or that π_1 is less than π_2. In either case, the more the resulting sample proportions differ from one another, the more likely we are to reject the null hypothesis.

It is assumed that the two samples are independently and randomly drawn from their respective populations (i.e., the assumption of independence) and that the normal distribution is the appropriate sampling distribution. The next step is to compute the test statistic z as

$$z = \frac{p_1 - p_2}{s_{p_1 - p_2}} = \frac{p_1 - p_2}{\sqrt{(p)(1-p)\left(\dfrac{1}{n_1} + \dfrac{1}{n_2}\right)}}$$

where n_1 and n_2 are the sample sizes for samples 1 and 2 respectively, and

$$p = \frac{f_1 - f_2}{n_1 + n_2}$$

where f_1 and f_2 are the number of observed frequencies for samples 1 and 2 respectively. The denominator of the z test statistic $s_{p_1 - p_2}$ is known as the **standard error of the difference between two proportions** and provides an index of how variable the sample statistic (in this case, the sample proportion) is when multiple samples of the same size are drawn. This test statistic is conceptually similar to the test statistic for the independent t test.

The test statistic z is then compared to a critical value(s) from the unit normal distribution. For a two-tailed test, the critical values are denoted as $\pm_{\alpha/2} z$ and are found in Table A.1 in the Appendix. If the test statistic z falls into either critical region, then we reject H_0; otherwise, we fail to reject H_0. For a one-tailed test, the critical value is denoted as $\pm_{\alpha} z$ for the alternative hypothesis $H_1: \pi_1 - \pi_2 > 0$ (i.e., a right-tailed test) and as $-_{\alpha} z$ for the alternative hypothesis $H_1: \pi_1 - \pi_2 < 0$ (i.e., a left-tailed test). If the test statistic z falls into the appropriate critical region, then we reject H_0; otherwise, we fail to reject H_0. It should be noted that other alternatives to this test have been proposed (e.g., Storer & Kim, 1990).

For the two-tailed test, a $(1 - \alpha)\%$ confidence interval can also be examined. The confidence interval is formed as follows:

$$\left(p_1 - p_2\right) \pm {}_{\alpha/2} z \left(s_{p_1 - p_2}\right)$$

If the confidence interval contains zero, then the conclusion is to fail to reject H_0; otherwise, we reject H_0. Alternative methods are described by Beal (1987) and Coe and Tamhane (1993).

8.1.1.2.1 An Example

Let us consider an example to illustrate use of the test of two independent proportions. Suppose a researcher is taste-testing a new chocolate candy ("chocolate yummies") and wants to know the extent to which individuals would likely purchase the product. As taste in candy may be different for adults versus children, a study is conducted where independent samples of adults and children are given "chocolate yummies" to eat and asked whether they would buy them or not. The researcher would like to know whether the population proportion of individuals who would purchase "chocolate yummies" is different for adults and children. Thus, a nondirectional, two-tailed alternative hypothesis is utilized. The null and alternative hypotheses are denoted as follows:

$$H_0: \pi_1 - \pi_2 = 0$$
$$H_1: \pi_1 - \pi_2 \neq 0$$

If the null hypothesis is rejected, this would indicate that interest in purchasing the product is different in the two groups, and this might result in different marketing and packaging strategies for each group. If the null hypothesis is not rejected, then this would indicate the product is equally of interest to both adults and children, and different marketing and packaging strategies are not necessary.

A random sample of 100 children (sample 1) and a random sample of 100 adults (sample 2) are independently selected. Each individual consumes the product and indicates whether or not he or she would purchase it. Sixty-eight of the children and 54 of the adults state they would purchase "chocolate yummies" if they were available. The level of significance is set at $\alpha = .05$.

The test statistic z is computed as follows. We know that $n_1 = 100$, $n_2 = 100$, $f_1 = 68$, $f_2 = 54$, $p_1 = .68$, and $p_2 = .54$. We compute the sample proportion, p, to be

$$p = \frac{f_1 + f_2}{n_1 + n_2} = \frac{68 + 54}{100 + 100} = \frac{122}{200} = .61$$

This allows us to compute the test statistic z as

$$z = \frac{p_1 - p_2}{\sqrt{(p)(1-p)\left(\dfrac{1}{n_1} + \dfrac{1}{n_2}\right)}} = \frac{.68 - .54}{\sqrt{(.61)(1-.61)\left(\dfrac{1}{100} + \dfrac{1}{100}\right)}} =$$

$$z = \frac{.14}{\sqrt{(.61)(.39)(.02)}} = \frac{.14}{.069} = 2.0290$$

The denominator of the z test statistic, $s_{p1 - p2} = .0690$, is the standard error of the difference between two proportions, which we will need for computing the confidence interval.

The test statistic z is then compared to the critical values from the unit normal distribution. As this is a two-tailed test, the critical values are denoted as $\pm_{\alpha/2} z$ and are found in Table A.1 of the Appendix to be $\pm_{\alpha/2} z = \pm_{.025} z = \pm 1.96$. In other words, this is the z value that is closest to a $P(z)$ of .975. As the test statistic z falls into the upper-tail critical region, we reject H_0 and conclude that the proportion of adults and children are *not* equally interested in the product.

Finally, we can compute the 95% confidence interval as follows:

$$\left(p_1 - p_2\right) \pm \left(_{\alpha/2} z\right)\left(s_{p_1 - p_2}\right) = (.68 - .54) \pm (1.96)(.0690) = (.14) \pm (.1352) = (.0048, .2752)$$

Because the confidence interval does not include zero, we would again reject H_0 and conclude that the proportion of adults and children are not equally interested in the product. As previously stated, the conclusion derived from the test statistic is always consistent with the conclusion derived from the confidence interval at the same level of significance. We can interpret the confidence interval as follows: for 95% of similarly constructed CIs, the true population proportion difference will not include zero.

8.1.1.3 Inferences About Two Dependent Proportions

In our third inferential testing situation for proportions, the researcher would like to know whether the population proportion for one group is different from the population proportion for a second dependent group. This is comparable to the dependent t test described in Chapter 7 where one population mean was compared to a second dependent population mean. Once again we have two dependently drawn samples as discussed in Chapter 7. For example, we may have a pretest–posttest situation where a comparison of proportions over time for the same individuals is conducted. Alternatively, we may have pairs of matched individuals (e.g., spouses, twins, brother–sister) for which a comparison of proportions is of interest.

First, the hypotheses to be evaluated for detecting whether two dependent population proportions differ are as follows. The *null hypothesis*, H_0, is that there is no difference between the two population proportions π_1 and π_2, which we denote as

$$H_0: \pi_1 - \pi_2 = 0$$

Here there is no difference, or a "null" difference, between the two population proportions. For example, a political analyst may be interested in determining whether the approval rating of the president is the same just prior to and immediately following his annual State of the Union address (i.e., a pretest–posttest situation). As a second example, a marriage counselor wants to know whether husbands and wives equally favor a particular training program designed to enhance their relationship (i.e., a couple situation).

The *nondirectional, scientific, or alternative hypothesis, H_1,* is that there is a difference between the population proportions, π_1 and π_2, which we denote as follows:

$$H_1: \pi_1 - \pi_2 \neq 0$$

The null hypothesis, H_0, will be rejected here in favor of the alternative hypothesis, H_1, if the population proportions are different. As we have not specified a direction on H_1, we are willing to reject either if π_1 is greater than π_2 or if π_1 is less than π_2. This alternative hypothesis results in a two-tailed test. Directional alternative hypotheses can also be tested if we believe either that π_1 is greater than π_2 or that π_1 is less than π_2. The more the resulting sample proportions differ from one another, the more likely we are to reject the null hypothesis.

Before we examine the test statistic, let us consider a table in which the proportions are often presented. As shown in Table 8.1, the **contingency table** lists proportions for each of the different possible outcomes. *The columns indicate the proportions for sample 1.* The left column contains those proportions related to the "unfavorable" condition (or disagree or no, depending on the situation), and the right column those proportions related to the "favorable" condition (or agree or yes, depending on the situation). At the bottom of the

TABLE 8.1

Contingency Table for Two Samples

	Sample 1		
Sample 2	**"Unfavorable"**	**"Favorable"**	**Marginal Proportions**
"Favorable"	a	b	p_2
"Unfavorable"	c	d	$1 - p_2$
Marginal proportions	$1 - p_1$	p_1	

columns are the marginal proportions shown for the "unfavorable" condition, denoted by $1 - p_1$, and for the "favorable" condition, denoted by p_1. *The rows indicate the proportions for sample 2.* The top row contains those proportions for the "favorable" condition, and the bottom row contains those proportions for the "unfavorable" condition. To the right of the rows are the marginal proportions shown for the "favorable" condition, denoted by p_2, and for the "unfavorable" condition, denoted by $1 - p_2$.

Within the box of the table are the proportions for the different combinations of conditions across the two samples. The *upper left-hand cell* is the proportion of observations that are "unfavorable" in sample 1 and "favorable" in sample 2 (i.e., dissimilar across samples), denoted by a. The *upper right-hand cell* is the proportion of observations who are "favorable" in sample 1 and "favorable" in sample 2 (i.e., similar across samples), denoted by b. The *lower left-hand cell* is the proportion of observations who are "unfavorable" in sample 1 and "unfavorable" in sample 2 (i.e., similar across samples), denoted by c. The *lower right-hand cell* is the proportion of observations who are "favorable" in sample 1 and "unfavorable" in sample 2 (i.e., dissimilar across samples), denoted by d.

The next step is to compute the test statistic z as

$$z = \frac{p_1 - p_2}{s_{p_1 - p_2}} = \frac{p_1 - p_2}{\sqrt{\dfrac{d + a}{n}}}$$

where n is the total number of pairs. The denominator of the z test statistic, $s_{p_1 - p_2}$, is again known as the **standard error of the difference between two proportions** and provides an index of how variable the sample statistic (i.e., the difference between two sample proportions) is when multiple samples of the same size are drawn. This test statistic is conceptually similar to the test statistic for the dependent t test.

The test statistic z is then compared to a critical value(s) from the unit normal distribution. For a two-tailed test, the critical values are denoted as $\pm_{\alpha/2}z$ and are found in Table A.1 in the Appendix. If the test statistic z falls into either critical region, then we reject H_0; otherwise, we fail to reject H_0. For a one-tailed test, the critical value is denoted as $+_{\alpha}z$ for the alternative hypothesis H_1: $\pi_1 - \pi_2 > 0$ (i.e., right-tailed test) and as $-_{\alpha}z$ for the alternative hypothesis H_1: $\pi_1 - \pi_2 < 0$ (i.e., left-tailed test). If the test statistic z falls into the appropriate critical region, then we reject H_0; otherwise, we fail to reject H_0. It should be noted that other alternatives to this test have been proposed (e.g., the chi-square test as described in the following section). Unfortunately, the z test does not yield an acceptable confidence interval procedure.

8.1.1.3.1 An Example

Let us consider an example to illustrate use of the test of two dependent proportions. Suppose a medical researcher is interested in whether husbands and wives agree on the effectiveness of a new headache medication "No-Ache." A random sample of 100 husband–wife couples were selected and asked to try "No-Ache" for 2 months. At the end of 2 months, each individual was asked whether the medication was effective or not at reducing headache pain. The researcher wants to know whether the medication is differentially effective for husbands and wives. Thus, a nondirectional, two-tailed alternative hypothesis is utilized.

TABLE 8.2

Contingency Table for Headache Example

| | Husband Sample | | |
Wife Sample	Ineffective	Effective	Marginal Proportions
Effective	$a = .40$	$b = .25$	$p_2 = .65$
Ineffective	$c = .20$	$d = .15$	$1 - p_1 = .35$
Marginal proportions	$1 - p_1 = .60$	$p_1 = .40$	

The resulting proportions are presented as a contingency table in Table 8.2. The level of significance is set at $\alpha = .05$. The test statistic z is computed as follows:

$$z = \frac{p_1 - p_2}{s_{p_1 - p_2}} = \frac{p_1 - p_2}{\sqrt{\dfrac{d + a}{n}}} = \frac{.40 - .65}{\sqrt{\dfrac{.15 + .40}{100}}} = \frac{-.25}{.0742} = -3.3693$$

The test statistic z is then compared to the critical values from the unit normal distribution. As this is a two-tailed test, the critical values are denoted as $\pm\,_{\alpha/2}z$ and are found in Table A.1 in the Appendix to be $\pm\,_{\alpha/2}z = \pm\,_{.025}z = \pm 1.96$. In other words, this is the z value that is closest to a $P(z)$ of .975. As the test statistic z falls into the lower-tail critical region, we *reject* H_0 and conclude that the husbands and wives do not believe equally in the effectiveness of "No-Ache." In other words, there are dissimilar proportions of husbands and wives who believe in the effectiveness of "No-Ache."

8.1.2 Power

As stated elsewhere, in general, nonparametric procedures have lower power relative to sample size, in other words, rejecting the null hypothesis if it is false requires a larger sample size with nonparametric procedures. We encourage researchers to examine power prior, such as power tables or software (e.g., G*Power), to conducting their study so that the study is sufficiently powered to detect an effect.

8.1.3 Effect Size

Cohen's (1988) measure of effect size for proportion tests using z is known as h; thus, h is the effect size index for a difference in proportions. Unfortunately, h involves the use of arc-sin transformations of the proportions, which is beyond the scope of this text. In addition, standard statistical software, such as SPSS, does not provide measures of effect size for any of these tests. Using **R**, however, we can compute h, as shown in Figure 8.1. Using Cohen's (1988) conventions, a small difference between proportions is $h = 20$, medium effect is $h = 50$, and large effect is $h = .80$.

Working in **R**, we can compute the effect size *h* using the *pwr* package.

```
install.packages("pwr")
library(pwr)
```

With the *install.packages* function, we install the *pwr* package. Using the *library* function, we then load *pwr* into our library.

```
h<-ES.h(0.40,.65)
h
```

We use the *ES.h* function and include our proportions in parentheses, where the first value represents p_1 and the second value represents p_2. Using the data from the headache example, our proportions are .40 and .65. From the results, we create an object named "h." The second line of script is simply telling **R** to output the results, which we see here. Thus, $h = -.51$. Using Cohen's conventions, this represents a moderate effect.

```
[1] -0.5060506
```

```
pwr.p.test(h=h,n=100,sig.level=0.05,
alternative="two.sided")
```

The *pwr.p.test* function can be used to compute observed power given the observed *h*, sample size (i.e., "n=100"), alpha level ("sig.level=0.05"), and two-sided test (alternative = "two.sided"). In this example, we find power to be .999, which indicates very high power.

```
proportion power calculation for binomial distribution (arcsine transformation)

              h = 0.5060506
              n = 100
      sig.level = 0.05
          power = 0.9990342
    alternative = two.sided
```

FIGURE 8.1
Computing effect size *h* in **R**.

8.1.4 Assumptions

For inferences about proportions assuming the normal distribution, it is assumed that the sample (in the case of a single proportion) or samples (in the case of independent and dependent proportions) have been randomly selected from the population (i.e., the assumption of independence) and that the normal distribution is the appropriate sampling distribution.

8.2 What Inferences About Proportions Involving the Chi-Square Distribution Are and How They Work

This section deals with concepts and procedures for testing inferences about proportions that involve the chi-square distribution. Following a discussion of the chi-square distribution relevant to tests of proportions, inferential tests are presented for the chi-square goodness-of-fit test and the chi-square test of association.

8.2.1 Characteristics

The previous tests of proportions in this chapter were based on the *unit normal distribution*, whereas the tests of proportions in the remainder of the chapter are based on the **chi-square distribution**. Thus, we need to become familiar with this new distribution. Like the normal and *t* distributions, the chi-square distribution is really a *family of distributions*. Also, like the *t* distribution, the chi-square distribution family members depend on the number of degrees of freedom represented. As we shall see, the *degrees of freedom* for the chi-square goodness-of-fit test are calculated as *the number of categories (denoted as J) minus 1*. For example, the chi-square distribution for one degree of freedom (i.e., for a variable that has two categories) is denoted by χ_1^2, as shown in Figure 8.2. This particular chi-square distribution is especially positively skewed and leptokurtic (sharp peak).

Figure 8.2 also describes graphically the distributions for χ_5^2 and χ_{10}^2. As you can see in the figure, as the degrees of freedom increase, the distribution becomes less skewed and less leptokurtic; in fact, *the distribution becomes more nearly normal in shape as the number of degrees of freedom increase*. For extremely large degrees of freedom, the chi-square distribution is approximately normal. In general we denote a particular chi-square distribution with ν degrees of freedom as χ_ν^2. The *mean* of any chi-square distribution is ν, the *mode* is $\nu - 2$ when ν is at least 2, and the *variance* is 2ν. The value of chi-square can range from zero to positive infinity. A table of different percentile values for many chi-square distributions is given in Table A.3 in the Appendix. This table is utilized in the following two chi-square tests.

One additional point that should be noted about each of the chi-square tests of proportions developed in this chapter is that there are *no confidence interval procedures* for either the chi-square goodness-of-fit test or the chi-square test of association.

8.2.1.1 The Chi-Square Goodness-of-Fit Test

The first test to consider is the **chi-square goodness-of-fit test**. This test is used to determine whether the observed proportions in two or more categories of a categorical variable differ from what we would expect *a priori*. For example, a researcher is interested

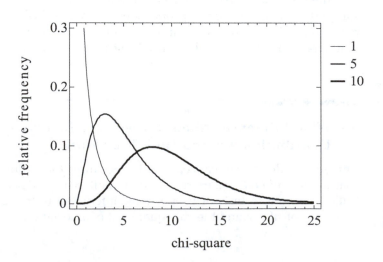

FIGURE 8.2
Several members of the family
of the chi-square distribution.

in whether the current undergraduate student body at Ivy-Covered University (ICU) is majoring in disciplines according to an *a priori* or expected set of proportions. Based on research at the national level, the expected proportions of undergraduate college majors are as follows: .20 Education; .40 Arts and Sciences; .10 Communications; and .30 Business. In a random sample of 100 undergraduates at ICU, the observed proportions are as follows: .25 Education, .50 Arts and Sciences, .10 Communications, and .15 Business. Thus, the researcher would like to know whether the sample proportions observed at ICU fit the expected national proportions. In essence, the chi-square goodness-of-fit test is used to test proportions for a single categorical variable (i.e., nominal or ordinal measurement scale) and in this way is akin to a one-sample *t* test.

The **observed proportions** are denoted by p_j, where p represents a sample proportion and j represents a particular category (e.g., Education majors), where $j = 1, \ldots, J$ categories. The **expected proportions** are denoted by π_j, where π represents an expected proportion and j represents a particular category. The null and alternative hypotheses are denoted as follows, where the null hypothesis states that the difference between the observed and expected proportions is zero for all categories.

$$H_0: \left(p_j - \pi_j \right) = 0 \, for \, all \, j$$
$$H_1: \left(p_j - \pi_j \right) \neq 0 \, for \, all \, j$$

The test statistic is a chi-square and is computed by

$$\chi^2 = n \sum_{j=1}^{J} \frac{\left(p_j - \pi_j \right)^2}{\pi_j}$$

where n is the size of the sample. The test statistic is compared to a critical value from the chi-square table (Table A.3 in the Appendix) $_\alpha \chi_v^2$, where $v = J - 1$. The degrees of freedom are one less than the total number of categories J, because the proportions must total to 1.00; thus, only $J - 1$ are free to vary.

If the test statistic is larger than the critical value, then the null hypothesis is rejected in favor of the alternative. This would indicate that the observed and expected proportions were *not* equal for all categories. The larger the differences are between one or more observed and expected proportions, the larger the value of the test statistic, and the more likely it is to reject the null hypothesis. Otherwise, we would fail to reject the null hypothesis (i.e., the test statistic is smaller than the critical value), indicating that the observed and expected proportions were approximately equal for all categories.

If the null hypothesis is rejected, one may wish to determine which sample proportions are different from their respective expected proportions, and one option is to conduct tests of a single proportion as described in the preceding section. If you would like to control the experiment-wise Type I error rate across a set of such tests, then the Bonferroni method is recommended where the alpha level is divided up among the number of tests conducted. For example, with an overall $\alpha = .05$ and five categories, one would conduct five tests of a single proportion, each at the .01 level of alpha.

Another way to determine which cells are statistically different in observed to expected proportions is to examine the **standardized residuals**, which can be computed as follows:

$$R = \frac{O - E}{\sqrt{E}}$$

Standardized residuals that are greater (in absolute value terms) than 1.96 (when $\alpha = .05$) or 2.58 (when $\alpha = .01$) have different observed to expected frequencies and are contributing to the statistically significant chi-square statistic. The sign of the residual provides information on whether the observed frequency is greater than the expected frequency (i.e., positive value) or less than the expected frequency (i.e., negative value).

Let us return to the example and conduct the chi-square goodness-of-fit test. The test statistic is computed as follows:

$$\chi^2 = n \sum_{j=1}^{J} \frac{\left(p_j - \pi_j\right)^2}{\pi_j}$$

$$\chi^2 = 100 \sum_{j=1}^{4} \left[\frac{(.25 - .20)^2}{.20} + \frac{(.50 - .40)^2}{.40} + \frac{(.10 - .10)^2}{.10} + \frac{(.15 - .30)^2}{.30} \right]$$

$$\chi^2 = 100 \sum_{j=1}^{4} [.0125 + .0250 + .0000 + .0750] = 100(.1125) = 11.25$$

The test statistic is compared to the critical value from Table A.3 in the Appendix, which is $_{.05}\chi^2_3 = 7.8147$. Because the test statistic is larger than the critical value, we *reject the null hypothesis* and conclude that the sample proportions from ICU are different from the expected proportions at the national level. Follow-up tests to determine which cells are statistically different in their observed to expected proportions involve examining the standardized residuals. In this example, the standardized residuals are computed as follows:

$$R_{Education} = \frac{O - E}{\sqrt{E}} = \frac{25 - 20}{\sqrt{20}} = 1.118$$

$$R_{Arts\ \&\ Sciences} = \frac{O - E}{\sqrt{E}} = \frac{50 - 40}{\sqrt{40}} = 1.581$$

$$R_{Communication} = \frac{O - E}{\sqrt{E}} = \frac{10 - 10}{\sqrt{10}} = 0$$

$$R_{Business} = \frac{O - E}{\sqrt{E}} = \frac{15 - 30}{\sqrt{30}} = -2.739$$

The standardized residual for Business is greater (in absolute value terms) than 1.96 ($\alpha = .05$), and thus *suggests that there are different observed to expected frequencies for students majoring in Business at ICU compared to national estimates, and that this category is the one which is contributing most to the statistically significant chi-square statistic.*

8.2.1.2 The Chi-Square Test of Association

The second test to consider is the chi-square test of association. This test is equivalent to the chi-square test of independence and the chi-square test of homogeneity, which are not discussed further. The chi-square test of association incorporates both of these tests (e.g., Glass & Hopkins, 1996). The **chi-square test of association** *is used to determine whether there is an association or relationship between two or more categorical (i.e., nominal or ordinal) variables.* Our discussion is, for the most part, restricted to the two-variable situation where each variable has two or more categories. The chi-square test of association is the logical extension to the chi-square goodness-of-fit test, which is concerned with one categorical variable. Unlike the chi-square goodness-of-fit test where the expected proportions are known *a priori*, for the chi-square test of association the expected proportions are not known *a priori*, but must be estimated from the sample data.

For example, suppose a researcher is interested in whether there is an association between level of education and stance on a proposed amendment to legalize gambling. Thus, one categorical variable is level of education with the categories being: (a) less than a high school education, (b) high school graduate, (c) undergraduate degree, and (d) graduate school degree. The other categorical variable is stance on the gambling amendment with the categories being: (a) in favor of the gambling bill and (b) opposed to the gambling bill. The null hypothesis is that there is no association between level of education and stance on gambling, whereas the alternative hypothesis is that there is some association between level of education and stance on gambling. The alternative would be supported if individuals at one level of education felt differently about the bill than individuals at another level of education.

The data are shown in the contingency table (or cross-tabulation table) in Table 8.3. Because there are two categorical variables, we have a two-way, or two-dimensional, contingency table. Each combination of the two variables is known as a **cell**. For example, the cell for row 1, "favor bill," and column 2, "high school graduate," is denoted as *cell 12*; the first value (i.e., 1) refers to the *row* and the second value (i.e., 2) to the *column*. Thus, the first subscript indicates the particular row r and the second subscript indicates the particular column c. The row subscript ranges from $r = 1, \ldots, R$ and the column subscript ranges from $c = 1, \ldots, C$, where R is the last row and C is the last column. This example contains a total of eight cells, two rows multiplied by four columns, denoted by $R \times C = 2 \times 4 = 8$.

Each cell in the table contains two pieces of information: the number (or count or frequencies) of observations in that cell and the observed proportion in that cell. Cell 12 has 13 observations, denoted by $n_{12} = 13$, and an observed proportion of .65, denoted by $p_{12} = .65$. The observed proportion is computed by taking the number of observations in the

TABLE 8.3

Contingency Table for Gambling Example

Stance on Gambling	Level of Education				Row Marginals
	Less Than High School	High School	Undergraduate	Graduate	
Favor	$n_{11} = 16$	$n_{12} = 13$	$n_{13} = 10$	$n_{14} = 5$	$n_{1.} = 44$
	$p_{11} = .80$	$p_{12} = .65$	$p_{13} = .50$	$p_{14} = .25$	$\pi_{1.} = 55$
Opposed	$n_{21} = 4$	$n_{22} = 7$	$n_{23} = 10$	$n_{24} = 15$	$n_{2.} = 36$
	$p_{21} = .20$	$p_{22} = .35$	$p_{23} = .50$	$p_{24} = .75$	$\pi_{2.} = .45$
Column marginals	$n_{.1} = 20$	$n_{.2} = 20$	$n_{.3} = 20$	$n_{.4} = 20$	$n_{..} = 80$

cell and dividing by the number of observations in the column. Thus for cell 12, 13 of the 20 high school graduates favor the bill, or $13/20 = .6$. The column information, known as the **column marginal**, is given at the bottom of each column. Here we are given the number of observations in a column, denoted by $n_{.c}$, where the "." indicates we have summed across rows and c indicates the particular column. For column 2 (reflecting high school graduates), there are 20 observations, denoted by $n_{.c} = 20$.

Row information is also provided at the end of each row, known as the **row marginals**. Two values are listed in the row marginals. First, the number of observations in a row is denoted by $n_{r.}$, where r indicates the particular row and the "." indicates we have summed across the columns. Second, the expected proportion for a specific row is denoted by $\pi_{r.}$, where again r indicates the particular row and the "." indicates we have summed across the columns. The expected proportion for a particular row is computed by taking the number of observations in row $n_{r.}$ and dividing by the number of total observations n. Note that the total number of observations is given in the lower right-hand portion of the figure and denoted as $n. = 80$. Thus for the first row, the expected proportion is computed as $\pi_1 = n_1/n = 44/80 = 55$.

The null and alternative hypotheses can be written as follows:

$$H_0 : (p_{rc} - \pi_{r.}) \neq 0 \text{ } f \text{ or all cells}$$
$$H_1 : (p_{rc} - \pi_{r.}) \neq 0 \text{ } f \text{ or all cells}$$

The test statistic is a chi-square and is computed by

$$\chi^2 = \sum_{r=1}^{R}\sum_{c=1}^{C} n_{.c} \frac{(p_{rc} - \pi_{r.})^2}{\pi_{r.}}$$

The test statistic is compared to a critical value from the chi-square table (Table A.3 in the Appendix) of $_{.05}\chi_v^2$, where $v = (R - 1)(C - 1)$. That is, the degrees of freedom are one less than the number of rows multiplied by one less than the number of columns.

If the test statistic is *larger* than the critical value, then the null hypothesis is *rejected* in favor of the alternative. This would indicate that the observed and expected proportions *were not* equal across cells such that the two categorical variables have some association. The larger the differences between the observed and expected proportions, the larger the value of the test statistic, and the more likely it is to reject the null hypothesis. Otherwise, we would fail to reject the null hypothesis, indicating that the observed and expected proportions were approximately equal, such that the two categorical variables have no association.

If the null hypothesis is rejected, then one may wish to determine for which combination of categories the sample proportions are different from their respective expected proportions. One way to do this is to construct 2×2 contingency tables as subsets of the larger table and conduct chi-square tests of association. If you would like to control the experiment-wise Type I error rate across the set of tests, then the Bonferroni method is recommended, where the α level is divided up among the number of tests conducted. For example, with $\alpha = .05$ and five 2×2 tables, one would conduct five tests each at the .01 alpha level. Another way to do this (i.e., to determine for which combination of categories the sample proportions are different from their respective expected proportions), as with the chi-square goodness of fit test, is to examine the standardized residuals to determine the cells that have statistically significantly different observed to expected proportions. Cells where the standardized residuals are greater (in absolute value terms) than 1.96 (when $\alpha = .05$) or 2.58 (when $\alpha = .01$) are statistically significantly different in observed to expected frequencies.

Finally, it should be noted that we have only considered two-way contingency tables here. Multiway contingency tables can also be constructed and the chi-square test of association utilized to determine whether there is an association among several categorical variables.

8.2.1.2.1 An Example

Let us complete the analysis of the example data. The test statistic is computed as

$$\chi^2 = \sum_{r=1}^{R} \sum_{c=1}^{C} (n_{.c}) \left[\frac{(p_{rc} - \pi_{r.})^2}{\pi_{r.}} \right]$$

$$\chi^2 = (20) \left[\frac{(.80 - .55)^2}{.55} \right] + (20) \left[\frac{(.20 - .45)^2}{.45} \right] + (20) \left[\frac{(.65 - .55)^2}{.55} \right] + (20) \left[\frac{(.35 - .45)^2}{.45} \right]$$

$$+ (20) \left[\frac{(.50 - .55)^2}{.55} \right] + (20) \left[\frac{(.50 - .45)^2}{.45} \right] + (20) \left[\frac{(.25 - .55)^2}{.55} \right] + (20) \left[\frac{(.75 - .45)^2}{.45} \right]$$

$$= 2.2727 + 2.778 + 0.3636 + 0.4444 + 0.0909 + 0.1111 + 3.2727 + 4.0000 = 13.3332$$

The test statistic is compared to the critical value, from Table A.3 in the Appendix, of $_{.05}\chi^2_3 = 7.8147$. Because the test statistic is larger than the critical value, we *reject the null hypothesis* and conclude that there is an association between level of education and stance on the gambling bill. In other words, stance on gambling is not the same for all levels of education.

Follow-up tests to determine which cells are statistically different in the observed to expected proportions can be conducted by examining the standardized residuals. As we will see later in Table 8.6, the standardized residual for the cell "do not support" and "graduate level of education" are statistically significant. Thus, this cell is contributing to the statistically significant association between stance on gambling and education level.

8.2.2 Power

As stated elsewhere, in general, nonparametric procedures (compared to parametric procedures) have lower power relative to sample size, in other words, rejecting the null hypothesis if it is false requires a larger sample size with nonparametric procedures. Researchers are encouraged to examine *a priori* power using power tables or software (e.g., G*Power) so that their study is sufficiently powered to detect a meaningful effect.

8.2.3 Effect Size

Different effect size indices can be computed depending on whether you are working with just one categorical variable or a cross-tabulation of two categorical variables. A summary

TABLE 8.4

Effect Sizes Indices for Chi-Square Tests and Interpretations

Chi-Square Test	Effect Size	Interpretation
Chi-square goodness-of-fit test	Cohen's w	Ranges from 0 (no difference between the sample and hypothesized proportions, and thus no effect) to +1.0 (maximum difference between the sample and hypothesized proportions and thus a large effect): • Small effect = .10 • Medium effect = .30 • Large effect = .50
Chi-square test of association with one nominal and one ordinal variable *or* two nominal variables	Phi (ρ_φ) Cramer's Phi (ϕ_c)	Degree of relationship between two variables. Zero indicates no association; +1.0 indicates a perfect relationship between the variables: • Small effect = .10 • Medium effect = .30 • Large effect = .50
Chi-square test of association with *two* *ordinal variables*	Spearman's rho (ρ_s) Kendall's tau (τ)	Degree of relationship between two variables. Zero indicates no relationship; +1.0 indicates a perfect relationship between the variables: • Small effect = .10 • Medium effect = .30 • Large effect = .50

of effect size indices is presented in Table 8.4, with details provided in the following sections.

8.2.3.1 Chi-Square Goodness-of-Fit Effect Size

An effect size for the chi-square goodness-of-fit test, Cohen's w (Cohen, 1988), can be computed as follows:

$$w = \frac{\chi^2}{N(J-1)}$$

where χ^2 is the computed chi-square test statistic value, N is the total sample size, and J is the number of categories in the variable. This effect size statistic, w, can range from 0 to 1, where 0 indicates no difference between the sample and hypothesized proportions (and thus no effect). A value of 1 indicates the maximum difference between the sample and hypothesized proportions (and thus a large effect). Given the range of this value (0 to +1.0) and the similarity to a correlation coefficient, it is reasonable to apply Cohen's interpretations for correlations as a rule of thumb. These include the following: small effect size = .10, medium effect size = .30, and large effect size = .50. For the previous example, the effect size would be calculated as follows and would be interpreted as a small effect:

$$w = \frac{\chi^2}{N(J-1)} = \frac{11.25}{100(4-1)} = \frac{11.25}{300} = .0375$$

8.2.3.2 Chi-Square Test of Association Effect Size

Several measures of effect size, such as correlation coefficients and measures of association, can be requested in SPSS or computed in **R**, and are commonly reported effect size indices for results from chi-square tests of association. Which effect size value is selected depends in part on the measurement scale of the variable. For example, researchers working with nominal data can select a contingency coefficient: phi (for 2×2 tables), Cramer's V (for tables larger than 2×2), lambda, or an uncertainty coefficient. Correlation options available for ordinal data include gamma, Somer's d, Kendall's tau-b, and Kendall's tau-c. From the contingency coefficient, C, we can compute Cohen's w as follows:

$$w = \sqrt{\frac{C^2}{1-C^2}}$$

Cohen's recommended subjective standard for interpreting w (as well as the other correlation coefficients presented) is as follows: small effect size, $w = .10$, medium effect size, $w = .30$, large effect size, $w = .50$. See Cohen (1988) for further details. We will later review how to compute confidence intervals for w.

8.2.4 Assumptions

8.2.4.1 Chi-Square Goodness-of-Fit Assumptions

Two assumptions are made for the chi square goodness-of-fit test: (a) observations are *independent* (which is met when a random sample of the population is selected) and (b) an *expected* frequency of at least five per cell (and in the case of the chi-square goodness-of-fit test, this translates to an expected frequency of at least five per category, as there is only one variable included in the analysis). When the expected frequency is less than five, that particular cell (i.e., category) has undue influence on the chi-square statistic. In other words, the chi-square goodness-of-fit test becomes too sensitive when the expected values are less than five.

8.2.4.1 Chi-Square Test of Association Assumptions

The same two assumptions that apply to the chi-square goodness-of-fit test also apply to the chi-square test of association: (a) observations are independent (which is met when a random sample of the population is selected) and (b) an *expected* frequency of at least five per cell. When the expected frequency is less than five, that particular cell has undue influence on the chi-square statistic. In other words, the chi-square test of association becomes too sensitive when the expected values are less than five.

8.3 Computing Inferences About Proportions Involving the Chi-Square Distribution Using SPSS

Once again we consider the use of SPSS for the example datasets. Although SPSS does not have any of the z procedures described in the first part of this chapter, it is capable of conducting both of the chi-square procedures described.

8.3.1 The Chi-Square Goodness-of-Fit Test

Step 1. To conduct the chi-square goodness-of-fit test, you need one variable that is either nominal or ordinal in scale. We will be using the college major data (Ch8_CollegeMajor. sav) and the nominal variable that represents college major. To conduct the chi-square goodness-of-fit test, go to "Analyze" in the top pulldown menu, then select "Nonparametric Tests," followed by "Legacy Dialogs," and then "Chi-Square." Following the screenshot for Step 1 shown in Figure 8.3 produces the "Chi-Square Goodness-of-Fit" dialog box.

FIGURE 8.3
Chi-square goodness-of-fit test: Step 1.

Step 2. Next, from the main "Chi-Square Goodness-of-Fit" dialog box, click the variable (e.g., "College major") and move it into the "Test Variable List" box by clicking the arrow button. In the lower right-hand portion of the screen is a section labeled "Expected Values." The default is to conduct the analysis with the expected values equal for each category (you will see that the radio button for "All categories equal" is preselected). Much of the time you will want to use different expected values. To define different expected values, click the "Values" radio button (see the screenshot for Step 2a in Figure 8.4). Enter each expected value in the box below "Values," in the same order as the categories (e.g., first enter the expected value for category 1, then the expected value for category 2, etc.), and then click "Add" to define the value in the box. This sets up an expected value for each category. Repeat this process for every category of your variable (see the screenshot for Step 2b in Figure 8.5). Then click on "OK" to run the analysis. The output is shown in Table 8.5

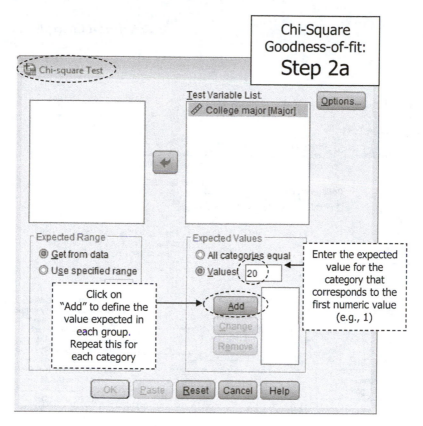

FIGURE 8.4
Chi-square goodness-of-fit test: Step 2a.

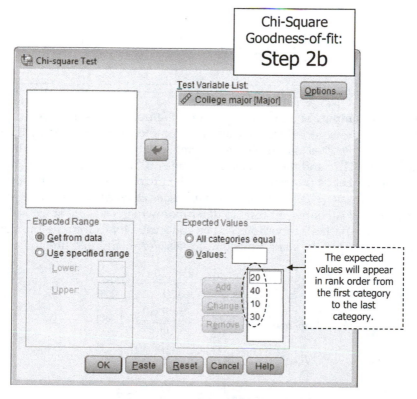

FIGURE 8.5
Chi-square goodness-of-fit test: Step 2b.

TABLE 8.5

SPSS Results for Undergraduate Majors Example

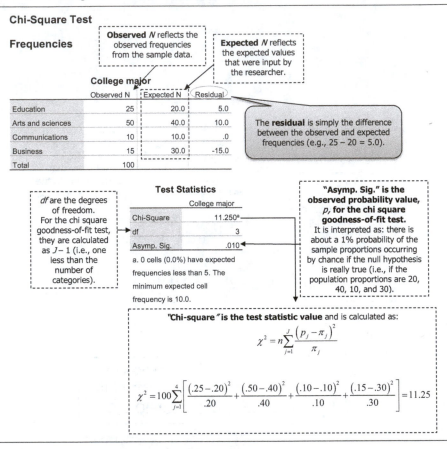

Chi-Square Test

Frequencies — Observed *N* reflects the observed frequencies from the sample data.

Expected *N* reflects the expected values that were input by the researcher.

College major

	Observed N	Expected N	Residual
Education	25	20.0	5.0
Arts and sciences	50	40.0	10.0
Communications	10	10.0	.0
Business	15	30.0	-15.0
Total	100		

The **residual** is simply the difference between the observed and expected frequencies (e.g., 25 − 20 = 5.0).

df are the degrees of freedom. For the chi square goodness-of-fit test, they are calculated as *J* − 1 (i.e., one less than the number of categories).

Test Statistics

	College major
Chi-Square	11.250[a]
df	3
Asymp. Sig.	.010

a. 0 cells (0.0%) have expected frequencies less than 5. The minimum expected cell frequency is 10.0.

"Asymp. Sig." is the observed probability value, *p*, for the chi square goodness-of-fit test. It is interpreted as: there is about a 1% probability of the sample proportions occurring by chance if the null hypothesis is really true (i.e., if the population proportions are 20, 40, 10, and 30).

"Chi-square" is the test statistic value and is calculated as:

$$\chi^2 = n \sum_{j=1}^{J} \frac{(p_j - \pi_j)^2}{\pi_j}$$

$$\chi^2 = 100 \sum_{j=1}^{4} \left[\frac{(.25 - .20)^2}{.20} + \frac{(.50 - .40)^2}{.40} + \frac{(.10 - .10)^2}{.10} + \frac{(.15 - .30)^2}{.30} \right] = 11.25$$

Interpreting the output. The top table provides the frequencies observed in the sample ("Observed *N*") and the expected frequencies based on the values defined by the researcher ("Expected *N*"). The "Residual" is simply the difference between the two *N*s. The chi-square test statistic value is 11.25 and the associated *p* value is .01. Because *p* is less than α, we *reject* the null hypothesis. Let us translate this back to the purpose of our null hypothesis statistical test. *The evidence suggests that the sample proportions observed differ from the proportions of college majors nationally.* Follow-up tests to determine which cells are statistically different in the observed to expected proportions can be conducted by examining the standardized residuals. In this example, the standardized residuals were computed previously as follows:

$$R_{Education} = \frac{O - E}{\sqrt{E}} = \frac{25 - 20}{\sqrt{20}} = 1.118$$

$$R_{Arts \& Sciences} = \frac{O - E}{\sqrt{E}} = \frac{50 - 40}{\sqrt{40}} = 1.581$$

$$R_{Communication} = \frac{O - E}{\sqrt{E}} = \frac{10 - 10}{\sqrt{10}} = 0$$

$$R_{Business} = \frac{O - E}{\sqrt{E}} = \frac{15 - 30}{\sqrt{30}} = -2.739$$

The standardized residual for business is greater (in absolute value terms) than 1.96 (given $\alpha = .05$), and thus suggests that there are different observed to expected frequencies for students majoring in business at ICU compared to national estimates. This category is the one contributing most to the statistically significant chi-square statistic.

The effect size can be calculated as follows and, using Cohen's conventions, is interpreted as a small effect:

$$w = \frac{\chi^2}{N(J-1)} = \frac{11.25}{100(4-1)} = \frac{11.25}{300} = .0375$$

8.3.2 The Chi-Square Test of Association

Step 1. To conduct a chi-square test of association, you need two categorical variables (nominal and/or ordinal) whose frequencies you wish to associate. We will use the Ch8_Gambling.sav data with two nominal variables: education level and stance on gambling. To compute the chi-square test of association, go to "Analyze" in the top pulldown, then select "Descriptive Statistics," and then select the "Crosstabs" procedure (see the screenshot of Step 1 in Figure 8.6).

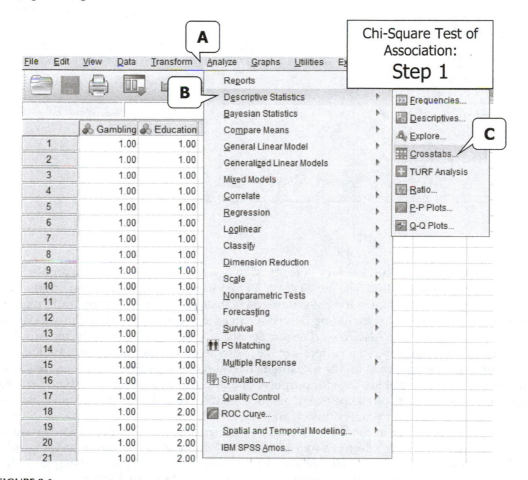

FIGURE 8.6
Chi-square test of association: Step 1.

Step 2. Select the *dependent variable* and move it into the "Row(s)" box by clicking the arrow key. Here we use "Stance on gambling" as the dependent variable (1 = support; 0 = not support). Then select the *independent variable* and move it into the "Column(s)" box. In this example, "Level of education" is the independent variable (1 = less than high school; 2 = high school; 3 = undergraduate; 4 = graduate) (see the screenshot of Step 2 in Figure 8.7).

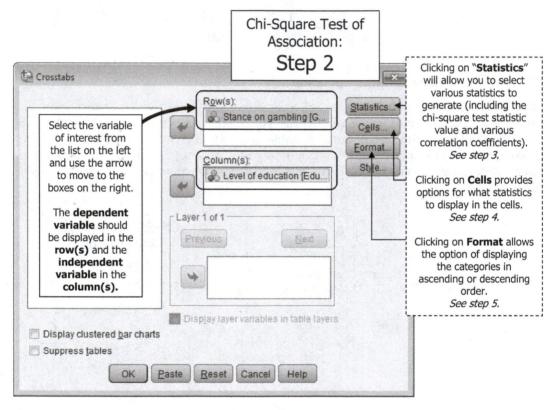

FIGURE 8.7
Chi-square test of association: Step 2.

Step 3. In the top-right corner of the "Crosstabs" dialog box (see the screenshot for Step 2 in Figure 8.7), click the button labeled "Statistics." From here, placing a checkmark in the box for "Chi-square" will produce the chi-square test statistic value and resulting null hypothesis statistical test results (including degrees of freedom and p value) (see the screenshot for Step 3 in Figure 8.8). Also from "Crosstab Statistics," you can select various measures of association that can serve as an effect size (i.e., correlation coefficient values). Which correlation is selected depends on the measurement scales of your variables. We are working with two nominal variables, thus for purposes of this example, we will select both "Phi and Cramer's V" and "Contingency coefficient" just to illustrate two different effect size indices (although it is standard practice to use and report only one effect size). We will use the contingency coefficient to compute Cohen's w. Had we had one nominal and one ordinal variable, we would have selected a statistic from the "Nominal" list. Had we had two ordinal variables, we would have selected a statistic from the "ordinal" list (see Chapter 10 for more on this!). Click "Continue" to return to the main "Crosstabs" dialog box.

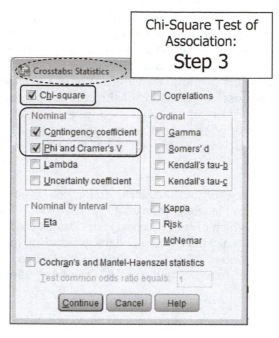

FIGURE 8.8
Chi-square test of association: Step 3.

Step 4. In the top-right corner of the "Crosstabs" dialog box (see the screenshot for Step 2 in Figure 8.7), click the button labeled "Cells." From the "Cells" dialog box, options are available for selecting counts and percentages (see the screenshot for Step 4 in Figure 8.9). We have requested "Observed" and "Expected" counts, "Column" percentages,

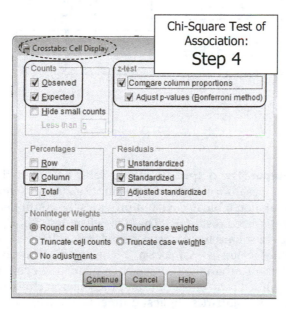

FIGURE 8.9
Chi-square test of association: Step 4.

and "Standardized" residuals. We will review the expected counts to determine if the assumption of five expected frequencies per cell is met. We will use the standardized residuals post hoc if the results of the test are statistically significant to determine which cell(s) are most influencing the chi-square value. We also select the z test to "Compare column proportions" and want to "adjust p values (Bonferroni method)." Selecting this option will produce pairwise comparisons of the column proportions and provides a subscript to denote which pairs of columns for a given row are statistically different. By selecting to apply the Bonferroni, we are making the adjustment to the p value to correct for multiple comparisons. Click "Continue" to return to the main "Crosstabs" dialog box.

Step 5. In the top-right corner of the "Crosstabs" dialog box (see the screenshot for Step 2 in Figure 8.7), click the button labeled "Format." From the "Format" dialog box, options are available for determining which order, "Ascending" or "Descending," you want the row values presented in the contingency table (we asked for descending in this example, such that row 1 was "gambling = 1" and row 2 was "gambling = 0") (see the screenshot for Step 5 in Figure 8.10). Click "Continue" to return to the main "Crosstabs" dialog box. Then click "OK" to run the analysis.

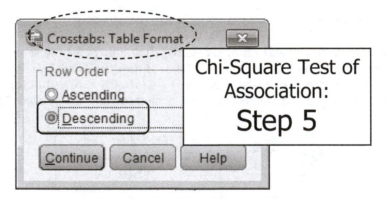

FIGURE 8.10
Chi-square test of association: Step 5.

   Interpreting the output. The output appears in Table 8.6 where the top box ("Case Processing Summary") provides information on the sample size and frequency of missing data (if any). The cross-tabulation table is next and provides the contingency table (i.e., counts, percentages, and standardized residuals). The "Chi-Square Tests" box gives the results of the procedure (including chi-square test statistic value labeled "Pearson Chi-Square," degrees of freedom, and p value labeled as "Asymp. Sig."). The likelihood ratio chi-square uses a different mathematical formula than the Pearson chi-square; however, for large sample sizes, the values for the likelihood ratio chi-square and the Pearson chi-square should be similar (and rarely should the two statistics suggest different conclusions in terms of rejecting or failing to reject the null hypothesis). The linear-by-linear association statistic, also known as the Mantel Haenszel chi-square, is based on the Pearson correlation and tests whether

TABLE 8.6

SPSS Results for Gambling Example

Case Processing Summary

	Cases					
	Valid		Missing		Total	
	N	Percent	N	Percent	N	Percent
Stance on gambling * Level of education	80	100.0%	0	0.0%	80	100.0%

> Review the standardized residuals to determine which cell(s) are contributing to the statistically significant chi-square value. Standardized residuals greater than an absolute value of 1.96 (critical value when alpha = .05) indicate that cell is contributing to the association between the variables.
> In this case, only one cell, **graduate/do not support,** has a standardized residual of 2.0 and thus is contributing to the relationship. *This is a slightly different result than reviewing the z test for the column comparisons (as denoted by the subscripts).*

Stance on gambling * Level of education Crosstabulation

> Observed and expected counts

> When analyzing the percentages in the crosstab table, compare the categories of the dependent variable (rows) across the columns of the independent variable (columns). *For example, of respondents with a high school diploma, 65% support gambling.*

			Less than high school	High school	Undergraduate	Graduate	Total
Stance on gambling	Support	Count	16$_a$	13$_{a,b}$	10$_{a,b}$	5$_b$	44
		Expected Count	11.0	11.0	11.0	11.0	44.0
		% within Level of education	80.0%	65.0%	50.0%	25.0%	55.0%
		Standardized Residual	1.5	.6	-.3	-1.8	
	Do Not Support	Count	4$_a$	7$_{a,b}$	10$_{a,b}$	15$_b$	36
		Expected Count	9.0	9.0	9.0	9.0	36.0
		% within Level of education	20.0%	35.0%	50.0%	75.0%	45.0%
		Standardized Residual	-1.7	-.7	.3	2.0	
Total		Count	20	20	20	20	80
		Expected Count	20.0	20.0	20.0	20.0	80.0
		% within Level of education	100.0%	100.0%	100.0%	100.0%	100.0%

Level of education

Each subscript letter denotes a subset of Level of education categories whose column proportions do not differ significantly from each other at the .05 level.

> The subscript letters allow us to interpret column comparisons with 'a' denoting 'less than high school' and 'b' denoting 'high school.' (Not seen, but 'c' would be undergraduate and 'd' would be graduate). The column proportions are compared using a z test, with Bonferonni adjustment, for each pair of columns. As noted by the footnote, each subscript denotes a subset of education whose column proportion is NOT statistically different. For example, 10ab tells us that the proportion of undergraduates who support versus do not support gambling is *not* statistically significantly different than 'less than high school' and high school'. In other words, there are similar proportions of undergraduates, less than high school, and high school who support and who do not support gambling. As another example, 5b tells us that the proportion of graduates who support versus do not support gambling is not statistically significant different than the proportion of high school (i.e., subscript b).

(continued)

TABLE 8.6 (continued)

SPSS Results for Gambling Example

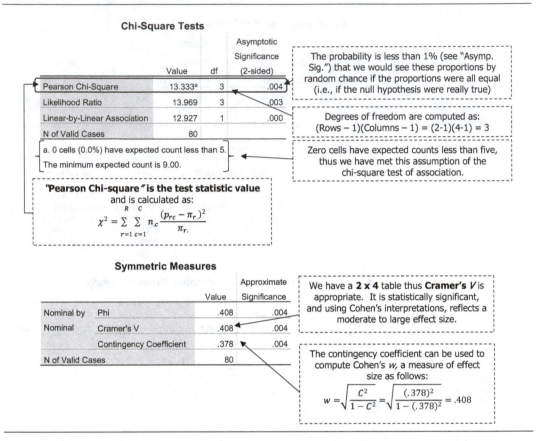

there is a linear association between the two variables (and thus should not be used for nominal variables).

We can use the *standardized residuals* to determine which cells are contributing to the statistically significant results by reviewing the value of the standardized residual to the z critical value. With alpha of .05, our critical value is ±1.96. Thus, based on the standardized residuals, individuals with a "graduate" level of education who "do not support" gambling are contributing to the statistically significant results. As you recall, we also requested the z test to compare column proportions. Based on the Bonferroni-corrected z test, we see both "less than high school" and "graduate" have statistically significantly different proportions of their stance on gambling.

For the contingency coefficient, C, of .378, we compute Cohen's w effect size as follows:

$$w = \sqrt{\frac{C^2}{1-C^2}} = \sqrt{\frac{.378^2}{1-.378^2}} = \sqrt{\frac{.143}{1-.143}} = \sqrt{.167} = .408$$

Cohen's w of .408 would be interpreted as a moderate to large effect. Cramer's V, as seen in the output, is .408 and would be interpreted similarly—a moderate to large effect.

8.4 Computing Inferences About Proportions Involving the Chi-Square Distribution Using R

We will illustrate computing both the chi-square goodness-of-fit and chi-square test of association using **R**.

8.4.1 The Chi-Square Goodness-of-Fit Test

Next we consider **R** for the chi-square goodness-of-fit test. The scripts are provided within the blocks with additional annotation to assist in understanding how the commands work. Should you want to write reminder notes and annotation to yourself as you write the commands in **R** (and we highly encourage doing so), remember that any text that follows a hashtag (i.e., #) is annotation only and not part of the **R** script. Thus, you can write annotations directly into **R** with hashtags. We encourage this practice so that when you call up the commands in the future, you'll understand what the various lines of code are doing. You may think you'll remember what you did. However, trust us. There is a good chance that you won't. Thus, consider it best practice when using **R** to annotate heavily!

8.4.1.1 Reading Data Into R

```
getwd()
```

R is always pointed to a directory on your computer. To find out which directory it is pointed to, run this "get working directory" function. We will assume that we need to change the working directory, and will use the next line of code to set the working directory to the desired path.

```
setwd("E:/Folder")
```

To set the working directory, use the *setwd* function and change what is in quotation marks here to your file location. Also, if you are copying the directory name, it will copy in slashes. You will need to change the slash (i.e., \) to a backslash (i.e., /). Note that you need your destination name within quotation marks in the parentheses.

```
Ch8_CollegeMajor <- read.csv("Ch8_CollegeMajor.csv")
```

The *read.csv* function reads our data into **R**. What's to the left of the <- will be what the data will be called in **R**. In this example, we're calling the R dataframe "Ch8_CollegeMajor." What's to the right of the <- tells **R** to find this particular .csv file. In this example, our file is called "Ch8_CollegeMajor.csv." Make sure the extension (i.e., .csv) is included in your script. Also note that the name of your file should be in quotation marks within the parentheses.

```
names(Ch8_CollegeMajor)
```

The *names* function will produce a list of variable names for each dataframe, as follows. This is a good check to make sure your data have been read in correctly.

FIGURE 8.11
Reading data into **R**.

```
[1] "Major"
```

```
View(Ch8_CollegeMajor)
```

The *View* function will let you view the dataset in spreadsheet format in RStudio.

```
Ch8_CollegeMajor$Major <- factor(Ch8_CollegeMajor$Major,
                        labels = c("education", "A&S",
                        "communication", "business"))
```

The *factor* function renames the variable "Major" that is in the "Ch8_CollegeMajor" dataframe as nominal with four groups or categories with labels of "education," "A&S," "communication," and "business."

```
summary(Ch8_CollegeMajor)
```

The *summary* function will produce basic descriptive statistics on all the variables in your dataframe. This is a great way to quickly check to see if the data have been read in correctly and to get a feel for your data, if you haven't already. The output from the summary statement for this dataframe looks like this. Because the variable "Major" is nominal, our output includes only the frequencies of cases within the categories.

```
            Major
education    :25
A&S          :50
communication:10
business     :15
```

FIGURE 8.11 (continued)
Reading data into **R**.

8.4.1.2 Generating the Chi-Square Goodness-of-Fit Test

```
install.packages("MASS")
```

The *install.packages* function will install the *MASS* package that will be used to generate our test.

```
library(MASS)
```

Next, we load the *MASS* package into our library using the *library* function.

```
major.freq = table(Ch8_CollegeMajor$Major)
```

We use the *table* function to create a frequency table from our variable "Major" and call this table "major.freq."

```
major.freq
```

This command will let us view the frequency table we just created:

```
    education        A&S communication business
           25         50            10       15
```

FIGURE 8.12
Generating the chi-square goodness-of-fit test.

```
major.prob = c(.20,.40,.10,.30)
```

The *major.prob* function creates an object called "major.prob" that defines the hypothesized proportions for the four categories in our variable of 20%, 40%, 10%, and 30%.

```
Chi2_major <- chisq.test(major.freq, p = major.prob)
Chi2_major
```

The *chisq.test* function generates the chi-square goodness-of-fit test using the frequencies in our table (i.e., "major.freq") and the hypothesized values (via the command p = *major.prob*). *Chi2_major* creates an object of the results of our chi-square test. Running the line for *Chi2_major* will present the output in the console in RStudio.

Our output looks like this, where chi-square = 11.25, with 3 degrees of freedom, and a statistically significant finding, $p = .01$.

```
        Chi-squared test for given probabilities

data:   major.freq
X-squared = 11.25, df = 3, p-value = 0.01045
```

```
Chi2_major$expected
```

Should we need a reminder on our expected frequencies, we can run this script that uses our chi square results (i.e., *Chi2_major*) and the respective expected frequencies.

```
  education      A&S   communication      business
         20       40              10            30
```

FIGURE 8.12 (continued)
Generating the chi-square goodness-of-fit test.

8.4.2 The Chi-Square Test of Association

Next we consider **R** for the chi-square test of association. The **R** script includes only those lines of text that are included in the boxes. The remainder is annotation, provided here to help you understand what the various lines of code are doing.

8.4.2.1 Reading Data Into R

```
getwd()
```

R is always pointed to a directory on your computer. To find out which directory it is pointed to, run this "get working directory" function. We will assume that we need to change the working directory, and will use the next line of code to set the working directory to the desired path.

```
setwd("E:/Folder")
```

FIGURE 8.13
Reading data into **R**.

To set the working directory, use the *setwd* function and change what is in quotation marks here to your file location. Also, if you are copying the directory name, it will copy in slashes. You will need to change the slash (i.e., \) to a forward slash (i.e., /). Note that you need your destination name within quotation marks in the parentheses.

```
Ch8_Gambling <- read.csv("Ch8_Gambling.csv")
```

The *read.csv* function reads our data into **R**. What's to the left of the <- will be what the data will be called in **R**. In this example, we're calling the **R** dataframe "Ch8_Gambling." What's to the right of the <- tells **R** to find this particular .csv file. In this example, our file is called "Ch8_Gambling.csv." Make sure the extension (i.e., .csv) is there. Also note that you need this in quotation marks.

```
names(Ch8_Gambling)
```

The *names* function will produce a list of variable names for each dataframe, as follows. This is a good check to make sure your data have been read in correctly.

```
[1] "Gambling" "Education"
```

```
Ch8_Gambling$Gambling <- factor(Ch8_Gambling$Gambling,
                        labels = c("do not support",
                                   "support"))
```

The *factor* function renames the variable "Gambling" as a categorical variable and defines the levels of gambling within our dataframe as "do not support" and "support."

```
Ch8_Gambling$Education <- factor(Ch8_Gambling$Education,
                        labels = c("less than high school",
                                   "high school",
                                   "undergraduate",
                                   "graduate"))
```

The *factor* function renames the variable "Education" as a categorical variable and defines the four levels of education within our dataframe.

```
View(Ch8_Gambling)
```

The *View* function will let you view the dataset in spreadsheet format in RStudio.

```
levels(Ch8_Gambling$Gambling)
levels(Ch8_Gambling$Education)
```

The *levels* function provides the names of the categories within each of our variables.

```
# levels(Ch8_Gambling$Gambling)
[1] "do not support" "support"
```

```
# levels(Ch8_Gambling$Education)
[1] "less than high school" "high school"
[3] "undergraduate"         "graduate"
```

FIGURE 8.13 (continued)
Reading data into **R**.

8.4.2.2 Generating the Chi-Square Test of Association

```
Chi2_gamble <- chisq.test(Ch8_Gambling$Gambling,
                          Ch8_Gambling$Education)
```

The *chisq.test* function generates the chi-square test of association with variables "Gambling" and "Education" from the "Ch8_Gambling" dataframe. It will name the object "Chi2_gamble."

```
Chi2_gamble
```

This script will generate the output from the chi-square test of association, which includes the following. We see we have a chi-squared value of 13.33 with 3 degrees of freedom. The *p* value is approximately .004. *Thus, we have a statistically significant relationship between the variables*. In Chapter 10, we will see how to generate measures of the correlation coefficient that can be used as indices of effect size for the chi-square test of association.

```
        Pearson's Chi-squared test

data:  Ch8_Gambling$Gambling and Ch8_Gambling$Education
X-squared = 13.3333, df = 3, p-value = 0.003969
```

```
round(Chi2_gamble$residuals,3)
```

We can request standardized residuals to see which cells are contributing to the statistically significant chi-square using this script. *Standardized residuals greater than an absolute value of 1.96 (i.e., the critical value when* α *= .05) are contributing to the statistically significant chi-square*. The only input that we include in the command is "Chi2gamble" to define the object for which we want the residual values. We see that category 4 ("graduate education") has a standardized residual for stance on gambling of 0 ("do not support") of 2.00, thus is contributing to the association between the variables.

```
                        Ch8_Gambling$Education
Ch8_Gambling$Gambling less than high school       high school
        do not support              -1.667         -0.667
        support                      1.508          0.603

                        Ch8_Gambling$Education
Ch8_Gambling$Gambling undergraduate             graduate
do not support               0.333              2.000
support                     -0.302             -1.809
```

```
Chi2_gamble$expected
```

Should we need a reminder on our expected frequencies, we can run this script that uses our chi-square results (i.e., *Chi2_gamble*) and the respective expected frequencies.

```
                        Ch8_Gambling$Education
Ch8_Gambling$Gambling less than high school high school
        do not support 9 9
        support 11 11

                        Ch8_Gambling$Education
Ch8_Gambling$Gambling undergraduate graduate
        do not support 9 9
        support 11 11
```

FIGURE 8.14
Generating the chi-square test of association.

8.5 Data Screening

Because it is a nonparametric procedure, fewer assumptions are associated with chi-square tests, and only one is actually tested when the procedure is generated (that being the assumption of expected frequencies). Examination of the assumptions for the examples have been provided in previous sections and presented with the statistical software computer output.

8.6 Power Using G*Power

A priori power can be determined using specialized software (e.g., Power and Precision, Ex-Sample, G*Power) or power tables (e.g., Cohen, 1988), as previously described. However, because standard statistical software does not provide power information for the results of the chi-square test of association just conducted, let us use G*Power to compute the post hoc power of our test.

8.6.1 Post Hoc Power for the Chi-Square Test of Association Using G*Power

The first thing that must be done when using G*Power for computing post hoc power is to select the correct test family. In our case, we conducted a chi-square test of association; therefore, the toggle button must be used to change the test family to χ^2 (see the screenshot in Figure 8.15). Next, we need to select the appropriate statistical test. We toggle to "Goodness-of-fit tests: Contingency tables." The "Type of power analysis" then needs to be selected. To compute post hoc power, we select "Post hoc: Compute achieved power—given α, sample size, and effect size."

The "Input Parameters" must then be specified. The first parameter is specification of the effect size w (this was computed by hand from the contingency coefficient and $w = .408$). The alpha level we tested at was .05, the sample size was 80, and the degrees of freedom were 3. Once the parameters are specified, simply click "Calculate" to generate the achieved power statistics.

The "Output Parameters" provide the relevant statistics given the input just specified. In this example, we were interested in determining post hoc power given a two-tailed test, with an observed effect size of .408, an alpha level of .05, and sample size of 80. Based on those criteria, the post hoc power was approximately .88. In other words, with a sample size of 80, testing at an alpha level of .05, and observing a moderate to large effect of .408, the power of our test was .88; thus, the probability of rejecting the null hypothesis when it is really false is 88%, which is very high power. Keep in mind that conducting power analysis *a priori* is recommended so that you avoid a situation where, post hoc, you find that the sample size was not sufficient to reach the desired level of power (given the observed effect size and alpha level).

8.7 Recommendations

Box 8.1 summarizes the tests reviewed in this chapter and the key points related to each (including the distribution involved and recommendations for when to use the test).

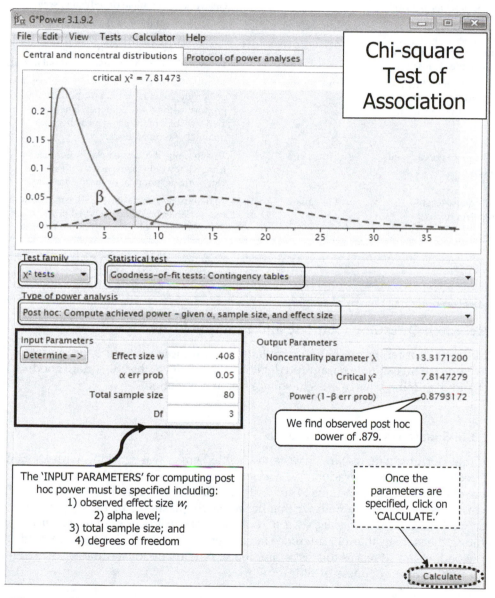

FIGURE 8.15
Chi-square test of association post hoc power.

BOX 8.1 Characteristics and Recommendations for Inferences About Proportions

Test	Distribution	When to Use
Inferences about a single proportion (akin to a one-sample mean test)	Unit normal, z	To determine if the sample proportion differs from a hypothesized proportion One variable, nominal or ordinal in scale
Inferences about two independent proportions (akin to the independent t test)	Unit normal, z	To determine if the population proportion for one group differs from the population proportion for a second independent group Two variables, both nominal or ordinal in scale
Inferences about two dependent proportions (akin to the dependent t test)	Unit normal, z	To determine if the population proportion for one group is different than the population proportion for a second dependent group Two variables of the same measure, both nominal or ordinal in scale
Chi-square goodness-of-fit test	Chi-square	To determine if observed proportions differ from what would be expected *a priori* One variable, nominal or ordinal in scale
Chi-square test of association	Chi-square	To determine association/relationship between two variables based on observed proportions Two variables, both nominal or ordinal in scale

8.8 Research Question Template and Example Write-Up

We finish the chapter by presenting templates and example write-ups for our examples. First we present an example paragraph detailing the results of the chi-square goodness-of-fit test and then follow this by the chi-square test of association.

8.8.1 Chi-Square Goodness-of-Fit Test

Recall that our graduate research assistant, Challie Lenge, was working with Dr. Senata, the Director of the Undergraduate Services Office at Ivy Covered University (ICU), to assist in analyzing the proportions of students enrolled in undergraduate majors. Challie's task was to assist Dr. Senata with writing her research question (*Are the sample proportions of undergraduate student college majors at ICU in the same proportions as those nationally?*) and generating the statistical test of inference to answer her question. Challie suggested a chi-square goodness-of-fit test as the test of inference. A template for writing a research question for a chi-square goodness-of-fit test follows:

Are the sample proportions of [units in categories] in the same proportions of those [identify the source to which the comparison is being made]?

It may be helpful to include in the results of the chi-square goodness-of-fit test information on an examination of the extent to which the assumptions were met (recall there are two assumptions: independence and expected frequency of at least five per cell). This assists the reader in understanding that you were thorough in data screening prior to conducting the test of inference.

A chi-square goodness-of-fit test was conducted to determine if the sample proportions of undergraduate student college majors at Ivy Covered University (ICU) were in the same proportions of those reported nationally. The test was conducted using an alpha of .05. The null hypothesis was that the proportions would be as follows: .20 education, .40 arts and sciences, .10 communications, and .30 business. The assumption of an expected frequency of at least five per cell was met. The assumption of independence was met via random selection.

There was a statistically significant difference between the proportion of undergraduate majors at ICU and those reported nationally ($\chi^2 = 11.250$, $df = 3$, $p = .010$). Thus the null hypothesis that the proportions of undergraduate majors at ICU parallel those expected at the national level was rejected at the .05 level of significance. The effect

size, w, $\left(\sqrt{\chi^2 / [(N)(J-1)]}\right)$ was .0375, and interpreted using Cohen's guide (1988) as a very

small effect.

Follow-up tests were conducted by examining the standardized residuals. The standardized residual for Business was -2.739 and thus suggests that there are different observed to expected frequencies for students majoring in Business at ICU compared to national estimates. Therefore, Business is the college major that is contributing most to the statistically significant chi-square statistic.

8.8.2 Chi-Square Test of Association

Addie Venture, our graduate research assistant, was working with Dr. Walnut, a lobbyist interested in examining the association between education level and stance on gambling. Addie was tasked with assisting Dr. Walnut in writing his research question (*Is there an association between level of education and stance on gambling?*) and generating the test of inference to answer his question. Addie suggested a chi-square test of association as the test of inference. A template for writing a research question for a chi-square test of association follows:

Is there an association between [independent variable] and [dependent variable]?

It may be helpful to include in the results of the chi-square test of association information on the extent to which the assumptions were met (recall there are two assumptions: independence and expected frequency of at least five per cell). This assists the reader in understanding that you were thorough in data screening prior to conducting the test of inference. It is also desirable to include a measure of effect size. Given the contingency coefficient, C, of .378, we computed Cohen's w effect size to be .408, which would be interpreted as a moderate to large effect.

A chi-square test of association was conducted to determine if there was a relationship between level of education and stance on gambling. The test was conducted using an alpha of .05. It was hypothesized that there was an association between the two variables. The assumption of an expected frequency of at least five per cell was met. The assumption of independence was not met because the respondents were not randomly selected; thus, there is an increased probability of a Type I error.

From Table 8.6 we can see from the row marginals that 55% of the individuals overall support gambling. However, lower levels of education have a much higher percentage of support, while the highest level of education has a much lower percentage of support. Thus, there appears to be an association or relationship between gambling stance and level of education. This is subsequently supported statistically from the chi-square test ($\chi^2 = 13.333$, $df = 3$, $p = .004$). Thus, the null hypothesis that there is no association between stance on gambling and level of education was rejected at the .05 level of significance. Examination of the standardized residuals suggests that respondents who hold a graduate degree are significantly more likely not to support gambling (standardized residual = 2.0) as compared to all other respondents. Further examination of column proportions using a Bonferroni-corrected z test suggests that individuals with less than a high school degree are statistically significantly different in proportions relative to all other education levels, proportions of those with a high school degree are also statistically different than undergraduate and graduate, and proportions of undergraduate and graduate also differ. The effect size, Cohen's w, was computed to be .408, which is interpreted to be a moderate to large effect (Cohen, 1988).

8.9 Additional Resources

In this chapter we described a third inferential testing situation, testing hypotheses about proportions. A number of resources have been provided throughout. For additional coverage of tests of proportion and analyzing categorical data, you may wish to consider Agresti (2013), among others. If you are interested in deeper coverage of chi-square, in particular, you may wish to consider Voinov, Balakrishnan, and Nikulin (2013) (which also includes an historical account and many other chi-square tests that are beyond the scope of this text) or Greenwood and Nikulin (1996).

Problems

Conceptual Problems

1. How many degrees of freedom are there in a 5 × 7 contingency table when the chi-square test of association is used?

    a. 12

    b. 24

    c. 30

    d. 35

2. True or false? The more that two independent sample proportions differ, all else being equal, the smaller the z test statistic.

3. True or false? The null hypothesis is a numerical statement about an unknown parameter.

4. True or false? In testing the null hypothesis that the proportion is .50, the critical value of z increases as degrees of freedom increase.

5. When the chi-square test statistic for a test of association is less than the corresponding critical value, I assert that I should reject the null hypothesis. Am I correct?

6. True or false? Other things being equal, the larger the sample size, the smaller the value of s_p.

7. In the chi-square test of association, as the difference between the observed and expected proportions increases:
   a. the critical value for chi-square increases.
   b. the critical value for chi-square decreases.
   c. the likelihood of rejecting the null hypothesis decreases.
   d. the likelihood of rejecting the null hypothesis increases.

8. When the hypothesized value of the population proportion lies outside of the confidence interval around a single sample proportion, I assert that the researcher should reject the null hypothesis. Am I correct?

9. Statisticians at a theme park want to know if the same proportions of visitors select the Jungle Safari as their favorite ride as compared to the Mountain Rollercoaster. They sample 150 visitors and collect data on one variable: favorite ride (two categories: Jungle Safari and Mountain Rollercoaster). Which statistical procedure is most appropriate to use to test the hypothesis?
   a. Chi-square goodness-of-fit test
   b. Chi-square test of association

10. Sophie is a reading teacher. She is researching the following question: Is there a relationship between a child's favorite genre of book and their socioeconomic status? She collects data from 35 children on two variables: (a) favorite genre of book (two categories: fiction, nonfiction) and (b) socioeconomic status (three categories: low, middle, high). Which statistical procedure is most appropriate to use to test the hypothesis?
   a. Chi-square goodness-of-fit test
   b. Chi-square test of association

11. Which of the following are assumptions for the chi-square test of association? Select all that apply.
   a. Balanced design
   b. Expected frequency of 5 per cell
   c. Independence
   d. Normality

12. Which of the following cannot be used when testing inferences about a single proportion?
   a. Counts
   b. Frequencies
   c. Means
   d. Relative frequency

13. After computing a chi-square test of association, the researcher has computed Cohen's w and found $w = .28$. What interpretation can the researcher make based on this using Cohen's subjective standards?
    a. Small effect
    b. Moderate effect
    c. Moderate to large effect
    d. Large effect
14. Which of the following are assumptions for the chi-square goodness-of-fit test? Select all that apply.
    a. Balanced design
    b. Expected frequency of 5 per cell
    c. Independence
    d. Normality

Answers to Conceptual Problems

1. **b** $(4 \times 6 = 24)$
3. **True** (By definition, the null hypothesis is a numerical statement about an unknown parameter.)
5. **No** (Reject when test statistic exceeds critical value.)
7. **d** (As the difference between the observed and expected proportions increases, the chi-square test statistic increases, and thus we are more likely to reject.)
9. **a** (Chi-square goodness-of-fit test given that there is only one variable and the goal is to determine if the proportions within the categories of that variable are the same.)
11. **b and c** (The two assumptions for chi-square tests are independence of observations and expected frequency of 5 per cell.)
13. **b** (Cohen's w values around .30 are interpreted to be a medium effect.)

Computational Problems

1. For a random sample of 40 widgets produced by the Acme Widget Company, 30 successes and 10 failures are observed. Test the following hypotheses at the .05 level of significance:

$$H_0 : \pi = .60$$

$$H_1 : \pi > .60$$

2. The following data are calculated for two independent random samples of male and female teenagers, respectively, on whether they expect to attend graduate school: $n_1 = 48, p_1 = 18 / 48, n_2 = 52, p_2 = 33 / 52$. Test the following hypotheses at the .05 level of significance:

$$H_0 : \pi_1 - \pi_2 = 0$$

$$H_1 : \pi_1 - \pi_2 \neq 0$$

3. The following frequencies of successes and failures are obtained for two dependent random samples measured at the pretest and posttest of a weight training program:

	Pretest	
Posttest	Success	Failure
Failure	18	30
Success	33	19

Test the following hypotheses at the .05 level of significance:

$$H_0 : \pi_1 - \pi_2 = 0$$

$$H_1 : \pi_1 - \pi_2 \neq 0$$

4. A chi-square goodness-of-fit test is to be conducted with six categories of professions to determine whether the sample proportions of those supporting the current government differ from *a priori* national proportions. The chi-square test statistic is equal to 16.00. Determine the result of this test by looking up the critical value and making a statistical decision, using $\alpha = .01$.

5. A chi-square goodness-of-fit test is to be conducted to determine whether the sample proportions of families in Florida who select various schooling options (five categories: "home school," "public school," "public charter school," "private school," and "other") differ from the proportions reported nationally. The chi-square test statistic is equal to 9.00. Determine the result of this test by looking up the critical value and making a statistical decision, using $\alpha = .05$.

6. A random sample of 30 voters was classified according to their general political beliefs (liberal vs. conservative) and also according to whether they voted for or against the incumbent representative in their town. The results were placed into the following contingency table:

	Liberal	Conservative
Yes	10	5
No	5	10

Use the chi-square test of association to determine whether political belief is independent of voting behavior at the .05 level of significance.

7. A random sample of 40 kindergarten children was classified according to whether they attended at least 1 year of preschool prior to entering kindergarten and also according to gender. The results were placed into the following contingency table:

	Boy	Girl
Preschool	12	10
No preschool	8	10

Use the chi-square test of association to determine whether enrollment in preschool is independent of gender at the .05 level of significance.

8. For a random sample of 30 athletes who completed an optional preseason training program, 80% ($n = 24$) were retained on their team and the rest were released. Test the following hypotheses, that the proportion retained was different than 75%, at the .05 level of significance:

$$H_0 : \pi = .75$$

$$H_1 : \pi \neq .75$$

9. A researcher followed a sample of 1000 registered nurses after their graduation and collected data on the type of employer and type of position in which they were employed. Using the Ch8_nurses.sav or Ch8-nurses.csv data, compute a chi-square test of association at alpha of .05 to determine the relationship between position and employer.

Answers to Computational Problems

1. $p = .75$, $z = 1.936$, critical values $= -1.96$ and $+1.96$, thus fail to reject H_0.
3. $z = -.1644$, critical values $= -1.96$ and $+1.96$, thus fail to reject H_0.
5. critical value $= 9.48773$, fail to reject H_0 as the test statistic does not exceed the critical value.
7. $\chi^2 = .404$, critical value $= 3.84$, thus fail to reject H_0.
9. Using SPSS, the crosstab of position by employer is:

Position * Employer Crosstabulation

Count

		Employer			Total
		General practitioner	Hospital	Traveling nurse	
Position	General care	190	238	72	500
	Special care	188	238	74	500
Total		378	476	146	1000

The results of the chi-square test are not statistically significant ($\chi^2 = .038$, $df = 2$, $p = .981$). We fail to reject the null hypothesis that there is no association between position and employer.

Chi-Square Tests

	Value	df	Asymptotic Significance (2-sided)
Pearson Chi-Square	.038[a]	2	.981
Likelihood Ratio	.038	2	.981
Linear-by-Linear Association	.034	1	.854
N of Valid Cases	1000		

a. 0 cells (0.0%) have expected count less than 5. The minimum expected count is 73.00.

Interpretive Problem

1. The survey1 dataset, which is accessible from the website, can be analyzed in several different ways, as there are several categorical variables. Here are some examples for the tests described in this chapter.

   a. Conduct a test of a single proportion: Is the sample proportion of females equal to .50?

   b. Conduct a test of two independent proportions: Is there a difference between the sample proportion of females who are right-handed and the sample proportion of males who are right-handed?

   c. Conduct a test of two dependent proportions: Is there a difference between the sample proportion of student's mothers who are right-handed and the sample proportion of student's fathers who are right-handed?

   d. Conduct a chi-square goodness-of-fit test: Do the sample proportions for the political view categories differ from their expected proportions (very liberal = .10, liberal = .15, middle of the road = .50, conservative = .15, very conservative = .10)? Determine if the assumptions of the test are met. Determine and interpret the corresponding effect size.

   e. Conduct a chi-square goodness-of-fit test to determine if there are similar proportions of respondents who can (vs. cannot) tell the difference between Pepsi and Coke. Determine if the assumptions of the test are met. Determine and interpret the corresponding effect size.

   f. Conduct a chi-square test of association: Is there an association between political view and gender? Determine if the assumptions of the test are met. Determine and interpret the corresponding effect size.

   g. Compute a chi-square test of association to examine the relationship between if a person smokes and their political view. Determine if the assumptions of the test are met. Determine and interpret the corresponding effect size.

2. Using the Integrated Postsecondary Education Data System dataset (IPEDS2017), which is accessible from the website, conduct a chi-square test of association to determine if there are similar proportions of institutions by level of institution [LEVEL] and control [CONTROL]. Determine if the assumptions of the test are met. Determine and interpret the corresponding effect size.

3. Using the Integrated Postsecondary Education Data System dataset (IPEDS2017), which is accessible from the website, conduct a chi-square goodness-of-fit test to determine if there are similar proportions of institutions by degree-granting status [DEGGRANT]. Determine if the assumptions of the test are met. Determine and interpret the corresponding effect size.

9

Inferences About Variances

Key Concepts

1. Sampling distributions of the variance

2. The F distribution

3. Homogeneity of variance tests

In the previous three chapters we looked at testing inferences about means (Chapters 6 and 7) and about proportions (Chapter 8). In this chapter we examine inferential tests involving variances. Tests of variances are useful in two applications: (a) as an inferential test by itself and (b) as a test of the homogeneity of variance assumption for another procedure (e.g., t test, analysis of variance).

First, a researcher may want to perform inferential tests on variances for their own sake, in the same fashion that we described for the one- and two-sample t tests on means. For example, we may want to assess whether the variance of undergraduates at Ivy-Covered University on an intelligence measure is the same as the theoretically derived variance of 225 (from when the test was developed and normed). In other words, is the variance at a particular university greater than or less than 225? As another example, we may want to determine whether the variances on an intelligence measure are consistent across two or more groups; for example, is the variance of the intelligence measure at Ivy-Covered University different from that at The Greatest University?

Second, for some procedures, such as the independent t test (Chapter 7) and the analysis of variance, it is assumed that the variances for two or more independent samples are equal (known as the homogeneity of variance assumption). Thus, we may want to use an inferential test of variances to assess whether this assumption has been violated or not. The following inferential tests of variance are covered in this chapter: (a) testing whether a single variance is different from a hypothesized value; (b) testing whether two dependent variances are different; and (c) testing whether two or more independent variances are different. We utilize many of the foundational concepts covered in Chapters 6, 7, and 8. New concepts to be discussed include the following: the sampling distributions of the variance, the F distribution, and homogeneity of variance tests. Our objectives are that by the end of this chapter, you will be able to (a) understand the basic concepts underlying tests of variances, (b) select the appropriate test, and (c) determine and interpret the results from the appropriate test.

9.1 Inferences About Variances and How They Work

As you remember, Oso Wyse is one of four extraordinarily talented graduate students who is working in the stats lab. Oso and colleagues have had the opportunity to work on quite a number of exciting statistical projects. We revisit the group again, with Oso getting ready to embark on another stats journey.

Another call has been fielded by the stats lab for assistance with statistical analysis. This time, it is Dr. Abraham, an elementary assistant principal within the community. Dr. Abraham shares with Oso that she is conducting a teacher research project related to achievement of first grade students at her school. Dr. Abraham wants to determine if the variances of the achievement scores differ when children begin school in the fall as compared to when they end school in the spring. Oso suggests the following research question: *Are the variances of achievement scores for first grade children the same in the fall as compared to the spring?* Oso suggests a test of variance as the test of inference. His task is then to assist Dr. Abraham in generating the test of inference to answer her research question.

This section deals with concepts for testing inferences about variances, in particular, the sampling distributions underlying such tests. Subsequent sections deal with several inferential tests of variances. Although the sampling distribution of the mean is a normal distribution (Chapters 6 and 7), and the sampling distribution of a proportion is either a normal or chi-square distribution (Chapter 8), the **sampling distribution of a variance** *is a chi-square distribution for a single variance, a* t *distribution for two dependent variances, or an* F *distribution for two or more independent variances.* Although we have already discussed the t distribution in Chapter 6 and the chi-square distribution in Chapter 8, we need to discuss the F distribution (named in honor of the famous statistician Sir Ronald A. Fisher) in some detail here.

9.1.1 Characteristics of the *F* Distribution

Like the normal, *t*, and chi-square distributions, the **F distribution** is really a family of distributions. Also, like the *t* and chi-square distributions, the *F* distribution family members depend on the number of degrees of freedom represented. However, unlike any previously discussed distribution, the *F* distribution family members actually depend on a *combination of two different degrees of freedom, one for the numerator and one for the denominator*. The reason is that the *F* distribution is a *ratio of two chi-square variables*. To be more precise, *F* with v_1 degrees of freedom for the numerator and v_2 degrees of freedom for the denominator is actually a ratio of the following chi-square variables:

$$F_{v_1, v_2} = \frac{\chi^2_{v_1} / v_1}{\chi^2_{v_2} / v_2}$$

For example, an *F* distribution for a numerator with 1 degree of freedom and a denominator with 10 degrees of freedom is denoted by $F_{1,10}$.

In terms of distributional shape, the *F* distribution is generally positively skewed and leptokurtic in shape (like the chi-square distribution) and has a mean of $\frac{v_2}{v_2 - 2}$ when $v_2 > 2$ (where v_2 represents the denominator degrees of freedom). A few examples of the *F* distribution are shown in Figure 9.1 for the following pairs of degrees of freedom (i.e., numerator, denominator): $F_{10,10}$, $F_{20,20}$, and $F_{40,40}$.

Critical values for several levels of alpha of the *F* distribution at various combinations of degrees of freedom are given in Table A.4 in the Appendix. The numerator degrees of freedom are given in the *columns* of the table (v_1) and the denominator degrees of freedom are shown in the *rows* of the table (v_2). Only the upper-tail critical values are given in the table (e.g., percentiles of .90, .95, .99 for α = .10, .05, .01, respectively). The reason is that most inferential tests involving the *F* distribution are *one-tailed tests* using the upper-tail critical

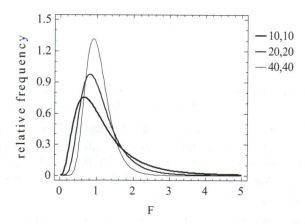

FIGURE 9.1
Several members of the family of *F* distributions.

region. Thus to find the upper-tail critical value for $_{.05}F_{1,10}$, look for the $\alpha = .05$ heading, in the first column of values for that heading for $v_1 = 1$, and where it intersects with the 10th row of values for $v_2 = 10$. There you should find $_{.05}F_{1,10} = 4.96$.

9.1.1.1 Inferences About a Single Variance

In our initial inferential testing situation for variances, the researcher would like to know whether the population variance is equal to some hypothesized variance or not—this represents a nondirectional, or two-tailed, test. First, the hypotheses to be evaluated for detecting whether a population variance differs from a hypothesized variance are as follows. The *nondirectional null hypothesis*, H_0, is that there is no difference between the population variance σ^2 and the hypothesized variance σ_0^2, which we denote as

$$H_0: \sigma^2 = \sigma_0^2$$

Here, there is no difference, or a "null" difference, between the population variance and the hypothesized variance. For example, if we are seeking to determine whether the variance on an intelligence measure at Ivy-Covered University is different from the overall adult population, then a reasonable hypothesized value would be 225, as this is the theoretically derived variance for the adult population.

The *nondirectional, scientific, or alternative hypothesis*, H_1, is that there is a difference between the population variance, σ^2, and the hypothesized variance, σ_0^2, which we denote as

$$H_1: \sigma^2 \neq \sigma_0^2$$

The null hypothesis, H_0, will be rejected here in favor of the alternative hypothesis, H_1, if the population variance is different from the hypothesized variance. As we have not specified a direction on H_1, we are willing to reject either if σ^2 is greater than σ_0^2 or if σ^2 is less than σ_0^2. This alternative hypothesis results in a two-tailed test. Directional alternative hypotheses can also be tested if we believe either that s^2 is greater than σ_0^2 or that σ^2 is less than σ_0^2. In either case, the more the resulting sample variance differs from the hypothesized variance, the more likely we are to reject the null hypothesis.

The next step is to compute the test statistic χ^2:

$$\chi^2 = \frac{vs^2}{\sigma_0^2}$$

where s^2 is the sample variance and $v = n - 1$. The test statistic χ^2 is then compared to a critical value(s) from the chi-square distribution. For a two-tailed test, the critical values are denoted as $_{\alpha/2}\chi_v^2$ and $_{1-\alpha/2}\chi_v^2$ and are found in Table A.3 in the Appendix (recall that unlike z and t critical values, two unique χ^2 critical values must be found from the table because the χ^2 distribution is not symmetric like z or t). If the test statistic c^2 falls into either critical region, then we reject H_0; otherwise, we fail to reject H_0. For a one-tailed test, the critical value is denoted as $_{\alpha}\chi_v^2$ for the alternative hypothesis $H_1: \sigma^2 < \sigma_0^2$ and as $_{1-\alpha/2}\chi_v^2$ for the alternative hypothesis $H_1: \sigma^2 > \sigma_0^2$. If the test statistic χ^2 falls into the appropriate critical region, then we reject H_0; otherwise, we fail to reject H_0.

For the two-tailed test, a $(1 - \alpha)\%$ confidence interval can also be examined and is formed as follows. The lower limit of the confidence interval is computed as:

$$\frac{vs^2}{_{1-\alpha/2}\chi^2_\nu}$$

The upper limit of the confidence interval is computed as:

$$\frac{vs^2}{_{\alpha/2}\chi^2_\nu}$$

If the confidence interval contains the hypothesized value σ_0^2, then the conclusion is to *fail to reject H_0*; otherwise, we *reject H_0*.

9.1.1.1.1 An Example

Now consider an example to illustrate use of the test of a single variance. We follow the basic steps for hypothesis testing that we applied in previous chapters. These steps include:

1. State the null and alternative hypotheses.
2. Select the level of significance (i.e., alpha, α).
3. Calculate the test statistic value.
4. Make a statistical decision (reject or fail to reject H_0).

A researcher at the esteemed Ivy-Covered University is interested in determining whether the population variance in intelligence at the university is different from the norm-developed hypothesized variance of 225. Thus, a nondirectional, two-tailed alternative hypothesis is utilized. If the null hypothesis is rejected, this would indicate that the intelligence level at Ivy-Covered University is more or less diverse or variable than the norm. If the null hypothesis is not rejected, this would indicate that the intelligence level at Ivy-Covered University is as equally diverse or variable as the norm of 225.

The researcher takes a random sample of 101 undergraduates from throughout the university and computes a sample variance of 149. The test statistic χ^2 is computed as follows:

$$\chi^2 = \frac{vs^2}{\sigma_0^2} = \frac{100(149)}{225} = 66.2222$$

From the Table A.3 in the Appendix and using an alpha level of .05, we determine the critical values to be $_{.025}\chi^2_{100} = 74.2219$ and $_{.975}\chi^2_{100} = 129.561$. Because the test statistic does exceed one of the critical values by falling into the lower-tail critical region (i.e., $66.2222 < 74.2219$), our decision is to *reject H_0*. *Our conclusion then is that the variance of the undergraduates at Ivy-Covered University is different from the hypothesized variance value of 225.*

The 95% confidence interval for the example is computed as follows. The lower limit of the confidence interval is computed as:

$$\frac{vs^2}{{}_{1-\alpha/2}\chi_\nu^2} = \frac{100(149)}{129.561} = 115.0037$$

and the upper limit of the confidence interval is computed as:

$$\frac{vs^2}{{}_{\alpha/2}\chi_\nu^2} = \frac{100(149)}{74.2219} = 200.7494$$

As the limits of the confidence interval (i.e., 115.0037, 200.7494) do not contain the hypothesized variance of 225, the conclusion is to *reject* H_0. As always, the confidence interval procedure leads us to the same conclusion as the hypothesis testing procedure for the same alpha level.

9.1.1.2 Inferences About Two Dependent Variances

In our second inferential testing situation for variances, the researcher would like to know whether the population variance for one group is different from the population variance for a second dependent group. This is comparable to the dependent *t* test described in Chapter 7 where one population mean was compared to a second dependent population mean. Once again we have two dependently drawn samples.

First, the hypotheses to be evaluated for detecting whether two dependent population variances differ (i.e., reflecting a nondirectional, or two-tailed, test) are as follows. The *nondirectional null hypothesis, H_0,* is that there is no difference between the two population variances σ_1^2 and σ_2^2, which we denote as

$$H_0: \sigma_1^2 - \sigma_2^2 = 0$$

Here there is no difference, or a "null" difference, between the two population variances. For example, we may be seeking to determine whether the variance of income of husbands is equal to the variance of their wives' incomes. Thus, the husband and wife samples are drawn as couples in pairs, or dependently, rather than individually, or independently.

The *nondirectional, scientific, or alternative hypothesis, H_1,* is that there is a difference between the population variances σ_1^2 and σ_2^2, which we denote as

$$H_1: \sigma_1^2 - \sigma_2^2 \neq 0$$

The null hypothesis, H_0, is rejected here in favor of the alternative hypothesis, H_1, if the population variances are different. As we have not specified a direction on H_1, we are willing to reject either if σ_1^2 is greater than σ_2^2 or if σ_1^2 is less than σ_2^2. This alternative hypothesis results in a two-tailed test. Directional alternative hypotheses can also be tested if we believe either that σ_1^2 is greater than σ_2^2 or that σ_1^2 is less than σ_2^2. In either case, the more the resulting sample variances differ from one another, the more likely we are to reject the null hypothesis.

The next step is to compute the test statistic t as follows:

$$t = \frac{s_1^2 - s_2^2}{2s_1 s_2 \sqrt{\dfrac{1 - r_{12}^2}{\nu}}}$$

where s_1^2 and s_2^2 are the sample variances for samples 1 and 2, respectively; s_1 and s_2 are the sample standard deviations for samples 1 and 2, respectively; r_{12} is the correlation between the scores from sample 1 and sample 2 (which is then squared); and ν is the number of degrees of freedom, $\nu = n - 2$, with n being the number of paired observations (not the number of total observations). Although correlations are not formally discussed until Chapter 10, conceptually the correlation is a measure of the relationship between two variables. This test statistic is conceptually somewhat similar to the test statistic for the dependent t test.

The test statistic t is then compared to a critical value(s) from the t distribution. For a two-tailed test, the critical values are denoted as $\pm_{\alpha_2} t_\nu$ and are found in Table A.2 in the Appendix. If the test statistic t falls into either critical region, then we reject H_0; otherwise, we fail to reject H_0. For a one-tailed test, the critical value is denoted as $+_{\alpha_1} t_\nu$ for the alternative hypothesis $H_0 : \sigma_1^2 - \sigma_2^2 > 0$ and as $-_{\alpha_2} t_\nu$ for the alternative hypothesis $H_0 : \sigma_1^2 - \sigma_2^2 < 0$. If the test statistic t falls into the appropriate critical region, then we reject H_0; otherwise, we fail to reject H_0. Some of the new procedures can also be used for testing inferences involving the equality of two or more dependent variances. In addition, note that acceptable confidence interval procedures are not currently available.

9.1.1.2.1 An Example

Let us consider an example to illustrate use of the test of two dependent variances. The same basic steps for hypothesis testing that we applied in previous chapters will be applied here as well. These steps include:

1. State the null and alternative hypotheses.
2. Select the level of significance (i.e., alpha, α).
3. Calculate the test statistic value.
4. Make a statistical decision (reject or fail to reject H_0).

A researcher is interested in whether there is greater variation in achievement test scores at the end of the first grade as compared to the beginning of the first grade. Thus, a directional, one-tailed alternative hypothesis is utilized. If the null hypothesis is rejected, this would indicate that first graders' achievement test scores are more variable at the end of the year than at the beginning of the year. If the null hypothesis is not rejected, this would indicate that first graders' achievement test scores have approximately the same variance at both the end of the year and at the beginning of the year.

A random sample of 62 first-grade children is selected and given the same achievement test at the beginning of the school year (September) and at the end of the school year (April). Thus, the same students are tested twice with the same instrument, thereby resulting in dependent samples at time 1 and time 2. The level of significance is set at a = .01. The test statistic t is computed as follows. We determine that $n = 62$, $\nu = 60$,

$s_1^2 = 100$, $s_1 = 10$, $s_2^2 = 169$, $s_2 = 13$, and $r_{12} = .80$ (thus squared $= .64$). We compute the test statistic t to be

$$t = \frac{s_1^2 - s_2^2}{2s_1 s_2 \sqrt{\frac{1 - r_{12}^2}{\nu}}} = \frac{100 - 169}{(2)(10)(13)\sqrt{\frac{1 - .64}{60}}} = -3.4261$$

The test statistic t is then compared to the critical value from the t distribution. Because this is a one-tailed test, the critical value is denoted as $-_{\alpha 1} t_\nu$ and is determined from Table A.2 in the Appendix to be $-_{.01} t_{60} = -2.390$. The test statistic t falls into the lower-tail critical region, as it is less than the critical value (i.e., $-3.4261 < -2.390$), so we reject H_0 and conclude that the variance in achievement test scores increases from September to April.

9.1.1.3 Inferences About Two or More Independent Variances (Homogeneity of Variance Tests)

In our third and final inferential testing situation for variances, the researcher would like to know whether the population variance for one group is different from the population variance for one or more other independent groups. In this section we first describe the somewhat cloudy situation that exists for the traditional tests. Then we provide details on two recommended tests, the Brown-Forsythe procedure and the O'Brien procedure.

9.1.1.3.1 Traditional Tests

One of the more heavily studied inferential testing situations in recent years has been for testing whether differences exist among two or more independent group variances. These tests are often referred to as **homogeneity of variance tests**. Here we briefly discuss the more traditional tests and their associated problems. In the sections that follow, we then recommend two of the "better" tests. As was noted in the previous procedures, the variable for which the variance(s) is computed must be interval or ratio in scale.

Several tests have traditionally been used to test for the equality of independent variances. An early simple test for two independent variances is to form a ratio of the two sample variances, which yields the following F test statistic:

$$F = \frac{s_1^2}{s_2^2}$$

This F ratio test assumes that the two populations are normally distributed. However, it is known that the F ratio test is not very robust to violation of the normality assumption, except for when the sample sizes are equal (i.e., $n_1 = n_2$). In addition, the F ratio test can only be used for the two-group situation.

Subsequently, more general tests were developed to cover the multiple-group situation. One such popular test is **Hartley's F_{max} test** (developed in 1950), which is simply a more general version of the F ratio test just described. The test statistic for Hartley's F_{max} test is the following:

$$F_{max} = \frac{s_{largest}^2}{s_{smallest}^2}$$

where $s^2_{largest}$ is the largest variance in the set of variances and $s^2_{smallest}$ is the smallest variance in the set. Hartley's F_{max} test assumes normal population distributions and requires equal sample sizes. We also know that Hartley's F_{max} test is not very robust to violation of the normality assumption. **Cochran's C test** (developed in 1941) is also an F test statistic and is computed by taking the ratio of the largest variance to the sum of all of the variances. Cochran's C test also assumes normality, requires equal sample sizes, and has been found to be even less robust to nonnormality than Hartley's F_{max} test. As seen for the analysis of variance, *it is when we have unequal sample sizes that unequal variances is a problem*; for these reasons none of these tests can be recommended, which is the same situation we encountered with the independent t test.

Bartlett's χ2 test (developed in 1937) does not have the stringent requirement of equal sample sizes; however, it does still assume normality. Bartlett's test is very sensitive to nonnormality, and is therefore not recommended either. Since 1950 the development of homogeneity tests has proliferated, with the goal being to find a test that is fairly robust to nonnormality. Seemingly as each new test was developed, later research would show that the test was not very robust.

Levene's test was developed in 1960 (Levene, 1960) and was developed as an alternative to the F test for homogeneity, which was problematic in the presence of nonnormality. Levene's test is essentially an analysis of variance on the transformed variable:

$$Z_{ij} = \left| Y_{ij} - \bar{Y}_{.j} \right|$$

where ij designates the ith observation in group j, and Z_{ij} is computed for each individual by taking their score Y_{ij}, subtracting from it the group mean $\bar{Y}_{.j}$ (the "." indicating we have averaged across all i observations in group j), and then taking the absolute value (i.e., by removing the sign). Unfortunately, Levene's test is not very robust to nonnormality, except when sample sizes are equal. In particular, the nominal alpha is maintained only for symmetric distributions. Thus, kurtosis may not be problematic as long as skew is minimal (i.e., distributions that show nonnormal kurtosis but are still symmetric) (Carroll & Schneider, 1985).

A nonparametric version of Levene's test was developed more recently (Zumbo & Nordstokke, 2010). One of the assumptions of the nonparametric Levene's test is that the samples are drawn from populations with equal means but not necessarily equal variances. However, recent simulation research suggests that sampling from populations with unequal and unknown means can lead to increased or decreased Type I error rates of the nonparametric Levene's test (Shear, Nordstokke, & Zumbo, 2018). Even more recently, Kim and Cribbie (2018) introduced a test for homogeneity of variance that incorporates an equivalence testing approach. Rather than testing the null hypothesis of equal variances, the proposed test examines a null hypothesis that the difference in the variances is beyond or at the border of a predetermined interval (with the alternative hypothesis being that the difference in variances is within the predetermined interval). This aligns the alternative hypothesis with the research hypothesis (i.e., equal variances).

Today, well over 60 such tests are available for examining homogeneity of variance. A recent simulation study by Wang et al. (2017) studied the performance of 14 homogeneity tests on controlling Type I error and power in one-way ANOVA. They found that the Ramsey conditional, O'Brien, Brown-Forsythe, bootstrap Brown-Forsythe, and Levene with squared deviation tests maintained adequate control of Type I errors and performed better than others reviewed, including maintaining acceptable power, across the simulated conditions. Recommendations for selecting a test for homogeneity of variance based on average cell size include the following: (a) when cell size is less than 10, O'Brien is the recommended test for homogeneity of variance as it maintains adequate Type I error control; (b) when cell size is greater than 10 but less than 20, the Ramsey conditional test is recommended as it also maintains adequate Type I error control; and (c) when the cell size is more than 20, the Brown-Forsythe, bootstrap Brown-Forsythe, or Ramsey conditional test are recommended as these tests provide maintains adequate Type I error control and greater power (around .80). Rather than engage in a protracted discussion of these tests and their associated limitations, we simply present a few additional tests that have been shown to be most robust to nonnormality in several recent studies and/or have become more widely available in standard statistical software.

9.1.1.3.2 The Brown-Forsythe Procedure

The Brown-Forsythe procedure is a variation of Levene's test. Developed in 1974, the Brown-Forsythe procedure has been shown to be quite robust to nonnormality in numerous studies (Olejnik & Algina, 1987; Ramsey, 1994). Based on this and other research, the Brown-Forsythe procedure is recommended for leptokurtic distributions (i.e., those with sharp peaks), as it is robust to nonnormality and provides adequate Type I error protection and excellent power. In the next section we describe the O'Brien procedure, which is recommended for other distributions (i.e., mesokurtic and platykurtic distributions). In cases where you are unsure of which procedure to use, Algina, Blair, and Coombs (1995) recommend using a maximum procedure, where both tests are conducted and the procedure with the maximum test statistic is selected.

Let us now examine in detail the Brown-Forsythe procedure. The null hypothesis is that the population variances of the groups are equal, $H_0 : \sigma_1^2 = \sigma_2^2 = \cdots = \sigma_J^2$, and the alternative hypothesis is that not all of the population group variances are the same. The Brown-Forsythe procedure is essentially an analysis of variance on the transformed variable

$$Z_{ij} = \left| Y_{ij} - Mdn_{.j} \right|$$

which is computed for each individual by taking their score on the dependent variable, Y_{ij}, subtracting from it the group median, $Mdn_{.j}$, and then taking the absolute value (i.e., by removing the sign). The test statistic is an F and is computed by the following equation:

$$F = \frac{\sum_{j=1}^{J} n_j \left(\bar{Z}_{.j} - \bar{Z}_{..} \right)^2 \Big/ (J-1)}{\sum_{i=1}^{n_j} \sum_{j=1}^{J} \left(Z_{ij} - \bar{Z}_{.j} \right)^2 \Big/ (N-J)}$$

where n_j designates the number of observations in group j, J is the number of groups (where j ranges from 1 to J), $\bar{Z}_{.j}$ is the mean for group j (computed by taking the sum of the observations in group j and dividing by the number of observations in group j, which is n_j), and $\bar{Z}_{..}$ is the overall mean regardless of group membership (computed by taking the sum of all of the observations across all groups and dividing by the total number of observations N). The test statistic F is compared against a critical value from the F table (Table A.4 in the Appendix) with $J - 1$ degrees of freedom in the numerator and $N - J$ degrees of freedom in the denominator, denoted by $\alpha F_{J-1,N-J}$. If the test statistic is greater than the critical value, we reject H_0; otherwise, we fail to reject H_0.

An example using the Brown-Forsythe procedure is certainly in order now. Three different groups of children—below-average, average, and above-average readers—play a computer game. The scores on the dependent variable Y are their total points from the game. We are interested in whether the variances for the three student groups are equal or not. The example data and computations are given in Table 9.1. First we compute the median for each group, and then compute the deviation from the median for each individual to obtain the transformed Z values. Then the transformed Z values are used to compute the F test statistic.

TABLE 9.1

Example Using the Brown-Forsythe and O'Brien Procedures

Group 1			Group 2			Group 3		
Y	Z	r	Y	Z	r	Y	Z	r
6	4	124.2499	9	4	143	10	8	704
8	2	14.2499	12	1	7	16	2	−16
12	2	34.2499	14	1	−7	20	2	−96
13	3	89.2499	17	4	43	30	12	1104
Mdn	$\bar{Z}$	$\bar{r}$	*Mdn*	$\bar{Z}$	$\bar{r}$	*Mdn*	$\bar{Z}$	$\bar{r}$
10	2.75	65.4999	13	2.50	68	18	6	424
		Overall $\bar{Z}$			Overall $\bar{r}$			
		3.75			185.8333			

Computations for the **Brown-Forsythe** procedure:

$$F = \frac{\left[\sum_{j=1}^{J} n_j \left(\bar{Z}_{.j} - \bar{Z}_{..} \right)^2 \right] \Big/ (J-1)}{\left[\sum_{i=1}^{n_j} \sum_{j=1}^{J} \left(\bar{Z}_{ij} - \bar{Z}_{.j} \right)^2 \right] \Big/ (N-J)}$$

$$F = \frac{\left[4(2.75 - 3.75)^2 + 4(2.50 - 3.75)^2 + 4(6 - 3.75)^2 \right] \Big/ (2)}{\left[(4 - 2.75)^2 + (2 - 2.75)^2 + \ldots + (12 - 6)^2 \right] \Big/ (9)} = 1.6388$$

(continued)

TABLE 9.1 (continued)

Example Using the Brown-Forsythe and O'Brien Procedures

Computations for the **O'Brien** procedure:

Sample means: $\bar{Y}_1 = 9.75$, $\bar{Y}_2 = 13.0$, $\bar{Y}_3 = 19.0$

Sample variances: $s_1^2 = 10.9167$, $s_2^2 = 11.3333$, $s_3^2 = 70.6667$

Example computation for r_{ij}:

$$r_{ij} = \frac{\left(n_j - 1.5\right)\left(n_j\right)\left(Y_{ij} - \bar{Y}_{.j}\right)^2 - \left(.5 s_j^2\right)\left(n_j - 1\right)}{\left(n_j - 1\right)\left(n_j - 2\right)}$$

$$r_{ij} = \frac{\left(4 - 1.5\right)\left(4\right)\left(6 - 9.75\right)^2 - \left(.5\right)\left(10.9167\right)\left(4 - 1\right)}{\left(4 - 1\right)\left(4 - 2\right)} = 124.249$$

Test statistic for the O'Brien:

$$F = \frac{\left[\sum_{j=1}^{J} n_j \left(\bar{r}_{.j} - \bar{r}_{..}\right)^2\right] \Big/ \left(J - 1\right)}{\left[\sum_{i=1}^{n_j} \sum_{j=1}^{J} \left(r_{ij} - \bar{r}_{.j}\right)^2\right] \Big/ \left(N - J\right)}$$

$$F = \frac{\left[\left(4\right)\left(65.4999 - 185.8333\right)^2 + \left(4\right)\left(68 - 185.8333\right)^2 + \left(4\right)\left(424 - 185.8333\right)^2\right] \Big/ \left(2\right)}{\left[\left(124.2499 - 65.4999\right)^2 + \left(14.2499 - 65.4999\right)^2 + \ldots + \left(1,104 - 424\right)^2\right] \Big/ \left(9\right)}$$

$$F = 1.4799$$

The Brown-Forsyth test statistic $F = 1.6388$ is compared against the critical value for $\alpha = .05$ of $_{.05}F_{2,9} = 4.26$. As the test statistic is smaller than the critical value (i.e., $1.6388 < 4.26$), we fail to reject the null hypothesis and conclude that the three student groups do not have different variances.

9.1.1.3.3 The O'Brien Procedure

The final test to consider in this chapter is the O'Brien procedure. While the Brown-Forsythe procedure is recommended for leptokurtic distributions, the O'Brien procedure is recommended for other distributions (i.e., mesokurtic and platykurtic distributions). Let us now examine in detail the O'Brien procedure. The null hypothesis is again that the population variances of the groups are equal, $H_0 : \sigma_1^2 = \sigma_2^2 = \cdots = \sigma_J^2$, and the alternative hypothesis is that not all of the population group variances are the same.

The O'Brien procedure is an analysis of variance on a *different* transformed variable:

$$r_{ij} = \frac{(n_j - 1.5)(n_j)(Y_{ij} - \overline{Y}_j)^2 - (.5)(s_j^2)(n_j - 1)}{(n_j - 1)(n_j - 2)}$$

$$r_{ij} = \frac{(n_j - 1.5)n_j(Y_{ij} - \overline{Y}_j)^2 - .5s_j^2(n_j - 1)}{(n_j - 1)(n_j - 2)}$$

which is computed for each individual, where n_j is the size of group j, $\overline{Y}_{.j}$ is the mean on the outcome for group j, and s_j^2 is the sample variance for group j.

The test statistic is an F statistic and is computed by the following equation:

$$F = \frac{\sum_{j=1}^{J} n_j \left(\overline{r}_{.j} - \overline{r}_{..}\right)^2 \Big/ (J-1)}{\sum_{i=1}^{n_j} \sum_{j=1}^{J} \left(r_{ij} - \overline{r}_{.j}\right)^2 \Big/ (N-J)}$$

where n_j designates the number of observations in group j, J is the number of groups (where j ranges from 1 to J), $\overline{r}_{.j}$ is the mean for group j (computed by taking the sum of the observations in group j and dividing by the number of observations in group j, which is n_j), and $r_{..}$ is the overall mean regardless of group membership (computed by taking the sum of all of the observations across all groups and dividing by the total number of observations N). The test statistic F is compared against a critical value from the F table (Table A.4 in the Appendix) with $J - 1$ degrees of freedom in the numerator and $N - J$ degrees of freedom in the denominator, denoted by $_{\alpha}F_{J-1,N-J}$. If the test statistic is greater than the critical value, then we reject H_0; otherwise, we fail to reject H_0.

Let us return to the example in Table 9.1 and consider the results of the O'Brien procedure. From the computations shown in the table, the test statistic $F = 1.4799$ is compared against the critical value for $\alpha = .05$ of $_{.05}F_{2,9} = 4.26$. Because the test statistic is smaller than the critical value (i.e., $1.4799 < 4.26$), we fail to reject the null hypothesis and conclude that the three student groups do not have different variances.

9.2 Assumptions

9.2.1 Assumptions for Inferences About a Single Variance

It is assumed that the sample is randomly drawn from the population (i.e., the assumption of independence) and that the population of scores is normally distributed. It has been noted by statisticians such as Wilcox (1996) that the chi-square distribution does not perform adequately when sampling from a nonnormal distribution, because the actual Type I error rate can differ greatly from the nominal alpha level (the level set by the researcher).

While not an assumption, because we are testing a variance, a condition of the test is that the variable must be *interval* or *ratio* in scale.

9.2.2 Assumptions for Inferences About Two Dependent Variances

It is assumed that the two samples are dependently and randomly drawn from their respective populations, that both populations are normal in shape, and that the t distribution is the appropriate sampling distribution. It is thought that this test is not particularly robust to nonnormality (Wilcox, 1987). As a result, other procedures have been developed that are thought to be more robust. However, little in the way of empirical results is known at this time.

While not an assumption, because we are testing a variance, a condition of the test is that the variable must be *interval* or *ratio* in scale. Recall that variances can only be computed with data that are interval or ratio in scale.

9.3 Sample Size, Power, and Effect Size

There is really not much we can report on that is available in published in the literature on sample size, power, and effect sizes for tests of variances.

9.4 Computing Inferences About Variances Using SPSS

Unfortunately, there is not much to report on tests of variances for SPSS. There are no unique (i.e., standalone) tests available for inferences about a single variance or for inferences about two dependent variances. For inferences about independent variances, SPSS does provide Levene's test as part of the "Independent t Test" procedure (discussed in Chapter 7) and as part of the "One Way ANOVA" and "Univariate ANOVA" procedures. While it is commonly reported as evidence for meeting the assumption of equal variances, given our previous concerns with Levene's test, use it with caution.

9.5 Computing Inferences About Variances Using R

Next we consider **R** for computing inferences about variances. We will examine both inferences about a single variance and inferences about two dependent variances.

Note that the scripts are provided within the blocks with additional annotation to assist in understanding how the command works. Should you want to write reminder notes and annotation to yourself as you write the commands in **R** (and we highly encourage doing so), remember that any text that follows a hashtag (i.e., #) is annotation only and not part of the **R** script. Thus, you can write annotations directly into **R** with hashtags. We encourage this practice so that when you call up the commands in the future, you'll understand what the various lines of code are doing. You may think you'll remember what you did. However, trust us. There is a good chance that you won't. Thus, consider it best practice when using **R** to annotate heavily!

9.5.1 Reading Data Into R for the Test of Inference About a Single Variance

```
getwd()
```

R is always pointed to a directory on your computer. To find out which directory it is pointed to, run this "get working directory" function. We will assume that we need to change the working directory, and will use the next line of code to set the working directory to the desired path.

```
setwd("E:/Folder")
```

To set the working directory, use the *setwd* function and change what is in quotation marks here to your file location. Also, if you are copying the directory name, it will copy in slashes. You will need to change the slash (i.e., \) to a forward slash (i.e., /). Note that you need your destination name within quotation marks in the parentheses.

```
Ch9_psychdistress <- read.csv("Ch9_psychdistress.csv")
```

The *read.csv* function reads our data into **R**. What's to the left of the <- will be what the data will be called in **R**. In this example, we're calling the R dataframe "Ch9_psychdistress." What's to the right of the <- tells **R** to find this particular .csv file. In this example, our file is called "Ch9_psychdistress. csv." Make sure the extension (i.e., .csv) is included in your script. Also note that the name of your file should be in quotation marks within the parentheses.

```
names(Ch9_psychdistress)
```

The *names* function will produce a list of variable names for each dataframe as follows. This is a good check to make sure your data have been read in correctly.

```
[1] "Sport" "Selection" "Distress"
Ch9_psychdistress$Sport <- factor(Ch9_psychdistress$Sport,
labels = c("movement", "target", "fielding", "territory"))
```

The *factor* function renames our "Sport" variable (which is in our "Ch9_psychdistress" dataframe) as nominal with four groups or categories with labels of "movement," "target," "fielding," and "territory."

```
View(Ch9_psychdistress)
```

The *View* function will let you view the dataset in spreadsheet format in RStudio.

```
summary(Ch9_psychdistress)
```

The *summary* function will produce basic descriptive statistics on all the variables in your dataframe. This is a great way to quickly check to see if the data have been read in correctly and to get a feel for your data, if you haven't already. The output from the summary statement for this dataframe looks like this. Because the variable "Sport" is nominal, our output includes only the frequencies of cases within the categories.

```
      Sport            Selection           Distress
movement :8       deselected:16      Min.    : 3.00
target   :8       selected  :16      1st Qu.:12.00
fielding :8                          Median :20.00
territory:8                          Mean   :18.41
                                     3rd Qu.:25.00
                                     Max.   :30.00
```

FIGURE 9.2
Reading data into **R**.

9.5.2 Generating the Test of Inference About a Single Variance

```
install.packages("EnvStats")
```

The *install.packages* function will be used to install the *EnvStats* package that we will use to test the inference about a single variance. We first install the package using this command. Note that the package name needs to be in quotation marks within the parentheses.

```
library(EnvStats)
```

Now we need to load EnvStats into our library using the *library* function.

```
varTest(Ch9_psychdistress$Distress, alternative = "two.sided",
conf.level = 0.95,
sigma.squared = 50)
```

We will use the *varTest* function to test the inference about a single variance. Let's look inside the parentheses. We first define the dataframe (i.e., "Ch9_psychdistress") and variable ("Distress") to compute the test. The *alternative* command specifies the alternative hypothesis that the true variance is different than the hypothesized variance. Had we wanted to test a one-directional hypothesis, we would have had the command *alternative = "greater"* or *alternative = "less,"* respectively. We test at an alpha of .05, so the confidence level is .95 (*conf.level = 0.95*). The command *sigma squared* is the hypothesized value to which we are testing, which is 50 in this example.

Using this script we are provided with the following results. We see that the variance of our variable, "Distress," is 56.44254. The results of the chi-squared test are not statistically significant ($\chi^2 = 34.99$, $df = 31$, $p = .57$).

```
Results of Hypothesis Test
--------------------------
```

Null Hypothesis:	variance = 50
Alternative Hypothesis:	True variance is not equal to 50
Test Name:	Chi-Squared Test on Variance
Estimated Parameter(s):	variance = 56.44254
Data:	Ch9_distress$Distress
Test Statistic:	**Chi-Squared = 34.99437**
Test Statistic Parameter:	df = 31
P-value:	**0.5680487**
95% Confidence Interval:	LCL = 36.27722
	UCL = 99.76309

FIGURE 9.3
Generating a test of inference about a single variance.

9.5.3 Reading Data Into R for the Test of Inference About Two Dependent Variances

```
getwd()
```

R is always pointed to a directory on your computer. To find out which directory it is pointed to, run this "get working directory" function. We will assume that we need to change the working directory, and will use the next line of code to set the working directory to the desired path.

```
setwd("E:/Folder")
```

To set the working directory, use the *setwd* function and change what is in quotation marks here to your file location. Also, if you are copying the directory name, it will copy in slashes. You will need to change the slash (i.e., \) to a forward slash (i.e., /). Note that you need your destination name within quotation marks in the parentheses.

```
Ch9_swimming <- read.csv("Ch9_swimming.csv")
```

The *read.csv* function reads our data into **R**. What's to the left of the <- will be what the data will be called in **R**. In this example, we're calling the dataframe "Ch9_swimming." What's to the right of the <- tells **R** to find this particular .csv file. In this example, our file is called "Ch9_swimming.csv." Make sure the extension (i.e., .csv) is included in your script. Also note that the name of your file should be in quotation marks within the parentheses. Note that this is the same data that we used in our discussion of dependent *t* tests.

```
names(Ch9_swimming)
```

The *names* function will produce a list of variable names for each dataframe as follows. This is a good check to make sure your data have been read in correctly.

```
[1] "pretest" "posttest"
```

```
View(Ch9_swimming)
```

The *View* function will let you view the dataset in spreadsheet format in RStudio.

```
summary(Ch9_swimming)
```

The *summary* function will produce basic descriptive statistics on all the variables in your dataframe. This is a great way to quickly check to see if the data have been read in correctly and to get a feel for your data, if you haven't already. The output from the summary statement for this dataframe looks like this.

```
    pretest             posttest
Min.   :58.00      Min.   :54.00
1st Qu.:61.25      1st Qu.:56.25
Median :63.50      Median :59.50
Mean   :64.00      Mean   :59.00
3rd Qu.:65.75      3rd Qu.:61.75
Max.   :72.00      Max.   :64.00
```

FIGURE 9.4
Reading data into **R** for the test of inference about two dependent variances.

9.5.4 Generating the Test of Inference About Two Dependent Variances

```
var(Ch9_swimming$pretest)
var(Ch9_swimming$posttest)
```

Before we compute the test for the inference about two dependent variances, let's generate the values of the variances for both the pretest and posttest. Using the *var* function for the two variables of interest, the variances are, respectively:

```
[1] 17.77778 #pretest
[1] 13.11111 #posttest
```

```
var.test(Ch9_swimming$pretest, Ch9_swimming$posttest,
        paired=TRUE,
        alternative = "two.sided",
        conf.level = 0.95)
```

We will use the *var.test* function to test the inference about two dependent variances. Let's review what is inside the parentheses. We first define the dataframe ("Ch9_swimming") and variables to compute the test ("Ch9_swimming$pretest" and "Ch9_swimming$posttest). This test is comparable to the dependent *t* test, comparing one population variance to another, and thus we define this as *paired=TRUE*. The *alternative* command specifies the alternative hypothesis the variance for the pretest is different than the variance for the posttest. Had we wanted to test a one-directional hypothesis, we would have had the command *alternative = "greater"* or *alternative = "less,"* respectively. We test at an alpha of .05, so the confidence level is .95 (*conf.level = 0.95*). Using this command, we are provided with the following results. We see the ratio of the variances is about 1.36. The results of the *F* test are not statistically significant ($F = 1.36, p = .68$).

```
Results of Hypothesis Test
--------------------------
```

Null Hypothesis:	ratio of variances = 1
Alternative Hypothesis:	True ratio of variances is not equal to 1
Test Name:	F test to compare two variances
Estimated Parameter(s):	ratio of variances = 1.355932
Data:	Ch9_swimming$pretest and Ch9_swimming$posttest
Test Statistic:	**F = 1.355932**
Test Statistic Parameters:	num df = 9
	denom df = 9
P-value:	**0.6574637**
95% Confidence Interval:	LCL = 0.3367944
	UCL = 5.4589751

FIGURE 9.5
Generating a test of inference about two dependent variances.

9.6 Research Question Template and Example Write-Up

Consider an example paragraph for one of the tests described in this chapter, more specifically, testing inferences about two dependent variances. As you may remember, our graduate research assistant, Oso, was working with Dr. Abraham, an assistant principal, to assist in analyzing the variances of first grade students. Oso's task was to assist Dr. Abraham with writing her research question (*Are the variances of achievement scores for first grade children the same in the fall as compared to the spring?*) and generating the test of inference to answer her question. Oso suggested a dependent variances test as the test of inference. A template for writing a research question for the dependent variances follows:

Are the variances of [variable] the same in [time 1] as compared to [time 2]?

The following is an example write-up:

A test of dependent variances was conducted to determine if variances of achievement scores for first grade children were the same in the fall as compared to the spring. The test was conducted using an alpha of .05. The null hypothesis was that the variances would be the same.

There was a statistically significant difference in variances of achievement scores of first grade children in the fall as compared to the spring ($t = -3.4261$, $df = 60$, $p < .05$). Thus the null hypothesis that the variances would be equal at the beginning and end of the first grade was rejected. The variances of achievement test scores significantly increased from September to April.

9.7 Additional Resources

We have offered a number of resources within the chapter and refer readers who are interested in learning more to those resources. Because homogeneity of variance is an integral assumption to tests of means, readers may also find coverage of tests of inference in texts that deal with ANOVA and related designs (e.g., Maxwell, Delaney, & Kelley, 2018).

Problems

Conceptual Problems

1. Which of the following tests of homogeneity of variance is most robust to assumption violations?
   a. F ratio test
   b. Bartlett's chi-square test
   c. O'Brien procedure
   d. Hartley's F_{max} test
2. True or false? Cochran's C test requires equal sample sizes.
3. I assert that if two dependent sample variances are identical, I would not be able to reject the null hypothesis. Am I correct?

4. The 90% CI for a single variance extends from 25.7 to 33.6 and the hypothesized value is 22.0. If the level of significance is .10, do I reject the null hypothesis?

    a. Yes

    b. No

    c. Cannot be determined

5. The 95% CI for a single variance ranges from 82.0 to 93.5, and the hypothesized value is 87.2. If the level of significance is .05, do I reject the null hypothesis?

    a. Yes

    b. No

    c. Cannot be determined

6. If the mean of the sampling distribution of the difference between two variances equals 0, I assert that both samples probably represent a single population. Am I correct?

7. Which of the following is an example of two dependent samples?

    a. Pretest scores of males in one course and posttest scores of females in another course

    b. Husbands and their wives in your neighborhood

    c. Softball players at your school and football players at your school

    d. Professors in education and professors in psychology

8. True or false? The mean of the F distribution increases as the degrees of freedom in the denominator (v_2) increase.

9. A researcher is testing whether the population variance for a treatment group differs than the population variance for a control group. The distribution is nonnormal and relatively peaked. Which of the following procedures would you recommend to the researcher?

    a. Brown-Forsythe procedure

    b. Hartley's F_{max} test

    c. O'Brien procedure

    d. Ratio of the sample variances

10. A researcher is testing whether the population variance for a treatment group differs than the population variance for a comparison group. The distribution is nonnormal and relatively flat. Which of the following procedures would you recommend to the researcher?

    a. Brown-Forsythe procedure

    b. Hartley's F_{max} test

    c. O'Brien procedure

    d. Ratio of the sample variances

11. Tests of inferences about variances are appropriate in all but which of the following situations?

    a. To examine linearity between two variances

    b. To examine the extent to which the assumption of equal variances has been met

c. To determine whether a variance differs from a hypothesized value

d. To determine whether two variances that are dependent are different from each other

Answers to Conceptual Problems

1. c (The O'Brien procedure has been shown to be more robust to nonnormality than the others listed here.)

3. **Yes** (Cannot reject if sample variances are equal.)

5. **b** (The hypothesized value is 87.2 with a 95% CI for a single variance ranging from 82.0 to 93.5, and the level of significance is .05; the hypothesized values falls within the CI, so fail to reject the null hypothesis.)

7. **Yes** (If the mean difference is 0, then there really is only one population.)

9. **False** (The mean decreases as v_2 increases, as it moves closer and closer to 1.0.)

11. c (The O'Brien procedure is recommended for nonnormal distributions that are mesokurtic or platykurtic.)

Computational Problems

1. The following random sample of scores on a preschool ability test is obtained from a normally distributed population of 4-year-olds:

20	22	24	30	18	22	29	27
25	21	19	22	38	26	17	25

a. Test the following hypotheses at the .10 level of significance:

$$H_0: \sigma^2 = 75$$

$$H_1: \sigma^2 \neq 75$$

b. Construct a 90% CI.

2. The following two independent random samples of number of books owned are obtained from two populations of undergraduate (sample 1) and graduate students (sample 2), respectively:

Sample 1 data						Sample 2 data				
42	36	47	35	46		45	50	57	58	43
37	52	44	47	51		52	43	60	41	49
56	54	55	50	40		44	51	49	55	56
40	46	41								

Test the following hypotheses at the .05 level of significance using the Brown-Forsythe and O'Brien procedures:

$$H_0 : \sigma_1^2 - \sigma_2^2 = 0$$

$$H_1 : \sigma_1^2 - \sigma_2^2 \neq 0$$

3. The following summary statistics are available for two dependent random samples of brothers and sisters, respectively, on their allowance for the past month: $s_1^2 = 49$, $s_2^2 = 25$, $n = 32$, $r_{12} = .60$.

   Test the following hypotheses at the .05 level of significance:

$$H_0: \sigma_1^2 - \sigma_2^2 = 0$$

$$H_1: \sigma_1^2 - \sigma_2^2 \neq 0$$

4. The following summary statistics are available for two dependent random samples of first-semester college students who were measured on their high school and first semester college GPAs, respectively: $s_1^2 = 1.56$, $s_2^2 = 4.42$, $n = 62$, $r_{12} = .72$.

   Test the following hypotheses at the .05 level of significance:

$$H_0: \sigma_1^2 - \sigma_2^2 = 0$$

$$H_1: \sigma_1^2 - \sigma_2^2 \neq 0$$

5. A random sample of 21 statistics exam scores is collected with a sample mean of 50 and a sample variance of 10. Test the following hypotheses at the .05 level of significance:

$$H_0: \sigma^2 = 25$$

$$H_1: \sigma^2 \neq 25$$

6. A random sample of 30 placement exam scores is collected with a sample mean of 525 and a sample variance of 16900. Test the following hypotheses at the .05 level of significance:

$$H_0: \sigma^2 = 10000$$

$$H_1: \sigma^2 \neq 10000$$

7. An employability assessment was given at the time individuals applied for work (i.e., pre-employment) and after employed for 6 months. The pre-employment variance is 36, the 6-month variance is 64, sample size is 31, and the pre–post correlation is .80. Test the null hypothesis that the two dependent variances are equal against a nondirectional alternative at the .01 level of significance.

8. A random sample of 25 adults completed the Big 5 personality test, and their emotional stability scores are provided here:

2.10	2.60	3.30
1.50	3.90	2.80
4.50	1.40	2.70
1.80	3.60	3.20
3.80	2.30	2.80
1.80	1.80	2.20
4.20	4.20	3.60
2.00	4.80	4.40
2.60	3.70	

Test the following hypotheses at the .05 level of significance:

$$H_0: \sigma^2 = 1.25$$

$$H_1: \sigma^2 \neq 1.25$$

9. The following summary statistics are available for two dependent random samples who have been measured on the Big 5 personality test, respectively: $s^2_{conscientiousness} = .503$, $s^2_{imagination} = .427$, $n = 25$, $r_{12} = .10$.

Test the following hypotheses at the .05 level of significance:

$$H_0: \sigma^2_1 - \sigma^2_2 = 0$$

$$H_1: \sigma^2_1 - \sigma^2_2 \neq 0$$

Selected Answers to Computational Problems

1. (a) sample variance = 27.9292, χ^2 = 5.5858, critical values = 7.2609 and 24.9958, thus reject H_0. (b) (16.7603, 57.6978), thus reject H_0 as the interval does not contain 75.

3. $t = 2.3474$, critical values = −2.042 and +2.042, thus reject H_0.

5. $\chi^2 = 8.0$, critical values = 9.59078 and 34.1696, thus reject H_0.

7. $t = -2.6178$, critical values = −2.756 and +2.756, thus fail to reject H_0.

9. Given $s^2_{conscientiousness} = s^2_1 = .50$, $s^2_{imagination} = s^2_2 = .43$, $n = 25$, $r_{12} = .10$.

$$t = \frac{s^2_1 - s^2_2}{2 s_1 s_2 \sqrt{\dfrac{1 - r^2_{12}}{\nu}}} = \frac{100 - 169}{(2)(10)(13)\sqrt{\dfrac{1 - .64}{60}}} = -3.4261$$

Interpretive Problem

1. Use the survey1 dataset from the website to determine if there are gender differences among the variances for any items of interest that are at least interval or ratio in scale. Some example items might include the following:

   a. Height in inches [HEIGHT]

   b. Amount spent at last hair appointment [HAIRAPPT], number of songs downloaded to your phone [SONGS]

   c. Current GPA [GPA]

   d. Amount of exercise per week [EXERCISE]

   e. Number of alcoholic drinks per week [DRINKS]

   f. Number of hours studied per week [STUDYHRS]

2. Use the survey1 dataset from the website to determine if there are differences between the variances for left- versus right-handed individuals on any items of interest that are at least interval or ratio in scale. Some example items might include the following:

   a. Height in inches [HEIGHT]

b. Amount spent at last hair appointment [HAIRAPPT], number of songs downloaded to your phone [SONGS]

c. Current GPA [GPA]

d. Amount of exercise per week [EXERCISE]

e. Number of alcoholic drinks per week [DRINKS]

f. Number of hours studied per week [STUDYHRS]

10

Bivariate Measures of Association

Chapter Outline

Key Concepts

1. Scatterplot

2. Strength and direction

3. Covariance

4. Correlation coefficient

5. Fisher's Z transformation

6. Linearity assumption, causation, and restriction of range issues

We have considered various inferential tests in the last four chapters, specifically those that deal with tests of means, proportions, and variances. In this chapter we examine measures of association as well as inferences involving measures of association. Methods for directly determining the relationship among two variables are known as **bivariate analysis**, rather than **univariate analysis**, which is only concerned with a single variable. The indices used to directly describe the relationship among two variables are known as *correlation coefficients* (in the old days known as co-relation) or as *measures of association*.

These measures of association allow us to determine how two variables are related to one another and can be useful in two applications: (a) as a descriptive statistic by itself and (b) as an inferential test. First, a researcher may want to compute a correlation coefficient for its own sake, simply to tell the researcher precisely how two variables are related or associated. For example, we may want to determine whether there is a relationship between the GRE-Quantitative Reasoning (GRE-Q) subtest and performance on a statistics exam. Do students who score relatively high on the GRE-Q perform higher on a statistics exam than do students who score relatively low on the GRE-Q? In other words, as scores increase on the GRE-Q, do they also correspondingly increase their performance on a statistics exam?

Second, we may want to use an inferential test to assess whether (a) a correlation is significantly different from zero or (b) two correlations are significantly different from one another. For example, is the correlation between GRE-Q and statistics exam performance significantly different from zero? As a second example, is the correlation between GRE-Q and statistics exam performance the same for younger students as it is for older students?

The following topics are covered in this chapter: scatterplot; covariance; Pearson product-moment correlation coefficient; inferences about the Pearson product-moment correlation coefficient; some issues regarding correlations; other measures of association; SPSS and **R**; and power. We utilize some of the basic concepts previously covered in Chapters 6 through 9. New concepts to be discussed include the following: scatterplot, strength and direction, covariance, correlation coefficient, Fisher's Z transformation, linearity assumption, causation, and restriction of range issues. Our objectives are that by the end of this chapter, you will be able to (a) understand the concepts underlying the correlation coefficient and correlation inferential tests, (b) select the appropriate type of correlation, and (c) determine and interpret the appropriate correlation and inferential test.

10.1 What Bivariate Measures of Association Are and How They Work

Challie Lenge, along with her accomplished cohort of graduate research assistants working in the statistics lab, continues to assist with various research projects. We now find her embarking on exciting challenge with a community partner.

The faculty advisor for the stats lab received a telephone call from Dr. Amberly, the director of marketing for the local animal shelter. Based on a recent survey of donors to the shelter, it appears that the donors who contribute the largest donations also have children and pets. In an effort to attract more donors to the animal shelter, Dr. Amberly is targeting select groups—one of which she believes may be families that have children at home and who also have pets. Dr. Amberly believes if there is a relationship between these variables, she can more easily reach the intended audience with her marketing materials, which will then translate into increased donations to the animal shelter. However, Dr. Amberly wants to base her decision on solid evidence and not just a hunch. Having built a good knowledge base with previous consulting work, the faculty advisor puts Dr. Amberly in touch with the graduate students in the statistics lab. After consulting with Dr. Amberly, Challie suggests a Pearson correlation as the test of inference to test her research question: *Is there a correlation between the number of children in a family and the number of pets?* Challie's task is then to assist in generating the test of inference to answer Dr. Amberly's research question.

10.1.1 Characteristics

10.1.1.1 Scatterplot

This section deals with an important concept underlying the relationship among two variables, the scatterplot. Later sections move us into ways of measuring the relationship among two variables. First, however, we need to set up the situation where we have data on two different variables for each of N individuals in the population. Table 10.1 displays such a situation. The first column is simply an index of the individuals in the population, from $i = 1, \ldots, N$, where N is the total number of individuals in the population. The second column denotes the values obtained for the first variable X. Thus, $X_1 = 10$ means that the first individual had a score of 10 on variable X. The third column provides the values for the second variable Y. Thus, $Y_1 = 20$ indicates that the first individual had a score of 20 on variable Y. In an actual data table, only the scores would be shown, not the X_i and Y_i notation. Thus, we have a tabular method for depicting the data of a two-variable situation in Table 10.1.

A graphical method for depicting the relationship among two variables is to *plot the pair of scores* on X and Y for each individual on a two-dimensional figure known as a **scatterplot** (or *scattergram*). Each individual has two scores in a two-dimensional coordinate system, denoted by (X, Y). For example, our individual 1 has the paired scores of (10, 20). An example scatterplot is shown in Figure 10.1. The **X axis** (the *horizontal axis* or *abscissa*) represents the values for variable X, and the **Y axis** (the *vertical axis* or *ordinate*) represents the values for variable Y. Each point on the scatterplot represents a pair of scores (X, Y) for a particular individual. Thus, individual 1 has a point at $X = 10$ and $Y = 20$ (the circled point). Points for other individuals are also shown. In essence, the scatterplot is actually

TABLE 10.1

Layout for Correlational Data

Individual	X	Y
1	$X_1 = 10$	$Y_1 = 20$
2	$X_2 = 12$	$Y_2 = 28$
3	$X_3 = 20$	$Y_3 = 33$
.	.	.
.	.	.
.	.	.
N	$X_N = 44$	$Y_N = 65$

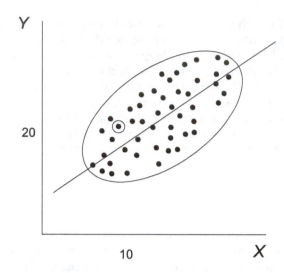

FIGURE 10.1
Scatterplot.

a bivariate frequency distribution. When there is a moderate degree of relationship, the points may take the shape of an ellipse (i.e., a football shape where the direction of the relationship, positive or negative, may make the football appear to point up to the right—as with a positive relation depicted in this figure), as in Figure 10.1.

The scatterplot allows the researcher to evaluate both the direction and the strength of the relationship among X and Y. The **direction** of the relationship has to do with whether the relationship is positive or negative. A *positive relationship* occurs when as scores on variable X increase (from left to right), scores on variable Y also increase (from bottom to top). Thus, Figure 10.1 indicates a positive relationship among X and Y. Examples of different scatterplots are shown in Figure 10.2. Figures 10.2a and 10.2d both display positive relationships.

A *negative relationship*, sometimes called an *inverse relationship*, occurs when as scores on variable X increase (from left to right), scores on variable Y decrease (from top to bottom). Figures 10.2b and 10.2e are examples of negative relationships. There is no relationship between X and Y when for a large value of X, a large or a small value of Y can occur, and for a small value of X, a large or a small value of Y can also occur. In other words, X and Y are not related, as shown in Figure 10.2c.

The **strength** of the relationship among X and Y is determined by the scatter of the points (hence the name *scatterplot*). First, we draw a straight line through the points that cuts the bivariate distribution in half, as shown in Figures 10.1 and 10.2. When you later learn about regression, we will note that this line is known as the **regression line**. If the scatter is such that the points tend to fall close to the line, then this is indicative of a strong relationship among X and Y. Both Figures 10.2a and 10.2b denote strong relationships. If the scatter is such that the points are widely scattered around the line, then this is indicative of a weak relationship among X and Y. Both Figures 10.2d and 10.2e denote weaker relationships. To summarize Figure 10.2, part (a) represents a strong positive relationship, part (b) a strong negative relationship, part (c) no relationship, part (d) a weaker positive relationship, and part (e) a weaker negative relationship. Thus the scatterplot is useful for providing a quick visual indication of the nature of the relationship among variables X and Y.

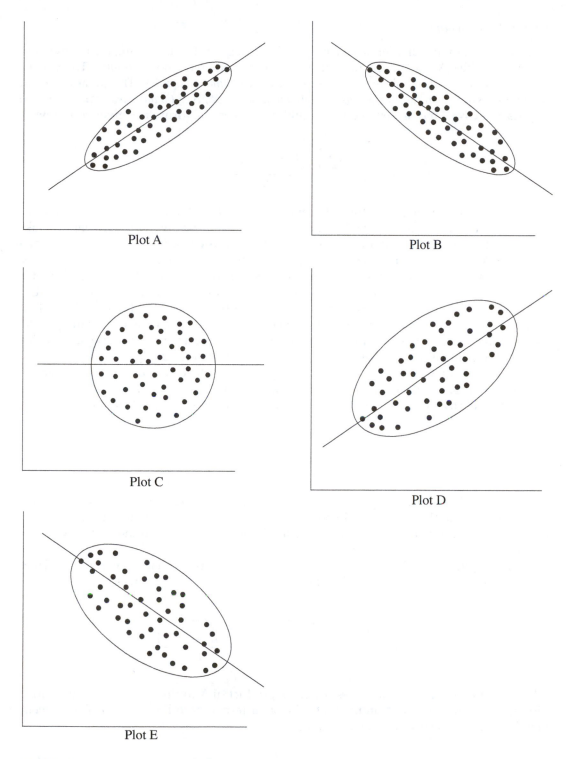

FIGURE 10.2
Examples of possible scatterplots.

10.1.1.2 Covariance

The remainder of this chapter deals with statistical methods for measuring the relationship among variables X and Y. The first such method is known as the *covariance*. The **covariance**, conceptually, *is the shared variance (or covariance) among X and Y*. The covariance and correlation share commonalities, *as the correlation is simply the standardized covariance*. The **population covariance** is denoted by σ_{XY} and the conceptual formula is given as follows:

$$\sigma_{XY} = \frac{\sum_{i=1}^{N}(X_i - \mu_X)(Y_i - \mu_Y)}{N}$$

where X_i and Y_i are the scores for individual i on variables X and Y, respectively, and μ_X and μ_Y are the population means for variables X and Y, respectively. This equation looks similar to the computational formula for the variance presented in Chapter 3 where deviation scores from the mean are computed for each individual. *The conceptual formula for the covariance is essentially an average of the paired deviation score products*. If variables X and Y are *positively related*, then the deviation scores will tend to be of the same sign, their products will tend to be positive, and the covariance will be a positive value (i.e., $\sigma_{XY} > 0$). If variables X and Y are *negatively related*, then the deviation scores will tend to be of opposite signs, their products will tend to be negative, and the covariance will be a negative value (i.e., $\sigma_{XY} < 0$). Finally, if variables X and Y are *not related*, then the deviation scores will consist of both the same and opposite signs, their products will be both positive and negative and sum to zero, and the covariance will be a zero value (i.e., $\sigma_{XY} = 0$).

The **sample covariance** is denoted by s_{XY}, and the conceptual formula becomes:

$$s_{XY} = \frac{\sum_{i=1}^{n}(X_i - \bar{X})(Y_i - \bar{Y})}{n-1}$$

where $\bar{X}$ and $\bar{Y}$ are the sample means for variables X and Y, respectively, and n is the sample size. Note that the denominator becomes $n - 1$ so as to yield an unbiased sample estimate of the population covariance (i.e., similar to what we did in the sample variance situation).

The conceptual formula is unwieldy and error-prone for other than small samples. Thus, a *computational formula for the population covariance* has been developed, as seen here:

$$\sigma_{XY} = \frac{N\left(\sum_{i=1}^{N} X_i Y_i\right) - \left(\sum_{i=1}^{N} X_i\right)\left(\sum_{i=1}^{N} Y_i\right)}{N^2}$$

where the first summation involves the cross-product of X multiplied by Y for each individual summed across all N individuals; the other terms should be familiar. The *computational formula for the sample covariance* is:

$$s_{XY} = \frac{n\left(\sum_{i=1}^{n} X_i Y_i\right) - \left(\sum_{i=1}^{n} X_i\right)\left(\sum_{i=1}^{n} Y_i\right)}{n(n-1)}$$

TABLE 10.2

Example Correlational Data (X = number of children, Y = number of pets)

Individual	X	Y	XY	X^2	Y^2	Rank X	Rank Y	(Rank X – Rank Y)^2
1	1	2	2	1	4	1	1	0
2	2	6	12	4	36	2	3	1
3	3	4	12	9	16	3	2	1
4	4	8	32	16	64	4	4	0
5		5	10	50	25	100	5	5	0
Sums	15	30	108	55	220			2

where the denominator is $n(n-1)$ so as to yield an unbiased sample estimate of the population covariance.

Table 10.2 gives an example of a population situation where a strong positive relationship is expected because as X (number of children in a family) increases, Y (number of pets in a family) also increases. Here σ_{XY} is computed as:

$$\sigma_{XY} = \frac{N\left(\sum_{i=1}^{N} X_i Y_i\right) - \left(\sum_{i=1}^{N} X_i\right)\left(\sum_{i=1}^{N} Y_i\right)}{N^2} = \frac{5(108) - (15)(30)}{5^2} = 3.6000$$

The sign indicates that the relationship between X and Y is indeed positive; that is, the more children a family has, the more pets they tend to have. However, like the variance, the value of the covariance depends on the scales of the variables involved. Thus, interpretation of the magnitude of a single covariance is difficult, as it can take on literally any value. We see shortly that the correlation coefficient takes care of this problem. For this reason you are only likely to see the covariance utilized in the analysis of covariance and advanced techniques such as structural equation modeling and multilevel modeling (beyond the scope of this text).

10.1.1.3 Pearson Product-Moment Correlation Coefficient

Other methods for measuring the relationship among X and Y have been developed that are easier to interpret than the covariance. We refer to these measures as **correlation coefficients**. The first correlation coefficient we consider is the **Pearson product-moment correlation coefficient**, developed by the famous statistician Karl Pearson, and simply referred to as the Pearson here. The Pearson can be considered in several different forms, where the *population value* is denoted by ρ_{XY} (rho) and the *sample* value by r_{XY}. One conceptual form of the Pearson is a product of standardized z scores (previously described in Chapter 4). This formula for the population Pearson is given as:

$$\rho_{XY} = \frac{\sum_{i=1}^{N} (z_X z_Y)}{N}$$

where z_X and z_Y are the z scores for variables X and Y, respectively, whose product is taken for each individual, and then summed across all N individuals.

Because z scores are standardized versions of raw scores, then the Pearson correlation is simply a standardized version of the covariance. The *sign* of the Pearson denotes the direction of the relationship (e.g., positive or negative), and the *value* of the Pearson denotes the strength of the relationship. The Pearson falls on a scale from −1.00 to +1.00, where −1.00 indicates a perfect negative relationship, 0 indicates no relationship, and +1.00 indicates a perfect positive relationship. Values near .50 or −.50 are considered as moderate relationships, values near 0 as weak relationships, and values near +1.00 or −1.00 as strong relationships (although these are subjective terms). Cohen (1988) also offers conventions, which are presented later in this chapter, for interpreting the value of the correlation. As you may see as you read more statistics and research methods textbooks, there are other guidelines offered for interpreting the value of the correlation.

There are other forms of the Pearson. A second conceptual form of the Pearson is in terms of the covariance and the standard deviations, and the *population formula*, denoted by $\rho_{XY,}$ is given as:

$$\rho_{XY} = \frac{\sigma_{XY}}{\sigma_X \sigma_Y}$$

This form is useful when the covariance and standard deviations are already known. A final form of the Pearson is the *computational formula*, written as follows:

$$\rho_{XY} = \frac{N\left(\sum_{i=1}^{N} X_i Y_i\right) - \left(\sum_{i=1}^{N} X_i\right)\left(\sum_{i=1}^{N} Y_i\right)}{\sqrt{\left[N\left(\sum_{i=1}^{N} X_i^2\right) - \left(\sum_{i=1}^{N} X_i\right)^2\right]\left[N\left(\sum_{i=1}^{N} Y_i^2\right) - \left(\sum_{i=1}^{N} Y_i\right)^2\right]}}$$

where all terms should be familiar from the computational formulas of the variance and covariance. This is the formula to use for hand computations, as it is more error-free than the other previously given formulas.

For the example children–pet data given in Table 10.2, we see that the Pearson correlation is computed as follows:

$$\rho_{XY} = \frac{N\left(\sum_{i=1}^{N} X_i Y_i\right) - \left(\sum_{i=1}^{N} X_i\right)\left(\sum_{i=1}^{N} Y_i\right)}{\sqrt{\left[N\left(\sum_{i=1}^{N} X_i^2\right) - \left(\sum_{i=1}^{N} X_i\right)^2\right]\left[N\left(\sum_{i=1}^{N} Y_i^2\right) - \left(\sum_{i=1}^{N} Y_i\right)^2\right]}}$$

$$\rho_{XY} = \frac{5(108) - (15)(30)}{\sqrt{\left[5(55) - (15)^2\right]\left[5(220) - (30)^2\right]}} = .900$$

Thus, there is a very strong positive relationship among variables X (the number of children) and Y (the number of pets).

The **sample correlation** is denoted by r_{XY}. The formulas are essentially the same for the sample correlation, r_{XY}, and the population correlation, ρ_{XY}, except that n is substituted for N. For example, the computational formula for the sample correlation is noted here:

$$r_{XY} = \frac{n\left(\sum_{i=1}^{n} X_i Y_i\right) - \left(\sum_{i=1}^{n} X_i\right)\left(\sum_{i=1}^{n} Y_i\right)}{\sqrt{\left[n\left(\sum_{i=1}^{n} X_i^2\right) - \left(\sum_{i=1}^{n} X_i\right)^2\right]\left[n\left(\sum_{i=1}^{n} Y_i^2\right) - \left(\sum_{i=1}^{n} Y_i\right)^2\right]}}$$

Unlike the sample variance and covariance, the sample correlation has no correction for bias.

10.1.1.4 Inferences about the Pearson Product-Moment Correlation Coefficient

Once a researcher has determined one or more Pearson correlation coefficients, it is often useful to know whether the sample correlations are significantly different from zero. Thus, we need to visit the world of inferential statistics again. In this section we consider two different inferential tests: first for testing *whether a single sample correlation is significantly different from zero*, and second for testing *whether two independent sample correlations are significantly different*.

10.1.1.4.1 Inferences for a Single Sample

Our first inferential test is appropriate when you are interested in determining whether the correlation among variables X and Y for a *single sample* is significantly different from zero. For example, is the correlation between the number of years of education and current income significantly different from zero? The test of inference for the Pearson correlation will be conducted following the same steps as those in previous chapters. The null hypothesis is written as follows:

$$H_0 : \rho = 0$$

A nondirectional alternative hypothesis, where we are willing to reject the null if the sample correlation is either significantly greater than or less than zero, is nearly always utilized. Unfortunately, the sampling distribution of the sample Pearson r is too complex to be of much value to the applied researcher. For testing whether the correlation is different from zero (i.e., where the alternative hypothesis is specified as $H_1 : \rho \neq 0$), a transformation of r can be used to generate a t distributed test statistic. The test statistic is:

$$t = r\sqrt{\frac{n-2}{1-r^2}}$$

which is distributed as t (i.e., follows a t distribution) with $v = n - 2$ degrees of freedom, assuming that both X and Y are normally distributed. Note, however, even if one variable is normal and the other is not, the t distribution may still apply (see Hogg and Craig, 1995).

It should be noted for inferential tests of correlations that sample size plays a role in determining statistical significance. For instance, this particular test is based on $n - 2$ degrees of freedom. If the sample size is small (e.g., 10), then it is difficult to reject the null hypothesis except for very strong correlations. If the sample size is large (e.g., 200), then it is easier to reject the null hypothesis for all but very weak correlations. Thus, the statistical significance of a correlation is definitely a function of sample size, both for tests of a single correlation and for tests of two correlations.

From the example children–pet data, we want to determine whether the sample Pearson correlation is significantly different from zero, with a nondirectional alternative hypothesis and at the .05 level of significance. The test statistic is computed as follows:

$$t = r\sqrt{\frac{n-2}{1-r^2}} = .9000\sqrt{\frac{5-2}{1-.8100}} = 3.5762$$

The critical values from Table A.2 in the Appendix are $\pm_{\alpha_2} t_3 = \pm 3.182$. Thus we would *reject the null hypothesis*, as the test statistic exceeds the critical value, and conclude the correlation among variables X and Y is significantly different from zero. In summary, a strong, positive, statistically significant correlation exists between the number of children and the number of pets.

10.1.1.4.2 Inferences for Two Independent Samples

In a second situation, the researcher may have collected data from two different independent samples. It can be determined whether the correlations among variables X and Y are equal for these two independent samples of observations. For example, is the correlation among height and weight the same for children and adults? Here the null and alternative hypotheses are written as:

$$H_0: \rho_1 - \rho_2 = 0$$
$$H_1: \rho_1 - \rho_2 \neq 0$$

where ρ_1 is the correlation among X and Y for sample 1 and ρ_2 is the correlation among X and Y for sample 2. However, because correlations are not normally distributed for every value of ρ, a transformation is necessary. This transformation is known as **Fisher's Z transformation**, named after the famous statistician Sir Ronald A. Fisher, which is approximately normally distributed regardless of the value of ρ. Table A.5 in the Appendix is used to convert a sample correlation r to a Fisher's Z transformed value. Note that Fisher's Z is a totally different statistic from any z score or z statistic previously covered. The test statistic for this situation is the following:

$$z = \frac{Z_1 - Z_2}{\sqrt{\dfrac{1}{n_1 - 3} + \dfrac{1}{n_2 - 3}}}$$

where n_1 and n_2 are the sizes of the two samples, and Z_1 and Z_2 are the Fisher's Z transformed values for the two samples. The test statistic is then compared to critical values from the z distribution in Table A.1 in the Appendix. For a nondirectional alternative hypothesis where the two correlations may be different in either direction, then the critical values are $\pm_{\alpha_2} z$. Directional alternative hypotheses where the correlations are different in a particular direction can also be tested by looking in the appropriate tail of the z distribution (i.e., either $\pm_{\alpha_2} z$ or $-\pm_{\alpha_2} z$).

Consider the following example. Two samples have been independently drawn of 28 children (sample 1) and 28 adults (sample 2). For each sample, the correlations among height and weight were computed to be $r_{children} = .80$ and $r_{adults} = .40$. A nondirectional alternative hypothesis is utilized where the level of significance is set at .05. From Table A.5 in the Appendix, we first determine the Fisher's Z transformed values to be $Z_{children} = 1.099$ and $Z_{adults} = .4236$. Then the test statistic z is computed as follows:

$$z = \frac{Z_1 - Z_2}{\sqrt{\dfrac{1}{n_1 - 3} + \dfrac{1}{n_2 - 3}}} = \frac{1.099 - .4236}{\sqrt{\dfrac{1}{25} + \dfrac{1}{25}}} = 2.3878$$

From Table A.1 in the Appendix, the critical values are $\pm_{\alpha_2} z = \pm 1.96$. Our decision then is to *reject the null hypothesis* and conclude that height and weight do not have the same correlation for children and adults. In other words, there is a statistically significant difference of the height–weight correlation between children and adults with a strong effect size (as we will see later, the effect size q is computed as $q = Z_1 - Z_2 = 1.099 - .4236 = .6754$). This inferential test assumes both variables are normally distributed for each population and that scores are independent across individuals; however, the procedure is not very robust to nonnormality, because the Fisher's Z transformation assumes normality (Duncan & Layard, 1973; Wilcox, 2003; Yu & Dunn, 1982). Thus, caution should be exercised in using the z test when data are nonnormal (e.g., Yu & Dunn recommend the use of Kendall's τ, as discussed later in this chapter).

10.1.1.5 Issues Regarding Correlations

In the discussion of correlations, there are many concepts that are important, but two in particular that we will note. These include *causality* and *restriction of range*. See Box 10.1 for a summary.

BOX 10.1 Causality and Restriction of Range

Issue	Misinterpretation	Correct Interpretation
Causality	A correlation between X and Y equates to X *causes* Y	A correlation between X and Y equates to evidence of a relationship between X and Y that may be a result of any number of situations including: a. X causing Y b. Y causing X c. A third variable Z causing both X and Y d. Even more variables causing both X and Y
Restriction of range	A weak correlation between X and Y equates to little or no relationship between X and Y	A weak correlation between X and Y *may* equate to little or no relationship between X and Y *or* it may equate to scores on one or both variables being restricted due to the nature of the sample or population

10.1.1.5.1 Correlation and Causality

An important matter to consider is an often-made misinterpretation of a correlation. Many individuals (e.g., researchers, the public, and the media) often infer a causal relationship from a strong correlation. However, a correlation by itself should never be used to infer **causation**. In particular, a high correlation among variables X and Y does not imply that one variable is causing the other; it simply means that these two variables are related in some fashion. Variables X and Y may be highly correlated for a number of different reasons. A high correlation could be the result of (a) X causing Y, or (b) Y causing X, or (c) a third variable Z causing both X and Y, or (d) even more variables being involved in creating the relationship between X and Y. The only methods that can strictly be used to infer cause are experimental methods that employ random assignment where one variable is manipulated by the researcher (the cause), a second variable is subsequently observed (the effect), and all other variables are controlled. Note, however, that there are some excellent quasi-experimental methods—propensity score analysis and regression discontinuity—that can be used in some situations and that mimic random assignment and increase the likelihood of speaking to causal inference (Shadish, Cook, & Campbell, 2002).

10.1.1.5.2 Restriction of Range

A final issue to consider is the effect of **restriction of the range** of scores on one or both variables. For example, suppose that we are interested in the relationship among GRE scores and graduate grade point average (GGPA). In the entire population of students, the relationship might be depicted by the scatterplot shown in Figure 10.3. Say the Pearson correlation is found to be .60 as depicted by the entire sample in the full scatterplot. Now we take a more restricted population of students, those students at highly selective Ivy-Covered University (ICU). ICU only admits students whose GRE scores are above the cutoff score shown in Figure 10.3. Because of restriction of range in the scores of the GRE variable, the strength of the relationship among GRE and GGPA at ICU is reduced to a Pearson correlation of .20, where only the subsample portion of the plot to the right of the cutoff score is involved. Thus, when scores on one or both variables are restricted due to the nature of the sample or population, then the magnitude of the correlation will usually be reduced [although see an exception in Figure 6.3 from Wilcox (2003)].

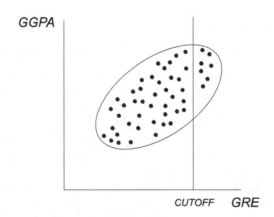

FIGURE 10.3
Restriction of range example.

It is difficult for two variables to be highly related when one or both variables have little variability. This is due to the nature of the formula. Recall that one version of the Pearson formula consisted of standard deviations in the denominator. Remember that the standard deviation measures the distance of the sample scores from the mean. When there is restriction of range, the distance of the individual scores from the mean is minimized. In other words, there is less variation or variability around the mean. This translates to smaller correlations (and smaller covariances). *If the size of the standard deviation for one variable is reduced, everything else being equal, then the size of correlations with other variables will also be reduced.* In other words, we need sufficient variation for a relationship to be evidenced through the correlation coefficient value. Otherwise the correlation is likely to be reduced in magnitude and you may miss an important correlation. If you must use a restrictive subsample, we suggest you choose measures of greater variability for correlational purposes.

Outliers, observations that are different from the bulk of the observations, also reduce the magnitude of correlations. If one observation is quite different from the rest such that it fell outside of the ellipse, then the correlation would be smaller in magnitude (e.g., closer to zero) than the correlation without the outlier.

10.1.1.5.3 Confidence Intervals

Confidence intervals for correlation coefficients have been proposed (e.g., Bonett & Wright, 2000) but the computations for such are not as straightforward as the confidence intervals with which we have worked previously given that the sampling distribution of r is not normally distributed. Thus, confidence intervals for Pearson's correlation, for example, require transformation of the correlation coefficient to Fisher's z to obtain the confidence limits and then back transformations to the correlation scale. As such, rather than spend time in hand calculations, we will rely on a number of tools now available that make computing confidence intervals for correlations quite easy. We will later illustrate the use of an online calculator as well as **R** for computing confidence intervals.

10.1.1.6 Other Measures of Association

Thus far we have considered one type of correlation, the Pearson product-moment correlation coefficient. The Pearson is most appropriate when both variables are at least interval level. That is, both variables X and Y are interval and/or ratio level variables. The Pearson is considered a parametric procedure given the distributional assumptions associated with it. If both variables are not at least interval level, then other measures of association, considered *nonparametric procedures*, should be considered because they do not have distributional assumptions associated with them. In this section we examine in detail the Spearman's rho and phi types of correlation coefficients and briefly mention several other types. While a distributional assumption for these correlations is not necessary, the assumption of independence still applies (and thus a random sample from the population is assumed).

10.1.1.6.1 Spearman's Rho

Spearman's rho's rank correlation coefficient is appropriate when *both variables are ordinal in scale*. This type of correlation was developed by Charles Spearman, the famous quantitative psychologist. Recall from Chapter 1 that ordinal data are where individuals have been rank ordered, such as class rank. Thus, for both variables, either the data are already available in ranks, or the researcher (or computer) converts the raw data to ranks prior to the analysis.

The equation for computing Spearman's rho's correlation is:

$$\rho_s = 1 - \frac{6\left[\sum_{i=1}^{N}(X_i - Y_i)^2\right]}{N(N^2 - 1)}$$

where ρ_s denotes the population Spearman's rho correlation and $(X_i - Y_i)$ represents the difference between the ranks on variables X and Y for unit i. The sample Spearman's rho correlation is denoted by r_s where n replaces N, but otherwise the equation remains the same. In case you were wondering where the 6 in the equation comes from, you will find interesting an article by Lamb (1984). Unfortunately, this particular computational formula is only appropriate when there are no ties among the ranks for either variable. An example of a tie in rank would be if two cases scored the same value on either X or Y. With ties, the formula given is only approximate, depending on the number of ties. In the case of ties, particularly when there are more than a few, many researchers recommend using Kendall's τ (tau) as an alternative correlation (e.g., Wilcox, 1995).

As with the Pearson correlation, Spearman's rho ranges from -1.0 to $+1.0$. Conventions that we use for interpreting the Pearson correlation (e.g., Cohen, 1988) can be applied to Spearman's rho correlation values as well. The sign of the coefficient can be interpreted as with the Pearson. A *negative sign* indicates that as the values for one variable increase, the values for the other variable decrease. A *positive sign* indicates that as one variable increases in value, the value of the second variable also increases.

As an example, consider the children–pets data again in Table 10.2. To the right of the table, you see the last three columns labeled as rank X, rank Y, and (*rank X – rank Y*)^2. The raw scores were converted to ranks, where the lowest raw score received a rank of 1. The last column lists the squared rank differences. As there were no ties, the computations are as follows:

$$\rho_s = 1 - \frac{6\left[\sum_{i=1}^{N}(X_i - Y_i)^2\right]}{N(N^2 - 1)} = 1 - \frac{6(2)}{5(24)} = .9000$$

Thus again there is a strong positive relationship among variables X and Y. It is a coincidence that $\rho = \rho_s$ for this dataset, but not so for computational problem 1 at the end of this chapter.

To test whether a sample Spearman's rho correlation is significantly different from zero, we examine the following null hypothesis (the alternative hypothesis would be stated as $H_1: \rho_s \neq 0$):

$$H_0: \rho_s = 0$$

The test statistic is given as follows:

$$t = \frac{r_s\sqrt{n-2}}{\sqrt{1-r_s^2}}$$

which is approximately distributed as a t distribution with $v = n - 2$ degrees of freedom (Ramsey, 1989). The approximation works best when n is at least 10. A nondirectional hypothesis, where we are willing to reject the null if the sample correlation is either significantly greater than or less than zero, is nearly always utilized. From the example, we want to determine whether the sample Spearman's rho correlation is significantly different from zero at the .05 level of significance. For a nondirectional hypothesis, the test statistic is computed as we see here:

$$t = \frac{r_s\sqrt{n-2}}{\sqrt{1-r_s^2}} = \frac{.9000\sqrt{5-2}}{\sqrt{1-.81}} = 3.5762$$

where the critical values from Table A.2 in the Appendix are $\pm_{\alpha_2} t_3 = \pm 3.182$ Given that the test statistic (3.5762) is greater than our critical value (+3.182), we *reject the null hypothesis* and conclude that the correlation is significantly different from zero, *strong in magnitude* (suggested by the value of the correlation coefficient; using Cohen's guidelines for interpretation as an effect size, this would be considered a large effect), and *positive in direction* (evidenced from the sign of the correlation coefficient). The exact sampling distribution for when $3 \leq n \leq 18$ is given by Ramsey (1989).

10.1.1.6.2 Kendall's Tau

Another correlation that can be computed with ordinal data is Kendall's tau, τ, which also uses ranks of data to calculate the correlation coefficient (and has an adjustment for tied ranks). The ranking for Kendall's tau differs from Spearman's rho in the following way. With Kendall's tau, the values for one variable are rank ordered and then the order of the second variable is examined to see how many pairs of values are out of order. A *perfect positive correlation* (+1.0) is achieved with Kendall's tau when *no* scores are out of order, and a *perfect negative correlation* (−1.0) is obtained when *all* scores are out of order. Values for Kendall's tau range from −1.0 to +1.0. Conventions for interpreting the Pearson correlation (e.g., Cohen, 1988) can be applied to Kendall's tau correlation values as well. The sign of the coefficient can be interpreted as with the Pearson: A *negative sign* indicates that as the values for one variable increase, the values for the second variable decrease. A *positive sign* indicates that as one variable increases in value, the value of the second variable also increases.

While similar in some respects, Spearman's rho and Kendall's tau are based on different calculations and thus finding different results is not uncommon. While both are appropriate when ordinal data are being correlated, it has been suggested that Kendall's tau (rather than Spearman's rho) provides a better estimation of the population correlation coefficient value given the sample data (Howell, 2010), especially with smaller sample sizes (e.g., $n < 10$).

10.1.1.6.3 Phi

The phi coefficient, ρ_φ, is appropriate when *both variables are dichotomous in nature* (and is statistically equivalent to the Pearson). Recall from Chapter 1 that a dichotomous variable is one consisting of only two categories (i.e., binary), such as sex, pass/fail, or enrolled/dropped out. Thus, the variables being correlated would be either nominal or ordinal in scale. When correlating two dichotomous variables, one can think of a 2 × 2 contingency

TABLE 10.3

Contingency Table for Phi Correlation

	Enrollment Status		
Student Gender	Dropped Out (0)	Enrolled (1)	
Female (1)	$a = 5$	$b = 20$	$a + b = 25$
Male (0)	$c = 15$	$d = 10$	$c + d = 25$
	$a + c = 20$	$b + d = 30$	$a + b + c + d = 50$

table as previously discussed in Chapter 8. For instance, to determine if there is a relationship among gender and whether students are still enrolled since their freshman year, a contingency table like Table 10.3 can be constructed. Here the columns correspond to the two levels of the enrollment status variable, "enrolled" (coded 1) or "dropped out" (0), and the rows correspond to the two levels of the gender variable, "female" (1) or "male" (0). The cells indicate the frequencies for the particular combinations of the levels of the two variables. If the frequencies in the cells are denoted by letters, then a represents females who dropped out, b represents females who are enrolled, c indicates males who dropped out, and d indicates males who are enrolled.

The equation for computing the phi coefficient is

$$\rho_\phi = \frac{(bc - ad)}{\sqrt{(a+c)(b+d)(a+b)(c+d)}}$$

where ρ_ϕ denotes the population phi coefficient (for consistency's sake, although typically written as ϕ), and r_ϕ denotes the sample phi coefficient using the same equation. Note that the bc product involves the *consistent cells*, where both values are the same, either both 0 or both 1, and the ad product involves the *inconsistent cells*, where both values are different.

Conventions for interpreting the magnitude of Pearson correlation (e.g., Cohen, 1988) can be applied to the phi coefficient as well. However, given the binary nature of the data, the *sign* of the coefficient *cannot* be interpreted as with the Pearson.

Using the example data from Table 10.3, we compute the phi coefficient to be the following:

$$\rho_\phi = \frac{(bc - ad)}{\sqrt{(a+c)(b+d)(a+b)(c+d)}} = \frac{(300 - 50)}{\sqrt{(20)(30)(25)(25)}} = .4082$$

Thus, there is a moderate, positive relationship between gender and enrollment status. We see from the table that a larger proportion of females than males are still enrolled.

To test whether a sample phi correlation is significantly different from zero, we test the following null hypothesis (the alternative hypothesis would be stated as H_1: $\rho_\phi \neq 0$):

$$H_0: \rho_\phi = 0$$

The test statistic is given as:

$$\chi^2 = nr_\phi^2$$

which is distributed as a χ^2 distribution with 1 degree of freedom. From the example, we want to determine whether the sample phi correlation is significantly different from zero at the .05 level of significance. The test statistic is computed as

$$\chi^2 = nr_\phi^2 = (50)(.4082)^2 = 8.3314$$

and the critical value from Table A.3 in the Appendix is $_{.05}\chi_1^2 = 3.84$. Thus, we would *reject the null hypothesis* and conclude that the correlation among gender and enrollment status is significantly different from zero.

10.1.1.6.4 Cramer's Phi

When the variables being correlated have more than two categories, Cramer's phi (Cramer's *V* in SPSS) can be computed. Thus, Cramer's phi is appropriate when *both variables are nominal (and at least one variable has more than two categories)* or *when one variable is nominal and the other variable is ordinal (and at least one variable has more than two categories)*. As with the other correlation coefficients that we have discussed, values range from −1.0 to +1.0. Conventions for interpreting the magnitude of Pearson correlation (e.g., Cohen, 1988) can be applied to Cramer's phi coefficient as well. However, given the nominal nature of one or both of the variables being correlated, the *sign* of Cramer's phi coefficient *cannot* be interpreted as with the Pearson.

10.1.1.6.5 Other Correlations

Other types of correlations have been developed for different combinations of types of variables, but these are rarely used in practice and are unavailable in most statistical packages (e.g., rank biserial and point biserial). Table 10.4 provides suggestions for when different types of correlations are most appropriate. We mention briefly the two other types of correlations in the table: the rank biserial correlation is appropriate when one variable is dichotomous and the other variable is ordinal, whereas the point biserial correlation is appropriate when one variable is dichotomous and the other variable is interval or ratio (statistically equivalent to the Pearson, thus the Pearson correlation can be computed in this situation).

In reviewing Table 10.4, we see that when one variable is ordinal and the second variable is interval or ratio, researchers may choose Pearson, Spearman, or Kendall's tau. In this situation, a researcher using Pearson with an ordinal item is essentially treating the ordinal item as continuous. *Thus, we caution readers in using Pearson with ordinal variables, particularly if there are a small number of levels within the variable.* Our professional opinion when one variable is ordinal and the second interval/ratio is to use Spearman or Kendall's tau unless you have good evidence to support the case that the ordinal variable has properties of a continuous variable (e.g., skew and kurtosis within normality; bell-shaped histogram) and the assumption of linearity for the Pearson correlation coefficient has been met. An ordinal item with five or fewer categories (and many times more than five categories) will likely *not* provide evidence to support the use of Pearson in this situation.

TABLE 10.4

Different Types of Correlation Coefficients

Variable Y	Variable X		
	Nominal	Ordinal	Interval/Ratio
Nominal	Phi (when both variables are dichotomous) or Cramer's V (when one or both variables have more than two categories)	Rank biserial or Cramer's V	Point biserial (Pearson in lieu of point biserial)
Ordinal	Rank biserial or Cramer's V	Spearman or Kendall's tau	Spearman or Kendall's tau or Pearson*
Interval/ratio	Point biserial (Pearson in lieu of point biserial)	Spearman or Kendall's tau or Pearson*	Pearson

*See cautionary note in text when using Pearson in this situation.

10.1.2 Power

Cohen (1988) has a nice series of power tables for determining power and sample size when planning a correlational study. We will later illustrate the use of G*Power for conducting power analysis in correlational studies.

10.1.3 Effect Size

We will preface the discussion of effect size as it relates to correlations by saying that correlation coefficients are, by default, effect size indices. A correlation coefficient provides, for example in the case of the Pearson correlation, the strength and direction of a relationship. We can also interpret that correlation coefficient as a measure of effect.

10.1.3.1 Effect Size for Pearson Correlation Coefficient

Effect size and power are always important, particularly here where sample size plays such a large role. Cohen (1988) proposed using r as a measure of effect size, using the subjective standard (ignoring the sign of the correlation) of $r = .1$ as a weak effect, $r = .3$ as a moderate effect, and $r = .5$ as a strong effect. These standards were developed for the behavioral sciences, but other standards may be used in other areas of inquiry.

10.1.3.2 Effect Size for Two Independent Samples

Cohen (1988) proposed a measure of effect size for the difference between two independent correlations as $q = Z_1 - Z_2$. The subjective standards proposed (ignoring the sign) are $q = .1$ as a weak effect, $q = .3$ as a moderate effect, and $q = .5$ as a strong effect (these are the standards for the behavioral sciences, although standards vary across disciplines).

10.1.3.3 Effect Size for Other Correlations

Cohen's guidelines (1988) for interpreting the correlation in terms of effect size can be applied to Spearman's rho, Kendall's tau, phi, and Cramer's phi correlations, as they can

TABLE 10.5

Correlation Coefficients as Effect Sizes and Interpretations

Effect Size	Interpretation
• Pearson correlation coefficient (r) • Spearman's rho (ρ_s) • Kendall's tau (τ) • Phi (ρ_φ) • Cramer's phi (ϕ_c)	Degree of relationship between two variables: 　• Small effect = .10 　• Medium effect = .30 　• Large effect = .50
Cohen's q	Standardized difference between Fisher's z_r transformed correlations: 　• Small effect = .10 　• Medium effect = .30 　• Large effect = .50

with any other correlation examined. These are, where r denotes other correlation coefficient measures: $r = .1$ as a weak effect, $r = .3$ as a moderate effect, and $r = .5$ as a strong effect.

10.1.4 Assumptions

The Pearson correlation has two assumptions. First, the Pearson correlation is appropriate only when there is a linear relationship assumed between the variables (given that both variables are at least interval in scale). Also, and as we have seen with the other inferential procedures discussed in previous chapters, we need to again assume that the scores of the individuals are independent of one another.

First, as mentioned previously, the Pearson correlation assumes that the relationship among X and Y is a *linear relationship*. In fact, the Pearson correlation, as a measure of relationship, is really a *linear* measure of relationship. Recall from earlier in the chapter the scatterplots to which we fit a straight line. The linearity assumption means that a straight line provides a reasonable fit to the data. *If the relationship is not a linear one, then the linearity assumption is violated.* However, these correlational methods can still be computed, fitting a straight line to the data, albeit inappropriately. The result of such a violation is that the strength of the relationship will be reduced. In other words, the linear correlation will be much closer to zero than the true nonlinear relationship.

For example, there is a perfect curvilinear relationship shown by the data in Figure 10.4 where all of the points fall precisely on the curved line. Something like this might occur if you correlate age with time in the mile run, as younger and older folks would take longer to run this distance than others. If these data are fit by a straight line, then the correlation will be severely reduced, in this case, to a value of zero (i.e., the horizontal straight line that runs through the curved line). This is another good reason to always examine your data. The computer may determine that the Pearson correlation among variables X and Y is small or around zero. However, on examination of the data, you might find that the relationship is indeed nonlinear; thus, you should get to know your data.

Second, the assumption of *independence* applies to correlations. This assumption is met when units or cases are randomly sampled from the population.

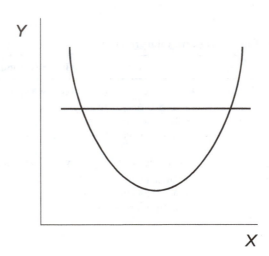

FIGURE 10.4
Nonlinear relationship.

10.2 Computing Bivariate Measures of Association Using SPSS

Next let us see what SPSS has to offer in terms of measures of association using the children–pets example dataset. SPSS has two tools for obtaining measures of association, dependent on the measurement scale of your variables: the Bivariate Correlation program (for computing the Pearson, Spearman's rho, and Kendall's tau) and the Crosstabs program (for computing the Pearson, Spearman's rho, Kendall's tau, phi, Cramer's phi, and several other types of measures of association).

10.2.1. Bivariate Correlations

Step 1. To locate the Bivariate Correlations program, we go to "Analyze" in the top pull-down menu, then select "Correlate," and then "Bivariate." Following the screenshot of Step 1 in Figure 10.5 produces the "Bivariate" dialog box.

   Step 2. Next, from the main "Bivariate Correlations" dialog box, click the variables to correlate (i.e., "Number of children" and "Number of pets") and move them into the "Variables" box by clicking the arrow button. In the bottom half of this dialog box options are available for selecting the type of correlation (*this is where it's important that you understand the measurement scales of your variables so that you are computing the correct correlation coefficient given the scale of measurement of your variables*), one- or two-tailed test (i.e., directional or nondirectional test), and whether to flag statistically significant correlations. For illustrative purposes, we will place a checkmark to generate the "Pearson," "Kendall's tau-b," and "Spearman's rho" correlation coefficients. We will also select the radio button for a "Two-tailed" test of significance and at the very bottom check "Flag significant correlations" (which simply means an asterisk will be placed next to significant correlations in the output). See the screenshot of Step 2 in Figure 10.6.

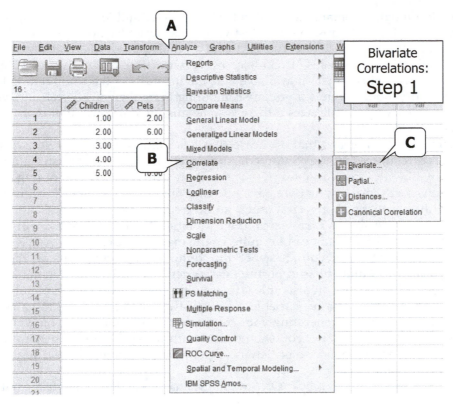

FIGURE 10.5
Bivariate correlations: Step 1.

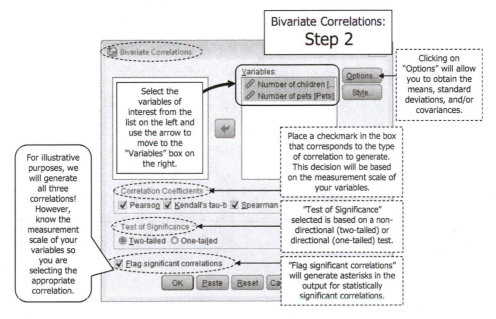

FIGURE 10.6
Bivariate correlations: Step 2.

Step 3 (optional). To obtain means, standard deviations, and/or covariances, as well as options for dealing with missing data (listwise or pairwise deletion), click the "Options" button located in the top-right corner of the main dialog box. Note that the default for dealing with missing values is "Exclude cases pairwise" (see the screenshot of Step 3 in Figure 10.7). This means that all available data are included in the computation for each bivariate correlation, and thus if you are computing more than one correlation, you will end up with varying sample sizes if there is some missing data on one or more variables being correlated.

Listwise deletion means that any case that has missing data is excluded from *all* bivariate correlations that are computed. As an example, let's say we have a total sample size of 10 with three variables (*X*, *Y*, and *Z*) on which we are computing bivariate correlations. Let's also say that we have one case missing a score on *X*. With pairwise deletion, the correlation between *X* and *Y* and the correlation between *X* and *Z* will be based on a sample size of 9. However, the correlation between *Y* and *Z* will be based on a sample size of 10. This can be quite confusing, particularly if you have quite a bit of missing data and if you are generating quite a few correlations, as the sample for the correlations differs based on the missingness! With listwise deletion, all three correlations will be based on a sample size of 9. In essence, you've completely lost the case that has missing data on variable *X* with listwise deletion. As a researcher, you need to consider *prior* to generating your correlation coefficients how you want to deal with missing data. Generally, you should deal with missing prior to generating your correlations as neither pairwise or listwise deletion are considered ideal strategies for addressing missing data.

From the main dialog box, click "OK" to run the analysis and to generate the output.

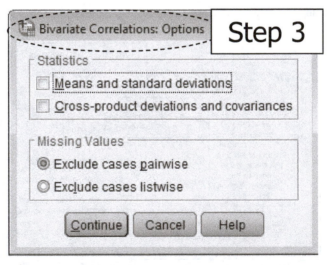

FIGURE 10.7
Bivariate correlations: Step 3.

10.2.1.1 Interpreting the Output

The output for generation of the Pearson and Spearman's rho bivariate correlations between number of children and number of pets appears in Table 10.6. For illustrative purposes, we asked for all three correlations: the Pearson, Kendall's tau-b, and Spearman's rho correlations (although the Pearson is the appropriate correlation given the measurement scales of our variables, we have also generated Kendall's tau-b and Spearman's rho so that the output can be reviewed). Thus, the top Correlations box gives the Pearson results and the bottom Correlations box provides Kendall's tau and Spearman's rho results. In both cases the output presents the correlation, sample size (N in SPSS language, although usually denoted as n by everyone else), observed level of significance, and asterisks denoting statistically significant correlations. In reviewing Table 10.6, we see that SPSS does not provide any output in terms of confidence intervals (illustrated in the next section), power, or effect size. Later in the chapter, we illustrate the use of G*Power for computing power.

TABLE 10.6

SPSS Results for Pearson's Correlation Coefficient

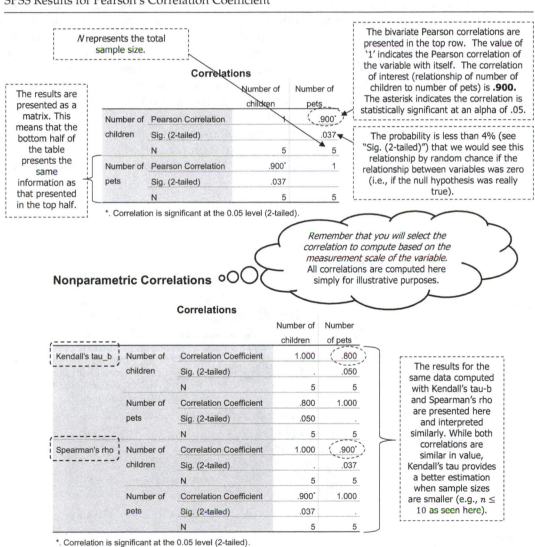

*. Correlation is significant at the 0.05 level (2-tailed).

Effect size is easily interpreted from the correlation coefficient value utilizing Cohen (1988) subjective standards previously described.

10.2.1.2 *Generating Confidence Intervals for the Effect Size (Pearson Correlation Coefficient)*

Confidence intervals (CI) can be computed for correlations. *Larger CI suggest lower precision, and smaller CI reflect higher precision.* An excellent online calculator for computing all types of effect sizes and their confidence intervals is provided by Dr. David B. Wilson and is available through the Campbell Collaboration (see https://campbellcollaboration.org/research-resources/effect-size-calculator.html). Although designed for use when conducting meta-analyses, the online calculator comes in handy whenever an effect size and its CI are desired.

Let's look at the example using the correlation we just generated with children and pets. Correlating the number of children and the number of pets, we find a Pearson correlation of .900. Using Campbell's effect size calculator for a correlation, along with the sample size, we find the 95% CI of (.0861, .9934) (see Figure 10.8). Because the confidence interval does not contain 0, our null value (i.e., reflecting no relationship), this provides evidence to suggest a statistically significant relationship between the number of children and the number of pets. Also on the output, we see Fisher's Z_r and its related confidence interval. The sampling distribution of Pearson is not normally distributed. Thus, to compute confidence intervals for a Pearson correlation, r is converted to Fisher's Z_r, the confidence interval using Fisher's Z_r is then computed, and the Fisher's Z_r confidence interval values are then converted back to Pearson's r. Fisher's Z_r may sound familiar as we discussed this in relation to inferences for two independent samples as well!

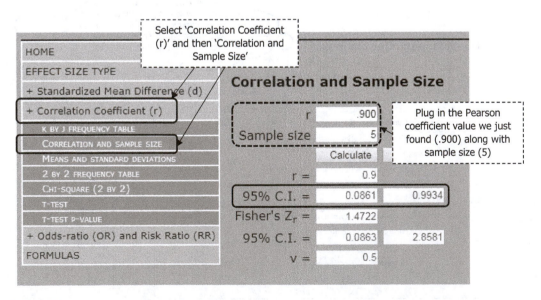

FIGURE 10.8
Confidence interval for the Pearson correlation coefficient.

10.2.2 Using Crosstabs to Compute Correlations

The Crosstabs program has already been discussed in Chapter 8, but it can also be used for obtaining many measures of association (specifically Spearman's rho, Kendall's tau, Pearson, phi and Cramer's phi). We will illustrate the use of Crosstabs for two nominal variables, thus generating phi and Cramer's phi.

Step 1. To compute phi or Cramer's phi correlations, go to "Analyze" in the top pulldown, then select "Descriptive Statistics," and then select the "Crosstabs" procedure. See the screenshot for Step 1 in Figure 10.9.

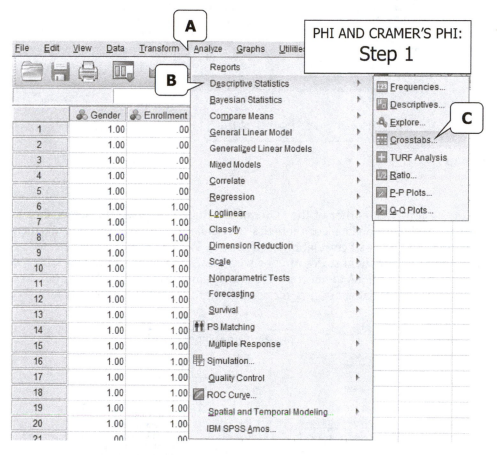

FIGURE 10.9
Phi and Cramer's phi: Step 1.

Step 2. Select the dependent variable (if applicable; many times there is not a dependent and independent variable, per se, with bivariate correlations, and in those cases which variable is *X* and which variable is *Y* is largely irrelevant) and move it into the "Row(s)" box by clicking the arrow key. Here we have used enrollment status as the dependent variable (1 = enrolled; 0 = not enrolled). Then select the independent variable and move it into the "Column(s)" box. In this example, gender is the independent variable (0 = male; 1 = female). See the screenshot for Step 2 in Figure 10.10.

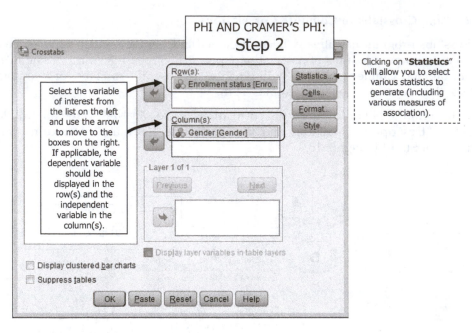

FIGURE 10.10
Phi and Cramer's phi: Step 2.

Step 3. In the top-right corner of the "Crosstabs" dialog box (see the screenshot in Figure 10.10), click the button labeled "Statistics." From here, you can select various measures of association (i.e., types of correlation coefficients). Which correlation is selected should depend on the measurement scales of your variables. With two nominal variables, one of the appropriate correlations to select is "Phi and Cramer's *V*." Click "Continue" to return to the main Crosstabs dialog box. See the screenshot for Step 3 in Figure 10.11.

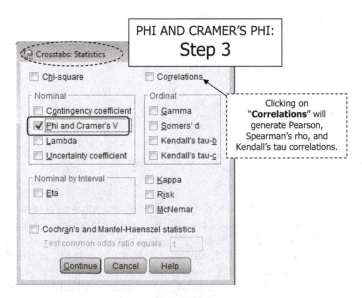

FIGURE 10.11
Phi and Cramer's phi: Step 3.

From the main dialog box, click on "OK" to run the analysis and generate the output.

10.2.2.1 Interpreting the Output

The output for generation of the phi and Cramer's phi correlation coefficients using gender and enrollment status data appears in Table 10.7. Because we generated this using the Crosstab feature, our first output includes a cross-tabulation of gender by enrollment status. We see the cell, marginal, and total sample sizes. For example, there were 15 males who dropped out and 15 females who enrolled. The next table provides the correlation coefficient values. We have a 2 × 2 table, so phi and Cramer's phi results in the same value: .350. At an alpha of .05, this is a statistically significant correlation ($p = .019$). In reviewing Table 10.7, we see that SPSS does not provide any output in terms of confidence intervals (which will be discussed in the next section), power, or effect size. Later in the chapter, we illustrate the use of G*Power for computing power, however G*Power does not have a direct way to estimate power for phi or Cramer's phi. Effect size is easily interpreted from the correlation coefficient value utilizing Cohen (1988) subjective standards previously described. Remember that the sign for phi and Cramer's phi is irrelevant given the nominal nature of the data.

TABLE 10.7

SPSS Results for Phi and Cramer's Phi Correlations

Enrollment status * Gender Crosstabulation

Count

| | | Gender | | |
		Male	Female	Total
Enrollment status	Dropped out	15	5	20
	Enrolled	10	15	25
Total		25	20	45

> Since we computed our correlation using the Crosstab feature, we are provided a crosstab of our variables showing the sample sizes per cell as well as marginal and total sample sizes.

Symmetric Measures

		Value	Approximate Significance
Nominal by Nominal	Phi	.350	.019
	Cramer's V	.350	.019
N of Valid Cases		45	

> The 'approximate significance' is our *p* value. In this case, we have a 2 x 2 table so phi and Cramer's phi results in the same correlation coefficient value (.350), and this is statistically significant at an alpha of .05 ($p = .019$).

> Remember that you will select the correlation to compute based on the measurement scale of the variable and generally will only present results from one procedure. In other words, we would present either phi or Cramer's phi but not generally both.

10.2.2.2 Generating Confidence Intervals for the Effect Size (Phi and Cramer's Phi)

Confidence intervals (CI) can be computed for correlations. *Larger CI suggest lower precision, and smaller CI reflect higher precision.* An excellent online calculator for computing all types of effect sizes and their confidence intervals is provided by Dr. David B. Wilson and is available through the Campbell Collaboration (see https://campbellcollaboration.org/research-resources/effect-size-calculator.html). Although designed for use when conducting meta-analyses, the online calculator comes in handy whenever an effect size and its CI are desired.

Let's look at the example using the correlation we just generated with gender and enrollment. Correlating the gender and enrollment, a 2 × 2 table, we find phi and Cramer's phi of .350. Using Campbell's effect size calculator for a correlation, along with the sample size, we find the 95% CI of (.0519, .5908) (see Figure 10.12). Because the confidence interval does not contain 0, our null value (i.e., reflecting no relationship), this provides evidence to suggest a statistically significant relationship between gender and enrollment status. Also on the output, we see Fisher's Z_r and its related confidence interval. As noted previously, Fisher's Z_r transformation is applied so that the confidence interval can be computed.

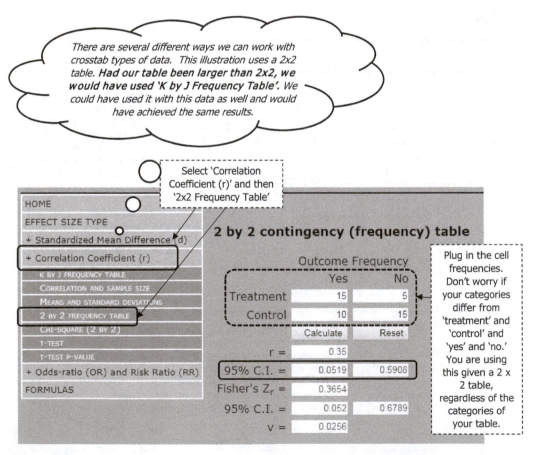

FIGURE 10.12
Confidence interval for phi or Cramer's phi correlation coefficient.

10.3 Computing Bivariate Measures of Association Using R

Next we consider **R** for a bivariate measures of association model. Note that the scripts are provided within the blocks with additional annotation to assist in understanding how the command works. Should you want to write reminder notes and annotation to yourself as you write the commands in **R** (and we highly encourage doing so), remember that any text that follows a hashtag (i.e., #) is annotation only and not part of the **R** script. Thus, you can write annotations directly into **R** with hashtags. We encourage this practice so that when you call up the commands in the future, you'll understand what the various lines of code are doing. You may think you'll remember what you did. However, trust us. There is a good chance that you won't. Thus, consider it best practice when using **R** to annotate heavily!

10.3.1 Reading Data Into R

```
getwd()
```

R is always pointed to a directory on your computer. To find out which directory it is pointed to, run this "get working directory" function. We will assume that we need to change the working directory, and will use the next line of code to set the working directory to the desired path.

```
setwd("E:/FolderName")
```

To set the working directory, change what is in quotation marks to your file location. Also, if you are copying the directory name, it will copy in slashes. You will need to change the slash (i.e., \) to a forward slash (i.e., /). Note that you need your destination name within quotation marks in the parentheses.

```
Ch10_kidspets <- read.csv("Ch10_kidspets.csv")
```

The *read.csv* function reads our data into **R**. What's to the left of the <- will be what the data will be called in **R**. In this example, we're calling the R dataframe "Ch10_kidspets." What's to the right of the <- tells **R** to find this particular .csv file. In this example, our file is called "Ch10_kidspets.csv." Make sure the extension (i.e., .csv) is included in your script. Also note that the name of your file should be in quotation marks within the parentheses.

```
names(Ch10_kidspets)
```

The *names* function will produce a list of variable names for each dataframe as follows. This is a good check to make sure your data have been read in correctly.

```
[1] "Children" "Pets"
View(Ch10_kidspets)
```

The *View* function will let you view the dataset in spreadsheet format in RStudio.

```
summary(Ch10_kidspets)
```

The *summary* function will produce basic descriptive statistics on all the variables in your dataframe. This is a great way to quickly check to see if the data have been read in correctly and to get a feel for your data, if you haven't already. The output from the summary statement for this dataframe looks like this.

```
   Children        Pets
Min.   :1     Min.   : 2
1st Qu.:2     1st Qu.: 4
Median :3     Median : 6
Mean   :3     Mean   : 6
3rd Qu.:4     3rd Qu.: 8
Max.   :5     Max.   :10
```

FIGURE 10.13
Reading data into **R**.

10.3.2 Generating Correlation Coefficients

```
cor.test(Ch10_kidspets$Children, Ch10_kidspets$Pets,
use = "everything",
method = "pearson",
conf.level = 0.95)
```

The *cor.test* function will compute a Pearson (i.e., *method = "pearson"*) correlation coefficient for variables children and pets (i.e., "Ch10_kidspets$Children," "Ch10_kidspets$Pets") and related *p* value using an alpha of .05 (i.e., *conf.level* = .95). The *use = "everything"* command will compute the correlation using all available data ("NA" will be the output if any variables have missing data; we could have used *complete.obs* for listwise deletion or *pairwise.complete.obs* for pairwise deletion, among other options). Because we have no missing data, the method for "use" will not matter; however, if you have missing data, be thoughtful in how you approach this!

Note: To compute Spearman or Kendall's tau, simply change the method (i.e., *method = "pearson"*) to *method = "kendall"* or *method = "spearman,"* using all lowercase letters.

Our output looks like this. We see our observed probability, *p* = .037, which is statistically significant at alpha of .05. We have a 95% confidence interval of the correlation coefficient (.086, .993), and our Pearson correlation coefficient, *r*, is .90.

Pearson's product-moment correlation

data: Ch10_kidspets$Children and Ch10_kidspets$Pets

t = 3.5762, df = 3, **p-value = 0.03739**

alternative hypothesis: true correlation is not equal to 0

95 percent confidence interval:
0.08610194 0.99343752

sample estimates:
cor
0.9

FIGURE 10.14
Generating correlation coefficients in **R**.

10.4 Data Screening

As noted previously, the assumptions of the Pearson correlation coefficient are linearity and independence. While the assumption of independence is based on how the data are sampled (with random sampling meeting the assumption of independence), we can use our data to examine the extent to which we meet the assumption of linearity.

10.4.1 Scatterplots to Examine Linearity Using SPSS

Step 1. As alluded to earlier in the chapter, understanding the extent to which linearity is a reasonable assumption is an important first step prior to computing a Pearson correlation coefficient. To generate a scatterplot, go to "Graphs" in the top pulldown menu. From there, select "Legacy Dialogs," then "Scatter/Dot" (see the screenshot for Step 1 in Figure 10.15).

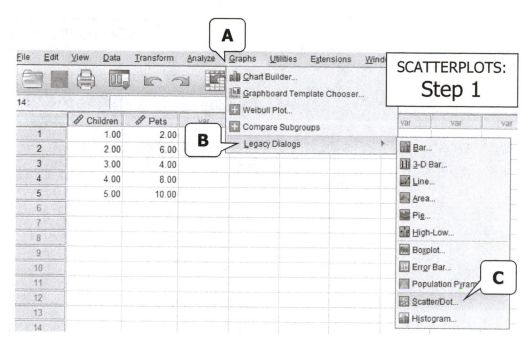

FIGURE 10.15
Generating a scatterplot: Step 1.

Step 2. This will bring up the "Scatter/Dot" dialog box (see the screenshot for Step 2 in Figure 10.16). The default selection is "Simple Scatter," and this is the option we will use. Then click "Define."

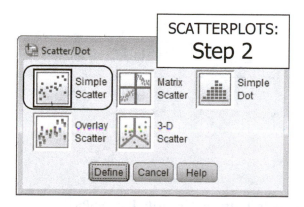

FIGURE 10.16
Generating a scatterplot: Step 2.

Step 3. This will bring up the "Simple Scatterplot" dialog box (see the screenshot for Step 3 in Figure 10.17). Click the dependent variable (e.g., number of pets) and move it into the "Y Axis" box by clicking on the arrow. Click the independent variable (e.g., number of children) and move it into the "X Axis" box by clicking on the arrow. Then click "OK."

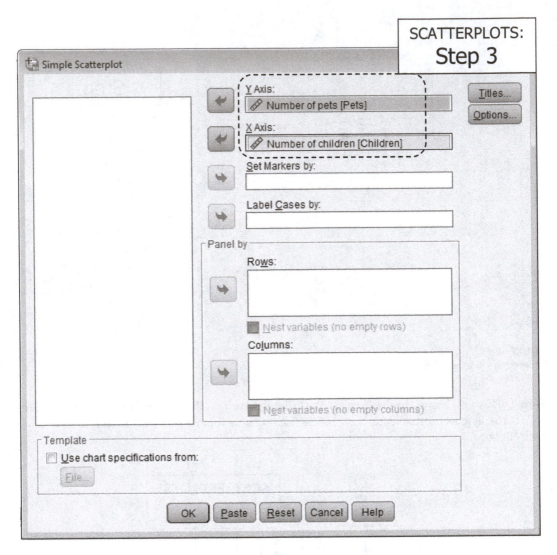

FIGURE 10.17
Generating a scatterplot: Step 3.

10.4.2 Hypothesis Tests to Examine Linearity Using SPSS

Another way to test for linearity is to conduct a hypothesis test using curve estimation to determine if there is a statistically significant linear (versus quadratic or cubic) relationship.

Step 1. To conduct curve estimation, go to "Analyze" in the top pulldown, then select "Regression," and then select the "Curve estimation" procedure (see the screenshot for Step 1 in Figure 10.18).

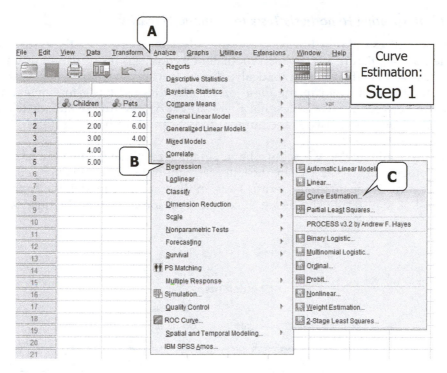

FIGURE 10.18
Hypothesis test for linearity: Step 1.

Step 2. In many cases, there may not be a dependent and independent variable, per se, when conducting a bivariate correlation. In this case, that's fine as we are simply checking the assumption of linearity. Thus, move one variable to the "**Dependent(s)**" box and the second variable to the "**Independent Variable**" box. Under "**Models**," select "Linear," "Quadratic," and "Cubic" (see the screenshot for Step 2 in Figure 10.19).

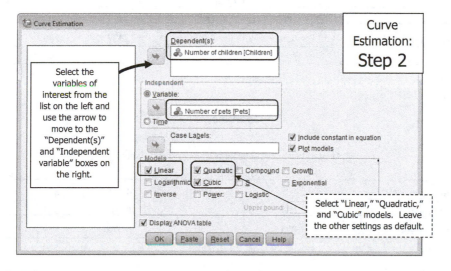

FIGURE 10.19
Hypothesis test for linearity: Step 2.

10.4.2.1 Interpreting Hypothesis Tests to Examine Linearity

For purposes of examining linearity, we are only concerned with the output for the "coefficients" (see Figure 10.20). Each coefficient hypothesis test is estimating whether the standardized coefficient is statistically different from zero. Finding statistical significance for the coefficient in the *linear model* provides evidence to suggest a linear relationship between the variables. For this illustration, we find a statistically significant linear relationship between the number of pets and number of children, $t = 3.576$, $p = .037$.

For the quadratic model, we see we have parameter estimates for number of pets as well as "Number of pets ** 2," where the latter term indicates the number of pets has been squared (i.e., this is the quadratic term). Thus, in the quadratic model, the squared term is of interest. A statistically significant quadratic term indicates that the quadratic trend

Linear

Coefficients

| | Unstandardized Coefficients | | Standardized Coefficients | | |
	B	Std. Error	Beta	t	Sig.
Number of pets	.450	.126	.900	3.576	**.037**
(Constant)	.300	.835		.359	.743

Quadratic

Coefficients

| | Unstandardized Coefficients | | Standardized Coefficients | | |
	B	Std. Error	Beta	t	Sig.
Number of pets	.236	.781	.471	.302	.791
Number of pets ** 2	.018	.064	.437	.280	**.806**
(Constant)	.800	2.051		.390	.734

Cubic

Coefficients

| | Unstandardized Coefficients | | Standardized Coefficients | | |
	B	Std. Error	Beta	t	Sig.
Number of pets	2.202	3.843	4.405	.573	.669
Number of pets ** 2	-.357	.713	-8.737	-.501	.704
Number of pets ** 3	.021	.039	5.372	.529	**.690**
(Constant)	-2.000	5.880		-.340	.791

FIGURE 10.20
Hypothesis test for linearity: Results.

(i.e., quadratic relationship) is statistically significant beyond the linear relationship. In this illustration, we find a nonstatistically significant quadratic relationship, $t = .280$, $p = .806$, which provides evidence to suggest there is *not* a quadratic relationship between our variables.

Next, we examine the results of the cubic model. We find that a new term has been estimated in this model, specifically "Number of pets ** 3." This term represented the cubic term. This model is estimating the extent to which there is a cubic trend, above and beyond the linear and quadratic relationships. A statistically significant cubic term suggests evidence that there is a cubic relationship between the variables. In this illustration, find a nonstatistically significant relationship, $t = .529$, $p = .690$. Thus, we have evidence to suggest that there is not a cubic relationship between our variables.

Looking at all three models—linear, quadratic, and cubic—we have evidence to suggest linearity between our variables given the nonstatistically significant nonlinear quadratic and cubic trends.

10.4.3 Scatterplots to Examine Linearity Using R

```
plot(Ch10_kidspets$Children, Ch10_kidspets$Pets,
xlab = "Number of Children",
ylab = "Number of Pets",
main = "Scatterplot")
```

The *plot* function can be used to generate a scatterplot of the variables "Children" and "Pets" from the "Ch10_kidspets" dataframe (i.e., using the command *Ch10_kidspets$Children, Ch10_kidspets$Pets* will define the variables to plot). We can label the *X* and *Y* axis as "Number of Children" and "Number of Pets," respectively, using the *xlab* and *ylab* commands. Using the *main* command, we can title the graph "Scatterplot."

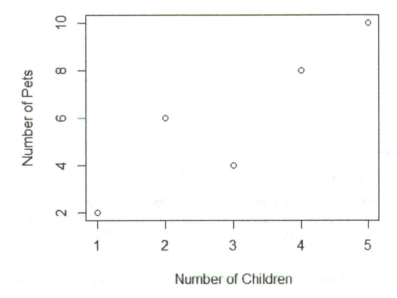

Figure 10.21
Generating scatterplots in **R**.

10.4.3.1 Interpreting Linearity Evidence

Scatterplots are also often examined to determine visual evidence of linearity prior to computing Pearson correlations. Scatterplots are graphs that depict coordinate values of X and Y. *Linearity is suggested by points that fall in a straight line or relatively straight line.* This line may suggest a *positive relation* (as scores on X increase, scores on Y increase, and vice versa), a *negative relation* (as scores on X increase, scores on Y decrease, and vice versa), *little or no relation* (relatively random display of points), or a *polynomial relation* (e.g., curvilinear). In this example, our scatterplot generally suggests evidence of linearity and, more specifically, a positive relationship between number of children and number of pets (see Figure 10.21, generated in **R,** and Figure 10.22, generated in SPSS). Thus, proceeding to compute a bivariate Pearson correlation coefficient is reasonable.

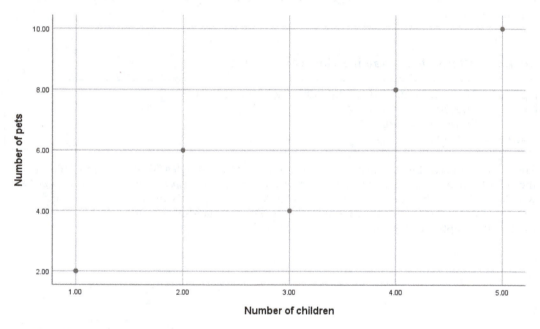

FIGURE 10.22
Scatterplot.

10.5 Power Using G*Power

A priori and post hoc power could again be determined using the specialized software described previously in this text (e.g., G*Power), or you can consult *a priori* power tables (e.g., Cohen, 1988). As an illustration, we use G*Power to compute the post hoc power of our test.

10.5.1.1 Post Hoc Power for the Pearson Bivariate Correlation Using G*Power

The first thing that must be done when using G*Power for computing post hoc power is to select the correct test family. In our case, we conducted a Pearson correlation.

To find the Pearson, we will select "Tests" in the top pulldown menu, then "Correlations and regression," and then "Correlations: Bivariate normal model." Once that selection is made, the "Test family" automatically changes to "Exact." See the screenshot for Step 1 in Figure 10.23.

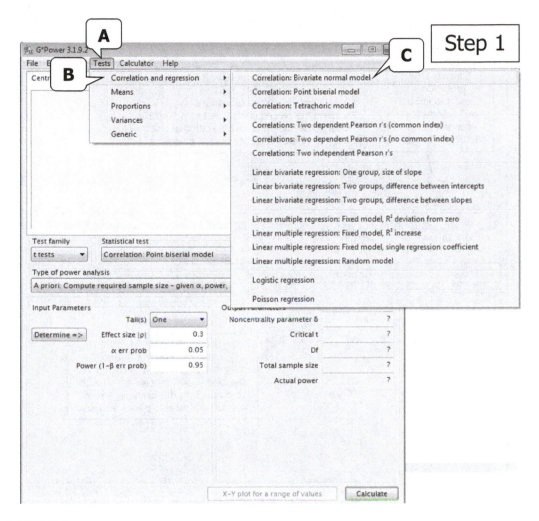

FIGURE10.23
Power: Step 1.

The "Type of power analysis" desired then needs to be selected. To compute post hoc power, select "Post hoc: Compute achieved power—given α, sample size, and effect size." See the screenshot for Step 2 in Figure 10.24.

The "Input Parameters" must then be specified. The first parameter is specification of the number of tail(s). For a directional hypothesis, "One" is selected, and for a nondirectional hypothesis, "Two" is selected. In our example, we chose a nondirectional hypothesis and thus will select "Two" tails. We then input the observed correlation coefficient value in the box for "Correlation ρ H1." In this example, our Pearson correlation coefficient value was .90.

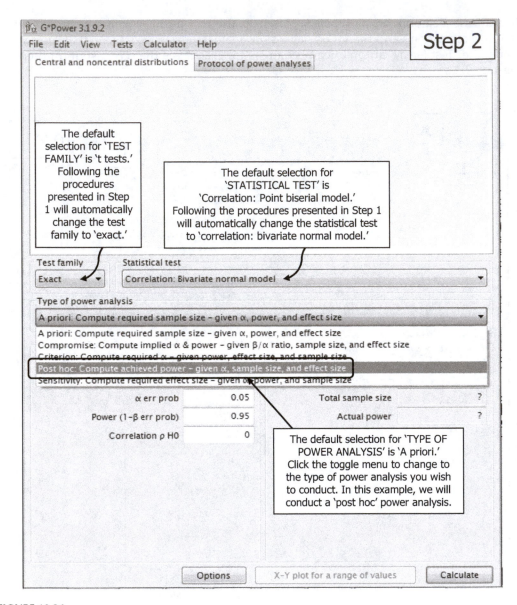

FIGURE 10.24
Power: Step 2.

The alpha level we tested at was .05, the total sample size was 5, and the "Correlation ρ H0" will remain as the default 0 (this is the correlation value expected if the null hypothesis is true; in other words, there is zero correlation between variables given the null hypothesis). Once the parameters are specified, simply click "Calculate" to generate the power results. See the screenshot for Step 3 in Figure 10.25.

The "Output Parameters" provide the relevant statistics given the input just specified. In this example, we were interested in determining post hoc power for a Pearson correlation given a two-tailed test, with a computed correlation value of .90, an alpha level of .05, total sample size of 5, and a null hypothesis correlation value of zero.

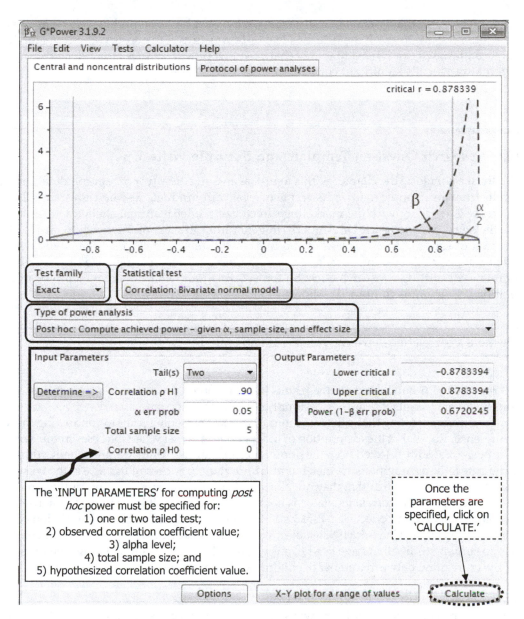

FIGURE 10.25
Post hoc power results.

Based on those criteria, the post hoc power was .67 (see Figure 10.25). In other words, with a two-tailed test, an observed Pearson correlation of .90, an alpha level of .05, sample size of 5, and a null hypothesis correlation value of zero, the power of our test was approximately .67—the probability of rejecting the null hypothesis when it is really false (in this case, the probability that there is *not* a zero correlation between our variables) was 67%, which is slightly less than what would be usually considered sufficient power (sufficient power is often .80 or above). Keep in mind that conducting power analysis *a priori* is recommended so that you avoid a situation where, post hoc, you find that the sample size was not sufficient to reach the desired level of power (given the observed parameters). In our situation, we don't need to worry that post hoc power was less than desirable as we found a statistically significant correlation.

10.6 Research Question Template and Example Write-Up

Finally, we conclude the chapter with a template and an APA-style paragraph detailing the results from an example dataset. As you may recall, our graduate research assistant, Challie Lenge, was working with the marketing director of the local animal shelter, Dr. Amberly. Challie's task was to assist Dr. Amberly in generating the test of inference to answer her research question, *"Is there a relationship between the number of children in a family and the number of pets?"* A Pearson correlation was the test of inference suggested by Challie. A template for writing a research question for a correlation (regardless of which type of correlation coefficient is computed) follows:

Is there a correlation between [variable 1] and [variable 2]?

It may be helpful to include in the results information on the extent to which the assumptions were met (recall there are two assumptions: independence and linearity). This assists the reader in understanding that you were thorough in data screening prior to conducting the test of inference. Recall that the assumption of independence is met when the cases in our sample have been randomly selected from the population. One or two sentences are usually sufficient to indicate if the assumptions are met. It is also important to address effect size in the write-up. Correlations are unique in that they are already effect size measures, so computing an effect size in addition to the correlation value is not needed. However, it is desirable to interpret the correlation value as an effect size. Effect size is easily interpreted from the correlation coefficient value utilizing Cohen's (1988) subjective standards previously described or in comparison to similar studies that have used like variables. Here is an example paragraph of results for the correlation between number of children and number of pets.

A Pearson correlation coefficient was computed to determine if there is a relationship between the number of children in a family and the number of pets in the family. The test was conducted using an alpha of .05. The null hypothesis was that the relationship would be zero. The assumption of independence was met via random selection. The assumption of linearity was reasonable given a visual review of a scatterplot of the variables along with hypothesis tests to examine quadratic and cubic trends (neither of which were statistically significant).

The Pearson correlation coefficient between children and pets is .90 (*CI* .09, .99), which is positive, is interpreted as a large effect size (Cohen, 1988), and is statistically different from zero ($r = .90, n = 5, p = .037$). Thus, the null hypothesis that the correlation is zero was rejected at the .05 level of significance. There is a strong, positive correlation between the number of children in a family and the number of pets in the family.

10.7 Additional Resources

This chapter has provided an introduction to conducting correlational analysis. However, there are a number of areas related to correlation, particularly as it relates to correlation as a precursor to regression, that space limitations prevent us from delving into. Those who are interested in general coverage of correlation as a precursor to regression may wish to review Sahay (2016).

Problems

Conceptual Problems

1. The variance of X is 9, the variance of Y is 4, and the covariance between X and Y is 2. What is r_{XY}?
    a. .039
    b. .056
    c. .233
    d. .333

2. The standard deviation of X is 20, the standard deviation of Y is 50, and the covariance between X and Y is 30. What is r_{XY}?
    a. .030
    b. .080
    c. .150
    d. .200

3. Which of the following correlation coefficients, each obtained from a sample of 1000 children, indicates the *weakest* relationship?
    a. −.90
    b. −.30
    c. +.20
    d. +.80

4. Which of the following correlation coefficients, each obtained from a sample of 1000 children, indicates the *strongest* relationship?
    a. −.90
    b. −.30
    c. +.20
    d. +.80

5. If the relationship between two variables is linear, which of the following is necessarily true?
    a. The relation can be most accurately represented by a straight line.
    b. All the points will fall on a curved line.
    c. The relationship is best represented by a curved line.
    d. All the points must fall exactly on a straight line.

6. True or false? In testing the null hypothesis that a correlation is equal to zero, the critical value decreases as α decreases.

7. True or false? If the variances of X and Y are increased, but their covariance remains constant, the value of r_{XY} will be unchanged.

8. We compute $r_{XY} = .50$ for a sample of students on variables X and Y. I assert that if the low-scoring students on variable X are removed, then the new value of r_{XY} would most likely be less than .50. Am I correct?

9. Two variables are linearly related such that there is a perfect relationship between X and Y. I assert that r_{XY} must be equal to either +1.00 or −1.00. Am I correct?

10. True or false? If the number of credit cards owned and the number of cars owned are *strongly positively* correlated, then those with more credit cards tend to own more cars.

11. True or false? If the number of credit cards owned and the number of cars owned are *strongly negatively* correlated, then those with more credit cards tend to own more cars.

12. True or false? If X correlates significantly with Y, then X is necessarily a cause of Y.

13. A researcher wishes to correlate the grade students earned from a pass/fail course (i.e., pass or fail) with their cumulative grade point average. Which of the following is the most appropriate correlation coefficient to examine this relationship?

    a. Pearson

    b. Spearman's rho or Kendall's tau

    c. Phi

    d. None of the above

14. True or false? If both X and Y are ordinal variables, then the most appropriate measure of association is the Pearson.

15. A researcher is correlating a 5-point Likert item with a binary variable. Which of the following correlation coefficients is appropriate?

    a. Cramer's phi

    b. Kendall's tau

    c. Pearson

    d. Phi

16. A researcher is correlating home ownership (own or do not own) with the number of hours worked per week (measured in whole numbers). Which of the following correlation coefficients is appropriate?

    a. Cramer's phi

    b. Kendall's tau

    c. Pearson

    d. Phi

17. True or false? When restriction of range occurs, the strength of the correlation is usually stronger.

18. Which of the following reduce the magnitude of a correlation coefficient? Select all that apply.

    a. Outliers

    b. Restriction of range

c. Variables that have little variability

d. Variables that are causally related

Answers to Conceptual Problems

1. **d** $(2/(3)(2) = .3333)$

3. **c** (Weakest means correlation nearest to 0.)

5. **a** (A linear relationship will fall into a reasonably linear scatterplot, although not necessarily a perfectly straight line.)

7. **False** (The correlation will become smaller; see the correlation equation involving covariance.)

9. **Yes** (A perfect relationship implies a perfect correlation, assuming linearity.)

11. **False** (In negative relationships, the *higher* the score on one variable, the *lower* the score on the other variable tends to be.)

13. **a** (The Pearson can be used when one variable is dichotomous, such as pass/fail, and the other variable is at least interval in scale, such as GPA.)

15. **a** (Cramer's phi is appropriate when one variable is nominal, such as a binary variable, and the other variable is ordinal, like a 5-point Likert item.)

17. **False** (When scores on one or both variables that are being correlated are restricted based on the nature of the sample or population, the strength of the correlation is usually decreased.)

Computational Problems

1. You are given the following pairs of sample scores on X (number of credit cards in your possession) and Y (number of those credit cards with balances):

X	Y
5	4
6	1
4	3
8	7
2	2

   e. Graph a scatterplot of the data.

   f. Compute the covariance.

   g. Determine the Pearson product-moment correlation coefficient.

   h. Determine the Spearman's rho correlation coefficient.

2. If $r_{XY} = .17$ for a random sample of size 84, test the hypothesis that the population Pearson is significantly different from 0 (conduct a two-tailed test at the .05 level of significance).

3. If $r_{XY} = .60$ for a random sample of size 30, test the hypothesis that the population Pearson is significantly different from 0 (conduct a two-tailed test at the .05 level of significance).

4. The correlation between vocabulary size and mother's age is .50 for 12 rural children and .85 for 17 inner-city children. Does the correlation for rural children differ from that of the inner-city children at the .05 level of significance?

5. You are given the following pairs of sample scores on X (number of coins in possession) and Y (number of bills in possession):

X	Y
2	1
3	3
4	5
5	5
6	3
7	1

a. Graph a scatterplot of the data.

b. Describe the relationship between X and Y.

c. What do you think the Pearson correlation will be?

6. Six adults were assessed on the number of minutes it took to read a government report (X) and the number of items correct on a test of the content of that report (Y). Use the data below to determine the Pearson correlation and the effect size.

X	Y
10	17
8	17
15	13
12	16
14	15
16	12

7. Ten kindergarten children were observed on the number of letters written in proper form (given 26 letters) (X) and the number of words that the child could read (given 50 words) (Y). Use the data below to determine the Pearson correlation and the effect size.

X	Y
10	5
16	8
22	40
8	15
12	28
20	37
17	29
21	30
15	18
9	4

8. Ten adults responded to "I am the life of the party" (X) and "I start conversations" (Y), both based on 5-point Likert scales. Use the data below to determine Kendall's tau correlation, and the strength of the correlation as an effect size.

X	Y
3	5
1	2
5	5
3	3
4	5
2	4
3	2
1	5
3	4
1	5

9. Ten adults responded to "I pay attention to detail" (X) and "I get things done right away" (Y), both based on 5-point Likert scales. Use the data below to determine Kendall's tau correlation, and the strength of the correlation as an effect size.

X	Y
4	5
2	1
5	5
5	1
4	3
3	5
3	3
5	5
4	2
4	5

Answers to Computational Problems

1. (a) Scatterplot shown below; (b) covariance = 3.250; (c) *r* = .631; (d) *r* = .400.

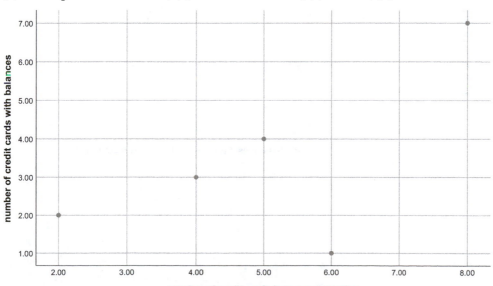

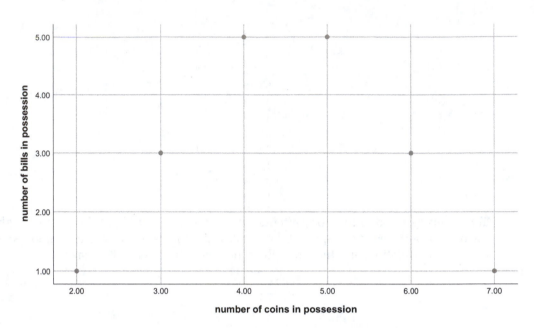

3. $t = 3.9686$, critical values are approximately -2.048 and $+2.048$, reject H_0.

5. (a) Scatterplot shown below; (b) nonlinear relationship; (c) $r =$ approximately zero.

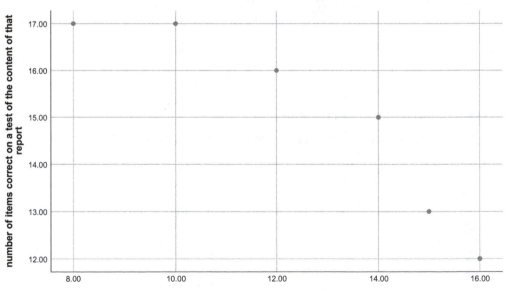

7. (a) $r = .78$; (b) strong effect.

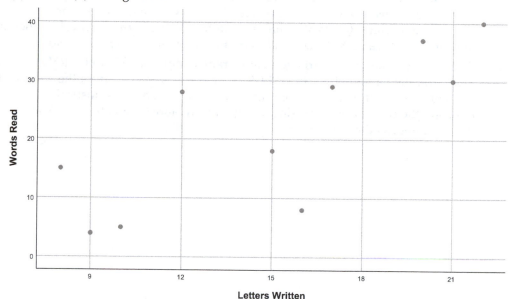

9. Kendall's tau = .206, p = .475. This is not a statistically significant correlation. Using Cohen's criteria, this is a weak to moderate relationship.

Interpretive Problem

1. Select two interval/ratio variables from the survey1 dataset accessible from the website. Use SPSS or **R** to generate the appropriate correlation, determine statistical significance, interpret the correlation value (including interpretation as an effect size), and examine and interpret the scatterplot.

2. Select two interval/ratio variables from the IPEDS2017 dataset accessible from the website. Use SPSS or **R** to generate the appropriate correlation, determine statistical significance, interpret the correlation value (including interpretation as an effect size), and examine and interpret the scatterplot.

3. Select two ordinal variables from the survey1 dataset accessible from the website. Use SPSS or **R** to generate the appropriate correlation, determine statistical significance, interpret the correlation value (including interpretation as an effect size), and examine and interpret the scatterplot.

4. Select one ordinal variable and one interval/ratio variable from the survey1 dataset accessible from the website. Use SPSS or **R** to generate the appropriate correlation, determine statistical significance, interpret the correlation value (including interpretation as an effect size), and examine and interpret the scatterplot.

5. Select one dichotomous variable and one interval/ratio variable from the survey1 dataset accessible from the website. Use SPSS or **R** to generate the appropriate correlation, determine statistical significance, interpret the correlation value (including interpretation as an effect size), and examine and interpret the scatterplot.

6. Select the dichotomous variable "land grant institution" [LANDGRNT] and one interval/ratio variable from the IPEDS2017 dataset accessible from the website. Use SPSS or **R** to generate the appropriate correlation, determine statistical significance, interpret the correlation value (including interpretation as an effect size), and examine and interpret the scatterplot.

Appendix

TABLE A.1

Standard Unit Normal Distribution.

Z	P(z)	Z	P(z)	Z	P(z)	Z	P(z)
0.00	0.5000000	0.31	0.6217195	0.62	0.7323711	0.93	0.8238145
0.01	0.5039894	0.32	0.6255158	0.63	0.7356527	0.94	0.8263912
0.02	0.5079783	0.33	0.6293	0.64	0.7389137	0.95	0.8289439
0.03	0.5119665	0.34	0.6330717	0.65	0.7421539	0.96	0.8314724
0.04	0.5159534	0.35	0.6368307	0.66	0.7453731	0.97	0.8339768
0.05	0.5199388	0.36	0.6405764	0.67	0.7485711	0.98	0.8364569
0.06	0.5239222	0.37	0.6443088	0.68	0.7517478	0.99	0.8389129
0.07	0.5279032	0.38	0.6480273	0.69	0.7549029	1.00	0.8413447
0.08	0.5318814	0.39	0.6517317	0.70	0.7580363	1.01	0.8437524
0.09	0.5358564	0.40	0.6554217	0.71	0.7611479	1.02	0.8461358
0.10	0.5398278	0.41	0.659097	0.72	0.7642375	1.03	0.848495
0.11	0.5437953	0.42	0.6627573	0.73	0.7673049	1.04	0.85083
0.12	0.5477584	0.43	0.6664022	0.74	0.77035	1.05	0.8531409
0.13	0.5517168	0.44	0.6700314	0.75	0.7733726	1.06	0.8554277
0.14	0.55567	0.45	0.6736448	0.76	0.7763727	1.07	0.8576903
0.15	0.5596177	0.46	0.6772419	0.77	0.7793501	1.08	0.8599289
0.16	0.5635595	0.47	0.6808225	0.78	0.7823046	1.09	0.8621434
0.17	0.5674949	0.48	0.6843863	0.79	0.7852361	1.10	0.8643339
0.18	0.5714237	0.49	0.6879331	0.80	0.7881446	1.11	0.8665005
0.19	0.5753454	0.50	0.6914625	0.81	0.7910299	1.12	0.8686431
0.20	0.5792597	0.51	0.6949743	0.82	0.7938919	1.13	0.8707619
0.21	0.5831662	0.52	0.6984682	0.83	0.7967306	1.14	0.8728568
0.22	0.5870644	0.53	0.701944	0.84	0.7995458	1.15	0.8749281
0.23	0.5909541	0.54	0.7054015	0.85	0.8023375	1.16	0.8769756
0.24	0.5948349	0.55	0.7088403	0.86	0.8051055	1.17	0.8789995
0.25	0.5987063	0.56	0.7122603	0.87	0.8078498	1.18	0.8809999
0.26	0.6025681	0.57	0.7156612	0.88	0.8105703	1.19	0.8829768
0.27	0.6064199	0.58	0.7190427	0.89	0.8132671	1.20	0.8849303
0.28	0.6102612	0.59	0.7224047	0.90	0.8159399	1.21	0.8868606
0.29	0.6140919	0.60	0.7257469	0.91	0.8185887	1.22	0.8887676
0.30	0.6179114	0.61	0.7290691	0.92	0.8212136	1.23	0.8906514

(*continued*)

417

TABLE A.1 (continued)

Standard Unit Normal Distribution.

Z	P(z)	Z	P(z)	Z	P(z)	Z	P(z)
1.24	0.8925123	1.62	0.9473839	2.00	0.9772499	2.38	0.9913437
1.25	0.8943502	1.63	0.9484493	2.01	0.9777844	2.39	0.9915758
1.26	0.8961653	1.64	0.9494974	2.02	0.9783083	2.40	0.9918025
1.27	0.8979577	1.65	0.9505285	2.03	0.9788217	2.41	0.9920237
1.28	0.8997274	1.66	0.9515428	2.04	0.9793248	2.42	0.9922397
1.29	0.9014747	1.67	0.9525403	2.05	0.9798178	2.43	0.9924506
1.30	0.9031995	1.68	0.9535213	2.06	0.9803007	2.44	0.9926564
1.31	0.9049021	1.69	0.954486	2.07	0.9807738	2.45	0.9928572
1.32	0.9065825	1.70	0.9554345	2.08	0.9812372	2.46	0.9930531
1.33	0.9082409	1.71	0.9563671	2.09	0.9816911	2.47	0.9932443
1.34	0.9098773	1.72	0.9572838	2.10	0.9821356	2.48	0.9934309
1.35	0.911492	1.73	0.9581849	2.11	0.9825708	2.49	0.9936128
1.36	0.913085	1.74	0.9590705	2.12	0.982997	2.50	0.9937903
1.37	0.9146565	1.75	0.9599408	2.13	0.9834142	2.51	0.9939634
1.38	0.9162067	1.76	0.9607961	2.14	0.9838226	2.52	0.9941323
1.39	0.9177356	1.77	0.9616364	2.15	0.9842224	2.53	0.9942969
1.40	0.9192433	1.78	0.962462	2.16	0.9846137	2.54	0.9944574
1.41	0.9207302	1.79	0.963273	2.17	0.9849966	2.55	0.9946139
1.42	0.9221962	1.80	0.9640697	2.18	0.9853713	2.56	0.9947664
1.43	0.9236415	1.81	0.9648521	2.19	0.9857379	2.57	0.9949151
1.44	0.9250663	1.82	0.9656205	2.20	0.9860966	2.58	0.99506
1.45	0.9264707	1.83	0.966375	2.21	0.9864474	2.59	0.9952012
1.46	0.927855	1.84	0.9671159	2.22	0.9867906	2.60	0.9953388
1.47	0.9292191	1.85	0.9678432	2.23	0.9871263	2.61	0.9954729
1.48	0.9305634	1.86	0.9685572	2.24	0.9874545	2.62	0.9956035
1.49	0.9318879	1.87	0.9692581	2.25	0.9877755	2.63	0.9957308
1.50	0.9331928	1.88	0.969946	2.26	0.9880894	2.64	0.9958547
1.51	0.9344783	1.89	0.970621	2.27	0.9883962	2.65	0.9959754
1.52	0.9357445	1.90	0.9712834	2.28	0.9886962	2.66	0.996093
1.53	0.9369916	1.91	0.9719334	2.29	0.9889893	2.67	0.9962074
1.54	0.9382198	1.92	0.9725711	2.30	0.9892759	2.68	0.9963189
1.55	0.9394292	1.93	0.9731966	2.31	0.9895559	2.69	0.9964274
1.56	0.9406201	1.94	0.9738102	2.32	0.9898296	2.70	0.996533
1.57	0.9417924	1.95	0.9744119	2.33	0.9900969	2.71	0.9966358
1.58	0.9429466	1.96	0.9750021	2.34	0.9903581	2.72	0.9967359
1.59	0.9440826	1.97	0.9755808	2.35	0.9906133	2.73	0.9968333
1.60	0.9452007	1.98	0.9761482	2.36	0.9908625	2.74	0.996928
1.61	0.9463011	1.99	0.9767045	2.37	0.991106	2.75	0.9970202

Z	P(z)	Z	P(z)	Z	P(z)	Z	P(z)
2.76	0.9971099	3.08	0.998965	3.40	0.9996631	3.72	0.9999004
2.77	0.9971972	3.09	0.9989992	3.41	0.9996752	3.73	0.9999043
2.78	0.9972821	3.10	0.9990324	3.42	0.9996869	3.74	0.999908
2.79	0.9973646	3.11	0.9990646	3.43	0.9996982	3.75	0.9999116
2.80	0.9974449	3.12	0.9990957	3.44	0.9997091	3.76	0.999915
2.81	0.9975229	3.13	0.999126	3.45	0.9997197	3.77	0.9999184
2.82	0.9975988	3.14	0.9991553	3.46	0.9997299	3.78	0.9999216
2.83	0.9976726	3.15	0.9991836	3.47	0.9997398	3.79	0.9999247
2.84	0.9977443	3.16	0.9992112	3.48	0.9997493	3.80	0.9999277
2.85	0.997814	3.17	0.9992378	3.49	0.9997585	3.81	0.9999305
2.86	0.9978818	3.18	0.9992636	3.50	0.9997674	3.82	0.9999333
2.87	0.9979476	3.19	0.9992886	3.51	0.9997759	3.83	0.9999359
2.88	0.9980116	3.20	0.9993129	3.52	0.9997842	3.84	0.9999385
2.89	0.9980738	3.21	0.9993363	3.53	0.9997922	3.85	0.9999409
2.90	0.9981342	3.22	0.999359	3.54	0.9997999	3.86	0.9999433
2.91	0.9981929	3.23	0.999381	3.55	0.9998074	3.87	0.9999456
2.92	0.9982498	3.25	0.9994024	3.56	0.9998146	3.88	0.9999478
2.93	0.9983052	3.25	0.999423	3.57	0.9998215	3.89	0.9999499
2.94	0.9983589	3.26	0.9994429	3.58	0.9998282	3.90	0.9999519
2.95	0.9984111	3.27	0.9994623	3.59	0.9998347	3.91	0.9999539
2.96	0.9984618	3.28	0.999481	3.60	0.9998409	3.92	0.9999557
2.97	0.998511	3.29	0.9994991	3.61	0.9998469	3.93	0.9999575
2.98	0.9985588	3.30	0.9995166	3.62	0.9998527	3.94	0.9999593
2.99	0.9986051	3.31	0.9995335	3.63	0.9998583	3.95	0.9999609
3.00	0.9986501	3.32	0.9995499	3.64	0.9998637	3.96	0.9999625
3.01	0.9986938	3.33	0.9995658	3.65	0.9998689	3.97	0.9999641
3.02	0.9987361	3.34	0.9995811	3.66	0.9998739	3,98	0.9999655
3.03	0.9987772	3.35	0.9995959	3.67	0.9998787	3.99	0.999967
3.04	0.9988171	3.36	0.9996103	3.68	0.9998834	4.00	0.9999683
3.05	0.9988558	3.37	0.9996242	3.69	0.9998879		
3.06	0.9988933	3.38	0.9996376	3.70	0.9998922		
3.07	0.9989297	3.39	0.9996505	3.71	0.9998964		

Values computed by the author using **R**.

TABLE A.2

Percentage Points of the *t* Distribution.

v	$\alpha_1 = 10$ $\alpha_2 = .20$	.05 .10	.025 .050	.01 .02	.005 .010	.0025 .0050	.001 .002	.0005 .0010
1	3.077684	6.313752	12.7062	31.82052	63.65674	127.3213	318.3088	636.6192
2	1.885618	2.919986	4.302653	6.964557	9.924843	14.08905	22.32712	31.59905
3	1.637744	2.353363	3.182446	4.540703	5.840909	7.453319	10.21453	12.92398
4	1.533206	2.131847	2.776445	3.746947	4.604095	5.597568	7.173182	8.610302
5	1.475884	2.015048	2.570582	3.36493	4.032143	4.773341	5.89343	6.868827
6	1.439756	1.94318	2.446912	3.142668	3.707428	4.316827	5.207626	5.958816
7	1.414924	1.894579	2.364624	2.997952	3.499483	4.029337	4.78529	5.407883
8	1.396815	1.859548	2.306004	2.896459	3.355387	3.832519	4.500791	5.041305
9	1.383029	1.833113	2.26215	2.821438	3.249836	3.689662	4.296806	4.780913
10	1.372184	1.812461	2.228139	2.763769	3.169273	3.581406	4.1437	4.586894
11	1.36343	1.795885	2.200985	2.718079	3.105807	3.496614	4.024701	4.436979
12	1.356217	1.782288	2.178813	2.680998	3.05454	3.428444	3.929633	4.317791
13	1.350171	1.770933	2.160369	2.650309	3.012276	3.372468	3.851982	4.220832
14	1.34503	1.76131	2.144787	2.624494	2.976843	3.325696	3.78739	4.140454
15	1.340606	1.75305	2.13145	2.60248	2.946713	3.286039	3.732834	4.072765
16	1.336757	1.745884	2.119905	2.583487	2.920782	3.251993	3.686155	4.014996
17	1.333379	1.739607	2.109816	2.566934	2.898231	3.22245	3.645767	3.965126
18	1.330391	1.734064	2.100922	2.55238	2.87844	3.196574	3.610485	3.921646
19	1.327728	1.729133	2.093024	2.539483	2.860935	3.173725	3.5794	3.883406
20	1.325341	1.724718	2.085963	2.527977	2.84534	3.153401	3.551808	3.849516
21	1.323188	1.720743	2.079614	2.517648	2.83136	3.135206	3.527154	3.819277
22	1.321237	1.717144	2.073873	2.508325	2.818756	3.118824	3.504992	3.792131
23	1.31946	1.713872	2.068658	2.499867	2.807336	3.103997	3.484964	3.767627
24	1.317836	1.710882	2.063899	2.492159	2.79694	3.090514	3.466777	3.745399
25	1.316345	1.708141	2.059539	2.485107	2.787436	3.078199	3.450189	3.725144
26	1.314972	1.705618	2.055529	2.47863	2.778715	3.066909	3.434997	3.706612
27	1.313703	1.703288	2.051831	2.47266	2.770683	3.05652	3.421034	3.689592
28	1.312527	1.701131	2.048407	2.46714	2.763262	3.046929	3.408155	3.673906
29	1.311434	1.699127	2.04523	2.462021	2.756386	3.038047	3.39624	3.659405
30	1.310415	1.697261	2.042272	2.457262	2.749996	3.029798	3.385185	3.645959
40	1.303077	1.683851	2.021075	2.423257	2.704459	2.971171	3.306878	3.550966
60	1.295821	1.670649	2.000298	2.390119	2.660283	2.914553	3.231709	3.4602
120	1.288646	1.657651	1.97993	2.357825	2.617421	2.859865	3.159539	3.373454
∞	1.281552	1.644854	1.959964	2.326348	2.575829	2.807034	3.090232	3.290527

Values computed by the author using **R**.

TABLE A.3

Percentage Points of the χ^2 Distribution.

	Alpha							
υ	0.990	0.975	0.950	0.900	0.100	0.050	0.025	0.010
1	0.000157088	0.000982069	0.00393214	0.01579077	2.705543	3.841459	5.023886	6.634897
2	0.02010067	0.05063562	0.1025866	0.210721	4.60517	5.991465	7.377759	9.21034
3	0.1148318	0.2157953	0.3518463	0.5843744	6.251389	7.814728	9.348404	11.34487
4	0.2971095	0.4844186	0.710723	1.063623	7.77944	9.487729	11.14329	13.2767
5	0.5542981	0.8312116	1.145476	1.610308	9.236357	11.0705	12.8325	15.08627
6	0.8720903	1.237344	1.635383	2.204131	10.64464	12.59159	14.44938	16.81189
7	1.239042	1.689869	2.16735	2.833107	12.01704	14.06714	16.01276	18.47531
8	1.646497	2.179731	2.732637	3.489539	13.36157	15.50731	17.53455	20.09024
9	2.087901	2.700389	3.325113	4.168159	14.68366	16.91898	19.02277	21.66599
10	2.558212	3.246973	3.940299	4.865182	15.98718	18.30704	20.48318	23.20925
11	3.053484	3.815748	4.574813	5.577785	17.27501	19.67514	21.92005	24.72497
12	3.570569	4.403789	5.226029	6.303796	18.54935	21.02607	23.33666	26.21697
13	4.106915	5.008751	5.891864	7.041505	19.81193	22.36203	24.7356	27.68825
14	4.660425	5.628726	6.570631	7.789534	21.06414	23.68479	26.11895	29.14124
15	5.229349	6.262138	7.260944	8.546756	22.30713	24.99579	27.48839	30.57791
16	5.812212	6.907664	7.961646	9.312236	23.54183	26.29623	28.84535	31.99993
17	6.40776	7.564186	8.67176	10.08519	24.76904	27.58711	30.19101	33.40866
18	7.014911	8.230746	9.390455	10.86494	25.98942	28.8693	31.52638	34.80531
19	7.63273	8.906516	10.11701	11.65091	27.20357	30.14353	32.85233	36.19087
20	8.260398	9.590777	10.85081	12.44261	28.41198	31.41043	34.16961	37.56623
21	8.897198	10.2829	11.59131	13.2396	29.61509	32.67057	35.47888	38.93217
22	9.542492	10.98232	12.33801	14.04149	30.81328	33.92444	36.78071	40.28936
23	10.19572	11.68855	13.09051	14.84796	32.0069	35.17246	38.07563	41.6384
24	10.85636	12.40115	13.84843	15.65868	33.19624	36.41503	39.36408	42.97982
25	11.52398	13.11972	14.61141	16.47341	34.38159	37.65248	40.64647	44.3141
26	12.19815	13.8439	15.37916	17.29188	35.56317	38.88514	41.92317	45.64168
27	12.8785	14.57338	16.1514	18.1139	36.74122	40.11327	43.19451	46.96294
28	13.56471	15.30786	16.92788	18.93924	37.91592	41.33714	44.46079	48.27824
29	14.25645	16.04707	17.70837	19.76774	39.08747	42.55697	45.72229	49.58788
30	14.95346	16.79077	18.49266	20.59923	40.25602	43.77297	46.97924	50.89218
40	22.16426	24.43304	26.5093	29.05052	51.80506	55.75848	59.34171	63.69074
50	29.70668	32.35736	34.76425	37.68865	63.16712	67.50481	71.4202	76.15389
60	37.48485	40.48175	43.18796	46.45889	74.39701	79.08194	83.29767	88.37942
70	45.44172	48.75756	51.73928	55.32894	85.52704	90.53123	95.02318	100.4252
80	53.54008	57.15317	60.39148	64.27784	96.5782	101.8795	106.6286	112.3288
90	61.75408	65.64662	69.12603	73.29109	107.565	113.1453	118.1359	124.1163
100	70.06489	74.22193	77.92947	82.35814	118.498	124.3421	129.5612	135.8067

Values computed by the author using **R**.

TABLE A.4

Percentage Points of the F Distribution.

alpha = .10

v_2	| v_1																		
	1	2	3	4	5	6	7	8	9	10	12	15	20	24	30	40	60	120	Infinity
1	39.86346	49.5	53.59324	55.83296	57.24008	58.20442	58.90595	59.43898	59.85759	60.19498	60.70521	61.22034	61.74029	62.00205	62.26497	62.52905	62.79428	63.06064	63.32812
2	8.526316	9	9.16179	9.243416	9.292626	9.32553	9.349081	9.36677	9.380544	9.391573	9.408132	9.424711	9.441309	9.449616	9.457927	9.466244	9.474565	9.482891	9.491222
3	5.538319	5.462383	5.390773	5.342644	5.309157	5.284732	5.266195	5.251671	5.239996	5.230411	5.215618	5.200313	5.184482	5.176365	5.168111	5.159719	5.15187	5.142513	5.133695
4	4.544771	4.324555	4.19086	4.10725	4.050579	4.009749	3.978966	3.95494	3.935671	3.919876	3.895527	3.87036	3.844338	3.830994	3.817422	3.803615	3.789568	3.775275	3.76073
5	4.060420	3.779716	3.619477	3.520196	3.452982	3.404507	3.367899	3.339276	3.316281	3.297402	3.268239	3.238011	3.20665	3.190523	3.174084	3.157324	3.14023	3.122792	3.104996
6	3.77595	3.463304	3.288762	3.180763	3.107512	3.054551	3.014457	2.983036	2.957741	2.936935	2.904721	2.871222	2.83634	2.818345	2.79996	2.781169	2.761952	2.74229	2.722162
7	3.589428	3.257442	3.074072	2.960534	2.883344	2.827392	2.78493	2.75158	2.724678	2.70251	2.668111	2.63223	2.594732	2.575327	2.555457	2.535096	2.514218	2.492792	2.470786
8	3.457919	3.113118	2.923796	2.806426	2.726447	2.668335	2.624135	2.589349	2.561238	2.538037	2.501958	2.464216	2.424637	2.404097	2.383016	2.361362	2.339097	2.316181	2.292566
9	3.360303	3.006452	2.812863	2.69268	2.610613	2.550855	2.505313	2.469406	2.44034	2.416316	2.378885	2.339624	2.298322	2.276827	2.25472	2.231958	2.208493	2.18427	2.159227
10	3.285015	2.924466	2.727673	2.605336	2.521641	2.460582	2.413965	2.37715	2.347306	2.322604	2.284051	2.243515	2.200744	2.178426	2.155426	2.131691	2.107161	2.081765	2.055422
11	3.225202	2.859511	2.660229	2.536188	2.451184	2.389067	2.341566	2.303997	2.273502	2.24823	2.208725	2.167094	2.123046	2.100005	2.076214	2.05161	2.026118	1.999652	1.972109
12	3.176549	2.806796	2.605525	2.480102	2.394022	2.331024	2.28278	2.244575	2.213525	2.187635	2.147437	2.104851	2.059677	2.035993	2.011492	1.986102	1.959732	1.932278	1.903615
13	3.136205	2.763167	2.560273	2.433705	2.346724	2.282979	2.234103	2.19535	2.16382	2.137635	2.096588	2.05316	2.006982	1.982718	1.957575	1.931466	1.904287	1.875915	1.846196
14	3.102213	2.726468	2.522224	2.394692	2.306943	2.242559	2.193134	2.153904	2.121955	2.095396	2.053714	2.009535	1.962453	1.937663	1.911933	1.885163	1.857234	1.828001	1.797283
15	3.073186	2.695173	2.489788	2.361433	2.273022	2.208082	2.158178	2.11853	2.086209	2.059319	2.01707	1.972216	1.924314	1.899044	1.872774	1.845393	1.816764	1.78672	1.755052
16	3.04811	2.668171	2.461811	2.332745	2.243758	2.178329	2.128003	2.087982	2.055331	2.028145	1.985386	1.939921	1.891272	1.865561	1.838792	1.810841	1.781557	1.750747	1.718169
17	3.026232	2.644638	2.437434	2.30747	2.218253	2.152392	2.101689	2.061336	2.028388	2.000936	1.957716	1.911695	1.862361	1.836242	1.80901	1.780528	1.750627	1.71909	1.685641
18	3.006977	2.623947	2.416005	2.285772	2.195827	2.129581	2.078541	2.037889	2.004674	1.97698	1.93334	1.886811	1.836845	1.810348	1.782685	1.753706	1.723222	1.690993	1.656706
19	2.9899	2.605612	2.397022	2.266303	2.175956	2.109364	2.05802	2.017098	1.983639	1.955725	1.911702	1.864705	1.814155	1.787307	1.759241	1.729793	1.698758	1.665869	1.630774
20	2.974653	2.589254	2.380087	2.248934	2.158227	2.091322	2.039703	1.998534	1.964853	1.936738	1.892363	1.844935	1.793843	1.766667	1.738223	1.708334	1.676676	1.643256	1.60738
21	2.960956	2.574569	2.364888	2.233345	2.142311	2.075123	2.023252	1.981858	1.947974	1.919674	1.874975	1.827148	1.77551	1.748068	1.719268	1.688962	1.656907	1.622782	1.586151
22	2.948585	2.561314	2.35117	2.219274	2.127944	2.060497	2.008397	1.966796	1.932725	1.904255	1.859255	1.811057	1.758989	1.731217	1.702083	1.671382	1.638853	1.604147	1.566785
23	2.937356	2.54929	2.338727	2.206512	2.114911	2.047227	1.994915	1.953124	1.91888	1.890252	1.844921	1.796431	1.743921	1.715878	1.686428	1.655352	1.622371	1.587107	1.549035
24	2.927117	2.538332	2.32739	2.194882	2.103033	2.035132	1.982625	1.940658	1.906255	1.87748	1.831942	1.783076	1.730152	1.701854	1.672104	1.640673	1.60726	1.571459	1.532696
25	2.917745	2.528305	2.317017	2.184242	2.092165	2.024062	1.971376	1.929246	1.894693	1.865782	1.820003	1.770834	1.71752	1.688981	1.658947	1.627177	1.59335	1.557031	1.517597
26	2.909132	2.519096	2.307491	2.174469	2.082182	2.013893	1.961039	1.918758	1.884067	1.855028	1.809023	1.759571	1.70589	1.677122	1.646819	1.614725	1.580502	1.543683	1.503595
27	2.901192	2.510609	2.298712	2.165463	2.072981	2.004519	1.95151	1.909087	1.874267	1.845109	1.798891	1.749173	1.695144	1.66616	1.635601	1.603198	1.568595	1.531293	1.490568
28	2.893846	2.502761	2.290595	2.157136	2.064473	1.995851	1.942696	1.900141	1.865199	1.83593	1.789513	1.739543	1.685187	1.655997	1.625193	1.592496	1.557527	1.519759	1.478412
29	2.887033	2.495483	2.283069	2.149415	2.056583	1.987811	1.934521	1.891842	1.856786	1.827412	1.780807	1.7306	1.675932	1.646547	1.615511	1.582531	1.54721	1.50899	1.467036
30	2.880695	2.488716	2.276071	2.142235	2.049246	1.980333	1.926916	1.884121	1.848958	1.819485	1.772272	1.722272	1.667309	1.637737	1.606479	1.573228	1.537569	1.498912	1.456365
40	2.835354	2.440369	2.226092	2.09095	1.99682	1.926879	1.872522	1.828863	1.792902	1.762686	1.714563	1.662411	1.605151	1.574111	1.541076	1.505625	1.467157	1.424757	1.376912
60	2.791068	2.393255	2.177411	2.040986	1.94571	1.87472	1.819393	1.774829	1.73802	1.707009	1.657429	1.603368	1.543486	1.510718	1.475539	1.437342	1.395201	1.347568	1.291464
120	2.747807	2.347338	2.129991	1.992302	1.895875	1.823812	1.767476	1.721959	1.684248	1.652379	1.601204	1.545002	1.482072	1.447226	1.409379	1.367602	1.32034	1.264573	1.192563
Infinity	2.705543	2.302585	2.083796	1.94486	1.847271	1.774107	1.71672	1.670196	1.631517	1.598718	1.545779	1.487142	1.420599	1.383177	1.341867	1.295126	1.23995	1.168605	1.000018

									v_1										
v_2	1	2	3	4	5	6	7	8	9	10	12	15	20	24	30	40	60	120	Infinity
alpha = .05																			
1	161.4476	199.5	215.7073	224.5832	230.1619	233.986	236.7684	238.8827	240.5433	241.8817	243.906	245.9499	248.0131	249.0518	250.0951	251.1432	252.1957	253.2529	254.3144
2	18.51282	19	19.16429	19.24679	19.29641	19.32953	19.35322	19.37099	19.38483	19.3959	19.41251	19.42914	19.44577	19.45409	19.46241	19.47074	19.47906	19.48739	19.49573
3	10.12796	9.552094	9.276628	9.117182	9.013455	8.940645	8.886743	8.845238	8.8123	8.785525	8.744641	8.70287	8.66019	8.638501	8.616576	8.594411	8.572004	8.549351	8.52645
4	7.708647	6.944272	6.591382	6.388233	6.256057	6.163132	6.094211	6.041044	5.998779	5.964371	5.911729	5.857805	5.802542	5.774389	5.745877	5.716998	5.687744	5.658105	5.628072
5	6.607891	5.786135	5.409451	5.192168	5.050329	4.950288	4.875872	4.81832	4.772466	4.735063	4.677704	4.618759	4.558131	4.527153	4.495712	4.463793	4.43138	4.398454	4.364997
6	5.987378	5.143253	4.757063	4.533677	4.387374	4.283866	4.206658	4.146804	4.099016	4.059963	3.999935	3.938058	3.874189	3.841457	3.808164	3.774286	3.739797	3.704667	3.668866
7	5.591448	4.737414	4.346831	4.120312	3.971523	3.865969	3.787044	3.725725	3.676675	3.636523	3.574676	3.51074	3.444525	3.410494	3.375808	3.34043	3.304323	3.267445	3.229751
8	5.317655	4.45897	4.066181	3.837853	3.687499	3.58058	3.500464	3.438101	3.38813	3.347163	3.283939	3.218406	3.150324	3.11524	3.079406	3.042778	3.005303	2.966923	3.229751
9	5.117355	4.256495	3.862548	3.633089	3.481659	3.373754	3.292746	3.229583	3.178893	3.13728	3.072947	3.006102	2.936455	2.900474	2.863652	2.825933	2.787249	2.747525	2.927575
10	4.964603	4.102821	3.708265	3.47805	3.325835	3.217175	3.135465	3.071658	3.020383	2.978237	2.912977	2.845017	2.774016	2.737248	2.699551	2.660855	2.621077	2.580122	2.537878
11	4.84336	3.982298	3.587434	3.35669	3.203874	3.094613	3.01233	2.94799	2.896223	2.853625	2.787569	2.71864	2.646445	2.608974	2.570489	2.530905	2.490123	2.448024	2.40447
12	4.747225	3.885294	3.490295	3.259167	3.105875	2.99612	2.913358	2.848565	2.796375	2.753387	2.686637	2.616851	2.543588	2.505482	2.466279	2.42588	2.384166	2.340995	2.296198
13	4.667193	3.805565	3.410534	3.179117	3.025438	2.915269	2.832098	2.766913	2.714356	2.671024	2.603661	2.53311	2.458882	2.420196	2.380334	2.33918	2.296596	2.252414	2.206432
14	4.60011	3.738892	3.343889	3.11225	2.958249	2.847726	2.764199	2.698672	2.645791	2.602155	2.534243	2.463003	2.387896	2.348678	2.308207	2.26635	2.22295	2.177811	2.130693
15	4.543077	3.68232	3.287382	3.055568	2.901295	2.790465	2.706627	2.640797	2.587626	2.543719	2.475313	2.403447	2.327535	2.287826	2.246789	2.204276	2.160105	2.114056	2.065847
16	4.493998	3.63723	3.238872	3.006917	2.852409	2.741311	2.657197	2.591096	2.537667	2.493513	2.42466	2.352223	2.27557	2.235405	2.193841	2.150711	2.105813	2.058895	2.009635
17	4.451322	3.591531	3.196777	2.964708	2.809996	2.69866	2.614299	2.547955	2.494291	2.449916	2.380654	2.307693	2.230354	2.189766	2.147708	2.103998	2.058411	2.010663	1.960386
18	4.413873	3.554557	3.159908	2.927744	2.772853	2.661305	2.576722	2.510158	2.456281	2.411702	2.342067	2.268622	2.190648	2.149665	2.107143	2.062885	2.016643	1.9681	1.91684
19	4.38075	3.521893	3.12735	2.895107	2.740058	2.628318	2.543534	2.47677	2.422699	2.377934	2.307954	2.234063	2.155497	2.114143	2.071186	2.02641	1.979544	1.930237	1.878025
20	4.351244	3.492828	3.098391	2.866081	2.71089	2.598978	2.514011	2.447064	2.392814	2.347878	2.277581	2.203274	2.124155	2.082454	2.039086	1.993819	1.946358	1.896318	1.84318
21	4.324794	3.4668	3.072467	2.8401	2.684781	2.572712	2.487578	2.420462	2.366048	2.320953	2.250362	2.17567	2.096033	2.054004	2.010248	1.964515	1.916486	1.865739	1.811703
22	4.30095	3.443357	3.049125	2.816708	2.661274	2.549061	2.463774	2.396503	2.341937	2.296696	2.225831	2.150778	2.070656	2.028319	1.984195	1.938018	1.889445	1.838018	1.783107
23	4.279344	3.422132	3.027998	2.795539	2.639999	2.527655	2.442226	2.374812	2.320105	2.274728	2.203607	2.128217	2.047638	2.005009	1.960537	1.913938	1.864844	1.81276	1.756997
24	4.259677	3.402826	3.008787	2.776289	2.620654	2.508189	2.422629	2.355081	2.300244	2.254739	2.18338	2.107673	2.026664	1.98376	1.938957	1.891955	1.84236	1.789642	1.733049
25	4.241699	3.38519	2.991241	2.75871	2.602987	2.49041	2.404728	2.337057	2.282097	2.236474	2.164891	2.088887	2.007471	1.964306	1.919188	1.871801	1.821727	1.768395	1.710992
26	4.225201	3.369016	2.975154	2.742594	2.58679	2.474109	2.388314	2.320527	2.265453	2.219188	2.147926	2.071642	1.989842	1.946428	1.90101	1.853255	1.802719	1.748795	1.6906
27	4.210008	3.354131	2.960351	2.727765	2.571886	2.459108	2.373208	2.305313	2.250131	2.204292	2.132303	2.055755	1.97359	1.9294	1.884236	1.836129	1.785149	1.73065	1.671682
28	4.195972	3.340386	2.946685	2.714076	2.558128	2.445259	2.35926	2.291264	2.235982	2.190044	2.117869	2.041071	1.958561	1.914686	1.868709	1.820263	1.768857	1.7138	1.654076
29	4.182964	3.327654	2.93403	2.701399	2.545386	2.432434	2.346342	2.278251	2.222874	2.176844	2.104493	2.027458	1.94462	1.900531	1.854293	1.805523	1.753704	1.698107	1.63764
30	4.170877	3.31583	2.922277	2.689628	2.533555	2.420523	2.334344	2.266163	2.210697	2.16458	2.092063	2.014804	1.931653	1.88736	1.840872	1.79179	1.739574	1.683452	1.622265
40	4.084746	3.231727	2.838745	2.605975	2.449466	2.335852	2.249024	2.18017	2.124029	2.077248	2.003459	1.924463	1.838859	1.792937	1.744432	1.692797	1.637252	1.57661	1.508904
60	4.001191	3.150411	2.758078	2.525215	2.36827	2.254053	2.166541	2.096968	2.040098	1.992592	1.917396	1.836437	1.747984	1.700117	1.649141	1.594273	1.534314	1.467267	1.389276
120	3.920124	3.071779	2.680168	2.447237	2.289851	2.175006	2.08677	2.016426	1.958763	1.910461	1.833695	1.750497	1.65868	1.608437	1.554343	1.495202	1.429013	1.351886	1.253858
Infinity	3.841459	2.995732	2.604909	2.371932	2.2141	2.098598	2.009591	1.938414	1.879886	1.830704	1.752172	1.666386	1.570522	1.517293	1.459099	1.393962	1.318032	1.221395	1.000023

(continued)

TABLE A.4 (continued)

Percentage Points of the F Distribution.

alpha = .01

v_2	v_1 1	2	3	4	5	6	7	8	9	10	12	15	20	24	30	40	60	120	Infinity
1	4052.181	4999.5	5403.352	5624.583	5763.65	5858.986	5928.356	5981.07	6022.473	6055.847	6106.321	6157.285	6208.73	6234.631	6260.649	6286.782	6313.03	6339.391	6365.864
2	98.50251	99	99.1662	99.24937	99.2993	99.33259	99.35637	99.37421	99.38809	99.3992	99.41585	99.43251	99.44917	99.4575	99.46583	99.47416	99.4825	99.49083	99.49916
3	34.11622	30.81652	29.4567	28.7099	28.23708	27.91066	27.6717	27.48918	27.34521	27.22873	27.05182	26.87219	26.68979	26.59752	26.50453	26.41081	26.31635	26.22114	26.12517
4	21.19769	18	16.69437	15.97702	15.52186	15.20686	14.97576	14.79889	14.65913	14.5459	14.37359	14.1982	14.01961	13.92906	13.83766	13.74538	13.6522	13.5581	13.46305
5	16.25818	13.27393	12.05995	11.39193	10.96702	10.67225	10.45551	10.28931	10.15776	10.05102	9.888275	9.722219	9.552646	9.466471	9.379329	9.291189	9.202015	9.111771	9.020417
6	13.74502	10.92477	9.779538	9.148301	8.745895	8.466125	8.259995	8.101651	7.976121	7.874119	7.718333	7.558994	7.395832	7.312721	7.228533	7.143222	7.056737	6.969022	6.880021
7	12.24638	9.54578	8.451285	7.846645	7.460435	7.191405	6.992063	6.840049	6.718752	6.620063	6.469091	6.314331	6.155438	6.074319	5.99201	5.908449	5.823566	5.737286	5.649525
8	11.25862	8.649111	7.590992	7.006077	6.631825	6.370681	6.177624	6.02887	5.910619	5.814294	5.666719	5.515125	5.359095	5.279264	5.19813	5.11561	5.031618	4.946052	4.858799
9	10.56143	8.021517	6.991917	6.422085	6.056941	5.8017	5.612865	5.467123	5.351129	5.256542	5.111431	4.962078	4.807995	4.728998	4.648582	4.566649	4.483087	4.397769	4.31055
10	10.04429	7.559432	6.552313	5.994339	5.636326	5.38581	5.200172	5.056693	4.942421	4.849147	4.70587	4.55814	4.405395	4.326929	4.246933	4.165287	4.081855	3.996481	3.90898
11	9.64034	7.205713	6.21673	5.6683	5.316009	5.06921	4.886072	4.744468	4.63154	4.539282	4.397401	4.250867	4.099046	4.02091	3.941132	3.859573	3.776071	3.690436	3.602442
12	9.330212	6.926608	5.952545	5.411951	5.064343	4.820574	4.639502	4.499365	4.38751	4.296054	4.155258	4.009619	3.858433	3.780485	3.700789	3.619181	3.535473	3.44944	3.360809
13	9.07806	6.700965	5.73938	5.20533	4.861621	4.620363	4.440997	4.302062	4.191078	4.100267	3.960326	3.815365	3.664609	3.586753	3.507042	3.425293	3.341287	3.25476	3.165393
14	8.861593	6.514884	5.563886	5.035378	4.694964	4.45582	4.277882	4.139946	4.02968	3.939396	3.800141	3.655697	3.505222	3.427387	3.347596	3.265641	3.181274	3.094191	3.004018
15	8.683117	6.355873	5.416965	4.89321	4.555614	4.318273	4.141546	4.004453	3.894788	3.80494	3.66624	3.522194	3.371892	3.294029	3.21411	3.131906	3.047135	2.959453	2.868426
16	8.530965	6.226235	5.292214	4.772578	4.4374	4.201634	4.025947	3.889572	3.780415	3.690931	3.552687	3.408947	3.258737	3.180811	3.100731	3.018248	2.933046	2.844737	2.752824
17	8.39974	6.112214	5.185	4.668968	4.335939	4.101505	3.926719	3.790964	3.682242	3.593066	3.455198	3.311694	3.161518	3.083502	3.003241	2.920458	2.834806	2.745852	2.663033
18	8.28542	6.012905	5.09189	4.579036	4.247882	4.014637	3.840639	3.705422	3.597074	3.508162	3.370608	3.227286	3.077097	2.998974	2.918516	2.83542	2.749309	2.659701	2.565963
19	8.184947	5.92579	5.010287	4.500258	4.170685	3.938673	3.765269	3.630525	3.522503	3.433817	3.296527	3.153343	3.003109	2.924866	2.844201	2.760786	2.674211	2.583944	2.48928
20	8.095958	5.848932	4.938193	4.43069	4.102685	3.871427	3.69874	3.564412	3.456676	3.368186	3.23112	3.088041	2.937735	2.859363	2.778485	2.694749	2.607708	2.516783	2.421191
21	8.016597	5.780416	4.874046	4.368815	4.042144	3.811725	3.63959	3.505632	3.398147	3.30983	3.172953	3.029951	2.879556	2.80105	2.719955	2.635896	2.548393	2.456813	2.360294
22	7.945386	5.719022	4.816606	4.313429	3.987963	3.758301	3.58666	3.453034	3.345773	3.257606	3.120891	2.977946	2.82747	2.748802	2.66749	2.583111	2.495149	2.402919	2.305477
23	7.881134	5.663699	4.764877	4.263567	3.939195	3.710218	3.539024	3.405695	3.298634	3.210599	3.074025	2.931118	2.780504	2.70172	2.620191	2.535496	2.447081	2.354209	2.25585
24	7.822871	5.613591	4.718051	4.218445	3.89507	3.666717	3.495928	3.362867	3.255985	3.168069	3.031615	2.888732	2.737997	2.659072	2.577329	2.492321	2.403461	2.309955	2.210685
25	7.769798	5.567997	4.675465	4.1742	3.854957	3.627174	3.456754	3.323937	3.217217	3.129406	2.993056	2.850186	2.699325	2.62026	2.538305	2.45299	2.363691	2.269562	2.16939
26	7.721254	5.526335	4.63657	4.13996	3.818336	3.591075	3.420993	3.288399	3.181824	3.094108	2.957848	2.814982	2.663991	2.584787	2.502624	2.417007	2.327279	2.232536	2.131471
27	7.676684	5.488118	4.600907	4.105622	3.78477	3.557991	3.388219	3.255827	3.149385	3.061754	2.925573	2.782703	2.63158	2.552239	2.469872	2.38396	2.293812	2.198465	2.096517
28	7.635619	5.452937	4.568091	4.074032	3.753895	3.527559	3.358073	3.225868	3.119547	3.031992	2.895881	2.753	2.601744	2.522268	2.439701	2.353501	2.262941	2.167001	2.06418
29	7.597663	5.420445	4.537795	4.044873	3.725399	3.499475	3.330252	3.198219	3.092009	3.004524	2.866472	2.725577	2.574188	2.494579	2.411817	2.325335	2.234372	2.137851	2.034166
30	7.562476	5.390346	4.50974	4.017877	3.699019	3.473477	3.304499	3.172624	3.066516	2.979094	2.843095	2.70018	2.548659	2.468921	2.385967	2.299211	2.207854	2.110762	2.006225
40	7.3141	5.178508	4.312569	3.828294	3.51384	3.291012	3.123757	2.992981	2.88756	2.800545	2.664827	2.521616	2.368876	2.287998	2.203382	2.114232	2.019411	1.917191	1.804707
60	7.077106	4.977432	4.125892	3.649047	3.338884	3.118674	2.953049	2.82328	2.718454	2.631751	2.496116	2.352297	2.197806	2.115364	2.028479	1.936018	1.836259	1.72632	1.600647
120	6.850893	4.78651	3.9491	3.479531	3.173545	2.955854	2.791764	2.662906	2.558574	2.472077	2.3363	2.191504	2.034588	1.950018	1.860005	1.762849	1.655693	1.532992	1.380528
Infinity	6.63897	4.60517	3.781622	3.319176	3.017254	2.801982	2.63933	2.511279	2.407333	2.320925	2.184747	2.038528	1.878312	1.790826	1.696406	1.592268	1.47299	1.324585	1.000033

Values computed by the author using **R**.

TABLE A.5

Fisher's Z Transformed Values.

r	Z	r	Z	r	Z	r	Z
0.00	0.000000	0.25	0.2554128	0.50	0.5493061	0.75	0.9729551
0.01	0.01000033	0.26	0.2661084	0.51	0.5627298	0.76	0.9962151
0.02	0.02000267	0.27	0.2768638	0.52	0.5763398	0.77	1.020328
0.03	0.030009	0.28	0.2876821	0.53	0.5901452	0.78	1.045371
0.04	0.04002135	0.29	0.2985663	0.54	0.6041556	0.79	1.071432
0.05	0.05004173	0.30	0.3095196	0.55	0.6183813	0.80	1.098612
0.06	0.06007216	0.31	0.3205454	0.56	0.6328332	0.81	1.127029
0.07	0.07011467	0.32	0.3316471	0.57	0.6475228	0.82	1.156817
0.08	0.08017133	0.33	0.3428283	0.58	0.6624627	0.83	1.188136
0.09	0.09024419	0.34	0.3540925	0.59	0.6776661	0.84	1.221174
0.10	0.1003353	0.35	0.3654438	0.60	0.6931472	0.85	1.256153
0.11	0.1104469	0.36	0.3768859	0.61	0.7089214	0.86	1.293345
0.12	0.120581	0.37	0.3884231	0.62	0.7250051	0.87	1.33308
0.13	0.1307399	0.38	0.4000597	0.63	0.7414161	0.88	1.375768
0.14	0.1409256	0.39	0.4118	0.64	0.7581737	0.89	1.421926
0.15	0.1511404	0.40	0.4236489	0.65	0.7752987	0.90	1.472219
0.16	0.1613867	0.41	0.4356112	0.66	0.7928136	0.91	1.527524
0.17	0.1716667	0.42	0.447692	0.67	0.8107431	0.92	1.589027
0.18	0.1819827	0.43	0.4598967	0.68	0.829114	0.93	1.65839
0.19	0.1923372	0.44	0.4722308	0.69	0.8479558	0.94	1.738049
0.20	0.2027326	0.45	0.4847003	0.70	0.8673005	0.95	1.831781
0.21	0.2131713	0.46	0.4973113	0.71	0.8871839	0.96	1.94591
0.22	0.2236561	0.47	0.5100703	0.72	0.907645	0.97	2.092296
0.23	0.2341895	0.48	0.5229843	0.73	0.9287274	0.98	2.29756
0.24	0.2447741	0.49	0.5360603	0.74	0.9504794	0.99	2.646652

Values computed by the author using **R**.

References

Agresti, A. (2013). *Categorical data analysis*. Hoboken, NJ: Wiley-Interscience.

Algina, J., Blair, R. C., & Coombs, W. T. (1995). A maximum test for scale: Type I error rates and power. *Journal of Educational and Behavioral Statistics*, 20(1), 27–39.

Algina, J., & Keselman, H. J. (2003). Approximate confidence intervals for effect sizes. *Educational and Psychological Measurement*, 63(4), 537–553.

Algina, J., Keselman, H. J., & Penfield, R. D. (2005). Effect sizes and their intervals: The two-level repeated measures case. *Educational and Psychological Measurement*, 65(2), 241–258.

American Psychological Association. (2010). *Publication manual of the American Psychological Association*. Washington, DC: American Psychological Association.

Amrhein, V., & Greenland, S. (2018). Remove, rather than redefine, statistical significance. *Nature Human Behaviour*, 2(1), 4.

Basu, S., & DasGupta, A. (1995). Robustness of standard confidence intervals for location parameters under departure from normality. *The Annals of Statistics*, 23(4), 1433–1442.

Batanero, C., & Chernoff, E. J. (2018). Teaching and learning stochastics: Advances in probability education research. Cham, Switzerland: Springer.

Beal, S. L. (1987). Asymptotic confidence intervals for the difference between two binomial parameters for use with small samples. *Biometrics*, (4), 941–950. doi:10.2307/2531547

Benjamin, D. J., Berger, J. O., Johannesson, M., Nosek, B. A., Wagenmakers, E. J., Berk, R., . . . Fehr, E. (2018). Redefine statistical significance. *Nature Human Behaviour*, 2(1), 6–10.

Blanca, M. J., Alarcón, R., Arnau, J., Bono, R., & Bendayan, R. (2018). Effect of variance ratio on ANOVA robustness: Might 15 be the limit? *Behavior Research Methods*, 50(3), 937–962. doi:10.3758/s13428-017-0918-2

Bonett, D. G., & Seier, E. (2002). A test of normality with high uniform power. *Computational Statistics and Data Analysis*, 40, 435–445. doi:10.1016/S0167-9473(02)00074-9

Bonett, D. G., & Wright, T. A. (2000). Sample size requirements for estimating Pearson, Kendall and Spearman correlations. *Psychometrika*, 65(1), 23–28. doi:10.1007/BF02294183

Carroll, R. J., & Schneider, H. (1985). A note on levene's tests for equality of variances. *Statistics and Probability Letters*, 3, 191–194. doi:10.1016/0167-7152(85)90016-1

Chakravart, I. M., Laha, R. G., & Roy, J. (1967). *Handbook of methods of applied statistics* (Vol. 1). New York: Wiley.

Chambers, J. M. (1983). *Graphical methods for data analysis*. Belmont, CA: Wadsworth.

Cleveland, W. S. (1994). *The elements of graphing data* (Rev. ed.). Murray Hill, NJ: AT&T Bell Laboratories.

Coe, P. R., & Tamhane, A. C. (1993). Small sample confidence intervals for the difference, ratio, and odds ratio of two success probabilities. *Communications in Statistics-Simulation and Computation*, 22, 925–938.

Cohen, J. (1988). *Statistical power analysis for the behavioral sciences* (2nd ed.). Hillsdale, NJ: Lawrence Erlbaum.

Conover, W. J., & Iman, R. L. (1981). Rank transformations as a bridge between parametric and nonparametric statistics. *The American Statistician*, (3), 124–129. doi:10.2307/2683975

Cortina, J. M., & Nouri, H. (2000). *Effect size for ANOVA designs*. Thousand Oaks, CA: Sage.

Cowles, M., & Davis, C. (1982). On the origins of the .05 level of statistical significance. *American Psychologist*, 37(5), 553–558. doi:10.1037/0003-066X.37.5.553

Crane, H. (2018). The impact of *p*-hacking on "redefine statistical significance". *Basic & Applied Social Psychology*, 40(4), 219–235. doi:10.1080/01973533.2018.1474111

Crawley, M. J. (2013). *The R book* (2nd ed.). Hoboken, NJ: John Wiley & Sons.

Cressie, N. A. C., & Whitford, H. J. (1986). How to use the two sample t-test. *Biometrical Journal*, 28(2), 131–148.

Cristea, I. A., & Ioannidis, J. P. A. (2018). P values in display items are ubiquitous and almost invariably significant: A survey of top science journals. *PLoS One, 13*(5), 1–15. doi:10.1371/journal.pone.0197440

Cumming, G., & Calin-Jageman, R. (2017). *Introduction to the new statistics: Estimation, open science, and beyond.* New York, NY: Routledge.

Cumming, G., & Finch, S. (2001). A primer on the understanding, use, and calculation of confidence intervals that are based on central and noncentral distributions. *Educational and Psychological Measurement, 61*(4), 532–574.

D'Agostino, R. B. (1970). Transformation to normality of the null distribution of g1. *Biometrika, 57*(3), 679–681.

D'Agostino, R. B., Belanger, A., & D'Agostino, R. B. J. (1990). A suggestion for using powerful and informative tests of normality. *The American Statistician,* (4), 316–321. doi:10.2307/2684359

Duncan, G. T., & Layard, M. W. J. (1973). A Monte-Carlo study of asymptotically robust tests for correlation coefficients. *Biometrika, 60*(3), 551–558.

Finch, S., & Cumming, G. (2009). Putting research in context: Understanding confidence intervals from one or more studies. *Journal of Pediatric Psychology, 34*(9), 903–916.

Fink, A. (2002). *How to sample in surveys* (2nd ed.). Thousand Oaks, CA: Sage.

Fisher, R. A. (1925). *Statistical methods for research workers* (2nd rev. and enl. ed.). Edinburgh, London: Oliver and Boyd.

Fisher, R. A. (1926). The arrangement of field experiments. *Journal of the Ministry of Agriculture, 33*, 503–513.

Fisher, R. A. (1935). Statistical tests. *Nature, 136*(3438), 474.

Gabor, A. (1990). *The man who discovered quality: How W. Edwards Deming brought the quality revolution to America: The stories of Ford, Xerox, and GM* (1st ed.). New York, NY: Times Books.

Ghosh, B. K. (1979). A comparison of some approximate confidence intervals for the binomial parameter. *Journal of the American Statistical Association, 74*, 894–900.

Glass, G. V. (1976). Primary, secondary, and meta-analysis of research. *Educational Researcher, 5*(10), 3–8.

Glass, G. V., & Hopkins, K. D. (1996). *Statistical methods in education and psychology* (3rd ed.). Boston, MA: Allyn and Bacon.

Glass, G. V., Peckham, P. D., & Sanders, J. R. (1972). Consequences of failure to meet assumptions underlying the fixed effects analyses of variance and covariance. *Review of Educational Research,* (3), 237–288.

Greenwood, P. E., & Nikulin, M. S. (1996). *A guide to chi-squared testing.* New York, NY: John Wiley & Sons.

Grissom, R. J., & Kim, J. J. (2005). *Effect sizes for research: A broad practical approach.* Mahway, NJ: Lawrence Erlbaum Associates.

Grissom, R. J., & Kim, J. J. (2012). *Effect sizes for research: Univariate and multivariate applications* (2nd ed.). New York NY: Routledge.

Hahs-Vaughn, D. L. (2005). A primer for using and understanding weights with national datasets. *Journal of Experimental Education, 73*(3), 221–248.

Hahs-Vaughn, D. L. (2006a). Analysis of data from complex samples. *International Journal of Research & Method in Education, 29*(2), 163–181.

Hahs-Vaughn, D. L. (2006b). Weighting omissions and best practices when using large-scale data in educational research. *Association for Institutional Research Professional File,* (101), 1–9.

Hahs-Vaughn, D. L., McWayne, C. M., Bulotskey-Shearer, R. J., Wen, X., & Faria, A. (2011a). Complex sample data recommendations and troubleshooting. *Evaluation Review, 35*(3), 304–313. doi:10.1177/0193841X11412070

Hahs-Vaughn, D. L., McWayne, C. M., Bulotskey-Shearer, R. J., Wen, X., & Faria, A. (2011b). Methodological considerations in using complex survey data: An applied example with the head start family and child experiences survey. *Evaluation Review, 35*(3), 269–303.

Hancock, G. R., & Mueller, R. O. (2010). *The reviewer's guide to quantitative methods in the social sciences.* New York, NY: Routledge.

Harlow, L. L., Mulaik, S. A., & Steiger, J. H. (Eds.). (1997). *What if there were no significance tests?* Mahwah, NJ: Lawrence Erlbaum Associates.

Hartley, J. (1992). A postscript to Wainer's "Understanding graphs and tables". *Educational Researcher, 21*, 25–26. doi:10.2307/1176844

Hedges, L. V. (1981). Distribution theory for Glass's estimator of effect size and related estimators. *Journal of Educational Statistics, 6*(2), 107–128.

Hedges, L. V., & Olkin, I. (1985). *Statistical methods for meta-analysis.* Orlando, FL: Academic Press.

Heyde, C. C., Seneta, E., Crepel, P., Feinberg, S. E., & Gain, J. (Eds.). (2001). *Statisticians of the centuries.* New York, NY: Springer.

Hoenig, J. M., & Heisey, D. M. (2001). The abuse of power: The pervasive fallacy of power calculations for data analysis. *The American Statistician, 55*(1), 19–24.

Hogg, R. V., & Craig, A. T. (1995). *Introduction to mathematical statistics* (5th ed.). Englewood Cliffs, NJ: Prentice Hall.

Howard, W. (1984). How to display data badly. *The American Statistician, 38*(2), 137–147. doi:10.2307/2683253

Howell, D. C. (2010). *Statistical methods for psychology* (7th ed.). Belmont, CA: Thomson Wadsworth.

Hsu, L. M. (1989). Random sampling, randomization, and equivalence of contrasted groups in psychotherapy outcome research. *Journal of Consulting and Clinical Psychology, 57*(1), 131–137.

Huberty, C. J. (2002). A history of effect size indices. *Educational and Psychological Measurement, 62*(2), 227–240.

Huck, S. W. (2000). *Reading statistics and research* (3rd ed.). New York, NY: Longman.

Huck, S. W. (2012). *Reading statistics and research* (6th ed.). Boston, MA: Pearson.

Huck, S. W. (2016). *Statistical misconceptions.* New York, NY: Routledge.

Jaeger, R. M. (1984). *Sampling in education and the social sciences.* New York, NY: Longman.

Joanes, D. N., & Gill, C. A. (1998). Comparing measures of sample skewness and kurtosis. *Journal of the Royal Statistical Society. Series D (The Statistician)*(1), 183–189.

Kalton, G. (1983). *Introduction to survey sampling.* Thousand Oaks, CA: Sage.

Keller, D. K. (2006). *The tao of statistics: A path to understanding (with no math).* Thousand Oaks, CA: Sage.

Kim, Y. J., & Cribbie, R. A. (2018). ANOVA and the variance homogeneity assumption: Exploring a better gatekeeper. *British Journal of Mathematical and Statistical Psychology, 71*(1), 1–12. doi:10.1111/bmsp.12103

Kinney, J. J. (2015). *Probability an introduction with statistical applications* (2nd ed.). Hoboken, NJ: John Wiley & Sons, Inc.

Kish, L., & Frankel, M. R. (1973, October 17). *Inference from complex samples.* Paper presented at the annual meeting of the Royal Statistical Society.

Kish, L., & Frankel, M. R. (1974). Inference from complex samples. *Journal of the Royal Statistical Society, Series B, 36*, 1–37.

Koren, J. (Ed.). (1970). *The history of statistics, their development and progress in many countries, in memoirs to commemorate the seventy fifth anniversary of the American statistical association.* New York, NY: Macmillan.

Korn, E. L., & Graubard, B. I. (1995). Examples of differing weighted and unweighted estimates from a sample survey. *American Statistician, 49*, 291–305.

Lamb, G. S. (1984). What you always wanted to know about six but were afraid to ask. *Journal of Irreproducible Results, 29*, 18–20.

Lance, C. E., & Vandenberg, R. J. (2009). *Statistical and methodological myths and urban legends: Doctrine, verity and fable in the organizational and social sciences.* New York, NY: Routledge.

Lee, E. S., Forthofer, R. N., & Lorimor, R. J. (1989). *Analyzing complex survey data.* Newbury Park, CA: Sage.

Levene, H. (1960). Robust tests for equality of variances. In I. Olkin (Ed.), *Contributions to probability and statistics: Essays in honor of Harold Hotelling* (pp. 278–292). Palo Alto, CA: Stanford University Press.

Levy, P. S., & Lemeshow, S. (2011). *Sampling of populations: Methods and applications* (4th ed.). Hoboken, NJ: John Wiley & Sons.

Lilliefors, H. (1967). On the Kolmogorov-Smirnov test for normality with mean and variance unknown. *Journal of the American Statistical Association, 62*, 399–402.

Lumley, T. (2004). Analysis of complex survey samples. *Journal of Statistical Software, 9*(8), 1–19.

Maxwell, S. E., Delaney, H. D., & Kelley, K. (2018). *Designing experiments and analyzing data*. New York, NY: Routledge.

Neyman, J. (1950). First course in probability and statistics. New York, NY: Holt.

Neyman, J., & Pearson, E. S. (1933). The testing of statistical hypotheses in relation to probabilities a priori. *Proceedings of the Cambridge Philosophical Society: Mathematical & Physical Sciences, 29*(4), 492–510.

Noreen, E. W. (1989). Computer-intensive methods for testing hypotheses: An introduction. New York, NY: Wiley.

Olejnik, S. F., & Algina, J. (1987). Type I error rates and power estimates of selected parametric and nonparametric tests of scale. *Journal of Educational Statistics*, (1), 45–61. doi:10.2307/1164627

Olejnik, S., & Algina, J. (2000). Measures of effect size for comparative studies: Applications, interpretations, and limitations. *Contemporary Educational Psychology, 25*, 241–286.

Olofsson, P. (2007). *Probabilities: The little numbers that rule our lives*. Hoboken, NJ: Wiley-Interscience.

Pearson, E. S. (1978). The history of statistics in the 17th and 18th centuries. New York, NY: Macmillan.

Pfeffermann, D. (1993). The role of sampling weights when modeling survey data. *International Statistical Review, 61*(2), 317–337.

Rahlf, T. (2017). *Data visualisation with R: 100 examples*. Cham, Switzerland: Springer International Publishing.

Ramsey, P. H. (1989). Critical values of Spearman's rank order correlation. *Journal of Educational Statistics, 14*, 245–253.

Ramsey, P. H. (1994). Testing variances in psychological and educational research. *Journal of Educational Statistics*, (1), 23–42. doi:10.2307/1165175

Robbins, N. B. (2005). *Creating more effective graphs*. Hoboken, NJ: Wiley-Interscience.

Rosenthal, R., & Rubin, D. B. (2003). R-sub(equivalent): A simple effect size indicator. *Psychological Methods, 8*(4), 492–496.

Rudas, T. (2004). *Probability theory a primer*. Thousand Oaks, CA: Sage.

Sahay, A. (2016). *Applied regression and modeling: A computer integrated approach* (1st ed.). New York, NY: Business Expert Press.

Sawilowsky, S. S., & Blair, R. C. (1992). A more realistic look at the robustness and type II error properties of the t test to departures from population normality. *Psychological Bulletin*, (2), 352–360.

Schmid, C. F. (1983). Statistical graphics: Design principles and practices. New York, NY: Wiley.

Shadish, W. R., Cook, T. D., & Campbell, D. T. (2002). *Experimental and quasi-experimental designs for generalized causal inference*. Boston: Houston Mifflin.

Shapiro, S. S., & Wilk, M. B. (1965). An analysis of variance test for normality (complete samples). *Biometrika, 52*(3–4), 591–611.

Shear, B. R. B. S. C. E., Nordstokke, D. W., & Zumbo, B. D. (2018). A note on using the nonparametric Levene test when population means Are unequal. *Practical Assessment, Research & Evaluation, 23*(13), 1–11.

Skinner, C. J., Holt, D., & Smith, T. M. F. (Eds.). (1989). *Analysis of complex samples*. New York: Wiley.

Smithson, M. (2003). Noncentral confidence intervals for standardized effect sizes. In *Confidence intervals* (pp. 33–41). Thousand Oaks, CA: Sage.

Stigler, S. M. (1986). *The history of statistics: The measurement of uncertainty before 1900*. Cambridge, MA: Belknap Press of Harvard University Press.

Storer, B. E., & Kim, C. (1990). Exact properties of some exact test statistics for comparing two binomial proportions. *Journal of the American Statistical Association*, (409), 146–155. doi:10.2307/2289537

Sudman, S. (1976). *Applied sampling*. New York, NY: Academic Press.

Tijms, H. (2004). *Understanding probability: Chance rules in everyday life*. New York, NY: Cambridge University Press.

Tiku, M. L., & Singh, M. (1981). Robust test for means when population variances are unequal. *Communications in Statistics: Theory and Methods, 10*(20), 2057–2071.

Trafimow, D., Amrhein, V., Areshenkoff, C. N., Barrera-Causil, C. J., Beh, E. J., Bilgic, Y. K., . . . Marmolejo-Ramos, F. (2018). Manipulating the alpha level cannot cure significance testing. *Frontiers in Psychology, 9*, 1–7. doi:10.3389/fpsyg.2018.00699

Tufte, E. R. (2001). *The visual display of quantitative information* (2nd ed.). Cheshire, CT: Graphics Press.

Tukey, J. W. (1977). *Exploratory data analysis*. Reading, MA: Addison-Wesley.

Uanhoro, J. O. (2017). *Effect size calculators*. Retrieved from https://effect-size-calculator.herokuapp.com/

Van Belle, G. (2002). *Statistical rules of thumb*. New York, NY: Wiley-Interscience.

Vogt, W. P. (2005). Dictionary of statistics and methodology: A nontechnical guide for the social sciences (3rd ed.). Los Angeles, CA: Sage.

Voinov, V., Balakrishnan, N., & Nikulin, M. S. (2013). *Chi-squared goodness of fit tests with applications* (1st ed.). Waltham, MA: Academic Press.

Wainer, H. (1992). Understanding graphs and tables. *Educational Researcher, 21*(1), 14–23.

Wainer, H. (2000). Visual revelations: Graphical tales of fate and deception from Napoleon Bonaparte to Ross Perot. Mahwah, NJ: Lawrence Erlbaum Associates.

Wallgren, A., Wallgren, B., Persson, R. S., Jorner, U., & Haaland, J-A. (1996). *Graphing statistics and data: Creating better charts*. Thousand Oaks, CA: Sage.

Wang, Y., Rodríguez de Gil, P., Chen, Y-H., Kromrey, J. D., Kim, E. S., Pham, T., . . . Romano, J. L. (2017). Comparing the performance of approaches for testing the homogeneity of variance assumption in one-factor ANOVA models. *Educational and Psychological Measurement, 77*(2), 305–329. doi:10.1177/0013164416645162

Wickham, H., & Grolemund, G. (2017). *R for data science*. Sebastopol, CA: O'Reilly Media.

Wilcox, R. R. (1986). Controlling power in a heteroscedastic ANOVA procedure. *British Journal of Mathematical and Statistical Psychology, 39*(1), 65–68. doi:10.1111/j.2044-8317.1986.tb00845.x

Wilcox, R. R. (1987). New statistical procedures for the social sciences: Modern solutions to basic problems. Hillsdale, NJ: Lawrence Erlbaum Associates.

Wilcox, R. R. (1993). Comparing one-step M-estimators of location when there are more than two groups. *Psychometrika, 58*(1), 71–78. doi:10.1007/BF02294471

Wilcox, R. R. (1995). *Statistics for the social sciences*. San Diego, CA: Academic Press.

Wilcox, R. R. (1996). *Statistics for the social sciences*. San Diego, CA: Academic.

Wilcox, R. R. (2003). *Applying contemporary statistical procedures*. San Diego, CA: Academic Press.

Wilcox, R. R. (2012). *Introduction to robust estimation and hypothesis testing* (3rd ed.). Boston, MA: Academic Press.

Wilcox, R. R. (2017). *Introduction to robust estimation and hypothesis testing* (4th ed.). Burlington, MA: Elsevier.

Wilkinson, L. (2005). *The grammar of graphics* (2nd ed.). New York, NY: Springer.

Yu, M. C., & Dunn, O. J. (1982). Robust tests for the equality of two correlation coefficients: A Monte Carlo study. *Educational & Psychological Measurement, 42*, 987–1004.

Yuan, K-H., & Maxwell, S. (2005). On the post hoc power in testing mean differences. *Journal of Educational and Behavioral Statistics, 30*(2), 141–167. doi:10.3102/10769986030002141

Zimmerman, D. W. (1997). A note on interpretation of the paired-samples t test. *Journal of Educational and Behavioral Statistics, 22*(3), 349–360. doi:10.2307/1165289

Zimmerman, D. W. (2003). A warning about the large-sample Wilcoxon-Mann-Whitney test. *Understanding Statistics, 2*(4), 267–280.

Zumbo, B. D., & Nordstokke, D. W. (2010). A new nonparametric Levene test for equal variances. *Psicológica, 32*(2), 401–430.

Name Index

Subject Index

Note: Page numbers in *italics* indicate figures, and those in **bold** type indicate tables